Secure and Intelligent IoT-Enabled Smart Cities

Sushil Kumar Singh
Marwadi University, India

Sudeep Tanwar
Nirma University, India

Rajendrasinh Jadeja
Marwadi University, India

Saurabh Singh
Woosong University, South Korea

Zdzislaw Polkowski
Wroclaw University of Economics, Poland

IGI Global
PUBLISHER of TIMELY KNOWLEDGE

A volume in the Advances in Computational Intelligence and Robotics (ACIR) Book Series

Published in the United States of America by
IGI Global
Engineering Science Reference (an imprint of IGI Global)
701 E. Chocolate Avenue
Hershey PA, USA 17033
Tel: 717-533-8845
Fax: 717-533-8661
E-mail: cust@igi-global.com
Web site: http://www.igi-global.com

Library of Congress Cataloging-in-Publication Data

Names: Singh, Sushil, 1983- editor. | Tanwar, Sudeep, editor. | Jadeja, Rajendrasinh, 1977- editor. | Singh, Saurabh, 1989- editor. | Polkowski, Zdzislaw, editor.
Title: Secure and intelligent IOT-enabled smart cities / edited by Sushil Singh, Sudeep Tanwar, Rajendrasinh Jadeja, Saurabh Singh, Zdzislaw Polkowski.
Description: Hershey, PA : Engineering Science Reference, [2024] | Includes bibliographical references and index. | Summary: "This book provides qualitative and theoretical knowledge about security and privacy in IoT and Smart City applications with advanced emerging technologies such as Blockchain, Artificial Intelligence, and Deep and Federated Learning"-- Provided by publisher.
Identifiers: LCCN 2023059498 (print) | LCCN 2023059499 (ebook) | ISBN 9798369323731 (h/c) | ISBN 9798369323748 (ebook)
Subjects: LCSH: Smart cities--Technological innovations. | Internet of things--Security measures. | Computer security--Technological innovations.
Classification: LCC TD159.4 .S429 2024 (print) | LCC TD159.4 (ebook) | DDC 005.8--dc23/eng/20240329
LC record available at https://lccn.loc.gov/2023059498
LC ebook record available at https://lccn.loc.gov/2023059499

This book is published in the IGI Global book series Advances in Computational Intelligence and Robotics (ACIR) (ISSN: 2327-0411; eISSN: 2327-042X)

British Cataloguing in Publication Data
A Cataloguing in Publication record for this book is available from the British Library.

For electronic access to this publication, please contact: eresources@igi-global.com.

Advances in Computational Intelligence and Robotics (ACIR) Book Series

Ivan Giannoccaro
University of Salento, Italy

ISSN:2327-0411
EISSN:2327-042X

Mission

While intelligence is traditionally a term applied to humans and human cognition, technology has progressed in such a way to allow for the development of intelligent systems able to simulate many human traits. With this new era of simulated and artificial intelligence, much research is needed in order to continue to advance the field and also to evaluate the ethical and societal concerns of the existence of artificial life and machine learning.

The **Advances in Computational Intelligence and Robotics (ACIR) Book Series** encourages scholarly discourse on all topics pertaining to evolutionary computing, artificial life, computational intelligence, machine learning, and robotics. ACIR presents the latest research being conducted on diverse topics in intelligence technologies with the goal of advancing knowledge and applications in this rapidly evolving field.

Coverage

- Natural Language Processing
- Automated Reasoning
- Artificial Intelligence
- Neural Networks
- Fuzzy Systems
- Artificial Life
- Robotics
- Algorithmic Learning
- Pattern Recognition
- Intelligent Control

IGI Global is currently accepting manuscripts for publication within this series. To submit a proposal for a volume in this series, please contact our Acquisition Editors at Acquisitions@igi-global.com or visit: http://www.igi-global.com/publish/.

The Advances in Computational Intelligence and Robotics (ACIR) Book Series (ISSN 2327-0411) is published by IGI Global, 701 E. Chocolate Avenue, Hershey, PA 17033-1240, USA, www.igi-global.com. This series is composed of titles available for purchase individually; each title is edited to be contextually exclusive from any other title within the series. For pricing and ordering information please visit http://www.igi-global.com/book-series/advances-computational-intelligence-robotics/73674. Postmaster: Send all address changes to above address.

Titles in this Series

For a list of additional titles in this series, please visit:
http://www.igi-global.com/book-series/advances-computational-intelligence-robotics/73674

Artificial Intelligence of Things (AIoT) for Productivity and Organizational Transition
Sajad Rezaei (University of Worcester, UK) and Amin Ansary (University of the Witwatersrand, South Africa)
Business Science Reference • © 2024 • 368pp • H/C (ISBN: 9798369309933) • US $275.00

Internet of Things and AI for Natural Disaster Management and Prediction
D. Satishkumar (Nehru Institute of Technology, India) and M. Sivaraja (Nehru Institute of Technology, India)
Engineering Science Reference • © 2024 • 334pp • H/C (ISBN: 9798369342848) • US $345.00

AI Applications for Business, Medical, and Agricultural Sustainability
Arshi Naim (King Khalid University, Saudi Arabia)
Engineering Science Reference • © 2024 • 322pp • H/C (ISBN: 9798369352663) • US $315.00

Innovative Machine Learning Applications for Cryptography
J. Anitha Ruth (SRM Institute of Science and Technology, India) G.V. Mahesh Vijayalakshmi (BMS Institute of Technology and Management, India) P. Visalakshi (SRM Institute of Science and Technology, India) R. Uma (Sri Sai Ram Engineering College, India) and A. Meenakshi (SRM Institute of Science and Technology, India)
Engineering Science Reference • © 2024 • 294pp • H/C (ISBN: 9798369316429) • US $300.00

The Ethical Frontier of AI and Data Analysis
Rajeev Kumar (Moradabad Institute of Technology, India) Ankush Joshi (COER University, Roorkee, India) Hari Om Sharan (Rama University, Kanpur, India) Sheng-Lung Peng (College of Innovative Design and Management, National Taipei University of Business, Taiwan) and Chetan R. Dudhagara (Anand Agricultural University, India)
Engineering Science Reference • © 2024 • 456pp • H/C (ISBN: 9798369329641) • US $365.00

Empowering Low-Resource Languages With NLP Solutions
Partha Pakray (National Institute of Technology, Silchar, India) Pankaj Dadure (University of Petroleum and Energy Studies, India) and Sivaji Bandyopadhyay (Jadavpur University, India)
Engineering Science Reference • © 2024 • 314pp • H/C (ISBN: 9798369307281) • US $300.00

Computational Intelligence for Green Cloud Computing and Digital Waste Management
K. Dinesh Kumar (Amrita Vishwa Vidyapeetham, India) Vijayakumar Varadarajan (The University of New South Wales, Australia) Nidal Nasser (College of Engineering, Alfaisal University, Saudi Arabia) and Ravi Kumar Poluru (Institute of Aeronautical Engineering, India)
Engineering Science Reference • © 2024 • 405pp • H/C (ISBN: 9798369315521) • US $300.00

IGI Global
PUBLISHER of TIMELY KNOWLEDGE

701 East Chocolate Avenue, Hershey, PA 17033, USA
Tel: 717-533-8845 x100 • Fax: 717-533-8661
E-Mail: cust@igi-global.com • www.igi-global.com

Table of Contents

Detailed Table of Contents

The convergence of cutting-edge technologies in the age of digital transformation has created a phenomenon that has the potential to redefine the very structure of our urban environments. The convergence of the internet of things (IoT) and the revolutionary features of 5G connectivity is set to bring about a transformative phase in urban living. This chapter determines how the convergence of IoT, smart cities, and 5G technology is reshaping our cities and fostering innovation, improving quality of life, and addressing current challenges. When IoT, smart cities, and 5G work together, they can make cities better, more sustainable, and more responsive to what people need. The chapter envisions convergence of the internet of things, smart cities, and 5G technology representing a transformative force that is reshaping the urban environment. This powerful combination has the potential to enhance the efficiency, sustainability, and overall quality of life in cities around the world.

Federated and deep learning are changing every field in today's era; these technologies are making devices, citizens, homes, buildings, cars, etc. Before these technologies, we used normal machine learning that has some cons. To counter those cons, federated and deep learning emerged. Federated and deep learning work on the same concept of machine learning, but with advanced methods. Using these technologies, we make work easier; and companies are using them to enhance their productivity, to grow the business, etc. Current smart city applications offer various facilities to ensure more effective, time-saving services like traffic management, environmental and public safety and security, energy management, healthcare services, etc. The smart city's components first collect data by using different IoT and other sensors. It requires processing the data to perform several actions to achieve the system's benefits. Deep learning and federated learning methods that use artificial intelligence to make cities smarter. In this chapter, the authors explore the cons of normal machine learning, and what the roles are of federated learning and deep learning in the making of cities smarter, as well as what is needed and how these technologies work.

The idea of smart cities is significant because it seeks to improve a city's infrastructure, traffic, governance, water and waste management, power management, health, safety and security, education, and other systems in order to raise the standard of living for its citizens. This chapter explains the idea of "smart cities" and lists all of the advantages. It explains the many services and applications needed to create a smart city, as well as the part ICT technologies play in putting them into practice. In addition, the difficulties with the current ICT systems are examined in relation to the deployment of smart cities. The chapter explores the anticipated characteristics of 5G technologies and explains why they might be the most effective solution for implementing smart cities successfully. Researchers and practitioners in the field can both benefit from this research, which offers a reflection on the state of the art, the use of 5G in smart cities.

The rise of 5G technology marks a significant shift in smart city development, bringing unprecedented connectivity and transformative opportunities. This chapter explores its profound impact on urban evolution, focusing on creating intelligent cityscapes. It examines key 5G components like the radio access network, core network, network slicing, edge computing, and IoT devices, enabling real-time monitoring, efficient resource management, and innovation in transportation, healthcare, public safety, and energy sectors. 5G facilitates intelligent transportation, enhances public safety via high-resolution video surveillance, and revolutionizes healthcare through telemedicine. Augmented reality (AR) and virtual reality (VR) experiences, enabled by 5G, drive innovative urban solutions. The economic and societal implications, including economic growth, job creation, and civic engagement, are discussed. Overall, 5G fosters sustainable, efficient, and citizen-centric urban environments.

Cloud computing for secure smart cities beyond 5G represents a cutting-edge approach to urban development and technology integration. It involves leveraging advanced cloud computing infrastructure and 5G connectivity to create highly secure, efficient, and interconnected smart city systems. In this context, cloud computing enables the centralized management of data and services, facilitating real-time analytics, resource optimization, and the seamless operation of various IoT devices and sensors throughout the city. The integration of 5G technology further enhances data transmission speed and capacity, ensuring rapid, reliable communication between devices and cloud resources. By prioritizing security, this approach safeguards sensitive data and ensures that smart city services operate within robust cybersecurity frameworks.

Manoj Kumar Patra, GITAM University, Hyderabad, India
Sampa Sahoo, C. V. Raman Global University, Bhubaneswar, India
Bibhudatta Sahoo, National Institute of Technology, Rourkela, India
Ashok Kumar Turuk, National Institute of Technology, Rourkela, India

As the evolution of technology ushers in an era beyond 5G, integrating cloud computing into the landscape of smart cities becomes paramount. This chapter delves into the foundational concept of cloud computing and elucidates its pivotal role in shaping the future of secure and connected smart cities. With its on-demand services, scalability, and cost-effectiveness, cloud computing emerges as a key enabler for handling the intricate demands of urban environments. The chapter begins by defining cloud computing and providing an overview of its essential characteristics. It then pivots to the dynamic context of smart cities, where an intricate web of internet of things (IoT) devices, sensors, and urban systems generate copious amounts of data. Cloud computing offers a robust solution for storing, processing, and analyzing this data, empowering smart cities with real-time insights and informed decision-making capabilities. This chapter explores the synergy between cloud computing and 5G networks, emphasizing the importance of high-speed connectivity and low latency in the smart city paradigm. The integration of edge computing further enriches the smart city infrastructure, enabling rapid local processing and reducing latency for time-sensitive applications. Security, a paramount concern in smart city environments, is addressed as the chapter delves into the challenges and solutions provided by cloud computing. The role of cloud platforms in safeguarding citizen data, managing cyber-physical threats, and ensuring compliance with regulatory frameworks is thoroughly examined. This chapter also explores emerging trends, such as the integration of artificial intelligence and blockchain technologies, offering a glimpse into the future of cloud computing in the smart city landscape. In conclusion, this chapter not only defines the synergy between cloud computing and smart cities but also provides a comprehensive understanding of how cloud computing, in the context of 5G and beyond, is instrumental in fostering secure, connected, and resilient urban environments.

Bhupinder Singh, Sharda University, India
Vishal Jain, Sharda University, India
Christian Kaunert, Dublin City University, Ireland
Komal Vig, Sharda University, India

The highly intelligent internet of things (IoT) and wireless sensor technologies are set to reshape the directions of safe and intelligent parking and transportation in the dynamic field of urban development. Sustainable and effective transportation solutions are critical as cities struggle with the effects of growing populations and rising urbanization. Sustainability is the key to the transportation of the future as the development of electric mobility solutions and environmentally friendly transportation choices is facilitated by highly intelligent IoT. By reducing the negative effects of transportation systems on the

Rapid IoT device integration in smart cities is transforming urban environments, delivering unparalleled efficiency, sustainability, and connection. This book chapter tackles smart city IoT infrastructure security, a top priority. It begins with an exploration of how IoT technologies are changing urban living and the pros and cons of their widespread adoption. IoT equipment including sensors, actuators, connected vehicles, and public infrastructure pose security vulnerabilities. IoT implementations, the chapter examines smart city cyber and privacy concerns. The next section presents a technical and policy-based framework for smart city IoT infrastructure security. Collaboration between government, industry, and the public is key to this framework's success. Blockchain for secure transactions, machine learning for anomaly detection, and encryption protocols are also explored in smart city IoT installations. The chapter finishes with a look ahead at smart city IoT infrastructure security, emphasizing the necessity for constant adaptation and improvement to combat new threats.

Smart cities offer the usage of digital technology to enhance the quality of life for city residents. The goal of these cities is to deal with some of the issues that are projected to arise in future cities, enabling more efficient and sustainable resource management, among other benefits. Through technology innovation and data-driven decision-making, smart cities have the potential to make societies safer, more efficient, and more resilient. Healthcare is important for the thriving growth of smart cities, and providing high-quality medical care is the municipal government's most difficult duty. Smart healthcare is a realistic solution for the health care industry to intelligently manage patient flow systems. Adoption of smart healthcare reduces costs and improves illness management. However, as the scale of wearable medical devices increases, preserving privacy and security becomes more difficult. However, clever security measures will be required to ensure that these advancements are not jeopardized. This chapter aims to examine the role of cyber security in the development of smart city healthcare, as well as the key challenges and benefits of the cyber security in the smart city healthcare systems.

This study examines the complex array of impediments and potential advantages of internet of things (IoT)-enabled secure and intelligent smart healthcare devices (IESISHDs) associated with the shift towards enabling smart cities, motivated by the pressing necessity to address climate change and promote sustaining smart healthcare systems. This study looks at the technological, economic, and social problems that need to be solved in order to make cities smarter with IoT. It does this by reading a lot of scholarly sources. Most stupendously, it emphasizes the environmentally sustainable merits, potential for economic growth, and improvements in societal well-being that can arise from this transition. It further depicts selected case studies to demonstrate sustainable empirical evidence and provide policy recommendations. The paradigm is to assist governments and other stakeholders in effectively managing human-associated challenges to attain maximum sustainable value and an innovative healthcare future that guarantees worldwide prosperity and ecological welfare.

The amalgamation of healthcare, sustainability, and internet of things (Io T) technology offers a significant prospect for effectively tackling urgent issues in the provision of healthcare services in metropolitan areas inside smart cities. The present research investigates the incorporation of IoT technology in order to advance environmental sustainability, augment healthcare accessibility, and boost health outcomes within the framework of smart city endeavors. This study seeks to enhance our comprehension of the interconnections between green healthcare and smart city development by employing a comprehensive strategy that includes healthcare delivery, technology innovation, urban planning, and community involvement. The research taxonomy encompasses multiple dimensions of the study, such as the examination of environmental sustainability in healthcare, the use of IoT applications, the integration of smart city infrastructure, policy and governance considerations, community participation, health equity, and effect evaluation. This research aims to clarify the intricacies of green healthcare in smart cities and develop strategies for improving sustainability, equality, and resilience in urban healthcare systems by analyzing these characteristics. This study's findings represent a valuable contribution to the academic conversation surrounding green healthcare, IoT technology, and the development of smart cities. The study provides practical recommendations that may be implemented by policymakers, healthcare practitioners, technology developers, urban planners, and community stakeholders. This project seeks to facilitate sustainable transformation in healthcare delivery and enhance holistic well-being in the rapidly urbanizing settings of smart cities through the promotion of interdisciplinary collaboration, stakeholder involvement, and evidence-based decision-making.

In smart city planning and development, smart transportation integrates advanced technology with traditional transportation systems to maximise sustainability, safety, and efficiency. Intelligent transportation systems collect and analyse vehicle movement, traffic patterns, and other data using sensors, data analytics, and AI. This data can then be utilised to optimise transport systems, decreasing emissions, enhancing safety, alleviating traffic, and boosting quality of life. Intelligent transport, which improves transport network sustainability, efficiency, and security, could transform urban mobility, and elevate living standards. In this chapter, intelligent transportation systems and their benefits are extensively covered. Mobility-as-

Preface

This book embarks on a journey into the realm of secure and intelligent IoT-enabled smart cities, where cutting-edge technology converges with visionary urban planning. Through a multidisciplinary lens, we delve into the intricacies of building cities that are not only smart but also safe, sustainable, and inclusive. Established and emerging technologies such as 5G, Internet of Things (IoT), Artificial Intelligence (AI), and blockchain play an increasingly significant role in innovative city applications, reinforcing the importance of designing security and privacy-aware / preserving solutions. Smart City already provides various human life advantages in advanced applications such as Smart Parking, Smart Healthcare, Smart Manufacturing, and others. These applications depend on IoT and Sensor devices such as humidity, current, temperature, etc. These IoT devices connect to the network using gateways that act as processing nodes. The nodes mentioned above, and sensors transfer the information data to the cloud, analyze it, and utilize it to improve and optimize smart applications. 5G is the fifth-generation communication technology for transferring information data from device to device and layer to layer in advanced IoT applications. It offers high-speed connectivity as specified by 3GPP cellular networks. Artificial Intelligence provides an automatic and privacy-preserved environment in advanced applications with deep and federated learning. However, security and privacy are the major issues in IoT-enabled Smart City Applications. In the smart city and IoT security Intelligence paradigms, there is a need for an edited collection of original research in this area. The primary objective of this book is to provide relevant theoretical frameworks and the latest empirical research findings in the area. It will be written for professionals who want to improve their understanding of the strategic role of a secure and intelligent environment in an IoT-enabled Smart City beyond 5G. In this book, we categorized many chapters based on the title and provided qualitative and theoretical knowledge about security and privacy in IoT and Smart City applications with advanced emerging technologies such as Blockchain, Artificial Intelligence, Deep and Federated Learning. The target audience of this book will be professionals and researchers working in secure and intelligent environments in IoT-enabled Smart City Applications such as Smart Healthcare, Smart Parking, Smart Manufacturing, Smart Transportation, and others with the emergence of advanced technologies. Moreover, the book will provide insights and support executives concerned with the Smart City and IoT Security and intelligent privacy preserved paradigms with federated and deep learning. The book proposes novel architectures that drive economically viable healthcare businesses. The book would serve key research directions in academia, healthcare industry professionals, and researchers.

The book is organized into three sections. The first section, which includes four chapters, is focused on the background and preliminaries. The second part, which includes four well-structured chapters, illustrates the Security case of an IoT-enabled Smart City. Finally, the last section, which includes ten chapters, focuses on Advanced Technologies for IoT-enabled Smart Cities.

SECTION 1: BACKGROUND AND PRELIMINARIES

The chapter "Emerging Horizons - IoT, 5G, and the Evolution of Smart Cities" determines how the convergence of IoT, Smart Cities, and 5G technology is reshaping our cities and fostering innovation, improving quality of life, and addressing current challenges. The chapter envisions convergence of the Internet of Things (IoT), Smart Cities, and 5G technology, representing a transformative force that is reshaping the urban environments. This powerful combination has the potential to enhance the efficiency, sustainability, and overall quality of life in cities around the world.

The chapter "Emergence of Federated and Deep Learning for Smart City" explores the cons of normal machine learning and the roles of federated learning and deep learning in making cities smarter, what is needed, and how these technologies work. Deep learning and federated learning methods use artificial intelligence to make intelligent to make cities smarter. Federated and deep learning are changing every field in today's era; these technologies are making devices, citizens, homes, buildings, cars, etc..

The chapter "Smart City And 5G" explores and discusses the anticipated characteristics of 5G technologies and explains why they might be the most effective solution for implementing smart cities successfully. Researchers and practitioners in the field can both benefit from this research, which offers a reflection on the state of the art in the use of 5G in smart cities. It explains the many Services and Applications needed to create a Smart City as well as the part ICT technologies play in putting them into practice, explains the idea of "smart cities," and lists all of its advantages.

The chapter "5G Cityscape Unleashing Seamless Connectivity for Smart Urban Evolution" explores its profound impact on urban evolution, focusing on creating intelligent cityscapes. It examines key 5G components like the Radio Access Network, Core Network, network slicing, edge computing, and IoT devices, enabling real-time monitoring, efficient resource management, and innovation in transportation, healthcare, public safety, and energy sectors.

SECTION 2: SECURITY USE-CASE OF IOT-ENABLED SMART CITY

The chapter "Enhancing Smart City Resilience Integrating Cloud Computing and 5G for Secure and Sustainable Urban Environments" presents that cloud computing enables the centralized management of data and services, facilitating real-time analytics, resource optimization, and the seamless operation of various IoT devices and sensors throughout the city. Cloud computing for secure smart cities beyond 5G represents a cutting-edge approach to urban development and technology integration. It involves leveraging advanced cloud computing infrastructure and 5G connectivity to create highly secure, efficient, and interconnected smart city systems.

The chapter "Cloud Computing for a Secure Smart City beyond 5G explores the synergy between cloud computing and 5G networks, emphasizing the importance of high-speed connectivity and low latency in the smart city paradigm. The integration of edge computing further enriches the Smart City infrastructure, enabling rapid local processing and reducing latency for time-sensitive applications. This chapter also explores emerging trends, such as integrating artificial intelligence and blockchain technologies, offering a glimpse into the future of cloud computing in the smart city landscape.

The chapter "Shaping Highly Intelligent Internet of Things (IoT) and Wireless Sensors for Smart Cities: Trajectories Smart and Secure Transportation and Parking Lensing Sustainable Future" presents and explores how highly intelligent Internet of Things (IoT) and wireless sensor technologies are developing and how they will affect urban transportation in the future to solve the difficulties of contemporary urban life, a focus is put on security measures, real-time data analytics and sustainable practices.

The chapter "Unveiling the Layered Architecture of IoT A Comprehensive Overview" presents an extensive exploration of the multi-layered framework constituting the IoT infrastructure. This abstract encapsulates a detailed examination of the fundamental layers' integral to IoT's functionality. Starting with the foundational Perception Layer, encompassing sensors and actuators, it progresses to the Network Layer facilitating seamless data transmission. Delving deeper, it explores the Middleware Layer, pivotal in data processing, and the diverse functionalities of the Application Layer across various domains. Moreover, the abstract sheds light on the Security and Management Layer, emphasizing its critical role in safeguarding IoT systems.

The chapter "Exploring the Layered Architecture of Internet of Things (IoT)" provides a comprehensive exploration of the layered architecture in the Internet of Things (IoT) ecosystem. IoT has become integral to modern life, touching industries from healthcare to smart cities. The chapter begins with an introduction to IoT's significance and evolution. It then breaks down the architecture into key layers - Perception, Network, Middleware, and Application, explaining their roles, interactions, and security considerations. Real-world case studies offer practical insights, while discussions on emerging technologies and challenges provide a glimpse into IoT's future. This chapter equips readers with a fundamental understanding of IoT's layered architecture, encouraging them to participate in this dynamic field.

SECTION 3: ADVANCED TECHNOLOGIES FOR IOT-ENABLED SMART CITY

The chapter "Blockchain's Motivation for IoT-enabled Smart City" examines the fusion of Blockchain technology with the Internet of Things (IoT) in Smart Cities, exploring how Blockchain's traits like immutability, decentralization, and consensus can address smart cities' concerns. It scrutinizes IoT's applications in Smart Cities like traffic management and waste control, highlighting data's critical role. It accentuates Blockchain's significance in device authentication, securing data integrity, and transactions in a decentralized network.

The chapter "Generative AI Enabled IoT Applications for Smart Cities, Unleashing Innovation and Paving the Way for the Future" explores the intricate balance of dynamic resource allocation and optimization facilitated by generative AI algorithms within intelligent city IoT networks. The chapter underscores the pivotal role of predictive analytics, behavior prediction, and cybersecurity measures in steering decision-making for optimal urban functioning. Real-world case studies illuminate successful generative AI-IoT integrations, providing tangible lessons for stakeholders, and conclude by urging ongoing collaborative research to address evolving challenges and chart future directions for a more interconnected and resilient urban future.

The chapter "Strategies for Mitigating Security Concerns in IoT-Enabled Smart Cities" comprehensively analyzes the security concerns inherent in smart cities enabled by the IoT. This paper presents a range of practical techniques and best practices that may be used to manage risks effectively, focusing on enhancing cybersecurity awareness, improving incident response capabilities, and fostering collaboration among stakeholders. In summary, this chapter provides a crucial resource for understanding and tackling security concerns within the ever-evolving domain of IoT-enabled smart cities.

The chapter "Securing the Foundations: IoT Infrastructure in Smart Cities" tackles smart city IoT infrastructure security, a top priority. It begins with an exploration of how IoT technologies are changing urban living and the pros and cons of their widespread adoption. IoT equipment, including sensors, actuators, connected vehicles, and public infrastructure, pose security vulnerabilities. IoT implementations, the chapter examines smart city cyber and privacy concerns. The next section presents a technical and policy-based framework for smart city IoT infrastructure security.

The chapter "Security and its Implications on Healthcare in an IoT-enabled Smart City" aims to examine the role of cyber security in developing smart city healthcare and the key challenges and benefits of cyber security in smart city healthcare systems. Adoption of smart healthcare reduces costs and improves illness management. However, as the scale of wearable medical devices increases, preserving privacy and security becomes more difficult. However, clever security measures will be required to ensure these advancements are not jeopardized.

The chapter "IoT-enabled Secure and Intelligence Smart Healthcare Beyond 5G in Enabling Smart Cities" offers insights into the transformative potential of IoT-enabled secure and intelligent smart healthcare in the context of future smart cities beyond the 5G era. It underscores the importance of adopting a holistic approach that addresses technical, regulatory, and ethical considerations to fully realize the benefits of IoT in healthcare while ensuring privacy, security, and inclusivity for all stakeholders.

The chapter "Green Healthcare in Smart Cities: Harnessing IoT for Sustainable Transformation of Healthcare System" investigates the incorporation of Internet of Things (IoT) technology to advance environmental sustainability, augment healthcare accessibility, and boost health outcomes within the framework of smart city endeavors. This study seeks to enhance our comprehension of the interconnections between green healthcare and smart city development by employing a comprehensive strategy that includes healthcare delivery, technology innovation, urban planning, and community involvement.

The chapter "Sustainable Smart Transportation-Technologies, Benefits, Challenges to Urbanization Concept" provides an overview of key technologies driving the evolution of smart transportation, including electric vehicles, autonomous vehicles, intelligent transportation systems, and mobility-as-a-service platforms. It examines the potential benefits of these technologies, such as improved air quality, reduced greenhouse gas emissions, enhanced safety, and increased accessibility for all members of society.

The chapter "A Comprehensive Exploration of the 'Umber' Mobile App's IoT-Infused Revolution in Umbrella Technology" explains the 'Umber' mobile app stands as a pioneering technological advancement, reshaping the traditional usage of umbrellas. This abstract encapsulates the app's diverse objectives, emphasizing elevated user convenience, technological innovation, environmental sustainability, and increased accessibility. Through seamless technology integration, 'Umber' revolutionizes the umbrella experience, introducing on-demand services, reducing forgetfulness, and promoting sustainability.

Chapter 1
Emerging Horizons: IoT, 5G, and the Evolution of Smart Cities

Ketaki Anandkumar Pattani
https://orcid.org/0000-0002-7942-8637
Institute of Advanced Research, Gandhinagar, India

Sunil Gautam
Nirma University, India

Ahsan Rizvi
Institute of Advanced Research, Gandhinagar, India

ABSTRACT

The convergence of cutting-edge technologies in the age of digital transformation has created a phenomenon that has the potential to redefine the very structure of our urban environments. The convergence of the internet of things (IoT) and the revolutionary features of 5G connectivity is set to bring about a transformative phase in urban living. This chapter determines how the convergence of IoT, smart cities, and 5G technology is reshaping our cities and fostering innovation, improving quality of life, and addressing current challenges. When IoT, smart cities, and 5G work together, they can make cities better, more sustainable, and more responsive to what people need. The chapter envisions convergence of the internet of things, smart cities, and 5G technology representing a transformative force that is reshaping the urban environment. This powerful combination has the potential to enhance the efficiency, sustainability, and overall quality of life in cities around the world.

INTRODUCTION

It is because of this that communication and intellect are being transformed by fast-moving technological advancements in our lives, jobs, and interactions within the world. Our communities have been changing due to digital evolution through the combination of smart cities' concepts, Internet of Things (IoT), and 5G technology. Positioned between connectivity, information and intelligence, this technology is

DOI: 10.4018/979-8-3693-2373-1.ch001

poised to change how we perceive and interact with the world. This chapter addresses how well these things interact, examining their individual importance and collective potential to transform the various aspects of modern life Three highly interrelated trends are leading this transformation: the Internet of Things (IoT), 5G technology, and the concept of smart cities. They provide a powerful synergy that can transform different parts of our everyday life. In this introduction we will examine the main drivers of this technological development and its profound impact on society.

The Internet of Things is a technological phenomenon that redefines how devices interact with things. It enables a vast platform for linking everyday wearables, wearable and industrial devices as well as accessories. This implies that the IoT has an extensive influence on practical operations, ranging from smart thermostats that learn user preference to cooperative robots employed in industries to enhance performance. This linked network can create immense productivity gains, reduce waste and promote evidence-based decision-making capability. The author points out what will drive next generation IoT connectivity encompassing all from consumer convenience to technical advancements (Li, Xu, & Zhao, 2015). In this case, different sensors are attached on each node in the network to enable this data sharing among intelligent systems. Thus, it can be said that there is potentiality of IoT in increasing efficiency as well as resource efficiency and creation of new possibilities in several sectors.

The reliability and dependability of IOT-focused solutions are supported by emerging technologies. IoT-enabled things and applications use real-time data for smart decision-making. Gartner estimates that the market growth of these things will surpass $20, 4 billion by 2020 (Meulen, 2017). The iOT is also expected to grow at a CAGR of 16.9% globally, reaching around $1,7 trillion in 2020 from about $655,8 billion in 2014 (Mehmood et al., 2017, pp. 16).

The Internet of Things (IoT) is growing and the rise of 5th generation wireless technology, generally referred to as 5G. Computer networks with these latest designs provide incredible speed, low latency and increased capacity while paving the way for a more connected future compared to previous generations as observed (Andrews et al., 2014). 5G has the potential to transformative support several applications including augmented reality, real-time communication and Internet of Everything (IoE). The use of 5G networks enables IoT devices' seamless communication as well as innovative solutions across industries. It also makes it possible to send and receive data at unprecedented speeds thus improving processes in the business world. With the combination of IoT and 5G, the dawn of a new era of connectivity begins, enabling advanced features such as autonomous cars, augmented reality and remote healthcare. Figure 1 shown below represents various IoT components.

Going forward, smart cities represent a crossover of these technological advances, combining IoT gadgets with 5G connectivity to enhance city residing. With increasing urbanization, the idea of clever towns emerges as a complete method to the complicated demanding situations faced via contemporary cities (Caragliu et al., 2011), clever towns are urban regions that use technologies, specially IoT and 5G, to enhance infrastructure, services, and the distribution of products. From clever transportation systems that cater to crowds to information-driven healthcare systems, clever cities feature synergies among technology and concrete design.This imaginative and prescient extends beyond sensor's use of sorts; It focuses on growing an city atmosphere being efficient, sustainable, and cares for the network. As a result, clever cities use records-pushed insights to streamline infrastructure, enhance public services, and improve the general fine of existence for residents.

In six noticeably short years, the usage of Internet of Things (IoT) devices increased surprisingly from 2012 to 2018, increasing from eight.7 billion to an amazing 50.1 billion (Rajendran et al., 2019; Zikria et al., 2019) That increase was huge across sectors but changed into particularly outstanding in factories

Figure 1. Representation of IoT platform

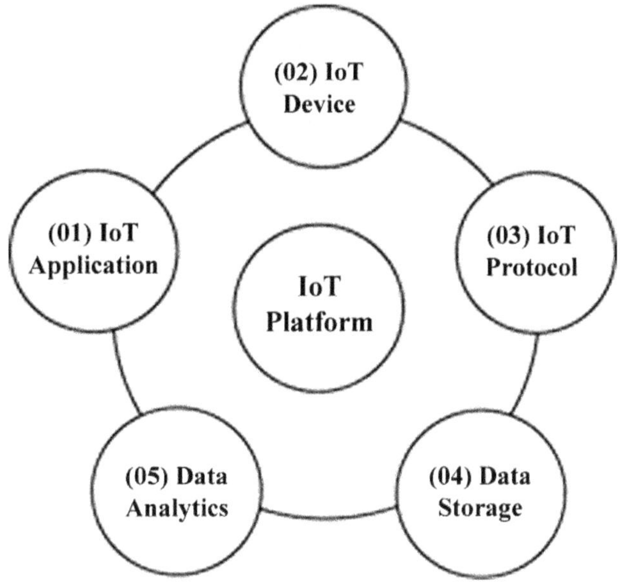

and industries. Although adoption of IoT in homes and retail was surprisingly low throughout this era, big-scale deployments in other industries highlighted the ability of these linked devices (Rajendran et al.).

Smartphones have moved beyond their traditional role as private communique tools and features become crucial for commercial enterprise. The impact of smartphones extends past character advantages, helping to enhance workplace autonomy, verbal exchange, and expertise sharing (Pitichat, 2013) Their integration into enterprise strategies will increase activity delight and productivity, acting as flexible tools that simplifies responsibilities and presents seamless conversation.

Productivity apps have grown to be the dominant organization of applications on customers' smartphones in the place of business (Lellis, 2020). This fashion displays the shift in the use of IoT gadgets for daily business activities, to improve efficiency and agility in extraordinary business environments Given the recognition of the vital position of smartphones, IT extra executives recognize their contributions in updating enterprise procedures and enabling real-time collaboration.

However, the large use of IoT devices within the corporation offers a number of challenges. The increasing reliance on these connected devices has raised concerns about capacity cyber threats, attacks, and exploitation (Xu, Wendt, & Potkonjak, 2014; Yang et al., 2017; Qin et al., 2021; Gebremichael et al., 2020; Kim & Na, 2016; Zhang et.al, 2019a). Connecting extra devices to the Internet creates security vulnerabilities that cybercriminals can be exploited for, ensuing in capacity facts corruption, unauthorized get right of entry to, and compromised communications. It is vital to establish as we adopt the developing fashion of related technologies in enterprises.

The combination of IoT, 5G, and smart towns is going beyond infrastructure and services; It has a profound impact at the day by day lives of people. From green visitors management and electricity-saving buildings to more efficient healthcare systems, clever cities are leveraging IoT and 5G to create a sustainable and linked city environment Real-time the connectivity supplied by using 5G enables IoT devices to immediately supply personalized reports. For example, smart houses with IoT devices can regulate lights, heating, and security settings primarily based on user options, as suggested (Zanella et al., 2014) . Additionally, clever healthcare is leveraging the networking and records processing talents of those technologies for far flung tracking personalized healthcare answers.

In conclusion, the collaboration of the Internet, 5G technology and clever towns heralds a transformational level in our generation adventure. As those traits retain to unfold, their blended effect at the manner we live, paintings and have interaction with our city environments will form the future of societies round the sector. The referred to studies gives a foundational know-how of those technologies and their implications, and serves as a starting point for similarly studies on this dynamic and rapidly evolving field.

The following sections offer a comprehensive knowledge of the IoT foundation, which include its improvement, key capabilities, and programs in numerous industries. This is followed by a detailed evaluation of the software of 5G generation, specializing in its function as a hyperlink between IoT and clever cities after which the dialogue delves into the interaction between IoT and 5G, addressing challenges and the possibilities provided by using this collaboration. Moving ahead, the focal point shifts to smart cities and their classifiers, imparting an in depth evaluation of the man or woman impacts of IoT and 5G on these urban spaces after which the bankruptcy explores ability challenges and analyzes a number of present tasks and programs that meet unique constraints. Conclusion The chapter sets the degree for destiny developments and changes, and gives a forward-looking method to the subject.

FOUNDATION OF IoT

The Internet of Things (IoT) is a paradigm shift that has developed considerably and had a long-lasting effect on many elements of our ordinary lives and industries. This chapter explores the evolution of the Internet of Things historically, explaining its fundamental factors and architectural framework. It additionally examines the diverse uses of IoT in crucial fields, focusing specifically on how deeply integrated it's far in enterprise, healthcare, and agriculture.

Evolution of IoT

The evolution of the Internet of Things (IoT) over the course of several a long time tells a captivating tale of a transformative journey from the initial conception to the extensively allotted networked surroundings that we see today. An modern concept that laid the foundation for the Internet of Things emerged within the overdue 20th century. It was first of all centered at the idea of connecting gadgets to the net. This progressive concept recounted the possibility of device communique, establishing up new avenues for efficiency and automation. This idea's concept signaled the begin of a revolution in how we view and have interaction with technology.

The early ranges of system-to-device conversation became crucial to the improvement of the Internet of Things. This stage marked the start of the Internet of Things (IoT) era by emphasizing the establishment of easy communication among devices without the need for direct human intervention. This helped pave the way for the development of automated structures capable of independent information alternate and undertaking execution.

Key technologies fashioned the course of the Internet of Things. Notably, sensor networks and radio-frequency identity (RFID) stand out as essential pillars. RFID generation have become a key thing for connecting physical objects to the virtual global by means of the usage of radio waves for specific item identity and monitoring. Simultaneously, the growth of IoT competencies turned into further fueled through sensor networks, which are made of networked sensors that accumulate and transmit real-international information (Atzori et al., 2010) .

The historical trajectory of the Internet of Things demonstrates several pivotal moments that demonstrate the gradual integration of IoT concepts into technology. Beginning with simple machine-to-machine communication and progressing to more complex and networked gadgets, the Internet of Things (IoT) is a reflection of a steadfast push towards a more intelligent and connected society. Given that IoT is now a part of many aspects of everyday life, it is critical to acknowledge the innovative ideas, revolutionary discoveries, and incremental advancements that have made IoT go from a theoretical notion to a pervasive reality.

Key Components and Architecture of IoT Systems

Systems for the Internet of Things (IoT) are delicately built to work as a meticulously arranged symphony of separate components, each of which is essential to facilitating smooth communication, data sharing, and the realization of the transformational potential that the IoT promises. In order to provide readers with a knowledge of the dynamic interaction that determines the operation of Internet of Things systems, this section examines the basic components and architectural intricacies of these systems.

Sensors and Actuators

The essential set of sensors and actuators lies at the heart of any Internet of Things system. Sensors gather information from the external environment, including motion, temperature, humidity, and other pertinent factors, acting as the system's eyes and ears. Actuators, on the other hand, translate digital orders into physical actions that enable the Internet of Things system to interact with its physical environment. The vast array of sensors and actuators, which ranges from basic temperature sensors to intricate robotic actuators, is designed to meet the unique requirements of diverse applications.

Communication Protocols

Effective communication is at the heart of Internet of Things systems, and standardizing protocols is crucial to fostering device interoperability. Numerous communication protocols, like MQTT (Message Queuing Telemetry Transport), CoAP (Constrained Application Protocol), and HTTP (Hypertext Transfer Protocol), make it simple for devices to communicate data. Scalability, security, and reliability are ensured by these protocols, which regulate data flow in the Internet of Things network (Zhang et al., 2016).

Edge Computing Devices

The need for efficient data processing is increasing due to the growing volume of data produced by Internet of Things devices. Real-time data processing is made feasible at the network's edge by carefully positioning edge computing devices near to the data source. A decentralized strategy lowers latency, consumes less bandwidth, and improves system efficiency overall (Shi et al., 2016). Analytics apps are frequently housed on edge computing hardware, enabling instantaneous insights without transferring data to centralized cloud servers.

Figure 2. Architecture of IoT central management system
(Aleksandrovičs et al., 2016)

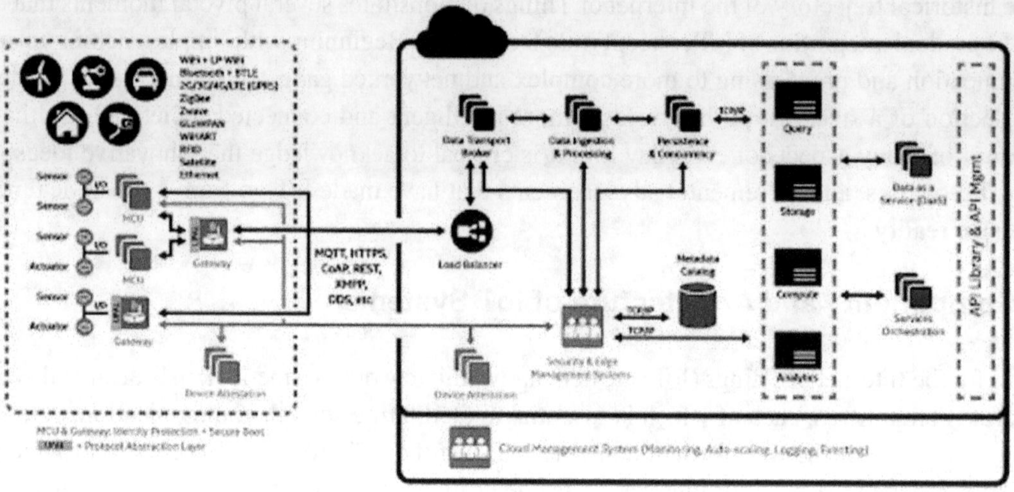

Cloud-Based Platforms

Because cloud computing provides centralized, scalable storage solutions and high processing capability, cloud computing plays a major role in IoT design. Storage facilities for massive volumes of data generated by Internet of Things devices are provided by cloud-based systems. Additionally, they make sophisticated analytics, machine learning, and data processing easier, allowing businesses to get insightful knowledge from the data they acquire (Fernandez-Carames & Fraga-Lamas, 2018).

Figure 2 above illustrates the various parts of the IoT central administration system. The well thought-out relationships between these elements form the foundation of the IoT ecosystem.

According to the results of a study conducted, these components are essential for the creation of a working Internet of Things system that combines data collection, processing, and communication (Li, Da Xu, & Zhao). Moreover, the incorporation of edge computing into the architectural framework (Shi et al.) addresses the novel problems arising from the increasing volume of data in Internet of Things contexts. The Internet of Things systems' architecture is essentially a sophisticated fusion of hardware and software components that are specifically engineered to optimize the capabilities of networked devices. As IoT develops further, the optimisation and enhancement of these architectural elements will have a substantial impact on its future.

However, there is no exact number of layers specified for IoT architecture w.r.t. cloud infrastructure. Below figure 3 represents the number of layers depicted by different researchers:

Here,

L1: The physical layer pertaining to the linked items is the first layer.

L2: The virtualization of linked objects is covered in this layer.

L3: The virtualization infrastructure layer, which covers the many technologies utilized to create virtual objects, is covered in this layer.

L4: The fourth layer deals with how various things are connected to one another and share information.

Figure 3. Rate of Articles Covering Identified Layers
(Bouaouad et al., 2020)

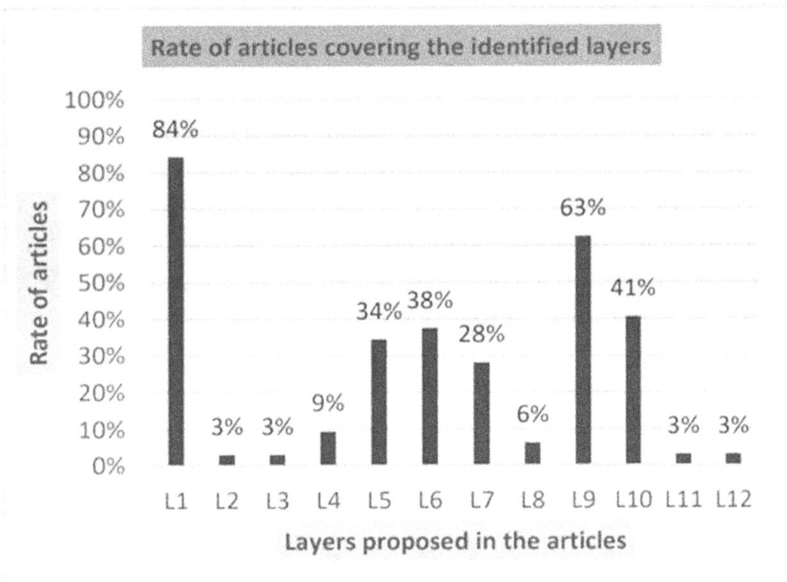

L5: Referring to the many gateways and aggregators that centralize the linked items, the access layer is the fifth layer.

L6: The network layer, which is the sixth layer, maintains communication between the cloud portion and the linked items.

L7: The Middleware layer is the seventh layer, and it is crucial for enabling interoperability via the APIs across the various platforms of the linked objects.

L8: The Business layer, the eighth layer, is in charge of displaying business applications to end users.

L9: The Cloud layer, which makes up the ninth layer, is responsible for processing, storing, and analyzing the data that is returned by the IoT component.

L10: The Application layer (Xu, Wendt, & Potkonjak), the tenth layer, gives the user the services and apps he needs to fulfill his demands;

L11: The application layer for virtualization is the eleventh layer;

L12: The twelfth layer comprises apps that are especially designed to meet the demands of the user about security and access control.

Thereby, a generic architecture should always be a requirement and further can be utilized to build context-specific architectures (Bouaouad et al.).

Examples of IoT Applications in Various Domains

i. Healthcare:

The healthcare business has entered a revolutionary period marked by the Internet of Things (IoT), which has revolutionized patient care, monitoring, and administration. By gathering real-time health data, wearable technology such as smartwatches and fitbits has become an essential tool for proactive health management. IoT is also critical to remote patient monitoring systems since it allows medical staff to respond promptly when needed and allows continuous vital sign tracking (Majeed, 2018).

ii. Agriculture:

Traditional agricultural methods have drastically transformed as a result of Internet of Things (IoT) enabled solutions in agriculture. Field-installed smart sensors detect critical data including soil moisture content and meteorological conditions. Then, with the aid of the real-time data collected, crop yields are raised and resource utilization is optimized. Precision agricultural techniques facilitated by the Internet of Things (IoT) allow farmers to make data-driven choices, reducing water wastage and promoting sustainable farming practices (Gubbi et al., 2013).

iii. Industry (IIoT - Industrial Internet of Things):

One major factor boosting operating efficiency in the industrial sector is the Industrial Internet of Things, or IIoT. A few examples of how Internet of Things applications facilitate industrial processes include predictive maintenance systems, smart logistics systems to optimize supply chain management, and sensor-machine links for real-time performance data collecting. Industry 4.0, which leverages IoT-enabled smart factories to automate intelligently, cannot be realized without these apps (Lee, Bagheri, & Kao, 2015).

iv. Smart Cities:

IoT is a natural fit for the concept of smart cities as it can be used for efficient waste disposal, intelligent transportation systems, and intelligent grid management. By using networked devices and systems, smart cities seek to reduce their negative environmental effects, raise overall living standards, and enhance urban living (Caragliu).

v. Retail:

Traditional retail business models have fundamentally transformed as a result of IoT applications. These applications include consumer insights to customize shopping experiences, networked sensor-based inventory management, and innovative ideas to boost overall retail efficiency (Perera et al., 2014).

vi. Energy:

IoT applications are essential to the energy sector's efforts to construct smart grids, monitor energy use, and deploy demand response systems. This results in more affordable energy consumption, improved grid management, and higher sustainability (Syed et al., 2021).

vii. Transportation:

Because it provides technologies like networked transportation systems, traffic control, and vehicle monitoring, the Internet of Things is crucial to the transportation industry. These apps seek to improve traffic flow, boost safety, and offer practical solutions for public transport (Truong, Dohler, & Charbonnier, 2013).

viii. Education:

Applications of IoT in education include smart classroom development, campus administration systems, and student tracking. These advancements facilitate the creation of a more coherent and productive learning environment (Khedekar & Murthy, 2015).

ix. Home Automation:

Smart thermostats, security systems, and linked appliances are a few examples of IoT uses in home automation. This enhances convenience, energy efficiency, and overall house management (Atzori et al.).

x. Environmental Monitoring:

Applications for the Internet of Things are used to track animals and keep an eye on the quality of the air and water in the environment. Both environmental preservation and sustainable resource management are aided by these uses (Silva, Khan, & Han, 2019).

The cited studies highlight the flexibility and transformative potential of this technology across a variety of sectors by describing the distinct contributions and benefits of IoT applications in each of these disciplines.

Flexible components with a long history and intricate topologies form the foundation of the Internet of Things. Meanwhile, IoT's practical applications in industry, healthcare, and agriculture show how transformative technology can be across a range of industries. The IoT foundation is changing as we go further into the areas of connection, data exchange, and intelligent decision-making.

5G TECHNOLOGY: CONNECTING ENDS

The introduction of 5G technology represents a significant advancement in wireless communication and has the capacity to fundamentally alter how we connect, interact, and utilize technology. 5G, in contrast to its predecessors, is a paradigm change with revolutionary capabilities that go beyond incremental gains and basic speed boosts. 5G, which is being hailed as the next big thing in wireless technology, promises to improve connection overall and deliver quicker data rates. Enhanced performance, reduced latency, and simultaneous support for many devices are all included in this comprehensive perspective.

One important differentiator of 5G networks is their capacity to operate over three distinct frequency bands, each of which is intended to meet a certain set of connection needs. Low-band technology may be utilized to reach isolated and rural locations because of its extensive coverage. The mid-band balances speed and coverage, making it versatile in both urban and suburban environments. Because high-band, also known as millimeter-wave, or mmWave, spectrum provides outstanding data speeds over shorter distances, it is most suitable for highly populated metropolitan regions (Boccardi et al., 2014). Because of its trifold band structure, 5G offers a versatile and adaptive network architecture that can handle a wide range of connection demands in a wide range of scenarios.

Figure 4. 5G Challenge, Facilitators, and Design Fundamental
(Gupta & Jha, 2015)

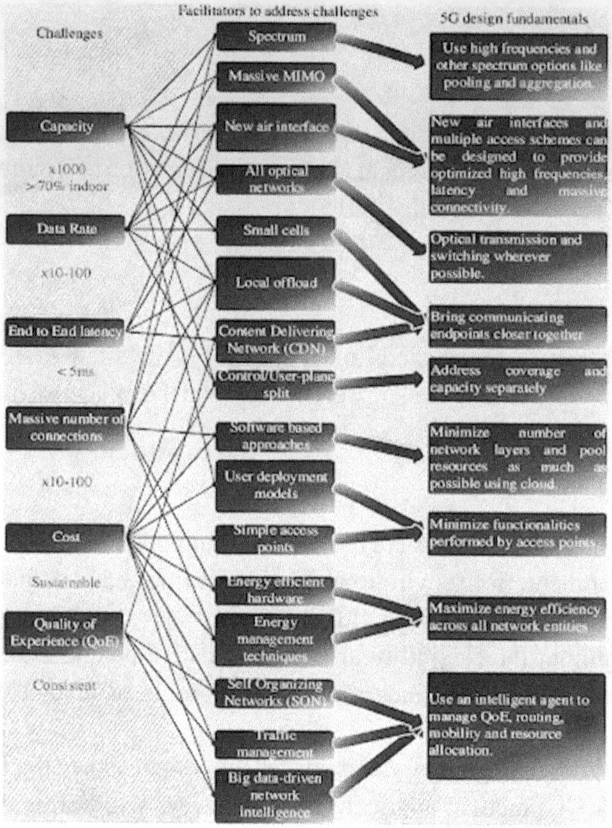

In the low band, 5G demonstrates a long-range capability that offers wide coverage even in challenging-to-reach areas. With its balanced approach, the mid-band achieves a harmonic balance between coverage and speed, ensuring stable connectivity in both urban and suburban contexts. However, only in a limited region will 5G attain hitherto unheard-of data speeds because of the high-band mmWave spectrum. This separation of frequency bands demonstrates the flexibility of 5G, which allows it to satisfy a range of connectivity requirements in a number of contexts (Park et al., 2021).

The versatility of 5G extends beyond its frequency spectrum. The technology introduces advanced antenna technologies, such as massive MIMO (Multiple Input, Multiple Output), which combines numerous antennas for simultaneous data transmission and reception. Massive MIMO enhances spectral efficiency, enabling 5G networks to manage several connections concurrently. This reduces interference and boosts network dependability by enabling focused and efficient signal transmission when paired with beamforming methods.

5G networks mark a paradigm shift in the evolution of wireless communication. 5G sets itself apart with its trifold band structure and state-of-the-art antenna technology, making it a versatile and adaptable connection solution. Global rollout of 5G is anticipated to continue, with its revolutionary capabilities poised to transform industries, allow cutting-edge apps, and provide customers an unparalleled wireless experience (Park et al.).

The aforementioned graphic illustrates the challenges that 5G must surmount, the tactics employed to assist them, and the architecture of the system. The issues include those related to capacity, data rate, large numbers of connections, end-to-end latency, cost, and Quality of Experience (QoE). Facilitators are established to overcome these problems, and the 5G system is developed using the specified current facilities.

Comparison With Previous Generations of Wireless Technology

When comparing 5G to its predecessors, especially 4G LTE, the level of progress is apparent. While 4G brought about considerable improvements in data speeds, 5G pushes this development to unprecedented levels. Data transmission speeds, latency, and capacity are the primary forces behind this advancement. With data speeds that may exceed gigabits per second, latency that is reduced to milliseconds, and the capacity to connect a large number of devices in a given area, 5G performs better than its predecessors (Andrews et al.). This makes 5G the cornerstone of a new age of connectivity that breaks free from the limitations of previous wireless technologies.

Implications of 5G for IoT Applications

5G has a huge and revolutionary impact on Internet of Things (IoT) applications. 5G networks' increased speed and exceptionally low latency open up new possibilities for IoT devices, particularly when responsiveness in real time is critical. Sectors that stand to benefit greatly include manufacturing, healthcare, and autonomous car technology. In the healthcare industry, for example, 5G enables real-time and extremely precise patient monitoring as well as remote surgeries (Bennis et al., 2018). The synchronization of machines and processes in manufacturing can reach previously unheard-of levels, greatly increasing productivity and efficiency. The scalability issues that prior generations faced are also addressed by 5G's greater capacity, which is important given the exponential growth in the number of connected devices in our increasingly interconnected world.

In conclusion, 5G technology is a revolutionary connectivity enabler rather than merely a minor improvement. Its revolutionary qualities raise the bar for Internet of Things applications and portend a time when connectedness and real-time communication will revolutionize markets and improve everyday life.

Synergy Between IoT and 5G

The convergence of 5G and the Internet of Things (IoT) presents a game-changing opportunity for connectivity, data sharing, and technological advancement. The Internet of Things (IoT) depends on seamless communication between various devices, and 5G, the fifth generation of wireless technology, provides the best infrastructure to support this networked environment. This partnership isn't just additive; rather, it's synergistic, meaning that each technology's strengths enhance and complement the other's potential.

5G improves IoT device connectivity through a number of crucial mechanisms. First of all, it offers much faster data transfer rates, allowing Internet of Things devices to send and receive data at previously unheard-of speeds. 5G's low latency guarantees nearly instantaneous communication, which is essential for applications like remote healthcare monitoring as well as autonomous cars that require real-time responsiveness (Andrews et al.). Moreover, 5G's broad device connectivity capabilities enable the concurrent connection of a large number of IoT devices within a designated area, resolving a major issue that previous wireless technology generations encountered.

Several examples demonstrate the effective use of 5G-powered IoT. 5G's high data transfer rates and low latency are used in health care facilities for remote patient monitoring, which allow medical professionals to monitor patients' vital signs in real-time and respond quickly (Bennis et al., 2018; Zhang et al., 2019b). 5G-enabled IoT applications are advantageous for the manufacturing industry, as smart factories use connected devices to improve productivity and streamline production processes.

However, this convergence also offers hitherto unseen possibilities. 5G's low latency and fast data rates make it possible for creative applications across a range of industries, from the creation of smart cities to augmented reality in education. 5G's smooth connectivity between IoT devices creates opportunities for increased automation, efficiency, and well-being. As these technologies progress, tackling obstacles and seizing chances, IoT and 5G convergence will be crucial in determining the direction of connectivity in the future, bringing in an era of never-before-seen opportunities and breakthroughs.

SMART CITIES: IDEA AND COMPONENTS

Smart cities are the embodiment of an all-encompassing urban development strategy that leverages technology and data-driven solutions to improve sustainability, efficiency, and the general quality of life for their citizens. Information and communication technologies (ICT) are used in these cities to optimize utilities, services, and infrastructure. Smart cities' core characteristics include using data and technology to improve mobility, sustainability, governance, and the overall well-being of residents (Caragliu).

Key Components of a Smart City Infrastructure (Sensors, Data Analytics, Connectivity)

Sensors

A network of sensors positioned carefully throughout the urban landscape is essential to smart cities. These sensors collect data in real time on a variety of parameters, including waste management, energy consumption, traffic flow, and air quality. Effective resource management and well-informed decision-making are predicated on this data (Caragliu).

Data Analytics

Advanced data analytics tools are used to process and analyze the gathered data. This helps city officials to see trends, obtain new perspectives, and make data-driven choices. Proactive urban planning is made possible by the use of predictive analytics to foresee needs and obstacles in the future (Manyika et al., 2013).

Connectivity

For smart cities to function, they require a reliable and fast connectivity infrastructure. To ensure seamless communication between devices and systems, this calls for the deployment of 5G technology in addition to high-speed broadband. The real-time exchange of data, which is necessary for the efficient operation of smart city operations, is based on connectivity (Boccardi et al.).

In Singapore, the Smart Nation Initiative integrates technology and data to elevate urban living, employing sensors for environmental monitoring, efficient energy management, and intelligent transportation systems (Yuen & Jiang, 2019). Meanwhile, Barcelona has established a comprehensive smart city infrastructure with widespread Wi-Fi hotspots, integrated waste management sensors, and smart lighting systems, utilizing data analytics to enhance traffic flow and public services (Nam & Pardo, 2011). South Korea's Songdo, a green and smart city, prioritizes sustainability with advanced technologies in waste management, energy efficiency, and smart building construction, facilitated by an extensive sensor network (Lee & Lee, 2015). Copenhagen employs smart traffic management systems to optimize transport effectiveness, monitoring traffic flow, adjusting signal timings, and enhancing overall mobility through sensors and real-time data analytics (Jensen et al., 2015). In Dubai, the Smart Dubai Initiative aims to position the city as a global leader in smart city innovation, encompassing projects such as blockchain technology for secure transactions, e-governance, and smart transportation (Alawadhi & Aldama-Nalda, 2019).

Therefore, smart cities represent a paradigm-shifting approach to urban planning, fusing data and technology to create more sustainable, efficient, and livable urban environments. The potential of these technologies in addressing urban challenges and improving the quality of life for residents is highlighted by the global success of smart city initiatives.

IoT IN SMART CITIES

The integration of Internet of Things (IoT) devices and sensors into smart cities represents a paradigm shift in the organization and design of urban spaces. With sensors built in and a network connecting them, Internet of Things (IoT) devices create a dynamic ecosystem that can gather and process data in real time. This network of interconnected devices, strategically placed throughout urban environments, provides a comprehensive view of city operations. Within the transportation sector, smart cities make use of IoT-enabled sensors to monitor traffic patterns, enhance signal timings, and enhance overall mobility. Roads, traffic lights, and automobiles all incorporate these sensors to create a seamless network that makes real-time traffic management possible (Zanella et al.). Below mentioned are a few roles of IoT in smart cities that are needed.

Traffic Management

A key component of traffic management optimization is the use of IoT devices. Sensor-equipped intelligent traffic lights modify their signal timings in response to current traffic conditions. By averting collisions, vehicle-to-vehicle communication improves safety, and intelligent parking systems direct cars to open spots, which eases traffic.

Waste Management

IoT-enabled waste bin sensors track fill levels and improve waste collection routes. As a result, operating expenses are reduced and resources are used more effectively. Urban environments can become cleaner and more sustainable by allowing cities to adapt dynamically to the demand for waste collection services.

Public Safety

IoT devices are essential for improving public safety because they provide real-time response and monitoring systems. IoT-enabled surveillance cameras can recognise unexpected activity or emergencies, allowing emergency services or law enforcement to react quickly. Additionally, by ensuring well-lit areas and adapting to changing environmental conditions, smart street lighting with sensors can improve public safety.

IoT integration transforms urban environments by increasing overall efficiency and optimizing services. The potential advantages of a connected and data-driven urban landscape are substantial, contributing to more sustainable, livable, and resilient cities, even though addressing issues like security and interoperability is crucial (Perera et al.).

IMPACT OF 5G ON SMART CITIES

5G, in contrast to its predecessors, supports a large number of connected devices at once, dramatically lowers latency, and offers faster data speeds. These qualities support smart city projects in a number of ways.

Enhanced Connectivity and Communication Infrastructure

Better connection in smart cities is made possible by 5G. Because of the technology's faster data transfer speeds and lower latency, real-time communication between devices is made possible, allowing for quick and effective decision-making. The vast network capacity of 5G meets the needs of connectivity for a multitude of sensors, devices, and applications placed all over the city (Boccardi et al.).

Smart Traffic Management

5G enables real-time traffic condition monitoring via a network of cameras and sensors. Instantaneous processing of this data allows for dynamic rerouting to reduce congestion and adaptive traffic signal control. The ability of vehicles with 5G connectivity to communicate with one another improves safety and traffic flow overall (Andrews et al.).

Public Safety and Surveillance

By enabling high-resolution video surveillance and analytics, 5G enhances public safety. In an emergency, 5G-capable surveillance cameras allow for quicker response times. Furthermore, real-time data exchange makes it easier for first responders to coordinate, improving public safety as a whole (Andrews et al.).

Smart Infrastructure Maintenance

5G makes it easier to install Internet of Things sensors to keep an eye on the state of vital infrastructure, like roads and bridges. Real-time detection of anomalies and structural problems by these sensors lowers the likelihood of failures and allows for proactive maintenance.

IoT-enabled Smart Grids

Within the utilities sector, 5G makes it easier to integrate IoT devices into smart grids. By improving resource management, optimizing energy use, and facilitating the integration of renewable energy sources, these devices improve the monitoring and control of energy distribution.

EXISTING PROJECTS AND THEIR COMPARISON

Cisco Kinetic for Cities

Cisco Kinetic for Cities is a notable IoT project, offering a unified platform designed for data aggregation, processing, and application enablement in smart cities. The platform leverages edge computing to process data closer to the source, reducing latency and enhancing real-time decision-making capabilities. This approach ensures scalability and interoperability, allowing seamless integration with Cisco's networking infrastructure (Cisco Kinetic for Cities, n.d.).

IBM Watson IoT for Smart Cities

IBM Watson IoT for Smart Cities is distinguished by its use of artificial intelligence and machine learning algorithms to analyze extensive datasets generated by city sensors. The platform employs edge computing strategies to process data locally, minimizing the need for extensive cloud processing and enhancing efficiency. With its integration capabilities and support for various IoT devices, IBM Watson IoT offers a comprehensive solution for smart city development (IBM Watson IoT for Smart Cities, n.d.).

Siemens City Performance Tool

Siemens City Performance Tool takes a modular approach, incorporating advanced analytics and simulation models to address urban challenges. Integrated with Siemens MindSphere, an industrial IoT platform, the tool facilitates data storage, analytics, and connectivity in real-time. The modular design enhances adaptability, allowing cities to tailor the solution to their specific requirements (Siemens City Performance Tool, n.d.).

Microsoft Azure IoT for Smart Cities

Microsoft Azure IoT for Smart Cities leverages cloud-based services for data storage, analytics, and application development. Using Azure IoT Hub for device connectivity and Azure Stream Analytics for real-time data processing, Microsoft's platform demonstrates scalability and global reach. Azure Digital Twins further enhances the platform's capabilities by allowing the creation of virtual models for simulation and analysis (Microsoft Azure IoT for Smart Cities, n.d.).

Barcelona's Smart City Initiatives

Barcelona's smart city initiatives involve an extensive deployment of sensors and smart meters powered by low-power wide-area networks (LPWAN) like LoRaWAN. These technologies enable real-time monitoring of waste levels, parking spaces, and lighting conditions, contributing to effective urban management. The integration of LPWAN ensures efficient and cost-effective communication among devices across the city (Barcelona's Smart City Initiatives, n.d.).

Singapore's Smart Nation Initiative

Singapore's Smart Nation Initiative integrates various cutting-edge technologies, including the Internet of Things, artificial intelligence, and data analytics. The city-state emphasizes the adoption of 5G and a robust network infrastructure to support an array of connected devices. The use of sensors and smart devices across sectors such as transportation and healthcare demonstrates a commitment to data-driven decision-making for urban development (Singapore's Smart Nation Initiative, n.d.).

Amsterdam Smart City

Amsterdam Smart City prioritizes sustainability and citizen engagement, employing technologies like smart grids, IoT devices, and mobile applications. The city utilizes smart grids for efficient energy management, IoT devices for environmental monitoring, and mobile applications to encourage citizen participation. The integration of various data sources, including social media and open data, contributes to a holistic understanding of urban dynamics (Amsterdam Smart City, n.d.).

Common Technological Challenges Across Projects

Despite the technological advancements in these smart city projects, common challenges persist. Ensuring interoperability standards among diverse IoT devices, implementing robust security measures, optimizing edge computing, and establishing privacy mechanisms to safeguard citizen data are critical challenges that require ongoing attention. Addressing these challenges is essential to the continued success and sustainability of smart city initiatives globally (Cisco Kinetic for Cities; IBM Watson IoT for Smart Cities; Siemens City Performance Tool; Microsoft Azure IoT for Smart Cities; Barcelona's Smart City Initiatives; Singapore's Smart Nation Initiative; Amsterdam Smart City, n.d.)

CHALLENGES AND CONSIDERATIONS IN DEPLOYMENT

Security and Privacy Concerns

Complex security and privacy issues are introduced by the combination of 5G, IoT, and smart city technologies. Because of their wide network of interconnectedness, these devices are attractive targets for cyberattacks due to the potential vulnerabilities they present. Protecting data from malicious activities and unauthorized access requires ensuring its confidentiality, integrity, and availability.

Table 1. Projects and research addressing IoT key challenges (Shah & Yaqoob, 2016)

IoT Challenge	Project/Protocols
Architecture	IoT-A, IoT @ Work, EBBITS, BETaaS, CALIPSO, VITAL, SENSEI
Availability	-
Reliability	PERUM, RELY on IT
Mobility	IoT6, Open IoT, APEC IoV
Performance	Smart Santander, RELY on IT
Management	OMA Device Management (OMA-DM), LWM2M, NETCONF Light, Kura, MASHPlatform
Scalability	IoT-iCore, IoT6, SENSEI
Interoperability	IoT-iCore, PROBE-IT, Open IoT, Link Smart
Security and Privacy	IETF SOLACE, BUTLER, Codo, SVELTE

Regulatory Challenges and Policy Considerations

The deployment of 5G, IoT, and smart city technologies presents regulatory challenges related to data governance, spectrum allocation, and interoperability standards. To maintain fair competition, defend consumer rights, and handle matters like data ownership and cross-border data flows, regulatory frameworks must change to keep up with the rapidly evolving nature of these technologies (Chourabi et al., 2012).

Environmental Considerations

Environmental challenges may arise from the widespread use of IoT devices and the deployment of 5G infrastructure. Electronic waste (e-waste) is a result of the production, use, and disposal of electronic devices. Furthermore, questions concerning sustainability are raised by the energy consumption of the data centers that power these technologies. Smart cities that are both technologically cutting edge and environmentally sustainable must strike a balance between environmental responsibility and technological advancement (Williams, 2019).

Ethical Considerations

Concerns about consent, privacy, and surveillance are raised by the collection and use of large amounts of data in smart cities. Ensuring the protection of citizens' rights and freedoms requires the implementation of strong policies and transparent, ethical data management practices. Building trust in smart city initiatives requires striking a balance between the benefits of data-driven technologies and ethical considerations (Kitchin, 2016).

In addition to the challenges mentioned above, the following are some of the IoT challenges related to the projects/protocols employed.

Therefore, addressing security, privacy, regulatory, environmental, and ethical issues is critical to the effective deployment and long-term expansion of 5G, IoT, and smart city technologies. To overcome these obstacles and guarantee that the advantages of these technologies are used responsibly, a thorough and multidisciplinary strategy involving technology developers, legislators, and the general public is required.

CONCLUSION AND FUTURE DIRECTIONS

In summary, the convergence of 5G technology, smart cities, and the Internet of Things heralds a significant revolution in urban development. Populations in cities around the world are increasing at an accelerated rate, and this trend is predicted to continue for some time. People moving to cities in search of the many benefits of urban living are the cause of this demographic shift from rural to urban areas. The growing number of people living in cities necessitates the extension and possible enhancement of current public infrastructure and services to handle this influx. Urban planners will therefore have to work hard to come up with practical ways to meet the changing needs of city dwellers while raising living standards all around.

With the help of 5G connectivity's wide range of capabilities, the integration of IoT devices turns cities into dynamic ecosystems driven by real-time data insights. Smart cities use this integration to improve governance, maximize services, and raise the standard of living for citizens. A significant amount of research is still required to handle IoT concerns including privacy, edge computing, cloud computing, participatory sensing, energy efficiency, and visualization, according to the study of the papers. This calls for ongoing cooperation between governmental agencies, commercial enterprises, and academic institutions. To support the Internet of Things, more attention should be paid to creating smart city infrastructures. In the near future, IoT will also have a significant impact on human behaviors and physical well-being. Thus, while planning, designing, and implementing IoT-based technologies, it is crucial to take their social effects on people and communities into account.

REFERENCES

Alawadhi, S., & Aldama-Nalda, A. (2019). The impact of smart city applications on the quality of life in Smart Dubai city. *Telematics and Informatics*, *44*, 101271.

Aleksandrovičs, V., Filičevs, E., & Kampars, J. (2016). Internet of things: Structure, features and management. *Information Technology and Management Science*, *19*(1), 78–84. doi:10.1515/itms-2016-0015

Andrews, J. G., Buzzi, S., Choi, W., Hanly, S. V., Lozano, A., Soong, A. C. K., & Zhang, J. C. (2014). What will 5G be? *IEEE Journal on Selected Areas in Communications*, *32*(6), 1065–1082. doi:10.1109/JSAC.2014.2328098

Atzori, L., Iera, A., & Morabito, G. (2010). The Internet of Things: A survey. *Computer Networks*, *54*(15), 2787–2805. doi:10.1016/j.comnet.2010.05.010

Bennis, M., Taleb, T., & Debbah, M. (2018). Ultra-reliable and low latency wireless communication: Tail, risk, and scale. *Proceedings of the IEEE*, *106*(10), 1834–1853. doi:10.1109/JPROC.2018.2867029

Boccardi, F., Heath, R. W., Lozano, A., Marzetta, T. L., & Popovski, P. (2014). Five disruptive technology directions for 5G. *IEEE Communications Magazine*, *52*(2), 74–80. doi:10.1109/MCOM.2014.6736746

Bouaouad, A. E., Cherradi, A., Assoul, S., & Souissi, N. (2020). The key layers of IoT architecture. In *2020 5th International Conference on Cloud Computing and Artificial Intelligence: Technologies and Applications (CloudTech)* (pp. 1-4). IEEE. 10.1109/CloudTech49835.2020.9365919

Caragliu, A., Del Bo, C., & Nijkamp, P. (2011). Smart cities in Europe. *Journal of Urban Technology, 18*(2), 65–82. doi:10.1080/10630732.2011.601117

Chourabi, H., Nam, T., Walker, S., Gil-Garcia, J. R., Mellouli, S., Nahon, K., & Scholl, H. J. (2012). Understanding smart cities: An integrative framework. *2012 45th Hawaii international conference on system sciences* (pp. 2289-2297). IEEE.

Fernandez-Carames, T. M., & Fraga-Lamas, P. (2018). A review on the use of blockchain for the Internet of Things. *IEEE Access : Practical Innovations, Open Solutions*, *6*, 32979–33001. doi:10.1109/ACCESS.2018.2842685

Gebremichael, T., Ledwaba, L. P., Eldefrawy, M. H., Hancke, G. P., Pereira, N., Gidlund, M., & Akerberg, J. (2020). Security and privacy in the industrial internet of things: Current standards and future challenges. *IEEE Access : Practical Innovations, Open Solutions*, *8*, 152351–152366. doi:10.1109/ACCESS.2020.3016937

Gubbi, J., Buyya, R., Marusic, S., & Palaniswami, M. (2013). Internet of Things (IoT): A review. *Future Generation Computer Systems*, *29*(7), 1645–1660. doi:10.1016/j.future.2013.01.010

Gupta, A., & Jha, R. K. (2015). A survey of 5G network: Architecture and emerging technologies. *IEEE Access : Practical Innovations, Open Solutions*, *3*, 1206–1232. doi:10.1109/ACCESS.2015.2461602

Jensen, C. S., Toftkjær, T., Larsen, A., & Hansen, T. R. (2015). Smart City in a box: Understanding strategic approaches to the smart city concept. In *2015 48th Hawaii international conference on system sciences* (pp. 2334-2343). IEEE.

Khedekar, I., & Murthy, G. (2015). Internet of Things: A new backbone for education system. *Procedia Computer Science*, *45*, 545–551.

Kim, S., & Na, W. (2016). Safe data transmission architecture based on cloud for Internet of Things. *Wireless Personal Communications*, *86*(1), 287–300. doi:10.1007/s11277-015-3063-1

Kitchin, R. (2016). The ethics of smart cities and urban science. *Philosophical Transactions. Series A, Mathematical, Physical, and Engineering Sciences*, *374*(2083), 20160115. doi:10.1098/rsta.2016.0115 PMID:28336794

Lee, I., Bagheri, B., & Kao, H. A. (2015). A Cyber-Physical Systems architecture for Industry 4.0-based manufacturing systems. *Manufacturing Letters*, *3*, 18–23. doi:10.1016/j.mfglet.2014.12.001

Lee, J. Y., & Lee, J. H. (2015). A study on the planning process of ubiquitous city and the case of Songdo IBD in South Korea. *Habitat International*, *46*, 118–125.

Lellis, R. (2020). *How IT leaders are turning to employee experience in 2020.* CIO Dive. [Online Article]

Li, S., Da Xu, L., & Zhao, S. (2015). The Internet of Things: A survey. *Information Systems Frontiers*, *17*(2), 243–259. doi:10.1007/s10796-014-9492-7

Majeed, M. (2018). Internet of Things (IoT) applications in healthcare: A review. *Journal of King Saud University. Computer and Information Sciences.*

Manyika, J., Chui, M., Brown, B., Bughin, J., Dobbs, R., Roxburgh, C., & Byers, A. H. (2013). *Big data: The next frontier for innovation, competition, and productivity*. McKinsey Global Institute.

Mehmood, Y., Ahmad, F., Yaqoob, I., Adnane, A., Imran, M., & Guizani, S. (2017). Internet-of-things-based smart cities: Recent advances and challenges. *IEEE Communications Magazine*, *55*(9), 16–24. doi:10.1109/MCOM.2017.1600514

Meulen, R. (2017). *Gartner says 8.4 billion connected "things" will be in use in 2017, up 31 percent from 2016*. Gartner. gartner.com/en/newsroom/press-releases/2017-02-07-gartner-says-8-billion-connected-things-will-be-in-use-in-2017-up-31-percent-from-2016

Nam, T., & Pardo, T. A. (2011). Conceptualizing smart city with dimensions of technology, people, and institutions. In *Proceedings of the 12th Annual International Digital Government Research Conference: Digital Government Innovation in Challenging Times* (pp. 282-291). ACM. 10.1145/2037556.2037602

Park JH, Rathore S, Singh SK, Salim MM, Azzaoui AE, Kim TW, Pan Y, Park JH. A comprehensive survey on core technologies and services for 5G security: Taxonomies, issues, and solutions. Hum.-Centric Comput. Inf. Sci. 2021 Jan 29;11(3).

Perera, C., Zaslavsky, A., Christen, P., & Georgakopoulos, D. (2014). Context Aware Computing for The Internet of Things: A Survey. *IEEE Communications Surveys and Tutorials*, *16*(1), 414–454. doi:10.1109/SURV.2013.042313.00197

Pitichat, T. (2013). Smartphones in the workplace: Changing organizational behavior, transforming the future. *LUX: A Journal of Transdisciplinary Writing and Research from Claremont Graduate University*, *3*(1), 13.

Qin, X., Huang, Y., Yang, Z., & Li, X. (2021). LBAC: A lightweight blockchain-based access control scheme for the internet of things. *Information Sciences*, *554*, 222–235. doi:10.1016/j.ins.2020.12.035

Rajendran, G., Nivash, R. R., Parthy, P. P., & Balamurugan, S. (2019, October). Modern security threats in the Internet of Things (IoT): Attacks and Countermeasures. In *2019 International Carnahan Conference on Security Technology (ICCST)* (pp. 1-6). IEEE. 10.1109/CCST.2019.8888399

Shah, S. H., & Yaqoob, I. (2016). A survey: Internet of Things (IOT) technologies, applications and challenges. *2016 IEEE Smart Energy Grid Engineering (SEGE),* (pp. 381-385). IEEE.

Shi, W., Dustdar, S., & Pan, Y. (2016). Edge computing: Vision and challenges. *IEEE Internet of Things Journal*, *3*(5), 637–646. doi:10.1109/JIOT.2016.2579198

Silva, B. M., Khan, M. A., & Han, K. (2019). *Environmental Internet of Things: Building Smart Environmental Management Systems*. Springer.

Syed, A. S., Sierra-Sosa, D., Kumar, A., & Elmaghraby, A. (2021). IoT in smart cities: A survey of technologies, practices and challenges. *Smart Cities*, *4*(2), 429–475. doi:10.3390/smartcities4020024

Truong, H. L., Dohler, M., & Charbonnier, D. (2013). Low-cost and highly scalable urban transportation: A market-oriented approach. *IEEE Communications Magazine*, *51*(12), 36–43.

Williams, K. (2019). *Smart cities and climate change: Digital low carbon cities*. Routledge.

Xu, T., Wendt, J. B., & Potkonjak, M. (2014, November). Security of IoT systems: Design challenges and opportunities. In *2014 IEEE/ACM International Conference on Computer-Aided Design (ICCAD)* (pp. 417-423). IEEE. 10.1109/ICCAD.2014.7001385

Yang, Y., Wu, L., Yin, G., Li, L., & Zhao, H. (2017). A survey on security and privacy issues in Internet-of-Things. *IEEE Internet of Things Journal*, *4*(5), 1250–1258. doi:10.1109/JIOT.2017.2694844

Yuen, B., & Jiang, Y. (2019). Singapore's smart nation initiative: A critical perspective. *Cities (London, England)*, *87*, 80–90.

Zanella, A., Bui, N., Castellani, A., Vangelista, L., & Zorzi, M. (2014). Internet of things for smart cities. *IEEE Internet of Things Journal*, *1*(1), 22–32. doi:10.1109/JIOT.2014.2306328

Zhang, P., Yang, X., Chen, J., & Huang, Y. (2019). A survey of testing for 5G: Solutions, opportunities, and challenges. *China Communications*, *16*(1), 69–85.

Zhang, Y., Zhang, J., Chen, W., & You, I. (2016). A survey on the edge computing for the Internet of Things. *IEEE Access : Practical Innovations, Open Solutions*, *4*, 2169–2179.

Zhang, Y., Zhang, J., Chen, W., & You, I. (2019). Security and privacy in the era of IoT and 5G: Challenges and solutions. *IEEE Internet of Things Journal*, *6*(3), 1606–1616.

Zikria, Y. B., Kim, S. W., Hahm, O., Afzal, M. K., & Aalsalem, M. Y. (2019). Internet of Things (IoT) operating systems management: Opportunities, challenges, and solution. *Sensors (Basel)*, *19*(8), 1793. doi:10.3390/s19081793 PMID:30991658

Chapter 2
Emergence of Federated and Deep Learning for Smart City

Shashi
CCS University, Meerut, India

Vasu Kumar Rana
CCS University, Meerut, India

ABSTRACT

Federated and deep learning are changing every field in today's era; these technologies are making devices, citizens, homes, buildings, cars, etc. Before these technologies, we used normal machine learning that has some cons. To counter those cons, federated and deep learning emerged. Federated and deep learning work on the same concept of machine learning, but with advanced methods. Using these technologies, we make work easier; and companies are using them to enhance their productivity, to grow the business, etc. Current smart city applications offer various facilities to ensure more effective, time-saving services like traffic management, environmental and public safety and security, energy management, healthcare services, etc. The smart city's components first collect data by using different IoT and other sensors. It requires processing the data to perform several actions to achieve the system's benefits. Deep learning and federated learning methods that use artificial intelligence to make cities smarter. In this chapter, the authors explore the cons of normal machine learning, and what the roles are of federated learning and deep learning in the making of cities smarter, as well as what is needed and how these technologies work.

INTRODUCTION

A city is called a smart city if the infra of the city is smart, transport is smart, smart mobility, smart healthcare, smart technology and smart citizen etc. To make all these things smarter we need the technology like machine learning, deep learning, federated learning, computer vision, NLP but the emergence of federated and deep learning becomes more important because AI models trained on millions of data points from sensors, smart phones, and cameras across the city, but without ever collecting raw data

DOI: 10.4018/979-8-3693-2373-1.ch002

from individuals. That's federated learning, like a city brain learning from its citizens without invading their privacy. Deep learning then takes the reins, processing this vast, decentralized knowledge to predict traffic jams, optimize energy grids, and even anticipate crimes (Lin et al., 2017). It's a potent cocktail of privacy-preserving insights and powerful AI, paving the way for smarter, safer, and more livable urban landscapes. Get ready for the evolution of smart cities, where federated and deep learning join forces to shape the future of urban living.

Background and Related Work

Federated Learning

Federated learning is also known as collaborative learning. it is also a part of machine learning. The role of federated learning in a smart city is very important because it optimize various fields, federated learning learns patterns form the different areas by using their corporative network and different audience from different locations and helps them according to the information that the model gained from their data.

Example-.training the models form the different locations of a city and suggesting the user to most frequents words in their chat keyboard and the words model is suggesting these words are the most used words on that location.

If a person goes to a different location of a city because of federated learning, his keyboard will suggest the most used words on that location according to the user need.

Deep Learning

Deep learning is a subfield of machine learning. Machine Learning trains the model on the past data and according to the features of the data. For example, we want to make a model that classified the tomato and cherry, so we need to provide the data that contains features like size of leaf, color and more and so that model can differentiate between the tomato and cherry.

But deep learning works on neural networks, that's why deep learning is also known as deep neural network (Mohammadi & Al-Fuqaha, 2018). Neural networks learn patterns from the data itself and solve almost all kinds of problems from education to medicine field, e.g. training a model for a smart door for an organization and the goal of the model is to classify authorized and unauthorized people and if the coming person is authorized the door will open automatically. To achieve this goal, we must train neural networks on the staff's data.

This is the reason the why emergence of federated and deep learning is becoming more necessary.

The concept of federated learning (FL) has been proposed for building intelligent and privacy-enhanced IoT systems. Technically, FL is a distributed collaborative AI approach that allows for data training by coordinating multiple devices with a central server without sharing actual datasets. For instance, multiple IoT devices can act as workers to communicate with an aggregator (e.g., a server) for performing neural network training in intelligent IoT networks. More specifically, the aggregator first initiates a global model with learning parameters (). Each worker down loads the cur-rent model from the aggregator, computes its model update, e.g., via stochastic gradient descent (SGD), by using its local dataset, and off loads the computed local update to the aggregator. Then, the aggregator combines all local model updates and constructs an improved global model. By using the computing power of distributed workers, the aggregator can enhance the training quality while minimizing user privacy leakage.

FL can offer various important benefits for IoT applications as follows:

- In FL, the raw data are not required for the training at the aggregator. Therefore, the leakage of sensitive user information to the external third-party is minimized and a degree of data privacy is provided. Following the increasingly stringent data privacy protection legislation such as the General Data Protection Regulation (GDPR) (Bacon, 2017), the privacy protection feature makes FL an ideal solution for building intelligent and safe IoT systems.
- Since there is no requirement for transmitting IoT data to the server, the use of FL helps reduce communication latencies caused by data offloading. In return, it also saves network resources, e.g., spectrum and transmit power, in the data training (Nguyen, 2021).

Enhanced Learning Quality: By attracting much computation resources and diverse datasets from a network of IoT devices, FL has the potential to enhance the convergence rate of the overall training process and achieve better learning accuracy rates (Goddard, 2017), which might not be achieved by using centralized AI approaches with insufficient data and constrained computational capabilities.

Type of FL-

We present several Federated Learning framework types in this section.

Vertical Federated Learning: This method is applied when each device has a dataset made up of sample instances with varying attributes. For example, using Vertical FL, two organizations with distinct feature sets and data about the same population can create a shared machine learning model (Sheller et al., 2019).

Horizontal Federated Learning: This method is applied when there are datasets on all devices that have the same feature space but distinct sample instances. This kind of learning is used in the initial FL use case, the Google keyboard, wherein the participating mobile phones have different training data but the same characteristics.

Federated Transfer Learning: This method is comparable to classical machine learning in that it involves adding a new feature to a model that has already been trained. The greatest illustration would be expanding vertical federated learning if we wanted to apply machine learning to a greater number of sample instances that aren't available in every partner organization.

Cross-Silo Federated Learning: This type of learning is employed when there are fewer participating devices that are accessible across all rounds. Both horizontal and vertical FL formats are possible for the training data. Cross-silo is mostly utilized in scenarios involving organizations. Cross-silo FL is used in works like (Sohn, 2016) to build their model.

Device Federated Learning - Scenarios with a large number of participating devices use Cross-device Feder- atedLearning. Client-selection and incentive designs (Misra & van der Maaten, 2020) are some notable techniques needed to facilitate this type of FL.

Why Federated Learning

Normal machine learning or centralized machine learning techniques and other algorithms are good and fulfilling requirements that are needed to make a city smarter but Normal machine learning ability is limited because it is not able to work on unstructured data, can't make pattern itself because they need structured data for model training and also it is not able to make features itself from the data.

In centralized learning an organization or companies or governess collect the data from their audience on their server and applied machine learning on the data that is collected by the organization or other

Figure 1. Training a model using simple machine learning technique

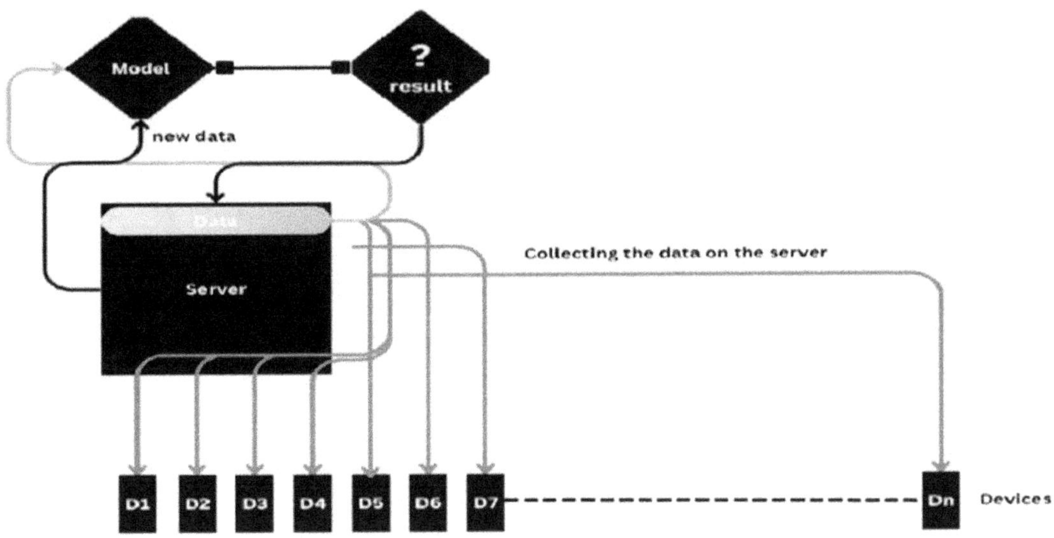

parties, and other parties or organization make the Machine learning model by using the different- different algorithms according to their need, these model gives the results on the new data for that is needed for an organization or other parties are looking.

As shown in the diagram server is collecting the data from the devices of a city (red line) after aggregation of the data, data will be sent for model training (grey line) when the new data comes from the devices model gives the result and that result will be sent to the device by the server (black line).

These results are not very useful to make a city smarter. We require technology like federated learning to help citizens, business, healthcare sector, retail sector etc. to become smarter and this is not an easy task to solve these issues federated learning has emerged (Park, 2020).

Federated Learning also used in scenarios where there is distributed data, and the goal is to train machine learning or deep learning models while protecting data privacy (Liu et al., 2020). It is particularly effective in addressing network training under local data heterogeneity and can improve the speed of model aggregation by taking similarity into account as an influence factor. Additionally, Federated Learning can be applied in real-world scenarios with rapidly changing environments and heterogeneous hardware settings, where a synchronous protocol may be inflexible. Asynchronous Federated Learning combined with a novel asynchronous model aggregation protocol has been shown to significantly improve prediction performance while maintaining the same level of accuracy as centralized machine learning. Furthermore, Federated Learning can be used in extensive heterogeneous settings, providing excellent convergence speed, accuracy, and computation/communication efficiency.

Why Deep Learning

deep learning is the advanced version of machine learning or we can say it is the deep version of the machine learning because it'stoo hard to train audio, video and text data on machine learning and the accuracy is also compromised by using the normal machine learning. If the data is very complex, then it is too difficult to find the best hyper parameters for the algorithms that have been used to train models. That's why we need deep learning. Deep learning can handle very complex and high amounts of data very easily and deep learning gives better results on video, audio and text data as compared to normal machine learning. Machine learning works on different-different algorithms and deep learning works on neural networks; neural networks inspired by human brain that's why deep learning is more reliable.

How Federated Learning for Smart City Can Be Used

Federated learning can be used in smart cities to address data privacy concerns and improve the performance of AI models. It allows multiple edge nodes to collaboratively train a global model while keeping their raw data local, protecting data privacy, and integration with smart city applications for privacy preservation and sensitive information protection. In the context of smart cities, federated learning enables the development of local, deep learning-based classifiers for data streams, which can be shared among vehicles or devices to improve accuracy and reduce communication overhead.

Federated learning is also used to find the strength of bridges via collecting the output from the sensors, building and other infrastructure of the city and gives prediction according to the data if there is bridge, long pipeline or any other infra is weak or break from somewhere then we can get that information very easily with help of federated learning and if there miss happening happened in the city then sensor will send data to the model and model will alert to the authorities and authorities can take action quickly. Authorities can stop accidents with the help of federated learning.

How Deep Learning for Smart City Can Be Used

Deep learning is the key to unlocking this intelligent future for smart cities. Think of it as the city's brain, trained on a vast network of sensors and cameras that gather data on traffic, energy use, public safety, and more. This data is then fed to deep learning algorithms, which learn to recognize patterns, predict trends, and make informed decisions. The result Traffic lights that adjust to congestion, energy grids that optimize power flow, and even crime prevention systems that anticipate and deter potential threats. Deep learning is the invisible hand, weaving a tapestry of efficiency, sustainability, and well-being into the very fabric of the urban landscape. It's the dawn of a new era for cities.

Workflow of Federated Learning in a Smart City

In federated learning or collaborative learning corporative server sends the very first version to all the devices and these models performs individual learning according to their devices and when model becomes efficient to learn from the data of the devices, devices send data or result to the corporative server and the corporative server aggregate all the data and train the model on the that data that send by all the devices and after that server sends the updated version of model to the all the devices those are coming under the server network.

This process works in a loop, and it is not necessary for devices to send the data at same time devices can send the data according to their network, battery or other requirements that are needed.

Let's taken an example -

A company wants to know the interests of the people of a city in different, different areas.

Figure 2. Model training using federated learning technique

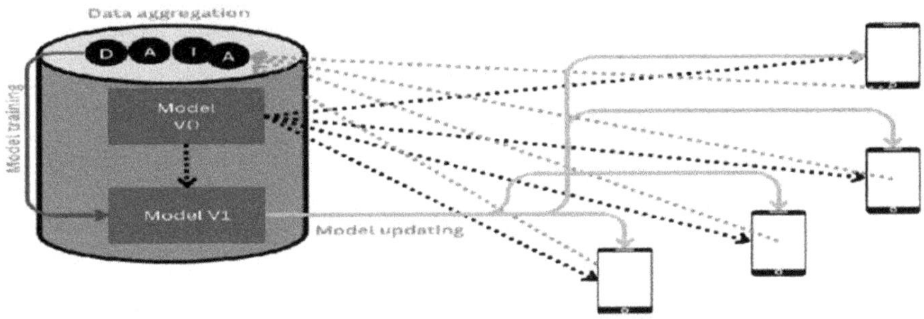

Company sends their V0 model to all mobiles phone of the city through their corporative server and these models will start learning from mobiles and when the model become efficient by continuously learning from activity of the mobile it will send data to the corporative server, corporative server aggregates the data and trained a new model V1 send to the mobiles or updated the V1 model into the devices and these process runs in epochs.

- Black line shows model installation
- Redline shows sending the trained data to the corporative server
- Green line showing installing updated model in mobiles

This process works in iteration. This diagram shows only one iteration.

MOST FAMOUS ALGORITHM IN FEDERATED LEARNING:

Fed Avg Algorithm: -

```
Clients collaboratively train a shared model
Fed Avg Loss-
Where
K = no of clients (k clients)
```

Fκ(w) = clients k's loss function = weighted by size of clients' dataset

Algorithm: - The k clients are indexed by K; B is local mini batch size, E is the number of local epochs, is the learning rate.

```
Server executes:
Initialize w0
For each round t = 1, 2,.....do
M <- max (C, K,1)
St <- (random set of m clients)
For each client k St in parallel do
```

```
t+1 <- client update (k, wt)
Wt+1 <-
Client Update(k,w): // Run on client k
B <- (Split into batches of size B)
for each local epoch I from to E to do
for batch b B do
ww-(w;b)
return w to server
```

First train no of rounds, then sample a fraction c of k clients (M <- max (C, K,1)), so in this case suppose k =6, c= 0.5 then send the current rounds weights to each client k (client update (k, wt)) and run SGD (stochastic gradient descent) for E epochs locally (for each local epoch I from to E to do) after that all clients weights are updated and then the weights are send to the server and once server received all the weights, it aggregate and take weighted average and then repeat to next round and soon.

How Federated Learning is Making Different Sectors Smart

Finance

Fraud Detection: -With the help of federated learning we can analyze transaction data from different banks and financial institutions to identify fraudulent activities without sharing sensitive customer information.

Personalized financial services: - Develop models tailored to individual needs and preferences based on personal financial data and these models give suggestions according to their requirements, while ensuring their security.

Credit and loan approval: - Build fairer and more accurate credit models by leveraging data from multiple lenders and optimize the banking loan system, federated learning helps banks to make decisions for a customer regarding the loan, without compromising data privacy.

Enhanced Language Models in Mobile Devices

Federated learning enhanced the accuracy of the server model by collecting the outputs from millions of devices, Federated learning offers substantial benefits for predictive text and language modeling in smartphones and communication apps as it enhances the accuracy of language models by gaining diverse user inputs across various devices. Crucially, federated learning does this without compromising the privacy of personal conversations.

On top of this, federated learning enables continuous improvement of models, as they can learn from new user inputs over time, thereby adapting to evolving language use and preferences. This results in more efficient and accurate predictive text capabilities and boosts the overall user experience in communication apps.

Personalization in eCommerce

e-commerce platforms can resort to federated learning to streamline customer shopping experiences. Thistechnology analyzes user interaction data on local devices and empowers retailers to provide personalized product recommendations tailored to individual preferences. It helps users to get the best product which they are looking for with similar products and helps companies to reach the right customers. Companies like Flipkart, Amazon, Myntra, Nykaa, Ajio etc. These companies use federated learning to show the advertisement to the right customer, if their model started giving the wrong outputs then company can lose crores of money .federated machine earnings streamline inventory management, which helps.

Businesses better predict and manage stock levels.

Urban Planning and Safety in Smart Cities

Urban areas are very populated so managing the traffic and rules and the safety of the citizens becomes a difficult task, so authorities use federated learning, deep learning to manage all these tasks. With smart city initiatives gaining momentum, federated machine learning is emerging as a crucial technology for enhancing traffic management and public safety systems. It processes data from diverse urban sensors and cameras locally and helps authorities regarding traffic flow and emergency responses. Urban areas are very populated so managing the traffic and rules and the safety of the citizens becomes a difficult task, so authorities use federated learning, deep learning to manage all these tasks. Thus, through federated learning, smart cities can achieve a delicate balance between advanced urban management and individual privacy.

FRAMEWORK OF FEDERATED LEARNING

TensorFlow Federated (TFF): Developed by Google, TFF is a powerful and flexible framework for building and deploying federated learning models. It offers a high level of abstraction, making it easy for developers to focus on the logic of their algorithms without getting bogged down in the nitty-gritty of communication protocols.

PySyft: This Python library takes a security-first approach to federated learning, offering features like secure aggregation and differential privacy to protect sensitive data. It's popular for research and experimentation, particularly in healthcare and finance.

Flower: This open-source framework from OpenAI emphasizes ease of use and accessibility. It provides a simple API for building and running federated learning experiments, making it a good choice for beginners and rapid prototyping.

FedML: This versatile framework supports a wide range of federated learning algorithms and communication protocols, making it ideal for research and experimentation. It's also actively maintained and well-documented, making it a good choice for developers looking for flexible and powerful federated learning too.

FATE (Federated AI Technology Platform): Developed by Huawei, FATE is a comprehensive federated learning platform with a focus on scalability and robustness. It's well-suited for large-scale deployments in enterprise and government settings.

Challenges and limitations of federated learning

As with any newly developed technology, federated learning meets with a few crucial challenges. Let's go through a few examples.

Communication Efficiency

Federated learning involves millions of devices in one network. The transfer of messages becomes slow due to several reasons: low bandwidth, lack of resources, or geographical location.

To keep the communication channels efficient, the total number of message passes and the size of a message in a single pass should be reduced. We can achieve it by using

- local updating methods (to reduce the number of rounds)
- model compression schemes (to reduce the size of the message)
- decentralized training (to operate in low bandwidth)

Privacy and Data Protection

Privacy and data security are some of the biggest concerns with federated learning. Although the local data stays on the user device, there's a risk for the information to be revealed from the model updates shared in the network.

Some of the common privacy-preserving techniques that can solve this problem include:

- Differential privacy—adding noisy data that makes it difficult to discern real information in case of data leaks
- Homomorphic encryption—performing computation on encrypted data
- Secure multiparty computation—spreading the sensitive data to different data owners so that they can collaboratively perform computation and reduce the risk of privacy breach

Systems Heterogeneity

System heterogeneity is also a big concern in federated learning because different devices have different configurations like storage, computational, and communication capabilities of the devices that are part of a federated network may differ significantly. Differences usually occur due to variability in hardware (CPU, memory), network connectivity (3G, 4G, 5G, Wi-Fi), and power supply (battery level).

Statistical Heterogeneity

This problem is posed by the multiple variations of data present across the client devices.

For example, some devices may have high-resolution image data, while others can only store low-resolution pictures, or languages might vary based on geographical location.

These instances denote that data is non-i.i.d(independent and identically distributed) in a federated learning setting, which is in contrast with the assumption of i.i.d data in normal algorithms. This might cause problems in the data structuring, modeling, and inferencing phases.

Figure 3. Training of a neural network

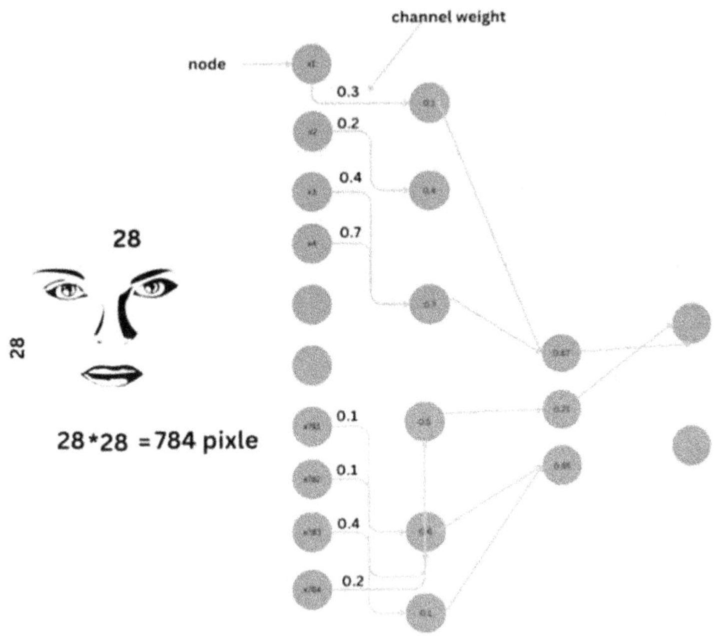

WORKFLOW OF DEEP LEARNING

deep learning works on neural networks and the neural network works like the human brain neuron works. Neural networks can learn from the data and make pattern itself; neural networks can learn from environment.

Neural networks have mainly three types layers called input layer, hidden layer, output layer, input layer has values of input data in large no of nodes and these nodes are connected to multiple hidden layers via channel and these channels are assigned a numerical value known as weights and inputs are multiply by corresponding of weights and send to hidden layer node and add the value of the corresponding node after that some those are selected, select the next nodes of next hidden layer by using the same process and in the end last layer of hidden layers select the node of the output layer and that node is the output value.

Most common example of deep learning in the smart city is Face recognition.

First layer of neural network has 784 nodes because image is contained total 784 pixels and each pixel's value are showing the darkness of the grey color and these nodes values are multiply by the value of channel weight and also add the value next corresponding layer node (x1*channel_weight + next_node_value) and the process goes into the forward direction until it reaches to the output.

Development Process of Deep Learning Model

1. Data Acquisition: Imagine collecting seashells on a beach – you gather a diverse variety, big and small, smooth and rough. Deep learning needs a similar collection: a vast and varied data set relevant to your problem. Think traffic camera footage for self-driving cars or medical scans for disease detection.

2. Data Preprocessing: Not all seashells are created equal – some might be broken, others covered in sand. Deep learning needs clean and organized data. This step involves cleaning, formatting, and structuring the data to feed it smoothly into the model.
3. Model Building: craft a deep learning model, by stacking building blocks called layers. Each layer learns specific features from the data, like edges in an image or patterns in medical scans. The more layers, the more complex the features the model can grasp.
4. Training & Optimization: The model is fed the prepped data, and with each iteration, it adjusts its internal parameters like a sculptor refining their clay. This "learning" process minimizes errors and refines the model's ability to recognize patterns and make predictions.
5. Evaluation & Testing:Deep learning models are evaluated on unseen data to gauge their accuracy and generalizability. If they stumble, you go back to training or refine the model's architecture.
6. Deployment & Refinement: Deep learning models are deployed in real-world applications, like self-driving cars navigating city streets or medical AI assisting diagnoses. But the process isn't over – the model continuously learns from new data and feedback, evolving and improving like a human.

MOST COMMONLY USED NEURAL NETWORK

Convolutional Neural Networks (CNNs)

Convolutional Neural network also known as convent or CNNs are a special kind of neural network for processing data that has a known grid –like topology like time series data (1D) or images 2D.

CNN works differently as compared to the other neural networks. CNN has an extra layer called convolution layer. Convolution layer work as filtering layer this layer filters the data and the next layers got a filtered data so that picking or making the pattern from the data is became easy for the next layers of neural network and with help of convolution layer output will be more accurate. A total of three types of layer CNN contains first one is convolution layer and the second one is polling layer and the last one is fully connected layer. CNN is used to solve a variety of problems like image classification, pattern recognition, object localization, object detection, image segmentation etc.

As shown on the image input is an image, so in CNN first convolution layer filter the pixels of the image and then next layer of neural network calculates all the to make patterns from the data after the fully connected layer understand the classification and shows the output with probabilities value, these probabilities are confidence value of the neural network.

CNN Approach to Solve Image Classification

You tell CNN what you're looking for, maybe a serene beach scene or a vibrant city panorama. CNN then springs into action, its internal filters scanning each image like meticulous art critics. They analyze edges, textures, colors, and even the composition, building a nuanced understanding of each picture's content. Based on this analysis, CNN ranks the images, presenting you with a curated selection that bestmatches your desires. It's like having a tireless, expert assistant constantly on the lookout for the visuals that resonate with you, saving you precious time and effort in your search.

Figure 4. Workflow of convolution neural network

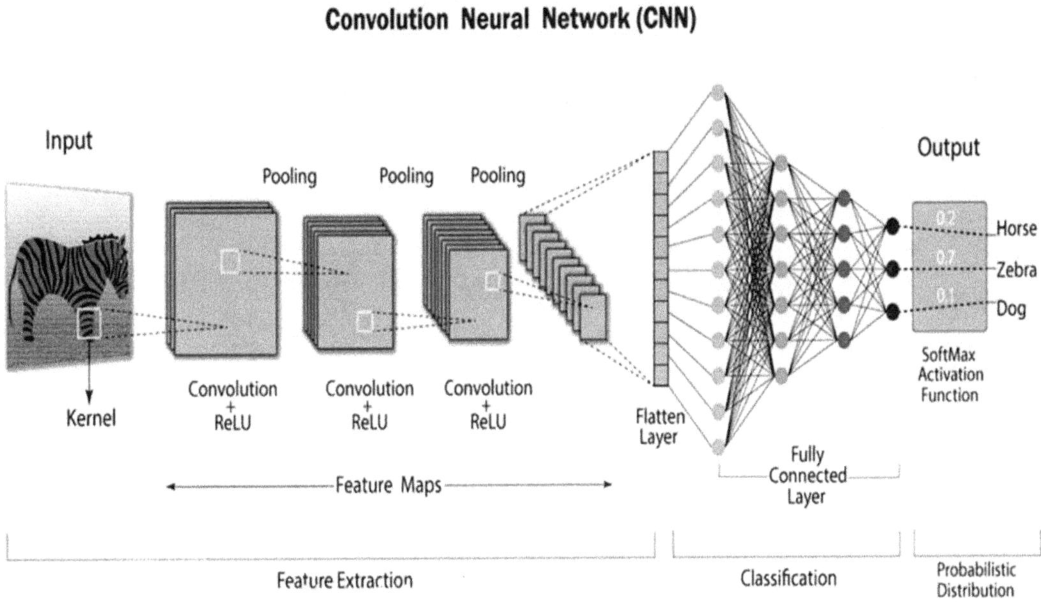

CNN Approach to Solve Object Detection

They have special filters that act like magnifying glasses, scanning images for specific objects. These filters work like layers, each one picking out different clues. For example, the first layer might look for edges and shapes, the next for textures and colors, and the final layer might put all the clues together to shout, "Aha! There's a cat in that picture!"

This ability to find objects in images is incredibly useful for all sorts of things, from helping self-driving cars avoid obstacles to letting doctors scan X-rays for abnormalities. So next time you see a car identify a stop sign or a doctor use AI to analyze a medical image, remember, it's object-detecting superpowers of CNNs and these powers are making citizens and cities smarter.

Architecture of CNN

This is the simple architecture of CNN; passing a RGB image as an input and the first layer of neural network in this architecture is convolutional layer that means it is a convolutional neural network, convolutional layer making a feature map from the data (image)

How Deep Learning is Making Different Sector's Smart

Manufacturing

Deep learning can analyze sensor data from industrial equipment to predict potential failures and schedule preventive maintenance, reducing downtime and costs.

Figure 5. CNN training steps

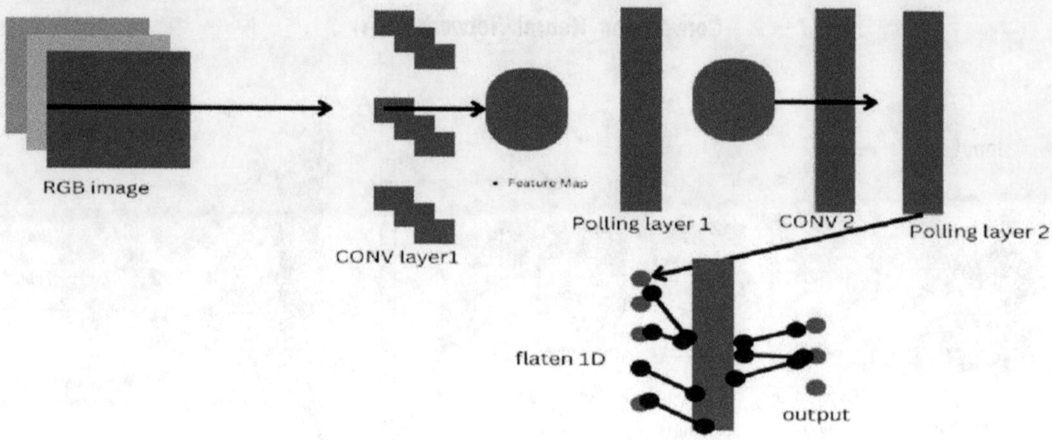

Deep learning is transforming manufacturing into a symphony of precision and efficiency. Imagine factories where machines hum with the intelligence of AI, predicting equipment failures before they happen, optimizing production lines in real-time, and even designing bespoke products based on customer needs. Deep learning algorithms analyze vast datasets of sensor data, production logs, and even images to identify patterns, predict maintenance needs, and adjust processes for optimal output. From defect detection to automated quality control, deep learning empowers manufacturers to minimize waste, maximize efficiency, and personalize production like never before.

Transportation

Imagine roads that predict and adjust traffic flow and red lights that switch according to the traffic on road, self-driving cars navigating with superhuman vision, and public transport systems optimized for real-time demand. Deep learning algorithms analyze data from cameras, sensors, and GPS to understand traffic patterns, predict congestion, and suggest alternative routes. They power self-driving cars by recognizing objects, pedestrians, and even weather conditions, enabling safe and efficient navigation. Public transportation systems leverage deep learning to analyze ridership patterns and optimize routes and schedules, reducing wait times and maximizing efficiency. It's a new era of smart transportation, where deep learning plays the conductor, ensuring everyone reaches their destination smoothly and efficiently.

Healthcare and Research

Deep learning is transforming healthcare and research into a detective, uncovering hidden patterns and secrets in mountains of data. Imagine medical images bursting with clues to diseases, genomic landscapes whispering tales of genetic predispositions, and research papers unlocking a wealth of untapped knowledge. Deep learning algorithms analyze these vast troves of information, deciphering subtle patterns and correlations invisible to the human eye. They can detect tumors in scans with razor-sharp precision, predict disease outbreaks before they even begin, and personalize treatment plans for optimal outcomes. In research, deep learning automates the analysis of massive datasets, accelerating discoveries and leading the way to cutting-edge breakthroughs. It's like having a tireless, super-powered research assistant, tirelessly sifting through data and illuminating the path to better health and scientific understanding.

Framework and Libraries of Deep Learning

TensorFlow: Developed by Google, TensorFlow is a widely used, open-source framework known for its flexibility, scalability, and vast community. It supports various programming languages like Python, C++, and Java, making it accessible to a broad range of developers. TensorFlow offers pre-built libraries for common tasks like image recognition and natural language processing, accelerating development. However, its complexity can be daunting for beginners.

Keras: Often considered the "friendly wrapper" of TensorFlow, Keras simplifies deep learning development by providing a high-level API. It focuses on conciseness and readability, making it perfect for beginners and quick experimentation. However, Keras lacks some of the advanced features and flexibility of TensorFlow and Py Torch.

PyTorch: Another open-source framework, PyTorch, is known for its simplicity and dynamic computational graph. Unlike TensorFlow's static graph, PyTorch allows for on-the-fly experimentation and debugging, making it ideal for research and rapid prototyping. Its Python-first approach makes it user-friendly, but it may not be as performant as TensorFlow for large-scale deployments

Scikit-learn: - scikit-learn also known as sk learn, it is used for applications such as computer vision and natural language processing, originally developed by Meta AI and now part of the Linux Foundation umbrella.

CORE CHALLENGES OF DEEP LEARNING

Data Dependency: Deep learning models often require massive amounts of data to train effectively. Acquiring, labeling, and cleaning such large datasets can be expensive, time-consuming, and impractical for certain applications.

Computational Cost: Training complex deep learning models can be computationally expensive, requiring specialized hardware like GPUs or TPUs. This limits accessibility for researchers and developers with limited resources.

Interpretability and Explainability: Deep learning models can be challenging to interpret, making it difficult to understand how they arrive at their decisions. This lack of transparency raises concerns about bias, fairness, and accountability.

Conclusion: Federated learning and deep learning are both relatively new technologies, but they are rapidly being adopted in smart cities. The combination of these two technologies has the potential to revolutionize the way that cities operate and the potential benefits of federated and deep learning for smart cities are vast. These technologies have the potential to make cities more efficient, sustainable, and livable.

Infrastructure, education, hospital, hotels, transport, tourism and citizen or other things are required technology like federated and deep learning to became smart, to make things smarter we need deep learning because of deep learning we can make smart door, smart lift, smart fire alarms, smart classes, smart switches, smart car or self-driving car on the other hand we can help citizens by using federated learning like we can help tourist in suggesting the hotels, language translation, landmark, suggesting words on their keyboard according to the location and federated learning. Deep and federated learning helps in many more things, federated and deep learning arethe brain &backbone of the smart cities. The emergence of federated and deep learning was necessary for smarter cities and the combination of federated and deep learning has the capability to provide an artificial brain to a city. So, the cities are becoming smarter because of federated and deep learning.

REFERENCES

BaconD. (2017). Federated learning: Strategies for improving communication efficiency. Available:arXiv:1610.05492.

Cisco. (2020). *Cisco Global Cloud Index: Forecast and Methodology, 2016-2021* (White Paper). Cisco. https://www.cisco.com/c/en/us/solutions/executive-perspectives/annual-internet-report/index.html

Goddard, M. (2017, November). The EU general data protection regulation (GDPR): European regulation that has global impact. *International Journal of Market Research*, *59*(6), 703–705. doi:10.2501/IJMR-2017-050

Lin, J., Yu, W., Zhang, N., Yang, X., Zhang, H., & Zhao, W. (2017, October). Asur-vey on Internet of Things: Architecture, enabling technologies, security and privacy, and applications. *IEEE Internet of Things Journal*, *4*(5), 1125–1142. doi:10.1109/JIOT.2017.2683200

LiuY.YuanX.XiongZ.KangJ.WangX. (2020). Federated learning for 6G communications: Challenges, methods, and future directions. Available:arXiv:2006.02931.

Misra & van der Maaten. (2020). Self-supervised learning of pretext-invariant representations. *Proceedings of the IEEE/CVF Conference on Computer Vision and Pattern Recognition*, 6707–6717.

Mohammadi, M., & Al-Fuqaha, A. (2018, February). Enabling cognitive smart cities using big data and machine learning: Approaches and challenges. *IEEE Communications Magazine*, *56*(2), 94–101. doi:10.1109/MCOM.2018.1700298

Nguyen. (2021). Federated learning meets blockchain in edgecomputing: Opportunities and challenges. *IEEE Internet Things J.* . doi:10.1109/JIOT.2021.3072611

ParkJ. (2020). *Communication-efficient and distributed learning over wireless networks: Principles and applications.* arXiv:2008.02608.

Sheller, M. J., Reina, G. A., Edwards, B., & Martin, J. (2019). Multi-Institutional Deep Learning Modeling Without Sharing Patient Data: A Feasibility Study on Brain Tumor Segmentation. Brainlesion.

Sohn. (2016). Improved deep metric learning with multi- class n-pair loss objective. Advances in neural information processing systems, 1857–1865.

Chapter 3
Smart City and 5G

Roheen Qamar
https://orcid.org/0000-0003-4169-9455
Quest Nawabshah, Pakistan

Baqar Ali Zardari
Quest Nawabshah, Pakistan

ABSTRACT

The idea of smart cities is significant because it seeks to improve a city's infrastructure, traffic, governance, water and waste management, power management, health, safety and security, education, and other systems in order to raise the standard of living for its citizens. This chapter explains the idea of "smart cities" and lists all of the advantages. It explains the many services and applications needed to create a smart city, as well as the part ICT technologies play in putting them into practice. In addition, the difficulties with the current ICT systems are examined in relation to the deployment of smart cities. The chapter explores the anticipated characteristics of 5G technologies and explains why they might be the most effective solution for implementing smart cities successfully. Researchers and practitioners in the field can both benefit from this research, which offers a reflection on the state of the art, the use of 5G in smart cities.

INTRODUCTION

5G is the fifth generation wireless network, with a set of characteristics, such as high bandwidth and data rates, massive connectivity, broad coverage, and low latency. Approximately 55% of people on Earth currently reside in cities, and by 2030, that percentage is predicted to rise to 66% (United Nations, 2016). Resources are limited as the city expands and new issues (such as traffic congestion, waste management, pollution, parking allotment, etc.) surface. As a result, everyone should prioritize helping the city adapt to its present and future demands, and researchers are no different. Around the world, a variety of efforts are being sparked by the pressing need to improve urban areas as places to live in quality (European Commission, U.S. Department of Transportation, n.d.). These projects range from businesses and municipal councils to research laboratories. People from many fields, backgrounds, cultures, and

DOI: 10.4018/979-8-3693-2373-1.ch003

passions are coming together to make the city smarter. A few years ago, "ideas about how information and communication technologies might improve the functioning of cities" came together to establish the notion of the Smart City (SC). Although more cities are being classified as "smart" every day, the term "smart cities" (SC) is becoming increasingly widely used, yet the idea is still in its early stages. The elements and traits of a smart city are enumerated. Smart buildings, smart energy, smart transportation, smart health care, smart technology, smart governance, smart education, and smart citizens are some of the constituents (Alahi, M. et al., 2023, pp.5206).

. A few of them will be quickly covered in the sections that follow. Depending on their focus, different smart cities feature varying degrees of these smart elements. The smart city's infrastructure consists of services, ICT, and physical elements. The actual structural components of the smart city are its buildings, roadways, train tracks, electricity supply lines, and water supply systems. These make up the physical infrastructure. The no smart part of smart cities is usually the physical infrastructure. The ICT infrastructure serves as the central nervous system of the smart city, connecting all the other elements together and serving as its central nervous system. Physical infrastructure serves as the foundation for the service infrastructure, which may also include certain ICT elements. A smart city's four main focuses are government, the environment, the economy, and society. A smart city's social theme emphasizes that the city is run by and for its residents, or citizens. A smart city's economics theme indicates that it may prosper with steady increases in both employment and GDP.

A smart city's environmental theme suggests that it will be able to continue operating for both the present and the future generations. A smart city's governance theme implies that the area is strong in its capacity to implement laws and integrate the other components. The expectation of living standards has grown along with the world population in the last few decades. By 2050, it is estimated that almost 70% of people on Earth would reside in cities. Currently, cities account for 75% of global resource and energy consumption, which produces 80% of greenhouse gas emissions. There could have a serious detrimental effect on the ecosystem in the upcoming decades. For this reason, the idea of smart cities is essential. Building smart cities is a logical response to the issues brought on by increasing urbanization and population density. Even with its related expenses, smart cities may lower energy, water, and carbon emissions consumption as well as transportation needs and urbanization (Chrysikos et al., 2023, pp.156).

SMART CITIES

The term "smart cities" first arose in print in the late 1990s, and since then, other strategies have been created. The term "smart city" is still used to refer to a variety of urban situations rather than a specific city. Examples include virtualized cities or city guides on the web, knowledge bases that serve local needs, business relocation-attracting ICT-enabled agglomerations, ubiquitous environments, metropolitan-wide ICT infrastructures that provide e-services to citizens, and most recently, ICT infrastructure for ecological use (Car et al., 2023, pp 377-389).

Though they approach smart cities from various angles, researchers, practitioners, businesspeople, and policymakers generally agree on a model that assesses the urban economy, mobility, environment, living, people, and government. However, the ICT and building sectors emphasize the need to capitalize (Al Sharif et al., 2022, pp 103542).

Figure 1. Smart city structure

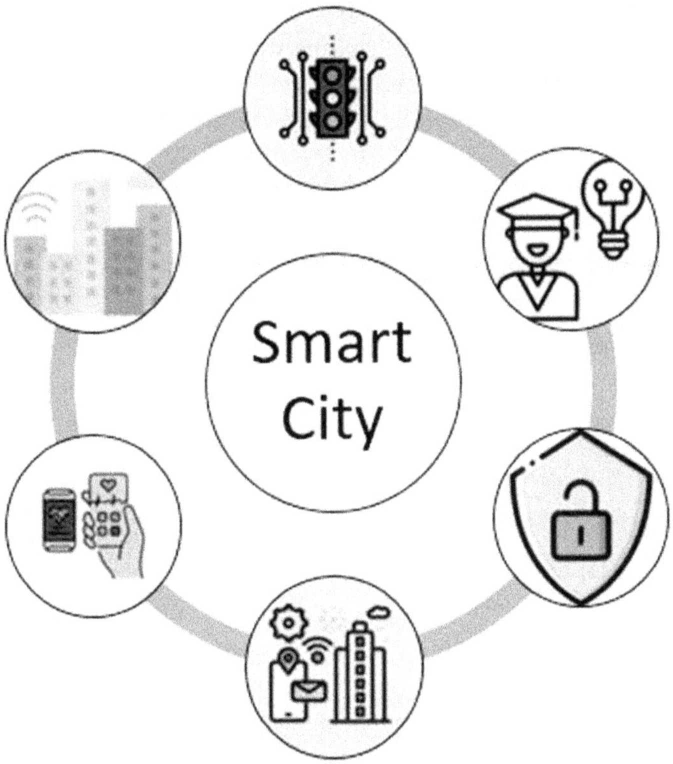

Personal assistants like Google Home and Amazon's Alexa are making life easier, and now that a new generation of smart apps is changing how we approach daily tasks, the concept has been extended to smart cities, which are seen as the future of urbanism. These cities ought to integrate infrastructure and technology in ways that aren't yet apparent, enhancing both the standard of living and how people interact with their surroundings. Cities are ranked according to nine main criteria that indicate how intelligent they are:

Infrastructure based on technology

- Eco-friendly initiatives
- Seamless public transportation system
- Responsible urban planning
- Smart government
- Intelligent grid and energy utilities
- Machine learning
- Telemedicine and smart healthcare
- Personal data privacy (Huseien et al., 2022, pp. 100116)

5G, an IoT enabling technology, is critical to the idea of a smart city. It will be crucial to the collection of data from sensors and the real-time transmission of that data to the central monitoring site.

Smart city initiatives will be impacted by 5G-based technology known as multi-access edge computing (MEC). In contrast to traditional centralized network architectures, where traffic had to travel through the entire network to a central point and then back to the end user hardware, MEC architecture allows computing and storage capabilities for applications at the edge of its internal network (Tan, L et al., 2021, pp. 103517).

SMART CITY: TRENDS OF PUBLICATIONS

The issues posed by growing urban populations in the areas of energy, transportation, security, and healthcare have been recognized as perfect opportunities for smart city development. Many smart city academics have concentrated on developing novel technologies and new regulations throughout the past ten years.

Absorb the swiftly evolving research trends in the field of smart cities Thus far, we have conducted a thorough analysis of smart city publications by utilizing relevant terms in the Scopus database, an international search engine for academic papers.

The information was gathered between 2008 and 2019.Based on the research publications that have been published throughout the years, the top ten keywords in the field of smart cities. The arc-shaped area's size is not depicted to scale. ''Smart city'' or ''smart cities'' is the most used term, with almost 17,393 usages in the published articles. This indicates that the word is the most popular. Keywords like "IoT," "big data," "ubiquitous computing," "information management," and "big data" have been used 6,286, 2,565, 1,393, and 977 times, respectively. Big data is a vast collection of data that can be analyzed to identify patterns; Internet of Things (IoT) is a system made up of billions of sensors and gadgets that are linked to the Internet and function as a significant Data processing is associated with both information management and ubiquitous computing. The four data collecting and processing methods listed above need widely dispersed sensor technologies and a ubiquitous power source. Afterwards, the terms "sustainable development," "smart power grids," "electric power transmission networks," "energy efficiency," and "energy utilization" were utilized 1,217, 1,117, 1,050, 1,080, and 976 times, respectively. These five keywords indicate that energy conversion and usage have received a lot of attention lately from researchers, which highlights the need for more sophisticated energy solutions in the field of smart cities.: Compared to 2008, there were around 78 times as many articles in 2019 that have the term "smart city" in their title, abstract, or keywords (TAK). Additionally, we limited our search to the article title. Specifically, we looked for the term "smart city" in the titles of the published articles. The steady growth in the number of published articles from 2008 to 2019. Consequently, the sharp rise in publications pertaining to "smart city" and the top ten keywords suggest that an increasing number of scholars from many scientific fields are becoming interested in this concept (Zhao et al., 2021, pp, 1391-1431).

A smart city's key components are energy, transportation, automobiles, human-machine interface, and healthcare.48, 52 Furthermore, creating smart cities—which run on renewable energy—would be a very successful way to slow down global warming and climate change. We have searched for published articles with the terms "smart city" + "climate change," "smart city" + "global warming," "smart city"

+ "energy," "smart city" + "transportation," "smart city" + "vehicle," "smart city" + "human-machine interface," and "smart city" + "healthcare" in their TAK in order to illustrate the current state of publication trends with an emphasis on these parts. The number of published publications grows significantly throughout all five areas, the number of publications with "energy" + "smart city" in their TAK is growing at the fastest rate. In conclusion, a great deal of study over the past 12 years has shown that energy-related issues for smart cities are a worry. Interestingly, NGs primarily contribute to the energy sector by resolving issues with the ubiquitous power supply for sensors and wireless devices (Borcoci et al., 2021, pp. 156624-156646)

THE EVOLUTION OF 5G

The fifth generation (5G) wireless cellular network is anticipated to meet the demands of the future generation of networks. Three key features of 5G are absent from networks of earlier generations. First of all, a vast quantity of data is produced. The International Telecommunication Union (ITU) estimates that there were over 7.5 billion mobile devices in use globally in 2017. The integrity and confidentiality of data being transported from a sender to a recipient via a mobile communication device are crucial. A system that enables the processing of encrypted messages in mobile communication devices may be employed to achieve 5G credibility. The message will be encrypted and contain both the encrypted content and the encryption accessing information. This way, when a mobile device receives a message, it can store the encryption accessing information in its memory for later use (Tang et al., 2021, pp. 105895)

The memory will be retrieved to allow for the decryption and reading of the received message after it has been encrypted. The newest advancement in cellular technology, known as fifth-generation wireless (5G), is designed to significantly boost the speed and responsiveness of wireless networks. Data sent over wireless internet connections may now move at multigigabit rates thanks to 5G, with some estimates putting peak speeds as high as 20 gigabits per second (Gbps). For applications that need real-time input, these speeds are advantageous since they give latency of less than 5 milliseconds (ms) or less, which is faster than landline network rates. A significant increase in data transmission over wireless systems will be possible with 5G thanks to improved antenna technology and increased accessible capacity (Gebremariam et al., 2021, pp. 1-6)

1. 1G

The analog mobile network, or 1G, was first available in 1979. Phone numbers were encoded into the phones itself; SIM cards were not used by the phones. The phones cost a ton of money.

2. 2G

Digital mobile technology, which included CDMA(2), GSM(3), and TDMA(4), was the first generation. It's intriguing that the 1Generation didn't have a name until recently. In 1991, it was introduced in Finland and has the following derivatives:

2.5 (GPRS(5)) is the two and a half generation, which refers to the 2G network that has package data transmission enabled. Additionally, there existed a 2.75 network where GPRS developed into EDGE.

Figure 2. Fifth generation

3. 3G

The Internet connection speed improved with 3G, going from 200 kbps to several Mbps. Upon its introduction in 1998, it was crucial for the advancements in wireless voice communication using mobile, video calls, and the Internet on-screen (Delson et al., 2021, pp.1-6).

4. 4G

In 2008, 4G technologies including were formally unveiled. They represented the next development in mobile network technology, enabling several hundred Mbps and even gigabit-speed Internet connections.

5. 5G

Three new features of 5G include faster speeds, reduced latency, and the ability to link many devices, including sensors and Internet of Things devices.

Since 5G systems still require active 4G support for the initial connection, they are not stand-alone networks. A few more years of work are still required for it to become a stand-alone system. Similar to earlier networks, 5G makes use of the cells system, which divides a region into sectors and uses radio waves to transmit encoded messages between hotspots. All of the cells have to be wired or wirelessly linked to the network spine. 5G operates at frequencies greater than 4G, often operating in two frequency bands: below and above 6 GHz.

While 5G networks are now being tested in Argentina and Columbia and developed in the USA (Chicago, Minneapolis), Asia continues to lead the world in the development and use of 5G technology. While Singapore, Turkey, and the United Arab Emirates have already put the pilot programs into action, China, Japan, and South Korea went the furthest. Numerous European nations, including Norway,

Germany, Great Britain, Italy, Switzerland, Spain, Austria, Russia, and Finland, have declared their intention to test the 5G signal.

Since artificial intelligence opens up new avenues for communication in both business and academic research, it is critical to the development of 5G networks (Ateya et al., 2021, pp.910)

Three primary technical issues with 5G may be handled by AI: detection (minimized error rate), estimate (channel estimation challenge), and optimization (allocation problem).

With the use of this technology, robotics will be able to explore new frontiers and enable intelligent robots to function in a wider range of "smart" environments (Knieps et al., 2022, pp. 102261)

The improvements this will bring to health technology outweigh the worries that it may be exploited for population tracking and military uses.

With the help of 5G connection, various automated systems with IoT sensors that have a few years' lifespan may access more real-time data while consuming significantly less power (Yang, et al., 2022, pp. 200065)

WHAT IS THE OPERATION OF 5G?

Cell sites that have been separated into sectors and transmit data via radio waves make up wireless networks. 5G is built on top of Fourth-Generation (4G) Long-Term Evolution (LTE) wireless technology. In contrast to 4G, which uses a lot of big, powerful cell towers to send information farther, 5G uses a lot of tiny cell stations that are positioned on things like building rooftops and light poles to transfer messages. The millimeter wave spectrum, which is the band of spectrum between 30 and 300 gigahertz (Ghz) that 5G uses to generate high speeds, can only travel over short distances and is susceptible to interference from weather and physical obstacles like buildings and trees. This makes the use of multiple small cells necessary. Previous generations of wireless technology have used lower-frequency bands of spectrum. To offset the challenges relating to distance and interference with Wave, the wireless industry is also considering the use of a lower-frequency spectrum for 5G networks so network operators could use spectrum they already own to build out their new networks. Lower-frequency spectrum reaches greater distances but has lower speed and capacity than Wave (Zhou et al., 2021, pp. 306-310)

WHAT IS THE SPEED OF 5G?

Currently, 5G download rates are as high as 1,000 megabits per second (Mbps) or even as high as 2.1 Gbps. This may be seen by someone using a 5G handset to stream a 1080p YouTube video without any buffering. Currently, downloading an episode of a Netflix show or an app may take several minutes, but now it only takes a few seconds. Moreover, 4K wireless streaming becomes far more feasible. These samples, now need to be a straight city block away from a 5G node in order for the download speed to return to 4G (Lu et al., .2021, pp. 2348-2356).

Longer ranges allow low band to remain locked at 5G speeds, and while low-band 5G may not be as fast overall as low band should still be quicker than what is thought to be a solid 4G connection. 5G download rates across low bands might reach 30 to 250 Mbps. More remote areas are expected to have access to low-band 5G. With potential download rates of 100 to 900 Mbps, 5G mid band technology is expected to be deployed in large cities (Tsakyridis et al., 2021, pp. 2816-2826)

WHAT ADVANTAGES DOES 5G OFFER?

5G offers several worthwhile advantages, such as the following, even though its drawbacks are less evident when considering radio frequency (RF) exposure restrictions or more evident when considering how readily may be prevented.

higher data rates, which will enable new technology options over 5G networks, such as 4K streaming or near-real-time virtual reality (VR) streaming; the use of higher frequencies; high bandwidth; improved mobile broadband; a lower latency of 5 ms; and the potential for a 5G mobile network composed of low-band, mid band, and mmWave frequencies (Gkagkas et al., 2021. pp. 1-7)

ICT AS A FUNDAMENTAL ENABLER FOR SMART CITIES

Cities throughout the globe are constantly expanding. 86% of the developed world and 64% of the developing world are expected to be urbanized by 2050. The structural integrity of cities is severely strained by this. Urban infrastructure is frequently overworked and poorly maintained, including housing, transportation, utilities, and environmental services. It gets harder to fund social services, healthcare, and education. These are legitimate issues that impact all cities. The conventional approaches of increasing funding or creating a new department within the municipality to handle the issue are no longer effective in addressing these problems. We need to implement a new, more sophisticated approach to urban management (Wen et al., 2021, pp. 7-25).

A smart city is an integrated urban development concept that prioritizes resource management that is intelligently used to address urban problems. Through the dissemination of knowledge and citizen participation, information and communication technology (ICT) is a potent instrument that has the potential to empower individuals. ICT is utilized in smart cities to save costs and resource consumption, increase communication between residents and city stakeholders, and improve the performance, quality, and interactivity of urban services. ICT is a smart city's lifeblood. The concept of a "smart city" is impossible without it. As a result, smart ICT infrastructure design is essential for smart cities. It's critical to give this network intelligence in addition to scalability, resilience, and adaptability (Ahvar, E et al., 2021, pp. 28-49)

The topic of discussion for this panel is ICTs and their uses in smart cities, with an emphasis on the challenges facing India as it attempts to implement these technologies. Among the topics to be covered include, but are not restricted to:

- Automated and Streamlined Network Administration
- Automated Identification and Mitigation of Security Risks
- GPS-enabled networks and IOT
- Sturdiness and Expandability
- Policies and Laws.
- Current water, energy, and transportation system infrastructure.
- Digital Gap
- Repair and upkeep of an intricate infrastructure for every service
- Interoperability and Data Integration: Overcoming Language Barriers ICT's Fundamental Enabler Role in all the Above Issues

Figure 3. Smart cities areas

ICTs have grown at an exponential rate over the past few years as a result of improvements in software and hardware architecture. The efficacy of cities has risen as a result of the usage of ICT in various forms for diverse purposes.

Activities, and a variety of words, including "cyberville," "digital city," "electronic city," "flexicity," "information city," "telicity," "wired city," and "smart city," have been used to describe these towns. Among the terms used for cities, "smart city" is the most abstract because it includes all other terms.

In a smart city, digital technology lead to improved citizen services, more efficient use of resources, and less negative environmental effects.

The following is one official definition of a smart city: In order to maximize the city's collective intelligence, a city must "connect the physical infrastructure, the information-technology infrastructure, the social infrastructure, and the business infrastructure." "An innovative city that uses information and communication technologies (ICTs) and other means to improve quality of life, efficiency of urban operations and services, and competitiveness, while ensuring that it meets the needs of present and future generations with respect to economic, social, and environmental aspects" is another formal and comprehensive definition of a "smart sustainable city."

The expectation of living standards has grown along with the world population in the last few decades. By 2050, it is estimated that almost 70% of people on Earth would reside in cities. Currently, cities account for 75% of global resource and energy consumption, which produces 80% of greenhouse gas emissions. There may be a serious detrimental effect on the ecosystem in the next decades. For this reason, the idea of smart cities is essential. Building smart cities is a logical response to the issues brought on by increasing urbanization and population density. Despite its related expenses, smart cities have the potential to decrease energy and water use, carbon emissions, transportation needs, and city (Belli et al., 2020, pp. 1039-1071)

SMART CITIES AND 5G APPLICATIONS

1) Traffic Control

In cities, traffic management is crucial to preventing massive traffic bottlenecks in busy areas and deserted streets elsewhere. This is likewise dependent on the layout and construction of the roadways, although it is controllable with intelligent traffic signals. For instance, the traffic lights have to be programmed to automatically change based on the volume of traffic, extending the duration of green lights during periods of high traffic and shortening them during periods of low traffic. In order to monitor their states and repair them when there is significant wear and tear, sensors can also be incorporated into highways and bridges. After all, one of the main contributors to traffic pollution are potholed roads (Barros et al., 2023, pp. 227-232)

2) Air Contamination

In many large cities, air pollution is a serious issue due to excessive levels of particulate matter in the air that can eventually harm lungs. However, air pollution may be decreased with the use of IoT and machine intelligence. This is made feasible by utilizing the Internet of Things (IoT) to gather data on city pollution, such as car emissions, pollen levels, airflow direction, weather, traffic volumes, etc., and then generating pollution predictions to identify patterns in pollution so that they may be managed (Mollel et al., 2021, pp. 45770-45802).

3) Visual Monitoring

It is among the most well regarded apps for smart cities that are currently in use. This kind of program and technologies provide simple tracking and surveillance, which contributes to improved upkeep and security. Using a CCTV camera and video camera allows for activity monitoring and the disruption of any disruptive behavior.

4) Security and Access

In locations where security is a top priority, these apps and technologies aid in improving accessibility and security through the usage of closed-circuit television systems and integrated systems. The use of alerting systems contributes to a decrease in theft, break-ins, and other actions endangering human life. Theft may be prevented by using appropriate sensor systems in parking lots as well (Gai et al., 2021, pp. 858-863)

5) Sensors For Fire

By using fire alarm systems, fire accidents and events may be controlled, which can lessen the harm that fire does to both the environment and people (Fang, H et al., 2021, pp. 643)

6) Meters of Water

Since water is a finite resource in the natural world, protecting it is crucial. Water warning systems are integrated into meters that are internet-connected, which helps minimize water waste. Additionally, it tracks the water's entry and outflow, which may be utilized to identify activities that involve excessive consumption.

7) Sensors of Occupancy

When individuals are not using the resources, these kinds of occupancy sensors aid in achieving the best possible use of those resources. For instance, when no one is present in a room or area, light control sensors are used to automatically switch off the lights and fans.

5G is faster than 4G and offers remote-controlled operation over a reliable network with zero delays. It provides down-link maximum throughput of up to 20 Gbps. In addition, 5G also supports 4G WWWW (4th Generation World Wide Wireless Web) and is based on Internet protocol version 6 (IPv6) protocol. 5G provides unlimited internet connection at your convenience, anytime, anywhere with extremely high speed, high throughput, low-latency, higher reliability, greater scalability, and energy-efficient mobile communication technology (Deebak et al., 2021.pp. 293-308.)

8) High-Speed Mobile Network

5G enables extremely fast download rates of up to 10 to 20 Gbps, which is an improvement above all prior mobile network technologies. The 5G wireless network functions similarly to a fiber-optic internet link. In contrast to all previous mobile transmission technologies, 5G provides efficient high-speed data and voice communication. 5G provides communication with a latency of less than one millisecond, making it ideal for mission-critical and autonomous driving applications. Compared to lower LTE bands, 5G will employ millimeter waves for data transmission, offering a larger data throughput and better bandwidth. Since 5G is a quick mobile network technology, it will provide for safe and secure access to cloud services and business resources as well as virtual access to powerful computing capacity (Hsu et al., 2021, pp. 1-4).

9) Virtual Reality (VR) and Augmented Reality (AR)

Applications for AR and VR will become much more immersive and engaging thanks to 5G's reduced latency. In industrial settings, for instance, a technician donning 5G augmented reality goggles may view an overlay of a machine that indicates parts, offers instructions for repairs, or indicates portions that should not be touched. There will be plenty of chances for highly responsive industrial apps to handle complicated jobs (Nazim et al., 2021, pp. 19-30).

10) Drone Applications for 5G IoT

Beyond the consumer applications of videography and photography, drones have a wide range of expanding applications nowadays. Drones are currently being used by utilities, for instance, to examine equipment. Drone deliveries of goods are being considered by logistics and retail organizations. This tendency will continue, and 5G will enable us to push the boundaries of current drone technology, particularly in terms of range and interaction (Ometov et al., 2021, pp. 185-190).

11) Wearable's and Mobile Are Two Applications That Will Benefit From the Massive IoT

What may cause the number of linked IoT devices to soar? The Massive IoT element of 5G will see a significant market for wearable's, trackers, and sensors. Think of a day when, in addition to your current phones, tablets, and laptops, all of the devices, appliances, and equipment you use on a daily basis will be directly connected via a cellular connection. Many more gadgets will be able to function in any given location with 5G without experiencing apparent delays, lost signals, etc. (Kaur, et al., 2021, pp. 012011).

12) 5G Healthcare

Use cases will make it possible for patients and physicians to communicate more than before. When a patient exhibits symptoms, wearable medical equipment might notify medical professionals. For example, an internal defibrillator could immediately notify an ER cardiology team to prepare for a new patient, and the device would keep a detailed track of all the data it collects.

13) Shop

A key consideration for 5G retail applications will be the user experience. Future retail spaces could not resemble the aisles of fully filled shelves of today. Consider a store that functions more like a showroom, where you may place products in a virtual trolley as opposed to using a real one to make purchases.

5G may potentially be used by retailers to instantly control stock levels and inventories. Customers may even see developments such as the replacement of the conventional checkout line with cashier less businesses that just keep track of the items placed in your basket (Khujamatov et al., 2021, pp 1-6).

14) Agriculture

Agriculture Future farms will rely less on pesticides and more on data. With the use of data from sensors placed directly in fields, farmers are able to determine very precisely which regions require pest control, watering, or disease treatment.

Livestock health monitoring may also become more common as wearables grow more affordable and 5G makes it simpler to expand networks with lots of IoT devices. Farmers are able to decrease antibiotic use without jeopardizing the safety of the food supply by using more precise health data (Mahamuni et al., 2021, pp 1324-1331).

15) Manufacturing

Convergence of 5G, AI, and IoT will completely change manufacturing floors. Factories will employ 5G technology to monitor and analyze industrial processes with unprecedented accuracy, in addition to using predictive maintenance to save costs and downtime.

Manufacturers may streamline traditional quality assurance procedures with sensor technologies and artificial intelligence (AI) in order to take advantage of the increased connectivity that 5G offers.

16) Logistics

Logistics Inventory tracking is costly, time-consuming, and challenging in the shipping and logistics industries. More connectivity between cars and the infrastructure itself, as well as between cars, is possible with 5G.

With 5G, fleet monitoring and navigation will be much simpler on a large scale. An augmented reality system that recognizes and indicates possible risks without taking the driver's focus off the road has the potential to power driver guidance (Mahmoud et al., 2021, pp. 4233).

LITERATURE REVIEW

(Guevara et al., 2021, pp. 12).This debate aims to provide, in a comprehensive manner, how 5G technology will effect on smart cities, intelligent transportation systems - including autonomous or semi-autonomous cars - and vehicular communications, as well as its technological, economic, and regulatory problems, in the next years The next mobile technology, 5G, challenges the present communications landscape by overcoming the shortcomings of the already operational 4G. Such innovative technology provides smart cities and intelligent transportation systems with a new path to complete integration by permitting large simultaneous connections and network ubiquity, especially in high-mobility or densely inhabited locations. As a result, 5G will play an important role in enabling the genuine Internet of Things and the associated Internet of Vehicles.

(Khanh et al., 2020, pp 1-12) This technology is transforming the Internet of Things (IoT) into a digital society, enabling applications like smart cities, agriculture, retail, and transportation systems. However, challenges like energy savings, security, performance, and QoS support remain. This study provides a comprehensive vision of the IoT, discussing communication technologies, challenges, and future research directions, aiming to guide future studies on IoT in 5G.

(Syed, A et al., 2021, pp 429-475) The Internet of Things (IoT) is a system that integrates various devices and technologies, reducing human intervention and enabling smarter cities worldwide. It facilitates sustainable living, increased comfort, and productivity for citizens. This paper provides a comprehensive overview of IoT in Smart Cities, discussing its fundamental components, technologies, architectures, networking, and Artificial Algorithms. It also reviews common practices and applications, and discusses challenges and mitigation measures.

(Ahmed et al., 2016, pp 10-16). The broad use of IoT-based technologies in smart city settings has been made possible by the notable advancements in wireless and sensor-based technologies .Key technologies such sensors, machine learning, IoT, big data, and GPS-based apps must be integrated for the smart city to function. These technologies pose serious risks to the security and integrity of data relating to citizens. Systems must have sufficient security measures and be technologically advanced in order to avoid data breaches and reveal flaws. Unmanned aerial vehicles (UAVs), building automation systems, smart grids, and electric vehicles (EVs) are examples of smart city infrastructure. These systems provide major hazards and inherent complications that need to be handled.

CHALLENGES OF 5G THAT MOTIVATE THE 6TH GENERATION NETWORK

The deployment and development of 5G networks were still proceeding as of my latest knowledge update in January 2022, and nothing was known about the unique issues driving the creation of 6G networks. I can provide you a few broad 5G problems, though, which can propel the progression towards 6G

1. **Network Congestion and Capacity:** As more devices join 5G networks, handling the resulting surge in data traffic and guaranteeing enough network capacity may present difficulties. The boundaries of what 5G can provide may be reached due to the desire for fast data speeds and minimal latency (Pérez-Romero et al., 2016, pp, 359-365).
2. **Coverage and Range:** 5G networks rely on a dense network of small cells, and the coverage in certain areas, especially in rural or remote locations, may be limited. Developing a network that can provide widespread coverage is a challenge.
3. **Interoperability and Standards:** Ensuring seamless interoperability between different 5G networks and devices can be complex. There could be a need for more standardized approaches to improve compatibility.

Energy Consumption: The deployment of 5G networks involves a significant number of small cells and infrastructure, which may lead to increased energy consumption. Developing more energy-efficient technologies could be a focus for future generations (Naaz et al., 2023, pp. 537-548)

CONCLUSION

A city is an ensemble of interconnected systems, each with its own history and distinct social and environmental setting. In order for a city to thrive, its major systems must cooperate with one another and pool their resources to meet the obstacles the city encounters. A city's capacity to pool all of its resources and run its operations as efficiently as possible in order to achieve the goals it has set for itself is referred to as "smartness." There are differing meanings of the term "smart city" among academics and industry experts. One or more of the following components can be found in a smart city: smart grid, smart transportation, smart health care, and smart government. .. For long-term sustainability, smart cities with low installation and operating costs are essential. Many smart cities with various smart components are currently operational in different regions of the world. The need for smart cities is rising daily due to population expansion and the depletion of earth's resources. This paper discusses the expected features of 5G technologies and argues that they may be the best option for putting smart cities into practice. This research provides a reflection on the state of the art regarding the usage of 5G in smart cities, which is beneficial to both researchers and practitioners in the field.

REFERENCES

Ahmed, E., Yaqoob, I., Gani, A., Imran, M., & Guizani, M. (2016). Internet-of-things-based smart environments: State of the art, taxonomy, and open research challenges. *IEEE Wireless Communications, 23*(5), 10–16. doi:10.1109/MWC.2016.7721736

Ahvar, E., Ahvar, S., Raza, S. M., Manuel Sanchez Vilchez, J., & Lee, G. M. (2021). Next generation of SDN in cloud-fog for 5G and beyond-enabled applications: Opportunities and challenges. *Network, 1*(1), 28-49.28-49. doi:10.3390/network1010004

Al Sharif, R., & Pokharel, S. (2022). Smart city dimensions and associated risks: Review of literature. *Sustainable Cities and Society, 77*, 103542. doi:10.1016/j.scs.2021.103542

Alahi, M. E. E., Sukkuea, A., Tina, F. W., Nag, A., Kurdthongmee, W., Suwannarat, K., & Mukhopadhyay, S. C. (2023). Integration of IoT-enabled technologies and artificial intelligence (AI) for smart city scenario: Recent advancements and future trends. *Sensors (Basel), 23*(11), 5206. doi:10.3390/s23115206 PMID:37299934

Ateya, A. A., Algarni, A. D., Hamdi, M., Koucheryavy, A., & Soliman, N. F. (2021). Enabling heterogeneous IoT networks over 5G networks with ultra-dense deployment—Using MEC/SDN. *Electronics (Basel), 10*(8), 910. doi:10.3390/electronics10080910

Barros, T., Silva, R., Quevedo, J., Corujo, D., & Aguiar, R. L. (2023, November). Flexible Aether Slice Provisioning for 5G Enterprise Connected Edge. In *2023 IEEE Conference on Network Function Virtualization and Software Defined Networks (NFV-SDN)* (pp. 227-232). IEEE. 10.1109/NFV-SDN59219.2023.10329728

Belli, L., Cilfone, A., Davoli, L., Ferrari, G., Adorni, P., Di Nocera, F., & Bertolotti, E. (2020). IoT-enabled smart sustainable cities: Challenges and approaches. *Smart Cities, 3*(3), 1039-1071.*3*(3), 1039-1071.

Borcoci, E., Drăgulinescu, A. M., Li, F. Y., Vochin, M. C., & Kjellstadli, K. (2021). An overview of 5G slicing operational business models for Internet of vehicles, maritime IoT applications and connectivity solutions. *IEEE Access : Practical Innovations, Open Solutions, 9*, 156624–156646. doi:10.1109/ACCESS.2021.3128496

Car, T., Stifanich, L. P., & Kovačić, N. (2022). The role of 5G and IoT in smart cities. *ENTRENOVA-ENTerprise REsearch InNOVAtion, 8*(1), 377–389. doi:10.54820/entrenova-2022-0032

Chrysikos, T., Gourna, S., & Skouroliakou, A. (2023). RF Coverage Design for the Implementation of a Broadband Monitoring Service in the Context of 5G-Enabled Smart Cities. *Information (Basel), 14*(3), 156. doi:10.3390/info14030156

Deebak, B. D., & Fadi, A. T. (2022). A robust and distributed architecture for 5G-enabled networks in the smart blockchain era. *Computer Communications, 181*, 293–308. doi:10.1016/j.comcom.2021.10.015

Delson, T. R., & Jose, I. (2022, October). Study on 5G Massive MIMO Technology Key Parameters for Spectral Efficiency Improvement Including SINR Mapping on Rural Area Test Case. In *2022 IEEE 3rd Global Conference for Advancement in Technology (GCAT)* (pp. 1-6). IEEE.

Fang, H., Lo, S., & Lo, J. T. (2021). Building fire evacuation: An IoT-aided perspective in the 5G era. *Buildings*, *11*(12), 643. doi:10.3390/buildings11120643

Gai, R., Du, X., Ma, S., Chen, N., & Gao, S. (2021, March). A Summary of 5G applications and prosprcts of 5G in the Internet of Things. In *2021 IEEE 2nd International Conference on Big Data, Artificial Intelligence and Internet of Things Engineering (ICBAIE)* (pp. 858-863). IEEE. 10.1109/ICBAIE52039.2021.9389985

Gebremariam, Y. E., Duguma, D. G., Park, H. Y., Kim, Y. N., Kim, B., & You, I. (2021, August). 5G and beyond telco cloud: architecture and cybersecurity challenges. In *2021 World Automation Congress (WAC)* (pp. 1-6). IEEE. 10.23919/WAC50355.2021.9559450

Gkagkas, G., Vergados, D. J., & Michalas, A. (2021, September). The advantage of the 5G network for enhancing the Internet of Things. In *2021 6th South-East Europe Design Automation, Computer Engineering, Computer Networks and Social Media Conference (SEEDA-CECNSM)* (pp. 1-7). IEEE. 10.1109/SEEDA-CECNSM53056.2021.9566239

Guevara, L., & Auat Cheein, F. (2020). The role of 5G technologies: Challenges in smart cities and intelligent transportation systems. *Sustainability (Basel)*, *12*(16), 6469. doi:10.3390/su12166469

Hsu, W. L., Wu, X., Yu, F. C., & Sun, K. S. (2021, December). Research on Shanghai smart city evaluation system in the era of 5G Internet of Things. In *2021 IEEE 3rd International Conference on Architecture, Construction, Environment and Hydraulics (ICACEH)* (pp. 1-4). IEEE.10.1109/ICACEH54312.2021.9768847

Huseien, G. F., & Shah, K. W. (2022). A review on 5G technology for smart energy management and smart buildings in Singapore. *Energy and AI*, *7*, 100116. doi:10.1016/j.egyai.2021.100116

Kaur, P., & Garg, R. (2021). A survey on key enabling technologies towards 5G. In IOP Conference Series: Materials Science and Engineering (Vol. 1033, No. 1, p. 012011). IOP Publishing. doi:10.1145/3457388.3458614

Khanh, Q. V., Hoai, N. V., Manh, L. D., Le, A. N., & Jeon, G. (2022). Wireless communication technologies for IoT in 5G: Vision, applications, and challenges. *Wireless Communications and Mobile Computing*, *2022*, 1–12. doi:10.1155/2022/3229294

Khujamatov, K. E., Toshtemirov, T. K., Lazarev, A. P., & Raximjonov, Q. T. (2021, November). IoT and 5G technology in agriculture. In *2021 International Conference on Information Science and Communications Technologies (ICISCT)* (pp. 1-6). IEEE. 10.1109/ICISCT52966.2021.9670037

Knieps, G., & Bauer, J. M. (2022). Internet of things and the economics of 5G-based local industrial networks. *Telecommunications Policy*, *46*(4), 102261. doi:10.1016/j.telpol.2021.102261

Lu, H. H., Li, C. Y., Tsai, W. S., Chang, P. S., Chen, Y. T., Liu, C. X., Ko, T., & Lin, Y. Y. (2021). Simultaneous transmission of 5G MMW and sub-THz signals through a fiber-FSO-5G NR converged system. *Journal of Lightwave Technology*, *40*(8), 2348–2356. doi:10.1109/JLT.2021.3139620

Mahamuni, C. V. (2023, November). Exploring IoT-Applications: A Survey of Recent Progress, Challenges, and Impact of AI, Blockchain, and Disruptive Technologies. In *2023 7th International Conference on Electronics, Communication and Aerospace Technology (ICECA),* (pp. 1324-1331). IEEE. 10.1109/ICECA58529.2023.10395064

Mahmoud, H. H. H., Amer, A. A., & Ismail, T. (2021). 6G: A comprehensive survey on technologies, applications, challenges, and research problems. *Transactions on Emerging Telecommunications Technologies*, *32*(4), e4233. doi:10.1002/ett.4233

Mollel, M. S., Abubakar, A. I., Ozturk, M., Kaijage, S. F., Kisangiri, M., Hussain, S., & Abbasi, Q. H. (2021). A survey of machine learning applications to handover management in 5G and beyond. *IEEE Access : Practical Innovations, Open Solutions*, *9*, 45770–45802. doi:10.1109/ACCESS.2021.3067503

Naaz, S., & Parveen, S. (2023, January). An In-Depth Study of 5G-Based Eco-Friendly Smart City. In *International Conference on Smart Trends in Computing and Communications* (pp. 537-548). Singapore: Springer Nature Singapore 10.1007/978-981-99-0769-4_47

Nazim, S. F., Danish, M. S. S., & Senjyu, T. (2022). A brief review of the future of smart mobility using 5G and IoT. *Journal of Sustainability Outreach*. doi:10.37357/1068/jso/3.1.02

Ometov, A., Chukhno, O., Chukhno, N., Nurmi, J., & Lohan, E. S. (2021, May). When wearable technology meets computing in future networks: A road ahead. In *Proceedings of the 18th ACM International Conference on Computing Frontiers* (pp. 185-190). ACM. 10.1145/3457388.3458614

Pérez-Romero, J., Sallent, O., Ferrús, R., & Agustí, R. (2016, September). Knowledge-based 5G radio access network planning and optimization. In *2016 International Symposium on Wireless Communication Systems (ISWCS)* (pp. 359-365). IEEE 10.1109/ISWCS.2016.7600929

Syed, A. S., Sierra-Sosa, D., Kumar, A., & Elmaghraby, A. (2021). IoT in smart cities: A survey of technologies, practices and challenges. *Smart Cities*, *4*(2), 429–475. doi:10.3390/smartcities4020024

Tan, L., Xiao, H., Yu, K., Aloqaily, M., & Jararweh, Y. (2021). A blockchain-empowered crowdsourcing system for 5G-enabled smart cities. *Computer Standards & Interfaces*, *76*, 103517. doi:10.1016/j.csi.2021.103517

Tang, Y., Dananjayan, S., Hou, C., Guo, Q., Luo, S., & He, Y. (2021). A survey on the 5G network and its impact on agriculture: Challenges and opportunities. *Computers and Electronics in Agriculture*, *180*, 105895. doi:10.1016/j.compag.2020.105895

Tsakyridis, A., Ruggeri, E., Kalfas, G., Oldenbeuving, R. M., van Dijk, P. W., Roeloffzen, C. G., Leiba, Y., Miliou, A., Pleros, N., & Vagionas, C. (2021). Reconfigurable fiber wireless IFoF fronthaul with 60 GHz phased array antenna and silicon photonic ROADM for 5G mmWave C-RANs. *IEEE Journal on Selected Areas in Communications*, *39*(9), 2816–2826. doi:10.1109/JSAC.2021.3064649

Wen, M., Li, Q., Kim, K. J., López-Pérez, D., Dobre, O. A., Poor, H. V., Popovski, P., & Tsiftsis, T. A. (2021). Private 5G networks: Concepts, architectures, and research landscape. *IEEE Journal of Selected Topics in Signal Processing*, *16*(1), 7–25. doi:10.1109/JSTSP.2021.3137669

Yang, C., Liang, P., Fu, L., Cui, G., Huang, F., Teng, F., & Bangash, Y. A. (2022). Using 5G in smart cities: A systematic mapping study. *Intelligent Systems with Applications*, *14*, 200065. doi:10.1016/j.iswa.2022.200065

Yang, C., Liang, P., Fu, L., Cui, G., Huang, F., Teng, F., & Bangash, Y. A. (2022). Using 5G in smart cities: A systematic mapping study. *Intelligent Systems with Applications*, *14*, 200065. doi:10.1016/j.iswa.2022.200065

Zhao, X., Askari, H., & Chen, J. (2021). Nanogenerators for smart cities in the era of 5G and Internet of Things. *Joule*, *5*(6), 1391–1431. doi:10.1016/j.joule.2021.03.013

Zhou, Y. (2021). Material foundation for future 5G technology. *Accounts of Materials Research*, 2(5), 306–310. doi:10.1021/accountsmr.0c00087

Chapter 4
5G Cityscape:
Unleashing Seamless Connectivity for Smart Urban Evolution

Manisha Koranga
Graphic Era Hill University, India

Tarun Kumar
MIET Kumaon, India

Sujata Negi Thakur
Graphic Era Hill University, India

Richa Pandey
Graphic Era Hill University, India

Mayurika Joshi
Graphic Era Hill University, India

ABSTRACT

The rise of 5G technology marks a significant shift in smart city development, bringing unprecedented connectivity and transformative opportunities. This chapter explores its profound impact on urban evolution, focusing on creating intelligent cityscapes. It examines key 5G components like the radio access network, core network, network slicing, edge computing, and IoT devices, enabling real-time monitoring, efficient resource management, and innovation in transportation, healthcare, public safety, and energy sectors. 5G facilitates intelligent transportation, enhances public safety via high-resolution video surveillance, and revolutionizes healthcare through telemedicine. Augmented reality (AR) and virtual reality (VR) experiences, enabled by 5G, drive innovative urban solutions. The economic and societal implications, including economic growth, job creation, and civic engagement, are discussed. Overall, 5G fosters sustainable, efficient, and citizen-centric urban environments.

DOI: 10.4018/979-8-3693-2373-1.ch004

INTRODUCTION

The evolution of urban landscapes is undergoing a revolutionary transformation propelled by the integration of advanced technologies, with smart cities emerging as the epitome of this paradigm shift. A smart city leverages technology and data-driven solutions to optimize performance, enhance well-being, and streamline resource consumption and costs (Singh *et al.,* 2022a). At the forefront of this transformative journey is the next iteration of wireless communication technology, often referred to as 5G. Representing a substantial leap beyond its predecessor, 4G (LTE), 5G introduces unparalleled advancements in data transfer speeds, network capacity, and connectivity capabilities (Rong *et al.,* 2020). The deployment of 5G technology holds profound implications across various sectors, playing a crucial role in advancing and improving of smart cities. This paper explores the multifaceted impact of 5G on the cityscape, delving into its potential to unleash seamless connectivity and foster innovation across diverse domains. The foundational elements of 5G, such as ultra-fast connectivity, minimal delay and capacity for connecting numerous devices, are examined for their transformative influence on urban environments (Xu & Jia, 2021). As urban populations burgeon, the demand for smarter, more connected cities intensifies. In response to this imperative, 5G technology emerges as a transformative force, promising unparalleled connectivity and catalyzing a new era in smart urban evolution. The research endeavors to comprehensively examine the role of 5G in shaping the smart city landscape, unraveling the intricacies of its technological underpinnings, applications, and societal implications. Understanding how 5G enables seamless connectivity becomes pivotal for city planners, policymakers, and technologists navigating the complexities of modern urban development (Singh *et al.*, 2023a). The integration of 5G technology facilitates real-time communication, supports a myriad of connected devices, and enables innovative applications (Guevara & Cheein, 2020). This positions 5G as a cornerstone for building smart cities that are not just interconnected but additionally, efficient, resilient, and adaptable to the changing needs of their residents. As cities grapple with challenges related to population growth, resource management, and sustainability, 5G technology emerges as a catalyst for positive change, offering the ability to monitor and manage utilities, transportation systems, and other critical urban components efficiently (Telsac &Yilmaz, 2021).

In the subsequent sections, this research paper will delve into the foundations of 5G technology, explore its components in smart city integration, and examine the transformative impact it exerts across various domains. By unraveling the complexities of the 5G cityscape, the paper aims to enhance comprehension of the possibilities and challenges involved in the pursuit of smart urban evolution.

LITERATURE REVIEW

In an era where urbanization is rapidly advancing, the role of 5G technology in influencing the future of smart cities is pivotal. This literature review delves into the scholarly discourse, aiming to elucidate the multifaceted dimensions of the "5G Cityscape."

A systematic mapping study conducted between January 2012 and December 2019, focusing on the utilization of 5G technology in smart cities. The study analyzes 32 selected works, summarizing and further examining various aspects such as scenarios, architecture, technologies, challenges, and lessons learned (Yang *et al.,* 2022). A comprehensive systematic review on the incorporation of 5G technology within smart cities, focusing on published papers spanning from 2020 to 2023 is conducted by authors. The examination relies on two primary databases, namely Google Scholar and Mendeley, as foundational references for the review. The research endeavors to highlight key insights from the identified literature and, upon culmination, elucidate the challenges encountered in integrating 5G technology into smart cities. Furthermore, the paper aims to propose viable solutions to enhance the seamless integration of 5G technology, thereby contributing to the advancement of smart city initiatives (Ejreaw, 2023). The authors explore the progression of smart city development in China, emphasizing the benefits of integrating 5G technology. It delves into the advantages of applying 5G across various sectors, namely smart transportation, environmental conservation, healthcare, security, and government operations. Furthermore, the article assesses the impact of 5G applications within these scenarios. Conclusively, it addresses the primary challenges confronting China's 5G smart cities and offers relevant recommendations (Xu & Jia, 2021). The authors examine several practical concerns associated with 5G-driven IoT applications, encompassing the necessity for small cells, transmission challenges at millimeter wave frequencies, constructing penetration issues, and the need for distributed antenna systems. Additionally, to cater to the specific requirements of smart cities, this study provides a concise overview of pre-5G IoT technologies like NB-IoT and LTE-M (Minoli & Occhiogrosso, 2019). The authors have initially provided a thorough examination of the foundational framework and features of the 5G system. Subsequently, authors offer a thorough examination of delineate characteristics and the hierarchical structure of the Internet of Things (IoT). They also highlighted the necessity of requisites of 5G-enabled IoT, Blockchain-integrated 5G IoT, and the convergence of 5G and artificial intelligence. They explore the potential possibilities of 5G IoT across diverse domains. Lastly, the paper scrutinizes and assesses the research gaps, challenges, and possible solutions presented in a detailed table format (Haque *et al.*, 2023). The authors draw attention on the significance of tackling interference and optimizing network performance within 5G networks to guarantee a dependable and efficient connectivity environment for IoT devices. The authors also highlighted the prospective benefits arising from the convergence of networks and services, amplifying internet accessibility speed and availability (Pons *et al.,* 2023). The authors in their paper delves into diverse architectures exploring the integration of hybrid 5G-LPWAN-IoT systems within the context of Smart Cities. They address security challenges and proposes solutions for both endogenous security concerns within 5G and LPWAN-IoT. The authors also introduce the concept of slicing virtual networks through software-based networking (SDN) and virtualized network functions (NFV). Additionally, a strategic approach is outlined, considering the simultaneous deployment of 5G and Weightless-N (TVWS) technologies for reducing interference at cell edges (Ogbodo *et al.,* 2023).

FOUNDATION OF 5G

The evolution of wireless communication has witnessed a succession of transformative leaps, progressing from 2G to 3G, 4G, and now, the much-anticipated fifth generation–5G. The technological transformation from 1G (First Generation) to 5G (Fifth Generation) represents a remarkable evolution in wireless communication, marked by significant improvements in speed, capacity, and functionality (Singh *et al.,* 2022c; Mendonca *et al.,* 2022; Zhou, 2021) as shown in figure 1. The key milestones in this transformation:

Figure 1. Technological transformation from 1G to 5G

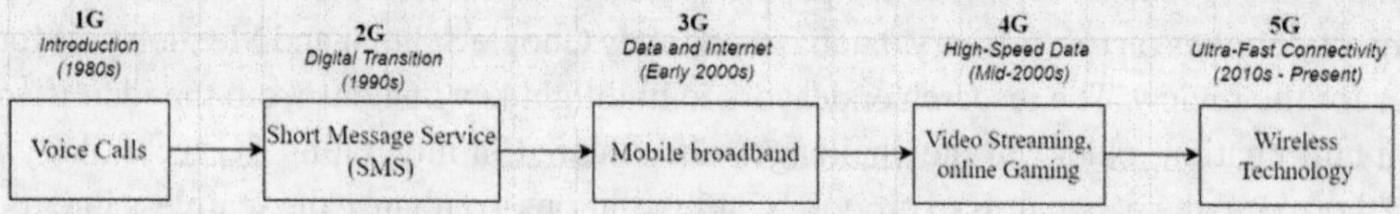

1G (First Generation)

Introduction (1980s): 1G marked the inception of mobile telephony, enabling basic voice communication. Analog technology was used, allowing users to make voice calls through the use of large, bulky devices.

2G (Second Generation)

Digital Transition (1990s): 2G marked the shift from analog to digital technology, providing enhanced voice quality and the introduction of Short Message Service (SMS). Digital cellular networks paved the way for smaller and more portable devices.

3G (Third Generation)

Data and Internet (Early 2000s): 3G introduced mobile data services, enabling internet connectivity on mobile devices. This generation marked the beginning of mobile broadband, allowing users to access email, browse the web, and use multimedia applications.

4G (Fourth Generation)

High-Speed Data (Mid-2000s): 4G significantly enhanced data transfer speeds, providing a basis for high-definition video streaming, online gaming, and other data-intensive applications. It introduced Long-Term Evolution (LTE) technology.

5G (Fifth Generation)

Ultra-Fast Connectivity (2010s - Present): 5G represents a revolutionary leap in wireless technology. Key characteristics involves:

- *Faster Data Transfer Speeds:* 5G offers exponentially higher data transfer speeds compared to its predecessors, facilitating quick downloads and low-latency communication.
- *Low Latency*: The latency in 5G is significantly reduced, enabling near-instantaneous communication. This is critical for real-time applications like autonomous vehicles and augmented reality.
- *Massive Device Connectivity*: 5G can support a massive quantity of connected devices simultaneously, making it instrumental for the Internet of Things (IoT) and smart city applications.

- *Increased Network Capacity:* 5G addresses network congestion issues and accommodates the growing demand for high-quality services by substantially expanding network capacity.
- *Multiple Frequency Bands*: 5G utilizes different frequency bands, such as sub-6 GHz and millimeter-wave (mmWave), each serving specific purposes in delivering enhanced connectivity.
- *Massive MIMO and Beamforming*: MIMO (Multiple Input, Multiple Output) and beamforming technologies are employed to improve data transfer rates and optimize signal strength.
- *Network Slicing*: 5G introduces network slicing, enabling the creation of virtual networks customized for specific applications or services, ensuring efficient resource allocation.

The transformation from 1G to 5G reflects a journey of continuous innovation, evolving from basic voice communication to a sophisticated, interconnected ecosystem capable of providing a wide array of applications and services, encompasses smart cities, IoT, augmented reality, and beyond (Dangi *et al.,* 2021; Georgiou *et al.,* 2021; Mendonca *et al.,* 2022; Attar *et al.,* 2022). The rapid advancements in each generation have contributed to the increasingly interconnected and data-centric nature of our modern communication landscape.

COMPONENTS OF 5G-ENABLED SMART CITIES

The components of 5G-enabled smart cities encompass a diverse range of technologies and infrastructure that collectively contribute to creating intelligent, connected, and efficient urban environments (Car *et al.,* 2022; Bibri & Jagatheesaperumal, 2023; Gracias *et al.,* 2023; Ogbodo *et al.,* 2023; Singh *et al.,* 2023a; Singh *et al.,* 2024) as shown in Figure 2. Here are the key components:

- *5G Radio Access Network (RAN):* The radio access network is an important component of 5G infrastructure that includes base stations and antennas. It facilitates wireless communication between devices and the core network, providing the necessary connectivity for 5G-enabled devices.
- *Core Network and Network Slicing:* The core network processes and manages data traffic. Network slicing is an innovative feature of 5G that enables the creation of virtual networks customized for specific applications or services. This ensures efficient resource allocation and optimal performance for diverse use cases.
- *Edge Computing:* Edge computing involves processing data closer to the source of generation rather than relying solely on centralized cloud servers. In smart cities, edge computing is integral for reducing latency and enabling real-time processing of data from IoT devices.
- *Internet of Things (IoT) Devices:* IoT devices, including sensors, actuators, and connected gadgets, form the backbone of a smart city's data-generating infrastructure. 5G's ability to support a massive number of connected devices facilitates the proliferation of IoT applications.
- *Smart Infrastructure:* Infrastructure elements such as smart grids, smart streetlights, and connected utilities leverage 5G connectivity for efficient monitoring and management. This leads to improved resource utilization and sustainability in urban areas.
- *Real-Time Monitoring and Analytics:* 5G enables real-time monitoring of various parameters, including traffic flow, air quality, and energy consumption. Advanced analytics powered by high data speeds and low latency allow for prompt analysis and response to data.

Figure 2. 5G-Enabled smart cities

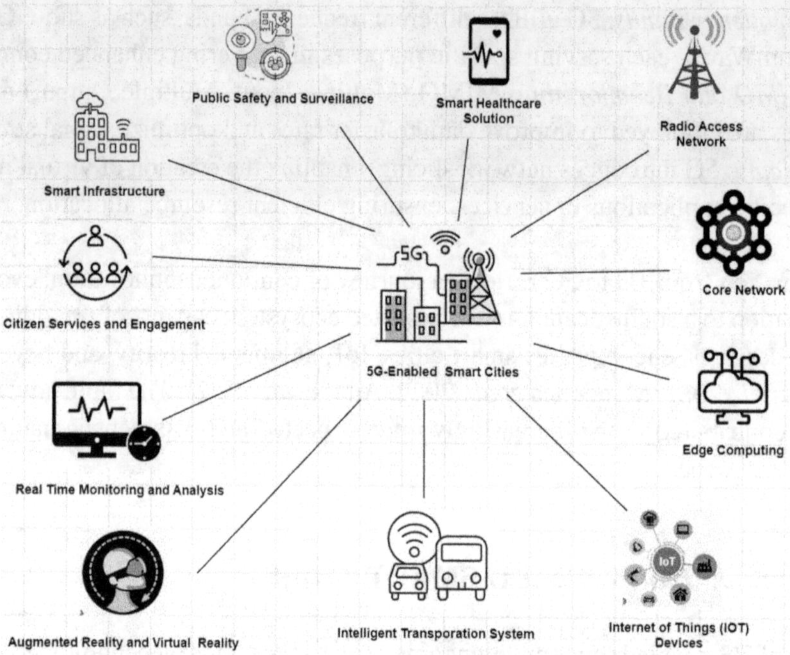

- *Intelligent Transportation Systems (ITS):* 5G plays a pivotal role in the development of ITS, enabling connected vehicles to communicate with each other and with smart infrastructure. This contributes to enhanced traffic flow, reduced congestion, and improved overall mobility.
- *Augmented Reality (AR) and Virtual Reality (VR):* The high-speed and low-latency capabilities of 5G support immersive AR and VR experiences. These technologies find applications in smart city planning, education, tourism, and other domains.
- *Smart Healthcare Solutions:* Telemedicine, remote patient monitoring, and other healthcare applications benefit from 5G connectivity. The technology ensures high-quality, real-time communication for healthcare professionals and patients.
- *Public Safety and Surveillance:* 5G enables advanced public safety systems, including high-resolution video surveillance and emergency response mechanisms. Real-time data transmission enhances the effectiveness of smart surveillance cameras and emergency services.
- *Citizen Services and Engagement:* 5G enhances citizen services through improved and responsive digital platforms. Citizens can access services more efficiently, contributing to an enhanced overall experience.
- *Network Slicing for Specific Use Cases*: 5G's network slicing capability allows the creation of virtual networks tailored to specific smart city applications. This ensures efficient resource allocation and optimal performance for various use cases.

The integration of these components forms a cohesive ecosystem, leveraging the capabilities of 5G to create smart cities that are not just connected but also intelligent, sustainable, and responsive to the needs of their residents (Gohar & Nencioni, 2021; Ejreaw, 2023; Ogbodo *et al.,* 2023).

TECHNOLOGICAL SYNERGIES FOR REAL-TIME SOLUTIONS IN 5G CITYSCAPE

The technological synergies for real-time solutions in the 5G cityscape are pivotal in realizing the vision of unleashing seamless connectivity for smart urban evolution (Gohar & Nencioni, 2021; Anantrasirichai & Bull, 2022; Haque *et al.,* 2023; Ogbodo *et al.,* 2023; Singh *et al.,* 2023). The convergence of cutting-edge technologies within the 5G ecosystem creates a dynamic environment where real-time solutions become not just possible but transformative for urban living (Guevara & Cheein, 2020). Key technological synergies include:

- *Ultra-Fast Connectivity:* The inherent high data transfer speeds of 5G lay the foundation for real-time solutions, enabling instant communication and rapid data exchange.
- *Low Latency:* 5G's minimal latency ensures near-instantaneous response times, crucial for applications demanding real-time interactions such as autonomous vehicles, smart traffic management, and emergency services.
- *Massive Device Connectivity:* The ability of 5G to support a massive number of connected devices simultaneously facilitates the proliferation of real-time solutions, from IoT sensors to smart devices and urban infrastructure.
- *Edge Computing:* Edge computing, coupled with 5G, brings processing closer to the data source. This synergy reduces latency, improving the feasibility of real-time analytics and decision-making in urban environments.
- *Internet of Things (IoT):* 5G's seamless integration with IoT devices creates a networked environment where real-time data from sensors and connected devices contribute to dynamic, responsive city systems.
- *Network Slicing:* In 5G, network slicing enables the creation of dedicated virtual networks for specific applications. This ensures optimal resource allocation and performance for real-time solutions.
- *Artificial Intelligence (AI) and Machine Learning (ML):* Integration of AI and ML algorithms with 5G data streams enables real-time analytics and insights. Smart algorithms can process and interpret data rapidly, contributing to intelligent decision-making in urban scenarios.
- *Augmented Reality (AR) and Virtual Reality (VR):* The high-speed, low-latency capabilities of 5G enable immersive Augmented Reality (AR) and Virtual Reality (VR) experiences in real-time, applicable in urban planning, education, tourism, and various other domains.
- *Smart Infrastructure Management:* Real-time monitoring and management of smart infrastructure, such as utilities, transportation systems, and public services, are facilitated by 5G connectivity. This contributes to efficiency, resilience, and responsiveness in city operations.

- *Intelligent Transportation Systems (ITS):* The real-time capabilities of 5G are crucial for the advancement of Intelligent Transportation Systems (ITS), which optimize traffic flow, reduce congestion, and enhance overall mobility through connected vehicles and smart traffic management.
- *Public Safety and Surveillance:* Advanced public safety systems, including high-resolution video surveillance and emergency response mechanisms, benefit from 5G's high-speed and reliable connectivity, enhancing security in real-time.
- *Citizen Services:* Real-time access to digital platforms and services, enabled by 5G, enhances the overall experience for residents. From instant information updates to responsive civic engagement, citizens benefit from seamless connectivity.

In the 5G cityscape, the synergy of these technologies unleashes a new era where real-time solutions become integral to the fabric of smart urban evolution (Bibri & Jagatheesaperumal, 2023). This interconnected ecosystem not only enhances efficiency but also fosters innovation, sustainability, and an improved quality of life for city dwellers.

REVOLUTIONIZING HEALTHCARE AND QUALITY OF LIFE IN 5G CITYSCAPE

The revolutionization of healthcare and the enhancement of quality of life within the 5G cityscape mark a transformative phase, leveraging seamless connectivity for smart urban evolution (Xiong *et al.,* 2022; Rahman *et al.,* 2022; Car *et al.,* 2022; Pons *et al.,* 2023; Singh *et al.,* 2023b). The integration of 5G technology with healthcare services and urban living contribute to a myriad of advancements, fostering improved well-being and accessibility to healthcare resources (Singh & Park, 2022; Singh *et al.,* 2022c; Cabanillas-Carbonell *et al.,* 2023). Key aspects include:

- *Telemedicine and Remote Patient Monitoring:* 5G enables the expansion of telemedicine services, allowing healthcare professionals to conduct remote consultations, monitor patients in real-time, and offer timely medical advice.
- *High-Resolution Imaging and Diagnostics:* The high data transfer speeds of 5G support the seamless transmission of large medical imaging files, facilitating high-resolution diagnostics, and enabling healthcare professionals to make more accurate assessments.
- *Real-Time Health Monitoring Wearables:* Wearable devices equipped with real-time health monitoring capabilities, such as heart rate and blood pressure sensors, benefit from 5G connectivity. This ensures continuous data transmission for immediate analysis and timely interventions.
- *Emergency Medical Services (EMS):* 5G enhances emergency response systems with real-time data transmission, enabling faster communication between ambulances, hospitals, and emergency personnel. This is crucial for prompt and effective emergency medical care.
- *IoT-Enabled Healthcare Devices:* The utilization of Internet of Things (IoT) devices in healthcare, from smart medical devices to health trackers, is facilitated by 5G connectivity. This interconnected ecosystem supports real-time data collection and analysis for personalized healthcare.
- *Remote Surgery and Telehealth Procedures:* 5G's low latency and high-speed connectivity open avenues for remote surgery and telehealth procedures, enabling surgeons to perform intricate operations with precision from a distance.

- *Augmented Reality (AR) for Medical Training:* The integration of 5G with AR technology enhances medical training by providing real-time, immersive experiences for healthcare professionals, improving their skills and knowledge.
- *Smart Health Infrastructure Management:* Real-time monitoring of healthcare facilities, equipment, and resources is facilitated by 5G. This ensures efficient management, predictive maintenance, and optimal utilization of healthcare infrastructure.
- *Data Security and Privacy in Healthcare:* 5G networks incorporate advanced security measures, ensuring the privacy and confidentiality of sensitive healthcare data, a critical aspect in the evolution of smart healthcare systems.
- *Enhanced Connectivity for Rural and Underserved Areas:* 5G's extended reach facilitates healthcare access in remote and underserved areas, overcoming geographical barriers and ensuring that residents in such regions receive quality medical services.
- *Patient-Centric Digital Platforms:* 5G enables the development of patient-centric digital platforms, providing seamless connectivity for accessing health records, scheduling appointments, and engaging in telehealth consultations, contributing to an empowered and informed patient experience.

In the 5G cityscape, the revolutionized healthcare ecosystem promotes not only efficiency and accessibility but also a proactive approach to well-being. The synergy of healthcare services with 5G connectivity exemplifies a future where urban living is characterized by smart, responsive, and inclusive healthcare solutions.

ECONOMIC AND SOCIETAL IMPLICATIONS IN 5G CITYSCAPE

The advent of the 5G cityscape brings forth significant economic and societal implications, shaping urban environments in transformative ways (Dutta & Hammad, 2020). This evolution is characterized by a host of opportunities and challenges that have profound effects on both economic structures and societal dynamics (El-Shorbagy, 2021; Humayun *et al.*, 2021; Park *et al.*, 2021; O'Connell *et al.*, 2020; Fabregue & Bogoni, 2023; Singh *et al.*, 2023a; Park *et al.*, 2024; Kumar *et al.*, 2024). Here are key considerations for the economic and societal implications in the 5G cityscape:

Economic Implications

- *Job Creation and Industry Growth:* The deployment and maintenance of 5G infrastructure contribute to job creation across various sectors, including telecommunications, technology, and construction. Additionally, the growth of new technologies and services in the 5G ecosystem fosters the emergence of new industries.
- *Innovation and Entrepreneurship:* The 5G cityscape serves as a catalyst for innovation, providing a fertile ground for entrepreneurs to develop and implement novel technologies and solutions. Startups focused on IoT, smart city applications, and 5G-enabled services become key drivers of economic growth.
- *Increased Productivity and Efficiency:* 5G's high-speed connectivity and low latency enhance productivity in various sectors, from manufacturing to healthcare. Businesses can leverage real-

time data analytics and efficient communication for streamlined operations, leading to increased efficiency.

- *Smart Infrastructure Investment:* Governments and private entities invest in smart infrastructure projects enabled by 5G technology. These investments, ranging from smart grids to intelligent transportation systems, stimulate economic growth and create opportunities for public-private partnerships.
- *Digital Economy Expansion:* The 5G cityscape accelerates the growth of the digital economy, with businesses and consumers relying on seamless connectivity for e-commerce, digital services, and data-driven applications. This shift further integrates digital technologies into everyday economic activities.
- *Global Competitiveness:* Cities that embrace and successfully implement 5G technologies enhance their global competitiveness. The ability to offer advanced digital services, attract investments, and foster innovation positions them as leaders in the global economic landscape.

Societal Implications

- *Improved Quality of Life:* The 5G cityscape enhances the overall quality of life for residents through improved connectivity, smart services, and efficient urban infrastructure. Real-time solutions in healthcare, education, and public services contribute to a more comfortable and connected living experience.
- *Enhanced Accessibility and Inclusivity:* 5G facilitates better accessibility to services and information, bridging gaps in connectivity. The technology contributes to inclusivity by ensuring that a wide spectrum of the population, encompassing those in remote areas, can access advanced digital services.
- *Smart Mobility and Reduced Congestion:* The implementation of intelligent transportation systems powered by 5G leads to reduced traffic congestion, improved traffic flow, and enhanced public transportation services. This positively impacts urban mobility and reduces environmental impact.
- *Digital Education and Remote Learning:* 5G enables advanced digital education platforms and remote learning opportunities. Students can access high-quality educational resources, participate in virtual classrooms, and engage in collaborative learning experiences, irrespective of geographical constraints.
- *Citizen Engagement and Participation:* 5G cityscapes encourage citizen engagement through digital platforms, enabling residents to actively participate in civic activities, provide feedback, and stay informed about local developments. This fosters a more engaged and empowered citizenry.
- *Data Privacy and Security Considerations:* The increased connectivity in the 5G cityscape necessitates robust measures for data privacy and security. Societal implications include the need for clear regulations, awareness programs, and mechanisms to safeguard individual privacy in an interconnected environment.
- *Addressing the Digital Divide:* Efforts to implement 5G technologies need to address the digital divide, ensuring that all segments of the population have access to the benefits of connectivity. Bridging this gap becomes crucial for fostering societal equity and preventing the marginalization of certain groups.

In essence, the 5G cityscape is a multifaceted transformation that not only drives economic prosperity but also reshapes the way society's function and interact with their urban environments (Sullivan *et al.,* 2021). It necessitates a thoughtful approach to ensure that the benefits are inclusive, and potential challenges are addressed for the overall betterment of communities.

CHALLENGES IN 5G CITYSCAPE AND ITS POSSIBLE SOLUTIONS

The 5G cityscape presents various challenges that must be addressed in order to successful deployment and optimal utilization (Singh *et al.,* 2021a; Sullivan *et al.,* 2021; Mendonca *et al.,* 2022; Attar *et al.,* 2022; Bibri & Jagatheesaperumal, 2023; Ejreaw, 2023; Singh *et al.,* 2023b). Here are some key challenges and possible solutions:

i. **Infrastructure Deployment Challenge:** The deployment of 5G infrastructure requires substantial investment and may face challenges related to zoning regulations, public acceptance, and collaboration with various stakeholders (O'Connell *et al.,* 2020; Dutta & Hammad, 2020; Fabregue & Bogoni, 2023).

The Possible Solution of Infrastructure Deployment

- *Strategic Planning:* Develop a comprehensive strategic plan for 5G deployment, considering factors such as coverage requirements, population density, and existing infrastructure. Prioritize areas based on demand and potential benefits to optimize deployment efforts.
- *Regulatory Streamlining:* Work with regulatory authorities to streamline processes related to permits, zoning, and approvals. Simplifying regulatory hurdles can significantly expedite the deployment of small cells and antennas.
- *Public-Private Partnerships:* Collaborate with private entities through public-private partnerships. This can involve sharing the cost of infrastructure deployment, leveraging private sector expertise, and aligning goals for faster implementation.
- *Community Engagement:* Engage with local communities to address concerns, provide information, and garner support for 5G deployment. Transparent communication about the benefits, potential disruptions, and safety measures can build public acceptance.
- *Digital Twin Technology:* Utilize digital twin technology to develop virtual replicas of the urban environment. This allows planners to assess the impact of infrastructure deployment, optimize locations for small cells, and minimize disruptions.
- *Incentives and Subsidies:* Provide incentives and subsidies for telecom operators and infrastructure providers to encourage 5G deployment. Financial incentives or reduced regulatory fees can motivate private entities to invest in infrastructure.
- *Infrastructure Sharing:* Encourage infrastructure sharing among multiple service providers. Shared infrastructure, such as towers and backhaul networks, can reduce costs and minimize the physical footprint of 5G infrastructure.
- *Fiber Optic Expansion:* Invest in the expansion of fiber optic networks, which serve as the backbone for 5G connectivity. Fiber backhauls is essential for connecting small cells to the core network and ensuring high-speed, reliable connectivity.

- *Utilize Existing Infrastructure:* Explore opportunities to co-locate 5G equipment on existing infrastructure, such as utility poles or streetlights. Leveraging existing structures reduces the need for additional physical space and accelerates deployment.
- *Standardization and Guidelines:* Establish standardized guidelines for 5G infrastructure deployment to ensure consistency and streamline the approval process. Clearly defined standards can simplify regulatory compliance and reduce delays.
- *Cross-Sector Collaboration:* Foster collaboration between telecom operators, city planners, utility companies, and other relevant stakeholders. A cross-sector approach can lead to coordinated efforts, resource sharing, and more efficient deployment.
- *Education and Awareness:* Educate local authorities, communities, and stakeholders about the benefits of 5G technology. Dispel myths, address health concerns with factual information, and emphasize the positive impact on urban living.
- *Adaptive Policies:* Develop adaptive policies that can evolve with technological advancements. Policies should be adaptable to accommodate changes in technology and support the continuous evolution of the 5G landscape.

ii. Interference and Spectrum Allocation Challenge: The spectrum for 5G is limited, and interference issues may arise, especially in densely populated areas. Efficient spectrum allocation is crucial to avoid conflicts and ensure optimal performance (Sullivan *et al.,* 2021; Singh *et al.,* 2022c; Mendonca *et al.,* 2022; Bibri & Jagatheesaperumal, 2023).

The Possible Solution of Infrastructure Deployment

- *Spectrum Auctions and Assignments:* Regulatory authorities can conduct well-organized spectrum auctions, ensuring fair and efficient allocation to telecom operators. Assigning specific frequency bands for 5G use and establishing clear rules for spectrum sharing can help optimize usage.
- *Harmonization and Standardization:* Promote international harmonization and standardization of spectrum bands for 5G. Aligning frequency bands globally facilitates economies of scale, encourages equipment interoperability, and enables seamless roaming for users.
- *Dynamic Spectrum Sharing:* Implement dynamic spectrum sharing (DSS) technologies that allow multiple services to share the same frequency bands dynamically. This enhances spectrum efficiency and enables more flexible use of available frequencies.
- *Flexible Licensing Models:* Adopt flexible licensing models that accommodate diverse use cases. For example, license-exempt or lightly licensed bands can be used for specific applications, encouraging innovation and fostering the growth of niche services.
- *Cognitive Radio Technology:* Explore cognitive radio technology, which enables devices to intelligently access and utilize available spectrum dynamically. Cognitive radio can help optimize spectrum use by identifying and leveraging unused frequencies in real-time.
- *Database-Driven Spectrum Access:* Implement database-driven spectrum access systems that enable dynamic sharing of spectrum based on real-time availability. These systems can efficiently allocate frequencies while preventing interference with existing users.
- *Encourage Private Networks:* Encourage the development of private 5G networks for specific industries or applications. Allocating dedicated spectrum for private networks can optimize usage and avoid congestion on public networks.

- *Millimeter Wave Spectrum Utilization:* Leverage millimeter-wave spectrum (e.g., 24 GHz, 28 GHz, and above) for 5G services. These high-frequency bands offer larger bandwidths, supporting high data rates, though they may require denser infrastructure deployment due to shorter range.
- *Spectrum Aggregation:* Allow spectrum aggregation, enabling operators to combine multiple frequency bands to achieve higher data rates and better network performance. This approach enhances the efficiency of spectrum use and provides a more robust network.
- *Spectrum Sharing Frameworks:* Establish spectrum sharing frameworks that promote collaboration among different entities, including government agencies, private enterprises, and service providers. Spectrum-sharing agreements can enhance overall spectrum utilization.
- *5G Spectrum Roadmaps:* Develop clear and forward-looking 5G spectrum roadmaps that outline the phased release of spectrum bands. This enables operators and manufacturers to plan their investments and deployments effectively.
- *Global and Regional Coordination*: Engage in international and regional coordination to address cross-border interference issues. Collaborative efforts with neighboring countries and regions can ensure efficient use of shared spectrum resources.
- *Research and Development*: Invest in research and development to investigate new frequency bands and technologies that can be utilized for 5G and future innovations. Continuous innovation can lead to the discovery of more efficient ways to use the spectrum.
- *Spectrum Re-Farming*: Consider re-farming existing spectrum bands, reallocating them from legacy technologies to 5G. This requires a coordinated approach with stakeholders to manage the transition without disrupting existing services.

iii. Coverage and Range Challenge: 5G's higher frequency bands have shorter ranges and are more prone to signal blockage, requiring more infrastructure to ensure comprehensive coverage, especially in dense urban areas (Yang *et al.*, 2022; Singh *et al.*, 2022c; Liu *et al.*, 2022).

The Possible Solution of Coverage and Range

- *Dense Small Cell Deployments:* Implement dense small cell deployments to enhance coverage in urban areas. This involves installing a large number of small cells in strategic locations to fill coverage gaps and improve overall network density.
- *Macrocell Expansion:* Expand macrocell coverage to reach a wider geographical area. Macrocells provide broader coverage compared to small cells, making them suitable for addressing range challenges in less densely populated or suburban areas.
- *Beamforming Technology*: Utilize beamforming technology to focus 5G signals in specific directions, improving coverage and range. This enables more efficient use of radio frequency resources and better penetration through obstacles.
- *Frequency Bands Optimization*: Optimize the use of different frequency bands to balance coverage and capacity. Lower frequency bands provide better coverage over long distances, while higher frequency bands offer increased capacity in dense urban areas.
- *Hybrid Networks:* Implement hybrid networks that combine different technologies, such as 5G and existing 4G LTE infrastructure. This approach allows for a gradual transition to 5G and ensures coverage continuity in areas where 5G deployment might be challenging.

- *Satellite Backhaul Solutions:* Explore satellite backhaul solutions to extend coverage to remote or challenging terrains. Satellite connectivity can act as a backhaul for 5G networks, enabling coverage in areas where traditional infrastructure is not feasible.
- *Strategic Site Selection*: Strategically select sites for base stations and small cells to optimize coverage. Consider geographical features, building structures, and population density to ensure that network elements are placed in locations that maximize coverage.
- *Urban Planning Collaboration:* Collaborate with urban planners and local authorities to integrate 5G infrastructure into city planning. This includes considering the placement of antennas and small cells in a way that minimizes obstacles and maximizes coverage.
- *Dynamic Spectrum Sharing:* Implement dynamic spectrum sharing mechanisms that allow for the flexible allocation of spectrum between 4G and 5G based on demand. This ensures efficient use of available resources and optimal coverage.
- *Community Engagement for Site Approval:* Engage with local communities to gain approval for site installations. Address concerns and communicate the benefits of 5G technology to foster community support, facilitating smoother site approval processes.
- *Airborne Platforms (Drones or Balloons):* Explore the use of airborne platforms, such as drones or balloons, equipped with 5G equipment to provide temporary coverage in specific areas. This can be especially useful in emergency situations or for events that require additional network capacity.
- *Mobile Edge Computing (MEC):* Deploy Mobile Edge Computing (MEC) to position computing resources nearer to the network edge. This reduces latency and enhances coverage by processing data closer to the end-user, especially in areas with high user density.
- *Government Incentives for Rural Deployment:* Provide government incentives to encourage telecommunication providers to extend 5G coverage to rural and underserved areas. Incentives could include subsidies, tax breaks, or regulatory benefits.
- *Continuous Network Optimization:* Continuously optimize the network based on real-time data and performance metrics. Regularly assess coverage gaps, adjust antenna configurations, and optimize signal propagation to address evolving coverage challenges.

iv. Security Concerns Challenge: The increased connectivity in a smart city introduces security concerns, including potential vulnerabilities in IoT devices and networks that need robust cybersecurity measures (Humayun *et al.,* 2021; Singh *et al.,* 2021b; Sullivan *et al.,* 2021; Dutta & Hammad, 2020; Choi *et al.,* 2022; Park *et al.,* 2022; Anantrasirichai & Bull, 2022; Fabreque & Bogoni, 2023).

The Possible Solution of Security Concerns Challenge

- *End-to-End Encryption:* Implement robust end-to-end encryption for data transmitted over the 5G network. This ensures that data remains protected and confidential, protecting it from unauthorized access or interception.
- *Network Function Virtualization (NFV) Security:* Strengthen the security of virtualized network functions by implementing NFV security measures. This includes secure hypervisors, regular security audits, and isolation of virtualized functions to prevent unauthorized access.

- *Multi-Factor Authentication (MFA):* Enforce multi-factor authentication for accessing critical infrastructure and systems. This adds an additional layer of security by necessitating multiple forms of verification, minimizing the risk of unauthorized access.
- *Secure Device Onboarding:* Implement secure processes for onboarding and connecting devices to the 5G network. Ensure that only authorized devices can access the network, preventing the inclusion of compromised devices.
- *Security-by-Design Principles:* Integrate security measures into the design and development of 5G infrastructure and devices. Following security-by-design principles ensures that security is a fundamental consideration from the outset.
- *Regular Security Audits and Penetration Testing:* Perform routine security audits and penetration testing to pinpoint vulnerabilities in the 5G network. Address any weaknesses promptly to proactively mitigate potential security threats.
- *Threat Intelligence and Information Sharing:* Establish mechanisms for collecting and sharing threat intelligence across stakeholders, including government agencies, network operators, and cybersecurity firms. Collaborative efforts enhance the ability to respond to emerging threats.
- *User Education and Awareness:* Educating users about best practices for security and potential risks associated with 5G technology. Awareness campaigns can help prevent common security issues stemming from user behavior, such as phishing attacks.
- *Secure Application Development:* Encourage secure coding practices for applications and services running on the 5G network. Vet third-party applications for security vulnerabilities before deployment to prevent potential threats.
- *Security Automation and Orchestration:* Implement automated security processes and orchestration to respond quickly to security incidents. Automation enhances the speed and efficiency of threat detection and mitigation.
- *Zero Trust Security Model:* Adopting a zero-trust security model, where trust is never assumed, and verification is required from everyone attempting to access resources in the network. This approach enhances the overall security posture.
- *Physical Security Measures:* Implement physical security measures to safeguard critical infrastructure components, such as data centers, base stations, and control centers. Restrict access to authorized personnel only.
- *Incident Response Plans:* Develop and maintain up-to-date incident response plans to promptly address security breaches. Clearly define roles and responsibilities, and conduct regular drills to ensure readiness.
- *Collaboration with Cybersecurity Agencies:* Collaborate with national and international cybersecurity agencies to stay informed about emerging threats and receive guidance on best practices. This collaboration strengthens the overall cybersecurity posture.
- *Continuous Monitoring and Anomaly Detection:* Implementing continuous monitoring and anomaly detection systems to identify unusual behavior or patterns in the network. Prompt detection enables rapid response to potential security incidents.

v. Regulatory and Privacy Issues Challenges: Addressing regulatory issues related to 5G deployment, spectrum allocation, and ensuring privacy protection is essential to gain public trust and compliance (Humayun *et al.,* 2021; Park *et al.,* 2021; Dutta & Hammad, 2020; Singh *et al.,* 2022b; Fabregue & Bogoni, 2023).

The Possible Solution of Regulatory and Privacy Issues Challenge

- *Clear Regulatory Frameworks*: Establish clear and comprehensive regulatory frameworks that provide guidelines for the deployment, operation, and management of 5G networks. Clarity in regulations helps all stakeholders understand their roles and responsibilities.
- *International Standardization*: Promote international standardization of 5G regulations to ensure consistency across borders. Collaborate with global organizations and regulatory bodies to develop standards that facilitate interoperability and compliance.
- *Collaboration with Regulatory Authorities*: Foster collaboration and open communication with regulatory authorities. Regular consultations and feedback sessions can help address concerns, align strategies, and ensure that regulations keep pace with technological advancements.
- *Privacy by Design:* Implement a privacy-by-design approach in the development and deployment of 5G infrastructure. Ensure that privacy considerations are integrated into the design process from the outset, addressing potential risks and concerns proactively.
- *Transparency in Data Collection and Use:* Establish transparent practices regarding data collection and usage. Clearly communicate to users the intended utilization of their data., providing options for consent and ensuring that data is only used for legitimate purposes.
- *Data Reduction and Anonymization:* Adopt data reduction principles, collecting only the essential data for specific purposes. Additionally, implementing anonymization techniques to safeguard individual privacy while still enabling valuable data analysis.
- *Regular Privacy Impact Assessments (PIAs):* Conduct regular Privacy Impact Assessments (PIAs) to identify and address potential privacy risks linked with 5G deployment. PIAs help ensure that privacy considerations are an integral part of the decision-making process.
- *User Empowerment and Control:* Empower users by giving them control over their personal data. Implement user-friendly interfaces that enable individuals to manage their privacy settings, including the option to opt in or out of specific data collection practices.
- *Education and Awareness Programs:* Launch education and awareness programs to inform the public about the privacy implications of 5G technology.
- *Legal Safeguards for Privacy:* Enact and enforce robust legal safeguards for privacy. Ensure that privacy laws and regulations align with the technological landscape, providing individuals with legal recourse in case of privacy violations.
- *Third-Party Audits and Certifications:* Engage third-party auditors to conduct privacy audits and certifications. This external validation helps build trust among stakeholders and ensures that privacy practices meet established standards.
- *Regulatory Sandboxes*: Establish regulatory sandboxes where innovative 5G applications and services can be tested in a controlled environment. This allows regulators to understand potential challenges and adjust regulations accordingly without impeding innovation.
- *Public-Private Collaboration on Policies:* Facilitate collaboration between public and private sectors in developing privacy policies. Engage in open dialogues to find common ground, balancing regulatory requirements with the need for innovation and economic growth.
- *Continuous Regulatory Updates:* Regularly update regulatory frameworks to adapt to evolving technologies and address emerging privacy concerns. A dynamic regulatory environment is essential to keep pace with the rapid advancements in the 5G landscape.

vi. Digital Divide: Ensuring equal access to 5G technology across all socioeconomic groups is a challenge, as the digital divide could exacerbate existing inequalities (Seung-Yoon *et al.* 2021; Shin *et al.*, 2021; Cabanillas-Carbonell *et al.*, 2023; Caragliu & Del Bo, 2023).

The Possible Solution of Digital Divide Challenge

- *Inclusive Infrastructure Planning:* Develop inclusive infrastructure plans that prioritize underserved and economically disadvantaged areas. Ensure that 5G deployment is not solely focused on urban centers but includes suburban and rural regions.
- *Public-Private Partnerships for Inclusive Deployment:* Foster public-private partnerships that specifically target the digital divide. Collaborate with telecommunication companies, government entities, and community organizations to ensure 5G infrastructure reaches marginalized communities.
- *Affordable Access Programs:* Implement affordable access programs to make 5G services accessible to low-income households. This could involve subsidized plans, discounted devices, or community initiatives that bridge the affordability gap.
- *Community Connectivity Projects:* Launch community-driven projects that focus on connectivity in underserved areas. Involve local communities in the planning and deployment of 5G infrastructure, tailoring solutions to meet their specific needs.
- *Digital Literacy Initiatives:* Invest in digital literacy programs to empower individuals in underserved communities with the skills and knowledge to utilize 5G technology effectively. This includes training on device usage, internet navigation, and online safety.
- *Mobile Connectivity Solutions*: Leverage mobile connectivity solutions, such as mobile broadband or fixed wireless access, to reach areas where traditional wired infrastructure is challenging. This can be a cost-effective way to bring 5G services to remote or economically disadvantaged regions.
- *Government Subsidies for Connectivity*: Provide government subsidies or grants to telecommunication providers willing to expand 5G coverage in underserved areas. This financial support can incentivize companies to invest in infrastructure where the business case might be less compelling.
- *Community Wi-Fi Initiatives:* Establish community Wi-Fi initiatives in public spaces, community centers, and libraries. This helps bridge the connectivity gap for individuals who may not have access at home, fostering digital inclusion.
- *Device Accessibility Programs:* Introduce programs that ensure affordable access to 5G-enabled devices. This may involve device subsidies, trade-in programs, or partnerships with manufacturers to produce cost-effective devices.
- *Digital Inclusion Grants:* Offer grants to community organizations and nonprofits working towards digital inclusion. These grants can support initiatives that address the digital divide, including technology training, access programs, and community outreach.
- *Network Infrastructure Sharing:* Encourage network infrastructure sharing among telecommunication companies. This collaborative approach can optimize resources and accelerate the expansion of 5G coverage to underserved areas.
- *Government-Community Collaboration:* Facilitate collaboration between government agencies and local communities. Engage community leaders, local governments, and grassroots organizations in the planning and execution of 5G initiatives to ensure they meet community needs.

- *Public Awareness Campaigns:* Initiate public outreach campaigns to educate underserved communities about the advantages of 5G technology and accessible access programs. Address concerns, dispel myths, and promote the positive impact of digital inclusion.
- *Inclusive Policy Development*: Develop policies that explicitly prioritize digital inclusion and address the unique challenges faced by underserved communities. Consider factors such as affordability, language diversity, and cultural sensitivity in policy formulation.

In conclusion, the 5G cityscape presents numerous challenges that necessitate strategic and collaborative efforts to ensure a successful and enduring implementation. Addressing these challenges is essential for realizing the full potential of 5G technology in smart urban evolution.

CONCLUSION

In the conclusion, the 5G cityscape stands for a transformative leap forward in the evolution of smart urban environments. This research paper has delved into the multifaceted impact of 5G technology, uncovering its potential to unleash seamless connectivity and foster innovation across diverse sectors. From the foundational aspects of 5G technology to its integration into smart city components, the journey has been one of discovery and exploration. The deployment of 5G technology brings forth a paradigm shift, not just in regards to increased data transfer speeds and lower latency but also in its capacity to connect an unprecedented quantity of devices simultaneously. This capability is instrumental in realizing the full potential of the Internet of Things (IoT) and enabling the seamless communication essential for real-time applications. The implications of 5G extend across critical domains, including transportation, public safety, immersive technologies, and smart grids, redefining the possibilities for smart city initiatives. As urban populations continue to grow, the imperative for smarter, more connected cities intensifies. In response to this demand, 5G technology emerges as a catalyst for change, promising unparalleled connectivity and ushering in a new era in smart urban evolution. The ability of 5G to facilitate real-time communication, support a myriad of connected devices, and enable innovative applications positions it as a cornerstone for building cities that are connected and also efficient, resilient, and responsive to the needs of their inhabitants.

REFERENCES

Anantrasirichai, N., & Bull, D. (2022). Artificial intelligence in the creative industries [review]. *Artificial Intelligence Review*, *55*(1), 589–656. doi:10.1007/s10462-021-10039-7

Attar, H., Issa, H., Ababneh, J., Abbasi, M., Solyman, A. A. A., Khosravi, M., & Agieb, R. S. (2022). 5G System Overview for Ongoing Smart Applications: Structure, Requirements, and Specifications. *Computational Intelligence and Neuroscience 2022*. doi:10.1155/2022/2476841

Bibri, S. E., & Jagatheesaperumal, S. K. (2023). Harnessing the Potential of the Metaverse and Artificial Intelligence for the Internet of City Things: Cost-Effective XReality and Synergistic AIoT Technologies. *Smart Cities*, *6*(5), 2397–2429. doi:10.3390/smartcities6050109

Cabanillas-Carbonell, M., Pérez-Martínez, J., & Yáñez, J. (2023). 5G Technology in the Digital Transformation of Healthcare, a Systematic Review. *Sustainability*, *15*, 3178. doi:10.3390/su15043178

Car, T., Pilepić Stifanich, L., & Kovačić, N. (2022). The Role of 5G and IoT in Smart Cities, In: *Proceedings of the ENTRENOVA - ENTerprise REsearch InNOVAtion Conference, Hybrid Conference*, (pp. 17-18). Society for Advancing Innovation and Research in Economy. 10.54820/entrenova-2022-0032

Caragliu, A., & Del Bo, C. (2023). Smart cities and the urban digital divide. *NPJ Urban Sustainability*, *3*(1), 43. doi:10.1038/s42949-023-00117-w

Choi, M., Azzaoui, A. E., Singh, S. K., Salim, M. M., Jeremiah, S. R., & Park, J. H. (2022). The future of metaverse: Security issues, requirements, and solutions. *Human-Centric Computing and Information Sciences*, *12*(60), 1–14.

Dangi, R., Lalwani, P., Choudhary, G., You, I., & Pau, G. (2021). Study and Investigation on 5G Technology: A Systematic Review. *Sensors (Basel)*, *22*(1), 26. doi:10.3390/s22010026 PMID:35009569

Dutta, A., & Hammad, E. (2020). 5G Security Challenges and Opportunities: A System Approach, *2020 IEEE 3rd 5G World Forum (5GWF)*, (pp. 109-114). IEEE. 10.1109/5GWF49715.2020.9221122

Ejreaw, A. M. A. (2023). The Integration of 5G Technology in Smart Cities: Challenges and Solutions. [AJAPAS]. *African Journal of Advanced Pure and Applied Sciences*, *2*(4), 289–297.

El-Shorbagy, A. (2021). 5G Technology and the Future of Architecture. *Procedia Computer Science*, *182*, 121–131. doi:10.1016/j.procs.2021.02.017

Fabrègue, B. F. G., & Bogoni, A. (2023). Privacy and Security Concerns in the Smart City. *Smart Cities*, *6*(1), 586–613. doi:10.3390/smartcities6010027

Georgiou, K. E., Georgiou, E., Satava, R. M. (2021). 5G Use in Healthcare: The Future is Present. *Journal of the Society of Laparoscopic & Robotic Surgeons*. *25*(4), e2021.00064. . doi:10.4293/JSLS.2021.00064

Gohar, A., & Nencioni, G. (2021). The Role of 5G Technologies in a Smart City: The Case for Intelligent Transportation System. *Sustainability (Basel)*, *13*(9), 5188. doi:10.3390/su13095188

Gracias, J. S., Parnell, G. S., Specking, E., Pohl, E. A., & Buchanan, R. (2023). Smart Cities—A Structured Literature Review. *Smart Cities*, *6*(4), 1719–1743. doi:10.3390/smartcities6040080

Guevara, L., & Cheein, F. A. (2020). The Role of 5G Technologies: Challenges in Smart Cities and Intelligent Transportation Systems. *Sustainability (Basel)*, *12*(16), 6469. doi:10.3390/su12166469

Haque, A. K. M. B., Zihad, M. O. M., & Hasan, M. R. (2023). 5G and Internet of Things-Integration Trends, Opportunities, and Future Research Avenues. In: Bhushan, B., Sharma, S.K., Kumar, R., Priyadarshini, I. (eds) 5G and beyond. Springer Tracts in Electrical and Electronics Engineering. Springer, Singapore. doi:10.1007/978-981-99-3668-7_11

Humayun, M., Hamid, B., Jhanjhi, N. Z., Suseendran, G., & Talib, M. N. (2021). 5G Network Security Issues, Challenges, Opportunities and Future Directions: A Survey. *Journal of Physics: Conference Series*, *979*(1), 012037. doi:10.1088/1742-6596/1979/1/012037

Kumar, M., Kim, C., Son, Y., Singh, S. K., & Kim, S. (2024). Empowering Cyberattack Identification in IoHT Networks with Neighborhood Component-based Improvised Long Short-Term Memory. *IEEE Internet of Things Journal*, 1. doi:10.1109/JIOT.2024.3354988

Liu, Q., Yang, Y., Meng, Q., Man, S., & Wang, Y. (2022). The Multiple Cooperative Mechanism and Globalization Path of Small Inland Cities in China: A Showcase Study of Dunhuang, China. *International Journal of Environmental Research and Public Health*, *19*(18), 11241. doi:10.3390/ijerph191811241 PMID:36141533

Mendonça, S., Damásio, B., Freitas, L., Oliveira, L., Cichy, M., & Nicita, A. (2022). The rise of 5G technologies and systems: A quantitative analysis of knowledge production. *Telecommunications Policy*, *46*(4), 102327. doi:10.1016/j.telpol.2022.102327

Minoli, D., & Occhiogrosso, B. (2019). Practical Aspects for the Integration of 5G Networks and IoT Applications in Smart Cities. Environments, Wireless Communications and Mobile Computing. Hindawi. doi:10.1155/2019/5710834

O'Connell, E., Moore, D., & Newe, T. (2020). Challenges Associated with Implementing 5G in Manufacturing. *Telecom.*, *1*(1), 48–67. doi:10.3390/telecom1010005

Ogbodo, E. U., Abu-Mahfouz, A. M., & Kurien, A. M. (2023). A Survey on 5G and LPWAN-IoT for Improved Smart Cities and Remote Area Applications: From the Aspect of Architecture and Security. *Sensors (Basel)*, *22*(16), 6313. doi:10.3390/s22166313 PMID:36016078

Park, J. H., Singh, S. K., Salim, M. M., Azzaoui, A. E., & Park, J. H. (2022). Ransomware-based Cyber Attacks: A Comprehensive Survey. *Wangji Wanglu Jishu Xuekan*, *23*(7), 1557–1564. doi:10.53106/160792642022122307010

Park, J. H., Yotxay, S., Singh, S. K., & Park, J. H. (2024). PoAh-Enabled Federated Learning Architecture for DDoS Attack Detection in IoT Networks. *Human Centric Computing and Information Science, 14*(3).

Park, S., Kim, D., Park, Y., Cho, H., Kim, D., & Kwon, S. (2021). 5G Security Threat Assessment in Real Networks. *Sensors (Basel)*, *21*(16), 5524. doi:10.3390/s21165524 PMID:34450971

Pons, M., Valenzuela, E., Rodríguez, B., Nolazco-Flores, J. A., & Del-Valle-Soto, C. (2023). Utilization of 5G Technologies in IoT Applications: Current Limitations by Interference and Network Optimization Difficulties—A Review. *Sensors (Basel)*, *23*(8), 3876. doi:10.3390/s23083876 PMID:37112216

Rahman, M. M., Khatun, F., Sami, S. I., & Uzzaman, A. (2022). The evolving roles and impacts of 5G enabled technologies in healthcare: The world epidemic COVID-19 issues. *Array (New York, N.Y.)*, *14*, 100178. doi:10.1016/j.array.2022.100178 PMID:35571870

Rong, B., Han, S., Kadoch, M., Chen, X., & Jara, A. (2020). Integration of 5G Networks and Internet of Things for Future Smart City, Wireless Communications and Mobile Computing. Hindawi. doi:10.1155/2020/2903525

Seung-Yoon, S., Dongwook, K., & Soon, A. C. (2021). Digital Divide in Advanced Smart City Innovations [April.]. *Sustainability, MDPI*, *13*(7), 1–22.

Shin, S.-Y., Kim, D., & Chun, S. A. (2021). Digital Divide in Advanced Smart City Innovations. *Sustainability (Basel), 13*(7), 4076. doi:10.3390/su13074076

Singh, S. K., Azzaoui, A. E., Choo, K. K. R., Yang, L. T., & Park, J. H. (2023b). A Comprehensive Survey on Blockchain for Secure IoT-enabled Smart City beyond 5G: Approaches, Processes, Challenges, and Opportunities. *Human Centric Computing and Information Science, 13*(51).

Singh, S. K., Azzaoui, A. E., Kim, T. W., Pan, Y., & Park, J. H. (2021b). DeepBlockScheme: A deep learning-based blockchain driven scheme for secure smart city. *Human-centric Computing and Information Sciences*, *11*(12), 1–13.

Singh, S. K., Kumar, M., Tanwar, S., & Park, J. H. (2024). GRU-based digital twin framework for data allocation and storage in IoT-enabled smart home networks. *Future Generation Computer Systems*, *153*, 391–402. doi:10.1016/j.future.2023.12.009

Singh, S. K., Pan, Y., & Park, J. H. (2021a). OTS scheme based secure architecture for energy-efficient iot in edge infrastructure. *Computers, Materials & Continua*, *66*(3), 2905–2922. doi:10.32604/cmc.2021.014151

Singh, S. K., Pan, Y., & Park, J. H. (2022c). Blockchain-enabled secure framework for energy-efficient smart parking in sustainable city environment. *Sustainable Cities and Society*, *76*, 103364. doi:10.1016/j.scs.2021.103364

Singh, S. K., & Park, J. H. (2022a). TaLWaR: Blockchain-based trust management scheme for smart enterprises with augmented intelligence. *IEEE Transactions on Industrial Informatics*, *19*(1), 626–634. doi:10.1109/TII.2022.3204692

Singh, S. K., Park, L., & Park, J. H. (2022b). Blockchain-based Federated Approach for Privacy-Preserved IoT-enabled Smart Vehicular Networks. In *2022 13th International Conference on Information and Communication Technology Convergence (ICTC)* (pp. 1995-1999). IEEE. 10.1109/ICTC55196.2022.9952835

Singh, S. K., Yang, L. T., & Park, J. H. (2023a). FusionFedBlock: Fusion of blockchain and federated learning to preserve privacy in industry 5.0. *Information Fusion*, *90*, 233–240. doi:10.1016/j.inffus.2022.09.027

Singh, T., Solanki, A., Sharma, S. K., Nayyar, A., & Paul, A. (2022a). A Decade Review on Smart Cities: Paradigms, Challenges and Opportunities. *IEEE Access : Practical Innovations, Open Solutions, 10*, 68319–68364. doi:10.1109/ACCESS.2022.3184710

Sullivan, S., Brighente, A., Kumar, S., & Conti, M. (2021). 5G Security Challenges and Solutions: A Review by OSI Layers. *IEEE Access : Practical Innovations, Open Solutions*, *495*, 116294–116314. https://engagedscholarship.csuohio.edu/enece_facpub/495. doi:10.1109/ACCESS.2021.3105396

Telsaç, C., & Yilmaz, V. (2021). *Smart City Components*. 10th International Conference on Social Sciences, Arapgir -Malatya, Turkey.

Xiong, C., Song, T., & Zhou, C. (2022). A Study on the Relationship between Artificial Intelligence and 5G Network Construction and the Level of Economic Development of Regional Cities. *Wireless Communications and Mobile Computing*, *2022*, 1–9. doi:10.1155/2022/8020388

Xu, Y., & Jia, S. (2021). Application of 5G to Smart City. *The 2nd International Conference on Civil, Architecture and Pollution Control (ICCAPC 2021).* IOP Conference Series: Earth and Environmental Science.

Yang, C., Liang, P., Fu, L., Cui, G., Huang, F., Teng, F., & Bangash, Y.A. (2022). Using 5G in Smart Cities: A Systematic Mapping Study. ArXiv, abs/*2202.04312*.

Zhou, Y. (2021). Material Foundation for Future 5G Technology. *Accounts of Materials Research*, *2*(5), 306–310. doi:10.1021/accountsmr.0c00087

Chapter 5
Enhancing Smart City Resilience:
Integrating Cloud Computing and 5G for Secure and Sustainable Urban Environments

Richa Pandey
Graphic Era Hill University, India

Ishwari Singh Rajput
Graphic Era Hill University, India

Sonam Tyagi
Graphic Era Hill University, India

Manisha Koranga
Graphic Era Hill University, India

Praveen Kumar Sharma
Seoul National University of Science and Technology, South Korea

ABSTRACT

Cloud computing for secure smart cities beyond 5G represents a cutting-edge approach to urban development and technology integration. It involves leveraging advanced cloud computing infrastructure and 5G connectivity to create highly secure, efficient, and interconnected smart city systems. In this context, cloud computing enables the centralized management of data and services, facilitating real-time analytics, resource optimization, and the seamless operation of various IoT devices and sensors throughout the city. The integration of 5G technology further enhances data transmission speed and capacity, ensuring rapid, reliable communication between devices and cloud resources. By prioritizing security, this approach safeguards sensitive data and ensures that smart city services operate within robust cybersecurity frameworks.

DOI: 10.4018/979-8-3693-2373-1.ch005

INTRODUCTION

In the realm of information technology, cloud computing represents a groundbreaking paradigm shift that has fundamentally altered the way individuals and institutions acquire and utilize computing resources. Cloud computing is essentially the internet-based distribution of different computer services, such as networking, processing power, storage, and software. Utilizing a shared pool of remotely hosted resources, users can perform computer tasks without depending on personal devices or local servers.

Cloud computing has become a cornerstone of modern IT infrastructure, fostering innovation, collaboration, and agility. It has empowered businesses of all sizes to focus on their core competencies while outsourcing the complexities of managing and maintaining hardware and software infrastructure to cloud service providers. This shift has had a profound impact on industries, enabling digital transformation and the rapid development of new technologies and services.

Cloud computing assumes a central role in the realm of smart cities, playing a crucial part in the creation, execution, and enhancement of various smart city applications. The interconnection between cloud computing and smart city initiatives is manifested in several ways:

Data Storage and Processing

i. **Data Centralization**: Smart cities generate vast amounts of data from sensors, devices, and other sources. Cloud computing allows for centralized storage, making it easier to manage and analyze diverse datasets.
ii. **Scalable Processing**: The scalable nature of cloud computing enables efficient processing of large volumes of data, facilitating real-time analytics and insights for smart city decision-making.

Smart City Infrastructure

i. **Resource Sharing:** Cloud infrastructure supports the sharing of computing resources among various smart city applications. This resource pooling enhances efficiency and reduces infrastructure costs.
ii. **Flexibility and Adaptability:** Cloud services provide the flexibility needed to adapt to changing requirements, allowing smart city planners to scale resources based on demand.

Internet of Things (IoT) Connectivity

i. **IoT Integration**: Cloud computing acts as a backbone for IoT devices in smart cities, providing a platform for the seamless integration of sensors, actuators, and other IoT components.
ii. **Data Processing at the Edge**: Cloud services often work in conjunction with edge computing to process and analyze data closer to the source (at the edge of the network), reducing latency and enhancing responsiveness.

Smart City Applications

i. **Urban Mobility:** Cloud-based solutions support intelligent transportation systems, traffic management, and real-time monitoring of public transit, contributing to optimized urban mobility.

ii. **Public Safety:** Cloud computing facilitates video analytics, predictive policing, and emergency response systems, enhancing public safety and security.
iii. **Energy Management:** Cloud platforms enable smart grids and energy management systems, promoting efficient energy distribution and consumption.

Collaboration and Interoperability

i. **Interconnected Systems:** Cloud services foster collaboration and interoperability among different smart city components and applications. This interconnectedness enhances the overall functionality and effectiveness of the smart city ecosystem.

Cost-Efficiency and Accessibility

i. **Cost Savings:** Utilizing cloud computing eliminates the necessity for significant upfront investments in hardware and infrastructure. Pay-as-you-go cloud services can be utilized by smart cities to optimize expenses.
ii. **Accessibility**: Cloud-based applications and services are accessible from various devices, allowing residents, businesses, and city administrators to access information and services easily.

Data Security and Privacy

i. **Security Measures:** Cloud service providers employ robust security measures to safeguard the data associated with smart city initiatives. Key elements of these security measures include encryption, authentication, and access controls, all of which are crucial for ensuring the security and privacy of smart city data.

In the rapidly evolving landscape of urban development, the convergence of cutting-edge technologies has emerged as a catalyst for transformative change. One of the most promising synergies lies in the seamless integration of Cloud Computing and 5G connectivity, heralding a new era of secure and sustainable urban environments. This innovative fusion not only addresses the escalating demands for high-speed, low-latency communication but also lays the foundation for intelligent and resource-efficient city management.

By harnessing the power of Cloud Computing and the lightning-fast capabilities of 5G networks, cities can unlock unprecedented opportunities for enhanced security, streamlined services, and the cultivation of sustainable practices. This introduction sets the stage for a comprehensive exploration of how the amalgamation of Cloud Computing and 5G is reshaping the urban landscape, ensuring a future that is not only technologically advanced but also resilient and environmentally conscious.

LITERATURE STUDY

This segment comprises 20 papers spanning the years 2020 to 2023, focusing on the convergence of IoT and 5G technologies. Each year witnesses diverse developments resulting from continuous technological advancements.

Figure 1. Blockchain in smart city

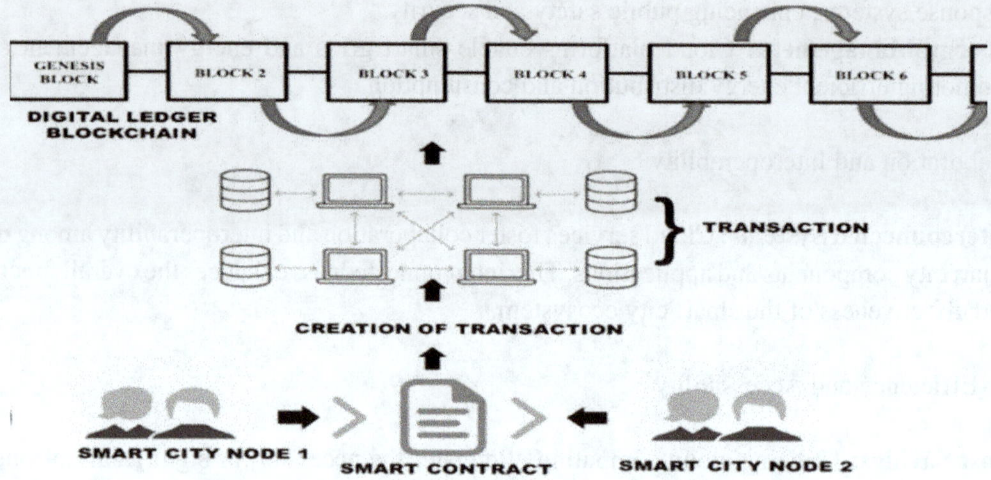

RECENT DEVELOPMENTS IN SMART CITY APPLICATIONS

This portion examines recent research achievements in the realm of blockchain-driven smart cities and their interconnected smart environments. The objective of this section is to thoroughly assess and categorize the latest advancements in research, identifying them as potential solutions for smart cities built on blockchain technology. The illustration depicts a smart city scenario, featuring multiple smart environments functioning simultaneously. Within each smart environment, various entities are responsible for upholding the distributed ledger on a blockchain network, with smart contracts executing the necessary business logic.

Decentralized Governance and Identity Management: Blockchain is being employed to establish decentralized systems for managing identities and governing smart city operations. This enhances security and privacy while allowing residents to have more control over their personal data.

Supply Chain and Logistics Optimization: Blockchain is being utilized to streamline supply chain and logistics processes within smart cities. The technology ensures transparency, traceability, and efficiency in the movement of goods, contributing to better urban planning and resource management.

Energy Management and Grid Optimization: Smart grids powered by blockchain facilitate efficient energy distribution and consumption. Through decentralized energy transactions and smart contracts, residents and businesses can participate in energy trading, promoting sustainability and reducing reliance on traditional energy sources.

Tokenization of Assets and Services: Blockchain enables the tokenization of assets and services within smart cities. This involves representing physical or digital assets as tokens on the blockchain, allowing for easier transfer, trading, and utilization of resources such as property, transportation services, and more.

Interoperability and Standardization: Efforts are being made to establish interoperability standards among different blockchain platforms to ensure seamless integration within the complex systems of a smart city. Standardization helps in the development of a cohesive and interconnected urban infrastructure.

Table 1. Literature survey

S.NO	Author Name	Paper Name	Conclusion
1.	Y. Jiang et al (2020)	Smart Urban Living: Enabling Emotion-Guided Interaction With Next Generation Sensing Fabric	• In this article, we introduce a novel sensing fabric integrated into the smart city infrastructure, presenting an architecture for emotion-guided interactions within the realm of smart urban living. However, The data collected in a smart city by different sensing fabrics often displays information redundancy in the temporal context. • Consequently, we propose a strategy for optimizing energy consumption in sensing fabrics, which involves identifying and minimizing redundancy within the collected data. We derive an effective data allocation method by evaluating the sensing fabric's remaining energy and current data collection capabilities. • The goal of this strategy is to improve the smart urban system's overall user experience. We ran simulated tests to confirm that our suggested model worked as intended.
2.	Sumit Pundir et al (2020)	Intrusion Detection Protocols in Wireless Sensor Networks Integrated to Internet of Things Deployment: Survey and Future Challenges	• This extensive survey article delves deeply into the threat model that is relevant to maintaining the security of Internet of Things and Wireless Sensor Networks communications. • In addition to clarifying security needs and describing potential assaults in WSN and IoT communication contexts, the study explores the intricacies of the threat landscape. The article also provides an overview of new initiatives that combine the Internet of Things with Wireless Sensor Networks.
3.	Yaqiong Liu et al (2020)	Toward Edge Intelligence: Multiaccess Edge Computing for 5G and Internet of Things	• This article provides an in-depth exploration of Mobile Edge Computing (MEC) in the context of 5G and the Internet of Things (IoT). It conducts a comprehensive analysis of MEC's key features within the framework of 5G and IoT, examining crucial technologies that facilitate MEC implementation in these domains. • This category of technologies includes cloud computing, virtual machines (VMs) and containers, compute offloading, Software-defined networking (SDN) and network function virtualization (NFV), information-centric networks (ICN), and intelligent or smart devices. • The paper also provides a summary of MEC's function in 5G and IoT, showcasing a number of applications made possible by MEC, and outlining potential future paths for MEC integration with these technologies.
4.	Hassan Rajaei et al (2020)	SBDC: Smart Building Data Center for Iot, Edge, and 5G	• In this research, A novel architectural concept named the Smart Building Data-Center (SBDC) is introduced. It functions as an edge cloudlet node that provides significant processing power and storage that is tailored for large amounts of IoT data stored in a building. • Moreover, this data center incorporates Fifth Generation (5G) Mobile Edge Computing (MEC) to support all 5G wireless devices utilized within the building. Each SBDC is linked to neighboring smart buildings, cloud data centers, and other networks within a Smart City. • The paper provides detailed insights into the design, architecture, and network connectivity of the proposed system.
5.	Huajun Chen et al (2020)	5G Boosting Smart Cities Development	• The fifth-generation mobile communication technology (5G), regarded as a major catalyst for the upcoming information technology revolution, boasts ultra-bandwidth, high reliability, low latency, and extensive connectivity features. • It has the potential to be a significant additional instrument for comprehensive urban development if used wisely. The seamless integration of various technologies, such as big data, blockchain, Internet of Things (IoT), artificial intelligence (AI), and Industrial Internet, through 5G heralds a new era in the advancement of smart cities.
6.	Zi Wang et al (2021)	Data-Augmentation-Based Cellular Traffic Prediction in Edge-Computing-Enabled Smart City	• Introducing ctGAN-S2S, a pioneering cellular traffic prediction model, our approach incorporates data augmentation and an inventive submodel rooted in generative adversarial networks (GANs). This not only enhances prediction accuracy but also ensures the preservation of data privacy. • Additionally, the model incorporates a sequence-to-sequence submodel based on long short-term memory (LSTM), offering adaptability for multi-step cellular traffic predictions. Our ctGAN-S2S model outperforms four common reference models in experiments conducted on a real-world city-scale cellular traffic dataset, with prediction accuracy increases of up to 48.49%.

continued on following page

Table 1. Continued

S.NO	Author Name	Paper Name	Conclusion
7.	Shuai Yu (2021)	When Deep Reinforcement Learning Meets Federated Learning: Intelligent Multitimescale Resource Management for Multiaccess Edge Computing in 5G Ultradense Network	• First, we present the Intelligent UDEC (I-UDEC) framework, which integrates 5G UDEC networks with blockchain technology and artificial intelligence (AI). Our methodology presents a novel Two-Timescale Deep Reinforcement Learning (2Ts-DRL) method that may be used to give real-time, low-overhead computing judgments and strategies for resource allocation. • This method entails learning on two different timescales: quickly and slowly. The main goal is to reduce overall offloading latency and network resource usage through simultaneous optimization of compute offloading, resource allocation, and placement of service caching. To safeguard data privacy on edge devices, a distributed approach is adopted, employing federated learning (FL) for training the 2Ts-DRL model. • The simulation results show that our suggested algorithm drastically cuts task execution time, highlighting the usefulness of both the 2Ts-DRL and FL within the I-UDEC framework.
8.	Afaq Muhammad et al (2021)	Sensor Virtualization and Data Orchestration in Internet of Vehicles (IoV)	• In order to preserve the state of the underlying network at the intermediate layer, the study presents a system that makes use of virtualization and Mobile Edge Computing (MEC). • The objective is to improve the efficiency of data processing and ensure that newly launched services can access pre-processed or real-time data from the vehicular network, even when vehicles are disconnected.
9.	Siya Xu et al (2021)	MECC: A Mobile Edge Collaborative Caching Framework Empowered by Deep Reinforcement Learning (Xu et al., 2021)	• Deep reinforcement learning (DRL) is a novel approach in the field of artificial intelligence that has made great strides in solving problems related to high-dimensional data and network resource management. As such, we have integrated DRL with collaborative caching to create an intelligent edge caching architecture that allows Edge Servers (ESs) and the cloud to cooperate in caching. • An early version for this caching technology uses a federated machine learning model to forecast user behavior. The purpose of this model is to describe mobile consumers' mobility patterns and content preferences.
10.	Yusuke Hirota at al (2021)	End-to-End Management of All Optical Disaggregated Network and Applications with Cloud Native Environment for the Smart World Network Infrastructure	• A network infrastructure for the Smart World is established on a multi-cloud basis, showcasing diverse forms of network control and services. • This encompasses Private LTE with Precision Time Protocol (PTP) devices, an Artificial Intelligence (AI)-driven Service Function Chaining (SFC) Platform, dependable routing utilizing WhiteBox technology, and a disaggregated Spatial Division Multiplexing (SDM) network.
11.	Shuai Yu et al (2022)	EC-SAGINs: Edge-Computing-Enhanced Space–Air–Ground-Integrated Networks for Internet of Vehicles	• The authors propose a framework for Smart Autonomous Ground Information Networks (EC-IoV) that is enabled by Edge Computing and allows for a variety of Internet of cars (IoV) services that are tailored for cars that are driven in remote areas. • This framework's main objectives are to reduce task completion times and maximize the use of satellite resources. Preclassification is used to reduce the size of the action space in order to accomplish this. • Furthermore, an offloading and caching technique driven by deep imitation learning is proposed for real-time decision making. Simulation findings show that the suggested approach is effective. The last sections of the article discuss technological issues and suggest possible future paths.
12.	Arslan Qadeer et al (2022)	DDPG-Edge-Cloud: A Deep-Deterministic Policy Gradient based Multi-Resource Allocation in Edge-Cloud System	• This study tackles the issue of resource allocation in an integrated Edge Computing (EC) and Blockchain (BC) setup. While machine learning methods are commonly used to handle such optimization challenges, traditional discrete action space techniques encounter scalability limitations in large-scale environments. • To address the constraints imposed by restricted wireless bandwidth and compute capacity in EC and BC contexts, we present DDPG-Edge-Cloud. • This framework, based on deep deterministic policy gradients, facilitates multi-resource allocation (MRA) within a continuous action space. Our approach integrates a pruning principle to boost efficiency.

continued on following page

Table 1. Continued

S.NO	Author Name	Paper Name	Conclusion
13.	Tingting Yang et al (2022)	Kubeedge Wireless for Integrated Communication and Computing Services Everywhere	• In order to accomplish integrated communication and computing services, the study presents the Network for AI (NET4AI) and edge-mesh computing architectures, extending cloud-native capabilities into the communication network. • Interestingly, the talk highlights a KubeEdge Wireless (KEW) platform that is flexible and offers insights into dynamic services like service migration. This contribution is important for academics and industry because it shows how computer and communication services may be improved and made more flexible.
14.	Min-Hwa Chi et al	IC Technologies and Systems for Green Future	• In the AI/IoT era, environmentally friendly or "green" IC technologies and systems encompass a wide array of concepts within smart systems (both hardware and software), emphasizing energy efficiency, reconfiguration, modularization, data centers, cloud/edge computing, and 5G communication. • This extends to IC designs and 3DIC (Three-Dimensional Integrated Circuits) for low power, reusable IPs (Intellectual Properties), reconfigurable and modularized devices/blocks, and 3DIC/SIP (System in Package).
15.	Fatema Elwy et al (2022)	Role of Fog Computing in Smart Spaces	• In addition to providing a thorough analysis, this study presents a 3-Tier, 3-Dimensions reference model for smart spaces. The edge, fog, and cloud tiers make up the 3-Tier structure. The compute, network, and application dimensions are the three dimensions that each tier is closely related to. The paper explores each dimension within every tier and outlines the existing technologies that fulfill specific roles within these dimensions. • To illustrate the practical application of this reference model, a case study is presented within the context of a smart healthcare application, demonstrating how the proposed model can be implemented in real-world scenarios.
16.	Shenghan Zhou et al (2023)	Short-Term Traffic Flow Prediction of the Smart City Using 5G Internet of Vehicles Based on Edge Computing	• The study presents a model that uses Edge Computing (EC) and Deep Learning (DL) to estimate short-term traffic flow in a 5G vehicle network. Through simulation, the suggested algorithm's performance is examined, with noteworthy outcomes. • The algorithm maintains a consistent average unloading utility at approximately 70% while displaying a decreased average delay cost. With respect to prediction performance, the suggested algorithm outperforms the sophisticated Convolutional Neural Network (CNN) technique put forth by previous researchers by a minimum of 1.14%, achieving a recognition accuracy of 98.06%. Furthermore, the suggested approach reaches a quicker rate of convergence.
17.	Qianli Zhao et al (2023)	Customizable Cloud-Native Infrastructure for Private 5G	• A methodology is put forth to address the difficulties in setting up cloud-native infrastructure for Private 5G deployments, with a focus on the performance benefits that come from containerized implementations, which are crucial for Private 5G platforms. This framework makes use of the Smart Edge's highly integrated open-source Edge services platform, the Private Wireless Experience Kit (PWEK). • In order to evaluate the viability, data plane performance, and practical applications of 5G, an End-to-End 5G testbed is utilized to enable User Equipment (UE) connectivity with Edge applications via 5G spectrum and containerized network functionalities. • The test findings show that virtual Radio Access Network (vRAN) functions on an Edge platform that are cloud-native and containerized, with deterministic latency, perform almost as well as their bare-metal equivalents after the necessary improvements.
18.	Pedro Rito et al (2023)	Aveiro Tech City Living Lab: A Communication, Sensing, and Computing Platform for City Environments	• The architecture, development, and deployment tactics used to operationalize a complete platform intended to integrate citizens and researchers are described in the paper. It also provides instances of performance indicators obtained in urban infrastructure. • The data collected is showcased for visualization and utilization in developing various services and applications for urban environments. The article concludes by presenting diverse use cases in mobility and safety scenarios, emphasizing the practical applications and benefits of the platform in enhancing city living.

continued on following page

Table 1. Continued

S.NO	Author Name	Paper Name	Conclusion
19.	Dongyang Ou et al (2023)	Container Power Consumption Prediction Based on GBRT-PL for Edge Servers in Smart City	• To forecast container power usage effectively, the proposed method introduces a Gradient Boosting Piecewise Linear Regression Tree (GBRT-PL). To model power consumption efficiently, performance metrics are selected for their strong correlation with server and container power usage. • Recognizing the nonlinear relationship between server power consumption and container performance metrics, the approach integrates the segmented linear model of each individual Regression Tree (RT) leaf node with the predictive capabilities of multiple RTs to enhance overall prediction accuracy.
20.	Mano Yadav et al (2023)	Exploring Synergy of Blockchain and 6G Network for Industrial Automation	• This paper explores the possible consequences of combining 6G with blockchain technologies with an emphasis on industrial automation. Through this integration, the goal is to imagine the future of intelligent supply chains and smart manufacturing. • The proposed work aims to provide a thorough understanding of the main advantages, difficulties, opportunities, and solutions related to this newly formed merger, as well as insights into its possible effects on the industrial landscape.

Figure 2. Smart cities challenges (Syed et al., 2021)

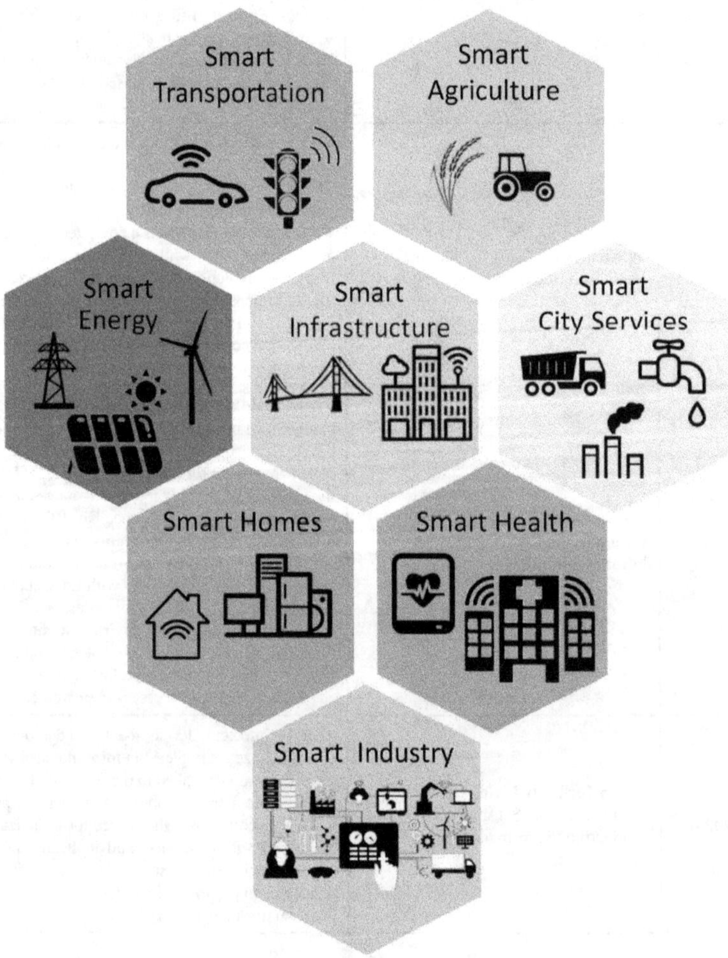

Figure 3. Future trends of integrating cloud computing and 5G for secure and sustainable urban environments

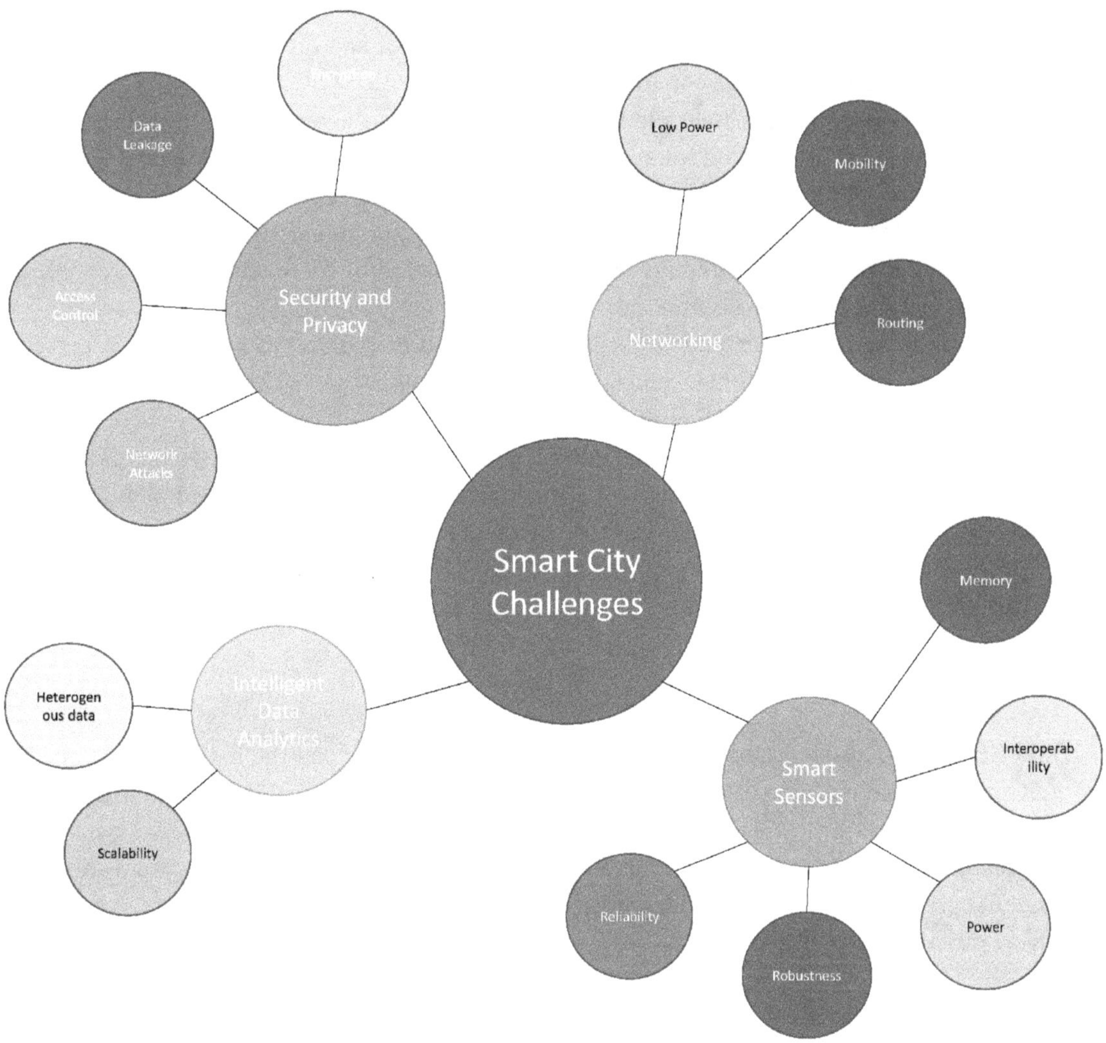

Smart Contracts for Urban Services: The use of smart contracts is expanding to automate various urban services such as waste management, traffic control, and public transportation. These self-executing contracts improve efficiency, reduce costs, and enhance the overall performance of smart city services.

Data Security and Privacy: Blockchain provides enhanced security for sensitive data in smart cities. The decentralized and cryptographic nature of blockchain helps in securing data integrity, preventing unauthorized access, and ensuring the privacy of citizens.

Smart City Infrastructure: Cloud Computing and 5G can be harnessed to create comprehensive smart city platforms. These platforms may integrate data from various sensors, devices, and systems to optimize city services, enhance public safety, and improve resource management (El Azzaoui et al., 2020).

Surveillance and Public Safety: The combination of Cloud Computing and 5G enables real-time processing and analysis of large volumes of data from surveillance cameras, sensors, and other sources.

This can enhance public safety through advanced video analytics, predictive policing, and rapid emergency response systems.

Traffic Management: Integrating Cloud Computing with 5G can improve traffic flow and reduce congestion by enabling real-time communication between vehicles and infrastructure. This can lead to more efficient transportation systems and lower emissions.

Environmental Monitoring: Cloud platforms can process and analyze data from environmental sensors, providing insights into air and water quality, noise levels, and other environmental factors. This information can contribute to sustainable urban planning and management.

Energy Efficiency: Cloud-based solutions combined with 5G connectivity can optimize energy consumption in buildings and infrastructure. Smart grids, powered by these technologies, enable more efficient energy distribution and consumption.

Healthcare Services: Cloud-based healthcare solutions, supported by 5G connectivity, can enable remote patient monitoring, telemedicine, and faster access to medical data. This can improve healthcare services and contribute to the overall well-being of urban residents.

Waste Management: Cloud platforms can optimize waste collection routes based on real-time data, reducing fuel consumption and improving overall efficiency. Smart waste management systems can enhance recycling efforts and contribute to a more sustainable urban environment.

4. While the integration of Cloud Computing and 5G in smart cities offers numerous benefits, it also poses certain challenges and potential adverse effects. Some of these include:

Security Concerns

i. **Data Security**: The increased reliance on cloud-based systems and the high-speed connectivity of 5G may expose sensitive data to potential security breaches. Ensuring robust security measures becomes crucial to protect against cyber threats (Singh et al., 2023).
ii. **Privacy Issues**: With the extensive collection and sharing of data in smart cities, there are concerns about the privacy of individuals. Unauthorized access to personal information or surveillance can lead to privacy breaches and legal issues.

Dependency and Reliability

i. **Service Dependency:** Smart city services heavily depend on the seamless functioning of both cloud computing and 5G networks. Any disruptions or outages in either of these technologies could lead to service downtime and affect critical urban functions.
ii. **Reliability Challenges**: While 5G promises high reliability, the actual performance may vary based on factors such as network congestion and signal interference. Inconsistent reliability can impact the effectiveness of smart city applications.

Infrastructure and Cost

i. **Infrastructure Costs:** Strong cloud and 5G infrastructure implementation and upkeep can be costly. It may be financially difficult for some communities, particularly those with little funding, to implement and maintain such cutting-edge technology.

ii. **Digital Divide:** The combination could worsen existing digital disparities, as specific regions or demographic groups might lack equitable access to high-speed internet or sophisticated cloud services.

Regulatory and Compliance Issues

i. **Data Governance:** Smart cities generate vast amounts of data, and managing this data in compliance with privacy regulations and governance standards is a complex task. Ensuring adherence to data protection laws and ethical considerations is crucial.
ii. **Regulatory Hurdles**: Navigating regulatory frameworks for cloud services and 5G deployment can be challenging. Regulatory barriers and uncertainties may slow down the implementation of these technologies.

Environmental Impact

i. **Increased Energy Consumption:** The expansion of cloud computing and 5G infrastructure may lead to higher energy consumption. Data centers and the operation of 5G networks can contribute to environmental concerns unless energy-efficient solutions are implemented.

Technological Maturity

i. **Integration Challenges**: The seamless integration of diverse technologies, including legacy systems, into a unified smart city framework can be technically challenging. Interoperability issues and compatibility concerns may arise.

Social Implications

i. **Job Displacement:** Automation and the integration of smart technologies may lead to job displacement in certain sectors. Preparing the workforce for these changes and addressing potential unemployment issues is essential.

FUTURE TRENDS OF INTEGRATING CLOUD COMPUTING AND 5G FOR SECURE AND SUSTAINABLE URBAN ENVIRONMENTS

The integration of cloud computing and 5G technology will play a pivotal role in creating secure, sustainable, and efficient urban environments in the future. Here are some potential future trends in this area:

Edge Computing Enhancements: With the proliferation of IoT devices in urban environments, there will be an increasing need for edge computing capabilities to process data closer to the source. Cloud computing integrated with 5G will enable more efficient and faster processing of data at the edge, reducing latency and enhancing real-time decision-making for various urban applications, such as traffic management, public safety, and energy optimization.

Enhanced Data Analytics: The combination of cloud computing and 5G will enable more advanced data analytics capabilities, allowing urban planners and administrators to gain deeper insights into various aspects of city operations. Predictive analytics, machine learning, and AI algorithms will be leveraged to optimize resource allocation, improve infrastructure efficiency, and enhance overall urban sustainability.

Smart Infrastructure Development: Cloud computing and 5G will facilitate the development of smarter and more interconnected urban infrastructure. For example, smart grids powered by 5G-connected sensors and cloud-based analytics will enable more efficient energy distribution and consumption. Similarly, intelligent transportation systems will utilize real-time data from cloud servers to optimize traffic flow, reduce congestion, and minimize emissions.

Enhanced Security Measures: The integration of cloud computing and 5G will enable more robust security measures to protect urban environments against cyber threats and physical breaches. Advanced encryption techniques, multi-factor authentication, and real-time threat detection systems will be implemented to safeguard critical infrastructure, sensitive data, and citizen privacy (Choi et al., 2022).

Virtual and Augmented Reality Applications: Cloud computing combined with 5G's high bandwidth and low latency will enable immersive virtual and augmented reality experiences in urban environments. These technologies will revolutionize urban planning, allowing stakeholders to visualize proposed developments in real-time and make more informed decisions. Additionally, AR-based navigation systems will enhance the urban mobility experience for residents and visitors alike.

Remote Work and Telemedicine: The COVID-19 pandemic has accelerated the adoption of remote work and telemedicine, and this trend is expected to continue in the future. Cloud computing and 5G will enable seamless connectivity and collaboration, allowing urban residents to work remotely and access healthcare services from anywhere. This will reduce the need for commuting, leading to reduced traffic congestion, lower carbon emissions, and improved air quality in cities (Singh, Park, & Park, 2022).

Data Privacy and Governance: As urban environments become more data-driven, ensuring data privacy and governance will be critical. Regulations and standards for data protection, transparency, and accountability will need to be developed and enforced to maintain public trust in cloud-based urban systems. Additionally, technologies such as blockchain may be employed to enhance data security and integrity in urban environments.

Conclusion: The integration of IoT and 5G technologies in smart cities represents a transformative paradigm shift with profound implications for urban development and sustainability. Through an in-depth exploration of the literature and empirical analysis, this research has highlighted the multifaceted advantages that arise from the seamless collaboration between IoT devices and the high-speed, low-latency capabilities of 5G networks (Singh, Pan, & Park, 2022).

The amalgamation of these technologies not only enhances the efficiency of urban services but also fosters a more connected, responsive, and intelligent urban environment. From smart infrastructure management to real-time data analytics and intelligent transportation systems, the synergies between IoT and 5G empower smart cities to address contemporary challenges such as traffic congestion, energy consumption, and resource allocation.

Furthermore, the findings of this study underscore the potential economic, social, and environmental benefits that accrue from the integration of IoT and 5G in smart cities. Improved resource utilization, enhanced public safety, and the creation of innovative services contribute to the overall well-being of urban dwellers.

REFERENCES

Chen, H., Yuan, L., & Jing, G. (2020). *5G Boosting Smart Cities Development.* 2020 2nd International Conference on Artificial Intelligence and Advanced Manufacture (AIAM), Manchester, UK. 10.1109/AIAM50918.2020.00038

Chi, M.-H. (2022). IC Technologies and Systems for Green Future. *2022 China Semiconductor Technology International Conference (CSTIC)*, Shanghai, China. 10.1109/CSTIC55103.2022.9856769

Choi, M., Azzaoui, A. E., Singh, S. K., Salim, M. M., Jeremiah, S. R., & Park, J. H. (2022). The future of metaverse: Security issues, requirements, and solutions. *Human-Centric Computing and Information Sciences*, *12*(60), 1–14.

El Azzaoui, A., Singh, S. K., Pan, Y., & Park, J. H. (2020). Block5GIntell: Blockchain for AI-enabled 5G networks. *IEEE Access : Practical Innovations, Open Solutions*, *8*, 145918–145935. doi:10.1109/ACCESS.2020.3014356

Elwy, F., Aburukba, R., & Al-Ali, A. R. (2022). Role of Fog Computing in Smart Spaces. *2022 IEEE International Conference on Edge Computing and Communications (EDGE)*, Barcelona, Spain. 10.1109/EDGE55608.2022.00021

Hirota, Y. (2021End-to-End Management of All Optical Disaggregated Network and Applications with Cloud Native Environment for the Smart World Network Infrastructure. *2021 Opto-Electronics and Communications Conference (OECC)*, Hong Kong, Hong Kong. 10.1364/OECC.2021.M4A.4

Jiang, Y., Xiao, W., Wang, R., & Barnawi, A. (2020). Smart Urban Living: Enabling Emotion-Guided Interaction With Next Generation Sensing Fabric. *IEEE Access : Practical Innovations, Open Solutions*, *8*, 28395–28402. doi:10.1109/ACCESS.2019.2961957

Liu, Y., Peng, M., Shou, G., Chen, Y., & Chen, S. (2020, August). Toward Edge Intelligence: Multiaccess Edge Computing for 5G and Internet of Things. *IEEE Internet of Things Journal*, *7*(8), 6722–6747. doi:10.1109/JIOT.2020.3004500

Muhammad, A., Saqib, M., & Song, W.-C. (2021). Sensor Virtualization and Data Orchestration in Internet of Vehicles (IoV). *IFIP/IEEE International Symposium on Integrated Network Management (IM)*, Bordeaux, France.

Ou, D., Jiang, C., Zheng, M., & Ren, Y. (2023). Container Power Consumption Prediction Based on GBRT-PL for Edge Servers in Smart City. *IEEE Internet of Things Journal, 10*(21), 18799-18807. doi:10.1109/JIOT.2023.3281368

Pundir, S., Wazid, M., Singh, D. P., Das, A. K., Rodrigues, J. J. P. C., & Park, Y. (2020). Intrusion Detection Protocols in Wireless Sensor Networks Integrated to Internet of Things Deployment: Survey and Future Challenges. *IEEE Access : Practical Innovations, Open Solutions*, *8*, 3343–3363. doi:10.1109/ACCESS.2019.2962829

Qadeer, A., & Lee, M. J. (2022). *DDPG-Edge-Cloud: A Deep-Deterministic Policy Gradient based Multi-Resource Allocation in Edge-Cloud System.* 2022 International Conference on Artificial Intelligence in Information and Communication (ICAIIC), Jeju Island, South Korea. 10.1109/ICAIIC54071.2022.9722676

Rajaei, H., Kanumuri, B., & Narreddi, N. (2020). SBDC: Smart Building Data Center for Iot, Edge, and 5G. *2020 Spring Simulation Conference (SpringSim)*, Fairfax, VA, USA. 10.22360/SpringSim.2020.CNS.004

Rito, P. (2023). Aveiro Tech City Living Lab: A Communication, Sensing, and Computing Platform for City Environments. *IEEE Internet of Things Journal, 10*(15), 13489-13510. . doi:10.1109/JIOT.2023.3262627

Singh, S. K., Azzaoui, A. E., Choo, K. K. R., Yang, L. T., & Park, J. H. (2023). A Comprehensive Survey on Blockchain for Secure IoT-enabled Smart City beyond 5G: Approaches, Processes, Challenges, and Opportunities. *Hum.-Centric Comput. Inf. Sci, 13*(51).

Singh, S. K., Pan, Y., & Park, J. H. (2022). Blockchain-enabled secure framework for energy-efficient smart parking in sustainable city environment. *Sustainable Cities and Society*, *76*, 103364. doi:10.1016/j.scs.2021.103364

Singh, S. K., Park, L., & Park, J. H. (2022, October). Blockchain-based Federated Approach for Privacy-Preserved IoT-enabled Smart Vehicular Networks. In *2022 13th International Conference on Information and Communication Technology Convergence (ICTC)* (pp. 1995-1999). IEEE. 10.1109/ICTC55196.2022.9952835

Syed, A. S., Sierra-Sosa, D., Kumar, A., & Elmaghraby, A. (2021). IoT in Smart Cities: A Survey of Technologies, Practices and Challenges. *Smart Cities.*, *4*(2), 429–475. doi:10.3390/smartcities4020024

Wang, Z., Hu, J., Min, G., Zhao, Z., & Wang, J. (2021, June). Data-Augmentation-Based Cellular Traffic Prediction in Edge-Computing-Enabled Smart City. *IEEE Transactions on Industrial Informatics*, *17*(6), 4179–4187. doi:10.1109/TII.2020.3009159

Xu, S., Liu, X., Guo, S., Qiu, X., & Meng, L. (2021, July/August). MECC: A Mobile Edge Collaborative Caching Framework Empowered by Deep Reinforcement Learning. *IEEE Network*, *35*(4), 176–183. doi:10.1109/MNET.011.2000663

Yadav, M., Agarwal, U., Rishiwal, V., Tanwar, S., Kumar, S., Alqahtani, F., & Tolba, A. (2023). Exploring Synergy of Blockchain and 6G Network for Industrial Automation. *IEEE Access : Practical Innovations, Open Solutions*, *11*, 137163–137187. doi:10.1109/ACCESS.2023.3338861

Yang, T., Ning, J., Lan, D., Zhang, J., Yang, Y., Wang, X., & Taherkordi, A. (2022, April). Kubeedge Wireless for Integrated Communication and Computing Services Everywhere. *IEEE Wireless Communications*, *29*(2), 140–145. doi:10.1109/MWC.004.2100038

Yu, S., Chen, X., Zhou, Z., Gong, X., & Wu, D. (2021). When Deep Reinforcement Learning Meets Federated Learning: Intelligent Multitimescale Resource Management for Multiaccess Edge Computing in 5G Ultradense Network. *IEEE Internet of Things Journal, 8*(4), 2238-2251. . doi:10.1109/JIOT.2020.3026589

Yu, S., Gong, X., Shi, Q., Wang X., & Chen, X. (2022). EC-SAGINs: Edge-Computing-Enhanced Space–Air–Ground-Integrated Networks for Internet of Vehicles. *IEEE Internet of Things Journal, 9*(8), 5742-5754. . doi:10.1109/JIOT.2021.3052542

Zhao, Q. (2023). *Customizable Cloud-Native Infrastructure for Private 5G*. 2023 26th Conference on Innovation in Clouds, Internet and Networks and Workshops (ICIN), Paris, France. 10.1109/ICIN56760.2023.10073479

Zhou, S., Wei, C., Song, C., Pan, X., Chang, W., & Yang, L. (2023, February). Short-Term Traffic Flow Prediction of the Smart City Using 5G Internet of Vehicles Based on Edge Computing. *IEEE Transactions on Intelligent Transportation Systems*, *24*(2), 2229–2238. doi:10.1109/TITS.2022.3147845

Chapter 6
Cloud Computing for a Secure Smart City Beyond 5G

Manoj Kumar Patra
https://orcid.org/0000-0002-7435-2282
GITAM University, Hyderabad, India

Bibhudatta Sahoo
https://orcid.org/0000-0001-8273-9850
National Institute of Technology, Rourkela, India

Sampa Sahoo
C. V. Raman Global University, Bhubaneswar, India

Ashok Kumar Turuk
National Institute of Technology, Rourkela, India

ABSTRACT

As the evolution of technology ushers in an era beyond 5G, integrating cloud computing into the landscape of smart cities becomes paramount. This chapter delves into the foundational concept of cloud computing and elucidates its pivotal role in shaping the future of secure and connected smart cities. With its on-demand services, scalability, and cost-effectiveness, cloud computing emerges as a key enabler for handling the intricate demands of urban environments. The chapter begins by defining cloud computing and providing an overview of its essential characteristics. It then pivots to the dynamic context of smart cities, where an intricate web of internet of things (IoT) devices, sensors, and urban systems generate copious amounts of data. Cloud computing offers a robust solution for storing, processing, and analyzing this data, empowering smart cities with real-time insights and informed decision-making capabilities. This chapter explores the synergy between cloud computing and 5G networks, emphasizing the importance of high-speed connectivity and low latency in the smart city paradigm. The integration of edge computing further enriches the smart city infrastructure, enabling rapid local processing and reducing latency for time-sensitive applications. Security, a paramount concern in smart city environments, is addressed as the chapter delves into the challenges and solutions provided by cloud computing. The role of cloud platforms in safeguarding citizen data, managing cyber-physical threats, and ensuring compliance with regulatory frameworks is thoroughly examined. This chapter also explores emerging trends, such as the integration of artificial intelligence and blockchain technologies, offering a glimpse into the future of cloud computing in the smart city landscape. In conclusion, this chapter not only defines the synergy between cloud computing and smart cities but also provides a comprehensive understanding of how cloud computing, in the context of 5G and beyond, is instrumental in fostering secure, connected, and resilient urban environments.

DOI: 10.4018/979-8-3693-2373-1.ch006

CLOUD COMPUTING AND SMART CITIES

Computing in the cloud is the practice of providing data storage, processing power, and software applications over the Internet. Remote data centers give users access to computer resources rather than requiring them to depend on local servers or personal devices. These services are often categorized into three main models (Darwish, 2024): Infrastructure as a Service (IaaS), Platform as a Service (PaaS), and Software as a Service (SaaS). Key Characteristics of cloud computing is as follows:

- *On-Demand Self-Service:* In the absence of human involvement, users can avail and manage computer resources on an as-needed basis.
- *Broad Network Access:* Many internet-connected devices, including desktop computers, mobile phones, and tablets, may access cloud services.
- *Resource Pooling:* Computer resources may be used more efficiently and effectively by combining and sharing resources across several users.
- *Rapid Elasticity:* On-demand, cloud resources may be quickly increased or decreased. This guarantees efficiency and adaptability.
- *Measured Service:* Computing resources are charged to users according to their actual use. Scalability and cost-effectiveness are hallmarks of this pay-as-you-go strategy.

Role of Cloud Computing in Smart Cities

Cloud Computing plays an important role in Smart Cities by offering scalable, flexible, and cost-effective solutions for data storage, processing, and analysis. It facilitates the integration of diverse urban systems, enabling cities to make informed decisions, enhance efficiency, and improve the overall quality of life for citizens (Sharma et al., 2024). Cloud computing role in Smart Cities is discussed below.

Data Storage and Processing

Smart Cities produce vast amounts of data through IoT devices, sensors, and various urban systems. The use of cloud computing provides options that are both scalable and cost-effective for the storage and processing of this data. Cloud-based storage ensures that Smart Cities can handle the massive volumes of information generated daily (Patel et al., 2023).

Real-Time Analytics

Cloud platforms offer the computing power required for real-time data analytics. Smart Cities can leverage cloud-based analytics to derive valuable details from the collected data, enabling more informed decision-making for urban planning, traffic management, and resource allocation.

Connectivity and Accessibility

Cloud services enhance connectivity in Smart Cities by providing a centralized platform accessible from various locations and devices. This fosters collaboration, efficiency, and seamless communication among different city components. Here, the advancement in wireless communication technology (4G, 5G) plays an important role (Joshi et al., 2023).

Resource Optimization

Cloud Computing enables Smart Cities to optimize resource usage. By utilizing the on-demand and scalable nature of cloud resources, cities can efficiently manage energy consumption, waste management, and other essential services.

Scalability and Flexibility

Smart Cities are dynamic and constantly evolving. Cloud Computing offers the scalability and flexibility needed to adapt to changing requirements. Cities can scale their computing infrastructure up or down based on the growth of IoT devices, population, or other factors.

Cost-Effective Solutions

Cloud services provide solutions that are both cost-effective and efficient for Smart Cities, removing the need for significant initial expenditures in information technology infrastructure. According to the pay-as-you-go concept, communities are only required to pay for the resources that they really use, which makes it a financially feasible alternative.

Security and Data Privacy

Cloud service providers invest heavily in security measures. Smart Cities can benefit from the robust security protocols implemented by cloud platforms, ensuring the protection of sensitive citizen data and critical infrastructure (Patra, 2017).

EVOLUTION OF WIRELESS TECHNOLOGY FROM 4G TO 5G

The transition from 4G to 5G marks a revolutionary leap in wireless communication technology, reshaping the landscape of connectivity and paving the way for unprecedented advancements. In the era of 4G, data speeds saw a considerable boost, allowing for faster internet access and improved mobile communication. However, the limitations of 4G, such as latency and scalability issues, prompted the need for a more sophisticated and efficient network infrastructure. Enter 5G, the fifth generation of wireless technology, promising not just incremental improvements but a paradigm shift in connectivity. 5G brings forth unparalleled data transfer speeds, reaching gigabit-per-second rates, and remarkably low latency, measured in milliseconds. This transformative technology doesn't merely promise faster downloads; it signifies a fundamental change in how devices communicate, unlocking the potential for innovations that were previously constrained by network limitations. The increased connectivity density of 5G facilitates the massive deployment of Internet of Things (IoT) devices, contributing to the realization of Smart Cities where an intricate web of interconnected sensors and systems communicate seamlessly

(Kumar & Kumar, 2023). Network slicing, a feature unique to 5G, allows the creation of customized virtual networks tailored to specific applications, ensuring optimal resource allocation and network efficiency. Moreover, the integration of 5G with edge computing brings processing capabilities closer to the data source, reducing latency and opening avenues for real-time applications like augmented reality and autonomous systems. As 5G networks continue to roll out globally, the implications extend beyond mere speed improvements, ushering in an era where connectivity becomes a catalyst for unprecedented advancements in diverse fields, from healthcare and transportation to smart infrastructure and beyond. The evolution from 4G to 5G is not just an incremental upgrade; it is a transformative journey towards a more connected, efficient, and technologically advanced future.

Implications of 5G for Smart City Development

The advent of 5G technology brings with it profound implications for the development of Smart Cities, transcending the boundaries of conventional urban planning. The enhanced connectivity, marked by ultra-fast speeds and minimal latency, establishes the backbone for a multitude of transformative applications. In the realm of transportation, Smart Cities can harness 5G to enable real-time traffic management, optimized routing, and support for autonomous vehicles, ushering in an era of safer and more efficient mobility. The proliferation of IoT devices, facilitated by 5G's scalability, forms the fabric of a Smart City's nervous system, allowing for the seamless integration of sensors in various domains, from healthcare and environmental monitoring to waste management and energy grids. Furthermore, the ability of 5G to support a massive number of simultaneous connections ensures that the vast array of interconnected devices in a Smart City can communicate effortlessly, fostering a dynamic and responsive urban ecosystem. The customization capabilities afforded by 5G's network slicing feature enable Smart Cities to tailor connectivity solutions for specific applications, optimizing resources and ensuring that diverse services receive the necessary network support. Additionally, the integration of edge computing with 5G infrastructure facilitates the processing of data closer to the source, decreasing latency and offering real-time decision-making. As Smart Cities evolve, 5G becomes the linchpin, not only for improving existing services but also for unlocking novel possibilities that were once confined by the limitations of previous generations of wireless technology. In essence, the implications of 5G for Smart City development transcend mere technological upgrades; they represent a paradigm shift towards a more interconnected, efficient, and responsive urban environment that holds the promise of enhancing the quality of life for citizens and fostering sustainable urban development (Yang et al., 2022). The evolution from 4G to 5G brings about a transformative shift in connectivity, enabling Smart Cities to harness the full potential of emerging technologies and providing the foundation for more advanced and efficient urban development (Mukherjee et al., 2022).

REQUIREMENTS FOR SMART CITY APPLICATIONS

Smart City applications, at the intersection of urban development and advanced technology, pose unique and intricate challenges that necessitate tailored solutions. Among the distinct requirements, three stand out prominently: high data volumes, low latency, reliability, and security and privacy.

High Data Volumes

Smart Cities are characterized by an extensive network of interconnected devices and systems, collectively generating massive volumes of data. This data emanates from diverse sources such as sensors, surveillance cameras, traffic management systems, and citizen-centric applications. The intricate web of IoT devices contributes to the continuous flow of real-time information, creating a rich data ecosystem. To harness the potential of this data, Smart City applications must accommodate and process high data volumes efficiently (Javed et al., 2022). This necessitates robust data storage solutions and scalable processing capabilities, often found in cloud computing infrastructure. Cloud-based storage systems enable the aggregation and management of vast datasets, ensuring that Smart Cities can extract meaningful insights for informed decision-making in areas like urban planning, traffic management, and environmental monitoring.

Low Latency

In the context of Smart City applications, especially those with real-time requirements, latency becomes a critical consideration. For applications like autonomous vehicles, smart grids, and emergency response systems, low latency is imperative to enable quick and accurate decision-making. Imagine a scenario where an autonomous vehicle needs to process sensor data rapidly to navigate through traffic or an emergency response system relies on swift data transmission to assess and address a crisis. In such instances, delays could lead to suboptimal performance or, in critical situations, result in adverse outcomes. The integration of 5G networks and edge computing addresses this need for low latency. 5G's ultra-fast speeds and edge computing's ability to process data closer to the source significantly reduce the time it takes for data to travel, ensuring timely and responsive Smart City applications.

Reliability

Reliability is a fundamental requirement for Smart City applications, considering the critical nature of many urban services. From transportation systems and energy grids to healthcare and public safety applications, the reliability of the underlying technology is paramount. Citizens and businesses alike depend on the continuous operation of these services for their daily activities. The challenge lies not only in ensuring the reliability of individual components but also in establishing a resilient and redundant infrastructure that can withstand failures or disruptions. Smart Cities often employ redundancy measures, such as backup power systems, multiple data centers, and failover mechanisms, to ensure continuous service availability. Additionally, the reliability of communication networks, particularly in the context of 5G, is crucial. A robust and reliable network infrastructure forms the backbone for Smart City applications, enabling seamless connectivity, systems, and users.

Security and privacy stand as pivotal and distinct requirements in the landscape of Smart City applications, highlighting the delicate balance between technological innovation and the protection of citizens' rights.

Security

The interconnected nature of Smart City systems, which often involve critical infrastructure and vast networks of sensors and devices, poses unique security challenges. Protecting against cyber threats is paramount, as the compromise of essential services could have severe consequences. Robust cyber security measures are essential to thwart unauthorized access, prevent data breaches, and ensure the integrity and availability of critical infrastructure. Smart City applications must address vulnerabilities in the complex ecosystem, incorporating encryption, authentication protocols, and regular security updates. Incident response planning is equally critical, enabling swift reactions to security breaches and minimizing potential disruptions.

Privacy

Smart City applications inherently involve the collection and analysis of large amount of data, often including sensitive personal information. Citizens entrust their data to the city for various services, necessitating stringent data protection measures. Surveillance technologies, such as cameras and sensors, require transparent policies to mitigate potential privacy concerns. Ethical considerations come into play, emphasizing fair and responsible data practices. Respecting data ownership, obtaining informed consent, and implementing anonymization techniques contribute to building and maintaining public trust. The convergence of security and privacy is particularly evident in technologies like the IoT. While IoT devices enhance the efficiency of Smart City operations, they expand the attack surface for potential security breaches. Simultaneously, these devices collect huge amounts of data, creating concerns about individual privacy. Striking the right balance involves securing IoT devices against cyber threats and implementing measures to safeguard the privacy of the data they generate. To navigate these challenges effectively, Smart Cities should adopt a comprehensive and proactive approach to security and privacy. This includes ongoing assessments of cyber security protocols, regular audits of data handling practices, and continuous engagement with citizens to ensure that their privacy concerns are addressed. By embedding security and privacy measures into the foundation of Smart City initiatives, urban environments can harness technological advancements while safeguarding the rights and trust of their residents.

The unique requirements of Smart City applications, encompassing high data volumes, low latency, reliability, and security and privacy underscore the need for sophisticated and resilient technological solutions. As Smart Cities continue to evolve, addressing these requirements will be essential to unlock the full potential of urban development through technology, ensuring efficiency, sustainability, and an enhanced quality of life for citizens. A possible architecture of IoT integrated smart city architecture is presented in Figure. 1.

Cloud Computing to Address Unique Requirements

Cloud Computing plays a pivotal role in addressing the unique requirement of high data volumes in Smart City applications. The ability of Smart Cities to efficiently manage, process, and derive insights from massive amounts of data is crucial for informed decision-making and the effective functioning of various urban services. Here's how Cloud Computing addresses this specific need:

i. **Cloud Storage:** Cloud platforms offer robust and scalable storage solutions that can accommodate the vast amounts of data produced by Smart City applications. These cloud-based storage systems enable efficient and cost-effective handling of large datasets, ensuring that historical and real-time data can be stored securely and accessed when needed. Cloud Computing serves as a foundational technology that addresses the unique requirement of high data volumes in Smart City applications

Figure 1. Architecture of IoT and cloud integrated smart city

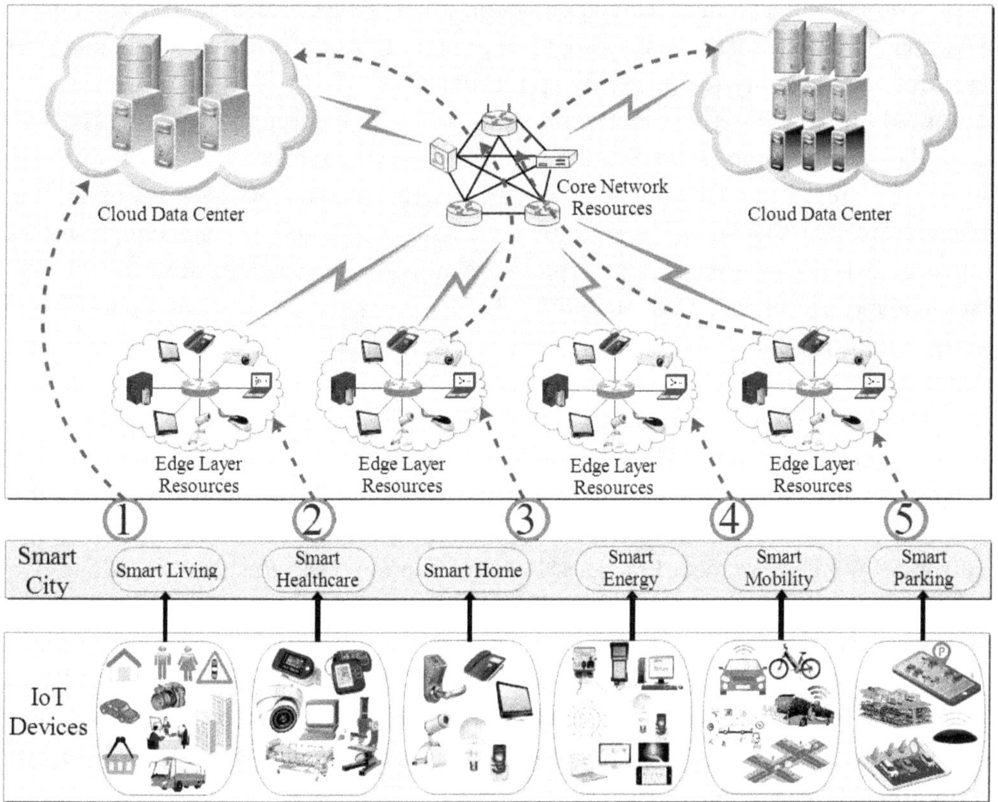

by providing scalable and efficient solutions for data storage, processing, and analysis. This, in turn, empowers Smart Cities to harness the full potential of data-driven insights for sustainable and intelligent urban development. Cloud Computing plays a crucial role in addressing the unique requirement of low latency in Smart City applications, ensuring that data processing and communication occur swiftly and responsively (Silva et al., 2018). Low latency is particularly essential for applications that need real-time interactions, such as autonomous vehicles, and emergency response systems. Here's how Cloud Computing addresses the challenge of low latency in Smart City scenarios.

ii. **Localized Processing:** Cloud computing platforms often integrate with edge computing, bringing computational power closer to the data source. Edge computing involves processing data locally, at or near the source of data generation. By reducing the physical distance that data needs to travel to reach a central data center, edge computing significantly minimizes latency. This is crucial for applications that demand quick responses, such as traffic signal optimization or real-time monitoring of critical infrastructure. Cloud Computing, with its integration of edge computing, use of Content Delivery Networks, reliance on high-speed networks, integration with 5G, and resource scaling capabilities, addresses the unique requirement of low latency in Smart City applications (Chen et al., 2021). This ensures that the vast array of interconnected devices and systems in a Smart City can operate seamlessly, providing real-time responsiveness and enhancing the overall efficiency of urban services. Cloud Computing serves as a foundational technology that effectively addresses the unique requirement of reliability in Smart City applications. The reliability of Smart City systems is crucial because these applications often involve critical services that impact public safety, transportation, energy management, and more. Here's how Cloud Computing contributes to ensuring the reliability of Smart City applications.

iii. **Automated Backup Systems:** Cloud Computing platforms incorporate automated backup systems that regularly duplicate and store data across multiple servers and locations. In the event of data loss or system failures, Smart City applications can quickly recover from backup copies, maintaining continuous operation and data integrity. By leveraging the reliability-enhancing features of Cloud Computing, Smart City applications can provide continuous, dependable services to residents, businesses, and city authorities. This reliability is fundamental to the success of Smart City initiatives, fostering public trust and ensuring the seamless operation of critical urban services (Coman et al., 2021). Cloud Computing also plays a pivotal role in addressing the unique and critical requirements of security and privacy in Smart City applications. The interconnected nature of Smart City systems, involving vast amounts of sensitive data, requires robust measures to safeguard against cyber threats and protect the privacy of citizens. The Cloud Computing addresses the specific needs such as Advanced Data Encryption, Identity and Access Management (IAM), Network Security, Secure Development Practices, Data Encryption, Data Residency Options, Transparent Data Handling Policies, User Consent Management, etc. In summary, Cloud Computing provides a comprehensive set of security and privacy features that empower Smart Cities to build and operate applications with the utmost protection for sensitive data and citizen privacy. By leveraging the security infrastructure and best practices offered by cloud providers, Smart City initiatives can instill confidence in residents and stakeholders, ensuring the responsible and secure use of technology for urban development.

INTEGRATION OF CLOUD COMPUTING AND 5G

The synergy between Cloud Computing and 5G networks represents a transformative combination that significantly enhances connectivity and performance across a myriad of applications and industries. Here's an examination of the key aspects of this synergy:

Ultra-Fast Speeds

5G Contribution: 5G networks are designed to deliver ultra-fast data speeds, reaching gigabit-per-second rates. This high-speed connectivity is fundamental for applications requiring real-time data transfer and low latency (Vilalta et al., 2017).

Cloud Impact: Cloud Computing leverages these high speeds by providing fast and efficient access to cloud-based resources and services. The synergy ensures that data-intensive tasks, such as large-scale data analytics or streaming high-definition content, can be seamlessly executed with minimal delays.

Low Latency

5G Contribution: 5G networks substantially reduce latency. 5G can achieve latency in the order of milliseconds, making it suitable for applications that demand near-instantaneous responses.

Cloud Impact: Cloud Computing complements low latency by offering edge computing capabilities. By placing processing power closer to the data source.

Massive Device Connectivity

5G Contribution: The needs of the Internet of Things and Smart City applications are satisfied by 5G networks, which are intended to accommodate a vast number of connected devices per square kilometer (Pham et al., 2020).

Cloud Impact: The scalability of cloud infrastructure ensures that the massive data volumes generated by IoT devices can be efficiently handled and analyzed.

Edge Computing Integration

5G Contribution: 5G networks seamlessly integrate with edge computing, bringing processing capabilities closer to the data source. This reduces the distance, minimizing latency and enhancing the performance of applications that need real-time data processing (Orabi et al., 2023).

Cloud Impact: Cloud providers extend their services to the edge, enabling seamless integration with edge computing. This synergy ensures that the benefits of cloud services, such as storage, analytics, and machine learning, are available at the edge for applications like smart manufacturing, healthcare, and augmented reality.

In summary, the synergy between cloud and 5G networks creates a powerful ecosystem that not only meets the growing demands for connectivity and performance but also acts as an enabler for unprecedented innovation across industries. As these technologies continue to evolve together, they will play a pivotal role in creating the future of digital experiences, smart cities, and advanced industrial applications.

SECURITY CHALLENGES IN SMART CITIES

Smart Cities, leveraging advanced technologies for urban development, face an array of security challenges that demand careful consideration and proactive solutions. As these cities integrate interconnected systems and data-driven applications, ensuring the security of sensitive information, safeguarding network infrastructure, and protecting against cyber-physical threats become paramount. This article identifies and analyzes the specific security challenges confronting Smart Cities, focusing on data privacy concerns, network security vulnerabilities, and the evolving landscape of cyber-physical threats.

Data Privacy in Smart Cities

Massive Data Collection and Handling

Smart Cities thrive on the collection of vast amounts of data from sensors, cameras, and various IoT devices. While this data is instrumental for optimizing city operations, the sheer volume poses challenges in terms of maintaining individual privacy (He & Zhang, 2023).

Consent Management

The sheer scope of data collection in Smart Cities necessitates clear and informed consent mechanisms. Ensuring that citizens are aware of how their data will be used and obtaining their explicit consent is crucial for building trust. Smart Cities must implement transparent policies and user-friendly interfaces for managing consent preferences.

Geographical Data and Location Privacy

Location-based services are integral to many Smart City applications, raising concerns about location privacy. Balancing the benefits of location data for services like traffic management with the need to protect individuals from unwarranted tracking requires careful consideration. Anonymization techniques and strict access controls are vital to mitigate location privacy risks.

Network Security Challenges

Proliferation of IoT Devices

The Internet of Things (IoT) is a cornerstone of Smart Cities, introducing a multitude of interconnected devices. However, the diverse nature of these devices, often with varying security postures, creates a complex attack surface. Ensuring the security of each IoT device and managing potential vulnerabilities is a significant challenge (Sharma & Arya, 2023).

Interconnected Infrastructure

Smart Cities rely on interconnected infrastructure where various systems and services communicate to enhance efficiency. This interconnectivity, while beneficial, introduces vulnerabilities. A breach in one system could potentially compromise the entire network. Implementing robust network segmentation and security protocols is crucial to prevent lateral movement by attackers.

5G Security Concerns

The integration of 5G networks enhances connectivity in Smart Cities but brings forth new security considerations. The higher data speeds and lower latency offered by 5G can attract more sophisticated cyber threats. Smart Cities must invest in robust security measures, including secure authentication and encryption protocols, to safeguard their 5G infrastructure.

Insider Threats

Internal actors, whether employees or third party service providers, can pose a significant security risk. Access to sensitive systems and data requires stringent access controls and continuous monitoring to detect and respond to any anomalous activities. Training programs and awareness initiatives can also play a crucial role in mitigating insider threats.

Cyber-Physical Threats

Critical Infrastructure Vulnerabilities

Cyber-physical threats targeting these systems can have severe consequences. Implementing robust cyber security measures for critical infrastructure is essential to prevent disruptions that could impact public safety (Demertzi et al., 2023).

Manipulation of Sensor Data

Sensors are the eyes and ears of Smart Cities, providing real-time data for decision-making. Manipulation of sensor data, whether through physical tampering or cyber attacks, can mislead city authorities and compromise the effectiveness of smart systems. Implementing integrity checks, secure communication protocols, and physical security measures for sensors are imperative.

Autonomous Vehicles Security

The deployment of autonomous vehicles in Smart Cities introduces a new dimension of cyber-physical security challenges. Hacking into vehicle systems or manipulating traffic signals could lead to accidents and traffic disruptions. Ensuring the cyber security of autonomous vehicles involves robust encryption, secure communication channels, and continuous monitoring for potential threats.

Emergency Services Disruption

Attacks on Smart City systems could target emergency services, leading to disruptions in response times and communication channels during critical situations. Protecting the integrity and availability of emergency services is crucial for public safety. Redundancy measures, secure communication networks, and regular security audits are essential components of a resilient emergency services infrastructure.

In navigating the security challenges specific to Smart Cities, a comprehensive and adaptive approach is indispensable. Protecting data privacy, securing network infrastructure, and mitigating cyber-physical threats require collaboration between city authorities, technology providers, and citizens. Implementing robust security measures, staying abreast of evolving cyber threats and fostering a culture of cyber security awareness are pivotal in building and sustaining secure and resilient Smart Cities. As these cities continue to evolve, addressing these challenges will be integral to ensuring that the promise of urban innovation is realized without compromising the safety and privacy of the citizens they serve.

Cloud Computing to Address Security Challenges

As Smart Cities grapple with the multifaceted security challenges encompassing data privacy, network vulnerabilities, and cyber-physical threats, the integration of Cloud Computing emerges as a key enabler for robust and comprehensive solutions. Cloud Computing offers a strategic framework to address these challenges by providing scalable, secure, and adaptable infrastructure that aligns with the dynamic nature of Smart City environments.

Enhancing Data Privacy in the Cloud:

Secure Data Storage and Processing

By leveraging encryption and access control mechanisms, sensitive information is safeguarded against unauthorized access. Cloud providers adhere to stringent security protocols, ensuring that data privacy remains a top priority (Singh et al., 2022).

Consent Management and Transparency

Cloud-based systems facilitate transparent consent management through user-friendly interfaces and clear communication channels. Smart Cities can implement consent mechanisms in the cloud, providing citizens with greater visibility and control over how their data is utilized. Cloud platforms support the development of transparent policies, fostering trust between city authorities and residents.

Strengthening Network Security with Cloud Infrastructure

Unified Security Management

Cloud Computing platforms provide centralized security management tools, allowing Smart Cities to monitor and secure their entire network infrastructure from a single interface. This centralized approach enhances visibility, making it easier to detect and respond to potential threats across interconnected systems.

Network Segmentation and Isolation

Cloud infrastructure supports network segmentation, enabling Smart Cities to isolate different components of their network. By segmenting systems, even in a connected environment, the impact of a security breach can be contained. This strategy prevents lateral movement by attackers, enhancing the overall resilience of the network.

Secure Integration with 5G Networks

The integration of Cloud Computing with 5G networks is instrumental in addressing the security concerns associated with enhanced connectivity. Cloud providers implement secure communication protocols and encryption mechanisms to safeguard data transmitted over 5G networks. This synergy ensures that the benefits of 5G, such as high-speed connectivity, are harnessed without compromising security.

Mitigating Cyber-Physical Threats through Cloud-Based Solutions

Resilient Critical Infrastructure Protection

Cloud Computing provides a resilient foundation for protecting critical infrastructure in Smart Cities. By hosting key systems in the cloud, cities can benefit from redundancy, backup capabilities, and disaster recovery services. In the event of a cyber-physical attack, the cloud infrastructure ensures the continuity of essential services.

Integrity Checks for Sensor Data

Cloud-based solutions enable Smart Cities to implement integrity checks for sensor data in real-time. By processing and validating sensor data in the cloud, cities can detect anomalies and potential manipulations. This enhances the reliability of data-driven decision-making and safeguards against cyber-physical threats that aim to manipulate sensor information.

Cloud Computing emerges as a pivotal technology in fortifying the security posture of Smart Cities. By addressing challenges related to data privacy, network security, and cyber-physical threats, the cloud provides a holistic and adaptable framework. Leveraging the scalability, centralized management, and advanced security features of cloud platforms; Smart Cities can navigate the evolving landscape of security threats with confidence.

DATA MANAGEMENT AND ANALYTICS

Cloud Computing plays a pivotal role in efficiently managing the massive datasets generated by Smart City sensors and devices, providing scalable storage, streamlined retrieval, and powerful analysis capabilities. The synergy between Smart Cities and Cloud Computing transforms the way data is handled, allowing for seamless integration, real-time insights, and effective decision-making. Here's how Cloud Computing enables these key aspects:

Scalable Storage Solutions

Massive Data Volumes: Smart City sensors and devices generate large volumes of data continuously, including information from IoT devices, surveillance cameras, environmental sensors, and more. Cloud computing platforms offer scalable storage solutions, allowing cities to dynamically expand their storage capacity to accommodate the ever-growing datasets (Patra et al., 2023, pp. 81-98).

Object Storage Services

Cloud providers offer object storage services that are well-suited for storing diverse data formats, including images, videos, and sensor readings. This allows Smart Cities to organize and store data efficiently, ensuring accessibility and flexibility in managing different types of information.

Data Tiering and Archiving

Cloud platforms often provide data tiering and archiving capabilities, making it possible for Smart Cities to reduce their storage expenses by shifting data that is accessed less often to storage tiers with reduced operating costs. This ensures that relevant data is readily available for analysis, while historical or less critical data is stored cost-effectively.

Streamlined Data Retrieval

a. *High-Speed Data Access:* Cloud computing offers high-speed data access through content delivery networks (CDNs) and optimized data retrieval mechanisms. Smart Cities can efficiently retrieve relevant data from the cloud, facilitating real-time applications such as traffic management, public safety monitoring, and environmental sensing.
b. *Global Accessibility:* Cloud storage provides global accessibility, allowing Smart Cities to access and retrieve data from anywhere. This is particularly beneficial for cities with distributed sensor networks, enabling centralized data access and management.

Powerful Data Analysis

a. *Scalable Computing Resources:* Cloud computing platforms offer scalable computing resources, allowing Smart Cities to deploy powerful data analysis tools and algorithms. This scalability ensures that real-time analytics, ML, and statistical modeling, can be performed efficiently even on massive datasets.
b. *Data Lakes and Warehouses:* Cloud providers offer services like data lakes and data warehouses that enable Smart Cities to consolidate and structure diverse datasets for analysis. This centralized approach simplifies data preparation and allows for comprehensive analysis across different data sources.

Real-Time Processing and Edge Computing

a. *Edge Computing Integration:* Cloud computing seamlessly integrates with edge computing architectures. Before transmitting pertinent data to the cloud, edge devices closer to the data source may execute preliminary processing and filtering. This reduces latency and ensures that only essential data is transmitted, optimizing bandwidth usage.
b. *Real-time Data Streams:* Cloud platforms support real-time data processing and analytics, allowing Smart Cities to derive insights from continuous streams of data. This capability is crucial for applications such as traffic management, where timely decisions based on current conditions are essential.
c. *Serverless Computing for Event-Driven Architectures:* Cloud providers offer serverless computing models that are well-suited for event-driven architectures. Smart Cities can leverage serverless functions to process events in real-time, trigger automated responses, and handle dynamic workloads without the need for manual scaling (Kumari et al., 2023).

Cloud Computing provides a robust foundation for efficiently managing and analyzing massive datasets generated by Smart City sensors and devices. From scalable storage solutions to streamlined data retrieval and powerful analysis capabilities, the cloud's versatility empowers Smart Cities to harness the full potential of their data for improved urban planning, enhanced services, and informed decision-making.

Cloud-Based Analytics in Deriving Actionable Insights

Cloud-based analytics plays a crucial role in converting raw data into usable insights for organizations across various industries. This paradigm shifts in data analysis leverages the scalability, flexibility, and computational power provided by cloud computing platforms. Here's a discussion on the key aspects of the role of cloud-based analytics in deriving actionable insights:

Scalability and Performance

Data Processing at Scale: Cloud-based analytics enables organizations to process and analyze huge datasets at scale. Cloud providers provide scalable resources, allowing for the efficient handling of diverse data sources, including structured and unstructured data.

High-Performance Computing: The cloud provides access to high-performance computing capabilities, reducing the time required for complex analytical tasks. This ensures faster insights, allowing organizations to make timely decisions based on the most current data.

Flexibility and Agility:

On-Demand Resources: Cloud-based analytics allows organizations to access computing resources on-demand. This flexibility enables them to increase during periods of high demand for processing and decrease during periods of lower demand, optimizing cost-efficiency.

Agile Analytics Workflows: Cloud platforms support agile analytics workflows, allowing organizations to experiment with different analytical models, algorithms, and approaches. This agility fosters innovation and continuous improvement in deriving insights from data.

Data Integration and Centralization

Unified Data Storage: Cloud-based analytics facilitates the centralization of diverse datasets in cloud data storage services. This unified data storage allows organizations to break down data silos, integrate information from various sources, and create a comprehensive view for analysis.

Integration with Data Warehouses: Cloud platforms offer data warehousing solutions that streamline the integration of structured data for analytical purposes. This integration simplifies the process of querying and analyzing data from multiple databases, enhancing the efficiency of analytics workflows.

Advanced Analytics and Machine Learning

Access to Advanced Analytical Tools: Cloud providers offer a suite of advanced analytics and machine learning tools. Organizations can leverage these tools to perform complex analyses, predictive modeling, and machine learning algorithms without the need for significant upfront investments in specialized hardware.

Managed Machine Learning Services

Cloud platforms provide managed machine learning services, making it easier for organizations to implement machine learning models. These services handle infrastructure management, model training, and deployment, allowing data scientists to focus on model development and optimization.

Real-Time Analytics and Streaming Data

Real-time Data Processing: Cloud-based analytics supports real-time data processing, offering organizations to extract insights from streaming data. This is mainly valuable for applications that need immediate responses to changing conditions, such as fraud detection, IoT analytics, and dynamic pricing.

Serverless and Event-Driven Architectures: Cloud platforms support serverless computing models and event-driven architectures, allowing organizations to build real-time analytics applications. Serverless functions can be triggered by events, enabling organizations to process data as it arrives and respond to events in real-time.

Collaboration and Accessibility

Collaborative Analytics Platforms: Cloud-based analytics platforms facilitate collaboration among teams by providing centralized and accessible environments for data analysis. Team members can work collaboratively on shared datasets, analytics models, and visualizations, fostering a culture of collaboration and knowledge sharing.

Accessibility from Anywhere: Cloud analytics solutions are accessible from anywhere with an internet connection. This accessibility ensures that stakeholders across different locations can access and interact with analytics dashboards and reports, promoting widespread use and adoption.

Cost-Efficiency and Pay-as-You-Go Models

Cost-Effective Resource Utilization: Cloud platforms offer cost-effective resource utilization through pay-as-you-go pricing models. A huge initial investment in hardware and infrastructure is unnecessary since organizations only pay for the computer resources that they actually utilize.

Resource Optimization: Cloud-based analytics allows organizations to optimize resource usage based on their specific analytical needs. They are able to optimize expenses without sacrificing performance by dynamically scaling resources during peak demand and scaling down during low demand.

In summary, cloud-based analytics transforms data into actionable insights by providing organizations with the tools and infrastructure needed to process, analyze, and derive value from their data assets. The scalability, flexibility, and advanced capabilities offered by cloud platforms empower organizations to harness and fostering innovation in a rapidly evolving digital landscape.

EDGE COMPUTING FOR SMART CITIES

Edge Computing in Smart Cities: Unleashing the Power of Proximity

When it comes to Smart City deployments, in particular, the arrival of Edge Computing has become a paradigm shifter. By relocating computing resources to the network's periphery, Edge Computing improves real-time processing, decreases latency, and opens up new opportunities for Smart Cities by processing data closer to its point of creation. The paper dives into the idea of Edge Computing and how it fits into the complex web of Smart City implementations (Khan et al., 2020).

Understanding Edge Computing

1. Proximity to Data Sources:

Edge Computing is proximity-based. Edge Computing processes data near its origins instead of transferring it to cloud servers. Reducing data transit distance decreases latency and speeds up real-time or near-real-time processing systems.

2. Decentralized Architecture:

Computing resources, such as servers and data storage, are distributed across the network, often at the periphery or "edge" of the network. This decentralized approach enhances scalability, resilience, and the ability to handle diverse workloads in Smart City environments.

Significance of Edge Computing in Smart Cities

1. Latency Reduction for Real-time Applications:

In smart cities, where making decisions in real-time is of the utmost importance, edge computing plays a crucial role in reducing latency. Instantaneous processing of data is required for applications such as intelligent traffic management, driverless cars, and public safety systems. Edge computing guarantees that crucial choices may be taken locally without the latency associated with transporting data to remote cloud servers (Patra et al., 2021).

2. Bandwidth Optimization:

Processing data locally allows edge computing to maximize the use of available bandwidth. When Internet of Things (IoT) devices and sensors produce enormous volumes of data, sending all of that data to centralized cloud servers may burden the network's capacity. Devices at the edge of the network filter and process data locally, transmitting only relevant information to the cloud. The network is less likely to get congested due to this, which also helps save bandwidth.

3. Enhanced Reliability and Redundancy:

Smart Cities demand high reliability in their systems, especially in critical applications like emergency services and infrastructure monitoring. Edge Computing introduces redundancy and reliability by ensuring that essential processing can occur even if there is a temporary loss of connectivity to the central cloud. This resilience is crucial for maintaining the continuity of services during network disruptions.

4. Privacy and Security Compliance:

Edge Computing addresses privacy and security concerns in Smart Cities by processing sensitive data locally. Certain data, especially in applications like video surveillance or health monitoring, can remain within specific geographical boundaries. This approach aligns with privacy regulations and compliance standards, mitigating the risk of unauthorized access to sensitive information.

5. Scalability for Dynamic Workloads:

Smart City environments often experience dynamic workloads, with fluctuating data volumes based on factors such as events, traffic patterns, and environmental conditions (Kang, et al., 2023). Edge Computing's scalability allows the network to adapt to these changing workloads by deploying additional edge devices as needed. This dynamic scalability enhances the overall flexibility and responsiveness of Smart City systems.

6. Support for Edge AI and Machine Learning:

This is particularly relevant in Smart Cities where AI-driven applications, such as predictive maintenance, anomaly detection, and intelligent surveillance, can benefit from local processing. Edge AI enables quick decision-making without relying heavily on central cloud resources.

Real-World Applications of Edge Computing in Smart Cities

1. Smart Traffic Management:

In Smart Traffic Management systems, edge devices at intersections process real-time data from cameras and sensors to optimize traffic light timings, reduce congestion, and enhance overall traffic flow. Edge Computing ensures swift decision-making without relying on centralized servers, contributing to efficient urban mobility.

2. Public Safety and Surveillance:

Edge Computing is instrumental in enhancing public safety through intelligent surveillance systems. Edge devices process video feeds locally to identify and respond to potential security threats in real-time. This rapid response is critical for preventing incidents and ensuring the safety of citizens.

3. Autonomous Vehicles:

Autonomous vehicles rely on Edge Computing for immediate decision-making. Edge devices in vehicles process sensor data locally to navigate and respond to their surroundings. This local processing is crucial for ensuring the safety and reliability of autonomous transportation systems.

4. Healthcare Monitoring:

In healthcare applications, Edge Computing supports real-time monitoring of patients. Devices that are worn and outfitted with the ability to do edge processing can analyze health metrics locally and transmit only relevant information to healthcare providers. This approach enhances the efficiency of remote patient monitoring (Patra et al., 2023, pp. 60-83).

5. Environmental Monitoring:

Edge Computing is employed in environmental monitoring systems to analyze data from sensors measuring air quality, temperature, and other environmental parameters. Localized processing enables quick detection of anomalies and facilitates timely interventions for environmental sustainability.

Edge Computing stands as a linchpin in the evolution of Smart Cities, offering a decentralized and responsive computing model that aligns with the demands of real-time applications and dynamic urban environments. By bringing processing capabilities closer to the data source, Edge Computing not only reduces latency and optimizes bandwidth but also enhances the reliability, security, and scalability of Smart City systems. As Smart Cities continue to evolve, the significance of Edge Computing is poised to grow, unlocking new possibilities for innovation, efficiency, and improved quality of life.

Edge Computing for Real-Time Processing and Low Latency

Edge computing is a transformative paradigm that significantly enhances real-time processing and reduces latency in various applications. By bringing computational capabilities closer to the source of data generation, edge computing minimizes the time it takes to process and analyze information, making it particularly crucial in scenarios where low latency is imperative. Here's a detailed discussion on how edge computing achieves these benefits:

1. Proximity to Data Sources:

Reduced Distance and Travel Time: Using edge computing, computational resources are brought into proximity to the data sources. This eliminates transferring data across vast distances to centralized cloud servers. This reduction in physical distance significantly decreases the travel time of data, resulting in lower latency for real-time processing.

2. Localized Processing:

Immediate Data Processing: Edge devices process data locally, enabling immediate processing and decision-making at the edge of the network. This localized approach eliminates the need to wait for data to traverse the network to distant cloud servers and back, ensuring real-time responses to dynamic situations.

3. Real-time Analytics:

Instantaneous Data Analysis: Edge computing supports real-time analytics, allowing organizations to analyze data as it is generated. This instantaneous data analysis is crucial for applications that require immediate insights, such as smart traffic management, where rapid decision-making based on real-time data is essential.

4. Low Latency Communication:

Optimized Communication: Edge computing optimizes communication by minimizing the distance data needs to travel. This is especially beneficial for applications with strict latency requirements, such as augmented reality (AR) or virtual reality (VR) applications, where delays in data transmission can result in a poor user experience.

5. Enhanced Responsiveness:

Quick Decision-Making: Edge computing enables quick decision-making by processing data locally. In scenarios like industrial automation or robotics, where swift responses to sensor data are critical, edge devices can analyze information on-site, ensuring a rapid and responsive system.

7. Edge AI and Machine Learning:

Local Model Inference: With the help of edge computing, ML and AI models may be deployed right at the edge of a network. This enables local model inference, allowing edge devices to make predictions and decisions without relying on distant cloud servers (Botez et al., 2023). This is particularly beneficial for applications like facial recognition or anomaly detection.

The ability of edge computing to enhance real-time processing and reduce latency is a game-changer in various industries and applications. Whether in smart cities, healthcare, industrial automation, or autonomous vehicles, the localized processing capabilities of edge computing contribute to quicker decision-making, improved responsiveness, and a more efficient utilization of computational resources.

FUTURE TRENDS AND INNOVATIONS

Emerging Trends in Cloud Computing and Smart Cities beyond 5G

Edge Computing Integration

Description: In order to improve real-time decision-making and decrease latency, edge computing brings processing of data closer to its point of creation. Beyond 5G, Smart Cities are increasingly integrating edge computing into their architectures for enhanced responsiveness and efficiency.

Impact: Edge computing reduces the reliance on centralized cloud resources, enabling quicker data processing for applications like autonomous vehicles, smart grids, and augmented reality.

AI and Machine Learning at the Edge

Description: Devices may make smart judgements locally without continuously depending on cloud servers when AI and ML algorithms are integrated at the edge. This trend is particularly relevant for Smart Cities aiming for autonomous systems and predictive analytics (Murshed et al., 2021).

Impact: Localized AI processing enhances the efficiency of smart devices, enabling faster and more context-aware decision-making. This is crucial for applications like traffic management, public safety, and energy optimization.

5G and Network Slicing

Description: With the advent of 5G networks comes lightning-fast connections with minimal latency, and with network slicing, specialized, virtualized networks can be built to meet the needs of individual applications. Smart Cities leverage 5G and network slicing to support diverse applications with varying connectivity requirements.

Impact: Enhanced connectivity supports a wide range of applications, from smart grids and autonomous vehicles to immersive augmented reality experiences, fostering a more connected and responsive urban environment.

Blockchain for Security and Trust

Description: Smart cities are increasingly embracing blockchain technology as a means to improve data transactions' security, transparency, and trustworthiness. It is used for secure data sharing, transparent record-keeping, and ensuring the integrity of smart contracts.

Impact: Blockchain enhances the security and integrity of data in Smart Cities, particularly in areas such as digital identity, supply chain management, and decentralized energy systems.

Digital Twins for Urban Planning

Description: Digital twins create virtual replicas of physical assets, infrastructure, or entire cities. Beyond 5G, Smart Cities leverage digital twins for advanced urban planning, monitoring, and simulation.

Impact: Digital twins enable city planners to model and simulate various scenarios, optimizing resource utilization, predicting the impact of changes, and facilitating data-driven decision-making for urban development.

These emerging trends indicate a shift towards more intelligent, efficient, and sustainable Smart Cities that leverage advanced technologies at the intersection of Cloud Computing and 5G networks. As technology continues to evolve, these trends are likely to shape the future of urban living, making cities more connected, resilient, and citizen-centric.

Innovative Technologies and Their Impact on Smart City Development

Artificial Intelligence (AI)

Description: Machine learning, reasoning, problem-solving, and decision-making are all examples of activities that are traditionally associated with human intellect. Artificial intelligence (AI) refers to the technologies that allow computers to accomplish these tasks.

Impact on Smart Cities:

- Traffic Management: AI-powered traffic management systems optimize traffic flow, reduce congestion, and enhance overall transportation efficiency.
- Public Safety: AI is used for predictive policing, video analytics, and emergency response optimization, enhancing public safety in urban areas.
- Energy Efficiency: AI-driven systems analyze energy consumption patterns, enabling cities to optimize energy distribution, reduce waste, and promote sustainability (Pandiyan et al., 2023).
- Smart Grids: AI facilitates adaptive and self-learning smart grids that enhance energy distribution, reduce downtime, and support renewable energy integration.

Blockchain Technology

Description: A distributed and decentralized ledger technology known as blockchain makes it possible to retain records in a way that is both secure and transparent. This is accomplished by using a chain of encrypted blocks that are connected together.

Impact on Smart Cities:

- Secure Transactions: Blockchain ensures secure and transparent transactions, enhancing trust in areas such as digital identity, financial transactions, and supply chain management.
- Smart Contracts: Self-executing smart contracts automate and enforce contractual agreements, streamlining processes like property transactions, permitting, and legal documentation.
- Data Security: Blockchain enhances data security and integrity, reducing the risk of data tampering and unauthorized access (Singh et al., 2020).
- Decentralized Energy Grids: Blockchain facilitates peer-to-peer energy transactions, enabling decentralized and transparent energy trading within communities.

Internet of Things (IoT)

Description: The Internet of Things (IoT) is the process of linking physical objects and sensors to the internet, which enables these devices to gather and share data.

Impact on Smart Cities:

- Smart Infrastructure: IoT sensors monitor and manage infrastructure, including roads, bridges, and buildings, allowing for predictive maintenance and improving overall infrastructure resilience.
- Waste Management: IoT sensors that are integrated into intelligent garbage bins allow for the optimization of waste collection routes, the reduction of operating costs, and the promotion of environmentally responsible waste management practices.
- Environmental Monitoring: IoT devices track air quality, water levels, and other environmental parameters, supporting data-driven decision-making for urban planning and sustainability.
- Smart Buildings: IoT-enabled smart buildings enhance energy efficiency, security, and occupant comfort through automated systems and real-time data analytics.

5G Connectivity

Description: 5G is the fifth generation of mobile networks, offering higher data speeds, lower latency, and increased device connectivity.

Impact on Smart Cities:

- Enhanced Connectivity: 5G enables faster and more reliable connectivity, supporting applications like augmented reality, autonomous vehicles, and real-time video analytics.
- Smart Mobility: 5G enhances communication in smart transportation systems, enabling seamless connectivity for connected vehicles, traffic management, and public transit.
- Remote Healthcare: High-speed and low-latency 5G connectivity facilitates remote healthcare services, including telemedicine, remote monitoring, and real-time patient data transmission (Alshammari & Fayez, 2023).
- Immersive Experiences: 5G supports augmented and virtual reality applications, offering immersive experiences for education, tourism, and urban planning.

These innovative technologies are reshaping the landscape of Smart Cities, fostering efficiency, sustainability, and improved quality of life for citizens. The integration of AI, blockchain, IoT, 5G, and digital twins represents a holistic approach to urban development, creating interconnected and intelligent ecosystems. As these technologies continue to evolve, Smart Cities are poised to become more resilient, responsive, and citizen-centric.

CONCLUSION AND FUTURE DIRECTIONS

The chapter delves into the confluence of Cloud Computing, emerging technologies, and the evolution of Smart Cities, with a specific focus on advancements beyond 5G. Key findings include the pivotal role of the 4G to 5G transition in laying the foundation for Smart City development, providing essential high-speed, low-latency connectivity. Innovations like AI, blockchain, IoT, 5G connectivity, AR/VR, RPA, and digital twins are identified as driving forces in shaping data-driven urban development. Emerging trends, such as edge computing, AI at the edge, 5G and network slicing, quantum computing exploration, decentralized networks, and sustainable computing practices, are highlighted. Ethical considerations and regulatory compliance, along with lessons learned and best practices, underscore the importance of security, transparency, citizen engagement, and responsible governance in successful Smart City initiatives. The chapter concludes by emphasizing the synergistic relationship between Cloud Computing and 5G networks, enabling enhanced connectivity, performance, and support for emerging technologies in the Smart City landscape.

The recommendations for future research and development at the intersection of Cloud Computing and Smart Cities encompass a multifaceted approach. They emphasize the critical need for advanced security and privacy solutions, including innovative encryption techniques and decentralized identity management systems. Further optimization of edge computing architectures, exploration of quantum computing applications, and advancement in intelligent traffic management systems are highlighted. The recommendations extend to investigating the broader use of blockchain for urban governance, researching decentralized and resilient network architectures, prioritizing human-centric and ethical AI practices, and addressing issues of inclusive technology adoption. Dynamic and adaptive cloud infrastructures, climate-resilient Smart Cities, collaborative data governance models, interdisciplinary collaboration, longitudinal studies, public perception, and citizen engagement are also underscored. The call for standardization and interoperability in Smart City technologies rounds out these comprehensive recommendations, aiming to guide future research toward building resilient, inclusive, and sustainable Smart Cities through the strategic integration of Cloud Computing and emerging technologies.

REFERENCES

Alshammari, A., & Fayez Alanazi, M. (2023). Use of Technology in Enhancing Learning Among Nurses in Saudi Arabia; a Systematic Review. *Journal of Multidisciplinary Healthcare*, *16*, 1587–1599. doi:10.2147/JMDH.S413281 PMID:37313273

Botez, R., Sferle, A. T., Ivanciu, I. A., & Dobrota, V. (2023, July). Work-in-Progress: KubeUT: A Cloud-Agnostic Kubernetes Management Platform. In *2023 IEEE International Black Sea Conference on Communications and Networking (BlackSeaCom)* (pp. 384-389). IEEE. 10.1109/BlackSeaCom58138.2023.10299745

Chen, X., Zhang, S., Ding, X., Kadry, S. N., & Hsu, C. H. (2021). IoT cloud platform for information processing in smart city. *Computational Intelligence*, *37*(3), 1428–1444. doi:10.1111/coin.12387

Coman, C. M., D'amico, G., Coman, A. V., & Florescu, A. (2021). Techniques to improve reliability in an IoT architecture framework for intelligent products. *IEEE Access : Practical Innovations, Open Solutions*, *9*, 56940–56954. doi:10.1109/ACCESS.2021.3072168

Darwish, D. (Ed.). (2024). *Emerging Trends in Cloud Computing Analytics*. Scalability, and Service Models.

Demertzi, V., Demertzis, S., & Demertzis, K. (2023). An Overview of Cyber Threats, Attacks and Countermeasures on the Primary Domains of Smart Cities. *Applied Sciences (Basel, Switzerland)*, *13*(2), 790. doi:10.3390/app13020790

He, Y., & Zhang, X. (2023). Retracted Article: Key technologies of massive concurrent data processing in smart city based on cloud computing. *International Journal of Computers and Applications*, *45*(2), 204–211. doi:10.1080/1206212X.2020.1743040

Javed, A. R., Shahzad, F., Rehman, S., Zikria, Y. B., Razzak, I., Jalil, Z., & Xu, G. (2022). Future smart cities: Requirements, emerging technologies, applications, challenges, and future aspects. *Cities (London, England)*, *129*, 103794. doi:10.1016/j.cities.2022.103794

Joshi, K., Sharma, R., Singh, N., & Sharma, B. (2023). Digital World of Cloud Computing and Wireless Networking: Challenges and Risks. In Applications of Artificial Intelligence in Wireless Communication Systems (pp. 36-47). IGI Global.

Kang, C. C., Lee, T. Y., Lim, W. F., & Yeo, W. W. Y. (2023). Opportunities and challenges of 5G network technology toward precision medicine. *Clinical and Translational Science*, *16*(11), 2078–2094. doi:10.1111/cts.13640 PMID:37702288

Khan, L. U., Yaqoob, I., Tran, N. H., Kazmi, S. A., Dang, T. N., & Hong, C. S. (2020). Edge-computing-enabled smart cities: A comprehensive survey. *IEEE Internet of Things Journal*, *7*(10), 10200–10232. doi:10.1109/JIOT.2020.2987070

Kumar, Y., & Kumar, V. (2023). A Systematic Review on Intrusion Detection System in Wireless Networks: Variants, Attacks, and Applications. *Wireless Personal Communications*, *133*(1), 1–58. doi:10.1007/s11277-023-10773-x

Kumari, A., Patra, M. K., & Sahoo, B. (2023). Data Controlling and Security Issues in Cloud: A Step Towards Serverless. In Perspectives on Social Welfare Applications' Optimization and Enhanced Computer Applications (pp. 105-124). IGI Global. doi:10.4018/978-1-6684-8306-0.ch007

Mukherjee, S., Gupta, S., Rawlley, O., & Jain, S. (2022). Leveraging big data analytics in 5G-enabled IoT and industrial IoT for the development of sustainable smart cities. *Transactions on Emerging Telecommunications Technologies*, *33*(12), e4618. doi:10.1002/ett.4618

Murshed, M. S., Murphy, C., Hou, D., Khan, N., Ananthanarayanan, G., & Hussain, F. (2021). Machine learning at the network edge: A survey. *ACM Computing Surveys*, *54*(8), 1–37. doi:10.1145/3469029

Orabi, M., Al Aghbari, Z., & Kamel, I. (2023). FogLBS: Utilizing fog computing for providing mobile Location-Based Services to mobile customers. *Pervasive and Mobile Computing*, *94*, 101832. doi:10.1016/j.pmcj.2023.101832

Pandiyan, P., Saravanan, S., Usha, K., Kannadasan, R., Alsharif, M. H., & Kim, M. K. (2023). Technological advancements toward smart energy management in smart cities. *Energy Reports*, *10*, 648–677. doi:10.1016/j.egyr.2023.07.021

Patel, R. K., Gidwani, P., & Patel, N. R. (2023). Privacy Preservation and Cloud Computing. In Privacy Preservation and Secured Data Storage in Cloud Computing (pp. 88-107). IGI Global. doi:10.4018/979-8-3693-0593-5.ch004

Patra, M. K. (2017, February). An architecture model for smart city using Cognitive Internet of Things (CIoT). In *2017 Second International Conference on Electrical, Computer and Communication Technologies (ICECCT)* (pp. 1-6). IEEE. 10.1109/ICECCT.2017.8117893

Patra, M. K., Kumari, A., Sahoo, B., & Turuk, A. K. (2023). Challenges and Opportunities Toward Integration of IoT with Cloud Computing. *Integration of IoT with Cloud Computing for Smart Applications*, 81-98.

Patra, M. K., Kumari, A., Sahoo, B., & Turuk, A. K. (2023). Smart Healthcare System Using Cloud-Integrated Internet of Medical Things. In Exploring the Convergence of Computer and Medical Science Through Cloud Healthcare (pp. 60-83). IGI Global.

Patra, M. K., Sahoo, S., Sahoo, B., & Turuk, A. K. (2021). Cloud-Edge Centric Service Provisioning in Smart City Using Internet of Things. In Advances in Parallel & Distributed Processing, and Applications: Proceedings from PDPTA'20, CSC'20, MSV'20, and GCC'20 (pp. 619-631). Springer International Publishing. doi:10.1007/978-3-030-69984-0_44

Pham, Q. V., Fang, F., Ha, V. N., Piran, M. J., Le, M., Le, L. B., Hwang, W.-J., & Ding, Z. (2020). A survey of multi-access edge computing in 5G and beyond: Fundamentals, technology integration, and state-of-the-art. *IEEE Access : Practical Innovations, Open Solutions*, *8*, 116974–117017. doi:10.1109/ACCESS.2020.3001277

Sharma, M., Sharma, M., Sharma, N., & Boopathi, S. (2024). Building Sustainable Smart Cities Through Cloud and Intelligent Parking System. In Handbook of Research on AI and ML for Intelligent Machines and Systems (pp. 195-222). IGI Global.

Sharma, R., & Arya, R. (2023). Security threats and measures in the Internet of Things for smart city infrastructure: A state of art. *Transactions on Emerging Telecommunications Technologies*, *34*(11), e4571. doi:10.1002/ett.4571

Silva, B. N., Khan, M., Jung, C., Seo, J., Muhammad, D., Han, J., Yoon, Y., & Han, K. (2018). Urban planning and smart city decision management empowered by real-time data processing using big data analytics. *Sensors (Basel)*, *18*(9), 2994. doi:10.3390/s18092994 PMID:30205499

Singh, R., Singh, S. K., Kumar, S., & Gill, S. S. (2022). SDN-Aided Edge Computing-Enabled AI for IoT and Smart Cities. *SDN-Supported Edge-Cloud Interplay for Next Generation Internet of Things*, (pp. 41-70). Research Gate.

Singh, S., Sharma, P. K., Yoon, B., Shojafar, M., Cho, G. H., & Ra, I. H. (2020). Convergence of blockchain and artificial intelligence in IoT network for the sustainable smart city. *Sustainable Cities and Society*, *63*, 102364. doi:10.1016/j.scs.2020.102364

Vilalta, R., López, V., Giorgetti, A., Peng, S., Orsini, V., Velasco, L., Serral-Gracia, R., Morris, D., De Fina, S., Cugini, F., Castoldi, P., Mayoral, A., Casellas, R., Martinez, R., Verikoukis, C., & Munoz, R. (2017). TelcoFog: A unified flexible fog and cloud computing architecture for 5G networks. *IEEE Communications Magazine*, *55*(8), 36–43. doi:10.1109/MCOM.2017.1600838

Yang, C., Liang, P., Fu, L., Cui, G., Huang, F., Teng, F., & Bangash, Y. A. (2022). Using 5G in smart cities: A systematic mapping study. *Intelligent Systems with Applications*, *14*, 200065. doi:10.1016/j.iswa.2022.200065

Chapter 7
Shaping Highly Intelligent Internet of Things (IoT) and Wireless Sensors for Smart Cities

Bhupinder Singh
https://orcid.org/0009-0006-4779-2553
Sharda University, India

Christian Kaunert
https://orcid.org/0000-0002-4493-2235
Dublin City University, Ireland

Vishal Jain
https://orcid.org/0000-0003-1126-7424
Sharda University, India

Komal Vig
Sharda University, India

ABSTRACT

The highly intelligent internet of things (IoT) and wireless sensor technologies are set to reshape the directions of safe and intelligent parking and transportation in the dynamic field of urban development. Sustainable and effective transportation solutions are critical as cities struggle with the effects of growing populations and rising urbanization. Sustainability is the key to the transportation of the future as the development of electric mobility solutions and environmentally friendly transportation choices is facilitated by highly intelligent IoT. By reducing the negative effects of transportation systems on the environment, this path hopes to promote a greener and more sustainable urban environment. So, tackling issues with privacy and cybersecurity, this trajectory seeks to increase confidence in the accuracy and privacy of data. This chapter explores how these technologies are developing and how they will affect urban transportation in the future to solve the difficulties of contemporary urban life, a focus is put on security measures, real-time data analytics and sustainable practices.

DOI: 10.4018/979-8-3693-2373-1.ch007

INTRODUCTION AND BACKGROUND

The advent of Highly Intelligent Internet of Things (IoT) and the integration of wireless sensor technologies have ushered in a new era of urban development, with a specific focus on shaping Smart Cities. In this transformative landscape, the emphasis extends beyond mere connectivity and towards the creation of intelligent ecosystems that optimize various facets of urban living. The critical domain within this paradigm is the reimagining of transportation and parking systems to align with principles of intelligence, security, and sustainability. As urbanization accelerates globally, Smart Cities emerge as a visionary response to the challenges posed by rapid population growth, resource constraints, and environmental concerns (Minoli & Occhiogrosso, 2018).

Smart transportation systems augmented by the deployment of IoT devices and wireless sensors lays down the unprecedented opportunities for efficient and secure mobility within urban environments. Real-time monitoring and data analytics enable dynamic traffic management, providing insights that empower city planners and authorities to alleviate congestion, reduce commute times, and enhance overall transportation efficiency. The integration of intelligent technologies not only streamlines existing transportation infrastructure but also opens avenues for the development of innovative solutions such as autonomous vehicles and interconnected transit networks (Bibri, 2018).

Simultaneously, the transformation of parking systems through the infusion of IoT and wireless sensors contributes significantly to the fabric of Smart Cities. The conventional challenges of finding parking spaces, traffic congestion caused by aimless circling, and inadequate utilization of parking infrastructure are addressed through real-time data collection and smart analytics. Smart parking solutions leverage technology to offer real-time information on parking space availability, enable reservation systems, and enhance enforcement mechanisms, thereby optimizing parking resources and improving the overall urban experience (Belli et al., 2020). The trajectory towards a Smart and Secure Transportation and Parking infrastructure for a Sustainable Future is not devoid of challenges. The integration of highly intelligent IoT devices and wireless sensors brings forth concerns related to data security and privacy. As these systems collect and transmit vast amounts of sensitive information, ensuring the integrity and confidentiality of data becomes paramount. Addressing these challenges is imperative for the sustainable development of Smart Cities, fostering a balance between technological innovation and safeguarding individual privacy and security Al-(Turjman & Lemayian, 2020).

Importance of Intelligent Transportation and Parking Systems: Building Smart and Sustainable Cities

The imperative to shape highly intelligent Internet of Things (IoT) and wireless sensor technologies for Smart Cities stems from a profound recognition of the multifaceted challenges that contemporary urban centers face. As the global population gravitates towards urban areas, cities become crucibles of innovation and change. The importance of infusing intelligence into urban infrastructure, particularly in the realms of transportation and parking comes in the potential to alleviate the strain imposed by rapid urbanization (Bauer et al., 2021). With harnessing the capabilities of IoT and wireless sensors, Smart Cities can not only optimize existing systems but also lay the foundation for sustainable, secure and efficient urban living. The central pillars of this significance fall in the smart transportation because the conventional paradigm of urban mobility is fraught with challenges such as traffic congestion, inefficient transit systems, and a lack of real-time data for informed decision-making. Highly intelligent IoT applications and wireless sensor networks address these challenges by creating interconnected systems capable of monitoring, analyzing, and adapting to dynamic traffic conditions. The result is a transportation network that is not only more responsive to the needs of the populace but is also inherently more sustainable, reducing emissions and energy consumption (Javed et al., 2022).

The importance of smart and secure parking solutions cannot be overstated. Parking inefficiencies contribute significantly to urban congestion and environmental degradation. Traditional parking systems are often plagued by issues of inadequate space utilization, traffic bottlenecks caused by drivers searching for parking, and ineffective enforcement. The integration of IoT and wireless sensors transforms parking into a smart, data-driven ecosystem. Real-time information on parking space availability, coupled with reservation systems and efficient enforcement mechanisms, not only streamlines the parking experience for citizens but also optimizes the use of urban space, contributing to a more sustainable urban environment (Musa et al., 2023).

The overarching importance of shaping highly intelligent IoT and wireless sensor technologies lies in their capacity to drive sustainability in urban development. By enhancing the efficiency of transportation and parking systems, these technologies contribute to reduced fuel consumption, lower emissions, and a more judicious use of urban resources. This sustainability imperative aligns with global efforts to combat climate change and create urban environments that prioritize ecological harmony. In the context of a sustainable future, the integration of these technologies into the fabric of Smart Cities is not merely a technological choice; it is a strategic imperative (Yang et al., 2021). As cities strive to meet the challenges of population growth, resource constraints, and environmental stewardship, the transformative power of highly intelligent IoT and wireless sensors emerges as a beacon guiding urban development towards a more resilient, connected, and sustainable future. The importance lies not only in the optimization of transportation and parking systems but in the profound impact on the overall quality of urban life and the planet's well-being (Nguyen et al., 2020).

Significance of Smart and Secure Transportation and Parking for Sustainable Urban Development

Smart and secure transportation and parking solutions hold immense significance for sustainable urban development, addressing critical challenges posed by rapid urbanization and the increasing demands on transportation infrastructure. In the context of transportation, the implementation of smart systems, driven by Internet of Things (IoT) and wireless sensor technologies, contributes to the optimization of traffic flow, reduction of congestion, and improvement of overall mobility. By leveraging real-time data and intelligent algorithms, smart transportation systems enable more efficient route planning, reducing fuel consumption and greenhouse gas emissions (Kaur & Sharma, 2023). The integration of secure and interconnected transportation networks not only enhances the daily commute for residents but also aligns with broader environmental goals, promoting sustainable urban living. The equally crucial is the role of smart parking solutions in the context of sustainable urban development. Traditional parking systems often contribute to traffic congestion and wasted fuel as drivers search for available spaces. Smart parking, facilitated by IoT and wireless sensors, transforms this scenario by providing real-time data on parking space availability. This not only minimizes the time spent searching for parking but also reduces overall traffic congestion and associated emissions. Additionally, by encouraging the use of reserved and efficiently utilized parking spaces, smart parking solutions contribute to more sustainable land use planning and urban design (Rejeb et al., 2022).

The integration of secure protocols ensures the protection of sensitive data related to transportation and parking, fostering trust among users and stakeholders. Privacy considerations are addressed through anonymization techniques, and robust authentication mechanisms prevent unauthorized access, making these systems not only smart but also resilient against potential cyber threats. In essence, smart and secure transportation and parking are integral components of sustainable urban development. They enhance the efficiency of urban mobility, reduce environmental impact, and contribute to the creation of livable, resilient cities. With investing in these technologies, urban centers can foster a harmonious relationship between technology, the environment and the well-being of their inhabitants, paving the way for a more sustainable and intelligent urban future (Xie et al., 2023).

Objectives of the Chapter

The chapter aims to contribute valuable insights to the ongoing discourse on shaping Smart Cities through the incorporation of highly intelligent IoT and wireless sensors, specifically focusing on the domains of smart and secure transportation and parking for a sustainable future. It has the following objectives to:

- explore the current state of integration of Highly Intelligent Internet of Things (IoT) technologies in Smart Cities.
- scrutinize the deployment of wireless sensor technologies in optimizing and securing smart transportation systems.
- examine the implementation and impact of IoT and wireless sensors in transforming traditional parking systems into smart, efficient, and secure solutions.
- identify and analyze the security challenges associated with the integration of highly intelligent IoT devices and wireless sensor networks.
- assess the environmental impact of optimized transportation and parking systems, focusing on energy efficiency, reduced emissions, and overall resource conservation.
- identify and analyze challenges faced during the integration of highly intelligent IoT and wireless sensors in Smart Cities, particularly in the domains of transportation and parking.
- provide insights and recommendations for policymakers, urban planners, and decision-makers on leveraging the findings of the research to inform strategic planning for the development of Smart Cities.

Structure of the Chapter

This paper comprehensively explores the various dimensions of for Shaping the Highly Intelligent Internet of Things (IoT) and Wireless Sensors for Smart Cities for Smart and Secure Transportation and Parking concerning Sustainable Future. Section 2 elaborates the IoT and Wireless Sensors in Smart Transportation. Section 3 specifies the Smart Parking Solutions: IoT and Wireless Sensors in Smart Parking Solutions. Section 4 lays down the Intelligent IoT Infrastructure: Architecture and Design Considerations. Section 5 expresses the Security and Privacy Concerns: Challenges to Security of IoT Devices and Wireless Sensor Networks. Section 6 travels the Sustainable Future: Implementation of Highly Intelligent IoT and Wireless Sensor Technologies Contributes to Sustainability. And, finally Section 7 Conclude the Chapter with Future Scope.

Figure 1. Objectives of the chapter

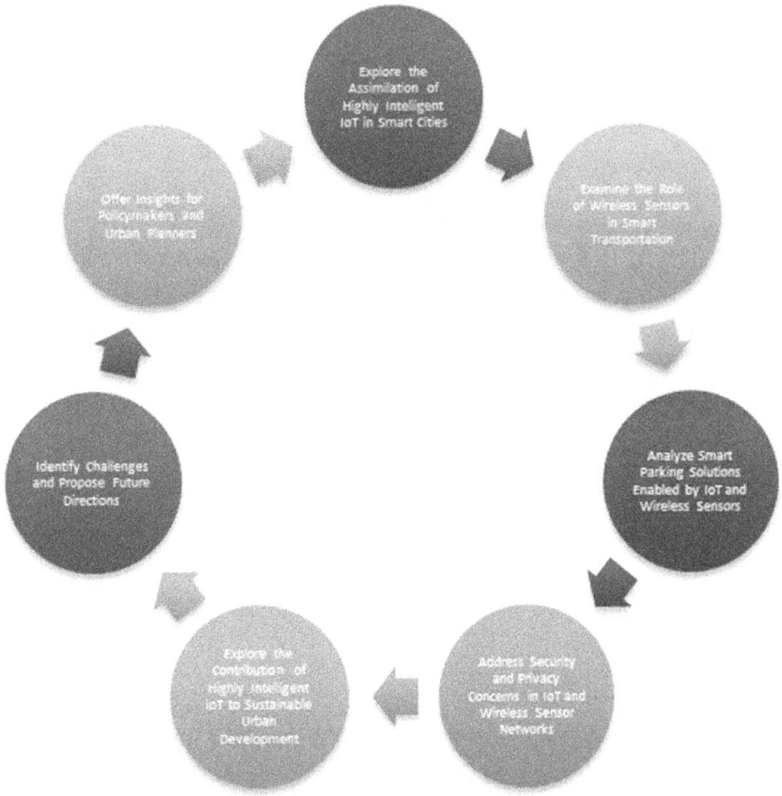

Figure 2. Structure of the chapter

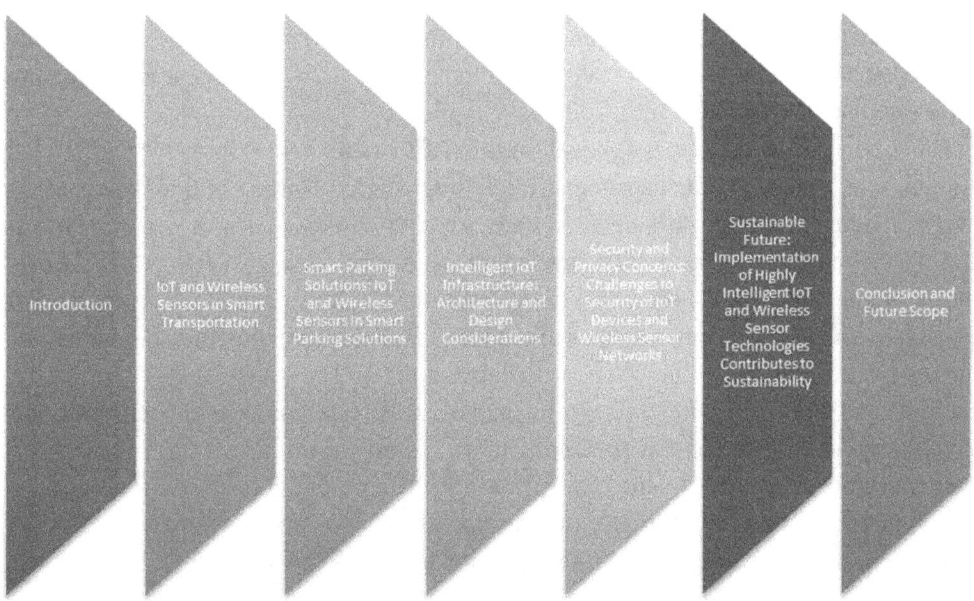

Figure 3. IoT and Wireless sensors in smart transportation benefits at a glance

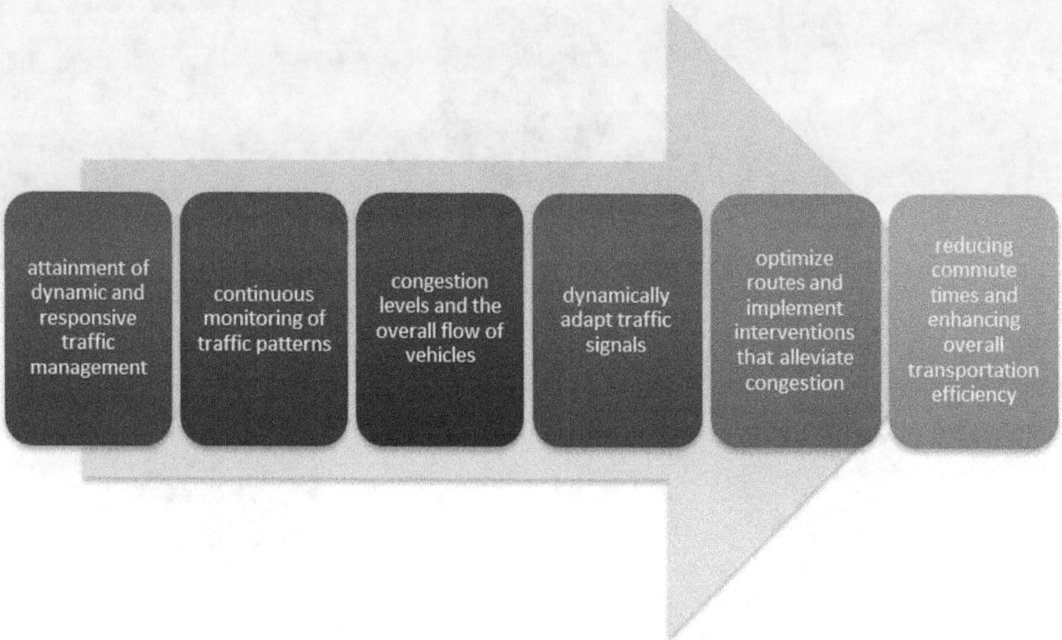

IOT AND WIRELESS SENSORS IN SMART TRANSPORTATION

The use of Highly Intelligent Internet of Things (IoT) and wireless sensor technologies has become a pivotal force in the optimization of transportation systems within Smart Cities. This amalgamation of cutting-edge technologies provides a transformative approach to urban mobility which addressing the intricate challenges posed by burgeoning populations and increasing demands on transportation infrastructure. The infusion of IoT in smart transportation involves the embedding of sensors in vehicles, roadways, and urban infrastructure to create an interconnected network capable of collecting and processing real-time data (Mishra & Singh, 2023).

The primary benefits of this use are the attainment of dynamic and responsive traffic management. As, traditional transportation systems often struggle with static planning and inefficient utilization of road networks. Highly intelligent IoT devices, together with wireless sensors, facilitate the continuous monitoring of traffic patterns, congestion levels and the overall flow of vehicles. This real-time data empowers city planners and transportation authorities with insights to dynamically adapt traffic signals, optimize routes and implement interventions that alleviate congestion, thereby reducing commute times and enhancing overall transportation efficiency (Paiva et al., 2021).

The integration of IoT and wireless sensors enables predictive analytics in transportation systems. With analyzing the historical and real-time data, these systems can forecast traffic patterns, anticipate peak hours, and proactively implement strategies to mitigate potential congestion points. This predictive capability not only improves the daily commute experience for citizens but also assists in long-term urban planning, allowing for the design of transportation infrastructure that aligns with future population growth and urban expansion (AlZubi et al., 2021).

The optimization of transportation systems through IoT and wireless sensors also extends to the realm of environmental sustainability. By facilitating the smooth flow of traffic, reducing idle times, and minimizing stop-and-go scenarios, smart transportation systems contribute to a reduction in fuel consumption and emissions. The environmental impact of these optimizations aligns with broader initiatives aimed at creating eco-friendly urban environments and mitigating the ecological footprint associated with traditional transportation models. The integration of IoT in smart transportation is a key enabler of emerging technologies such as autonomous vehicles. Wireless sensors play a crucial role in providing real-time data for autonomous vehicles to navigate through urban landscapes safely. This synergy between IoT and autonomous transportation heralds a future where intelligent, self-driving vehicles seamlessly interact with their environment, optimizing traffic flow and enhancing overall safety (Shahzad et al., 2021).

Highly Intelligent IoT and wireless sensors in smart transportation represents a paradigm shift in urban mobility. It transcends traditional models by creating adaptive, data-driven systems capable of addressing the dynamic nature of urban traffic. The optimization achieved through real-time monitoring, predictive analytics, and sustainability initiatives positions smart transportation as a cornerstone in the development of intelligent and resilient Smart Cities. As technology continues to advance, the trajectory of smart transportation fueled by IoT and wireless sensors is poised to redefine urban mobility, making it more efficient, sustainable, and responsive to the evolving needs of modern cities (Varadharajan, 2021).

Explore Real-Time Monitoring, Traffic Management, and Predictive Analytics

The integration of Highly Intelligent Internet of Things (IoT) and wireless sensors into smart transportation systems facilitates a comprehensive approach to urban mobility, encompassing real-time monitoring, traffic management, and predictive analytics. Real-time monitoring represents a fundamental shift from conventional, static traffic management models, offering an instantaneous and dynamic understanding of traffic conditions. Through the deployment of sensors in key locations, ranging from major intersections to thoroughfares, these systems continuously collect data on vehicle movements, traffic densities, and potential bottlenecks. This real-time stream of information empowers city authorities with a live, detailed overview of the urban traffic landscape. In the domain of traffic management, the insights gleaned from real-time monitoring become instrumental in optimizing the flow of vehicles through urban arteries. Intelligent traffic management systems leverage the data generated by IoT devices and wireless sensors to dynamically adjust traffic signals, synchronize traffic flows, and implement adaptive strategies to mitigate congestion (Singh & Kaunert, 2024).

This capability not only reduces the frustration of commuters stuck in traffic but also enhances the overall efficiency of transportation networks, facilitating smoother and more predictable travel experiences. Predictive analytics further elevates the intelligence of smart transportation systems by harnessing historical and real-time data to anticipate future traffic patterns. By analyzing trends, peak hours, and historical congestion data, these systems can forecast potential traffic bottlenecks and implement preemptive measures to prevent or alleviate congestion before it occurs. This forward-looking approach enhances the overall resilience of urban transportation, enabling city planners to proactively address issues and plan infrastructure improvements that align with the anticipated demands of a growing population (Ang et al., 2022).

The application of predictive analytics extends beyond immediate traffic concerns. By analyzing data over more extended periods, smart transportation systems can contribute to urban planning initiatives, helping authorities make informed decisions about the expansion and development of transportation infrastructure. This forward-thinking approach ensures that cities are equipped to handle future demands, minimizing the need for constant retrofitting and allowing for more sustainable, long-term solutions. The integration of real-time monitoring, traffic management, and predictive analytics in smart transportation systems marks a transformative leap towards more responsive, adaptive, and intelligent urban mobility. As cities continue to grow and evolve, these technologies offer a proactive solution to the challenges of congestion and inefficiency, providing a blueprint for sustainable and resilient transportation networks. The synergy between IoT and wireless sensors in these applications not only improves the daily lives of citizens but also lays the foundation for a smarter and more connected urban future (Hanes et al., 2017).

Integration of IoT in Traffic Management, Intelligent Traffic Lights and Vehicle-to-Everything (V2X) Communication

The integration of Highly Intelligent Internet of Things (IoT) in traffic management represents a paradigm shift in the way urban centers approach the optimization of transportation systems. One key facet of this transformation is the deployment of intelligent traffic lights, which are imbued with the capabilities of real-time data processing and decision-making. These smart traffic lights, embedded with IoT sensors, continuously gather data on traffic flow, vehicle volumes, and pedestrian movements. Through this real-time monitoring, traffic lights become dynamic entities capable of adapting signal timings based on the immediate needs of the road network. Intelligent traffic lights leverage the data collected through IoT sensors to optimize signal timings in response to changing traffic patterns. For instance, during peak hours or in the case of an unexpected traffic incident, these lights can dynamically adjust signal phases to alleviate congestion and enhance the overall flow of vehicles. This adaptive approach to traffic management ensures that signals respond in real-time to the dynamic nature of urban traffic, reducing wait times for commuters and enhancing the efficiency of transportation systems (Shen et al., 2018).

Vehicle-to-Everything (V2X) communication enhances the intelligence of traffic management systems by establishing a seamless connectivity framework between vehicles, traffic infrastructure, and even pedestrians. Through V2X communication, vehicles can transmit data about their location, speed, and direction to the surrounding infrastructure, including traffic lights equipped with IoT sensors. This bidirectional communication enables a more holistic approach to traffic management, where signals can prioritize the flow of emergency vehicles, adjust timings based on the density of approaching traffic, and enhance safety by alerting drivers to potential hazards or road conditions (Giourka et al., 2019).

The synergy between IoT-enabled traffic management, intelligent traffic lights, and V2X communication not only optimizes the efficiency of transportation systems but also contributes to overall safety and sustainability. The dynamic nature of these systems, driven by real-time data and adaptive algorithms, reduces congestion, minimizes fuel consumption, and lowers emissions. Moreover, the enhanced safety features provided by V2X communication contribute to accident prevention, as vehicles and infrastructure communicate to avoid collisions and provide timely warnings to drivers. IoT in traffic management, intelligent traffic lights, and V2X communication heralds a new era of responsive and interconnected urban mobility. These technologies not only address the immediate challenges of congestion and inefficiency but also pave the way for safer, more sustainable transportation systems. As cities continue to evolve, leveraging the power of IoT in traffic management becomes a cornerstone in the development of intelligent, adaptive, and resilient urban environments. The result is a transportation ecosystem that is not only more efficient but also safer, contributing to the overall well-being and satisfaction of urban citizens (Stratigea & Panagiotopoulou, 2015).

SMART PARKING SOLUTIONS: IOT AND WIRELESS SENSORS IN SMART PARKING SOLUTIONS

The role of Highly Intelligent Internet of Things (IoT) and wireless sensors in shaping smart parking solutions is pivotal in revolutionizing the way urban dwellers navigate and utilize parking infrastructure. Traditional parking systems are often plagued by inefficiencies, leading to increased traffic congestion, wasted time for drivers searching for parking spaces, and underutilization of available parking resources (Mitieka et al., 2023). The integration of IoT and wireless sensors addresses these challenges by infusing intelligence into parking infrastructure and providing real-time data on parking space availability, occupancy, and other relevant parameters. In the context of smart parking, IoT devices and wireless sensors are strategically deployed in parking spaces, garages, or street-side locations to monitor and relay information about their status. These sensors can detect the presence or absence of vehicles, and the data generated is communicated to a centralized system through IoT connectivity. This real-time information is then made accessible to drivers through mobile applications or electronic signage, enabling them to locate available parking spaces efficiently (Bagga et al., 2022).

IoT in smart parking solutions extends beyond mere space detection. These systems often include additional features, such as reservation capabilities and payment processing through mobile apps. Drivers can reserve parking spaces in advance, reducing uncertainty and minimizing the time spent searching for parking. The seamless integration of reservation and payment functionalities not only streamlines the user experience but also contributes to more efficient use of parking spaces and increased revenue for city authorities. Wireless sensors play a crucial role in ensuring the accuracy and reliability of the data collected in smart parking solutions. These sensors are designed to withstand various environmental conditions and can provide precise information about parking space occupancy. Furthermore, the deployment of wireless networks enables a scalable and flexible infrastructure that can be adapted to diverse urban landscapes, ranging from bustling city centers to residential areas (Abi Sen et al., 2023).

The significance of IoT and wireless sensors in smart parking solutions lies in their ability to transform parking from a traditionally static and inconvenient process into a dynamic, data-driven ecosystem. By optimizing parking space utilization, reducing traffic congestion, and enhancing the overall efficiency of parking infrastructure, these technologies contribute to the creation of more sustainable and user-friendly urban environments. As cities continue to grapple with the challenges of urbanization, the role of IoT and wireless sensors in smart parking emerges as a critical component in the broader effort to shape intelligent and livable urban spaces (Moir et al., 2014).

Exploring Real-Time Parking Availability, Reservation Systems, and Enforcement Mechanisms

The exploration of real-time parking availability, reservation systems, and enforcement mechanisms represents a critical dimension of the transformative impact of Highly Intelligent Internet of Things (IoT) and wireless sensors on modern urban living. Real-time parking availability, facilitated by IoT and wireless sensors, addresses one of the most common urban frustrations – the elusive search for an open parking space. Through strategically placed sensors in parking lots or on-street parking spaces, cities can collect and disseminate real-time data on the availability of parking spaces to drivers, either through mobile applications or digital signage. This instant accessibility to information empowers drivers to make informed decisions, reducing circling times and minimizing traffic congestion caused by aimlessly searching for parking (Cardullo, 2020).

The integration of reservation systems into smart parking solutions further optimizes the urban parking experience. Leveraging IoT connectivity, drivers can reserve parking spaces in advance, ensuring a designated spot upon arrival. Reservation systems not only enhance convenience for drivers but also contribute to a more efficient utilization of parking resources. This feature is particularly advantageous in high-demand areas or during peak hours, where securing a parking space in advance mitigates the uncertainty associated with traditional parking practices. The enforcement mechanisms, bolstered by IoT and wireless sensors, add a layer of efficiency and fairness to the management of urban parking spaces. Sensors can detect unauthorized or overstayed vehicles, and this data can trigger automated enforcement processes. Whether through automatic ticketing systems or alerts to parking attendants, the integration of enforcement mechanisms ensures that parking regulations are upheld consistently. This contributes to improved traffic flow and facilitates compliance with parking policies, ultimately enhancing the effectiveness of urban transportation systems (Bibri & Bibri, 2018).

So, enforcement mechanisms supported by IoT extend beyond punitive measures. Smart parking solutions can include features such as dynamic pricing, where parking fees adjust based on real-time demand. This approach not only encourages turnover in high-demand areas but also aligns with the broader goal of sustainable urban development by incentivizing more responsible use of parking spaces. The exploration of real-time parking availability, reservation systems, and enforcement mechanisms epitomizes the transformative potential of IoT and wireless sensors in reshaping urban infrastructure. By providing citizens with real-time information, streamlining the reservation process, and ensuring fair and efficient enforcement, these technologies contribute to the creation of more user-friendly and sustainable urban environments. As urbanization continues to accelerate, the role of IoT and wireless sensors in optimizing parking systems emerges as a fundamental aspect of the ongoing evolution towards smarter, more efficient, and livable cities (Miao et al., 2019).

Examination of Smart Parking Solutions- Impact on Urban Development

The examination of smart parking solutions and their impact on urban development reveals a profound shift in how cities address the challenges associated with increasing urbanization and the growing demands on transportation infrastructure. Smart parking, propelled by Highly Intelligent Internet of Things (IoT) and wireless sensors, represents a transformative approach that extends beyond the mere convenience of finding parking spaces. It encompasses a holistic reimagining of urban spaces, bringing forth efficiencies that ripple through various facets of city life and contribute to sustainable urban development (Shackelford, 2020).

The smart parking solutions leverage real-time data collected by IoT-enabled sensors to inform drivers about parking space availability. This seemingly simple innovation addresses a perennial urban woe – the time-consuming and frustrating search for parking. By providing drivers with up-to-the-minute information on available spaces, these solutions significantly reduce traffic congestion, carbon emissions, and the overall environmental impact associated with aimless circling for parking. The impact of smart parking solutions extends to the optimization of urban mobility. By reducing the time spent searching for parking, these systems contribute to smoother traffic flow and decreased vehicle idle times, resulting in a more efficient transportation network. The positive cascading effects extend to lower fuel consumption, reduced emissions, and a generally more sustainable urban environment (Chaloupkova & Janurova, 2019).

The integration of reservation systems in smart parking introduces an additional layer of efficiency and predictability. Through IoT connectivity, drivers can reserve parking spaces in advance, streamlining the parking process and enhancing the overall user experience. This feature not only caters to the needs of individuals but also facilitates planning for events, reducing the strain on parking infrastructure during peak times and minimizing the potential for traffic bottlenecks. Beyond the immediate benefits for drivers, the examination of smart parking solutions also reveals the potential for data-driven urban planning. The wealth of data generated by IoT sensors, encompassing parking patterns, demand peaks, and utilization rates, provides city planners with valuable insights. This data-driven approach allows for informed decision-making regarding the expansion of parking infrastructure, the allocation of resources, and the optimization of urban spaces. It aligns with the broader goals of creating sustainable, resilient cities capable of adapting to the evolving needs of their inhabitants (Silva et al., 2021).

The examination of smart parking solutions unveils a transformative force in urban development, fueled by the integration of IoT and wireless sensors. Beyond the immediate convenience for drivers, these solutions contribute to more efficient transportation networks, reduced environmental impact, and data-informed urban planning. As cities grapple with the challenges of rapid urbanization, the adoption of smart parking technologies emerges as a strategic and forward-thinking step towards creating intelligent, connected, and sustainable urban environments (Nasiri, 2016).

Wireless Sensors in Real-Time Parking Management

Wireless sensors play a pivotal role in providing accurate and up-to-the-minute information about parking space availability. Via detecting the presence or absence of vehicles, these sensors communicate their status wirelessly to a central management system. This real-time data is then made accessible to drivers through mobile applications, digital signage, or other communication channels. As drivers navigate urban environments, they can rely on this information to make informed decisions about where to find available parking spaces, drastically reducing the time spent searching for parking and minimizing traffic congestion caused by aimless circling (Zhao et al., 2022).

The role of wireless sensors in real-time parking management is paramount in reshaping the dynamics of urban mobility and addressing the persistent challenges associated with parking in densely populated areas. These wireless sensors, integral components of smart parking solutions, are strategically deployed in parking spaces, garages, and on-street locations to monitor and relay real-time data on space occupancy, availability, and turnover (McEwen & Cassimally, 2013). This deployment transforms static parking spaces into intelligent, connected nodes within the urban landscape, forming a dynamic ecosystem that responds in real-time to the ebb and flow of vehicle movements. The significance of wireless sensors in real-time parking management lies in their ability to offer a scalable and adaptable solution to the diverse landscapes of urban environments. Whether in bustling city centers, residential areas, or commercial districts, the wireless connectivity of these sensors ensures that parking data can be efficiently collected and disseminated. This adaptability is crucial in addressing the varying demands on parking infrastructure across different times of day, days of the week, or during special events (Fysarakis et al., 2017).

The data generated by wireless sensors serves as the backbone for analytics that can inform strategic urban planning. The insights derived from parking occupancy patterns, peak demand hours, and turnover rates empower city planners to optimize parking infrastructure, allocate resources effectively, and make informed decisions about future development. This data-driven approach enhances the overall efficiency and sustainability of urban spaces, aligning with the broader goals of creating intelligent and resilient cities (Jain et al., 2021). So, the role of wireless sensors in real-time parking management epitomizes the transformative potential of IoT technologies in urban development. By converting static parking spaces into dynamic, connected entities, these sensors contribute to more efficient transportation systems, reduced environmental impact, and enhanced overall urban mobility. As cities worldwide grapple with the challenges of population growth and urbanization, the deployment of wireless sensors in real-time parking management emerges as a critical component in the ongoing evolution towards smarter, more connected, and livable urban environments (Lefebvre, 2021).

Challenges in Implementing Smart Parking Systems

The implementing of smart parking systems presents a range of challenges and opportunities that reflect the complexities of integrating innovative technologies into urban infrastructure. So, understanding and navigating these factors is crucial for successful deployment and sustainable operation of smart parking solutions.

Infrastructure and Cost: Upgrading existing parking infrastructure to accommodate smart technologies can be capital-intensive.

Interoperability and Standards: Lack of standardized protocols can hinder interoperability among various smart parking systems.

Data Privacy and Security: Collecting and managing sensitive data, such as vehicle location, raises concerns about privacy and cybersecurity.

User Adoption and Education: Users may resist or be unaware of new technologies, leading to underutilization.

Regulatory Compliance: So, adhering to existing regulations and obtaining necessary approvals can be a bureaucratic hurdle.

While challenges exist, the opportunities presented by smart parking systems are extensive, offering the potential for more sustainable, efficient, and user-friendly urban environments. Successful implementation requires a strategic approach that addresses the challenges while capitalizing on the myriad opportunities these technologies bring to the forefront of modern urban development (Jeong & Shin, 2020).

INTELLIGENT IOT INFRASTRUCTURE: ARCHITECTURE AND DESIGN CONSIDERATIONS

The creation of highly intelligent Internet of Things (IoT) infrastructure demands meticulous architecture and design considerations to ensure its efficacy and resilience. At the core of this endeavor is the need for a scalable and adaptable framework capable of accommodating the diverse array of IoT devices and applications that contribute to a highly intelligent ecosystem. The architecture should prioritize modularity, allowing for the seamless integration of new devices and technologies as they emerge. A robust and secure communication protocol is paramount, ensuring efficient data exchange while safeguarding against cyber threats. Edge computing plays a pivotal role in enhancing the efficiency of highly intelligent IoT systems by enabling data processing closer to the source, reducing latency and optimizing bandwidth usage (Brunetta & Caldarice, 2020).

The considerations for data governance, privacy, and ethical use are integral, necessitating the implementation of rigorous security measures and compliance frameworks. The design of highly intelligent

Figure 4. Shows the challenges associated with smart parking systems implementation

IoT infrastructure must also account for interoperability, fostering compatibility across different devices and platforms to create a cohesive and collaborative ecosystem. The energy efficiency is crucial for sustainable operations, prompting the exploration of low-power communication protocols and energy-conscious device design. In essence, the architecture and design considerations for highly intelligent IoT infrastructure demand a holistic approach that balances technological innovation with security, scalability, and ethical considerations to create a resilient foundation for the future of intelligent connectivity (Maria de Fátima & Radwan, 2017).

Security Measures to Ensuring Integrity and Privacy of Data

Ensuring the integrity and privacy of data is paramount in the realm of Internet of Things (IoT), where interconnected devices continuously exchange sensitive information. Robust security measures are imperative to safeguard against potential threats and mitigate the risk of unauthorized access. Data encryption stands as a fundamental layer of defense, employing strong algorithms to protect data during transmission and storage. Authentication and authorization mechanisms play a crucial role in verifying the identities of both devices and users, ensuring that access privileges are granted based on a principle of least privilege. Secure device identity management, incorporating unique identifiers and secure lifecycle management, adds an additional layer of protection. Network security measures, such as firewalls and intrusion detection systems, secure communication channels and prevent unauthorized access. Regular software updates are essential to patch vulnerabilities and enhance overall security (Ullah et al., 2018).

Furthermore, data integrity checks, achieved through cryptographic hash functions lays a means to verify that data has not been tampered with during transit or storage. Privacy by design principles integrate privacy considerations from the initial stages of IoT system development, incorporating techniques like data anonymization and pseudonymization. Secure cloud services, if utilized, demand adherence to stringent security practices, including proper access controls and encryption for stored data (Horijon, 2017). A robust incident response plan and continuous monitoring with intrusion detection systems and security information and event management (SIEM) tools bolster the ability to detect and respond to security incidents promptly. Lastly, compliance with relevant data protection regulations, such as GDPR or HIPAA, ensures that the security measures align with legal standards, reinforcing the commitment to data integrity and privacy. These security measures constitute a comprehensive approach to fortify the integrity and privacy of data in the dynamic landscape of IoT (Leal Filho et al., 2020).

Scalability and Interoperability for Seamless Integration of IoT Devices

Scalability and interoperability are pivotal considerations for ensuring the seamless integration of various Internet of Things (IoT) devices within a dynamic and interconnected ecosystem. Scalability involves designing an IoT infrastructure that can effortlessly accommodate the growing number of devices and the escalating volume of data they generate. A scalable system can adapt and expand to meet the increasing demands of diverse applications and user requirements without compromising performance. This flexibility is crucial as IoT deployments evolve, accommodating new devices and technologies seamlessly (Krishnamurthy et al., 2017).

Interoperability is about creating a cohesive environment where different IoT devices can communicate and work together effectively. In a landscape with numerous devices from various manufacturers, standards for communication protocols and data formats are essential. Interoperability ensures that devices from different vendors can understand and respond to each other's data, commands, and queries. A lack of interoperability can lead to siloed, disjointed systems, limiting the potential for collaboration and synergy among devices. The standardizing of communication protocols facilitates a harmonized IoT ecosystem where devices, regardless of their origin, can function cohesively, providing users with a unified and efficient experience (Liu et al., 2022).

Together, scalability and interoperability form the backbone of a resilient and future-proof IoT infrastructure. Scalability ensures that the system can handle growth and increased complexity, while interoperability fosters a harmonious environment where diverse devices seamlessly communicate and collaborate. This synergy is crucial for unlocking the full potential of the IoT, enabling innovative applications, and driving the development of intelligent and interconnected systems that transcend the limitations of individual devices. As the IoT continues to evolve, the emphasis on scalability and interoperability becomes paramount for creating a truly integrated and efficient digital landscape (Kumar et al., 2021).

SECURITY AND PRIVACY CONCERNS: CHALLENGES TO SECURITY OF IOT DEVICES AND WIRELESS SENSOR NETWORKS

Security and privacy concerns loom large in the landscape of Internet of Things (IoT) devices and wireless sensor networks, posing significant challenges that demand robust solutions. One primary concern revolves around the vulnerability of IoT devices to cyber threats (Escap, 2022). Many of these devices are resource-constrained, lacking the computing power and memory to implement sophisticated security measures. As a result, they become attractive targets for malicious actors seeking to exploit vulnerabilities and gain unauthorized access to sensitive data. To mitigate these risks, it is imperative to prioritize secure-by-design principles, incorporating encryption, secure authentication, and regular software updates into the development lifecycle of IoT devices (Abdelhady et al., 2022).

Wireless sensor networks, which form the backbone of many IoT applications, face unique security challenges. The wireless nature of communication exposes these networks to eavesdropping, man-in-the-middle attacks, and unauthorized access (Mukhopadhyay et al., 2022). So, implementing the strong encryption protocols for data in transit and securing communication channels through technologies like Virtual Private Networks (VPNs) are essential safeguards. The deployment of intrusion detection systems and continuous monitoring helps identify and respond to security incidents promptly, enhancing the overall resilience of wireless sensor networks (Singh, 2023). The privacy concerns arise from the vast amount of data generated by IoT devices and sensors. The collection of sensitive information, such as location data or personal habits, raises questions about how this data is stored, processed, and shared. Transparent privacy policies, data anonymization techniques, and user-centric consent mechanisms are pivotal in addressing these concerns. Striking a balance between collecting valuable data for improving services and respecting user privacy is a delicate task that requires careful consideration (Singh, 2024).

The interconnected nature of IoT systems further amplifies security and privacy challenges. Compromised devices can potentially serve as entry points into larger networks, leading to cascading security breaches (Singh, 2023). A comprehensive and layered security approach that includes network segmentation, regular security audits, and incident response planning is crucial for fortifying the entire IoT ecosystem. As the deployment of IoT devices and wireless sensor networks continues to proliferate, addressing security and privacy concerns is imperative. A proactive stance that integrates security measures into the design, operation, and maintenance of these systems is essential for building trust among users and stakeholders while ensuring the longevity and sustainability of the IoT landscape (Singh, 2023).

Measures and Technologies Employed to Ensuring Data Privacy and Integrity

Ensuring data privacy and integrity is a critical aspect of managing and securing sensitive information, especially in the context of evolving technologies and increasing cyber threats. Several measures and technologies are employed to safeguard data privacy and integrity effectively. The fundamental measure is the implementation of robust encryption protocols (Sharma & Singh, 2022). The encryption transforms data into an unreadable format, and only those with the appropriate decryption key can access the original information. This safeguards data from unauthorized access during transmission and storage, providing a strong layer of protection against eavesdropping and cyberattacks (Marr, 2020).

Authentication and access control mechanisms play a pivotal role in ensuring data privacy. Multi-factor authentication, secure password policies, and role-based access control ensure that only authorized individuals or devices can access specific data. This not only protects against unauthorized access but also helps in maintaining a detailed audit trail for accountability (Gaur & Sahoo, 2022).

Blockchain technology has emerged as a powerful tool for ensuring data integrity. Blockchain creates an immutable and decentralized ledger where transactions or data modifications are recorded in a secure and transparent manner. This ensures that once data is entered into the blockchain, it cannot be altered or tampered with, providing a high level of assurance regarding data integrity (Grigg, 2010).

Regular software updates and patch management are essential measures to address vulnerabilities and enhance overall security. Keeping software, operating systems, and applications up-to-date ensures that known vulnerabilities are patched, reducing the risk of exploitation by malicious actors (Sartal et al., 2020).

Figure 5. Shows the ensuring data privacy and integrity: Measures and technologies

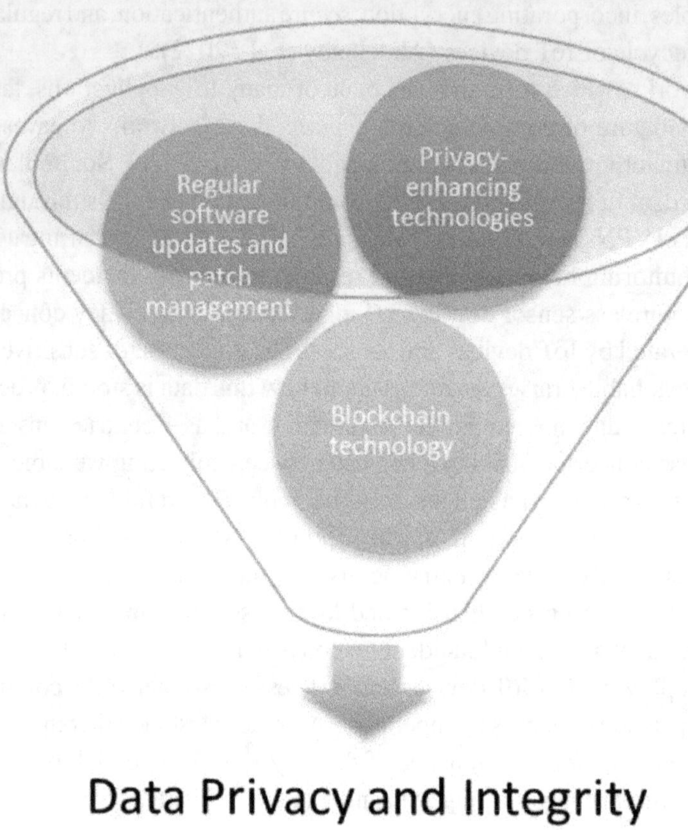

Privacy-enhancing technologies, such as differential privacy and homomorphic encryption, are designed to protect sensitive information while still allowing for meaningful analysis. These technologies add layers of privacy protection by anonymizing data or enabling computations on encrypted data without decrypting it (Obiako, I2022).

In addition to these measures, organizations often conduct privacy impact assessments, which evaluate the potential privacy risks associated with new technologies or data processing activities. This proactive approach helps identify and mitigate privacy concerns before they become issues (Ardakani & Cheshmehzangi, 2023). The adherence to data protection regulations and standards, such as GDPR (General Data Protection Regulation) or HIPAA (Health Insurance Portability and Accountability Act), ensures that organizations comply with legal requirements and industry best practices, fostering a culture of responsible data handling. The multi-faceted approach involving encryption, authentication, blockchain, privacy-enhancing technologies, regular updates, and regulatory compliance is crucial for ensuring the privacy and integrity of data. By adopting these measures and technologies, organizations can fortify their defenses against evolving cyber threats and build trust among users and stakeholders regarding the responsible handling of sensitive information (Gansky, 2010).

SUSTAINABLE FUTURE: IMPLEMENTATION OF HIGHLY INTELLIGENT IOT AND WIRELESS SENSOR TECHNOLOGIES CONTRIBUTES TO SUSTAINABILITY

The implementation of highly intelligent Internet of Things (IoT) and wireless sensor technologies plays a pivotal role in shaping a sustainable future across various domains. In the realm of smart cities, these technologies offer innovative solutions to optimize resource utilization and energy efficiency. Smart grids, enabled by IoT and wireless sensors, facilitate the real-time monitoring and management of electricity consumption, reducing waste and promoting a more sustainable energy infrastructure. Additionally, in urban mobility, intelligent transportation systems leverage these technologies to optimize traffic flow, reduce congestion, and minimize carbon emissions, contributing to environmentally friendly and efficient transportation networks (Ahuja et al., 2021).

In agriculture, the deployment of IoT and wireless sensors enables precision farming techniques. These technologies provide real-time data on soil conditions, weather patterns, and crop health, allowing farmers to optimize irrigation, minimize the use of pesticides, and enhance overall agricultural productivity. The result is not only improved yields but also a more sustainable and eco-friendly approach to farming (Knaap et al., 2022).

In industrial settings, IoT and wireless sensors facilitate predictive maintenance, minimizing downtime and optimizing energy consumption by identifying potential equipment failures before they occur. This approach not only enhances operational efficiency but also reduces resource waste and extends the lifespan of machinery, aligning with principles of sustainability (Mohring et al., 2018).

Smart buildings, equipped with IoT and wireless sensor technologies, contribute significantly to energy conservation. The automated systems for lighting, heating and cooling adjust based on occupancy and environmental conditions, minimizing energy consumption and reducing the ecological footprint of buildings. the implementation of smart waste management systems, incorporating sensors to monitor fill levels and optimize collection routes, promotes efficient waste disposal practices, further contributing to a sustainable urban environment (Kataray et al., 2023).

The deployment of highly intelligent IoT and wireless sensor technologies fosters a data-driven approach to sustainability. By providing real-time insights and enabling proactive decision-making, these technologies empower individuals, businesses, and city planners to adopt more sustainable practices across various sectors. The result is a harmonious integration of technology and environmental responsibility, paving the way for a sustainable future where efficiency, resource conservation, and eco-consciousness are at the forefront of technological advancements (Ashraf, 2021).

Energy Efficiency, Reduced Emissions, and Overall Environmental Impact

The integration of highly intelligent Internet of Things (IoT) and wireless sensor technologies into various sectors contributes significantly to energy efficiency, reduced emissions, and an overall positive environmental impact (Malini et al., 2021). The key area where this impact is notable is in the realm of smart cities. Intelligent transportation systems, powered by IoT and wireless sensors, optimize traffic flow, reduce congestion, and enhance public transportation efficiency. This not only minimizes fuel consumption but also leads to a substantial reduction in emissions, contributing to improved air quality and a healthier urban environment (Lv et al., 2019).

In the industrial sector, the implementation of IoT-driven smart manufacturing processes allows for precise control and monitoring of energy usage (Janani et al., 2021). The predictive maintenance made possible through IoT technologies, helps identify inefficiencies and potential failures in equipment, reducing downtime and preventing unnecessary energy consumption. The result is a more energy-efficient industrial landscape that lowers operational costs and mitigates environmental impact (Wang et al., 2020).

The energy efficiency is a cornerstone of smart building solutions, where IoT and wireless sensors regulate lighting, heating, and cooling systems based on occupancy and environmental conditions (Ponnusamy & Alagarsamy, 2023). Automated adjustments ensure that energy is used optimally, reducing waste and leading to substantial energy savings over time. This not only benefits building owners by lowering utility costs but also contributes to the global effort to mitigate climate change by curbing greenhouse gas emissions (Ramírez-Moreno et al., 2021). In the agricultural sector, precision farming made possible by IoT and wireless sensors enables targeted irrigation and fertilization based on real-time data. This optimized resource usage not only increases crop yields but also minimizes the environmental impact of excessive water and chemical usage, fostering a more sustainable and eco-friendly approach to agriculture (Nourildean et al., 2022).

The overall environmental impact of these technologies extends beyond individual sectors. With creating interconnected, data-driven ecosystems, highly intelligent IoT and wireless sensor technologies empower businesses, governments and individuals to make informed decisions that collectively contribute to a more sustainable future (Jha et al., 2020). The reduction in energy consumption, lower emissions, and efficient resource utilization underscore the transformative potential of these technologies in creating a more environmentally conscious and resilient global landscape (Sharma & Arya, 2023).

CONCLUSION AND FUTURE SCOPE

The endeavor to shape highly intelligent Internet of Things (IoT) and wireless sensors for smart cities, with a specific focus on smart and secure transportation and parking, marks a pivotal stride towards a sustainable future. The integration of these technologies into urban infrastructure has showcased immense potential in optimizing transportation systems, reducing traffic congestion, and enhancing overall mobility. Smart parking solutions, empowered by IoT and wireless sensors, have redefined the efficiency and user experience within urban parking spaces, minimizing search times and contributing to a more streamlined and sustainable transportation ecosystem. The emphasis on security measures ensures that the benefits of these advancements are not compromised, offering users confidence in the reliability and privacy of the data generated and processed. The future scope of these technologies is expansive. Further advancements in machine learning, artificial intelligence, and edge computing will refine the capabilities of IoT and wireless sensors, providing even more sophisticated solutions for urban challenges. The evolution towards connected and autonomous vehicles, coupled with the integration of 5G networks, holds the promise of more seamless and responsive transportation systems. The expansion of the smart city initiatives will likely lead to the incorporation of these technologies in broader urban planning strategies which contributing to holistic and sustainable city development. As smart cities continue to evolve, the synergy between highly intelligent IoT and wireless sensors, smart transportation, and secure parking solutions will play a pivotal role in defining the urban landscapes of the future. The ongoing commitment to innovation, coupled with a keen awareness of security and privacy considerations, ensures that these technologies will continue to shape urban environments towards greater efficiency, resilience and sustainability.

REFERENCES

Abdelhady, A. M., Amin, O., Alouini, M. S., & Shihada, B. (2022). Revolutionizing optical wireless communications via smart optics. *IEEE Open Journal of the Communications Society*, *3*, 654–669. doi:10.1109/OJCOMS.2022.3164790

Abi Sen, A. A., Aljohani, Y. M., Hakami, A. A. H., Bahbouh, N. M., Alkhodre, A., & Alghamdi, M. S. (2023, March). A Framework for Moving from Traditional to Smart University. In *2023 10th International Conference on Computing for Sustainable Global Development (INDIACom)* (pp. 562-569). IEEE.

Ahuja, N. J., Srikanth, P., Konstantinou, C., & Kaust, C. (2021). *Blockchain and Autonomous Vehicles: Recent Advances and Future Directions*. Research. Gate.

Al-Turjman, F., & Lemayian, J. P. (2020). Intelligence, security, and vehicular sensor networks in internet of things (IoT)-enabled smart-cities: An overview. *Computers & Electrical Engineering*, *87*, 106776. doi:10.1016/j.compeleceng.2020.106776

AlZubi, A. A., Alarifi, A., Al-Maitah, M., & Alheyasat, O. (2021). Multi-sensor information fusion for Internet of Things assisted automated guided vehicles in smart city. *Sustainable Cities and Society*, *64*, 102539. doi:10.1016/j.scs.2020.102539

Ang, K. L. M., Seng, J. K. P., & Ngharamike, E. (2022). Towards crowdsourcing internet of things (crowd-iot): Architectures, security and applications. *Future Internet*, *14*(2), 49. doi:10.3390/fi14020049

Ardakani, S. P., & Cheshmehzangi, A. (2023). *Big Data Analytics for Smart Urban Systems*. Springer Nature. doi:10.1007/978-981-99-5543-5

Ashraf, S. (2021). A proactive role of IoT devices in building smart cities. *Internet of Things and Cyber-Physical Systems*, *1*, 8–13. doi:10.1016/j.iotcps.2021.08.001

Bagga, P., Das, A. K., Chamola, V., & Guizani, M. (2022). Blockchain-envisioned access control for internet of things applications: A comprehensive survey and future directions. *Telecommunication Systems*, *81*(1), 125–173. doi:10.1007/s11235-022-00938-7 PMID:35879968

Bauer, M., Sanchez, L., & Song, J. (2021). IoT-enabled smart cities: Evolution and outlook. *Sensors (Basel)*, *21*(13), 4511. doi:10.3390/s21134511 PMID:34209436

Belli, L., Cilfone, A., Davoli, L., Ferrari, G., Adorni, P., Di Nocera, F., Dall'Olio, A., Pellegrini, C., Mordacci, M., & Bertolotti, E. (2020). IoT-enabled smart sustainable cities: Challenges and approaches. *Smart Cities*, *3*(3), 1039–1071. doi:10.3390/smartcities3030052

Bibri, S. E. (2018). The IoT for smart sustainable cities of the future: An analytical framework for sensor-based big data applications for environmental sustainability. *Sustainable Cities and Society*, *38*, 230–253. doi:10.1016/j.scs.2017.12.034

Bibri, S. E., & Bibri, S. E. (2018). Conceptual, theoretical, disciplinary, and discursive foundations: A multidimensional framework. *Smart Sustainable Cities of the Future: The Untapped Potential of Big Data Analytics and Context–Aware Computing for Advancing Sustainability*, (pp. 39-131). Research Gate.

Brunetta, G., & Caldarice, O. (2020). Spatial resilience in planning: Meanings, challenges, and perspectives for urban transition. *Sustainable Cities and Communities*, 628-640.

Cardullo, P. (2020). *Citizens in the'smart City': Participation, Co-production, Governance*. Routledge. doi:10.4324/9780429438806

Chaloupková, M., & Janurová, M. (2019, June). Applications of the Smart Cities Concept. In *Proceedings of FEB Zagreb International Odyssey Conference on Economics and Business* (Vol. 1, No. 1, pp. 532-546). University of Zagreb, Faculty of Economics and Business.

Fysarakis, K., Askoxylakis, I., Katos, V., Ioannidis, S., & Marinos, L. (2017). Security Concerns in Cooperative Intelligent Transportation Systems. *Intrusion Detection and Prevention for Mobile Ecosystems*, 487-522.

Gansky, L. (2010). *The mesh: Why the future of business is sharing*. Penguin.

Gaur, L., & Sahoo, B. M. (2022). *Explainable Artificial Intelligence for Intelligent Transportation Systems: Ethics and Applications*. Springer Nature. doi:10.1007/978-3-031-09644-0

Giourka, P., Sanders, M. W., Angelakoglou, K., Pramangioulis, D., Nikolopoulos, N., Rakopoulos, D., Tryferidis, A., & Tzovaras, D. (2019). The smart city business model canvas—A smart city business modeling framework and practical tool. *Energies*, *12*(24), 4798. doi:10.3390/en12244798

Grigg, N. S. (2010). *Infrastructure finance: the business of infrastructure for a sustainable future* (Vol. 536). John Wiley & Sons. doi:10.1002/9781118266182

Hanes, D., Salgueiro, G., Grossetete, P., Barton, R., & Henry, J. (2017). *IoT fundamentals: Networking technologies, protocols, and use cases for the internet of things*. Cisco Press.

Horijon, T. (2017). *Paving the road towards intelligent transportation systems: A governmentality analysis of smart traffic management in the Netherlands*. Wageningen University & Research.

Jain, S., Ahuja, N. J., Srikanth, P., Bhadane, K. V., Nagaiah, B., Kumar, A., & Konstantinou, C. (2021). Blockchain and autonomous vehicles: Recent advances and future directions. *IEEE Access : Practical Innovations, Open Solutions*, *9*, 130264–130328. doi:10.1109/ACCESS.2021.3113649

Janani, R. P., Renuka, K., & Aruna, A. (2021). IoT in smart cities: A contemporary survey. *Global Transitions Proceedings*, *2*(2), 187–193. doi:10.1016/j.gltp.2021.08.069

Javed, A. R., Shahzad, F., Rehman, S., Zikria, Y. B., Razzak, I., Jalil, Z., & Xu, G. (2022). Future smart cities: Requirements, emerging technologies, applications, challenges, and future aspects. *Cities (London, England)*, *129*, 103794. doi:10.1016/j.cities.2022.103794

Jeong, M., & Shin, H. H. (2020). Tourists' experiences with smart tourism technology at smart destinations and their behavior intentions. *Journal of Travel Research*, *59*(8), 1464–1477. doi:10.1177/0047287519883034

Jha, S., Nkenyereye, L., Joshi, G. P., & Yang, E. (2020). Mitigating and monitoring smart city using internet of things. *Computers, Materials & Continua*, *65*(2), 1059–1079. doi:10.32604/cmc.2020.011754

Kataray, T., Nitesh, B., Yarram, B., Sinha, S., Cuce, E., Shaik, S., & Roy, A. (2023). Integration of smart grid with renewable energy sources: Opportunities and challenges–A comprehensive review. *Sustainable Energy Technologies and Assessments*, *58*, 103363. doi:10.1016/j.seta.2023.103363

Kaur, S., & Sharma, S. (2023, April). Internet of Things Enabled Framework for Sustainable Mobility and Clean Environment in Smart Cities. In *International Conference on Recent Trends in Artificial Intelligence and IoT* (pp. 285-298). Cham: Springer Nature Switzerland. 10.1007/978-3-031-37303-9_21

Knaap, G. J., Lewis, R., Chakraborty, A., & June-Friesen, K. (2022). Toward a "Smart Growth 2.0". *Handbook on Smart Growth: Promise, Principles, and Prospects for Planning*, 324. Research Gate.

Krishnamurthy, R., Smith, K. L., & Desouza, K. C. (2017). Urban informatics: critical data and technology considerations. *Seeing Cities Through Big Data: Research, Methods and Applications in Urban Informatics*, (pp. 163-188). Research Gate.

Kumar, R. L., Pham, Q. V., Khan, F., Piran, M. J., & Dev, K. (2021). Blockchain for securing aerial communications: Potentials, solutions, and research directions. *Physical Communication*, *47*, 101390. doi:10.1016/j.phycom.2021.101390

Leal Filho, W., Marisa Azul, A., Brandli, L., Gökçin Özuyar, P., & Wall, T. (Eds.). (2020). *Sustainable cities and communities*. Springer International Publishing.

Lefebvre, M. (2021). *Reimagining Smart Cities: reconsidering pluralism and data subjectivities* [Doctoral dissertation, University of Oxford].

Liu, F., Fan, H. Y., & Qi, J. Y. (2022). Blockchain technology, cryptocurrency: Entropy-based perspective. *Entropy (Basel, Switzerland)*, *24*(4), 557. doi:10.3390/e24040557 PMID:35455220

Lv, Z., Hu, B., & Lv, H. (2019). Infrastructure monitoring and operation for smart cities based on IoT system. *IEEE Transactions on Industrial Informatics*, *16*(3), 1957–1962. doi:10.1109/TII.2019.2913535

Malini, P., Gowthaman, N., Gautami, A., & Thillaiarasu, N. (2021). Internet of Everything (IoE) in smart city paradigm using advanced sensors for handheld devices and equipment. In *IoT and IoE Driven Smart Cities* (pp. 121–141). Springer International Publishing.

Maria de Fátima, F. D., & Radwan, A. (2017). *Optical Fiber Sensors for LoT and Smart Devices*. Springer.

Marr, B. (2020). *Tech Trends in Practice: The 25 technologies that are driving the 4th Industrial Revolution*. John Wiley & Sons.

McEwen, A., & Cassimally, H. (2013). *Designing the internet of things*. John Wiley & Sons.

Miao, J. T., & Phelps, N. (2019). Smart City Report 1: The evolution of smart city: case studies of Barcelona, Spain and Helsinki, Finland. Research Gate.

Minoli, D., & Occhiogrosso, B. (2018). Internet of things applications for smart cities. *Internet of things A to Z: technologies and applications*, 319-358.

Mishra, P., & Singh, G. (2023). Energy management systems in sustainable smart cities based on the internet of energy: A technical review. *Energies*, *16*(19), 6903. doi:10.3390/en16196903

Mitieka, D., Luke, R., Twinomurinzi, H., & Mageto, J. (2023). Smart Mobility in Urban Areas: A Bibliometric Review and Research Agenda. *Sustainability (Basel), 15*(8), 6754. doi:10.3390/su15086754

Mohring, K. A. (2018). *Smart streetlights: a feasibility study* [Doctoral dissertation, James Cook University].

Moir, E., Moonen, T., & Clark, G. (2014). What are future cities? Origins, meanings and uses. Government Office for Science, 14.

Mukhopadhyay, D., Bhattacharyya, S., Krishnan, B., & Roy, S. (Eds.). (2022). *Blockchain for IoT*. CRC Press. doi:10.1201/9781003188247

Musa, A. A., Malami, S. I., Alanazi, F., Ounaies, W., Alshammari, M., & Haruna, S. I. (2023). Sustainable Traffic Management for Smart Cities Using Internet-of-Things-Oriented Intelligent Transportation Systems (ITS): Challenges and Recommendations. *Sustainability (Basel), 15*(13), 9859. doi:10.3390/su15139859

Nasiri, M. (2016). *Internet of Things as an enabler in disruptive innovation for sustainability*. Research Gate.

Nguyen, D. D., Rohács, J., Rohács, D., & Boros, A. (2020). Intelligent total transportation management system for future smart cities. *Applied Sciences (Basel, Switzerland), 10*(24), 8933. doi:10.3390/app10248933

Nourildean, S. W., Hassib, M. D., & Mohammed, Y. A. (2022). Internet of things based wireless sensor network: A review. *Indonesian Journal of Electrical Engineering and Computer Science, 27*(1), 246–261. doi:10.11591/ijeecs.v27.i1.pp246-261

Obiako, I. V. (2022). *Toward a Bio-Inspired System Architecting Framework: Simulation of the Integration of Autonomous Bus Fleets and Alternative Fueling Infrastructures in Closed Sociotechnical Environments* [Doctoral dissertation, University of South Alabama].

Paiva, S., Ahad, M. A., Tripathi, G., Feroz, N., & Casalino, G. (2021). Enabling technologies for urban smart mobility: Recent trends, opportunities and challenges. *Sensors (Basel), 21*(6), 2143. doi:10.3390/s21062143 PMID:33803903

Ponnusamy, M., & Alagarsamy, A. (2023). Traffic monitoring in smart cities using internet of things assisted robotics. *Materials Today: Proceedings, 81*, 290–294. doi:10.1016/j.matpr.2021.03.192

Ramírez-Moreno, M. A., Keshtkar, S., Padilla-Reyes, D. A., Ramos-López, E., García-Martínez, M., Hernández-Luna, M. C., & Lozoya-Santos, J. D. J. (2021). Sensors for sustainable smart cities: A review. *Applied Sciences (Basel, Switzerland), 11*(17), 8198. doi:10.3390/app11178198

Rejeb, A., Rejeb, K., Simske, S., Treiblmaier, H., & Zailani, S. (2022). The big picture on the internet of things and the smart city: A review of what we know and what we need to know. *Internet of Things : Engineering Cyber Physical Human Systems, 19*, 100565. doi:10.1016/j.iot.2022.100565

Sartal, A., Carou, D., & Davim, J. P. (Eds.). (2020). *Enabling technologies for the successful deployment of industry 4.0*. CRC Press. doi:10.1201/9780429055621

Shackelford, S. J. (2020). *The Internet of Things: What Everyone Needs to Know*. Oxford University Press. doi:10.1093/wentk/9780190943813.001.0001

ShahzadF.JavedA. R.ZikriaY. B.RehmanS.JalilZ. (2021). Future smart cities: requirements, emerging technologies, applications, challenges, and future aspects. TechRxiv.

Sharma, A., & Singh, B. (2022). Measuring Impact of E-commerce on Small Scale Business: A Systematic Review. *Journal of Corporate Governance and International Business Law*, *5*(1).

Sharma, R., & Arya, R. (2023). Security threats and measures in the Internet of Things for smart city infrastructure: A state of art. *Transactions on Emerging Telecommunications Technologies*, *34*(11), e4571. doi:10.1002/ett.4571

Shen, S., Wei, Z. Q., Sun, L. J., Su, Y. Q., Wang, R. C., & Jiang, H. M. (2018). The shared bicycle and its network—internet of shared bicycle (IOSB): A review and survey. *Sensors (Basel)*, *18*(8), 2581. doi:10.3390/s18082581 PMID:30087263

Silva, L., Magaia, N., Sousa, B., Kobusińska, A., Casimiro, A., Mavromoustakis, C. X., & De Albuquerque, V. H. C. (2021). Computing paradigms in emerging vehicular environments: A review. *IEEE/CAA Journal of Automatica Sinica, 8*(3), 491-511.

Singh, B. (2023). Tele-Health Monitoring Lensing Deep Neural Learning Structure: Ambient Patient Wellness via Wearable Devices for Real-Time Alerts and Interventions. *Indian Journal of Health and Medical Law*, *6*(2), 12–16.

Singh, B. (2023). Blockchain Technology in Renovating Healthcare: Legal and Future Perspectives. In Revolutionizing Healthcare Through Artificial Intelligence and Internet of Things Applications (pp. 177-186). IGI Global.

Singh, B. (2023). Federated Learning for Envision Future Trajectory Smart Transport System for Climate Preservation and Smart Green Planet: Insights into Global Governance and SDG-9 (Industry, Innovation and Infrastructure). *National Journal of Environmental Law*, *6*(2), 6–17.

Singh, B. (2024). Legal Dynamics Lensing Metaverse Crafted for Videogame Industry and E-Sports: Phenomenological Exploration Catalyst Complexity and Future. *Journal of Intellectual Property Rights Law*, *7*(1), 8–14.

Singh, B., & Kaunert, C. (2024). Integration of Cutting-Edge Technologies such as Internet of Things (IoT) and 5G in Health Monitoring Systems: A Comprehensive Legal Analysis and Futuristic Outcomes. *GLS Law Journal*, *6*(1), 13–20.

Stratigea, A., & Panagiotopoulou, M. (2015). 'Smart'Cities at the Service of Urban Sustainability-A Flavor of the Mediterranean Experience. *Journal of Regional & Socio-Economic Issues*, *5*(3).

Ullah, F., Sepasgozar, S. M., & Wang, C. (2018). A systematic review of smart real estate technology: Drivers of, and barriers to, the use of digital disruptive technologies and online platforms. *Sustainability (Basel)*, *10*(9), 3142. doi:10.3390/su10093142

Varadharajan, V. (2021). Next Generation of Intelligent Cities: Case Studies From Europe. In Developing and Monitoring Smart Environments for Intelligent Cities (pp. 87-111). IGI Global.

Wang, A., Wang, P., Miao, X., Li, X., Ye, N., & Liu, Y. (2020). A review on non-terrestrial wireless technologies for Smart City Internet of Things. *International Journal of Distributed Sensor Networks*, *16*(6), 1550147720936824. doi:10.1177/1550147720936824

Xie, H., Huang, R., Sun, H., Han, Z., Jiang, M., Zhang, D., Goh, H. H., Kurniawan, T. A., Han, F., Liu, H., & Wu, T. (2023). Wireless energy: Paving the way for smart cities and a greener future. *Energy and Building*, *297*, 113469. doi:10.1016/j.enbuild.2023.113469

Yang, Z., Jianjun, L., Faqiri, H., Shafik, W., Talal Abdulrahman, A., Yusuf, M., & Sharawy, A. M. (2021). Green internet of things and big data application in smart cities development. *Complexity*, *2021*, 1–15. doi:10.1155/2021/4922697

Zhao, W., Liang, Z., & Li, B. (2022). Realizing a Rural Sustainable Development through a Digital Village Construction: Experiences from China. *Sustainability (Basel)*, *14*(21), 14199. doi:10.3390/su142114199

Chapter 8
Unveiling the Layered Architecture of IoT:
A Comprehensive Overview

Purnima Gupta
IMS Ghaziabad, University Courses Campus, India

Deepak Kumar Verma
https://orcid.org/0000-0002-4745-1752
Marwadi University, India

Archana Gupta
IMS Ghaziabad, University Courses Campus, India

ABSTRACT

This chapter presents an extensive exploration of the multi-layered framework constituting the IoT infrastructure. This abstract encapsulates a detailed examination of the fundamental layers integral to IoT's functionality. Starting with the foundational Perception Layer, encompassing sensors and actuators, it progresses to the Network Layer facilitating seamless data transmission. Delving deeper, it explores the Middleware Layer, pivotal in data processing, and the diverse functionalities of the application layer across various domains. Moreover, the abstract sheds light on the security and management layer, emphasizing its critical role in safeguarding IoT systems. The interplay and interdependence among these layers are intricately examined, illustrating their collective significance in orchestrating IoT operations. Through this comprehensive overview, the abstract aims to elucidate the nuanced interactions within the layered architecture, providing a holistic understanding essential for leveraging the potential of IoT technologies across diverse industries and applications.

INTRODUCTION

The Internet of Things, or IoT, is a revolutionary force that is changing the face of technology by connecting systems and devices to form a networked web of data and functionality. At its core lies a layered architecture, a stratified framework essential for the seamless operation and efficiency of IoT ecosystems. This comprehensive analysis embarks on a meticulous journey to unravel, scrutinize, and comprehend the multifaceted layers constituting the bedrock of IoT technology.

DOI: 10.4018/979-8-3693-2373-1.ch008

The interconnection of various types of entities, which could include humans, sensors, or anything else that could inquire or offer a service, is known as the Internet of Things (IoT) (Hong, Y. G., et al. 2015). An isolated device can become a communicating thing due to the development of numerous communication protocols as well as the decrease in transceivers. Furthermore, though their sizes have significantly reduced, the computational power, energy capacity, and storage capabilities of small computing or sensing devices have substantially enhanced (Hong, Y. G., Choi, et al. 2015)12. The "Internet of Things" conceptualizes a digital world in which everything in the surrounding has a digital identity which is a part of a network, and exchanges information via communication (Ray, P. P. 2018). The Internet of Things (IoT) applications have grown significantly in the last several years thanks to advancements in WSN (Wireless Sensor Networks) and (RFID) Radio Frequency Identification. RFID, the Internet of Things' primary identifying technology, makes it possible to stamp or mark every item. WSN classifies all people and objects as things. It transforms into a wirelessly identifying object that can communicate with other physical, digital, and cyber objects (Dange S., Chatterjee M. (2020; Kushner, D. 2013).

IoT devices have embedded transceivers, processors, actuators, and sensors. IoT is considered to be a collection of numerous technologies that work together (Constantinos Kolias, G. K. (2017). Several Applications of the Internet of Things (IoT) are centered on automating different processes to give inanimate physical objects the ability to act without human intervention. The surviving and forthcoming IoT applications are extremely promising to increase the user's level of comfort, efficiency, and automation. To create a setting this comfortable, robust security, privacy, authentication, and attack recovery are required. Consequently, to accomplish end-to-end encryption and secure IoT settings, the IoT application architecture must be modified as needed. Interacting with the physical environment is made possible through sensors and actuators. To draw relevant inferences from the data collected by sensors, it must be accurately prepared, and stored. The action is performed by the device called an actuator whereas the changes are detected through the device called a sensor. Temperature, pressure, water quality, chemical reactions, smoke sensors, and other physical phenomena can all be measured by a sensor. The output is delivered which is based on the concept of the sensor that provided its internal state and environment referred to as current state. Similar to the temperature controller on an air conditioner, an actuator modifies the surrounding conditions. Data processing and storage might be carried out on a remote server or at the network's edge. The available resources also confine the storage and processing abilities of an IoT object. Lot many challenges are faced in data collection, communication, and security as well. The newer wireless networks are used among the IoT devices with high-ranking sensors and innovative computing abilities that guarantee to lead us to smarter and more comfortable lives. Security is the major concern in IOT applications with the speed increase in the role of IOT applications in most areas [Shen, Guicheng, and Bingwu Liu., 2011; Howell, J. 2017).

The security issues raised by IoT technology are gaining increasing attention due to the ongoing advancement of theoretical knowledge and the expansion of real-world application scenarios (Al-Kashoash, H. A., & Kemp, A. H. 2016).

From the introduction of the Internet of Things (IoT), this chapter discusses the security goal for IOT in various applications and architectures of IoT. As we all are aware IoT applications make our life comfortable and modern. The massive use of IoT applications leads to challenges of security and privacy. Without a reliability IoT application demand may lose all their prospective (Kushner, D. 2013). IoT architecture does not follow any unique architecture as well as there is no interoperability in communication, service as well as knowledge level (GOODIN, D. 2017). This chapter aims to discuss various industry-level architecture and the role of each layer.

IoT Technologies

A network of physical objects, the Internet of Things (IoT) is embedded with software, sensors, and other technologies to exchange data with other devices and systems over the Internet. (M, S. D. 2018). IoT technology can revolutionize how businesses and individuals engage with their surroundings and have a broad range of applications across multiple industries. Key IoT components and technologies include the following:

Sensors and Actuators: Sensors gather information about the surrounding conditions, including light, motion, temperature, and humidity. Actuators are parts of devices that allow them to do things like operate motors, open valves, or set off alarms based on the data they receive.

Connectivity: Wireless Technologies like WiFi, Bluetooth, Zigbee, Z-Wave, LTE, and 5G are the wireless communication protocols that Internet of Things devices frequently connect to and share data. Wired Technologies to provide more reliable and secure connectivity, Internet of Things devices occasionally make use of wired connections like Ethernet.

IoT Platforms: These are software frameworks that help with device administration, application development, data flow, and communication within the Internet of Things ecosystem (Kumar, S., et al. 2019).

Cloud Computing: The enormous volumes of data produced by IoT devices are processed, stored, and analyzed using cloud platforms. Solutions that are flexible and scalable are made possible by this.

Edge Computing: It is possible to reduce latency and bandwidth usage by processing data closer to the source. Applications requiring quick decisions and those that operate in real-time benefit greatly from edge computing.

Security: Device Security is used to stop unwanted access and safeguard sensitive data, it's imperative to make sure IoT devices are secure. Data Encryption is used to protect security and privacy, data must be encrypted both during transmission and storage. Authentication and Authorization is enforcing robust authentication protocols to confirm the legitimacy of users and devices.

Data Analytics and Machine Learning: Data analytics is done by examining the enormous volumes of data produced by Internet of Things devices, and valuable insights for making decisions can be extracted. Machine Learning is the predictive analysis and intelligent automation is made possible by applying machine learning algorithms to Internet of Things data.

Protocol and Standards: Message Queuing Telemetry Transport (MQTT) is a quick and effective communication system. Constrained Application Protocol (CoAP) is intended for devices with limited resources. Frequently used for web-based communication is HTTP/HTTPS.

Low Power Design: Low Power Internet of Things Devices is used to increase a device's battery life, particularly in situations where it is not practical to replace batteries frequently.

5G Technologies: High-Speed Connectivity 5G networks facilitate more effective communication between IoT devices by providing quicker and more dependable connections.

All of these technologies work together to support the development and application of IoT in several industries, including healthcare, smart homes, manufacturing, transportation, and agriculture.

Figure 1. Internet of things technologies

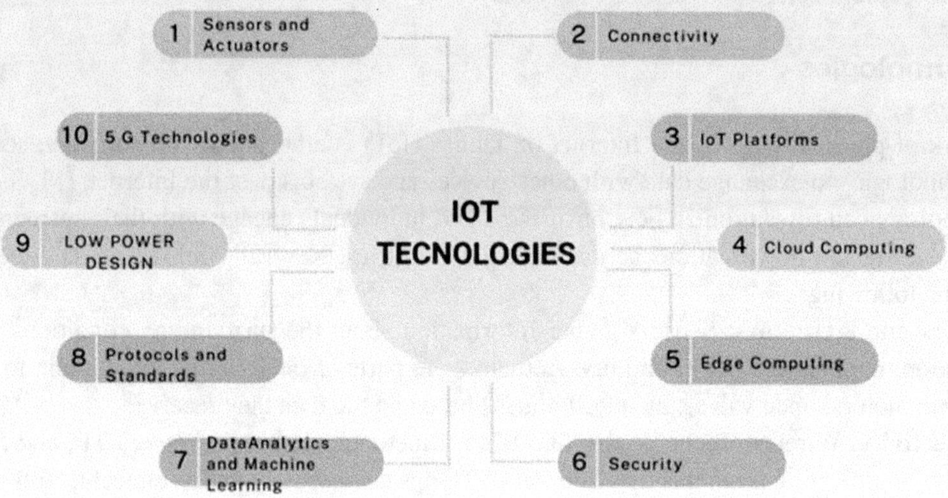

IOT SECURITY GOAL: CIA

IoT applications have the potential to significantly improve our lives. If we can get rid of the security threat barrier, the Internet of Things, with its improved sensors, more advanced computing power, and more modern wireless networks, may be the next big thing (Shen, Guicheng, and Bingwu Liu., 2011).

We talk about the design of security methods for Internet of Things systems in this chapter. IoT security aims to apply security by utilizing three primary domains: availability, integrity, and confidentiality of data. (CIA security model, shown in Figure 1).

Security Goals: CIA Security Framework The security triad is a well-known model for the creation of security mechanisms. Data confidentiality, on the other hand, is the capacity to give users confidence regarding the privacy of sensitive information by employing various mechanisms to prevent its disclosure to unauthorized parties and restrict access to authorized users only (Hudson, B.,2014). According to Narendra, Duquennoy, and Voigt (2015), strict access control, stringent authentication processes, and appropriate encryption are usually used to enforce this security objective, which is intended to safeguard assets from unauthorized access. Different mechanisms, like data encryption or access control, are typically used to support data confidentiality (Ech-Chaitami, T., Mrabet, R., & Berbia, H., 2011). The preservation of valuable information from external parties or cybercriminals is referred to as data integrity. Shen, Guicheng, and Bingwu Liu., 2011; Ray, P. P. 2018; Hudson, B. 2014).

ARCHITECTURE LAYERS AND PROTOCOLS IN IOT:

The architecture of IoT is not standardized yet. Some industry and many research groups are still working on the architecture of IoT. However, some of the basic ideas that will act as the platform for the Internet of Things development are already defined (Ray, P. P. 2018). A generic IoT system can be fully represented and described by using three main key players: 1) perception; 2) transportation; and 3) ap-

Figure 2. IOT security goals: CIA

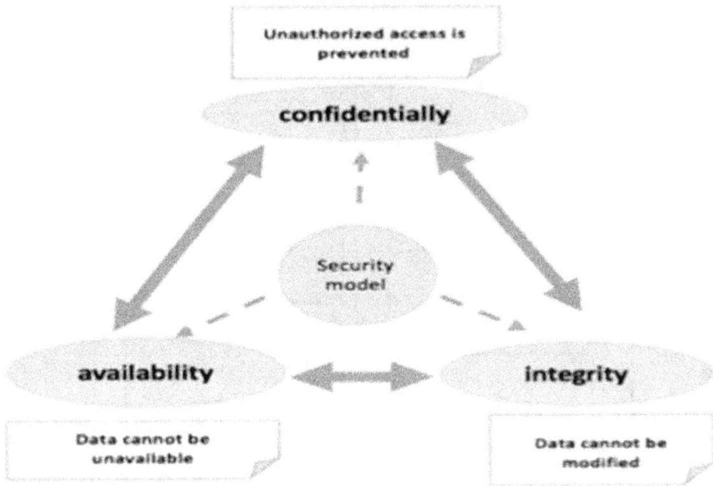

plication (Hudson, B., 2014). This architecture defines the basic minimal things needed for the devices to be connected to the internet (Fruhlinger, J. (2018, March). However, research always will be in search of finer things in the model and hence resulted in a five-layer [5-7] and then to seven-layer (Fruhlinger, J.2018). Hence, following the internet, IoT architecture was initially designed to have 3-layer architecture and went on to become 7-layer architecture currently based on protocol.

Three-Layered Architecture: In a simplified three-layered IoT architecture, security protocols play a crucial role in securing different aspects of the system. Here's an overview of each layer and the associated security protocols commonly used:

Perception Layer: This layer involves sensors, physical devices, and actuators that interact with the physical environs. Security protocols are given below:

(a) **SSL/TLS (Secure Sockets Layer/Transport Layer Security):** Ensures secure communication between devices and servers, encrypting data transmissions.
(b)Device Authentication Protocols: Protocols like OAuth (Open Authorization) or X.509 certificates help authenticate devices and Ensure that the network can only be accessed by authorized devices.
(b) **Secure Boot:** Verifies the integrity of device firmware during boot-up, preventing unauthorized modifications.

Network Layer: Manages communication between devices, gateways, and the broader network infrastructure. **Security Protocols:**

(a) **IPsec (Internet Protocol Security):** Provides secure communication and data transmission between devices over IP networks, ensuring data integrity, authentication, and encryption.
(b) **DTLS (Datagram Transport Layer Security):** Secures communication for UDP-based applications, ensuring secure data transmission.

Figure 3. IOT 3, 4, 5, and 6 layered architecture

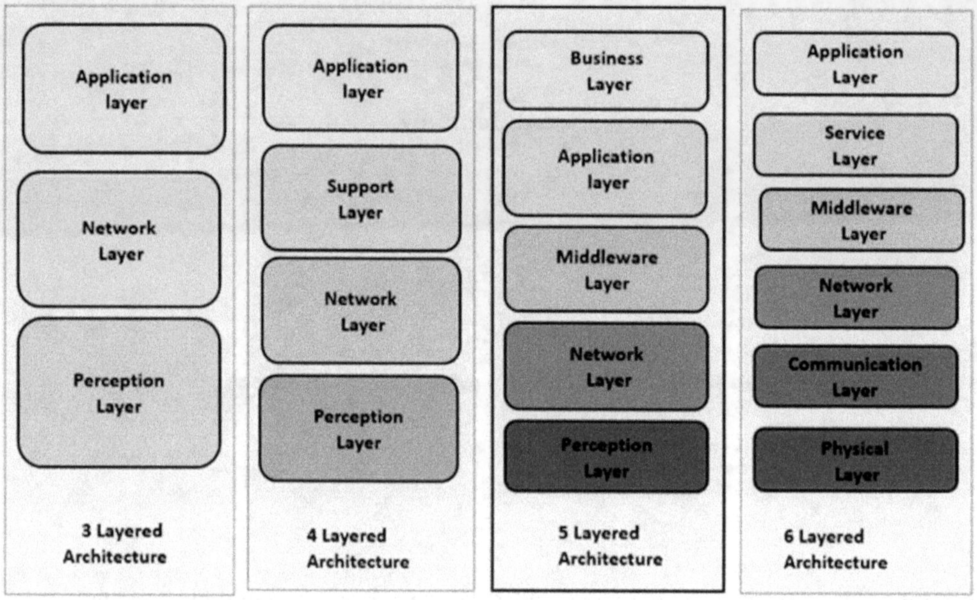

(c) **VPN (Virtual Private Network):** Enables secure, encrypted communication over public networks, allowing remote devices to connect securely to the main network.

Application Layer: Involves applications, services, and interfaces that interact directly with end-users or other systems. **Security Protocols are:**

(a) **OAuth (Open Authorization):** Manages access control and authorization between applications and devices, ensuring secure API access.
(b) **JWT (JSON Web Tokens):** Securely transmits information between parties as JSON objects, commonly used for authentication and information exchange in IoT applications.
(c) **Secure API Protocols:** Utilizes protocols like HTTPS and OAuth2.0 to secure interactions between IoT applications and APIs, ensuring data integrity and confidentiality.

These security protocols help address different security concerns at each layer of the simplified three-layered IoT architecture, covering aspects such as data encryption, authentication, secure communication, and access control. Implementing a combination of these protocols enhances the overall security posture of an IoT system (Mansour, M. et al. (2023)).

Four Layered Architecture

In a four-layered IoT architecture, each layer serves a specific function in managing data flow, communication, and application handling. Here's a breakdown of these layers and some associated protocols:

Device Layer (Perception Layer): Includes physical devices, sensors, and actuators. **Protocols are:**

(a) **MQTT (Message Queuing Telemetry Transport):** lightweight and effective for communicating between devices, particularly in settings with limited resources.
(b) **CoAP (Constrained Application Protocol):** Designed to facilitate RESTful communication over UDP on devices with limited resources.
(c) **Zigbee:** Low-power, low-data-rate wireless protocol commonly used in home automation and industrial applications.

Communication Layer: Manages data transmission between devices, gateways, and network infrastructure. **protocols:**

(a) **IPsec (Internet Protocol Security):** Provides secure communication and data transmission over IP networks, ensuring data integrity, authentication, and encryption.
(b) **DTLS (Datagram Transport Layer Security):** Secures communication for UDP-based applications, ensuring secure data transmission.
(c) **LoRaWAN (Long Range Wide Area Network):** Wide-area coverage is a frequent use case for IoT applications that need low power consumption and long-range communication. It is optimized for devices with constrained resources.

Processing Layer: Involves data processing, aggregation, and possibly basic analytics closer to the data source. **Protocols:**

(a) **HTTP/REST (Hypertext Transfer Protocol / Representational State Transfer):** Used for data transfer and API communication between devices or applications.
(b) **AMQP (Advanced Message Queuing Protocol):** Supports message-oriented middleware for reliable and secure data exchange between devices and applications.

Application Layer: Encompasses applications, services, and interfaces that utilize processed data. Security **Protocols are:**

(a) **HTTPS (Hypertext Transfer Protocol Secure):** offers encryption and authentication to provide safe connection between apps and APIs.
(b) **Web sockets:** Facilitates real-time, bidirectional communication between IoT applications and devices.

These protocols facilitate communication, secure data transmission, and ensure interoperability between devices and applications in a structured four-layered IoT system

Five Layer Architecture

Middleware Layer

serves as a bridge between application layers at lower levels and higher-level processes.

Protocols:

(a) **DDS (Data Distribution Service):** Middleware protocol for real-time data distribution and integration between various devices and applications.
(b) **CoAP, MQTT:** These lightweight protocols might also be used in the middleware layer for communication with devices or applications.

To summarize, the Processing Layer in a 5-layer Internet of Things architecture is presented to tackle the difficulties and prospects related to edge computing, offering benefits like lower latency, optimized bandwidth, heightened privacy, and the capacity to function in situations with sporadic or non-existent connectivity. (dos Santos, 2019).

Six-Layered Architecture

Certainly, a six-layered IoT architecture is designed to efficiently manage and process data while ensuring security and reliability. Here's a breakdown of each layer:

Business Layer

Aligns IoT strategies with broader business objectives. Protocols are:

(a) **Blockchain:** Used for securing and verifying transactions, ensuring data integrity and traceability in business processes.
(b) **Governance Frameworks:** Implement standards and policies to ensure security compliance and mitigate risks at the business level.

Seven Layers Architecture

While Cisco doesn't strictly adhere to a seven-layer model like the OSI model for its collaboration and edge computing solutions, we can attempt to map the layers you've mentioned to common elements in these technologies along with associated protocols:

Physical Device and Controller: This layer involves physical devices like IP phones, video conferencing endpoints, and controllers managing these devices. Protocols might include SIP (Session Initiation Protocol) for real-time communication and control and various device-specific protocols.

Connectivity: In the context of networking, Cisco employs various protocols for connectivity, including Ethernet for wired connections and Wi-Fi standards (such as 802.11ac) for wireless connections. Cisco devices often support standard networking protocols like TCP/IP.

Edge Computing: Processes at the network's edge are handled by the edge computing layer. A lightweight and effective protocol for communication between edge devices and servers is MQTT (Message Queuing Telemetry Transport).

Data Abstraction: Data abstraction is the process of arranging and displaying data in a useful manner. Standards like JSON (JavaScript Object Notation) and XML (eXtensible Markup Language) are frequently used for data representation and abstraction, even though specific protocols may not be linked to this layer.

Figure 4. Seven layer architecture

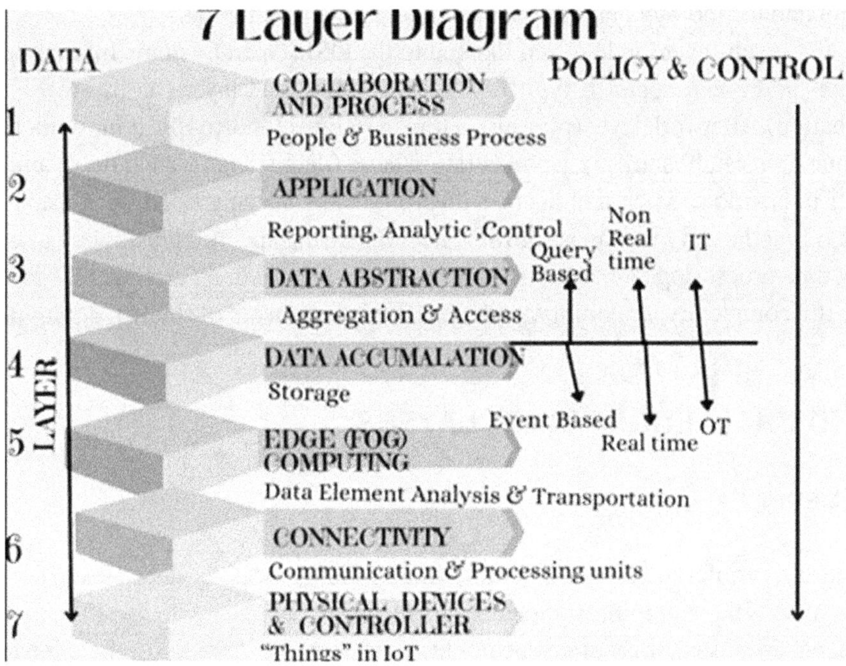

Application: Collaboration applications and platforms from Cisco may use various protocols. For example, Cisco Webex may use HTTPS for secure communication, while Cisco Unified Communications Manager (CUCM) might use SIP and H.323 for call signaling.

Collaboration and Process: This layer involves tools and solutions facilitating collaboration and integration with business processes. Protocols could include HTTPS for secure web communication, and APIs (Application Programming Interfaces) using REST or SOAP for integration with other applications.

Business Integration: Business integration focuses on aligning collaboration with broader business objectives. The protocols used here may vary based on specific integrations, potentially involving standards like OAuth for authentication and authorization.

It's crucial to note that this mapping is a conceptual representation, and Cisco's actual implementation and recommendations may differ. Cisco's collaboration and edge computing solutions often involve a combination of various technologies, services, and protocols to deliver comprehensive and efficient solutions. For the most accurate and up-to-date information, refer to Cisco's official documentation or consult directly with Cisco experts.

In a seven-layered IoT architecture, each layer serves distinct functions and requires specific security protocols to ensure the system's integrity, confidentiality, and availability. Here's an overview of the layers and associated security protocols:

The network layer (data transmission), the application layer (data usage), and the perception layer (devices) make up the three layers of the Internet of Things architecture. A middleware layer is added when the model is expanded to four levels, allowing data processing and analytics to occur between the network and application layers. Moving to a five-layer architecture, it adds a distinct device/thing layer, emphasizing device-specific functionalities, and a business layer that aligns IoT initiatives with strategic business goals. The six-layer architecture includes a communication layer, focusing on protocol and technology handling between devices and networks.

In comparison, the seven-layer model often likened to the OSI (Open Systems Interconnection) model, incorporates additional depth. It typically features a physical layer (hardware), a data link layer (frame creation), a network layer (routing), a transport layer (end-to-end communication), a session layer (connection establishment), a presentation layer (data format translation), and an application layer (user interaction). Each architecture layering offers varying degrees of granularity, specialization, and functionality in managing IoT data, addressing specific needs such as communication protocols, data processing, and user interaction. The selection of an architecture model is typically driven by the complexity, scalability, and specific requirements of the IoT deployment.

TRENDS AND CHALLENGES IN IOT LAYERS

Perception Layer

Trends: include the proliferation of edge computing, which processes data closer to the source, the miniaturization of sensors, and improved energy efficiency.

Challenges: ensuring sensor accuracy, reliability, and security. Arranging the enormous amount of data that sensors provide and drawing wise judgments fast.

Network Layer

Trends: Mesh networks are becoming more prevalent for increased scalability and dependability, low-power wide-area networks (LPWAN) are being more widely used, and 5G technology promises high-speed, low-latency connectivity.

Challenges: Vulnerabilities in network security, such as data interception and illegal access. Facilitating smooth communication between diverse networks. Controlling bandwidth constraints and network congestion.

Middleware Layer

Trends: AI-driven analytics, edge computing, cloud services, and IoT platform integration for real-time data processing and decision-making.

Challenges: Interoperability between different IoT platforms and protocols. Handling the complexities of data integration, transformation, and orchestration across diverse IoT devices and systems. Ensuring data privacy and compliance with regulations.

Application Layer

Trends: The use of IoT solutions across a range of sectors, including manufacturing, transportation, smart cities, healthcare, and agriculture. A focus on tailored experiences and user-centric design.

Difficulties: Creating user-friendly and intuitive interfaces for Internet of Things apps. Addressing issues with data security, privacy, and moral application of data created by the Internet of Things. Combining Internet of Things solutions with legacy systems and current IT infrastructure.

Business Layer

Trends: A move towards outcome-based business models powered by predictive analytics and data-driven insights, such as IoT as a service (IoTaaS) and predictive maintenance.

Difficulties: Finding clear-cut ROI IoT application cases that are feasible. Removing cultural and organizational hurdles to IoT adoption. Navigating legal obstacles and making sure data protection regulations are followed.

Security Layer

Trends: Blockchain technology adoption for identity management and safe data exchange. Application of encryption methods and security-by-design concepts to protect IoT networks and devices.

Difficulties: Handling the expanding array of threats, such as ransomware, malware, and DDoS assaults directed towards Internet of Things devices. Juggling resource limitations with security measures, especially in IoT devices with low memory and computational capability.

To fully use IoT while reducing related risks, tackling these trends and difficulties calls for an integrated strategy that includes technological innovation, stakeholder collaboration, and proactive risk management techniques.

STRATEGIES FOR OPTIMIZING ENERGY CONSUMPTION AT VARIOUS LAYERS

It's critical to optimize energy usage in Internet of Things (IoT) devices to increase overall efficiency, decrease environmental impact, and prolong battery life. Every layer of the IoT architecture, which usually comprises multiple levels, should take energy consumption optimization into account. The following techniques aim to maximize energy usage at various IoT architecture layers:

Device Layer

Hardware with Low Power: Make use of sensors and microcontrollers that use the least amount of energy when they are in sleep or active states.

Duty Cycling: Use duty cycling to periodically switch off non-essential parts of the device during times of low activity so that it can go into low power.

Energy-Aware Communication: Utilize energy-efficient wireless technologies, such as Bluetooth Low Energy (BLE) and Zigbee, and improve communication protocols.

Combining data from several sensors to minimize the need for continuous sensor activation.

Network Layer

Effective Protocols: Select energy-efficient protocols that minimize data transmission and cut down on communication energy.

Adaptive Transmission speeds: These lower energy consumption during idle times by dynamically adjusting transmission speeds based on the urgency of the data and the available resources.

Mesh networking: Use mesh networking to shorten communication paths between devices and boost productivity, which enables reduced transmission power. Sleep Scheduling: Plan your devices' wake and sleep cycles to lower network traffic when they're idle.

Level of Middleware: Data Aggregation: Reduce the amount of data sent to the cloud and instead gather and process data locally to reduce the amount of transmission energy used.

Edge Computing: Reduce the need for continuous contact with centralized servers by processing and analysing data on edge devices. Give programs the ability to dynamically adjust their behaviour in response to changing environmental circumstances and device statuses.

Application Layer: Optimized Algorithms: To reduce resource consumption apply energy-efficient algorithms for data processing, analysis, and decision-making. Utilize predictive analytics to foresee future occurrences, allowing for early intervention and the requirement for ongoing observation. Enable apps to adjust their behavior dynamically in response to shifting device statuses and ambient conditions.

Cloud Layer

Serverless Computing: Utilize serverless computing to scale resources dynamically and only consume energy when processing is required.

Green Data Centres: Choose cloud providers that prioritize sustainability and use energy-efficient data centres.

Data Compression: Implement data compression techniques to reduce the amount of data transmitted between edge devices and the cloud.

Security Layer: Energy-Efficient Cryptography: Use lightweight cryptographic algorithms to secure communication without significantly impacting energy consumption.

Role-Based Access Control: Implement fine-grained access control to ensure that only authorized devices access sensitive data, reducing unnecessary communication.

By incorporating these strategies at each layer of the IoT architecture, you can create a more energy-efficient and sustainable IoT ecosystem. Keep in mind that the specific strategies may vary based on the application, requirements, and constraints of the IoT deployment.

IOT COMMUNICATION PROTOCOLS

Wireless Technologies like WiFi, Bluetooth, Zigbee, Z-Wave, LTE, and 5G are the wireless communication protocols that Internet of Things devices frequently connect to and share data.

- **Wifi**: It is one of the IoT communication protocols, best suitable for LAN — a computer network that interconnects computers within a limited area environment, allowing for fast data transfer. It uses internet protocols (IP) to communicate between endpoint devices.

Table 1. Comparison table of communication protocol used by IoT devices

Protocol	Standard	Frequencies	Range	Data Rates
WiFi	Based on IEEE 802.11	2.4 GHz and 5 GHz bands	50 to 100 meters600 Mbps	600 Mbps 150-200 Mbps the most common
Bluetooth	Bluetooth 4.2 core specification	2.5 GHz	50 to 150 meters	1 Mbps
Zigbee	Zigbee 2.0 based on IEEE802.15	42.4 GHz	10 to 100 meters	250 Kbps
MQTTISO/IEC 20922				. ----Up to 256 Mbps in size
Cellular Data	GSM/GPRS/EDGE(2G), UMTS/ HSPA(3G), LTE(4G)	900/1800/1900/2100MHz	35km max for GSM; 200km max for HSPA	35-170 Kbps
Z Wave	Z-wave Alliance	Various	30 meters	0.3 to 50 Kbps
NFC (Narrowband IoT)	ISO/IEC 18000-3	13.56 MHz	10cm	100-420 Kbps
LoraWAN (Long Range Wide Area Network)	LoRaWAN	Various	2.5km (urban environment), 15km (suburban environment)	0.3 to 50 Kbps
Sigfox	Sigfox	900 Mhz	30-50 km (rural environments), 3-10 km (urban environments)	10-10000 Kbps

- **Bluetooth**: Bluetooth is a protocol used for short-range communication and exchanging of small amounts of data for personal products like smart watches or wireless speakers.
- **Zigbee**: Zigbee's advantage comes from low power consumption, wireless control, security, and scalability. Applications such as wireless thermostats and lighting systems are examples of devices using Zigbee for connection.
- **MQTT**: It handles the transfer of light and simple data from sensors to applications and middleware. It offers a reliable connection and is bandwidth-friendly.
- **Z Wave**: Z wave is based on low-power radio frequency (RF) communication technology. It's highly preferable for smart home products such as lamp controllers, door locks, electronic kettles, etc.
- **Cellular data**: Cellular networks are capable of handling large flows of data. Its high connectivity range makes it a good choice for connecting objects distanced from one another.
- **NFC (Near Field Communication)**: NFC uses electromagnetic communication between the antennas of two devices that are located next to each other. NFC is the technology used in contactless payment at shops today.
- **LoRaWAN**: Lora is a long-range, radio-wide network that has low power consumption and is capable of handling large networks consisting of multiple devices.
- **Sigfox**: Sigfox is a long-range network for machine-to-machine (M2M) applications, with less power consumption than others. That makes it a good choice for connecting remote devices that have to run on batteries for long periods without charging batteries.

This chapter can provide some general trends and advancements in sensor communication protocols and middleware technologies. 5G Connectivity: The rollout of 5G networks has been a significant development in the communication landscape. 5G's low-latency and high-bandwidth capabilities are expected to enhance communication between sensors and devices, enabling faster and more reliable data transfer. Edge Computing: Edge computing involves processing data closer to the source (sensors) rather than relying solely on centralized cloud servers. This reduces latency and enhances real-time data processing. Various middleware solutions are emerging to facilitate efficient edge computing for sensor networks. MQTT (Message Queuing Telemetry Transport): MQTT continues to be a popular lightweight and efficient protocol for IoT (Internet of Things) communication. It is widely used in sensor networks due to its low bandwidth overhead and support for unreliable networks. CoAP (Constrained Application Protocol): CoAP is a specialized web transfer protocol for use with constrained nodes and constrained networks in the Internet of Things. It is designed to be simple and lightweight, making it suitable for communication in resource-constrained environments. Bluetooth Low Energy (BLE): BLE has gained popularity for short-range communication in IoT devices, including sensors. It is energy-efficient and well-suited for applications such as wearables, home automation, and industrial IoT. OPC UA (Unified Architecture): OPC UA is a widely adopted industrial communication protocol that provides a platform-independent, service-oriented architecture for exchanging information in the industrial automation space. It aims to ensure interoperability and security. Time-Sensitive Networking (TSN): TSN standards enhance Ethernet to make it suitable for time-sensitive applications, such as industrial automation and control systems. TSN can provide precise synchronization and low-latency communication, critical for certain sensor applications. Apache Kafka: Kafka is a distributed event streaming platform that can be used as middleware for real-time data streaming and processing. It is being adopted in various industries, including IoT, for its ability to handle large volumes of data and provide scalable, fault-tolerant communication.

APPLICATIONS OF IOT TECHNOLOGY

The adoption of IOT has a significant social impact across various domain. The promise of IoT applications to boost productivity, make better decisions, and develop new business models is evident in their implementation across a wide range of industries. These noteworthy IoT uses span a variety of industries (Korade, A., et al. 2019). Internet of Things technology has already found commercial use in areas such as smart parking (Saini, P., et al. 2023), precision agriculture (Yarahmadi, H., et al. 2023), and water usage management (Ma, J., et al. 2023). Extensive research has also been conducted into the use of IoT for developing intelligent systems in areas including traffic congestion minimization (Shihab, S., et al.. 2023), structural health monitoring (Shourie, P., et al. 2023), crash-avoiding cars (Patil, R., et al. 2023) and smart grids (Manual, V., et al. 2023).

(a) **Smart home Automation**: Cameras and sensors connected to the Internet of Things in home security systems. Appliances that are automated like ovens, washing machines, refrigerators, and Smart thermostats for energy-efficient climate management are helpful for a smart life (Salman, A. 2020).
(b) **Healthcare**: IoT Devices are implemented for Monitoring Chronic illness remote patients. IoT Devices like Wearable gadgets for health monitoring and fitness tracking are used to monitor health. Sensitivity-enabled smart tablets that monitor drug compliance.

(c) **Industrial IoT**: Real-time product tracking combined with supply chain optimization. Robotics and automation in industry are implemented to increase productivity. Predictive maintenance for gear and apparatus is also done by IoT Devices.

(d) **Agriculture**: Precision farming that monitors soil conditions and uses Internet of Things sensors for irrigation. Monitoring makes it simple to analyze the health and behavior of livestock. Smart greenhouse controls adjust temperature and humidity.

(e) **Smart Cities**: Using technology to reduce traffic jams through traffic management systems. Energy-saving automated street lighting. IoT devices are managing garbage using connected containers to create effective routes for pickup.

(f) **Retails**: Internet of Things devices that use inventory management and RFID-based tracking. It is simple to use beacon technology to create personalized in-store marketing. To make shopping easier and more efficient, smart shelves and carts are used.

(g) **Energy Management**: Intelligent power distribution systems can be designed for this purpose. Consumer energy management systems could be implemented at home. Controlling and keeping an eye on renewable energy sources.

(h) **Transportation**: Vehicles that are networked for real-time navigation and traffic. Fleet management with Internet of Things-enabled diagnostics and tracking can be done properly. Smart parking options can be implemented to maximize the use of available parking spaces.

(i) **Logistics and supply chain**: IoT Technologies could be used for monitoring the cold chain for perishable items. Asset tracking for real-time shipping visibility can be enhanced. Inventory control with IoT and RFID sensors can be done.

(j) **Environmental Monitoring**: Water and air quality are tracked using Internet of Things devices. Wildlife monitoring and conservation can be aided by IoT devices. Early warning systems for natural disasters can be created. It would be simpler to implement building automation. HVAC (Heating, ventilation, and air conditioning) systems with intelligence are used to cut energy usage. It is also possible to implement occupancy- and daylight-based lighting control. IoT technology in security systems enables access control and cameras.

(k) **Wearable Technology**: Integrated sensors in smartwatches can be used to manage fitness and health tracking. Information can be accessed hands-free with augmented reality (AR) glasses. Smart grids oversee and manage the distribution of power. The system can be expanded to include renewable energy sources. Energy-efficient demand response systems would be simpler to implement. These illustrations show the broad diversity

Applications and Gadgets for the IoT Healthcare System

Current technologies demonstrate that a healthcare Internet of Things system also has to have effective communication. Short-range communications, such as Bluetooth are proposed in several current system models (Ramzan, R., et al. 2023, Alsaig, A., & Alagar, V., 2023, Sajjan, R., et al. 2023) for the processing of sensor data once it is transferred to a smartphone.

Now in this book chapter, we are going to discuss the several uses of Internet of Things (IoT) devices in the healthcare industry, which can lead to better patient care, more effective monitoring, and more efficient delivery of healthcare. The following are a few noteworthy uses of IoT devices in the medical field:

Figure 5. Applications of IoT

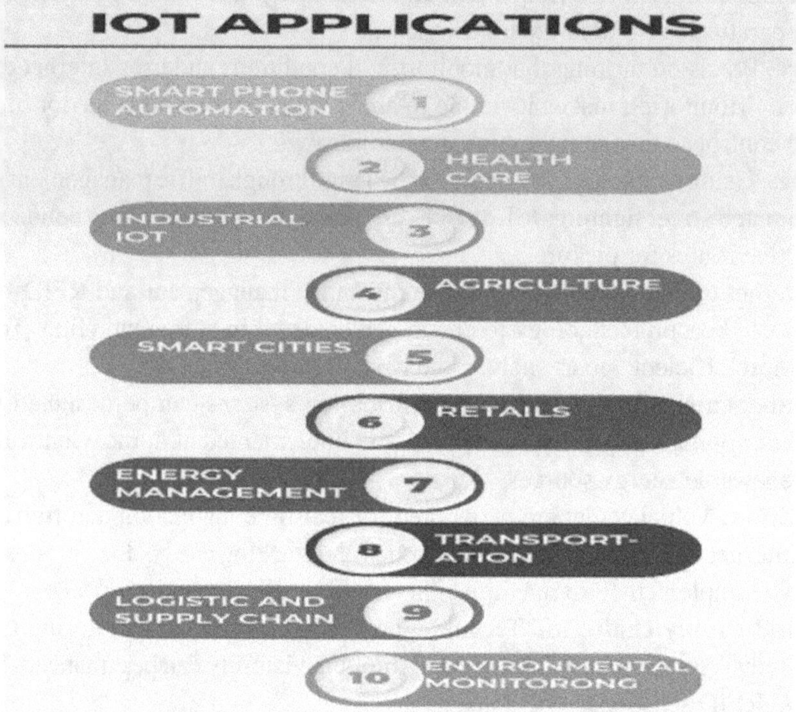

a. Remote Patient Monitoring: Wearable with the Internet of Things capabilities, including fitness trackers and smartwatches, may keep a watch on activity levels, vital signs, and other health indicators. This enables medical professionals to monitor patients' health problems from a distance and take appropriate action as needed.
b. Telehealth and Telemedicine: Internet of Things (IoT) permits patients and medical professionals to consult virtually, enabling instant access to medical advice and avoiding the need for in-person visits. Through connected medical devices like glucometers, blood pressure monitors, and scales, IoT devices enable remote monitoring of patients with chronic illnesses [Kumar, M. et al. 2024; Hong, Y. G., et al. 2015].
c. Adherence to Medication: Smart Internet of Things (IoT)-enabled pill dispensers have the ability to remind patients to take their prescriptions, distribute the right dosage, and inform caregivers or medical professionals in the event that adherence problems arise.
d. Elderly Care and Fall Detection: Wearable Sensors IoT gadgets can identify falls in senior citizens. In the case of a fall, wearable sensors can transmit notifications to emergency services or caregivers, guaranteeing prompt action.
e. Asset and Inventory Management: Internet of Things (IoT) technology, including RFID tags, support better inventory control by helping healthcare facilities track and manage medications, medical supplies, and equipment.

f. Hospital Operations and Efficiency: IoT devices help to build smart hospitals by maximizing energy use, boosting overall operational efficiency, and facilitating better equipment maintenance through predictive analytics.
g. Patient Engagement: Personalized health information, medication reminders, and lifestyle advice to promote better choices are just a few ways that IoT applications can help.
h. Biometric authentication: In the context of healthcare settings, biometric authentication is facilitated by IoT devices equipped with biometric sensors, which also improve security and access management. Systems for patient identity and safe data access can be implemented using fingerprint or face recognition.
i. Infection Control: These devices can track how medical equipment is used, keep it clean, and make sure that hygiene procedures are followed.
j. Clinical Trials and Research: These devices help collect real-time data during clinical trials, enabling researchers to monitor participants remotely and gather more thorough and timely information.
k. Emergency Response: IoT-enabled Emergency Services are provided by these devices, integrated into emergency response systems, assisting in the rapid location of patients, providing medical history information and facilitating a more effective response in times of need. The potential benefits of IoT devices are integration in healthcare.

In order to provide better medical treatment, IoT devices create an online medical decision support system for forecasting chronic kidney failure. Their method of forecasting chronic kidney illnesses involves several processes, including gathering, pre-processing, and classifying medical data (Rahul, A. 2015).

Stakeholders in IoT ecosystem: The Internet of Things (IoT) ecosystem involves a wide range of stakeholders who play different roles in the development, deployment, and use of IoT technologies. Here are some key stakeholders in the IoT ecosystem: Device Manufacturers: Companies that design, produce, and supply IoT devices such as sensors, actuators, and other connected hardware.

Network Providers: Telecom companies and Internet Service Providers (ISPs) that offer the connectivity infrastructure for IoT devices to communicate with each other and with the cloud. Platform Providers: Companies that develop and maintain IoT platforms, which serve as the backbone for managing and analyzing data from connected devices.

l. Cloud Service Providers: Organizations that offer cloud computing services for storage, processing, and analysis of large volumes of IoT data.
m. Application Developers: Individuals or companies that create software applications and services that leverage data from IoT devices to provide specific functionalities and solutions. Data Analytics and AI Providers: Companies that specialize in analyzing and deriving insights from the vast amount of data generated by IoT devices. Artificial Intelligence (AI) and Machine Learning (ML) play a crucial role in making sense of this data.
n. Regulatory Bodies: Government agencies and regulatory bodies that establish and enforce standards and regulations related to IoT to ensure security, privacy, and interoperability.
o. End Users: Individuals or organizations that use IoT devices and applications to gain specific benefits, such as improved efficiency, cost savings, or enhanced user experiences.
p. System Integrators: Companies that specialize in integrating various IoT components, including hardware, software, and networking, to create comprehensive solutions for specific industries or use cases.

Figure 6. Application and Gadgets for the IoT Healthcare System Industry

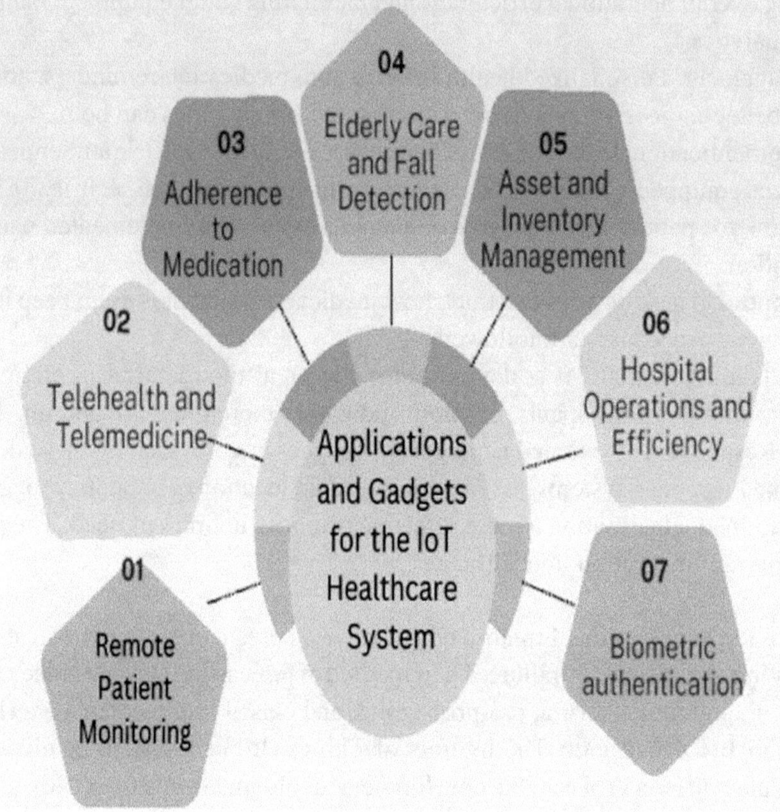

q. Security Providers: Organizations that focus on developing and implementing security solutions to safeguard IoT devices, networks, and data from cyber threats.
r. Privacy Advocates: Individuals or groups that advocate for user privacy and work towards ensuring that IoT systems are designed and implemented with privacy considerations in mind. Standards Organizations: Groups that develop and promote standards for IoT to facilitate interoperability, compatibility, and security across different devices and platforms.
s. Investors and Financial Institutions: Entities that provide funding and financial support for the development and growth of IoT-related businesses and initiatives.
t. Maintenance and Support Services: Companies that offer maintenance, support, and update services for IoT devices and systems to ensure their proper functioning over time.
u. Environmental and Sustainability Groups: Organizations concerned with the environmental impact of IoT technologies and work towards promoting sustainable practices in the design, manufacturing, and usage of IoT devices. The collaboration and effective interaction among these stakeholders are crucial for the successful development and deployment of IoT solutions.

This case study shows the implementation of a Smart City project in Barcelona showcases a comprehensive integration of IoT layers to enhance urban functionality. In the Sensing Layer, Barcelona deployed an extensive network of sensors, encompassing environmental sensors, traffic cameras, waste management sensors, and smart lighting systems. This layer systematically collected real-time data pertaining to air quality, traffic patterns, waste levels, and energy consumption.

In the Communication Layer, the city established high-speed communication networks, including Wi-Fi, LoRaWAN, and 4G/5G, ensuring seamless connectivity between sensors and central data processing units. The interplay within this layer facilitated the swift transfer of real-time data from sensors to the cloud, thereby enabling prompt decision-making.

The Data Processing and Analytics Layer employed a robust cloud-based platform to aggregate and process data collected from sensors. Utilizing advanced analytics tools and machine learning algorithms, this layer correlated information from diverse sources, identifying patterns and trends. For instance, it analyzed traffic data to optimize signal timings and alleviate congestion.

The Application and Service Layer featured the development of various applications and services accessible to citizens through mobile devices and online platforms. These offerings included real-time traffic updates, waste collection schedules, and smart parking solutions. Citizens could interact with these services based on insights derived from the data. For example, citizens received alerts on air quality, and traffic management services helped optimize commuting routes.

The Security and Privacy Layer implemented robust cybersecurity measures to safeguard data at each layer. Privacy policies were established to ensure the ethical use of citizens' information. The interplay within this layer was integral to maintaining citizen trust and compliance with data protection regulations.

The outcomes of this integrated approach were significant. Efficient Resource Management was achieved through optimized waste collection routes, reduced energy consumption via smart lighting, and improved traffic flow. Enhanced Quality of Life was realized as citizens benefited from real-time information, enabling informed decisions about transportation, air quality, and city services. Furthermore, the project fostered an Innovation Ecosystem, with businesses developing new applications and services based on the open data provided by the city. This case study underscores how the successful interplay among various IoT layers contributed to the transformation of Barcelona into a smart city, delivering tangible benefits to both the city administration and its residents.

Although there are some industry-specific IoT use cases, many of the most common deployments involving connected technologies transcend any particular vertical and can be found across a wide range of organizations.

The benefits that come with those deployments similarly across industries.

Industry feedback includes the following Lower operational costs, Enhanced productivity, Optimized output, increased security, improved safety, personalized service, Better quality control, Heightened understanding and visibility into real-world activities

CONCLUSION

In conclusion, the chapter highlights the significance of addressing security concerns in IoT systems and emphasizes the CIA security model, focusing on data confidentiality, integrity, and availability. Implementing robust security measures is crucial to unlock the full potential of IoT applications and ensure their positive impact on various aspects of our lives. The architecture of IoT, although not standardized, revolves around key layers such as perception, transportation, and application. The evolution from a 3-layer architecture to a 7-layer architecture demonstrates the ongoing refinement and adaptation of IoT models based on protocols and industry requirements.

The components and technologies that constitute IoT, including sensors and actuators, connectivity options, IoT platforms, cloud computing, edge computing, security measures, data analytics, machine learning, and various protocols and standards, collectively contribute to the versatility and efficiency of IoT applications. The latter part of the chapter delves into the extensive applications of IoT devices in the healthcare industry. From remote patient monitoring to telehealth, adherence to medication, elderly care, asset and inventory management, hospital operations, patient engagement, biometric authentication, infection control, clinical trials, and emergency response, IoT devices offer a wide array of benefits in healthcare. Notably, the integration of IoT devices in healthcare facilitates an online medical decision support system for forecasting chronic kidney failure, showcasing their potential to improve medical treatment.

Despite the promising outlook, the chapter underscores the importance of addressing security challenges in IoT to fully realize the benefits outlined. Overall, the potential of IoT applications in enhancing our lives, especially in healthcare, is significant, and continued research and development in security measures will play a crucial role in unlocking this potential.

REFERENCES

Al-Kahtani, M. S., Khan, F., & Taekeun, W. (2022). Application of internet of things and sensors in healthcare. *Sensors (Basel)*, *22*(15), 5738. doi:10.3390/s22155738 PMID:35957294

Al-Kashoash, H. A., & Kemp, A. H. (2016). Comparison of 6LoWPAN and LPWAN for the Internet of Things. *Australian Journal of Electrical and Electronics Engineering*, *13*(4), 268–274. doi:10.1080/1448837X.2017.1409920

Alsaig, A., & Alagar, V. (2023, August). Dependable Service-Oriented Design of Healthcare IoT. In *2023 IEEE International Conference on Smart Internet of Things (SmartIoT)* (pp. 257-264). IEEE. 10.1109/SmartIoT58732.2023.00046

Angrishi, K. (2017). Turning internet of things (iot) into internet of vulnerabilities (iov): Iot botnets. *arXiv preprint arXiv:1702.03681.*

Ashokrao, P. R., Radhakrishna, D. D., Sharma, M., & Bhad, S. (2023, May). Health Disease Prediction Using Machine Learning and Internet of Things. In *2023 4th International Conference on Intelligent Engineering and Management (ICIEM)* (pp. 1-6). IEEE. 10.1109/ICIEM59379.2023.10165903

Bruce, Z. (2017, February, 9). Overview of networking technologies used to build IoT solutions. *Intelligent CIO*. https://www.intelligenttechchannels.com/2017/02/09/overview-of-networking-technologies-used-to-build-iot-solutions/

Cekerevac, Z., Dvorak, Z., Prigoda, L., & Cekerevac, P. (2017). Internet of things and the man-in-the-middle attacks–security and economic risks. *MEST Journal*, *5*(2), 15–25. doi:10.12709/mest.05.05.02.03

Dange, S., & Chatterjee, M. (2019). IoT botnet: The largest threat to the IoT network. In *Data Communication and Networks* [Singapore: Springer Singapore.]. *Proceedings of GUCON*, *2019*, 137–157.

Dawood, M. S., Margaret, M. J., & Devika, R. (2018). Review on applications of internet of things (IoT). [IJARCET]. *International Journal of Advanced Research in Computer Engineering and Technology*, *7*(12).

dos Santos, Y. L., & Dias Canedo, E. (2019). On the design and implementation of an IoT based architecture for reading ultra high frequency tags. *Information (Basel)*, *10*(2), 41. doi:10.3390/info10020041

Ech-Chaitami, T., Mrabet, R., & Berbia, H. (2011). Interoperability of LoWPANs Based on the IEEE802. 15.4 Standard through IPV6. [IJCSI]. *International Journal of Computer Science Issues*, *8*(2), 315.

Ergen, S. C. (2004). ZigBee/IEEE 802.15. 4 Summary. *UC Berkeley, September, 10*(17), 11.

Fruhlinger, J. (2018). The Mirai botnet explained: How teen scammers and CCTV cameras almost brought down the internet. *CSO online, 9.*

Goodin, D. (2017, October 28). Assessing the threat, the Reaper botnet poses to the Internet—what we know now. *Ars Technica*. https://arstechnica.com/information-technology/2017/10/assessing-the-threat-the-reaper-botnet-poses-to-the-internet-what-we-know-now/

Gupta, P., Sinha, A., & Srivastava, Kr., P., Perti, A., & Singh, A. K. (2021). Security implementations in IoT using digital signature. In *Innovations in Electrical and Electronic Engineering: Proceedings of ICEEE 2020* (pp. 523-535). Springer Singapore. 22.

Howell, J. (2017). Number of connected iot devices will surge to 125 billion by 2030, ihs markit says. *IHS Markit Technology*, (Oct), 24.

Hudson, B. (2014). *Advanced persistent threats: Detection, protection and prevention. Sophos Ltd.* US February.

Iqbal, M. A., Olaleye, O. G., &Bayoumi, M. A. (2017). A review on the Internet of Things (IoT): security and privacy requirements and the solution approaches. *Global Journal of Computer Science and Technology*.

Kaur, M., Sandhu, M., Mohan, N., & Sandhu, P. S. (2011). RFID technology principles, advantages, limitations & its applications. *International Journal of Computer and Electrical Engineering*, *3*(1), 151–157. doi:10.7763/IJCEE.2011.V3.306

Kolias, C., Kambourakis, G., Stavrou, A., & Voas, J. (2017). DDoS in the IoT: Mirai and other botnets. *Computer*, *50*(7), 80–84. doi:10.1109/MC.2017.201

Korade, S., Kotak, V., & Durafe, A. (2019). A review paper on internet of things (IoT) and its applications. *Int. Res. J. Eng. Technol*, *6*(6), 1623–1630.

Kumar, M., Kim, C., Son, Y., Singh, S. K., & Kim, S. (2024). Empowering Cyberattack Identification in IoHT Networks With Neighborhood Component-based Improvised Long Short-Term Memory. *IEEE Internet of Things Journal*, 1. doi:10.1109/JIOT.2024.3354988

Kumar, S., Tiwari, P., & Zymbler, M. (2019). Internet of Things is a revolutionary approach.Salman, A. (2020, September 28). Internet of Things (IoT) and its Applications: A Survey. *International Journal of Computer Applications*. doi:10.5120/ijca202091991

Kushner, D. (2013). The real story of stuxnet. *ieee. IEEE Spectrum*, *50*(3), 48–53. doi:10.1109/MSPEC.2013.6471059

Ma, J., Zhang, J., Shen, G., Marshall, A., & Chang, C. H. (2023, May). White-Box Adversarial Attacks on Deep Learning-Based Radio Frequency Fingerprint Identification. In *ICC 2023-IEEE International Conference on Communications* (pp. 3714-3719). IEEE. 10.1109/ICC45041.2023.10278927

Madakam, S., & Date, H. (2016). Security mechanisms for connectivity of smart devices in the internet of things. *Connectivity Frameworks for Smart Devices: The Internet of Things from a Distributed Computing Perspective*. Research Gate.

Manjula, V., & Vijayabanu, C. (2023, April). Predicting the Application of Internet of Things (IoT) a New Wave of Technology for Smart Health Care. In *2023 International Conference on Inventive Computation Technologies (ICICT)* (pp. 1343-1350). IEEE. 10.1109/ICICT57646.2023.10134279

Mansour, M., Gamal, A., Ahmed, A. I., Said, L. A., Elbaz, A., Herencsar, N., & Soltan, A. (2023). Internet of Things: A Comprehensive Overview on Protocols, Architectures, Technologies, Simulation Tools, and Future Directions. *Energies*, *16*(8), 3465. doi:10.3390/en16083465

Mendez, D. M., Papapanagiotou, I., & Yang, B. (2017). Internet of things: Survey on security and privacy. *arXiv preprint arXiv:1707.01879.*

Narendra, P., Duquennoy, S., & Voigt, T. (2016). BLE and IEEE 802.15. 4 in the IoT: Evaluation and Interoperability Considerations. In *Internet of Things. IoT Infrastructures: Second International Summit, IoT 360° 2015, Rome, Italy, October 27-29, 2015, Revised Selected Papers, Part II* (pp. 427-438). Springer International Publishing.

Nordrum, A. (2016). *Popular Internet of Things Forecast of 50 Billion Devices by 2020 is Outdated*. IEEE.

Papapanagiotou, I., Toumpakaris, D., Lee, J., & Devetsikiotis, M. (2009). A survey on next generation mobile WiMAX networks: Objectives, features and technical challenges. *IEEE Communications Surveys and Tutorials*, *11*(4), 3–18. doi:10.1109/SURV.2009.090402

Park, J. H., Yotxay, S., Singh, S. K., & Park, J. H. (2024). PoAh-Enabled Federated Learning Architecture for DDoS Attack Detection in IoT Networks. *HumCentric Comput. Inf. Sci, 14*(3).

Parmar, J. K., & Desai, A. (2016). IoT: Networking technologies and research challenges. *International Journal of Computer Applications*, *154*(7), 1–6. doi:10.5120/ijca2016912181

Rahul, A., Rao, S., & Raghu, M. E. (2015). Near field communication (NFC) technology: A survey. [IJCI]. *International Journal on Cybernetics & Informatics*, *4*(2), 133–144. doi:10.5121/ijci.2015.4213

Ramzan, R., Beg, A., Jawed, S. A., Aaquib, M., & Junaid, M. (2023, September). Quadrature RF-Only Logic Family for Single-Chip Self-Powered Transceivers. In *2023 IEEE 36th International System-on-Chip Conference (SOCC)* (pp. 1-5). IEEE. 10.1109/SOCC58585.2023.10256996

Ray, P. P. (2018). A survey on Internet of Things architectures. *Journal of King Saud University. Computer and Information Sciences*, *30*(3), 291–319. doi:10.1016/j.jksuci.2016.10.003

Razzak, F. (2012). Spamming the Internet of Things: A Possibility and its probable Solution. *Procedia Computer Science*, *10*, 658–665. doi:10.1016/j.procs.2012.06.084

Rejeb, A., Rejeb, K., Treiblmaier, H., Appolloni, A., Alghamdi, S., Alhasawi, Y., & Iranmanesh, M. (2023). The Internet of Things (IoT) in healthcare: Taking stock and moving forward. *Internet of Things : Engineering Cyber Physical Human Systems, 22*, 100721. doi:10.1016/j.iot.2023.100721

Saini, P., Gupta, L., & Malhotra, S. (2023, June). Internet of Medical Things: Current Applications, Challenges and Future. In *2023 International Conference on IoT, Communication and Automation Technology (ICICAT)* (pp. 1-5). IEEE. 10.1109/ICICAT57735.2023.10263636

Sajjan, R., Chaturvedi, T., Bhanusghare, D., & Bansal, Y. (2023, April). ProHealth–Improvised E-Health Care System. In *2023 IEEE International Conference on Contemporary Computing and Communications (InC4)* (Vol. 1, pp. 1-6). IEEE.

Shen, G., & Liu, B. (2011, May). The visions, technologies, applications, and security issues of the Internet of Things. In *2011 International Conference on E-Business and E-Government (ICEE)* (pp. 1-4). IEEE. 10.1109/ICEBEG.2011.5881892

Shihab, S., & AlTawy, R. (2023). Lightweight Authentication Scheme for Healthcare with Robustness to Desynchronization Attacks. *IEEE Internet of Things Journal, 10*(20), 18140–18153. doi:10.1109/JIOT.2023.3279035

Shourie, P., Kumar, N., Kaushal, R. K., & Verma, S. (2023, May). IoT-based Hybrid Fitness Monitoring Device. In *2023 7th International Conference on Intelligent Computing and Control Systems (ICICCS)* (pp. 1527-1532). IEEE. 10.1109/ICICCS56967.2023.10142333

Singh, S. K., Azzaoui, A. E., Choo, K. K. R., Yang, L. T., & Park, J. H. (2023). A Comprehensive Survey on Blockchain for Secure IoT-enabled Smart City beyond 5G: Approaches, Processes, Challenges, and Opportunities. *Hum.-Centric Comput. Inf. Sci, 13*(51).

Singh, S. K., Kumar, M., Tanwar, S., & Park, J. H. (2024). GRU-based digital twin framework for data allocation and storage in IoT-enabled smart home networks. *Future Generation Computer Systems, 153*, 391–402. doi:10.1016/j.future.2023.12.009

Yarahmadi, H., Shiri, M. E., Challenger, M., Navidi, H., & Sharifi, A. (2023, June). On the Use of Multi-agent Reinforcement Learning in Cyber-physical and Internet of Thing Systems. In *2023 12th Mediterranean Conference on Embedded Computing (MECO)* (pp. 1-8). IEEE. 10.1109/MECO58584.2023.10154952

Chapter 9
Layered Architecture of IoT

Satish Kumar Maurya
U.V. Patel College of Engineering, Ganpat University, India

Om Prakash Pal
https://orcid.org/0000-0002-2074-6083
U.V. Patel College of Engineering, Ganpat University, India

Ketan Sarvakar
https://orcid.org/0000-0003-4486-0224
U.V. Patel College of Engineering, Ganpat University, India

ABSTRACT

This chapter provides a comprehensive exploration of the layered architecture on the internet of things (IoT) ecosystem. IoT has become integral to modern life, touching industries from healthcare to smart cities. The chapter begins with an introduction to IoT's significance and evolution. It then breaks down the architecture into key layers—perception, network, middleware, and application—explaining their roles, interactions, and security considerations. Real-world case studies offer practical insights, while discussions on emerging technologies and challenges provide a glimpse into IoT's future. This chapter equips readers with a fundamental understanding of IoT's layered architecture, encouraging them to participate in this dynamic field.

INTRODUCTION

Understanding the Significance of IoT Layered Architecture

As the Internet of Things (IoT) continues to revolutionize diverse industries, understanding its layered architecture becomes paramount. This chapter aims to demystify the intricacies of IoT systems by dissecting their architectural framework. By delving into the roles and interactions of key layers - Perception, Network, Middleware, and Application - readers gain insight into how IoT orchestrates seamless connectivity and data exchange. Real-world case studies illustrate the practical implications, while discussions on emerging technologies and challenges offer a glimpse into the evolving landscape of

DOI: 10.4018/979-8-3693-2373-1.ch009

IoT. Through this exploration, readers are empowered to grasp the fundamental concepts of IoT architecture, fostering their engagement and participation in this dynamic technological realm (Markendahl, Lundberg, Kordas, & Movin, 2017).

Definition of IoT (Internet of Things)

The Internet of Things, often abbreviated as IoT, is a revolutionary technological paradigm that has taken the world by storm. At its core, IoT is a network of interconnected physical objects or "things" embedded with sensors, software, and other technologies, enabling them to collect and exchange data with other devices and systems over the internet. These "things" can be anything from household appliances and industrial machines to wearable devices and vehicles. The essence of IoT lies in the seamless communication and collaboration between these devices, resulting in an unprecedented level of automation, data-driven decision-making, and connectivity.

Significance and Pervasiveness of IoT in Today's World

The significance and pervasiveness of IoT in the contemporary world cannot be overstated. IoT has transcended its initial promise to become an integral part of our daily lives, shaping industries, enhancing efficiency, and fostering innovation. In today's interconnected world, IoT manifests its importance in various domains, including:

1. Smart Cities: IoT is the backbone of smart city initiatives, enabling efficient traffic management, waste collection, and resource optimization. It enhances the quality of urban life by providing real-time information to city planners and residents.
2. Healthcare: Wearable health devices and IoT-enabled medical equipment are revolutionizing healthcare. Remote monitoring of patients, early disease detection, and personalized treatments are now possible, improving patient outcomes.
3. Agriculture: IoT facilitates precision agriculture by monitoring soil conditions, weather patterns, and crop health. Farmers can make data-driven decisions to increase yields and reduce resource usage.
4. Manufacturing: Industrial IoT (IIoT) has transformed manufacturing processes. Factories now operate with higher efficiency, reduced downtime, and predictive maintenance, resulting in cost savings and improved product quality.
5. Environmental Monitoring: IoT is used to monitor and combat climate change. Sensors collect data on air and water quality, helping us make informed decisions to protect the environment.
6. Retail: IoT enhances customer experiences by enabling smart shelves, inventory tracking, and personalized marketing. It's changing the way we shop both online and in physical stores.

The prevalence of IoT is evident in smart homes, connected cars, and wearable devices that have become ubiquitous. The global IoT market is experiencing exponential growth, with an ever-expanding ecosystem of devices and applications.

Purpose of the Chapter: Exploring the Layered Architecture of IoT

The purpose of this chapter is to provide readers with an in-depth understanding of the layered architecture of IoT. While the significance of IoT is clear, its underlying architecture is often overlooked. To comprehend the intricacies of IoT and harness its potential, one must explore its structural framework. This chapter serves as a guide, breaking down IoT architecture into layers, which include the Perception Layer, Network Layer, Middleware Layer, and Application Layer.

Readers will gain insights into how data flows across these layers, the importance of security at each level, and the role of gateways and edge computing. Real-world case studies offer tangible examples of how layered IoT architecture is applied in practice. Furthermore, the chapter addresses future trends and challenges, ensuring that readers are equipped not only to understand IoT but also to participate in its ongoing evolution. By the end of this chapter, readers will possess a foundational knowledge of IoT's architectural structure, empowering them to navigate this dynamic and transformative field with confidence.

UNDERSTANDING IOT SYSTEMS

What is IoT?

The Internet of Things, commonly referred to as IoT, is a transformative technological concept that has reshaped the way we connect, communicate, and interact with the world around us. At its core, IoT is a network of interconnected physical objects, or "things," embedded with various sensors, software, and other technologies, which enable them to collect and exchange data with other devices and systems over the internet. These objects can range from everyday household appliances and industrial machines to wearable devices and vehicles. IoT brings these diverse entities together to create a seamless, data-driven ecosystem where information flows freely and interactions occur without human intervention (Nandyala & Kim, 2016).

Brief History and Evolution of IoT

The history of IoT can be traced back to the early 1980s, with the concept of networked devices and smart systems. However, it was in the late 1990s and early 2000s that the term "Internet of Things" began to gain prominence. The evolution of IoT can be summarized in the following key phases:

1. Emergence of RFID and Sensor Technologies: RFID (Radio-Frequency Identification) and sensor technologies paved the way for IoT by allowing the identification and tracking of objects and environmental parameters. These technologies laid the foundation for object connectivity.
2. The Birth of IoT Standards: The need for interoperability and standards became evident as the number of connected devices grew. The development of communication protocols like MQTT, CoAP, and the IPv6 addressing scheme standardized IoT communications.
3. Proliferation of Smart Devices: The early 2010s witnessed the rapid proliferation of smart devices, such as smartphones, wearable technology, and connected appliances. This marked the expansion of IoT into daily life.

4. Industrial IoT (IIoT): The industrial sector adopted IoT technologies to improve automation, monitor equipment, and enhance operational efficiency. IIoT has transformed manufacturing, energy, and logistics.
5. Smart Cities and Environmental Monitoring: IoT has played a crucial role in the development of smart cities, enhancing urban services, sustainability, and citizen engagement. Environmental monitoring solutions, powered by IoT, help combat climate change.
6. Healthcare and Wearables: The healthcare industry has embraced IoT through the use of wearable health devices and remote monitoring, resulting in improved patient care and outcomes.

Key Characteristics of IoT Systems:

Understanding the key characteristics of IoT systems is vital for grasping their impact and potential. Several defining features set IoT apart:

1. Connectivity: IoT thrives on connectivity. Devices can communicate with each other, cloud platforms, and end-users, enabling real-time data exchange.
2. Sensors and Data: Sensors are the heart of IoT. They gather data on a wide range of parameters, from temperature and location to heart rate and machine status. This data is the lifeblood of IoT systems.
3. Automation: IoT allows for automation and intelligent decision-making. Devices can react to changing conditions, reducing human intervention and improving efficiency.
4. Scalability: IoT systems can scale easily to accommodate a growing number of devices and applications, making it adaptable to various use cases.
5. Security and Privacy: IoT faces significant security and privacy challenges. Protecting data, preventing unauthorized access, and ensuring privacy are critical considerations.
6. Interoperability: Ensuring that diverse devices and platforms can work together seamlessly is essential for IoT to achieve its full potential.

IoT represents a technological revolution that has transformed the way we interact with our environment, shaping industries, improving efficiency, and enhancing our daily lives. Its history and key characteristics underscore its significance in the contemporary digital landscape. As IoT continues to evolve, it promises a future where an even greater number of objects and systems will be connected, redefining the way we live and work.

IoT Applications

The Internet of Things (IoT) has transcended its status as a mere technological buzzword to become an integral and transformative force across numerous industries. This section explores the vast landscape of IoT applications, highlighting real-world use cases and its profound importance in various sectors, including healthcare, agriculture, and the development of smart cities11].

Figure 1 illustrates a conceptual representation of a smart city ecosystem, showcasing interconnected smart devices such as traffic lights, environmental sensors, and smart infrastructure. This visualization encapsulates the integration of various IoT technologies to enhance urban services and improve quality of life.

Figure 1. Interconnected IoT applications with smart city

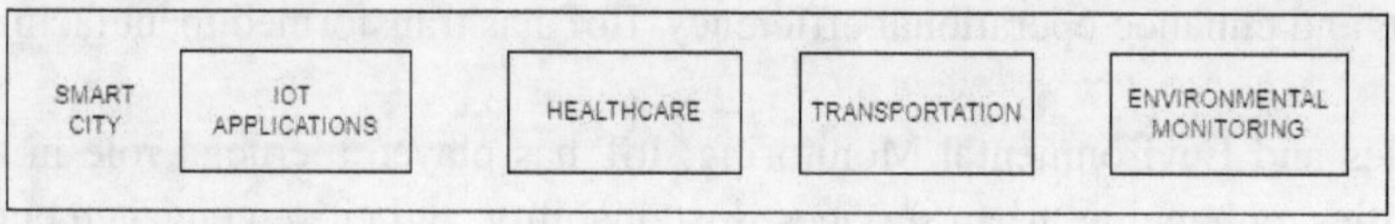

Real-World Applications and Use Cases

1. Smart Homes: One of the most visible and rapidly adopted applications of IoT is in smart homes. From connected thermostats and lighting to security systems and voice-activated assistants, IoT makes homes more efficient, secure, and convenient. For instance, a smart thermostat can learn user preferences and adjust the temperature accordingly, reducing energy consumption.
2. Wearable Technology: Wearables, such as fitness trackers and smartwatches, are revolutionizing personal health and fitness monitoring. These devices collect data on steps taken, heart rate, sleep patterns, and more, empowering individuals to make informed decisions about their health and lifestyle.
3. Industrial IoT (IIoT): In the industrial sector, IIoT plays a pivotal role in enhancing operational efficiency. IoT-enabled sensors and devices monitor equipment performance, predict maintenance needs, and optimize manufacturing processes. For instance, predictive maintenance in manufacturing can reduce downtime and save costs.
4. Agriculture: IoT is making its mark in agriculture with precision farming techniques. Farmers use IoT sensors to monitor soil conditions, weather patterns, and crop health, allowing for data-driven decisions that optimize crop yields and reduce resource usage.
5. Healthcare: IoT has transformed healthcare delivery. Remote patient monitoring, enabled by IoT, provides real-time data to healthcare providers. Wearable devices and connected medical equipment help monitor vital signs, detect anomalies, and ensure timely interventions.

Importance in Various Industries:

1. Healthcare: IoT's significance in healthcare is undeniable. The ability to monitor patients remotely, collect data on chronic conditions, and facilitate telemedicine is especially critical in an era of aging populations and the need for more accessible healthcare.
2. Agriculture: Precision agriculture not only increases crop yields but also helps to reduce the environmental impact of farming. IoT enables efficient resource utilization, reducing the need for excessive water, pesticides, and fertilizers.
3. Smart Cities: The development of smart cities relies on IoT for optimizing resource management, reducing energy consumption, and improving public services. Smart traffic management, waste collection, and environmental monitoring contribute to better urban living.
4. Manufacturing: In manufacturing, IIoT ensures equipment uptime, enhances product quality, and reduces operational costs. Predictive maintenance, data-driven process optimization, and supply chain visibility are just a few of the ways IoT is transforming the industry.

5. Transportation: IoT is changing the way we move people and goods. Connected vehicles, traffic management systems, and real-time transit information provide safer and more efficient transportation options.
6. Environmental Monitoring: IoT helps us understand and address environmental challenges, including air and water quality monitoring, climate change tracking, and wildlife conservation. This data is essential for informed decision-making.

IoT applications have infiltrated a multitude of industries, driving innovation, increasing efficiency, and improving the quality of life. From smart homes that offer convenience and energy savings to healthcare solutions that enhance patient care and well-being, the impact of IoT is profound. In agriculture, IoT is helping feed a growing global population more sustainably, while in manufacturing, it is ushering in a new era of productivity and quality. Smart cities are leveraging IoT to provide better services and a higher quality of life for urban residents, and environmental monitoring is helping us protect the planet. IoT's importance and adaptability are undeniable, making it a central player in shaping our connected future.

ARCHITECTURAL OVERVIEW

Layered Architecture Concept

The concept of layered architecture is fundamental in understanding the structure and functionality of complex systems, and in the context of the Internet of Things (IoT), it is of paramount importance. This section introduces the concept of layered architecture and explains why it is crucial in IoT (Gardašević, et al., 2017).

Introduction to the Concept of Layered Architecture:

Layered architecture, often referred to as a layered or tiered system, is a structural design pattern that divides a system into distinct, self-contained, and logically organized layers or tiers. Each layer has a specific role, and these layers work together to accomplish a common goal. This architectural approach provides several benefits, such as modularity, scalability, maintainability, and ease of understanding.

In the case of IoT, layered architecture is applied to structure and manage the complex interactions and functionalities that occur within an IoT system. An IoT system comprises a multitude of devices, sensors, networks, and applications, all of which must seamlessly collaborate. The layered architecture concept divides this system into well-defined layers, each with a specific function and level of abstraction.

Typically, an IoT layered architecture consists of four primary layers:

1. Perception Layer: This is the bottom layer, which deals with sensors and actuators. Sensors collect data from the physical world, while actuators allow the system to interact with it. The Perception Layer is responsible for gathering raw data and converting it into a digital format that can be processed.
2. Network Layer: Above the Perception Layer, the Network Layer handles data transmission and communication. It manages the connection between IoT devices and the central processing unit, often involving various communication protocols, such as Wi-Fi, Bluetooth, and cellular networks.
3. Middleware Layer: Positioned in the middle, the Middleware Layer serves as the bridge between the lower layers (Perception and Network) and the upper layer (Application). It handles data pro-

Figure 2. Layered architecture

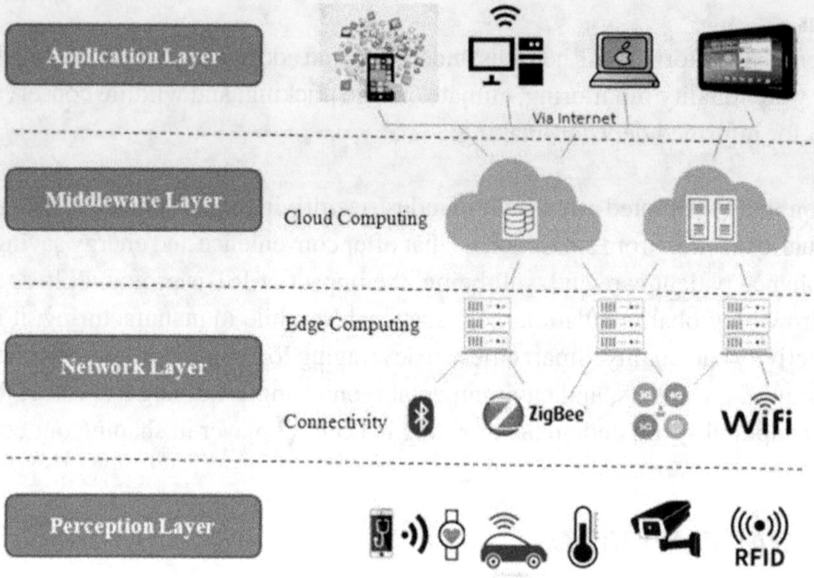

cessing, message brokering, and device management. This layer adds an abstraction that simplifies the interaction between devices and applications.

4. Application Layer: At the top of the hierarchy, the Application Layer is where end-users and external systems interact with the IoT system. This layer supports the development of IoT applications, data analysis, and user interfaces.

Why Layered Architecture is Crucial in IoT

Layered architecture is vital in the IoT context for several compelling reasons:

1. Modularization and Abstraction: By breaking down the system into well-defined layers, each layer can be developed and maintained independently. This modularity simplifies system management and allows for easier upgrades or replacements of specific components without affecting the entire system.
2. Scalability: IoT systems often need to scale up to accommodate a growing number of devices. Layered architecture supports scalability by allowing for the addition of more devices or resources at the appropriate layer without affecting the entire system.
3. Interoperability: IoT ecosystems frequently involve a variety of devices and technologies. Layered architecture, with its standardized interfaces between layers, ensures interoperability. Devices can work seamlessly with the rest of the system, regardless of their manufacturer or communication protocols.
4. Security: Security is a critical concern in IoT. Layered architecture allows for security measures to be implemented at each layer, from device-level encryption in the Perception Layer to network security and access control in the Network Layer.

Table 1. Comparison analysis of IoT layered architectures

Traditional IoT Layered Architecture	Event-Driven IoT Architecture	Three-Tier IoT Architecture	Microservices-Based IoT Architecture	Mesh IoT Architecture
This architecture typically consists of layers such as Perception, Network, Middleware, Application, and Business. It follows a hierarchical structure, ensuring a clear separation of concerns.	This architecture focuses on events or triggers, allowing devices to communicate based on specific occurrences. It emphasizes real-time responsiveness.	Comprising the Edge, Fog, and Cloud tiers, this architecture distributes processing tasks across different levels. Edge devices handle immediate processing, Fog provides intermediary processing, and Cloud manages storage and analytics.	Utilizing microservices for modular and independent components, this architecture enhances scalability and flexibility. Each function is encapsulated as a microservice.	Devices in this architecture communicate with each other, forming a mesh network. This approach is particularly beneficial for scenarios with device mobility.
Advantages: Well-established and widely used, offers simplicity and ease of understanding.	**Advantages:** Efficient in scenarios requiring quick reactions to events, suitable for time-sensitive applications.	**Advantages:** Offers a balance between local processing and centralized analytics, reducing latency.	**Advantages:** Scalable, adaptable to changing requirements, promotes system resilience.	**Advantages:** Enhanced reliability, as devices can communicate directly without relying on a centralized hub.
Limitations: May face challenges in handling the dynamic and heterogeneous nature of IoT devices.	**Limitations:** Complex event processing can introduce challenges in system complexity and resource utilization.	**Limitations:** Requires careful coordination and synchronization between tiers.	**Limitations:** Requires a robust communication infrastructure, and the management of numerous microservices can be complex.	**Limitations:** Potential challenges in scalability and managing communication overhead.

5. Flexibility and Adaptability: As technology evolves, IoT systems need to adapt. Layered architecture makes it easier to incorporate new technologies and protocols, keeping the system up to date and competitive.

Comparison Analysis of IoT Layered Architectures

Comparison Analysis

The concept of layered architecture is a cornerstone of IoT system design. It organizes the various components and functionalities, providing a structured framework for development and management. This approach ensures that IoT systems are modular, scalable, secure, and adaptable, which is essential in the dynamic and ever-expanding realm of the Internet of Things.

Table 2. Comparison analysis

Scalability	Latency	Flexibility	Resource Efficiency
Traditional and Three-Tier architectures offer good scalability, while Microservices and Mesh architectures excel in scalability due to their modular and distributed nature.	Event-Driven and Three-Tier architectures provide low-latency solutions, crucial for real-time applications.	Microservices architecture stands out for its flexibility, allowing easy adaptation to changing requirements.	Mesh architecture optimizes resource usage by enabling direct device-to-device communication.

The OSI Model and IoT

(Gupta, Tripathi, & Sharma, 2020) The OSI (Open Systems Interconnection) model is a conceptual framework that plays a crucial role in understanding network communication, including the communication processes within the Internet of Things (IoT). This section provides a brief explanation of the OSI model and explores how it can be applied to IoT (Vermesan, et al., 2022).

A Brief Explanation of the OSI Model

The OSI model is a standardized framework that defines the functions of a telecommunication or networking system. It was developed by the International Organization for Standardization (ISO) to facilitate communication between different systems and devices, regardless of their underlying technologies or protocols. The OSI model consists of seven distinct layers, each responsible for specific tasks and functions:

1. Physical Layer: This is the lowest layer, dealing with the physical connection between devices. It includes specifications for cables, connectors, and the transmission of raw binary data over a physical medium.
2. Data Link Layer: The data link layer is responsible for ensuring reliable point-to-point communication over a physical medium. It manages tasks such as addressing, error detection, and flow control.
3. Network Layer: The network layer focuses on routing data between devices in a network. It determines the best path for data packets to reach their destination and handles logical addressing and IP (Internet Protocol) addressing.
4. Transport Layer: The transport layer is responsible for end-to-end communication and ensures the integrity and reliability of data transmission. It uses protocols like TCP (Transmission Control Protocol) and UDP (User Datagram Protocol).
5. Session Layer: This layer manages and establishes sessions or connections between devices. It handles session establishment, maintenance, and termination.
6. Presentation Layer: The presentation layer is responsible for data translation, encryption, and data compression, making data from different sources compatible and secure for transmission.
7. Application Layer: The application layer is the topmost layer and provides application-specific services, such as file transfer, email, and web browsing. It interacts directly with end-user applications.

How the OSI Model Can Be Applied to IoT

The OSI model provides a structured and comprehensive approach to understanding the various layers involved in network communication, and it can be applied to IoT to illustrate the intricacies of communication within IoT systems.

1. Physical Layer: In the context of IoT, this layer involves the physical devices themselves, including sensors, actuators, and IoT endpoints. These devices collect and transmit data in their raw form, which is then prepared for communication.

2. Data Link Layer: The data link layer in IoT includes the protocols and mechanisms that ensure reliable data transfer over the physical medium. It manages addressing schemes, error checking, and ensures data integrity between devices and gateways.
3. Network Layer: In IoT, the network layer corresponds to the routing of data packets between devices and IoT gateways. This layer handles IP addressing, routing algorithms, and device discovery within the network.
4. Transport Layer: For IoT, the transport layer plays a role in ensuring the reliable and secure transfer of data between devices and applications. It may involve using protocols like MQTT (Message Queuing Telemetry Transport) for reliable messaging or CoAP (Constrained Application Protocol) for lightweight communication.
5. Session Layer: In IoT, the session layer manages the establishment and maintenance of connections between devices, gateways, and cloud-based platforms. It facilitates secure and persistent communication sessions.
6. Presentation Layer: The presentation layer in IoT is responsible for data transformation, encryption, and compression, ensuring that data is in the appropriate format and secure for transmission. Encryption and data format conversion are crucial in securing sensitive IoT data.
7. Application Layer: The application layer in IoT encompasses the various applications and services that interact with IoT devices. It includes IoT platforms, cloud-based services, and end-user applications that leverage IoT data for decision-making and control.

Applying the OSI model to IoT helps to visualize the complexity of IoT systems and the various components that work together to enable efficient and secure communication. It also highlights the importance of using appropriate protocols, addressing schemes, and security measures at each layer to ensure the reliability and functionality of IoT applications. By understanding the layered approach, developers and engineers can design IoT systems that are interoperable, secure, and scalable, while also ensuring data integrity and efficient communication between IoT devices and the wider network.

LAYERS IN IOT ARCHITECTURE

Perception Layer

The Perception Layer, a fundamental component in the layered architecture of the Internet of Things (IoT), serves as the point of entry for data from the physical world. This section delves into the definition and role of the Perception Layer, explaining the vital role of sensors and actuators within the context of IoT.

Definition and Role of the Perception Layer

The Perception Layer, often regarded as the lowest layer in the IoT architecture, is responsible for interacting with the physical world. It serves as the sensory interface, capturing data and events from the environment, and enabling IoT systems to gather information. This layer's primary function is to collect raw, real-world data and translate it into a digital format that can be processed, analyzed, and acted upon by higher layers of the IoT architecture (Aydin & Aydin, 2020).

Figure 3. Layered connectivity

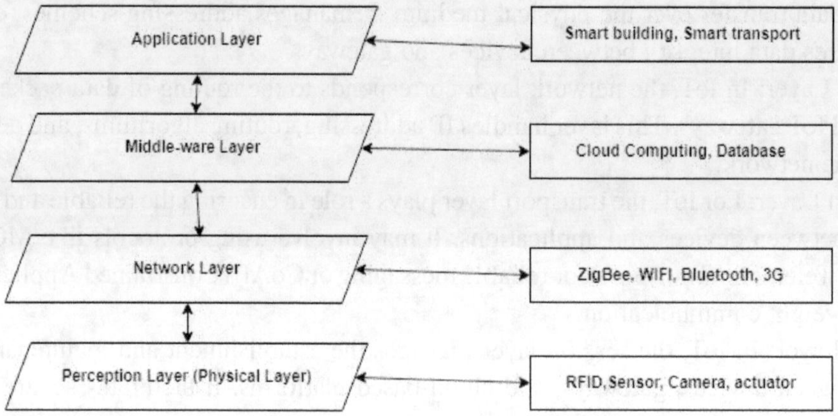

The Key Functions of the Perception Layer Include

1. Data Acquisition: Sensors and devices at this layer collect data through a variety of physical phenomena, including temperature, humidity, light, motion, pressure, and more. For example, a temperature sensor may collect data on room temperature, while a motion sensor detects movement in a space.
2. Event Detection: The Perception Layer is equipped to detect events or changes in the environment. For instance, it can recognize when a door is opened, a vehicle enters a specific area, or a light switch is turned on or off.
3. Data Conversion: The layer converts analog data, generated by sensors, into digital data that can be easily processed and transmitted by the IoT system. Analog-to-digital converters are often employed for this purpose.
4. Data Preprocessing: In some cases, data preprocessing occurs at this layer. For example, filtering or calibrating sensor data to remove noise or to ensure accuracy may be performed.

Sensors and Actuators in IoT

Sensors: Sensors are critical components in the Perception Layer. These devices are designed to detect and measure physical phenomena. There are various types of sensors employed in IoT applications, each tailored to specific use cases. Some common examples of sensors used in IoT include:

- Temperature Sensors: These sensors monitor temperature variations and are widely used for climate control in smart homes and environmental monitoring.
- Proximity Sensors: Proximity sensors detect the presence or absence of an object within a certain range. They are employed in applications such as automated doors and touchless faucets.
- Light Sensors: Light sensors, also known as photoresistors or photodiodes, detect light levels and are utilized in automatic lighting systems and outdoor lighting control.
- Motion Sensors: These sensors detect changes in motion and are used in security systems and automatic lighting systems.

- Gas Sensors: Gas sensors are employed for air quality monitoring and safety applications, such as detecting carbon monoxide or methane leaks.
- Pressure Sensors: Pressure sensors are used for measuring variations in pressure, useful in applications like tire pressure monitoring systems (TPMS) in vehicles.
- Actuators: While sensors collect data from the environment, actuators are devices within the Perception Layer responsible for taking actions based on the data received. Actuators bring the digital control provided by IoT systems into the physical world. Examples of actuators include:
- Relays: Relays are used to control high-voltage circuits or systems. They are often employed for tasks like switching lights on or off or controlling appliances.
- Motors: Electric motors are commonly used as actuators in applications such as home automation (e.g., motorized blinds) and industrial automation (e.g., conveyor belts).
- Solenoids: Solenoids are used to control linear motion. They can be found in applications like locking mechanisms or automated valve control.

Example:

Consider a smart home security system. In this system, motion sensors (a type of sensor) are strategically placed around the home to detect movement in various areas. When a motion sensor detects motion, it sends a signal to the Perception Layer of the IoT system. At this layer, the data from the sensor is processed and translated into a digital format that the IoT system can work with. The IoT system, in turn, triggers an actuator—an alarm system or camera—connected to the Perception Layer to take action based on the sensor's input. For example, the system may activate an alarm, send an alert to the homeowner's smartphone, or start recording video footage.

In this scenario, the Perception Layer plays a crucial role in collecting and processing data from the motion sensor and initiating an appropriate response through an actuator. It showcases how the Perception Layer bridges the physical world with the digital world, making IoT applications more interactive, responsive, and adaptable.

Network Layer

The Network Layer, a critical component within the layered architecture of the Internet of Things (IoT), plays a pivotal role in enabling the communication and connectivity of IoT devices. This section highlights the significance of the Network Layer in IoT and explores the protocols and communication technologies that underpin its operations, including MQTT, CoAP, and HTTP.

The Importance of the Network Layer in IoT

The Network Layer is a key element in IoT architecture, serving as the bridge between the Perception Layer (where sensors and actuators reside) and the Middleware Layer (responsible for data processing and management). Its importance in IoT can be summarized as follows:

1. Data Transmission: The Network Layer is responsible for establishing and managing connections between IoT devices and facilitating the transmission of data between them. It ensures that data collected by sensors can be efficiently transferred to other devices, gateways, and cloud platforms.

2. Interoperability: IoT devices often come from different manufacturers and may use diverse communication protocols. The Network Layer ensures interoperability, enabling devices with varying technologies to communicate seamlessly within the IoT ecosystem.
3. Reliability: In IoT, data reliability is critical. The Network Layer ensures that data packets are reliably transmitted and received, helping to prevent data loss or errors.
4. Scalability: IoT ecosystems are expected to grow, sometimes exponentially. The Network Layer must be capable of accommodating a rapidly increasing number of devices and connections, ensuring that the network remains stable and responsive.

Protocols and Communication Technologies

Various communication protocols and technologies are employed within the Network Layer of IoT to facilitate data exchange and connectivity. Here are some notable examples:

1. MQTT (Message Queuing Telemetry Transport): MQTT is a lightweight, publish-subscribe messaging protocol specifically designed for resource-constrained IoT devices. It operates on the principle of subscribing to specific topics and publishing messages to those topics. MQTT is known for its low overhead and efficient message delivery, making it suitable for remote monitoring, telemetry, and real-time applications. For instance, in a smart city application, streetlights could use MQTT to report their status, which is then subscribed to by a central control system for remote monitoring and management.
2. CoAP (Constrained Application Protocol): CoAP is a lightweight and efficient protocol designed for resource-constrained devices in IoT. It operates over the UDP (User Datagram Protocol) and is suitable for low-power, low-bandwidth devices. CoAP is commonly used in applications like smart agriculture, where sensors in the field communicate with a central server to transmit environmental data or control irrigation systems.
3. HTTP (Hypertext Transfer Protocol): While HTTP is widely known for web browsing, it is also used in IoT applications, especially when interacting with web-based services and APIs. For example, a smart home security camera may use HTTP to send video feed to a cloud storage service or to allow homeowners to access live camera streams through a web interface.
4. 6LoWPAN (IPv6 over Low-power Wireless Personal Area Networks): This protocol enables IPv6 communication over low-power wireless networks, which are commonly used in IoT. It allows IoT devices to have unique IP addresses and communicate over standard Internet protocols, making it suitable for IoT applications that require Internet connectivity, such as connected vehicles and industrial automation.

Example:

Imagine a smart agriculture application that uses IoT to monitor and control irrigation systems in a field. In this scenario, soil moisture sensors (Perception Layer) collect data on soil conditions, and actuators control irrigation valves to ensure optimal moisture levels.

The Network Layer plays a crucial role in this setup by enabling the communication between sensors and actuators. The IoT devices in the field communicate with a central irrigation controller using the CoAP protocol. The soil moisture sensors periodically send data to the controller, which, based on the received data, sends commands to the actuators to adjust the irrigation levels. The Network Layer ensures

Figure 4. MQTT architecture

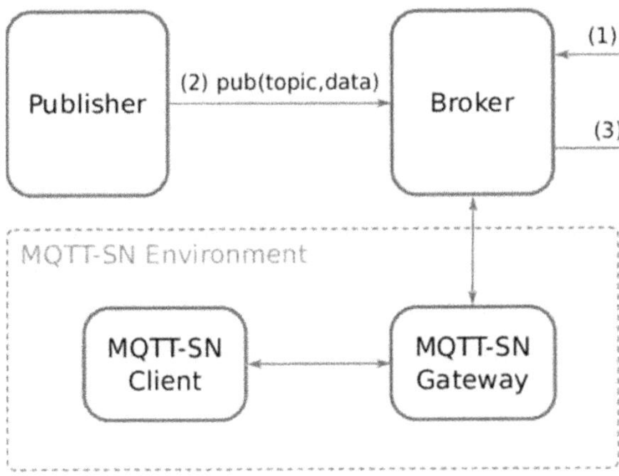

that the data from the sensors reaches the controller reliably and that the commands to the actuators are efficiently transmitted, maintaining the desired moisture levels in the field.

The use of CoAP in this example demonstrates the importance of selecting the right communication protocol for the specific needs of the IoT application, especially when dealing with resource-constrained devices and low-bandwidth networks, as is common in smart agriculture and many other IoT applications. The Network Layer's role is pivotal in orchestrating this communication and ensuring the reliability and efficiency of data transfer in IoT ecosystems.

Middleware Layer

(Singh, Pan, & Park, Blockchain-enabled Secure Framework for Energy-Efficient Smart Parking in Sustainable City Environment, 2022) The Middleware Layer, positioned between the Network Layer and the Application Layer in the layered architecture of the Internet of Things (IoT), plays a crucial role

Figure 5. CoAP and HTTP connectivity

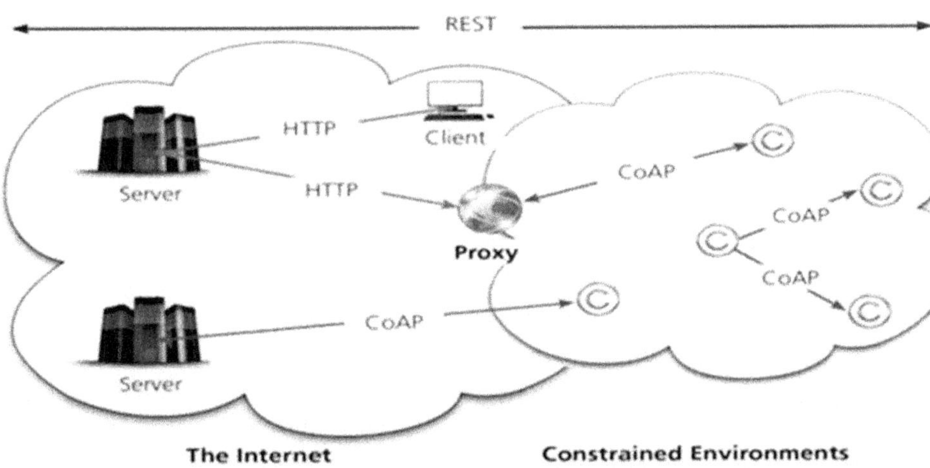

in processing and managing the data generated by IoT devices. This section delves into the functions of the Middleware Layer and its role in message brokering and data processing, illustrated with an example.

Functions of the Middleware Layer in IoT

The Middleware Layer in IoT performs a wide array of critical functions that are essential for the efficient and reliable operation of IoT ecosystems. Its primary functions include:

1. Data Processing: The Middleware Layer is responsible for processing the raw data collected from sensors in the Perception Layer. This processing may involve data aggregation, filtering, transformation, and normalization to ensure that the data is in a usable and consistent format for analysis and action.
2. Data Storage: Processed data is often stored in databases or other storage systems within the Middleware Layer. This allows for historical data analysis, trend monitoring, and retrieval when needed for decision-making or reporting.
3. Message Brokering: The Middleware Layer facilitates communication and message exchange between IoT devices, applications, and services. It acts as a message broker, routing messages to their intended destinations. This function is vital in enabling devices to communicate without needing direct connections to each other.
4. Device Management: IoT device management, such as configuration, updates, and security, is often handled by the Middleware Layer. It allows for remote device management and control, ensuring that devices operate efficiently and securely.
5. Security and Access Control: The Middleware Layer is responsible for implementing security measures, including authentication, authorization, and encryption, to protect the data and communication within the IoT ecosystem.
6. Scalability and Load Balancing: As the IoT ecosystem grows, the Middleware Layer can distribute the workload and manage the scalability of the system. It ensures that the system can handle an increasing number of devices and messages effectively.

Message Brokering and Data Processing

Message brokering and data processing are two core functions of the Middleware Layer that ensure data flows efficiently and is acted upon appropriately within IoT ecosystems.

Message Brokering: Message brokering involves routing messages between IoT devices, applications, and services. It operates on the publish-subscribe model, where devices publish messages to specific topics, and subscribers receive messages from those topics. This model decouples the sender and receiver, allowing for more flexible and efficient communication.

For example, in a smart city application, environmental sensors across the city may publish air quality data to specific topics. Different city departments, such as traffic management and environmental control, subscribe to these topics. When the sensors detect poor air quality, they publish this information to the relevant topic. Subscribers, in this case, can take action, such as adjusting traffic signals and activating air purification systems, based on the air quality data they receive.

Data Processing: Data processing involves transforming and analyzing the data collected from IoT devices. This can include real-time analytics to derive actionable insights and historical data analysis to identify trends and patterns.

In an industrial IoT (IIoT) setting, data from sensors on manufacturing equipment can be processed in real-time to detect anomalies and trigger maintenance alerts. Additionally, historical data analysis can reveal patterns that help optimize machine performance and reduce downtime.

Example:

Consider a smart building management system, where IoT sensors monitor temperature, occupancy, and lighting conditions within the building. The Middleware Layer in this system plays a pivotal role in data processing and message brokering.

- Data Processing: The Middleware Layer processes the raw sensor data, aggregating information from multiple sensors to provide a comprehensive view of building conditions. It may analyze the data to determine if temperature and lighting levels are within predefined ranges for energy efficiency. If not, the Middleware Layer can initiate actions, such as adjusting the HVAC system or lighting.
- Message Brokering: When an occupancy sensor detects that a meeting room is vacant, it publishes a message indicating room availability to a specific topic. Subscribers, such as the room booking system and facility management applications, receive this message. If someone schedules a meeting in the room, the room booking system subscribes to the topic and reserves the room accordingly, optimizing space utilization.

This example illustrates how the Middleware Layer processes data and facilitates communication between IoT devices and applications, enabling smart building management that improves energy efficiency and space utilization. It underscores the importance of these functions in ensuring IoT ecosystems are responsive and capable of taking informed actions based on the data collected from various sensors and devices.

Application Layer

How the application layer interfaces with end-users or other systems

Development of IoT applications

The Application Layer is the uppermost layer in the layered architecture of the Internet of Things (IoT). It is where the interaction between IoT systems and end-users or other external systems takes place. This section explores how the Application Layer interfaces with end-users and external systems and delves into the development of IoT applications, all illustrated with an example.

How the Application Layer Interfaces With End-Users or Other Systems

The Application Layer in IoT serves as the interface between the IoT ecosystem and its end-users or external systems. Its primary functions include:

1. User Interaction: The Application Layer provides a user-friendly interface through which end-users can interact with and control IoT devices and systems. This interface can take the form of web applications, mobile apps, or even voice-activated systems like virtual assistants.

2. Data Visualization: It presents data collected from IoT devices in a human-readable format. This can include charts, graphs, dashboards, and reports that help end-users make informed decisions based on the data.
3. Alerts and Notifications: The Application Layer can send alerts, notifications, and reports to end-users or external systems based on the data and events detected by IoT devices. For instance, in a smart home, if a security camera detects motion, an alert can be sent to the homeowner's smartphone.
4. Integration with External Systems: The Application Layer facilitates integration with external systems and services. This can include connecting with cloud platforms, databases, or third-party services to extend the capabilities of the IoT ecosystem.

Development of IoT Applications

Developing IoT applications at the Application Layer involves several key considerations:

1. Data Handling: IoT applications must be able to handle a large volume of data generated by sensors and devices. This requires efficient data storage, processing, and retrieval mechanisms to ensure that data is accessible when needed.
2. User Experience: The user interface of IoT applications should be intuitive, responsive, and user-friendly. This includes designing mobile apps or web interfaces that allow users to monitor and control IoT devices with ease.
3. Security: IoT applications must implement robust security measures to protect data and ensure the privacy and safety of users. This involves user authentication, data encryption, and access control.
4. Scalability: As IoT ecosystems grow, applications must be scalable to accommodate an increasing number of devices and users. This scalability is essential to maintain system performance and responsiveness.
5. Integration: IoT applications often need to integrate with other services and systems, including cloud platforms and external databases. This integration enables data analysis, automation, and external control.

Example:

Let's consider a smart city application that utilizes IoT technology to improve traffic management. In this scenario, the Application Layer interfaces with both end-users and external systems to enhance the overall traffic management experience.

- User Interaction: The smart city application provides a user interface accessible through a mobile app. Citizens and commuters can use the app to check real-time traffic conditions, find available parking spaces, and plan efficient routes for their daily commute. This user interface is intuitive and provides maps, traffic alerts, and estimated travel times.
- Data Visualization: The app visualizes data from various IoT sensors, including traffic cameras, vehicle detectors, and environmental sensors. Users can view live traffic camera feeds, check congestion levels on specific routes, and receive alerts about accidents or road closures.
- Alerts and Notifications: When a severe traffic incident occurs, such as a major accident or road closure, the smart city application sends instant notifications to affected commuters, helping them find alternative routes and avoid delays.

- Integration with External Systems: The Application Layer of the smart city application integrates with external services such as mapping platforms (e.g., Google Maps), weather services, and public transportation systems. This integration enhances the app's functionality, allowing users to access comprehensive information for their daily commute.

In this example, the Application Layer of the smart city IoT application serves as the interface between the IoT infrastructure and the end-users, providing them with valuable real-time traffic information and alerts. It also integrates with external systems to offer a complete transportation solution. The development of this IoT application involves creating a user-friendly interface, ensuring data visualization, and enabling seamless integration with external services, ultimately improving traffic management and the daily commuting experience for citizens.

INTERACTIONS BETWEEN LAYERS

Data Flow Across Layers

Understanding how data flows from the Perception Layer to the Application Layer is pivotal in comprehending the operation of an Internet of Things (IoT) system. This section explains the journey of data across the layers and the crucial role played by gateways and edge computing in this process, with the help of an example.

Data Flow From the Perception Layer to the Application Layer

Data in an IoT ecosystem typically starts its journey at the Perception Layer, where sensors and actuators are located. The process of data flow across the layers can be outlined as follows:

1. Data Collection at the Perception Layer: Sensors and actuators in the Perception Layer collect data from the physical environment. For example, in an industrial IoT application, sensors on manufacturing equipment collect data on temperature, pressure, and machine status.
2. Data Preprocessing: In some cases, data preprocessing may occur at the Perception Layer. This may involve data filtering, calibration, or aggregation to ensure data accuracy and consistency.
3. Data Transmission to the Network Layer: The data, in digital form, is transmitted from the Perception Layer to the Network Layer. This transmission can occur over various communication protocols, such as Wi-Fi, Ethernet, cellular networks, or low-power wireless protocols like Zigbee or LoRa.
4. Gateways and Edge Devices: In many IoT setups, data is then forwarded to a gateway or edge computing device, positioned at the boundary between the Network Layer and the Middleware Layer. Gateways and edge devices are essential components that play a pivotal role in data processing and management. These devices are equipped with the capability to preprocess, aggregate, and filter data, reducing the load on the central system and enhancing efficiency.
5. Data Processing at the Middleware Layer: Once data reaches the Middleware Layer, it undergoes further processing, including data storage, analysis, and distribution. Middleware systems are responsible for handling data from multiple sources and ensuring it is available for applications and end-users in a format suitable for decision-making.

6. Data Presentation at the Application Layer: Processed and relevant data is then made available to the Application Layer, where it can be visualized, analyzed, and presented to end-users or integrated with external systems. IoT applications at the Application Layer use this data to provide actionable insights and control IoT devices and systems.

The Role of Gateways and Edge Computing

Gateways and edge computing are critical components in the data flow across IoT layers. They serve several important functions:

1. Data Preprocessing: Gateways and edge devices can preprocess data locally before sending it to the central system. This preprocessing includes filtering out irrelevant data, aggregating data from multiple sensors, and applying simple analytics. For instance, in a smart home, an edge device can aggregate temperature readings from multiple rooms before sending the average temperature to the central system, reducing network traffic.
2. Low-Latency Processing: Edge computing allows for low-latency data processing, making it suitable for applications that require quick responses. In scenarios like autonomous vehicles or remote monitoring of critical infrastructure, edge devices can process data rapidly and make instant decisions, improving safety and efficiency.
3. Offline Operation: Edge devices can operate in offline or partially connected environments, ensuring that data processing and decision-making continue even when network connectivity is intermittent or unavailable. This is vital for applications like remote agriculture monitoring or oil rig operations.
4. Reduced Data Transfer: By preprocessing data at the edge, gateways and edge devices reduce the volume of data that needs to be transmitted to the central system. This minimizes the impact on network bandwidth, reduces data transmission costs, and speeds up response times.

Example:
Imagine a smart grid application that monitors and manages electricity distribution. In this scenario:

- Perception Layer: Sensors and smart meters collect data on electricity consumption and voltage levels at various points in the grid. These sensors and meters are located at substations and along power lines.
- Data Transmission: The collected data is transmitted to the Network Layer using communication protocols like cellular networks or powerline communication.
- Gateways and Edge Devices: At substations, edge devices known as intelligent gateways receive the data from the sensors and smart meters. These gateways preprocess the data, performing tasks such as aggregating consumption data from multiple meters and filtering out noise or irrelevant readings. This processed data is then transmitted to the Middleware Layer.
- Middleware Layer: In the Middleware Layer, the data from the edge devices is further processed and analyzed. Data from various substations is aggregated, and load analysis is performed to ensure a balanced distribution of electricity.
- Data Presentation: Processed data is made available to the Application Layer, where it can be visualized through a web-based utility management system. Utility operators and consumers can monitor electricity consumption, detect anomalies, and control the distribution system as needed.

In this example, gateways and edge devices serve to preprocess data at the edge, reducing the load on the central system and enabling faster responses to changing conditions in the smart grid. They play a crucial role in optimizing the operation of the IoT system and ensuring the reliability of the electricity distribution network.

Security and Privacy Considerations

(Shah & Ahmed, 2023) Security and privacy are paramount in the Internet of Things (IoT) landscape, given the vast amounts of data generated and exchanged. This section explores the security measures in place at each layer of IoT architecture and delves into data privacy concerns and encryption, with the aid of an example.

Security Measures at Each Layer

1. Perception Layer: Security measures at the Perception Layer include device authentication, ensuring that only authorized devices can collect or transmit data. Additionally, sensors and actuators should be physically secured to prevent tampering or unauthorized access. For example, in a smart healthcare application, wearable devices like heart rate monitors must be authenticated to connect to the user's smartphone.
2. Network Layer: At this layer, data encryption plays a significant role in securing data in transit. Communication protocols should use encryption mechanisms like SSL/TLS (Secure Sockets Layer/ Transport Layer Security) to protect data as it travels between devices and gateways. Network segmentation can also help isolate IoT devices from critical infrastructure, reducing the attack surface. In an industrial IoT setting, encrypted communication between sensors and a centralized control system ensures data integrity and confidentiality.
3. Middleware Layer: Security measures in the Middleware Layer encompass access control, ensuring that only authorized applications and services can access and process IoT data. This layer also handles data validation and normalization to prevent malicious data injection and exploitation. Role-based access control can be implemented to restrict access based on user roles. In a smart home application, only authorized users should be able to access and control smart devices within the home.
4. Application Layer: At the Application Layer, user authentication is paramount to protect against unauthorized access to IoT applications. Password policies, multi-factor authentication, and secure login processes should be in place. Additionally, secure API endpoints and proper input validation are essential to prevent injection attacks. In a connected car application, ensuring that only the vehicle owner can access and control the vehicle's functions through the mobile app is crucial for security.

Data Privacy Concerns and Encryption

(Singh & Park, TaLWaR: Blockchain-Based Trust Management Scheme for Smart Enterprises With Augmented Intelligence, 2023) Data privacy is a major concern in IoT, especially given the sensitive nature of data collected from various devices. Encryption plays a pivotal role in addressing these concerns:

1. End-to-End Encryption: Implementing end-to-end encryption ensures that data remains confidential during transmission. This means that data is encrypted at the sender's end, only to be decrypted by the authorized recipient. For example, in a healthcare IoT application, end-to-end encryption can protect patient data transmitted from wearable health monitors to a healthcare provider's server.
2. Data Encryption at Rest: Data storage within IoT systems should be encrypted to protect against unauthorized access to stored data. This is crucial in scenarios where historical data is archived or sensitive data is stored in databases. For instance, in a smart city's traffic management system, encrypted storage of video footage from surveillance cameras ensures that the footage remains secure.
3. Data Masking and Anonymization: To address privacy concerns, data can be masked or anonymized before storage. This involves replacing sensitive information with pseudonyms or masking parts of the data. For example, in a smart grid application, customer billing data may be anonymized to protect individual consumers' identities while still allowing grid analytics.
4. Consent Management: IoT applications should implement robust consent management systems to ensure that data is only collected, processed, and shared with the explicit consent of end-users. In a home automation application, users should have the ability to grant or revoke consent for data collection and sharing.

Example: (Singh, Yang, & Park, FusionFedBlock: Fusion of blockchain and federated learning to preserve privacy in industry 5.0, 2023)

Consider a wearable fitness tracker IoT application. In this scenario:

- Perception Layer: Fitness trackers collect data on a user's heart rate, steps taken, and sleep patterns. Security measures include device authentication, ensuring that only the user or authorized individuals can pair the wearable device with the mobile app.
- Network Layer: Data transmission between the wearable device and the user's smartphone should be encrypted to prevent eavesdropping during data transfer. Bluetooth connections should employ encryption to secure data in transit.
- Middleware Layer: Within the Middleware Layer, user data is stored and processed. Access control mechanisms ensure that only authorized healthcare professionals or applications can access the data for medical analysis or monitoring.
- Application Layer: The mobile app serves as the Application Layer, where user authentication and secure login are essential to protect against unauthorized access. Data privacy is a concern, and the app should include consent management features, allowing users to control what data is shared with third-party services.

(Jain, Laxmi, Tripathi, Gaur, & Bishnoi, 2020) Data privacy concerns are especially prevalent in healthcare applications. To address them, the IoT system should not only secure data transmission but also implement strong consent management and anonymization of data for research and analytics. These measures ensure that sensitive health data remains confidential while still allowing for meaningful analysis and monitoring of the user's well-being.

Figure 6. Smart agriculture IoT architecture

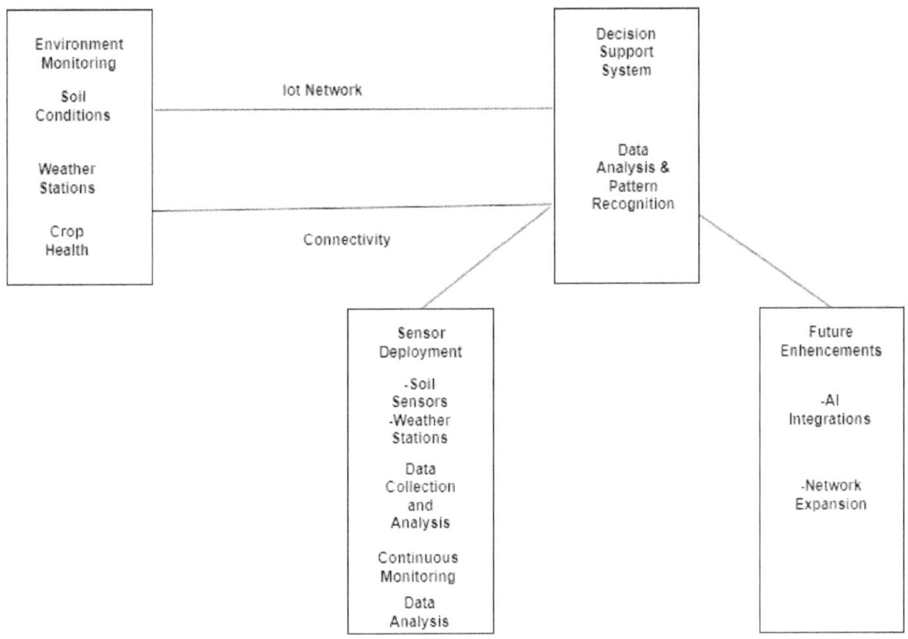

CASE STUDIES

Real-World Implementations

In the realm of the Internet of Things (IoT), real-world case studies demonstrate the practicality and impact of implementing layered architectures. Two noteworthy examples showcase successful IoT projects, each offering valuable lessons learned.

Case Study 1: Smart Agriculture for Precision Farming

Success Story:

Agriculture has greatly benefited from IoT applications that optimize farming processes. A precision farming project in California's Central Valley illustrates the power of layered IoT architecture.

Architecture diagram illustrating the layers and components of the Smart Agriculture IoT system.

Layered Architecture Overview

- Perception Layer: Soil moisture sensors, weather stations, and drones equipped with multispectral cameras collect data on soil conditions, weather patterns, and crop health.
- Network Layer: Data from sensors and drones is transmitted over a combination of cellular networks, satellite communications, and LoRaWAN (Low-Power Wide-Area Network) to gateways and edge devices in the field.

- Middleware Layer: Gateways and edge devices preprocess data by aggregating sensor readings and normalizing data. Middleware systems analyze this data, generating insights on irrigation needs, disease detection, and crop yield predictions.
- Application Layer: An intuitive web-based application allows farmers to access actionable insights. They can monitor real-time weather data, optimize irrigation schedules, and even receive automated alerts for disease outbreaks or unfavorable weather conditions.
- Lessons Learned:
- Data Accuracy: The Perception Layer's success depends on sensor calibration and accuracy. Regular maintenance and calibration are essential to ensure precise data collection.
- Network Resilience: The Network Layer's ability to use multiple communication methods (cellular, satellite, LoRaWAN) enhances data reliability and ensures connectivity even in remote areas.
- Edge Computing Benefits: Gateways and edge devices significantly reduce the data load on central systems, making data processing more efficient and cost-effective.

Case Study 2: Smart City Traffic Management (Singh, Lee, & Park, CoVAC: A P2P Smart Contract-Based Intelligent Smart City Architecture for Vaccine Manufacturing, 2022)

Success Story:

Smart cities worldwide are implementing IoT solutions to improve urban living. The city of Barcelona, Spain, has a remarkable traffic management system.

Layered Architecture Overview:

- Perception Layer: Traffic cameras, sensors embedded in the road, and parking space occupancy sensors collect data on traffic flow and parking availability.
- Network Layer: Data from these sensors is transmitted through wired and wireless networks to gateways strategically positioned throughout the city.
- Middleware Layer: Edge devices preprocess the data by filtering irrelevant information and aggregating it to reduce network congestion. Middleware systems analyze the data for traffic patterns, congestion prediction, and optimized traffic signal control.
- Application Layer: The city's traffic management system includes a user-friendly mobile app for commuters and a central control system for traffic operators. Commuters can access real-time traffic information, parking availability, and receive navigation recommendations to avoid congested routes.

Visualization of the intelligent road network in a smart city, showcasing the integration of traffic signals, sensor nodes, and a centralized control system. This system enhances urban mobility by optimizing traffic flow, reducing congestion, and providing real-time data for efficient city planning (Rejeb, Rejeb, Simske, Treiblmaier, & Zailani, 2022).

Lessons Learned:

- Real-Time Decision Making: The Middleware Layer plays a critical role in enabling real-time traffic decisions, such as adjusting traffic signal timing based on current traffic conditions.

Figure 7. Smart city traffic management network

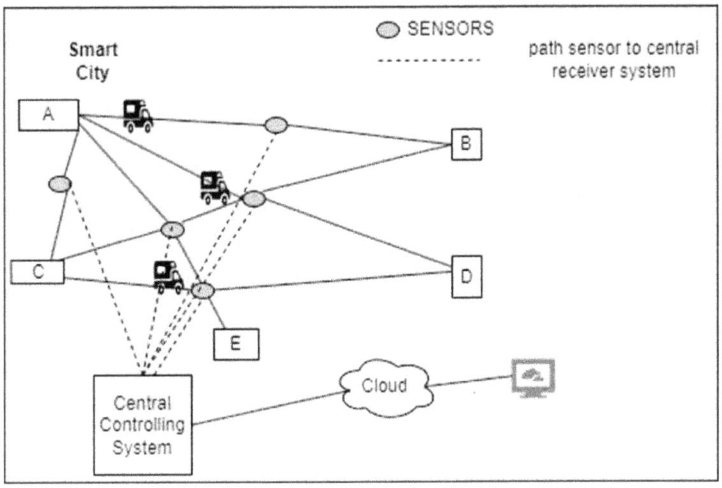

- Data Privacy: Privacy concerns are addressed through data anonymization and access control. The system provides aggregated data to the Application Layer while ensuring individual privacy.
- User Engagement: The success of the Application Layer relies on user engagement. An intuitive mobile app encourages users to access and contribute to the system's real-time traffic data.

These case studies exemplify how layered IoT architectures enable the development of successful applications across various domains, including agriculture and smart cities. By following lessons learned in these projects, future implementations can harness the full potential of IoT to improve efficiency, sustainability, and the quality of life.

RECENT TRENDS FOR IOT LAYERED ARCHITECTURE AND CHALLENGES

Emerging Technologies in IoT and Their Impact on Layered Architecture

(Vanzara, et al., 2018) The field of the Internet of Things (IoT) is continuously evolving, and emerging technologies are driving innovation across its layered architecture. These technologies not only enhance

Table 3. Comparison table based on existing research studies

Aspect	Case study-1	Case study-2
Significance and Evolution of IoT	✓	✓
Key Layers of IoT Architecture	✓	✓
Role and Interactions of Layers	✓	✓
Security Considerations	✓	✓
Real-world Case Studies	✓	✓
Emerging Technologies	✓	✓
Challenges and Future Outlook	✓	✓

the capabilities of IoT systems but also introduce new considerations and challenges. This section provides an overview of some key emerging technologies in IoT and their impact on the layered architecture (Singh, Park, Sharma, & Pan, 2022).

Edge Computing

Impact on Layered Architecture: Edge computing has a significant impact on the layered architecture of IoT. It introduces the concept of processing data closer to the source, at the edge of the network, rather than relying solely on centralized cloud processing in the Middleware Layer. This reduces latency, improves real-time processing, and minimizes the amount of data that needs to be transmitted to the Middleware Layer. Edge devices, positioned between the Network Layer and Middleware Layer, are crucial for preprocessing and filtering data, enhancing system efficiency.

5G Connectivity

Impact on Layered Architecture: The introduction of 5G networks significantly enhances the capabilities of the Network Layer. It provides higher bandwidth, lower latency, and increased network reliability. With 5G, IoT devices can transmit and receive data at faster rates, supporting real-time applications and high-resolution data streaming. This improves the overall responsiveness and performance of IoT systems.

AI and Machine Learning

Impact on Layered Architecture: AI and machine learning have a profound impact on the Middleware and Application Layers. AI algorithms can be deployed in the Middleware Layer to analyze data, detect patterns, and provide predictive insights. In the Application Layer, AI-driven applications can offer intelligent recommendations, automation, and personalized experiences for end-users. These technologies enable IoT systems to make informed decisions and offer advanced functionality.

Blockchain

Impact on Layered Architecture: Blockchain technology can be applied to enhance security and trust within the Middleware Layer. It can provide secure data storage, tamper-resistant audit trails, and secure access control. In IoT applications where data integrity and immutability are critical, such as supply chain management or healthcare, blockchain can be used to secure data and transactions (Singh, Azzaoui, Choo, Yang, & Park).

Quantum Computing

Impact on Layered Architecture: Quantum computing is still in its infancy, but it has the potential to disrupt existing cryptographic methods used for security in IoT. As quantum computers become more powerful, the security measures at all layers, especially in the Network and Middleware Layers, will need to adapt to quantum-resistant encryption methods to protect data.

Figure 8. Edge computing

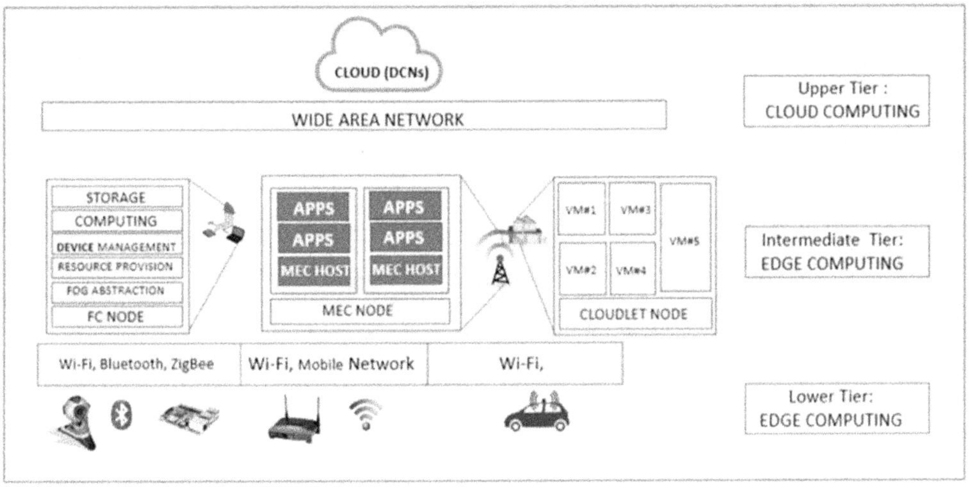

LPWAN Technologies

Impact on Layered Architecture: Low-Power Wide-Area Network (LPWAN) technologies like LoRaWAN and NB-IoT are designed to enable long-range, low-power communication for IoT devices. They are well-suited for applications in which devices need to operate for extended periods on battery power. LPWAN technologies expand the capabilities of the Network Layer by allowing IoT devices to communicate over longer distances with minimal energy consumption.

Digital Twins

Impact on Layered Architecture: Digital twins create virtual representations of physical objects or systems, allowing for real-time monitoring, analysis, and simulation. These virtual replicas impact the Middleware and Application Layers, enhancing data visualization and analysis. Digital twins can be used to create accurate models of IoT systems, improving predictive maintenance and control (Singh, Kumar, Tanwar, & Park, 2024).

Swarm Robotics and IoT Integration

Impact on Layered Architecture: Integrating swarm robotics with IoT allows for more collaborative and autonomous systems. In the Middleware Layer, coordination and control algorithms can be implemented to manage swarms of robots, while the Application Layer can offer intuitive interfaces for users to interact with these autonomous systems.

Biotechnology and IoT

Impact on Layered Architecture: The integration of biotechnology with IoT has far-reaching implications, especially in healthcare and agriculture. In the Perception Layer, biosensors collect data on biological processes, while the Middleware and Application Layers facilitate data analysis and interpretation. The impact is particularly significant in personalized medicine and precision agriculture.

3D Printing and IoT

Impact on Layered Architecture: 3D printing, when integrated with IoT, enables distributed manufacturing and remote control of 3D printers. The Application Layer can provide users with the ability to customize and print objects remotely, while the Middleware Layer can manage the distribution of printing tasks.

These emerging technologies are reshaping the landscape of IoT, offering new opportunities and challenges at every layer of the architecture. To fully harness the potential of these technologies, IoT developers and stakeholders must adapt their strategies, consider new security and privacy concerns, and continue to innovate in order to create smarter, more efficient, and more capable IoT systems.

Challenges in Layered IoT Architecture

(Solanki, Garg, & Chhikaniwala, 2022) Layered IoT architecture offers a structured approach to building IoT systems, but it comes with its own set of challenges. Addressing these challenges is essential to ensure the seamless operation of IoT ecosystems. This section highlights some common challenges and potential solutions, with a particular focus on scalability, interoperability, and standards.

Common Challenges (Park, Yotxay, Singh, & Park, 2024)

1. Scalability: IoT systems often need to scale to accommodate a growing number of devices and data. Scalability challenges may include handling a massive influx of data, managing an increasing number of devices, and ensuring that the system remains responsive.
2. Interoperability: IoT ecosystems comprise a variety of devices, each potentially using different communication protocols and data formats. Ensuring that these devices can work together seamlessly and share data is a significant challenge.
3. Security and Privacy: IoT systems are vulnerable to security breaches and privacy concerns. Protecting data and devices from unauthorized access and ensuring data privacy is a critical challenge.
4. Data Management: IoT systems generate vast amounts of data. Managing and processing this data efficiently and effectively can be challenging, especially for real-time applications.
5. Power Constraints: Many IoT devices operate on battery power, which introduces challenges in managing power consumption and ensuring devices have a long lifespan.

Potential Solutions

1. Scalability:
    - Edge Computing: Implementing edge computing at the Network Layer can reduce the load on centralized systems and enhance scalability. Edge devices can preprocess data locally, making it more manageable for the Middleware Layer.
    - Cloud Services: Utilizing cloud services can provide virtually unlimited resources, making it easier to scale IoT systems. Cloud platforms can handle data storage, processing, and analytics, alleviating the burden on the Middleware Layer.

2. Interoperability:
    - IoT Standards: Adhering to established IoT standards like MQTT, CoAP, and HTTP can promote interoperability. These standards define common communication protocols and data formats, making it easier for devices to communicate.
    - APIs and Middleware: Implementing APIs and middleware solutions that can translate between different data formats and communication protocols can bridge the interoperability gap. These components facilitate communication between devices with disparate specifications.
3. Security and Privacy:
    - End-to-End Encryption: Implementing end-to-end encryption ensures data remains secure during transmission. This is especially important in the Network Layer, where data is vulnerable to interception.
    - Access Control and Authentication: Robust access control measures, including user authentication and device authentication, should be enforced in the Middleware and Application Layers. This prevents unauthorized access to data and devices.
4. Data Management:
    - Data Analytics: Leveraging advanced analytics and machine learning in the Middleware Layer can help manage and analyze large datasets efficiently. These technologies enable real-time data processing and actionable insights.
    - Data Retention Policies: Implementing data retention policies in the Middleware Layer can help manage data storage. Historical data that is no longer useful can be archived or deleted to free up storage space.
5. Power Constraints:
    - Low-Power Protocols: Implementing low-power communication protocols like LoRaWAN or NB-IoT in the Network Layer can extend the lifespan of battery-powered devices.
    - Energy Harvesting: Leveraging energy harvesting solutions, such as solar panels or kinetic energy harvesters, can help recharge or extend the life of batteries in IoT devices.

Standards and Interoperability

Standards play a crucial role in addressing interoperability challenges. Various organizations and alliances, such as the Open Connectivity Foundation (OCF), the Industrial Internet Consortium (IIC), and the Internet Engineering Task Force (IETF), are working on standardizing communication protocols and data formats. Adhering to these standards ensures that devices and systems from different manufacturers can work together seamlessly (Kumar, Kim, Son, Singh, & Kim, 2024).

Additionally, organizations and industry bodies are developing reference architectures and frameworks to guide the development of IoT systems. These frameworks provide best practices and guidelines for designing scalable, secure, and interoperable IoT solutions.

while layered IoT architecture offers a structured approach to building IoT systems, it is not without its challenges. Scalability, interoperability, security, data management, and power constraints are common hurdles that need to be addressed. By implementing potential solutions and adhering to standards, IoT developers can overcome these challenges and build robust and efficient IoT ecosystems that meet the needs of various industries and applications.

CONCLUSION

- In this chapter, we have explored the layered architecture of IoT, highlighting its significance and the key points discussed throughout. Layered architecture is the backbone of IoT systems, providing a well-structured framework that enables efficient data flow, real-time processing, and scalability.
- We began by defining IoT and understanding its evolution, emphasizing its pivotal role in today's interconnected world. We delved into the layered architecture concept, which consists of the Perception Layer, Network Layer, Middleware Layer, and Application Layer. Each layer has a unique purpose, contributing to the overall functionality of an IoT system.
- We examined the role of the Perception Layer, where sensors and actuators collect data from the physical environment, and the Network Layer, which handles data transmission and communication protocols. The Middleware Layer was explored in detail, emphasizing its functions in data processing, message brokering, and ensuring data integrity. Lastly, we explored the Application Layer, which serves as the interface between the IoT system and end-users or external systems.
- Real-world applications and case studies demonstrated the practicality and impact of layered IoT systems, from precision farming in agriculture to traffic management in smart cities. These examples showcased how IoT is enhancing efficiency, sustainability, and the quality of life across various domains.
- As IoT continues to evolve, we discussed the significance of emerging technologies, such as edge computing, 5G connectivity, AI, and blockchain, in reshaping the IoT landscape. These technologies are enabling more powerful, efficient, and intelligent IoT systems.
- Lastly, we addressed the common challenges in layered IoT architecture, including scalability, interoperability, security, data management, and power constraints. We provided potential solutions and emphasized the importance of adhering to standards and best practices to ensure the successful development and deployment of IoT systems.

REFERENCES

Aydin, S., & Aydin, M. N. (2020). A sustainable multi-layered open data processing model for agriculture: IoT based case study using semantic web for hazelnut fields. *Adv. Sci. Technol. Eng. Syst. J*, *5*(2), 309–319. doi:10.25046/aj050241

Bhattacharjee, Y., Arief, I., & Bose, S. (2017). Recent trends in multi-layered architectures towards screening electromagnetic radiation: Challenges and perspectives. *Journal of Materials Chemistry. C, Materials for Optical and Electronic Devices*, *5*(30), 7390–7403. doi:10.1039/C7TC02172K

Gardašević, G., Veletić, M., Maletić, N., Vasiljević, D., Radusinović, I., Tomović, S., & Radonjić, M. (2017). The IoT architectural framework, design issues and application domains. *Wireless Personal Communications*, *92*(1), 127–148. doi:10.1007/s11277-016-3842-3

Gupta, A., Tripathi, M., & Sharma, A. (2020, July). A provably secure and efficient anonymous mutual authentication and key agreement protocol for wearable devices in WBAN. *Computer Communications*, *160*, 311–325. doi:10.1016/j.comcom.2020.06.010

Huh, M. A.-N. (2014). Fog computing and smart gateway based communication for cloud of things. *2nd IEEE Interenational Conference on Future Internet of Things and Cloud*. IEEE.

Jain, A., Laxmi, V., Tripathi, M., Gaur, M. S., & Bishnoi, R. (2020). TRACK: An algorithm for fault-tolerant, dynamic and scalable 2D mesh network-on-chip routing reconfiguration. *Integration (Amsterdam)*, *72*, 92–110. doi:10.1016/j.vlsi.2020.01.005

Kumar, M., Kim, C., Son, Y., Singh, S. K., & Kim, S. (2024). Empowering Cyberattack Identification in IoHT Networks With Neighborhood Component-based Improvised Long Short-Term Memory. *IEEE Internet of Things Journal*, 1–1. doi:10.1109/JIOT.2024.3354988

Markendahl, J., Lundberg, S., Kordas, O., & Movin, S. (2017). *On the role and potential of IoT in different industries: Analysis of actor cooperation and challenges for introduction of new technology. 2017 Internet of Things Business Models*. Users, and Networks.

Nandyala, C. S., & Kim, H.-K. (2016). Green IoT agriculture and healthcare application (GAHA). *International Journal of Smart Home*, *10*(4), 289–300. doi:10.14257/ijsh.2016.10.4.26

Park, J. H., Yotxay, S., Singh, S. K., & Park, J. H. (2024). PoAh-Enabled Federated Learning Architecture for DDoS Attack Detection in IoT Networks. *Human-Centric Computing And Information Sciences, 14*.

Rejeb, A., Rejeb, K., Simske, S., Treiblmaier, H., & Zailani, S. (2022, August). The big picture on the internet of things and the smart city: A review of what we know and what we need to know. *Internet of Things : Engineering Cyber Physical Human Systems*, *19*, 100565. doi:10.1016/j.iot.2022.100565

Shah, I. A., & Ahmed, M. (2023, March). $$F_K-meansRA$$: Fuzzy K-Means Clustering Routing Algorithm for Load Balancing in Wireless Sensor Networks. *Wireless Personal Communications*, *130*(2), 1071–1083. doi:10.1007/s11277-023-10320-8

Singh, S. K., Azzaoui, A. E., Choo, K.-K. R., Yang, L. T., & Park, J. H. (n.d.). *ArticlesA Comprehensive Survey on Blockchain for Secure IoT-enabled Smart City beyond 5G: Approaches*. Processes, Challenges, and Opportunities.

Singh, S. K., Kumar, M., Tanwar, S., & Park, J. H. (2024, April). GRU-based digital twin framework for data allocation and storage in IoT-enabled smart home networks. *Future Generation Computer Systems*, *153*, 391–402. doi:10.1016/j.future.2023.12.009

Singh, S. K., Lee, C., & Park, J. H. (2022, April). CoVAC: A P2P smart contract-based intelligent smart city architecture for vaccine manufacturing. *Computers &amp. Industrial Engineering (American Institute of Industrial Engineers)*, *166*, 107967. doi:10.1016/j.cie.2022.107967 PMID:35136280

Singh, S. K., Pan, Y., & Park, J. H. (2022, January). Blockchain-enabled Secure Framework for Energy-Efficient Smart Parking in Sustainable City Environment. *Sustainable Cities and Society*, *76*, 103364. doi:10.1016/j.scs.2021.103364

Singh, S. K., & Park, J. H. (2023, January). TaLWaR: Blockchain-Based Trust Management Scheme for Smart Enterprises With Augmented Intelligence. *IEEE Transactions on Industrial Informatics*, *19*(1), 626–634. doi:10.1109/TII.2022.3204692

Singh, S. K., Park, J. H., Sharma, P. K., & Pan, Y. (2022, November). BIIoVT: Blockchain-Based Secure Storage Architecture for Intelligent Internet of Vehicular Things. *IEEE Consumer Electronics Magazine*, *11*(6), 75–82. doi:10.1109/MCE.2021.3089992

Singh, S. K., Yang, L. T., & Park, J. H. (2023, February). FusionFedBlock: Fusion of blockchain and federated learning to preserve privacy in industry 5.0. *Information Fusion*, *90*, 233–240. doi:10.1016/j.inffus.2022.09.027

Solanki, P., Garg, S., & Chhikaniwala, H. (2022). Preserve Privacy on Streaming Data During the Process of Mining Using User Defined Delta Value. In *Innovative Data Communication Technologies and Application* [Springer.]. *Proceedings of ICIDCA*, *2021*, 197–212.

Vanzara, R., Sharma, P., Bhatt, H. S., Tanwar, S., Tyagi, S., Kumar, N., & Obaidat, M. S. (2018, November). ADYTIA: Adaptive and Dynamic TCP Interface Architecture for heterogeneous networks. *International Journal of Communication Systems*, *32*(2), e3855. doi:10.1002/dac.3855

Vermesan, O., Friess, P., Guillemin, P., Giaffreda, R., Grindvoll, H., Eisenhauer, M., & Tragos, E. Z. (2022, September). Internet of Things beyond the Hype: Research, Innovation and Deployment. In Building the Hyperconnected Society- Internet of Things Research and Innovation Value Chains, Ecosystems and Markets (pp. 15–118). River Publishers. doi:10.1201/9781003337454-3

Chapter 10
Blockchain's Motivation for IoT-Enabled Smart City

Wasswa Shafik
https://orcid.org/0000-0002-9320-3186
School of Digital Science, Universiti Brunei Darussalam, Brunei & Dig Connectivity Research Laboratory (DCRLab), Kampala, Uganda

Kassim Kalinaki
https://orcid.org/0000-0001-8630-9110
Islamic University in Uganda, Uganda

Rufai Yusuf Zakari
School of Digital Science, Universiti Brunei Darussalam, Brunei

ABSTRACT

This study examines the fusion of blockchain technology with the internet of things (IoT) in smart cities, exploring how Blockchain's traits like immutability, decentralization, and consensus can address smart cities' concerns. It scrutinizes IoT's applications in smart cities like traffic management and waste control, highlighting data's critical role. It accentuates blockchain's significance in device authentication, securing data integrity, and transactions in a decentralized network. Examining some case studies, it vitrines the benefits of integrating blockchain in smart cities such as optimized operations, enhanced security, and participant trust and confidence. Finally, it demonstrates privacy and security bottlenecks, including energy consumption, scalability, and regulations, emphasizing the need for solutions to overcome these challenges.

INTRODUCTION

Smart cities embody a paradigm shift in urban planning and governance, leveraging technology and data to augment the well-being of their inhabitants and foster sustainable economic and social progress (Dieye et al., 2023). The escalating process of urbanization in our society, wherein more than half of the global population now resides in urban areas, has created a pressing demand for inventive approaches to

DOI: 10.4018/979-8-3693-2373-1.ch010

tackle the intricate issues associated with urban living (Politou et al., 2021). Smart cities offer a proactive solution to these difficulties, promoting a novel phase of urban progress marked by effectiveness, connection, and sustainability.

The fundamental principle underlying the smart city concept is incorporating Information and Communication Technology (ICT) and the Internet of Things (IoT) into the very foundation of urban infrastructure using the big data era. This integration facilitates real-time data collection from a plethora of sources, such as sensors, cameras, and other IoT devices (Su et al., 2023). As a result, it institutes an all-encompassing digital neural network, augmenting decision-making, optimizing resource allocation, and elevating the holistic urban encounter (Alnssyan et al., 2023). Leveraging this vast reservoir of information, municipalities hold the potential to ameliorate the caliber and efficacy of public services, spanning various domains like transportation, healthcare, energy governance, and ecological resilience (Kushwaha et al., 2022).

The assimilation of these cutting-edge technologies seamlessly paves the way for constructing an all-encompassing digital framework that captures instantaneous data from diverse origins, such as sensors, cameras, and a myriad of IoT devices (Majeed et al., 2021). Incorporating Blockchain technology furnishes a resilient mechanism, safeguarding the sanctity and confidentiality of data, thereby adeptly shielding it against any illicit alterations or breaches (Shafik, 2023a). As a result, this procedural synergy furnishes invaluable insights for informed, data-driven decision-making, judicious resource allocation, and enhancing the holistic urban environment (Bansod & Ragha, 2022).

A diverse spectrum of technologies, from environmental sensors to intelligent traffic lights, constitutes IoT devices, collectively amassing considerable data. This data, in turn, yields invaluable insights into multifaceted aspects of urban existence (Bandara et al., 2022). Ensuring this data's integrity, visibility, and confidentiality is its secure storage on a Blockchain platform. Fundamental to Blockchain technology, smart contracts seamlessly facilitate automated, secure, and transparent transactions and agreements (Singh et al., 2021; Shafik, 2023b). Their applicability spans various domains, including energy consumption, waste management, and public transit services.

The smart city concept is grounded in inclusion and sustainability, prioritizing fair and equal access to technology and services for all community members. The capacity of Blockchain technology to grant individuals authority over their data and transactions is in accordance with the principles of inclusion and privacy (Majeed et al., 2021). IoT-enabled devices have the potential to actively include citizens in decision-making processes, enabling them to willingly contribute their data in return for enhanced services, all while safeguarding their privacy (Makani et al., 2022).

The need for secure data management is crucial in the context of smart cities, where large amounts of data are generated and utilized for urban growth and governance. Primarily, it guarantees the preservation of sensitive personal and civic data, hence upholding the privacy and security of individuals (Makhdoom et al., 2023). Data is gathered from several sources in a smart city, encompassing IoT devices, security cameras, and platforms that facilitate citizen interaction (Alqarni et al., 2023; Shafik, 2023c). The implementation of robust data security protocols, including encryption, access controls, and safe storage, is necessary to mitigate unauthorized access risks, cyberattacks, and data breaches that may potentially jeopardize the privacy of individuals and the overall integrity of the smart city ecosystem as depicted in Figure 1.

Moreover, implementing robust data management practices fosters confidence among citizens and stakeholders, promoting increased engagement in data-sharing endeavors essential for enhancing urban services and infrastructure (Alamri et al., 2022). The rationale behind integrating Blockchain technology

Figure 1. Smart cities and their components

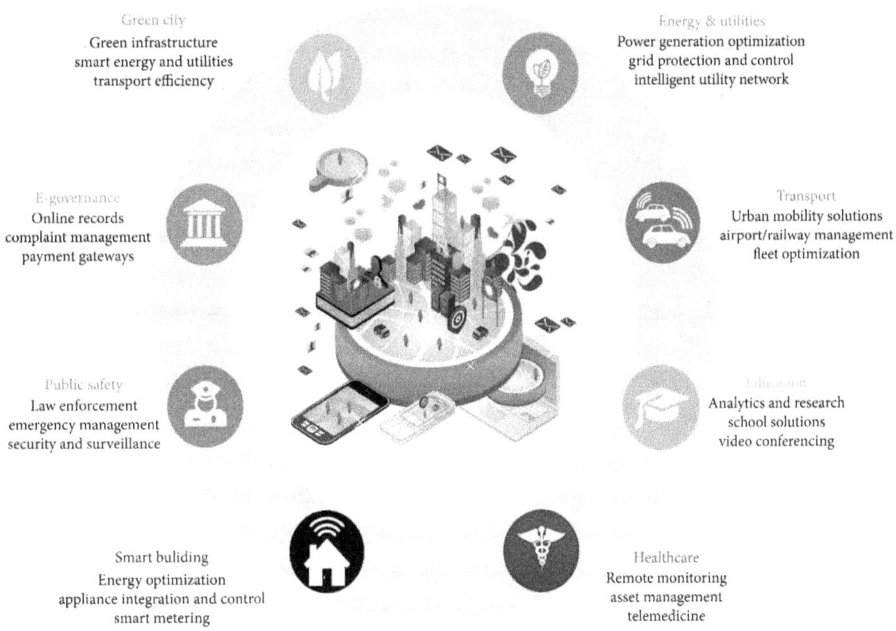

in smart cities is based on its ability to augment data security, transparency, and trust in urban development and government. Smart cities are dependent on extensive networks of IoT devices, sensors, and data collection stations, which generate substantial amounts of data pertaining to energy consumption, transportation, public services, and various other aspects (Shafik, 2024a; Dieye et al., 2023).

The decentralized and immutable ledger of Blockchain technology upholds data's integrity and privacy, effectively preventing any manipulation or illegal access. This practice not only cultivates increased assurance among residents and stakeholders regarding data precision but also strengthens the utilization of data-driven decision-making procedures (Kashif & Kalkan, 2024). Utilizing Blockchain technology enables the facilitation of secure, transparent, and auditable transactions through smart contracts, thereby enhancing the efficiency of urban operations, promoting cost-effective services, and fostering trust in digital interactions (Singh et al., 2021; Shafik, 2024b). Consequently, this advancement contributes to realizing the smart city concept, characterized by sustainable, efficient, and inclusive urban living.

The Chapter Contribution

This study contributes the following as summarized.

- The study elucidates the profound impact of the IoT on the transformation of urban landscapes. It also scrutinizes the diverse range of applications of the IoT in Smart Cities, explicitly exploring the utilization of IoT in areas like traffic control, waste management, and energy efficiency.
- Provides an overview of Blockchain technology, including its principles and features, explaining the concept of decentralization, immutability, and consensus mechanisms in Blockchain.

- Discusses on how Blockchain technology can enhance the security and reliability of IoT systems by exploring use cases of integrating Blockchain with IoT in smart cities, such as data integrity, device authentication, and secure transactions.
- Highlights the security and privacy challenges in IoT-enabled smart cities, enlightening on how Blockchain can address these concerns, including data encryption and access control.
- Demonstrate the security and privacy challenges in IoT-enabled Smart Cities, detailing how Blockchain can address these concerns, including data encryption and access control.
- It identifies the challenges and limitations of using Blockchain in smart cities, addressing scalability issues, energy consumption, and regulatory concerns.
- Finally, venture into the future of Blockchain and IoT in Smart Cities, discussing potential advancements and emerging trends.

The Chapter Organization

The remainder of this chapter is structured as follows. Section 2 presents the Internet of Things in Smart Cities, explains the significance of IoT in transforming urban environments and discusses the various applications of IoT in Smart Cities. Section 3 provides an overview of Blockchain technology, including its principles and features, and illustrates the concept of decentralization, immutability, and consensus mechanisms in Blockchain. Section 4 describes the security and privacy challenges in IoT-enabled smart cities and elucidates how Blockchain can address these concerns, including data encryption and access control. Section 5 Identifies the challenges and limitations of using Blockchain in smart cities and addresses scalability issues, energy consumption, and regulatory concerns. Section 6 speculates the future of Blockchain and IoT in Smart Cities and discusses potential advancements and emerging trends. Finally, Section 6 presents the conclusion.

INTERNET OF THINGS AND BLOCKCHAIN IN SMART CITIES

This section explains the significance of IoT in renovating sustainable urban and village environments with a simple discussion of the various applications of IoT in smart cities.

Internet of Things in Smart Cities

IoT is relevant in reshaping urban environments by revolutionizing how cities are built, administered, and experienced. Several crucial factors demonstrate its influence, as demonstrated below.

Data-Driven Decision-Making

Utilizing the IoT in data gathering and analysis provides city officials with the capability to make decisions based on empirical evidence, thus enhancing the efficacy of urban planning and management (Tang et al., 2023). By constantly monitoring and analyzing data collected from various sensors and devices, urban places promptly react to dynamic situations, such as optimizing traffic patterns to alleviate congestion or reallocating resources to areas requiring immediate attention (Bao et al., 2023). A data-driven approach enables urban areas to promptly respond to dynamic challenges, thus enhancing the overall well-being of its inhabitants.

Efficiency and Sustainability

The IoT plays a crucial role in enhancing urban sustainability through its capacity to optimize resource allocation effectively. One example of the potential benefits of smart waste management systems is the ability to optimize waste collection rounds by selectively collecting bins that have reached their full capacity (Nigmatov et al., 2023; Shafik et al., 2023). This approach results in cost savings and reduces fuel usage and carbon emissions. In a similar vein, intelligent lighting systems possess the capability to modulate brightness levels following the surrounding light environment, hence reducing energy use (Verma & Sheel, 2022). The efficiency improvements directly correlate with sustainability, as they effectively decrease a city's ecological impact and alleviate the resource burden, hence fostering an environmentally conscious urban setting (Singh et al., 2021).

Improved Public Services

The utilization of the IoT in public services brings about a significant transformation in how cities address the requirements of their residents. The utilization of real-time data obtained from IoT sensors enables the continuous monitoring of water quality, hence facilitating the early detection of potential concerns and ensuring safe drinking water (Alqarni et al., 2023). Similarly, implementing intelligent sensors within fire hydrants autonomously notifies relevant authorities of potential emergencies, enhancing the efficacy of emergency response operations (Kashif & Kalkan, 2024; Wang et al., 2023). The enhancements to public services ultimately contribute to an improved quality of life for urban people as they experience the advantages of faster, more dependable, and safer services. Figure 1 demonstrates approximations of IoTs and non-IoTs from 2015 through 2025.

Smart Transportation

The IoT has brought about a revolutionary transformation in the transportation sector, with its profound effects ranging from optimizing traffic flow to enhancing public transit systems (Makani et al., 2022). Smart traffic management systems utilize data collected from a multitude of sensors to dynamically adapt traffic signals and redirect traffic, thereby mitigating congestion and minimizing commute durations. Furthermore, integrating IoT technology into public transit systems provides passengers with timely and up-to-date information, thereby enhancing the efficiency and convenience of urban travel (Uchani Gutierrez & Xu, 2022). Smart transportation plays a crucial role in influencing the future of urban environments by mitigating traffic congestion and encouraging environmentally sustainable transportation alternatives (Bansod & Ragha, 2022).

Environmental Monitoring

The IoT significantly addresses critical environmental monitoring concerns, particularly in air and water quality. Sensors strategically deployed around the urban landscape consistently collect data about contaminants and ecological parameters (Singh et al., 2021). In instances where thresholds are surpassed,

Figure 2. Total active devices (non-IoT and IoT) connections worldwide
(Yang et al., 2021).

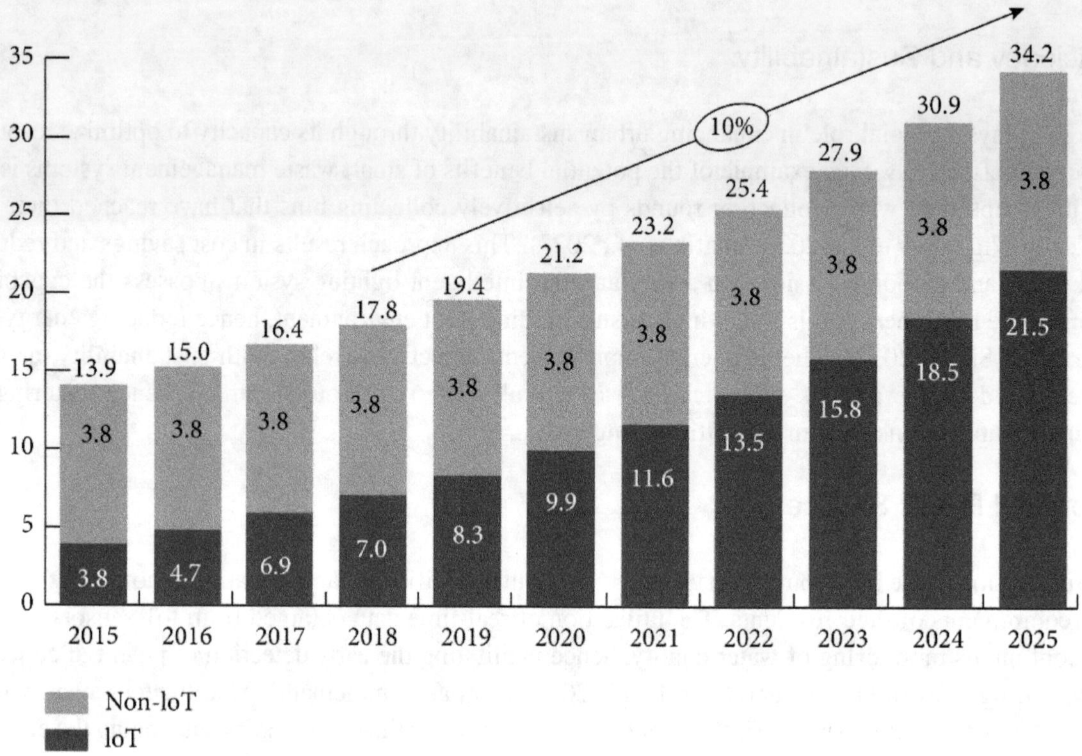

governmental entities can promptly implement measures to mitigate the adverse environmental consequences and safeguard the well-being of the general populace (Kashif & Kalkan, 2024). The continuous monitoring of environmental conditions serves the dual purpose of preserving the natural surroundings and safeguarding the welfare of urban inhabitants, thereby becoming a fundamental element in developing a healthier and more sustainable urban environment (Tang et al., 2023).

Security and Enhanced Safety

Implementing IoT technology has been found to significantly augment the levels of safety and security in metropolitan areas. This is mainly achieved through the utilization of IoT applications in the domains of surveillance and emergency response. Smart cameras with advanced image recognition technology detect and identify potential security risks (Zhu et al., 2023). These cameras promptly transmit real-time alerts to law enforcement agencies, enabling them to respond swiftly and effectively to potential threats. Furthermore, integrating IoT devices in emergency response systems allows precise identification of event locations and facilitates the efficient allocation of resources (Kushwaha et al., 2022). These advancements not only reduce the enhancement of physical safety but also cultivate a perception of security and overall well-being among inhabitants of metropolitan areas.

Sustainable Citizen Engagement

IoT empowers citizens to be active participants in their urban environments. Mobile apps, online platforms, and community engagement tools allow residents to report issues, access real-time information, and participate in decision-making processes (Tang et al., 2023). This engagement creates a more inclusive urban environment where residents have a direct stake in shaping their cities and improving the quality of services, fostering a sense of community involvement and ownership (Singh et al., 2021).

Sustainable Cost Savings

The long-term cost-saving potential of the IoT presents a notable advantage for metropolitan regions. Implementing efficient resource allocation strategies and the automation of operations, such as predictive maintenance for essential infrastructure, can generate significant cost reductions in the long run (Kashif & Kalkan, 2024). Cities can effectively mitigate the financial burden and operational delays associated with emergency repairs and service interruptions by taking proactive measures to restore infrastructure before it reaches a state of failure (Bandara et al., 2022). In a similar vein, implementing energy-efficient lighting and waste management systems diminishes operational expenses, hence facilitating the more effective allocation of resources by cities (Ma et al., 2023). This, in turn, allows for increased investments in other crucial services and infrastructure enhancement.

Blockchain Technology in Smart Cities

Within this subsection, an overview of Blockchain technology, including its principles and features, is provided. It elucidates the concept of decentralization, immutability, and consensus mechanisms in Blockchain.

Utilizing Blockchain technology revolutionizes numerous industries through its ability to augment transparency, fortify security measures, optimize operational efficiency, mitigate expenses, and cultivate trust (Verma & Sheel, 2022). The ideas and features of Blockchain have significant implications for the future of data management and digital trust, as seen by its notable implementation in cryptocurrencies. Nevertheless, it is imperative to confront obstacles such as scalability, energy consumption, and legal frameworks to fully use its inherent capabilities (Nigmatov et al., 2023).

Core Principles of Blockchain Technology

Blockchain technology functions on a decentralized computer network, often denoted as nodes. In contrast to conventional systems that rely on a central authority or intermediary to verify and record transactions, Blockchain technology operates through a decentralized network of participants.

Decentralization

The process of decentralization presents numerous advantages. Initially, utilizing Blockchain technology enhances transparency by ensuring that all participants within the network possess equal access to a shared ledger that is consistently updated in real time. Furthermore, it strengthens security by eliminating any potential failure points. Instead of depending on a singular entity, the verification of transactions is achieved through the network's consensus, thereby significantly impeding the ability of a malicious actor to control the system. The decentralized nature of Blockchain technology profoundly alters the mechanisms by which trust and authority are formed across various applications.

Distributed Ledger

The fundamental principle underlying Blockchain technology revolves around a decentralized ledger. The ledger serves as a comprehensive record of all transactions inside the network, organized consecutively through the formation of blocks, wherein each block encompasses a collection of transactions. Connecting blocks to form a sequential series is responsible for the term "Blockchain." Each individual within the network retains an identical replica of this ledger. The distributed ledger system guarantees uniform access to the transaction history for all participants, thereby significantly impeding any attempts to modify or delete data without obtaining consensus from the whole network. This capability offers unparalleled transparency, accountability, and data redundancy, which are of immense value in applications where trust and data integrity play a crucial role.

Immutability

Once a transaction is documented in a block and appended to the Blockchain, it becomes exceedingly arduous to alter or remove. The immutability of Blockchain technology can be attributed to the deployment of cryptographic hash functions. Every block comprises a collection of transactions and an exclusive cryptographic hash of the preceding block. The process generates a secure sequence of interconnected blocks that, once constructed, exhibit a high degree of resistance to any modification attempts. Modifying a single block necessitates altering all following blocks, a computationally impractical procedure. Consequently, the transaction history preserved on the Blockchain stays impervious to unauthorized modifications, thereby cultivating trust and assurance in the integrity of the data.

Consensus Mechanisms

Consensus algorithms play a crucial role in validating and recording transactions inside Blockchain networks. These mechanisms play a crucial role in establishing trust and consensus among participants in a network. The prevailing consensus mechanisms in Blockchain networks are Proof of Work (PoW) and Proof of Stake (PoS). In a Proof of Work (PoW) system, miners engage in a competitive process to solve intricate mathematical problems to append a new block to the Blockchain. In contrast, Proof of Stake (PoS) is a consensus mechanism that verifies transactions by considering the quantity of cryptocurrency tokens possessed by individuals involved. These techniques facilitate the confirmation of transactions through a consensus process that encompasses the entire network, thereby fostering equity, safeguarding against security threats, and enhancing the dependability of the Blockchain network.

Key Features of Blockchain Technology

Security

The high level of security in Blockchain is attributed to its decentralized and immutable characteristics. Modifying a single block would necessitate the modification of all subsequent blocks on the Blockchain, a computationally impractical task (Makhdoom et al., 2023). Utilizing Blockchain technology enhances its resilience against fraudulent activities and hacker attempts.

Transparency

The inherent transparency of Blockchain technology enables all participants to access and observe the complete transaction history. Although individual transactions are pseudonymous, meaning alphanumeric addresses identify them, the data remains accessible and verifiable (Makani et al., 2022). This feature can be advantageous for purposes like auditing and ensuring accountability.

Smart Contracts

The utilization of Blockchain technology enables the facilitation of smart contracts, which are contracts that are self-executing and possess terms that are explicitly encoded into the underlying code (Uchani Gutierrez & Xu, 2022). These contractual agreements are designed to execute autonomously upon the fulfillment of preset circumstances, thereby minimizing the requirement for intermediaries in diverse operational procedures.

Speed and Efficiency

The implementation of Blockchain technology can significantly improve the velocity and effectiveness of transactions, notably in cross-border payments and supply chain management (Alamri et al., 2022). Smart contracts and automated processes optimize operational efficiency by minimizing delays and decreasing expenses.

Accessibility

The promise of Blockchain technology extends beyond finance and brings about revolutionary changes in several areas, such as healthcare, supply chain management, voting systems, and others (Sabrina et al., 2022). The ideas of decentralization, immutability, and transparency, coupled with characteristics such as smart contracts, contribute to the bolstering of security, efficiency, and accountability in diverse applications (Makhdoom et al., 2023). Nevertheless, it is imperative to confront obstacles such as scalability, energy efficiency, and regulatory frameworks to actualize Blockchain technology's capabilities fully.

Figure 3. Blockchain and IoT integration in smart cities

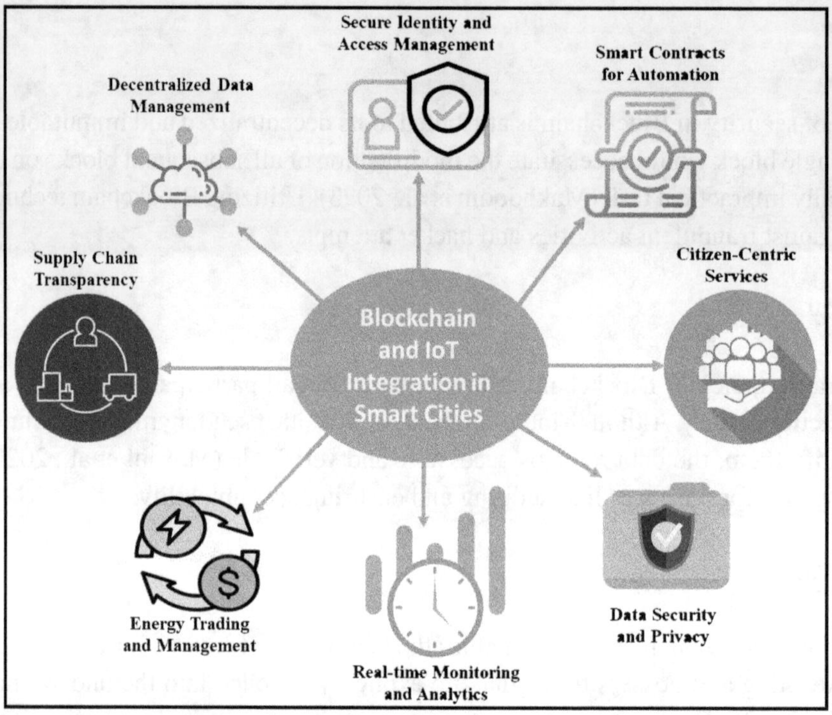

INTEGRATION OF BLOCKCHAIN AND IOT

In the 21st century, smart cities have emerged as a transformative force in modern urban planning. The escalating global urbanization trend demands innovative solutions to address the challenges of conventional urban infrastructure (Dieye et al., 2023). Challenges such as inefficient resource management, rapid population growth, increased resource demand, security and privacy concerns, and the imperative of sustainability have pushed cities to explore cutting-edge technologies. Among these, Blockchain and IoT have surfaced as promising technologies, holding immense potential to revolutionize smart city development (Alamri et al., 2022). Integrating Blockchain and the IoT in smart cities represents a paradigm shift in urban planning and development. As depicted in Figure 3, we explore the amalgamation of these two transformative technologies in this section, delving into their strengths and examining how their integration can address critical challenges conventional urban infrastructure faces. Through a comprehensive analysis of the benefits, this section aims to provide insights into the profound impact of amalgamating Blockchain and IoT in smart cities (Umran et al., 2023).

Decentralized Data Management

Blockchain represents an invaluable framework for decentralized and tamper-proof data management in smart cities (Hassanein et al., 2022). Integrating it with IoT guarantees that all transactions and data emanating from IoT devices are securely recorded on an immutable ledger, thus safeguarding data integrity and thwarting unauthorized modifications from malicious actors. Given the voluminous real-time data generated by IoT sensors and devices, Blockchain facilitates secure management without reliance on a central authority, mitigating data manipulation risk (Umran et al., 2023).

Secure Identity and Access Management

Blockchain's secure and decentralized identity management capability is a cornerstone for enhancing security and privacy within the smart city ecosystem (Khalil et al., 2022). A heightened level of security is achieved by allowing citizens, devices, and entities to store their identities on the Blockchain. This integration further addresses IoT devices' authentication and authorization requirements, providing a robust framework for managing identities and access permissions (Sabrina et al., 2022). This approach ensures secure interactions within the smart city network, reinforcing the system's overall resilience.

Smart Contracts for Automation

Integrating Blockchain and IoT introduces smart contracts that automate and enforce predefined rules, eliminating the need for intermediaries (Su et al., 2023). In smart cities, these contracts are pivotal in automating diverse processes such as utility payments, waste management, and traffic control (Makani et al., 2022; Uchani Gutierrez & Xu, 2022). IoT devices with sensors and actuators can trigger events based on real-world data. For example, combining IoT and Blockchain-based smart contracts in tourism finance can streamline processes, automatically executing actions when specific conditions are met. This integration enhances efficiency and ensures sustainable financial practices in the tourism industry (Demirel, 2023).

Supply Chain Transparency

Blockchain's transparent and traceable ledger finds application in supply chain management, ensuring the secure recording of transactions related to production, transportation, and distribution of goods (Centobelli et al., 2022). The synergy with IoT sensors in the supply chain enables real-time data generation on goods' location, condition, and status (Alqarni et al., 2023). When coupled with Blockchain, this data guarantees transparency and accountability, mitigating the risk of fraud and optimizing the overall efficiency of the supply chain (Madhwal et al., 2023).

Energy Trading and Management

Blockchain catalyzes peer-to-peer energy trading, establishing a decentralized and transparent avenue for energy transactions (Dong et al., 2022). In the IoT realm, smart meters and sensors monitor energy consumption and production in buildings (Chakravarthi et al., 2022). Integrating this data with Blockchain enables accurate and transparent billing and the implementation of dynamic pricing models. This encourages energy conservation and promotes using renewable energy sources, primarily indoors (Ma et al., 2023).

Data Security and Privacy

The secure and decentralized Blockchain architecture enhances data security, with cryptographic features ensuring encrypted access only for authorized parties (Khalil et al., 2022). The sensitivity of data collected by IoT devices makes preserving privacy paramount. Blockchain provides a decentralized control mechanism, substantially reducing the risk of unauthorized access or tampering (Kalinaki et al., 2023; Ullah et al., 2023).

Citizen-Centric Services

Blockchain enables transparent and secure citizen services, spanning activities like voting, property registration, and healthcare records (Nigmatov et al., 2023; Verma & Sheel, 2022). Blockchain's transparency enhances trust in government services by empowering citizens with greater control over their data. Citizen engagement is further augmented through IoT devices collecting feedback and real-time information, with Blockchain integration ensuring the authenticity of citizen input. This fosters more accountable and responsive governance (Testi et al., 2023).

Real-time Monitoring and Analytics

As a secure and transparent framework, Blockchain facilitates the recording and sharing of real-time data (Benedict et al., 2019). This becomes particularly beneficial in applications where data accuracy and integrity are paramount. IoT devices continuously generate real-time data on various city operations. Integration with Blockchain enables the utilization of this data for analytics, decision-making, and optimization of city services, especially in intelligent healthcare. Thus, collaboration between government agencies, private enterprises, and technology providers is essential to successfully integrate Blockchain and IoT in smart cities. Standards and protocols for interoperability, security, and data privacy must be established to ensure a seamless and secure smart city ecosystem.

SECURITY AND PRIVACY CONCERNS

Integrating Blockchain and IoT in smart cities promises to revolutionize data management and governance. However, this synergy introduces a spectrum of security and privacy challenges requiring meticulous examination. This section dissects these challenges, offering a scholarly exploration of the potential pitfalls and necessary safeguards.

Immutable Data and Access Controls

The inherent immutability of Blockchain technology, which ensures data integrity, becomes a double-edged sword when considering the integration of Blockchain and IoT in smart cities. While this feature safeguards against data tampering, it raises significant concerns regarding the permanence of sensitive information. Within the complex ecosystem of a smart city, the inability to modify or erase specific data introduces potential long-term privacy risks for individuals (Politou et al., 2022). Developing robust access controls and privacy-preserving mechanisms is imperative to navigate this challenge effectively. Establishing a delicate balance between the immutability of data and the necessity for data control is crucial to upholding individual privacy and security (Politou et al., 2021).

Smart Contract Vulnerabilities

Executing smart contracts, a foundational element of Blockchain-enabled IoT applications introduces vulnerabilities that malicious actors may exploit. In smart cities, flaws in smart contracts can lead to unauthorized access, manipulation of data, or disruptions in automated processes, mirroring the concerns observed in web applications (Kushwaha et al., 2022; Zhu et al., 2023). To fortify smart contracts against potential threats, a comprehensive approach involving rigorous code audits and implementing secure coding practices is essential. This proactive strategy is paramount in ensuring the integrity of the automated processes crucial for the seamless functioning of smart city infrastructures (Singh et al., 2021).

Scalability and Network Consensus

As the number of IoT devices and transactions surges, scalability issues and the selection of efficient consensus mechanisms become central concerns. Inefficient consensus algorithms and scalability bottlenecks can compromise smart city infrastructures' security and real-time responsiveness (Majeed et al., 2021). Addressing these challenges requires innovative solutions that enhance the scalability and efficiency of Blockchain networks. By continually evolving the technology underpinning these networks, we can better accommodate the increasing demands of a thriving smart city ecosystem (Bandara et al., 2022).

Network Security and Consensus Vulnerabilities

The reliance on consensus algorithms to validate transactions within Blockchain networks introduces vulnerabilities, particularly in large-scale IoT deployments. Malicious actors exploiting these vulnerabilities can compromise the integrity of transactions and stored data. Advanced consensus mechanisms and regular security audits are imperative to bolster network security to counteract this risk (Kashif & Kalkan, 2024; Singh et al., 2021; Tang et al., 2023). Proactive measures are vital to ensuring the robustness of the consensus mechanisms, safeguarding the smart city infrastructure from potential attacks on the Blockchain network.

Supply Chain Security for IoT Devices

Ensuring the security of the entire supply chain for IoT devices in smart cities is a multifaceted challenge. Tampering or compromising IoT devices at any stage of the supply chain can introduce vulnerabilities into the Blockchain network, undermining the overall security of intelligent city systems (Shafik & Kalinaki, 2023). Implementing stringent supply chain security measures and device attestation protocols is essential to mitigate this risk comprehensively. A proactive and vigilant approach across all supply chain stages is crucial to maintaining the integrity of the connected devices within the smart city landscape (Makhdoom et al., 2023).

Identity Management

Integrating IoT with Blockchain necessitates robust identity management systems, raising concerns about potentially exposing personally identifiable information. Inadequate identity protection measures may lead to the compromise of citizen privacy. Therefore, implementing privacy-centric identity solutions, such as zero-knowledge proofs, is crucial to mitigate these risks effectively (Alamri et al., 2022; Dieye et al., 2023). By incorporating cutting-edge privacy technologies, smart cities can strike a delicate balance between the advantages of identity management and the preservation of individual privacy.

Data Linkability

The transparent nature of Blockchain introduces the risk of data linkability, allowing entities to correlate and analyze transactional data. Persistent data linkability threatens citizen anonymity and privacy within the smart city landscape (Bansod & Ragha, 2022). Continuous innovations in cryptographic techniques and privacy-enhancing technologies are essential to counter this risk. These advancements are critical in thwarting the risks associated with data linkability, ensuring that smart cities can harness the benefits of Blockchain while safeguarding citizen privacy (Bao et al., 2023). Addressing these security and privacy concerns is imperative for researchers, developers, and policymakers to collaborate on innovative solutions that prioritize the ethical and responsible integration of Blockchain and IoT technologies in the evolving landscape of intelligent cities.

BLOCKCHAIN AND IOT INTEGRATION IN SMART CITIESCASE STUDIES

The integration of blockchain and IoT in smart cities promotes security, transparency, and efficiency, enabling a more connected, resilient, and sustainable urban environment, as illustrated in the following case studies.

Security and Trust: Dubai's Smart City Platform

Blockchain technology is being utilized by Dubai's Smart City[1] effort in order to enhance the level of security and trust in the data provided by Internet of Things devices in various industries such as transportation and healthcare (Tokkozhina et al., 2023). By utilizing a distributed ledger and smart contracts, the platform guarantees the authenticity of the data and makes it possible to conduct transactions securely. As a consequence of this, the infrastructure of the smart city has undergone an increase in overall security, which has fostered trust among city residents and other stakeholders (Alamri et al., 2022). Instilling faith in the dependability of information produced from a variety of IoT devices is made possible by the decentralized nature of blockchain, which contributes to data that is resistant to tampering.

Data Integrity and Transparency: Singapore's Project Ubin

Project Ubin[2], which the Monetary Authority of Singapore[3] is conducting, is investigating blockchain technology with the goal of improving data quality and transparency in financial transactions (Tokkozhina et al., 2023). This demonstrates blockchain's wider potential in smart cities. Through the utilization of blockchain technology, the project demonstrates the capacity of the technology to guarantee the integrity of data by establishing a platform that is both trustworthy and open to scrutiny for financial transactions (Kashif & Kalkan, 2024). Despite the fact that it is not focused on the IoT, the project illustrates that blockchain technology can improve the dependability of data exchanges, thereby setting the groundwork for more widespread applications in smart cities. It is possible to expand transparency and data integrity, which are essential for smart city services, to a variety of data created by the IoT.

Interoperability: Taipei's IOTA Integration

The city of Taipei[4] is working with the IOTA Foundation[5] to improve the interoperability of its smart city efforts. This is accomplished by employing IOTA's Tangle, which allows for safe and cost-free micro-transactions between Internet of Things devices (Liu et al., 2020). The technology developed by IOTA, which promotes standardized and interoperable communication among various devices, contributes to the development of a smart city ecosystem that is more efficient and connected. As a result of the incorporation of IOTA, transactions have become more simplified, which has fostered interoperability and standardization (Tiwari et al., 2019). This makes it possible for numerous IoTs devices to communicate with one another in a smooth manner, which contributes to the efficiency and efficacy of the smart city infrastructure in Taipei.

Decentralization and Resilience: Zug's Blockchain Digital ID

Zug, Switzerland, adopts a blockchain-powered digital identification system to strengthen decentralization and resilience, empowering residents with increased authority over their personal data (Astarita et al., 2020). Blockchain technology ensures the security and management of digital identities in a decentralized manner, hence minimizing the vulnerability of a single point of failure and improving the city's ability to withstand and recover from adverse events (Singh et al., 2021). The decentralized digital identification system enhances both resilience and security. This methodology may be extended to additional smart city services, guaranteeing a strong and resilient infrastructure by distributing control over crucial identity-related data.

Supply Chain and Resource Management: Shanghai's VeChain Implementation

Shanghai utilizes VeChain's[6] blockchain technology to augment the traceability of supply chains and the management of resources, guaranteeing transparency and genuineness in the tracking of products. VeChain's blockchain system documents and tracks the source of items, promoting transparency and responsibility in the supply chain (Tokkozhina et al., 2023). This notion can be expanded to oversee vital resources in the context of a smart city, fostering openness and effectiveness in the utilization of resources. The implementation has enhanced supply chain accountability, diminishing fraudulent activities and guaranteeing the genuineness of products (Astarita et al., 2020).

Efficient Resource Allocation: Barcelona's CityOS Platform

The CityOS platform in Barcelona incorporates blockchain and IoT technologies to automate governance procedures, enhancing the efficiency of resource distribution in sectors such as energy usage, waste disposal, and transportation (Andoni et al., 2019). Smart contracts used on the blockchain streamline governance procedures, enabling effective allocation and control of resources across diverse urban services. The implementation of the CityOS[7] platform has resulted in enhanced resource utilization, leading to cost reduction and less environmental footprint (H. Liu et al., 2023). Barcelona's smart city efforts employ blockchain and IoT technologies to guarantee transparency, accountability, and efficient resource allocation in governance processes.

Micropayments and Incentive Mechanisms: Austin, Texas - P2P Energy Trading

Austin[8], Texas, has introduced a platform that uses blockchain technology to facilitate direct energy trade between individuals. This network uses smart contracts to encourage citizens to produce and distribute surplus renewable energy (Jha, 2023). Blockchain enables transparent and secure peer-to-peer transactions between energy providers and consumers. It utilizes smart contracts to automate trading and encourage sustainable energy habits. The implementation promotes the generation of renewable energy, decreases reliance on centralized power networks, and cultivates a sustainable energy ecology (Plevris et al., 2022). The combination of blockchain and IoT offers a platform that enables transparent and motivation-based energy practices in Austin.

Energy Management: Power Ledger in Fremantle, Australia

Fremantle[9], an Australian city, is partnering with Power Ledger to deploy a blockchain-powered energy trading platform to oversee decentralized energy networks. Blockchain facilitates transparent and secure transactions among prosumers, while IoT devices, like smart meters, enable the real-time monitoring and selling of renewable energy (Bao et al., 2023). The decentralized energy trading market in Fremantle has improved energy efficiency, lowered expenses, and bolstered the utilization of renewable energy sources. The amalgamation of blockchain and IoT enhances the sustainability and efficacy of the urban energy management system (Kashif & Kalkan, 2024).

CHALLENGES, LIMITATIONS, AND IMPLICATIONS

Within this section, the challenges and limitations of using Blockchain in smart cities are presented, as well as some implications.

Challenges

Scalability

In smart cities, scalability poses a significant challenge for Blockchain and IoT technologies (Rejeb et al., 2021). On the Blockchain front, the issue lies in efficiently handling the large volume of transactions occurring within a smart city's dynamic and interconnected environment. As the city's infrastructure becomes increasingly digitized, the strain on the Blockchain network can hinder transaction processing speed and overall system performance (Rejeb et al., 2022). Simultaneously, the proliferation of IoT devices exacerbates scalability concerns. The growing number of these interconnected devices, ranging from sensors to smart appliances, intensifies the complexity of managing their interactions seamlessly (Plevris et al., 2022). They coordinate data exchange and communication among a vast array of real-time devices, demanding robust scalability solutions to prevent bottlenecks and ensure the smooth operation of smart city systems. Researchers and practitioners in this field are thus challenged to develop scalable architectures that can accommodate the evolving demands of both Blockchain and IoT components within the intricate landscape of smart cities (H. Liu et al., 2023).

Interoperability

This is a crucial challenge in integrating Blockchain and IoT within smart cities that revolve around the seamless communication between diverse IoT devices and Blockchain platforms (Nica et al., 2023; Tiwari et al., 2019). The intricate web of interconnected devices with unique protocols and specifications poses a significant hurdle. IoT devices generate vast amounts of data that must be efficiently and securely communicated to the Blockchain for processing. Achieving a standardized communication protocol that can accommodate the heterogeneity of IoT devices is essential. Without a common language, the potential benefits of the combined technologies may be compromised, hindering the smart city's ability to harness the full power of Blockchain and IoT synergies (Aghimien et al., 2022). Researchers and industry stakeholders are actively exploring solutions to establish universal standards, ensuring the smooth interoperability of these technologies in the complex landscape of smart urban environments (Rejeb et al., 2021).

Security Concerns

Security is a paramount concern when integrating Blockchain and IoT in smart cities. In the realm of Blockchain, the technology inherently offers robust security through its decentralized and cryptographic principles (Aggarwal et al., 2019). However, vulnerabilities can emerge in smart contracts, the self-executing codes on the Blockchain, or within the network's consensus algorithms. These vulnerabilities may be exploited, leading to potential breaches in the system (Andoni et al., 2019). On the other hand, IoT devices introduce another layer of security challenges. Device vulnerabilities, if not adequately addressed, can be exploited by malicious actors, jeopardizing the entire system's integrity. Furthermore, data security issues in the communication between IoT devices and the Blockchain network could expose sensitive information. Secure communication protocols and robust authentication mechanisms become imperative to mitigate these risks.

Energy Consumption

The energy consumption associated with Blockchain's Proof-of-Work (PoW) consensus algorithms is a significant concern, particularly when considering their potential implementation in smart cities. PoW involves complex mathematical puzzles miners must solve to validate transactions and create new blocks. This process requires substantial computational power, leading to high energy consumption. In the context of smart cities, where sustainability is a key focus, the environmental impact of PoW becomes a notable limitation. The energy-intensive nature of PoW can contribute to increased carbon footprints and undermine the goal of creating efficient and eco-friendly urban environments. Addressing this challenge requires exploring alternative consensus mechanisms, such as Proof-of-Stake (PoS)

Table 1. Summary of the research challenges along with their causes and possible solutions

Challenge	Causes	Guidelines
Scalability	- Blockchain: Inherent limitations in handling high transaction volume. - IoT: Managing interactions among a growing number of devices.	- Explore scalable consensus algorithms. - Investigate off-chain solutions. - Implement efficient IoT communication protocols.
Interoperability	Lack of standardized protocols and communication frameworks.	- Develop industry-wide standards for interoperability. - Create middleware solutions for communication between diverse systems.
Security concern	- Blockchain: Vulnerabilities in smart contracts and consensus. - IoT: Device vulnerabilities and potential data security issues.	- Conduct thorough security audits for smart contracts and nodes. - Implement robust encryption and authentication for IoT devices.
Energy consumption	Energy-intensive Proof-of-Work consensus algorithms in Blockchain.	- Explore and adopt energy-efficient consensus mechanisms (such as, Proof-of-Stake). - Implement sustainable practices in Blockchain network design.

or practical Byzantine fault tolerance (PBFT), known for their lower energy requirements. Additionally, ongoing research and development efforts in Blockchain technology aim to design consensus algorithms that balance security, decentralization, and energy efficiency, providing more sustainable options for smart city implementations.

Limitations

Cost

The cost implications of implementing and maintaining a Blockchain infrastructure pose a significant challenge for smart cities (Dlimi et al., 2021). The expenses incurred in setting up the necessary hardware, software, and network infrastructure, coupled with ongoing operational and maintenance costs, can strain the financial resources of municipal authorities (Khalil et al., 2022). Smart city projects often require substantial investments, and adopting Blockchain technology introduces additional financial commitment (Riđić et al., 2022). Costs are related to the initial deployment and include expenses for ensuring security, scalability, and compliance over time. Addressing these financial considerations is crucial for successfully integrating Blockchain in smart city initiatives, necessitating careful budgeting and strategic planning to balance technological innovation with fiscal responsibility.

Regulatory Uncertainty

This poses a significant obstacle to the widespread implementation of Blockchain and IoT in smart cities (Singh et al., 2020). The absence of transparent and standardized regulations creates an atmosphere of ambiguity, discouraging public and private sectors from fully embracing these transformative technologies. The intricate nature of Blockchain and IoT applications necessitates comprehensive legal frameworks to address data privacy, security, and interoperability issues. Without well-defined regulations, stakeholders may hesitate to invest in or adopt these innovations, fearing legal complications (Majeed et al., 2021).

Therefore, it is imperative for policymakers to collaboratively develop and establish clear regulatory guidelines that foster innovation while addressing the unique challenges presented by Blockchain and IoT integration in the context of smart cities (Nica et al., 2023). Such regulatory clarity will encourage investment and development and ensure the responsible and ethical implementation of these technologies for the benefit of urban environments and their residents.

Adoption Barriers

The adoption of Blockchain and IoT technologies in smart cities faces significant barriers, primarily rooted in resistance to change and the necessity for a comprehensive overhaul of existing systems (Singh et al., 2020). Cities and urban infrastructures often operate on well-established frameworks, and introducing disruptive technologies like Blockchain and IoT requires a fundamental shift in mindset and infrastructure. Stakeholders may be hesitant to embrace these changes due to concerns about the complexity of integration, potential disruptions during the transition, and the costs involved. Overcoming these adoption barriers necessitates strategic planning, clear communication of the benefits, and gradual implementation strategies that mitigate the perceived risks associated with such transformative technologies (Khalil et al., 2022). Collaborative efforts among policymakers, industry leaders, and the research community are crucial to developing frameworks that facilitate a smoother transition, address concerns, and foster a more receptive environment for adopting Blockchain and IoT in smart cities (Majeed et al., 2021).

Implications

Data Integrity

Data integrity is paramount in smart cities, where IoT devices continuously generate vast amounts of information (Andoni et al., 2019). The integration of Blockchain technology plays a pivotal role in fortifying data integrity within this dynamic ecosystem. Blockchain's inherent characteristic of immutability ensures that once data is recorded on the Blockchain, it cannot be altered or tampered with. In the context of IoT devices, this immutability feature is particularly crucial as it safeguards the authenticity and reliability of the data collected (Jha, 2023). Each transaction or piece of information from an IoT device is securely recorded in a block, and the decentralized and distributed nature of the Blockchain ensures that no single entity has control over the entire system, reducing the risk of unauthorized alterations. This establishes trust in the data generated by IoT devices and provides a robust foundation for various applications, such as smart contracts and transparent data-sharing mechanisms in smart city infrastructures (Zakari et al., 2021). The assurance of data integrity through Blockchain integration not only enhances the reliability of information but also contributes to the overall security and trustworthiness of smart city systems.

Decentralization

This plays a pivotal role in fortifying the resilience of smart city systems through implementing Blockchain technology (Khalid et al., 2020). By distributing the control and storage of data across a network of nodes rather than relying on a central authority, Blockchain mitigates the risk of a single point of failure (Tokkozhina et al., 2023). In the context of smart cities, this decentralized architecture ensures that if one node or component fails, the system as a whole remains operational. This increased robustness is particularly crucial in urban environments where the reliability of data and systems is paramount for various services, such as transportation, energy management, and public safety (Yu et al., 2022). The decentralized nature of Blockchain thus contributes significantly to smart city infrastructures' overall stability and dependability (Liu et al., 2020).

Efficiency Gains

Using Blockchain and IoT technologies in smart cities can significantly enhance operational efficiency (Majeed et al., 2021). With its decentralized and secure nature, Blockchain ensures the integrity and immutability of data collected from IoT devices. This is particularly crucial in a smart city context where vast amounts of data are generated from diverse sources such as sensors, cameras, and other connected devices (Bommu et al., 2023). One key aspect contributing to efficiency gains is the transparent and automated execution of smart contracts. These self-executing contracts, enabled by Blockchain, can automate various processes in smart cities, ranging from energy management and waste disposal to traffic control (Ahmed et al., 2022). For instance, smart contracts can facilitate automatic payments for energy usage based on real-time data from IoT-enabled meters, eliminating the need for intermediaries and streamlining the billing process (Shafik, 2024c). Moreover, the decentralized nature of Blockchain removes the reliance on a single central authority, reducing the risk of system failures or data breaches (Khrais, 2020). This decentralization, coupled with the secure and transparent audit trail provided by Blockchain, enhances the overall reliability of smart city operations.

Transparent Governance

Transparent governance is a pivotal aspect of integrating smart contracts on the Blockchain within the context of smart cities. Smart contracts, self-executing pieces of code with predefined rules, introduce transparency and automation that can revolutionize governance processes. The immutability of Blockchain ensures that the terms encoded in these contracts are tamper-proof, fostering trust among stakeholders (Astarita et al., 2020). This transparency mitigates the risk of fraudulent activities and allows citizens and authorities alike to trace and verify every step of a process. Automated execution of contracts further streamlines governance, reducing the need for intermediaries and minimizing the potential for human error (Liu et al., 2020). As smart cities evolve, implementing smart contracts becomes a cornerstone in establishing accountable and efficient governance structures, setting a precedent for a new era of transparent and automated public administration (Majeed et al., 2021).

FUTURE DIRECTIONS

The future directions in integrating Blockchain and IoT in smart cities hold immense potential for transformative advancements. Research endeavors should consider exploring hybrid Blockchain solutions that amalgamate the strengths of public and private Blockchains, providing a nuanced approach to scalability and privacy concerns. Investigating the synergy between Blockchain, IoT, and edge computing could mitigate latency issues and enhance real-time processing capabilities. Addressing security and privacy challenges remains pivotal, focusing on developing innovative protocols to safeguard the sensitive data generated by IoT devices.

Future research should also delve into energy-efficient consensus mechanisms to alleviate the environmental impact of Blockchain in smart city applications. Standardizing interoperability between diverse IoT devices and Blockchain platforms is crucial for seamless integration. Exploring the application of smart contracts for automating urban governance processes and enhancing transparency in supply chain management represents promising avenues. Furthermore, researchers should contribute to the development of adaptive regulatory frameworks to accommodate the evolving landscape of Blockchain and IoT technologies in smart cities. Attention to user-centric design, ethical considerations, and the integration of artificial intelligence will collectively shape a sustainable and inclusive future for smart city implementations.

CONCLUSION

Blockchain technology is leading a digital revolution, changing how we view and manage trust and data in a connected world. Decentralization, distributed ledger technology, immutability, and consensus processes are its cornerstones, transforming transaction verification and data security. Decentralization allows peer-to-peer networks to approve and record transactions without a central authority, challenging hierarchical structures. This move will enable people to trust one another directly, eliminating intermediaries. The distributed ledger maintains a synchronized and immutable transaction history, promoting transparency and discouraging fraud. Blockchain's immutable ledger and cryptographic security provide unmatched data integrity and cyber protection. Transparency and smart contracts increase accountability and automation across sectors, changing commercial transactions. Blockchain's efficiency can expedite procedures, reduce operational costs, and stimulate innovation in finance, supply chain management, healthcare, and governance. Blockchain is already transforming sectors, but scalability, energy consumption, and legal frameworks remain issues. It promises to create trust, transparency, and efficiency in our dynamic digital landscape. It is the foundation of a decentralized, secure, and trust-based future that will transform our digital age with lasting repercussions.

REFERENCES

Aggarwal, S., Chaudhary, R., Aujla, G. S., Kumar, N., Choo, K. K. R., & Zomaya, A. Y. (2019). Blockchain for smart communities: Applications, challenges and opportunities. In Journal of Network and Computer Applications, 144. doi:10.1016/j.jnca.2019.06.018

Aghimien, D. O., Aigbavboa, C., Edwards, D. J., Mahamadu, A. M., Olomolaiye, P., Nash, H., & Onyia, M. (2022). A fuzzy synthetic evaluation of the challenges of smart city development in developing countries. *Smart and Sustainable Built Environment*, *11*(3), 405–421. doi:10.1108/SASBE-06-2020-0092

Ahmed, I., Zhang, Y., Jeon, G., Lin, W., Khosravi, M. R., & Qi, L. (2022). A Blockchain- and artificial intelligence-enabled smart IoT framework for sustainable city. *International Journal of Intelligent Systems*, *37*(9), 6493–6507. doi:10.1002/int.22852

Alamri, B., Crowley, K., & Richardson, I. (2022). Blockchain-Based Identity Management Systems in Health IoT: A Systematic Review. *IEEE Access : Practical Innovations, Open Solutions*, *10*, 59612–59629. doi:10.1109/ACCESS.2022.3180367

Alnssyan, B., Ahmad, Z., Malela-Majika, J. C., Seong, J. T., & Shafik, W. (2023). On the identifiability and statistical features of a new distributional approach with reliability applications. *AIP Advances*, *13*(12), 125211. doi:10.1063/5.0178555

Alqarni, M. A., Alkatheiri, M. S., Chauhdary, S. H., & Saleem, S. (2023). Use of Blockchain-Based Smart Contracts in Logistics and Supply Chains. *Electronics (Basel)*, *12*(6), 1340. doi:10.3390/electronics12061340

Andoni, M., Robu, V., Flynn, D., Abram, S., Geach, D., Jenkins, D., McCallum, P., & Peacock, A. (2019). Blockchain technology in the energy sector: A systematic review of challenges and opportunities. In Renewable and Sustainable Energy Reviews, 100. doi:10.1016/j.rser.2018.10.014

Astarita, V., Giofrè, V. P., Mirabelli, G., & Solina, V. (2020). A Review of Blockchain-Based Systems in Transportation. *Information (Basel)*, *11*(1), 21. doi:10.3390/info11010021

Bandara, E., Shetty, S., Rahman, A., Mukkamala, R., & Liang, X. (2022). Moose: A Scalable Blockchain Architecture for 5G Enabled IoT with Sharding and Network Slicing. *IEEE Wireless Communications and Networking Conference, WCNC,* (pp. 1194–1199). IEEE. 10.1109/WCNC51071.2022.9771885

Bansod, S., & Ragha, L. (2022). Challenges in making Blockchain privacy compliant for the digital world: some measures. *Sadhana - Academy Proceedings in Engineering Sciences, 47*(3), 1–17. https://doi.org/. doi:10.1007/S12046-022-01931-1/FIGURES/9

Bao, Z., He, D., Wang, H., Luo, M., & Peng, C. (2023). A Group Signature Scheme with Selective Linkability and Traceability for Blockchain-Based Data Sharing Systems in E-health Services. *IEEE Internet of Things Journal*, *10*(23), 21115–21128. doi:10.1109/JIOT.2023.3284968

Benedict, S., Rumaise, P., & Kaur, J. (2019). IoT Blockchain Solution for Air Quality Monitoring in SmartCities. *International Symposium on Advanced Networks and Telecommunication Systems, ANTS, 2019-December.* IEEE. 10.1109/ANTS47819.2019.9118148

Bommu, S., M, A. K., Babburu, K., N, S., Thalluri, L. N., G, V. G., Gopalan, A., Mallapati, P. K., Guha, K., Mohammad, H. R., & S, S. K. (2023). Smart City IoT System Network Level Routing Analysis and Blockchain Security Based Implementation. *Journal of Electrical Engineering & Technology*, *18*(2), 1351–1368. doi:10.1007/s42835-022-01239-4 PMID:37521954

Centobelli, P., Cerchione, R., Del Vecchio, P., Oropallo, E., & Secundo, G. (2022). Blockchain technology for bridging trust, traceability and transparency in circular supply chain. *Information & Management*, *59*(7), 103508. doi:10.1016/j.im.2021.103508

Chakravarthi, P. K., Yuvaraj, D., & Venkataramanan, V. (2022). IoT-based smart energy meter for smart grids. *ICDCS 2022 - 2022 6th International Conference on Devices, Circuits and Systems,* 360–363. 10.1109/ICDCS54290.2022.9780714

Demirel, E. (2023). Application of Blockchain-Based Smart Contract in Sustainable Tourism Finance. *Blockchain for Tourism and Hospitality Industries,* 122–138. Springer.. doi:10.4324/9781003351917-9

Dieye, M., Valiorgue, P., Gelas, J. P., Diallo, E. H., Ghodous, P., Biennier, F., & Peyrol, E. (2023). A Self-Sovereign Identity Based on Zero-Knowledge Proof and Blockchain. *IEEE Access : Practical Innovations, Open Solutions*, *11*, 49445–49455. doi:10.1109/ACCESS.2023.3268768

Dlimi, Z., Ezzati, A., & Ben Alla, S. (2021). A Lightweight Blockchain for IoT in Smart City (IoT-SmartChain). *Computers, Materials & Continua*, *69*(2), 2687–2703. doi:10.32604/cmc.2021.018942

Dong, J., Song, C., Liu, S., Yin, H., Zheng, H., & Li, Y. (2022). Decentralized peer-to-peer energy trading strategy in energy Blockchain environment: A game-theoretic approach. *Applied Energy*, *325*, 119852. doi:10.1016/j.apenergy.2022.119852

Hassanein, A. A., El-Tazi, N., & Mohy, N. N. (2022). Blockchain, smart contracts, and decentralized applications: an introduction. *Implementing and leveraging Blockchain programming,* 97-114. Springer. . doi:10.1007/978-981-16-3412-3_6

Jha, S. K. (2023). Application of Blockchain technology in libraries and information centers services. *Library Hi Tech News*. doi:10.1108/LHTN-02-2023-0020

Kalinaki, K., Thilakarathne, N. N., Mubarak, H. R., Malik, O. A., & Abdullatif, M. (2023). Cybersafe Capabilities and Utilities for Smart Cities. In *Cybersecurity for Smart Cities* (pp. 71–86). Springer., doi:10.1007/978-3-031-24946-4_6

Kashif, M., & Kalkan, K. (2024). EPIoT: Enhanced privacy preservation based Blockchain mechanism for internet-of-things. *Computer Networks*, *238*, 110107. doi:10.1016/j.comnet.2023.110107

Khalid, U., Asim, M., Baker, T., Hung, P. C. K., Tariq, M. A., & Rafferty, L. (2020). A decentralized lightweight Blockchain-based authentication mechanism for IoT systems. *Cluster Computing*, *23*(3), 2067–2087. doi:10.1007/s10586-020-03058-6

Khalil, U., Malik, O. A., Uddin, M., & Chen, C. L. (2022). A Comparative Analysis on Blockchain versus Centralized Authentication Architectures for IoT-Enabled Smart Devices in Smart Cities: A Comprehensive Review, Recent Advances, and Future Research Directions. *Sensors (Basel)*, *22*(14), 5168. doi:10.3390/s22145168 PMID:35890848

Khalil, U., Mueen-Uddin, Malik, O. A., & Hussain, S. (2022). A Blockchain Footprint for Authentication of IoT-Enabled Smart Devices in Smart Cities: State-of-the-Art Advancements, Challenges and Future Research Directions. *IEEE Access : Practical Innovations, Open Solutions*, *10*, 76805–76823. Advance online publication. doi:10.1109/ACCESS.2022.3189998

Khrais, L. T. (2020). IoT and Blockchain in the development of smart cities. *International Journal of Advanced Computer Science and Applications*, *2*(2). doi:10.14569/IJACSA.2020.0110220

Kushwaha, S. S., Joshi, S., Singh, D., Kaur, M., & Lee, H. N. (2022). Systematic Review of Security Vulnerabilities in Ethereum Blockchain Smart Contract. *IEEE Access : Practical Innovations, Open Solutions*, *10*, 6605–6621. doi:10.1109/ACCESS.2021.3140091

Liu, H., Han, S., & Zhu, Z. (2023). Blockchain Technology toward Smart Construction: Review and Future Directions. *Journal of Construction Engineering and Management*, *149*(3), 03123002. Advance online publication. doi:10.1061/JCEMD4.COENG-11929

Liu, Y., Wang, K., Qian, K., Du, M., & Guo, S. (2020). Tornado: Enabling Blockchain in Heterogeneous Internet of Things Through a Space-Structured Approach. *IEEE Internet of Things Journal*, *7*(2), 1273–1286. doi:10.1109/JIOT.2019.2954128

Ma, N., Waegel, A., Hakkarainen, M., Braham, W. W., Glass, L., & Aviv, D. (2023). Blockchain + IoT sensor network to measure, evaluate and incentivize personal environmental accounting and efficient energy use in indoor spaces. *Applied Energy*, *332*, 120443. doi:10.1016/j.apenergy.2022.120443

Madhwal, Y., Yanovich, Y., Balachander, S., Poojaa, K. H., Saranya, R., & Subashini, B. (2023). Enhancing Supply Chain Efficiency and Security: A Proof of Concept for IoT Device Integration With Blockchain. *IEEE Access : Practical Innovations, Open Solutions*, *11*, 121173–121189. doi:10.1109/ACCESS.2023.3328569

Majeed, U., Khan, L. U., Yaqoob, I., Kazmi, S. M. A., Salah, K., & Hong, C. S. (2021). Blockchain for IoT-based smart cities: Recent advances, requirements, and future challenges. *Journal of Network and Computer Applications*, *181*, 103007. doi:10.1016/j.jnca.2021.103007

Makani, S., Pittala, R., Alsayed, E., Aloqaily, M., & Jararweh, Y. (2022). A survey of Blockchain applications in sustainable and smart cities. *Cluster Computing*, *25*(6), 3915–3936. doi:10.1007/s10586-022-03625-z

Makhdoom, I., Abolhasan, M., Franklin, D., Lipman, J., Zimmermann, C., Piccardi, M., & Moghadam, N. S. (2023). Detecting compromised IoT devices: Existing techniques, challenges, and a way forward. *Computers & Security*, *132*, 103384. doi:10.1016/j.cose.2023.103384

Nica, E., Popescu, G. H., Poliak, M., Kliestik, T., & Sabie, O. M. (2023). Digital Twin Simulation Tools, Spatial Cognition Algorithms, and Multi-Sensor Fusion Technology in Sustainable Urban Governance Networks. *Mathematics*, *11*(9), 1981. Advance online publication. doi:10.3390/math11091981

Nigmatov, A., Pradeep, A., & Musulmonova, N. (2023). Blockchain Technology in Improving Transparency and Efficiency in Government Operations. *15th International Conference on Electronics, Computers and Artificial Intelligence, ECAI 2023 - Proceedings*. IEEE. 10.1109/ECAI58194.2023.10194154

Plevris, V., Lagaros, N. D., & Zeytinci, A. (2022). Blockchain in Civil Engineering, Architecture and Construction Industry: State of the Art, Evolution, Challenges and Opportunities. In Frontiers in Built Environment, 8. doi:10.3389/fbuil.2022.840303

Politou, E., Alepis, E., Virvou, M., & Patsakis, C. (2022). Privacy in Blockchain. In *Privacy and Data Protection Challenges in the Distributed Era. Learning and Analytics in Intelligent Systems* (Vol. 26, pp. 133–149). Springer. doi:10.1007/978-3-030-85443-0_7

Politou, E., Casino, F., Alepis, E., & Patsakis, C. (2021). Blockchain Mutability: Challenges and Proposed Solutions. *IEEE Transactions on Emerging Topics in Computing*, *9*(4), 1972–1986. doi:10.1109/TETC.2019.2949510

Rejeb, A., Rejeb, K., Simske, S., Treiblmaier, H., & Zailani, S. (2022). The big picture on the internet of things and the smart city: A review of what we know and what we need to know. *Internet of Things : Engineering Cyber Physical Human Systems, 19*, 100565. doi:10.1016/j.iot.2022.100565

Rejeb, A., Rejeb, K., Simske, S. J., & Keogh, J. G. (2021). Blockchain technology in the smart city: A bibliometric review. *Quality & Quantity*. doi:10.1007/s11135-021-01251-2 PMID:34629554

Riđić, O., Jukić, T., Riđić, G., Mangafić, J., Bušatlić, S., & Karamehić, J. (2022). Implementation of Blockchain Technologies in Smart Cities, Opportunities and Challenges. In Environmental Footprints and Eco-Design of Products and Processes. Springer. doi:10.1007/978-981-16-6301-7_4

Sabrina, F., Li, N., & Sohail, S. (2022). A Blockchain Based Secure IoT System Using Device Identity Management. *Sensors, 22*(19), 7535. . doi:10.3390/s22197535

Shafik, W. (2023a). A Comprehensive Cybersecurity Framework for Present and Future Global Information Technology Organizations. In *Effective Cybersecurity Operations for Enterprise-Wide Systems* (pp. 56–79). IGI Global., doi:10.4018/978-1-6684-9018-1.ch002

Shafik, W. (2023b). Cyber Security Perspectives in Public Spaces: Drone Case Study. In Handbook of Research on Cybersecurity Risk in Contemporary Business Systems (pp. 79-97). IGI Global. doi:10.4018/978-1-6684-7207-1.ch004

Shafik, W. (2023c). Making Cities Smarter: IoT and SDN Applications, Challenges, and Future Trends. In Opportunities and Challenges of Industrial IoT in 5G and 6G Networks (pp. 73-94). IGI Global. doi:10.4018/978-1-7998-9266-3.ch004

Shafik, W. (2024a). Introduction to ChatGPT. In *Advanced Applications of Generative AI and Natural Language Processing Models* (pp. 1–25). IGI Global. doi:10.4018/979-8-3693-0502-7.ch001

Shafik, W. (2024b). Predicting Future Cybercrime Trends in the Metaverse Era. In *Forecasting Cyber Crimes in the Age of the Metaverse* (pp. 78–113). IGI Global. doi:10.4018/979-8-3693-0220-0.ch005

Shafik, W. (2024c). *Toward a More Ethical Future of Artificial Intelligence and Data Science. The Ethical Frontier of AI and Data Analysis*. IGI Global. doi:10.4018/979-8-3693-2964-1.ch022

Shafik, W., & Kalinaki, K. (2023). Smart City Ecosystem: An Exploration of Requirements, Architecture, Applications, Security, and Emerging Motivations. In Handbook of Research on Network-Enabled IoT Applications for Smart City Services (pp. 75–98). IGI Global. doi:10.4018/979-8-3693-0744-1.ch005

Shafik, W., Matinkhah, S. M., & Shokoor, F. (2023). Cybersecurity in unmanned aerial vehicles: A review. *International Journal on Smart Sensing and Intelligent Systems, 16*(1), 20230012. doi:10.2478/ijssis-2023-0012

Singh, S., Sanwar Hosen, A. S. M., & Yoon, B. (2021). Blockchain Security Attacks, Challenges, and Solutions for the Future Distributed IoT Network. *IEEE Access : Practical Innovations, Open Solutions, 9*, 13938–13959. doi:10.1109/ACCESS.2021.3051602

Singh, S., Sharma, P. K., Yoon, B., Shojafar, M., Cho, G. H., & Ra, I. H. (2020). Convergence of Blockchain and artificial intelligence in IoT network for the sustainable smart city. *Sustainable Cities and Society, 63*, 102364. doi:10.1016/j.scs.2020.102364

Su, X., Hu, Y., Liu, W., Jiang, Z., Qiu, C., Xiong, J., & Sun, J. (2023). A Blockchain-based smart contract model for secured energy trading management in smart microgrids. *Security and Privacy, 341*. doi:10.1002/spy2.341

Tang, Y., Yan, J., Chakraborty, C., & Sun, Y. (2023). Hedera: A Permissionless and Scalable Hybrid Blockchain Consensus Algorithm in Multi-Access Edge Computing for IoT. *IEEE Internet of Things Journal, 10*(24), 21187–21202. doi:10.1109/JIOT.2023.3279108

Testi, N., Marconi, R., & Pasher, E. (2023). Exploring the potential of Blockchain technology for citizen engagement in smart governance. *Open Research Europe*, *3*, 183. doi:10.12688/openreseurope.16153.2

Tiwari, P., Ilavarasan, P. V., & Punia, S. (2019). Content analysis of literature on big data in smart cities. *Benchmarking*, *28*(5), 1837–1857. doi:10.1108/BIJ-12-2018-0442

Tokkozhina, U., Mataloto, B. M., Martins, A. L., & Ferreira, J. C. (2023). Decentralizing Online Food Delivery Services: A Blockchain and IoT Model for Smart Cities. *Mobile Networks and Applications*. doi:10.1007/s11036-023-02119-5

Uchani Gutierrez, O. C., & Xu, G. (2023). Blockchain and Smart Contracts to Secure Property Transactions in Smart Cities. *Applied Sciences (Basel, Switzerland)*, *13*(1), 66. doi:10.3390/app13010066

Ullah, Z., Naeem, M., Coronato, A., Ribino, P., & De Pietro, G. (2023). Blockchain Applications in Sustainable Smart Cities. *Sustainable Cities and Society*, *97*, 104697. doi:10.1016/j.scs.2023.104697

Umran, S. M., Lu, S. F., Abduljabbar, Z. A., & Nyangaresi, V. O. (2023). Multi-chain Blockchain based secure data-sharing framework for industrial IoTs smart devices in petroleum industry. *Internet of Things : Engineering Cyber Physical Human Systems*, *24*, 100969. doi:10.1016/j.iot.2023.100969

Verma, S., & Sheel, A. (2022). Blockchain for government organizations: Past, present and future. *Journal of Global Operations and Strategic Sourcing*, *15*(3), 406–430. doi:10.1108/JGOSS-08-2021-0063

Wang, Y., Shafik, W., Seong, J. T., Al Mutairi, A., Mustafa, M. S., & Mouhamed, M. R. (2023). Service delay and optimization of the energy efficiency of a system in fog-enabled smart cities. *Alexandria Engineering Journal*, *84*, 112–125. doi:10.1016/j.aej.2023.10.034

Yang, Z., Jianjun, L., Faqiri, H., Shafik, W., Talal Abdulrahman, A., Yusuf, M., & Sharawy, A. M. (2021). Green internet of things and big data application in smart cities development. *Complexity*, *2021*, 1–15. doi:10.1155/2021/4922697

Yu, Z., Song, L., Jiang, L., & Khold Sharafi, O. (2022). Systematic literature review on the security challenges of Blockchain in IoT-based smart cities. *Kybernetes*, *51*(1), 323–347. doi:10.1108/K-07-2020-0449

Zakari, R. Y., Lawal, Z. K., & Abdulmumin, I. (2021). A Systematic Literature Review of Hausa Natural Language Processing. *International Journal of Computer and Information Technology*, *10*(4), 2279–0764. doi:10.24203/ijcit.v10i4.86

Zhu, L., Li, H., Dang, R., Yao, Y., & Wang, H. (2023). A Review of Approaches for Detecting Vulnerabilities in Smart Contracts within Web 3.0 Applications. *Blockchains, 1*(1), 3–18.

ENDNOTES

1 https://www.digitaldubai.ae/initiatives
2 https://www.mas.gov.sg/schemes-and-initiatives/project-ubin
3 https://www.mas.gov.sg/
4 https://english.gov.taipei/
5 https://www.iota.org/
6 https://www.vechain.com/aboutUs
7 https://ajuntament.barcelona.cat/imi/en/projects/city-os
8 https://www.habitat.energy/locations/usa/
9 https://fremantle.com/

Chapter 11
Generative AI-Enabled IoT Applications for Smart Cities:
Unleashing Innovation and Paving the Way for the Future

Anupriya Sharma Ghai
Graphic Era Hill University, India

Kapil Ghai
Graphic Era Hill University, India

Gulsun Kurubacak Cakir
Ankara Haci Bayram Veli University, Turkey

ABSTRACT

In the dynamic evolution of smart cities, the collaboration between generative artificial intelligence (AI) and internet of things (IoT) technologies is reshaping urban experiences and fostering sustainable urban development. This collaborative explores the intricate balance of dynamic resource allocation and optimization facilitated by generative AI algorithms within intelligent city IoT networks. It unfolds the transformative potential of generative design for smart city infrastructure, offering insights into energy efficiency and advanced AI processes. The chapter underscores the pivotal role of predictive analytics, behavior prediction, and cybersecurity measures in steering decision-making for optimal urban functioning. Real-world case studies illuminate successful generative AI-IoT integrations, providing tangible lessons for stakeholders, and conclude by urging ongoing collaborative research to address evolving challenges and chart future directions for a more interconnected and resilient urban future. This chapter serves as a valuable contribution, providing a comprehensive exploration of the transformative potential of this collaborative paradigm.

DOI: 10.4018/979-8-3693-2373-1.ch011

INTRODUCTION

Intelligent cities, distinguished by their utilization of digital technologies to elevate urban living, are intricately woven into the Internet of Things (IoT) fabric. The goal is to present a thorough exploration of the continuously evolving landscape of intelligent cities, with a specific emphasis on highlighting the crucial role played by IoT in connecting and optimizing diverse urban systems. IoT is the backbone of smart cities, acting as the connective tissue that links various components such as infrastructure, transportation, utilities, and public services. Its integration enables real-time data collection, analysis, and communication, forming the bedrock for informed decision-making and efficient resource management. Moreover, as we study the technological aspect more deeply, it becomes evident that the transformative potential of smart cities can be further enhanced by the strategic integration of Generative Artificial Intelligence (AI). Generative AI brings a new dimension to the capabilities of IoT, offering the ability to generate valuable insights, predict patterns, and dynamically optimize urban processes. Cappa's (2012) significant contributions particularly highlighted the intersection of technology and urban environments, emphasizing the transformative potential of data and technology in enhancing urban living. His research is pivotal in pioneering innovative approaches that leverage technology to create more responsive and efficient urban spaces, exploring concepts such as sensor networks and real-time data analytics. The technical aspects reflect a holistic view, considering the social dimensions of urban life and how technology can contribute to creating inclusive, accessible, and enjoyable cities through practical applications and forward-thinking initiatives. The influence extends beyond academia, inspiring a reimagining of urban spaces where technology is central in fostering positive, sustainable, and experientially prosperous urban environments. Alahi's (2023) collaboration between Generative AI and IoT promises innovative solutions that can address complex urban challenges. Whether optimizing traffic flow, managing energy consumption, or enhancing public safety, the collaborative interplay between these technologies opens avenues for creative problem-solving and improved urban experiences. By augmenting IoT capabilities with Generative AI, smart cities can evolve beyond mere connectivity to embody intelligence and adaptability. Singh (2023) in his research about the integration allows for the efficient collection of data and the generation of actionable intelligence, empowering urban planners and administrators to make informed decisions in real-time. As navigated by James (2021), the intricate landscape of smart cities makes it evident that the symbiotic relationship between IoT and Generative AI is instrumental in shaping the future of urban living. This collaboration holds the promise of not just connected cities but brilliant and responsive urban environments that cater to the evolving needs of their inhabitants. As evidenced in notable work, Korzun (2019) has emerged as an expert in ambient intelligence and the contributions of the Internet of Things (IoT), which revolve around advancing the understanding and application of IoT within intelligent environments. His emphasis on exploring the applications of IoT goes beyond conventional uses, focusing on the development of smart and adaptive spaces that dynamically respond to the needs of individuals. His work reflects a visionary perspective, positioning IoT not merely as a technological overlay but as an integral element in the quest to design environments that are not only smart but also intensely attuned to the nuanced requirements of individuals, thereby contributing to an elevated and adaptive quality of life. Cui (2018) has significantly contributed to the field of smart cities by addressing cybersecurity and privacy concerns related to IoT. Her expertise in ensuring secure and private technology integration in urban environments is crucial for the development and sustainability of smart cities. This expertise safeguards sensitive data, prevents cybersecurity threats, fosters citizen trust, ensures regulatory compliance, contributes to long-term sustainability, enables proactive risk management, and addresses the challenges of interconnected systems. Overall, it establishes a foundation of trust, resilience, and public support essential for the success of smart city initiatives. Bertino's (2018) work emphasizes the importance of safeguarding sensitive information and ensuring the responsible deployment of IoT technologies in urban contexts, underscores a commitment to protecting privacy and promoting ethical practices. This approach involves implementing robust security measures to protect sensitive data, conducting thorough risk assessments, and adhering to moral principles throughout the entire lifecycle of IoT deployment. It reflects a proactive stance toward addressing privacy concerns and contributing to the responsible and secure advancement of technology in urban environments. Bokhari (2022) has focused on applying artificial intelligence (AI) in smart cities, particularly urban planning and governance. His work aims to enhance city planning processes by strategically integrating AI technologies. His research addresses how AI can optimize urban governance structures and improve city planning. In this dynamic environment, IoT is essential, connecting and enhancing the efficiency of critical components within smart cities. Through its network of sensors, devices, and data analytics, IoT enables real-time monitoring, data collection, and communication, forming the backbone of informed decision-making and resource management in urban settings Singh (2024). This emphasis on IoT signifies a transformative shift in urban development, fostering connectivity and intelligent optimization to address the complexities of modern urban living. The convergence of Generative Artificial Intelligence (AI) with the Internet of Things (IoT) signifies a transformative step towards reshaping urban landscapes and enriching citizen experiences. In this integration, Generative AI plays a pivotal role in enhancing and augmenting the capabilities of IoT networks Park (2024) . Unlike traditional AI, which typically processes existing data, Generative AI can generate new content, insights, and even predictions based on the patterns it learns. In the context of smart cities, this collaboration unfolds a dynamic and intelligent layer within IoT networks. Englund (2021), Generative AI algorithms actively contribute to real-time decision-making processes, optimizing various urban systems. For instance, in traffic management, Generative AI can predict and adapt to changing patterns, optimizing traffic flow and minimizing congestion.

Similarly, these algorithms can dynamically adjust and allocate resources to ensure efficiency in energy consumption. One of the remarkable aspects of this integration is the generation of innovative solutions. Generative AI introduces a creative element by generating possibilities and solutions that may not be immediately apparent through traditional data analysis. This creative dimension is precious in addressing complex urban challenges that require adaptive and forward-thinking solutions. The integration of Generative Artificial Intelligence (AI) with the Internet of Things (IoT) represents a groundbreaking collaboration poised to redefine the trajectory of smart cities. The promise lies in optimizing urban systems and the creative solutions generated by Generative AI, addressing the intricate challenges of modern city living. This transformative alliance invites further exploration and application, offering a glimpse into a future where technology harmoniously shapes urban landscapes for the betterment of all.

Foundations of Generative AI and IoT

In the foundational exploration of Generative AI and IoT, we uncover the transformative potential when artificial intelligence, which can create and innovate autonomously, converges with the vast network of interconnected devices within the Internet of Things (IoT) landscape (Kumar, 2024). This collaboration goes beyond the traditional boundaries of urban development, constituting a dynamic partnership that reshapes the essence of cities. It transcends the pursuit of optimizing efficiency; instead, it undertakes a profound reimagination of urban landscapes, envisioning cities that are responsive and adaptable and intricately integrated with the diverse needs of their inhabitants. This foundational collaboration lays the groundwork for a paradigm shift in urban intelligence, marking the initiation of a journey toward more intelligent, interconnected, and citizen-centric urban environments.

Generative Artificial Intelligence

Generative Artificial Intelligence, commonly known as Generative AI, represents a category of artificial intelligence algorithms and models specifically engineered to produce new and original content. Unlike conventional AI systems primarily tasked with recognizing patterns within pre-existing datasets, generative AI can generate fresh outputs, spanning from images and text to entire scenarios, without direct exposure to the exact content during its training phase. Generative AI operates on the principle of learning underlying patterns and structures present within the provided data, subsequently leveraging this knowledge to construct entirely new instances that mimic the characteristics of the original dataset. This capability has propelled generative AI into various domains, from creative arts and entertainment to scientific research and industrial innovation. One of the key distinguishing features of generative AI is its capacity to foster creativity and innovation by producing content that transcends the confines of the input data. This transformative potential has led to breakthroughs in image synthesis, text generation, and music composition, revolutionizing how humans interact with technology and fostering new avenues for exploration and expression. However, deploying generative AI also presents ethical and societal challenges, particularly concerning authenticity, intellectual property rights, and misinformation (Singh, 2022). As generative AI becomes increasingly sophisticated, it is imperative to address these concerns through robust governance frameworks, ethical guidelines, and responsible usage practices to ensure its constructive integration into society while mitigating potential risks. In essence, Generative Artificial Intelligence embodies a paradigm shift in AI research and development, empowering machines to understand and replicate existing data and generate entirely new and innovative content, thereby reshaping the boundaries of human-machine interaction and creative expression.

Recent discourse on Generative Artificial Intelligence (AI) has focused on several pressing issues shaping its development and impact. Ethical considerations surrounding the use of generative AI, particularly regarding algorithmic bias, privacy infringement, and potential misuse of generated content, have been extensively discussed by author Floridi (2018). Of notable concern is the proliferation of deepfake technology, which employs generative AI to create highly realistic manipulated videos and images, raising alarm about the spread of misinformation and its implications for media integrity and democracy, Liao (2020). Additionally, there is a growing need for regulatory frameworks to govern the deployment and use of generative AI technologies, with discussions centering on transparency, accountability, and oversight by the Author Cath (2021). Security and cybersecurity challenges have emerged, as generative AI can be exploited to create sophisticated cyber threats such as phishing attacks and malware, Choi (2021). Harvey (2019) reported the issue of intellectual property rights in generative AI-generated content is also gaining attention, with debates on ownership, attribution, and licensing. Bolukbasi (2016) addressed bias and ensuring fairness in generative AI outputs is another critical area of research, aiming to mitigate biases inherited from training data and promote equity. Moreover, the environmental impact of large-scale generative AI models, including energy consumption and carbon emissions, has prompted investigations into more sustainable training methods reported by Schwartz (2019). Finally, exploring human-AI collaboration in creative endeavors such as art and design has become a focal point, with research focusing on understanding human-AI interaction dynamics and developing collaborative tools and interfaces reported by the Author Bernard (2020).

Bauer (2021) defines Generative AI in smart cities as a technology that requires robust security measures. This could involve safeguarding generated data, ensuring privacy, and addressing potential security vulnerabilities in deploying generative algorithms within urban environments. The hypothetical perspective attributed to Goundar (2019), an AI researcher at Google, envisions Generative AI in smart cities as a transformative technology. In this perspective, Generative AI is described as a tool with the creative ability to synthesize data, particularly for applications such as image generation and language synthesis. Its role is emphasized in contributing to creative solutions and innovative approaches to address the complex challenges inherent in urban environments. Generative AI's capacity to creatively synthesize data implies that it goes beyond replicating or analyzing existing information. Instead, it is portrayed as a technology that can generate novel and contextually relevant outputs. In smart cities, this creative potential holds promise for envisioning and implementing solutions that may not be immediately evident through traditional approaches. The application of Generative AI for image generation suggests creating visual content that could be utilized for urban planning, design simulations, or other visualizations relevant to innovative city initiatives Singh (2023).

Additionally, language synthesis implies generating textual content, which could find applications in areas such as natural language interfaces for citizen engagement or creating informative and engaging content related to urban developments. By characterizing Generative AI in this way, Jiang's (2023) perspective highlights its potential to bring a creative dimension to problem-solving within the smart city landscape. This creativity opens avenues for exploring unconventional and inventive strategies to enhance urban living and address the evolving needs of smart city inhabitants. Littmann (2022), a trailblazer in deep learning and artificial intelligence, brings insightful perspectives on applying generative AI in smart cities. Emphasizing machines' capacity to generate creative content, the author envisions generative models, such as GANs and VAEs, as pivotal tools for simulating and predicting urban scenarios. His research philosophy, rooted in recognizing patterns and generating meaningful content, aligns with the transformative potential of generative AI in smart cities. In data-driven decision-making, generative models offer valuable contributions, from simulating traffic patterns to predicting energy consumption, ultimately creating intelligent and responsive urban environments. In the field of generative AI, Naz (2023), particularly for his pioneering work on Generative Adversarial Networks (GANs), has significantly shaped the landscape of artificial intelligence. His contributions have laid the foundation for applications in smart cities. In the context of urban planning and resource optimization, GANs offer substantial potential. They can be instrumental in generating realistic simulations that aid planners and policymakers in visualizing and strategizing for optimal urban development. Ma (2020), an expert in reinforcement learning, is well-positioned to discuss the integration of generative AI with reinforcement learning techniques for optimizing urban systems. His insights may revolve around how these technologies work synergistically to adapt urban systems in response to changing conditions. Ma's expertise in reinforcement learning could provide valuable perspectives on the adaptive capabilities of generative AI in the context of smart city infrastructure and governance. The intricate world of advanced methodologies spotlights two prominent players: Generative Adversarial Networks (GANs) and Variational Autoencoders (VAEs). These techniques, akin to artistic maestros, possess the power to generate content, patterns, and predictions that challenge our perceptions of what AI can achieve.

Generative Adversarial Networks (GANs)

Generative Adversarial Networks (GANs) are innovative approaches to orchestrating a captivating wall between a generator and a discriminator. The generator creates synthetic data, while the discriminator is a keen critic, distinguishing between actual and generated data. Together, they engage in an adversarial process, pushing the boundaries of what AI can create. We unveil the nuances of this dynamic interplay and illuminate the creative potential locked within GANs. The journey into Generative Adversarial Networks (GANs) unfolds as a captivating exploration of artificial intelligence's creative prowess. Dwivedi (2021) said that the essence of GANs lies in their adversarial nature, a symbiotic relationship where these entities constantly push and pull, challenging and refining each other's abilities. This adversarial process becomes the ultimate obstacle to creativity, allowing the boundaries of what artificial intelligence can be conceived and produced. As we navigate through the nuances of this dynamic interplay, we unlock the latent creative potential embedded within GANs, showcasing their transformative impact on the landscape of AI-generated content. Generative Adversarial Networks (GANs) operate on a unique and adversarial principle involving two neural networks – a generator and a discriminator – engaged in a continuous, dynamic interaction. Here's a simplified explanation of how GANs work:

(i) Generator: The generator resembles an artist or a forger. Its task is to create synthetic data, such as images, that closely resemble accurate data. It starts with random noise as input and gradually refines its output through learning. Over time, the generator becomes adept at creating increasingly indistinguishable data from accurate data. A tangible generator application in intelligent cities creates synthetic urban data for simulation. Like an artist crafting a realistic portrayal, the generator starts with random inputs and gradually refines its output to generate synthetic data resembling natural urban environments. For instance, in optimizing traffic flow, the generator could simulate complex traffic patterns, considering factors like population density, road layouts, and public transportation systems. This synthetic data allows city planners to explore and evaluate various scenarios, enabling informed decision-making in urban development and smart city planning without relying solely on historical data, according to Andreani (2019).

(ii) Discriminator: The discriminator is like a detective or a critic. Its role is to evaluate data and determine whether it is real or generated. Initially, the discriminator is trained on a dataset of real examples and can effectively differentiate between authentic and synthetic data. As the generator improves, the discriminator's task becomes more challenging.

As per Lee (2010), the discriminator becomes adept at distinguishing between genuine traffic patterns and synthetic ones generated by the model. As the generator refines its ability to produce synthetic traffic data, incorporating population density, road layouts, and public transportation systems, the discriminator faces a progressively intricate task of determining whether the presented traffic scenarios align with actual urban dynamics or are skilfully crafted simulations. This evolving interplay between the generator and discriminator is pivotal for creating accurate and realistic synthetic traffic data, ensuring that the simulated scenarios effectively mirror the complexities of real-world traffic conditions in smart city planning and development.

(iii) Adversarial Process: The crux of GANs lies in the malicious process between the generator and discriminator. The generator strives to produce data that is so realistic that the discriminator cannot distinguish it from real data. Simultaneously, the discriminator aims to become more discerning, improving its ability to differentiate between real and generated data. In the intricate of smart city optimization, Ravindran (2022) envisions the adversarial process within a Generative Adversarial Network (GAN) as a captivating rivalry between a visionary traffic generator and an astute traffic discriminator. Simultaneously, the discriminator evolves into a discerning critic, sharpening its ability to unravel the nuances that distinguish genuine urban traffic from the generator's crafted compositions. This dynamic exchange propels a continuous refinement cycle, with the generator pursuing heightened authenticity and the discriminator aiming for heightened acumen. The result is an innovative cooperation that births remarkably lifelike synthetic data, offering a nuanced canvas for avant-garde intelligent city planning and traffic orchestration Ravindran (2022).

(iv) Training Iterations: The training process involves iterative feedback loops. The generator and discriminator are in a constant loop of improvement. As the generator gets better at creating realistic data, the discriminator adapts to become more effective in distinguishing between real and generated data. The discriminator adjusts in response, honing its discernment to better differentiate between authentic and generated traffic scenarios. This cyclical process of refinement and adaptation repeats iteratively, each iteration bringing the generator and discriminator closer to a harmonious equilibrium where the generated data becomes indistinguishable from real-world traffic dynamics. The training iterations, therefore, symbolize a continuous evolution akin to a captivating performance that propels the advancement of synthetic data for innovative smart city planning and traffic management, said Chakraborty (2023)

(v) Convergence: This adversarial process reaches a point of equilibrium where the generator produces data indistinguishable from real data, and the discriminator struggles to tell the difference. The discriminator faces a formidable challenge in distinguishing between authentic and generated traffic patterns. Lv (2022). This convergence signifies a breakthrough, where the generated data achieves realism that mirrors genuine urban traffic dynamics. In the landscape of smart city planning, this delicate balance attained during convergence becomes a pivotal milestone, providing decision-makers with highly accurate synthetic data for innovative and effective traffic management and urban development strategies.

(vi) Creative Output: The outcome is a generator capable of producing synthetic data that possesses the characteristics of the original dataset, showcasing the creative potential of GANs in generating diverse and realistic content, such as images, art, or even text.

GANs leverage a competitive and cooperative dynamic between a generator and a discriminator to enhance the ability to create realistic synthetic data iteratively, representing a remarkable advancement in generative artificial intelligence.

Variational Autoencoders (VAEs)

Variational Autoencoders (VAEs) are recognized for their ability to navigate latent spaces and create meaningful representations. Like skilled storytellers, VAEs encode data into a compressed yet expressive form and then decode it to generate diverse and novel outputs. As we unravel the workings of VAEs, we uncover how they contribute to the rich tapestry of generative AI, bringing forth not just replication but innovation. Variational Autoencoders (VAEs) represent a compelling chapter in the narrative of productive artificial intelligence, introducing a sophisticated approach to encoding and decoding data with a focus on meaningful representations. Law (2019) imagines VAEs as skilled storytellers adept at compressing information into a condensed yet highly expressive form, akin to summarizing a complex tale into its essence. The process begins with the encoder, which encapsulates the input data like a masterful storyteller into a latent space—a compressed representation capturing the essential features. This latent space is not just a reduction but a carefully crafted abstraction that captures the underlying structure and nuances of the input data.

Otter (2020) stated that the quality of VAEs lies in their inherent creativity during the decoding process. Like storytellers who can unfold myriad narratives from a condensed summary, VAEs decode the compressed representation into diverse and novel outputs. This generative aspect distinguishes VAEs, as they don't merely replicate input but generate variations, fostering innovation and creativity within the AI system. Gal (2022) on VAEs extends beyond mere data replication, offering a platform for exploration and generation within the latent space. Unraveling the workings of VAEs unveils their role in contributing to the expansive realm of generative AI. They stand as architects of diversity, enabling the creation of copies and imaginative renditions of input data. In this way, VAEs carve a niche in the generative landscape, where the emphasis shifts from replication to innovation, enriching the narrative of artificial intelligence with the capacity to generate, explore, and create. Variational Autoencoders (VAEs) function as sophisticated models within the domain of generative artificial intelligence, orchestrating a process that involves encoding data into a latent space and decoding it to generate diverse and novel outputs. Here's an elaboration on how VAEs work:

(i) Encoding Data: The process begins with the encoder, responsible for mapping input data, such as images or sequences, into a latent space. This latent space is a lower-dimensional representation that captures the essential features of the input data in a compressed form. Think of the encoder as a skilled storyteller summarizing a complex tale into a concise yet meaningful essence.
(ii) Latent Space Representation: The latent space is not merely a reduction of the input data but a carefully crafted abstraction that retains the underlying structure and nuances. It serves as a condensed and expressive representation, capturing the essential characteristics of the input in a reduced dimensionality.
(iii) Sampling and Generating: Once encoded into the latent space, the data can be sampled to generate novel outputs. This sampling process allows for the creation of diverse variations, introducing an element of creativity to the generative capabilities of VAEs. Like the storyteller unfolding narratives, the decoder transforms these sampled points into meaningful, novel data.
(iv) Generative Aspect: VAEs stand out for their productive nature, as they don't simply replicate input data but can generate new and innovative variations. The decoder plays a crucial role by transforming points in the latent space into diverse outputs, fostering creativity within the artificial intelligence system.
(v) Training Process: VAEs are trained by optimizing the model to reconstruct input data accurately while ensuring that the latent space follows a specific Gaussian distribution.

This dual objective of accurate reconstruction and structured latent space ensures that VAEs can encode data meaningfully and generate novel outputs. Hughes's (2021) explicit details about his work with GANs and VAEs in smart cities may need verification. His expertise suggests focusing on innovative applications in simulating and optimizing urban environments. Hughes's research likely delves into the intersection of generative models and urban design, contributing to advancements in computer-aided

Figure 1. Content processing using generative adversarial networks (GANs) and variational autoencoders (VAE)

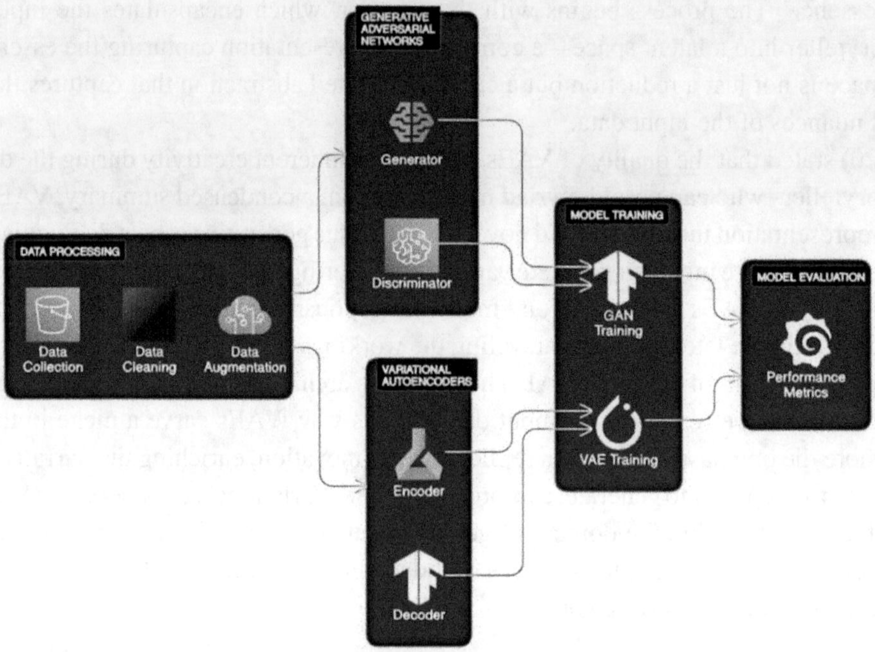

simulations for urban planning and development. The specific details of Gao's (2023) work with GANs and VAEs in smart cities may require further investigation into data-driven approaches pertinent to urban analytics. His research likely involves leveraging generative models to derive insights from large-scale urban datasets, fostering advancements in data-driven decision-making for city planning and management.

Li (2017) suggests utilizing GANs and VAEs to enhance decision-making processes in intelligent cities, potentially contributing to advancements in multi-agent systems for urban optimization and sustainability. Figure 1 shows a case of content processing using Generative Adversarial Networks (GANs) and Variational Autoencoders(VAE)

INTERNET OF THINGS (IOT) FOUNDATIONS IN SMART CITIES

In the ever-evolving landscape of smart cities, the Internet of Things (IoT) is a foundational and transformative element. At its core, IoT is a vast network of interconnected devices, ranging from sensors and actuators to everyday objects embedded with technology. These devices seamlessly communicate and share data, forming a dynamic web across urban environments. The backbone of IoT lies in its ability to enable real-time monitoring, data collection, and communication. In the context of smart cities, this interconnected network is pivotal in optimizing various urban systems, such as infrastructure, transportation, utilities, and public services, according to Sarwat (2018). The integration of IoT empowers cities with the capability to make informed decisions, enhance resource management, and address complex challenges. IoT acts as the connective tissue that weaves through the intricate fabric of smart cities, offering a comprehensive sensing and perception infrastructure. Through its network of sensors and devices,

IoT facilitates the continuous flow of data, providing valuable insights into the city's functioning. This data-driven approach forms the bedrock for informed decision-making, efficiency improvements, and the creation of intelligent urban solutions.

Furthermore, IoT enhances citizen experiences by fostering a more responsive and adaptive urban environment. Khan (2013) Applications range from smart traffic management systems that optimize flow and reduce congestion to intelligent energy grids that dynamically allocate resources based on demand. In essence, IoT transforms cities into living entities that can adapt and respond to the needs of their inhabitants in real time. As we explore the foundations of IoT in smart cities, we recognize its role as a catalyst for innovation, efficiency, and improved quality of life. IoT capabilities' continuous evolution and expansion promise a future where cities are interconnected and intelligent, offering a more sustainable and technologically advanced urban living experience.

Integration of Generative AI With IoT Architecture in Smart Cities

In the dynamic landscape of smart cities, the convergence of Generative Artificial Intelligence (AI) with the Internet of Things (IoT) architecture is a transformative force. At the heart of this integration lies the foundational components of IoT, forming a symbiotic relationship that enhances the responsiveness and intelligence of urban systems.

Sensors and Actuators Enhanced by Generative AI

Generative AI introduces a creative and anticipatory dimension to the sensory apparatus of smart cities. Generative AI algorithms generate insights and predictions beyond traditional analytics by dynamically interpreting sensors suggested Sarker (2021). This creative augmentation contributes to the adaptability of actuators, enabling them to respond not just to present conditions but also to anticipated changes, fostering a more proactive urban environment.

Communication Networks for Intelligent Data Exchange

Generative AI and IoT collaboration thrives on seamless communication networks. These networks, now imbued with the creative insights of Generative AI, facilitate the exchange of raw data and the dissemination of generative models and predictions, suggested Huzaifah (2021). This intelligent data exchange optimizes the efficiency of communication channels, ensuring that the entire urban ecosystem remains responsive and adaptable.

Cloud and Edge Computing for Real-Time Generative Insights

Generative AI finds a vast canvas for its creative endeavours in cloud computing. The cloud is a repository for generative models, allowing them to learn and evolve based on the continuously growing dataset. Simultaneously, integrating Generative AI with edge computing brings creativity to the forefront in real-time Rane (2019). This decentralized processing ensures that generative insights are not confined to cloud servers but can dynamically influence urban systems at the edge, promoting agility and immediate adaptation.

IoT Platforms Orchestrated by Generative AI

Generative AI, acting as an orchestrator of intelligence, finds its place within IoT platforms. Now infused with generative capabilities, these platforms streamline device management, monitoring, and control. Wen (2023) stated that Generative algorithms contribute to the customization of IoT applications, dynamically adjusting parameters based on real-time generative insights. A harmonious integration elevates the entire IoT architecture, making it data-centric and creatively intelligent.

Generative AI-Driven Sensing and Perception

Integrating Generative AI and IoT is pivotal for advancing sensory capabilities in IoT devices. By deploying sophisticated generative AI algorithms, the emphasis is on enhancing the devices' ability to perceive and interact with their surroundings. This combined effect holds excellent promise for reshaping decision-making processes in smart cities, offering a transformative impact on various applications. In the exploration of Generative AI, a key focus is on its application within computer vision, emphasizing its role in processing and deriving insights from visual data, fostering a new level of intelligence in IoT devices within smart city contexts. Generative AI algorithms with their respective examples in the context of IoT applications for smart cities: (i) In a smart city surveillance system, GANs enhance the quality of camera video feeds. By generating high-resolution and noise-free frames, GANs improve the accuracy of object detection and tracking. This is crucial for applications like public safety, where real-time and precise monitoring is essential. Rane (2023) has been at the forefront of integrating Generative AI with IoT in smart cities. The development of advanced Generative Adversarial Networks (GANs) tailored for urban environments. The researcher showcases how GANs can dynamically optimize energy consumption in smart buildings through extensive simulations, leading to substantial efficiency gains. His work has been influential in reshaping the discourse around sustainable urban development. (ii) A smart grid in a city with numerous sensors monitoring energy consumption VAEs can compress and efficiently represent this voluminous sensor data. By doing so, VAEs enable more economical transmission and storage of energy consumption patterns, facilitating better grid management and resource allocation, as suggested by Qolomany (2019). In a smart transportation system, autoencoders can analyze data from various vehicle sensors. Miglani (2019) stated that autoencoders contribute to real-time decision-making by extracting relevant features, such as traffic patterns, road conditions, and vehicle health. This aids in optimizing traffic flow, predicting maintenance needs, and enhancing overall transportation efficiency. Ahmad (2022) focuses on the practical applications of Generative AI in smart city transportation. His work introduces a novel predictive analytics model powered by generative models. By analyzing traffic patterns and human behavior, the model aids in adaptive decision-making for traffic management. This research has garnered attention for its potential to revolutionize urban mobility. In a citizen engagement platform, transformer models can process and understand textual feedback from residents Singh (2021). By analyzing sentiments and extracting meaningful insights, these models assist city officials in making informed decisions related to public services, infrastructure improvements, and policy changes Kumar (2022). These examples collectively showcase the diverse applications of generative AI algorithms in collaboration with IoT for enhancing various aspects of smart city functionalities. This symbiosis, marked by the fusion of generative AI and IoT, signifies a technological evolution and a profound shift in how smart city systems perceive and interact with their environment. The result is a new era of heightened intelligence, adaptability, and resilience, redefining the possibilities for the future of urban living.

Challenges of Integrating Generative AI and IoT in Smart Cities

This section focuses on the numerous challenges of integrating generative AI and IoT within the dynamic landscape of smart cities. These challenges encompass a spectrum of technical hurdles, ranging from ensuring seamless interoperability between diverse technologies to managing the sheer complexity of vast data generated by IoT devices. The chapter proposes strategies and potential solutions to navigate the identified challenges effectively. These solutions explore innovative technological approaches, adaptive algorithms, and comprehensive frameworks to enhance compatibility between generative AI and IoT systems. By exploring practical insights and case studies, the chapter aims to illustrate successful implementations of these strategies, offering valuable guidance to practitioners and researchers seeking to overcome hurdles and achieve seamless integration.

Furthermore, the chapter places a significant emphasis on ethical considerations inherent in the application of generative AI within smart cities. It scrutinizes the ethical implications surrounding data privacy, security, and the responsible deployment of AI technologies. The chapter highlights the importance of ensuring that generative AI and IoT integration is compatible with societal values, respects individual rights, and adheres to ethical standards.

EMERGING TRENDS IN THE INTERSECTION OF GENERATIVE AI AND IOT

The intersection of generative AI and the Internet of Things (IoT) is witnessing a paradigm shift marked by a convergence of cutting-edge technologies and innovative applications. AI algorithms are advancing rapidly, empowering IoT devices with enhanced predictive analytics capabilities. The utilization of Generative Adversarial Networks (GANs) for IoT security is a noteworthy trend, facilitating the creation of realistic simulated data to fortify security systems. Customized and contextual data generation through generative models addresses challenges in acquiring large datasets, which is particularly crucial for refining the performance of AI models in specific IoT applications. Energy-efficient edge computing is gaining prominence as generative AI optimizes local processing, addressing concerns related to power consumption in resource-constrained IoT devices. Furthermore, the collaboration between generative AI and IoT enhances human-machine collaboration, enhancing user experiences and interactions. Federated learning shapes the landscape by enabling collaborative model training across edge devices while preserving data privacy. Standardization efforts are underway to ensure interoperability and real-time generative AI processing is becoming imperative for time-sensitive IoT applications. The emphasis on explainability and trustworthiness in AI models addresses transparency concerns. Simultaneously, the evolving regulatory landscape underscores the need for ethical considerations in deploying generative AI within the IoT domain. These trends collectively guide researchers, policymakers, and industry stakeholders toward areas of exploration and investment, shaping the trajectory of this dynamic field with profound implications for the future of technology.

LIMITATIONS

Despite the immense potential and promising applications of Generative AI-enabled IoT in smart cities, several limitations and challenges must be acknowledged. Firstly, deploying such advanced systems requires substantial infrastructure investments, which may pose financial barriers for cities with limited resources. Additionally, Generative AI-enabled IoT applications rely heavily on vast amounts of data for training and operation, raising concerns about data privacy, security, and ownership. Ensuring the ethical and responsible use of data becomes paramount to prevent potential misuse and safeguard citizen rights. Moreover, the interoperability of diverse IoT devices and platforms remains a significant challenge, hindering seamless integration and collaboration among different stakeholders.

Furthermore, Generative AI algorithms may exhibit biases inherent in the training data, leading to unintended consequences and disparities in decision-making processes. Addressing these biases and ensuring fairness and equity in AI-enabled systems require ongoing research and development efforts. Lastly, the rapid pace of technological advancement and the dynamic nature of urban environments necessitate flexible and adaptive governance frameworks to regulate the deployment and operation of Generative AI-enabled IoT applications while promoting innovation and sustainability. Recognizing and mitigating these limitations is crucial for maximizing the benefits of Generative AI-enabled IoT in smart cities and fostering inclusive and equitable urban development.

REFERENCES

Abbeel, P., & Ng, A. Y. (2004, July). Apprenticeship learning via inverse reinforcement learning. In *Proceedings of the twenty-first international conference on Machine learning* (p. 1). ACM. 10.1145/1015330.1015430

Ahmad, T., Madonski, R., Zhang, D., Huang, C., & Mujeeb, A. (2022). Data-driven probabilistic machine learning in sustainable smart energy/smart energy systems: Key developments, challenges, and future research opportunities in the context of smart grid paradigm. *Renewable & Sustainable Energy Reviews*, *160*, 112128. doi:10.1016/j.rser.2022.112128

Alahi, M. E. E., Sukkuea, A., Tina, F. W., Nag, A., Kurdthongmee, W., Suwannarat, K., & Mukhopadhyay, S. C. (2023). Integration of IoT-Enabled Technologies and Artificial Intelligence (AI) for Smart City Scenario: Recent Advancements and Future Trends. *Sensors (Basel)*, *23*(11), 5206. doi:10.3390/s23115206 PMID:37299934

Andreani, S., Kalchschmidt, M., Pinto, R., & Sayegh, A. (2019). Reframing technologically enhanced urban scenarios: A design research model towards human centered smart cities. *Technological Forecasting and Social Change*, *142*, 15–25. doi:10.1016/j.techfore.2018.09.028

Bauer, M., Sanchez, L., & Song, J. (2021). IoT-enabled smart cities: Evolution and outlook. *Sensors (Basel)*, *21*(13), 4511. doi:10.3390/s21134511 PMID:34209436

Bernard, S., Mawad, F., & Kim, Y. (2020). From human-computer interaction to human- computer co-creation: A symbiotic approach to designing AI systems. *ACM Transactions on Interactive Intelligent Systems*, *10*(2), 1–29.

Bertino, E., & Jahanshahi, M. R. (2018). Adaptive and cost-effective collection of high- quality data for critical infrastructure and emergency management in smart cities—Framework and challenges. [JDIQ]. *ACM Journal of Data and Information Quality*, *10*(1), 1–6. doi:10.1145/3190579

Bokhari, S. A. A., & Myeong, S. (2022). Use of artificial intelligence in smart cities for smart decision-making: A social innovation perspective. *Sustainability (Basel)*, *14*(2), 620. doi:10.3390/su14020620

Bolukbasi, T., Chang, K.-W., Zou, J. Y., Saligrama, V., & Kalai, A. T. (2016). Man is to computer programmer as woman is to homemaker? Debiasing word embeddings. *Advances in Neural Information Processing Systems*.

Cappa, F., Franco, S., & Rosso, F. (2022). Citizens and cities: Leveraging citizen science and big data for sustainable urban development. *Business Strategy and the Environment*, *31*(2), 648–667. doi:10.1002/bse.2942

Cath, C., Wachter, S., Mittelstadt, B., Taddeo, M., & Floridi, L. (2021). Artificial intelligence and the 'good society': The US, EU, and UK approach. *Science & Public Policy*, *48*(1), 1–14.

Chakraborty, T., Naik, S. M., Panja, M., & Manvitha, B. (2023). Ten Years of Generative Adversarial Nets (GANs): A survey of the state-of-the-art. arXiv preprint arXiv:2308.16316. https://doi.org//arXiv.2308.16316 doi:10.48550

Chen, Y., Yao, Z., Zhao, Y., & Liu, K. (2018). A survey of big data architectures and machine learning algorithms in healthcare. *Journal of King Saud University. Computer and Information Sciences*.

Choi, Y., Lim, D., Kim, M., & Chung, J. (2021). DeepFake and AI-based multimedia forgery detection: A review. *IEEE Access : Practical Innovations, Open Solutions*, *9*, 3599–3622.

Cui, L., Xie, G., Qu, Y., Gao, L., & Yang, Y. (2018). Security and privacy in smart cities: Challenges and opportunities. *IEEE Access : Practical Innovations, Open Solutions*, *6*, 46134–46145. doi:10.1109/ACCESS.2018.2853985

Dwivedi, Y. K., Hughes, L., Ismagilova, E., Aarts, G., Coombs, C., Crick, T., Duan, Y., Dwivedi, R., Edwards, J., Eirug, A., Galanos, V., Ilavarasan, P. V., Janssen, M., Jones, P., Kar, A. K., Kizgin, H., Kronemann, B., Lal, B., Lucini, B., & Williams, M. D. (2021). Artificial Intelligence (AI): Multidisciplinary perspectives on emerging challenges, opportunities, and agenda for research, practice and policy. *International Journal of Information Management*, *57*, 101994. doi:10.1016/j.ijinfomgt.2019.08.002

Englund, C., Aksoy, E. E., Alonso-Fernandez, F., Cooney, M. D., Pashami, S., & Åstrand, B. (2021). AI perspectives in Smart Cities and Communities to enable road vehicle automation and smart traffic control. *Smart Cities*, *4*(2), 783–802. doi:10.3390/smartcities4020040

Englund, C., Aksoy, E. E., Alonso-Fernandez, F., Cooney, M. D., Pashami, S., & Åstrand, B. (2021). AI perspectives in Smart Cities and Communities to enable road vehicle automation and smart traffic control. *Smart Cities*, *4*(2), 783–802. doi:10.3390/smartcities4020040

Floridi, L., Cowls, J., Beltrametti, M., Chatila, R., Chazerand, P., Dignum, V., & Madelin, R. (2018). AI4People—an ethical framework for a good AI society: Opportunities, risks, principles, and recommendations. *Minds and Machines*, *28*(4), 689–707. doi:10.1007/s11023-018-9482-5 PMID:30930541

Gal, R., Alaluf, Y., Atzmon, Y., Patashnik, O., Bermano, A. H., Chechik, G., & Cohen-Or, D. (2022). *An image is worth one word: Personalizing text-to-image generation using textual inversion*. arXiv preprint arXiv:2208.01618.

Gao, X., Jiang, X., Zhuang, D., Chen, H., Wang, S., & Haworth, J. (2023). *Spatiotemporal graph neural networks with uncertainty quantification for traffic incident risk prediction.* arXiv preprint arXiv:2309.05072. https://doi.org//arXiv.2309.05072 doi:10.48550

Goundar, S., Purwar, A., & Singh, A. (Eds.). (2022). *Applications of Artificial Intelligence, Big Data and Internet of Things in Sustainable Development.* CRC Press. doi:10.1201/9781003245469

Harvey, A. C., Strong, R., & Liu, B. (2019). Generating Credible Fake News. *The Journal of Economic Perspectives*, *33*(2), 173–196. doi:10.48550/arXiv.2208.01618

Hughes, R. T., Zhu, L., & Bednarz, T. (2021). Generative adversarial networks–enabled human–artificial intelligence collaborative applications for creative and design industries: A systematic review of current approaches and trends. *Frontiers in Artificial Intelligence*, *4*, 604234. doi:10.3389/frai.2021.604234 PMID:33997773

Huzaifah, M., & Wyse, L. (2021). Deep generative models for musical audio synthesis. *Handbook of Artificial Intelligence for Music: Foundations, Advanced Approaches, and Developments for Creativity*, 639-678. Springer. https://link.springer.com/chapter/10.1007/978- 3-030-72116-9_22

James, P., Astoria, R., Castor, T., Hudspeth, C., Olstinske, D., & Ward, J. (2021). Smart cities: Fundamental concepts. Handbook of smart cities, (pp. 3-33). Springer. https://doi.org/ doi:10.1007/978-3-030 69698-6_2

Jiang, H., Geertman, S., & Witte, P. (2023). The contextualization of smart city technologies: An international comparison. *Journal of Urban Management*, *12*(1), 33–43. doi:10.1016/j.jum.2022.09.001

Khan, R. H., & Khan, J. Y. (2013). A comprehensive review of the application characteristics and traffic requirements of a smart grid communications network. *Computer Networks*, *57*(3), 825–845. doi:10.1016/j.comnet.2012.11.002

Korzun, D., Balandina, E., Kashevnik, A., Balandin, S., & Viola, F. (Eds.). (2019). Ambient Intelligence Services in IoT Environments: Emerging Research and Opportunities. Springer. doi:10.4018/978-1-5225-8973-0

Kumar, H., Singh, M. K., Gupta, M. P., & Madaan, J. (2020). Moving towards smart cities: Solutions that lead to the Smart City Transformation Framework. *Technological Forecasting and Social Change*, *153*, 119281. doi:10.1016/j.techfore.2018.04.024

Kumar, M., Kim, C., Son, Y., Singh, S. K., & Kim, S. (2024). Empowering Cyberattack Identification in IoHT Networks With Neighborhood Component-based Improvised Long Short-Term Memory. *IEEE Internet of Things Journal*, 1. doi:10.1109/JIOT.2024.3354988

Law, S., & Neira, M. (2019, November). An unsupervised approach to geographical knowledge discovery using street level and street network images. In *Proceedings of the 3rd ACM SIGSPATIAL International Workshop on AI for Geographic Knowledge Discovery* (pp. 56-65). ACM. 10.1145/3356471.3365238

Lee, J. G., Han, J., Li, X., & Cheng, H. (2010). Mining discriminative patterns for classifying trajectories on road networks. *IEEE Transactions on Knowledge and Data Engineering*, *23*(5), 713–726. doi:10.1109/TKDE.2010.153

Li, Y. (2017). Deep reinforcement learning: An overview. *arXiv preprint arXiv:1701.07274*. https://doi.org//arXiv.1701.07274 doi:10.48550

Liao, Y., & He, J. (2020). Deepfake Detection: A Review. *ACM Computing Surveys*, *53*(5), 1–35. doi:10.1145/3324473

Littman, M. L., Ajunwa, I., Berger, G., Boutilier, C., Currie, M., Doshi-Velez, F., & Walsh, T. (2022). Gathering strength, gathering storms: The one hundred year study on artificial intelligence (AI100) 2021 study panel report. *arXiv preprint arXiv:2210.15767*.

Lv, Z., & Xie, S. (2022). Artificial intelligence in the digital twins: State of the art, challenges, and future research topics. *Digital Twin*, *1*, 12. doi:10.12688/digitaltwin.17524.2

Ma, L., & Sun, B. (2020). Machine learning and AI in marketing–Connecting computing power to human insights. *International Journal of Research in Marketing*, *37*(3), 481–504. doi:10.1016/j.ijresmar.2020.04.005

Miglani, A., & Kumar, N. (2019). Deep learning models for traffic flow prediction in autonomous vehicles: A review, solutions, and challenges. *Vehicular Communications*, *20*, 100184. doi:10.1016/j.vehcom.2019.100184

Naz, H., Nijhawan, R., Ahuja, N. J., Al-Otaibi, S., Saba, T., Bahaj, S. A., & Rehman, A. (2023). Ensembled Deep Convolutional Generative Adversarial Network for Grading Imbalanced Diabetic Retinopathy Recognition. *IEEE Access : Practical Innovations, Open Solutions*, *11*, 120554–120568. doi:10.1109/ACCESS.2023.3327900

Otter, D. W., Medina, J. R., & Kalita, J. K. (2020). A survey of the usages of deep learning for natural language processing. *IEEE Transactions on Neural Networks and Learning Systems*, *32*(2), 604–624. doi:10.1109/TNNLS.2020.2979670 PMID:32324570

Park, J. H., Yotxay, S., Singh, S. K., & Park, J. H. (2024). PoAh-Enabled Federated Learning Architecture for DDoS Attack Detection in IoT Networks. *Hum.-Centric Comput. Inf. Sci*, *14*(3).

Qolomany, B., Al-Fuqaha, A., Gupta, A., Benhaddou, D., Alwajidi, S., Qadir, J., & Fong, A. C. (2019). Leveraging machine learning and big data for smart buildings: A comprehensive survey. *IEEE Access : Practical Innovations, Open Solutions*, *7*, 90316–90356. doi:10.1109/ACCESS.2019.2926642

RaneN. (2023) ChatGPT and Similar Generative Artificial Intelligence (AI) for Smart Industry: Role, Challenges and Opportunities for Industry 4.0, Industry 5.0 and Society 5.0. doi:10.2139/ssrn.4603234

Ravindran, A. (2022). *Will AI Dictate the Future?* Marshall Cavendish International Asia Pte Ltd.

Sarker, I. H. (2021). Data science and analytics: An overview from data-driven smart computing, decision-making and applications perspective. *SN Computer Science*, *2*(5), 377. https://link.springer.com/article/10.1007/s42979-021-00765-8. doi:10.1007/s42979-021-00765-8 PMID:34278328

Sarwat, A. I., Sundararajan, A., Parvez, I., Moghaddami, M., & Moghadasi, A. (2018). Toward a smart city of interdependent critical infrastructure networks. Sustainable Interdependent Networks: *From Theory to Application*, 21-45. Springer. https://link.springer.com/chapter/10.1007/978-3-319-74412-4_3

Schwartz, R., Dodge, J., Smith, N. A., & Etzioni, O. (2019). Green AI. *Proceedings of the 57th Annual Meeting of the Association for Computational Linguistics*. Springer.

Singh, S. K., Azzaoui, A. E., Choo, K. K. R., Yang, L. T., & Park, J. H. (2023). Articles A Comprehensive Survey on Blockchain for Secure IoT-enabled Smart City beyond 5G: Approaches, Processes, Challenges, and Opportunities. *Hum.-Centric Comput. Inf. Sci, 13*(51).

Singh, S. K., Kumar, M., Tanwar, S., & Park, J. H. (2024). GRU-based digital twin framework for data allocation and storage in IoT-enabled smart home networks. *Future Generation Computer Systems*, *153*, 391–402. doi:10.1016/j.future.2023.12.009

Singh, S. K., Pan, Y., & Park, J. H. (2022). Blockchain-enabled secure framework for energy-efficient smart parking in sustainable city environment. *Sustainable Cities and Society*, *76*, 103364. doi:10.1016/j.scs.2021.103364

Singh, S. K., & Park, J. H. (2022). TaLWaR: Blockchain-based trust management scheme for smart enterprises with augmented intelligence. *IEEE Transactions on Industrial Informatics*, *19*(1), 626–634. doi:10.1109/TII.2022.3204692

Singh, S. K., Park, J. H., Sharma, P. K., & Pan, Y. (2021). BIIoVT: Blockchain-based secure storage architecture for intelligent internet of vehicular things. *IEEE Consumer Electronics Magazine*, *11*(6), 75–82. doi:10.1109/MCE.2021.3089992

Singh, S. K., Yang, L. T., & Park, J. H. (2023). FusionFedBlock: Fusion of blockchain and federated learning to preserve privacy in industry 5.0. *Information Fusion*, *90*, 233–240. doi:10.1016/j.inffus.2022.09.027

Varoudis, T., & Penn, A. (2019, July). Variational Beauty of Space: Machine Intuition and Non-Linear Neural Aggregations. In *12th Space Syntax Symposium* (Vol. 12). IEEE.

Wen, J., Nie, J., Kang, J., Niyato, D., Du, H., Zhang, Y., & Guizani, M. (2023). *From generative ai to generative internet of things: Fundamentals, framework, and outlooks*. arXiv preprint arXiv:2310.18382.

Chapter 12
Strategies for Mitigating Security Concerns in IoT-Enabled Smart Cities

Ravikumar
Marwadi University, India

Shilpa Singhal
Marwadi University, India

Santushti Betgeri
Marwadi University, India

Sushil Kumar Singh
Marwadi University, India

ABSTRACT

This chapter explores security in IoT-enabled smart cities, focusing on dangers arising from interconnectivity. Emphasizing citizen data protection and infrastructure preservation, it analyzes hazards in sensor networks, edge computing, and cyber-physical systems. Addressing data security and privacy, it covers encryption, authentication, and the need for legal frameworks. Practical risk management techniques are presented, emphasizing cybersecurity awareness, incident response improvement, and stakeholder collaboration. This chapter is a vital resource for understanding and addressing security concerns in the evolving domain of IoT-enabled smart cities.

INTRODUCTION

The integration of the Internet of Things (IoT) into smart cities has become a revolutionary force as urban environments alter with technology breakthroughs. The idea covers an extensive network of interconnected devices, which includes sensors that capture environmental data and edge computing that enables real-time decision-making. According to Market Watch, the IoT security market achieved

DOI: 10.4018/979-8-3693-2373-1.ch012

a value of 3.35 billion in 2022 and is projected to see a Compound Annual Growth Rate (CAGR) of 26.36%. It is anticipated to reach a value of 13.36 billion by 2028. The incidence of malware assaults targeting Internet of Things (IoT) devices had a significant surge of 77% during the initial six months of 2022 (Watch, 2023). Gartner says that almost a quarter of all hacks targeting organization's would use IoT (Poy, 2023). Statista predicts that the market for endpoint security would exceed $29 billion by 2027 (Poy, 2022).

- **Definition and Scope of IoT in Smart Cities**

The *Internet of Things (IoT)* is a network including interconnected objects that engage in communication and data exchange. Smart cities have widely embraced the IoT. A *"smart city"* is an advanced metropolis that gathers information via the use of technological means and sensors. City operations are enhanced by the data's application to asset, resource, and service management. It aids in enhancing productivity, minimizing expenses, and elevating the quality of life for inhabitants. The system utilizes IoT-enabled devices, such as interconnected Bluetooth sensors, RFID tags, and meters, to gather data in real-time for further analysis. IoT enabled cities will benefit in many ways such as traffic management, environment safety, disaster management and much more (Ahmed et al., 2021). The scope of IoT in smart cities includes:

- **The Growing Significance of Security Concerns**

The networks utilized for connecting IoT devices in smart cities frequently exhibit inadequate security measures, rendering them susceptible to hacking and unauthorized intrusion. Metropolitan regions frequently experience interoperability challenges, meaning that the IoT devices and systems in use are typically not specifically intended to function flawlessly with one another. The significance of security issues is increasing due to several factors, such as: cyber security, cloud security, IoT attacks, weak passwords, identity management, compliance, insider threats, and malware.

Further, the rest of the chapter is organized as follows: components of smart city IoT, addressed data security and privacy, security challenges are discussed, strategies to mitigate risk, emerging technologies with case studies, and finally adaptive security measure are discussed followed by a conclusion.

FOUNDATIONAL COMPONENTS OF SMART CITY IOT

IoT implementation in smart cities necessitates the integration of several components, such as hardware sensors, data management, user interface, analytics, and security, computing devices, and networking with pre-existing systems.

- **Sensor Networks and Data Collection**

Sensor networks are the lifeblood of IoT smart city data collection. Critical to the provision of real-time data on environmental factors, traffic patterns, and a host of municipal services, these networks comprise a multitude of sensors integrated into urban infrastructure. Light, heat, motion, humidity, and pressure are just a few of the many variables that sensors can track and identify. Smart city sensors often detect the

Figure 1. Scope of IoT in smart cities
(Rai et al., 2023)

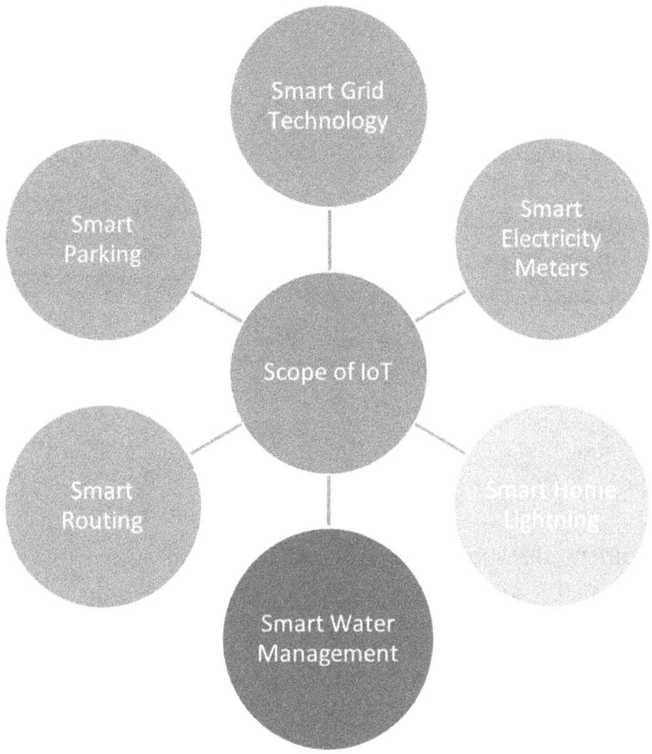

Figure 2. Security concerns
(Poy, 2009)

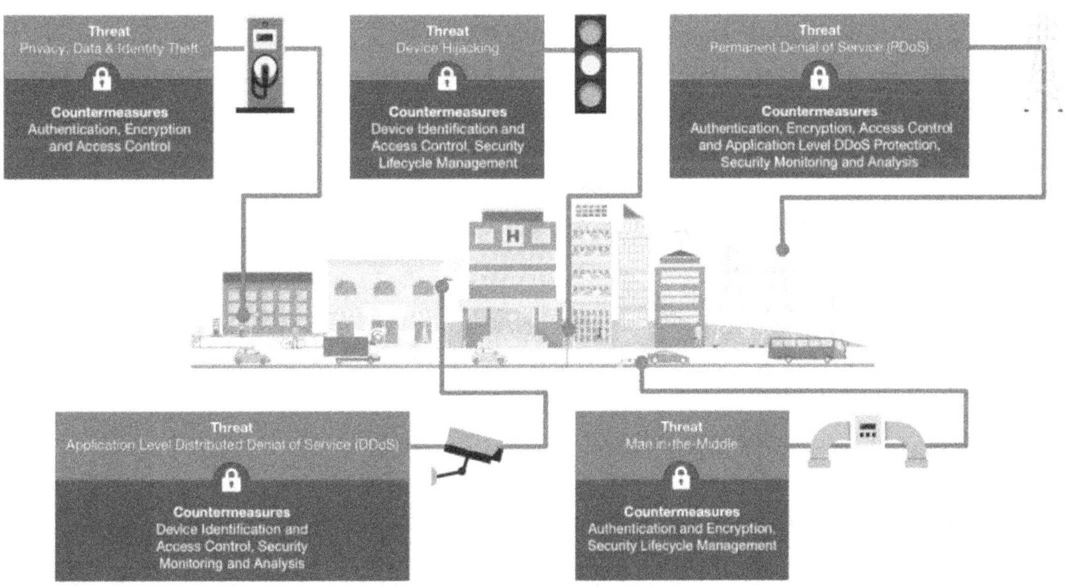

Figure 3. Edge layer and its connection
(Cooper, 2023)

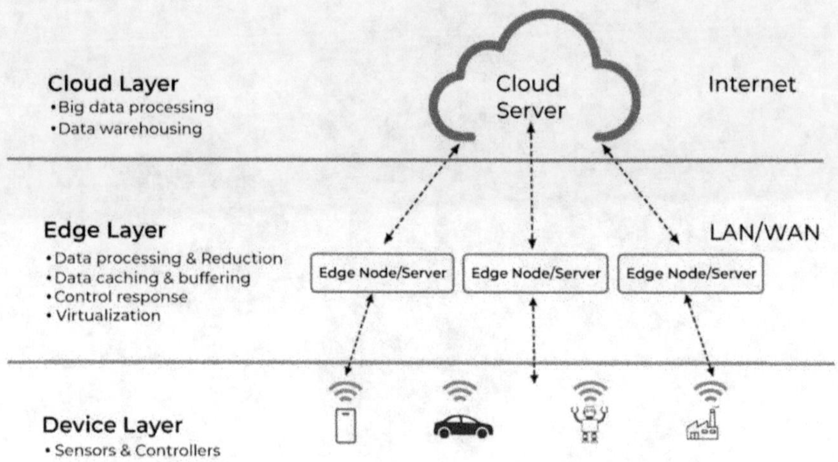

following: rotation, movement, threshold, proximity, infrared light, gases, smoke, alcohol, touch, color, and humidity (Wala et al., 2020). Several techniques exist for connecting sensors to the cloud, such as:

- Wireless cellular networks
- Direct Ethernet connections to the internet
- Bluetooth
- Low-Power Wide-Area Networks (LPWAN)
    - **Edge Computing and Decentralized Architectures**

Emerging as an essential part of smart city IoT, edge computing is at the crossroads of data processing and decision-making. One feature that has developed alongside the expansion of the Internet of Things is edge computing, a distributed computer architecture. It makes use of a decentralized network of IoT devices, desktops, laptops, and security cameras that each carry out calculations independently. Reduced latency allows for faster reaction times and enhanced system efficiency, which is achieved by moving processing workloads to the networks periphery (Khan et al., 2020). The following figure shoes the edge layer:

Among the many smart city applications of edge computing is the following:

- Enhanced data processing
- Deliver up-to-the-minute data
- Raise dependability
- Boost safety
- Use data to inform your choices
- Streamline offerings
- Raise the standard of living for all residents
    - **Cyber-Physical Systems and Interconnected Devices**

Cyber-Physical Systems (CPS) bring the digital and physical worlds together by integrating networked gadgets with the actual world in a seamless manner. In smart cities, CPS plays a crucial role as the foundation that coordinates the smooth functioning of many IoT devices. Medical devices, aerospace systems, transportation vehicles, and factory automation are just a few of the numerous areas that have used CPSs (Radanliev et al., 2021). Among the many advantages that CPSs may provide to businesses are:

- Enhanced dependability and productivity
- Increased security
- Increased adaptability
- Better oversight and management

In this section, components of IoT, edge computing and CPS are discussed with its use cases

DATA SECURITY AND PRIVACY TECHNIQUES

IoT devices from transportation systems to healthcare institutions can communicate and share data seamlessly, offering great potential. Connectivity provides many security risks that must be carefully examined. A multitude of hacking techniques, such as the Sybil attack, outside forgery attack, spam attack, identity attack, and eavesdropping attack, are capable of compromise nearly every application(Aslam et al., 2022; Ferrag et al., 2017). Additional instances where sensitive information can be compromised include smart homes and smart healthcare. This violation of information can be carried out by the service providers and the makers of the devices (Gong et al., 2015). Various data security and privacy techniques on development of smart cities are listed below in figure 4.

Encryption and Secure Communication:

Deploying persistent encryption algorithms to ensure the security of data transported across IoT networks. Encryption guarantees that, in the event of interception, the data will remain incomprehensible without the corresponding decryption key. Traditional algorithms and encryption standards are not entirely acceptable for devices with limited resources due to the complexity of the computations involved and the amount of energy that is used (Jing et al., 2014). The implementation of cryptographic technologies in practice has consequently resulted in the demand of lightweight encryption as a fundamental prerequisite. Figure 5 includes various Cryptography algorithms. In order to safeguard smart city applications, Li et al. (Li et al., 2017) recently presented a new lightweight authentication system that uses a public key encryption technique. Notably, there has been a rise in interest in homomorphic encryption (HE), which allows for calculations on encrypted data and the chaining of different services without revealing sensitive data (Talpur et al., 2015).

User Authentication and Access Control

For the purpose of verifying the identity of people or devices that interact with the Internet of Things ecosystem, the use of robust authentication mechanisms such as biometrics, two-factor authentication, or digital certificates is recommended. Biometrics are the highest standard for authentication in Internet

Figure 4. Data security and privacy techniques in IOT enabled smart cities

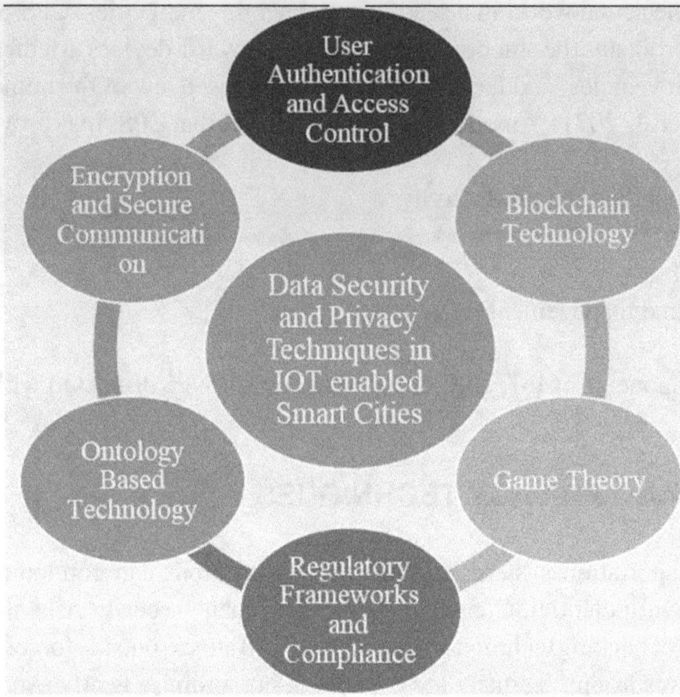

Figure 5. Cryptography algorithms

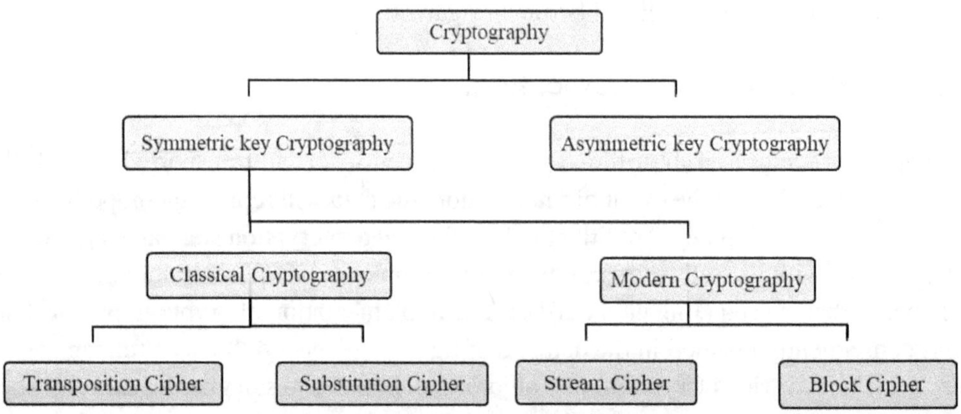

of Things (IoT) platforms. In particular, this technology can be employed to detect an individual automatically based on their distinct biological and behavioural traits. Many other types of bio-data, such as fingerprints, facial features, voice recordings, signatures, and so on, are retrieved. Among these methods, brainwave-based authentication (Zhou et al., 2020) stands out for its ability to both ensure efficiency and attain a high level of authentication accuracy. Note that improper usage of bio-based approaches can lead to increased privacy leakage risks. Wang et al.(Wang et al., 2018) developed privacy-preserving biometric schemes (PPBSs) to acknowledge the potential of biometrics in other fields, including e-commerce.

Figure 6. Biometric system

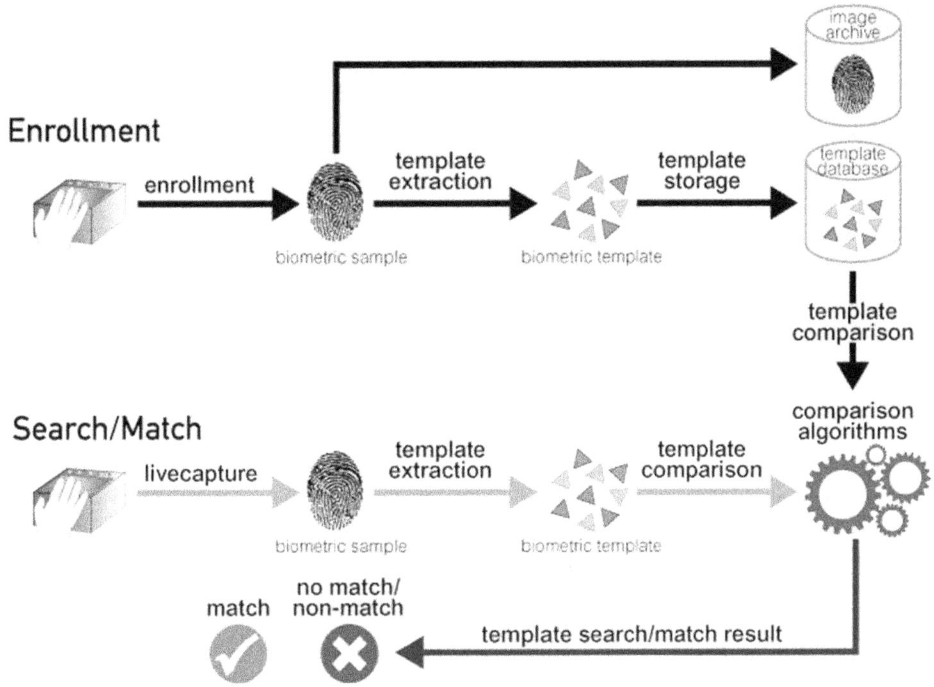

By implementing granular access control policies, which are designed to limit and manage rights, it is possible to guarantee that only authorized individuals or devices are able to access particular data or essential services. Figure 6 defines a biometric system and its different components.

Blockchain Technology

Blockchain strengthens IoT-enabled smart city security in a novel way. Blockchain ensures data integrity and transparency from many interconnected devices using its immutable ledger structure. A new security framework to ensure secure data communication has been developed integrating blockchain technology with devices used in smart cities (Biswas & Muthukkumarasamy, 2016). Encryption protects sensitive IoT data, and its decentralized nature spreads data among nodes, preventing single points of failure and strengthening cyber resilience. Blockchain can also be integrated with various technologies such as deep learning to provide a secure framework for smart cities. In (Shankar & Maple, 2023) a new framework SSCI-BDL, Secure Smart City Infrastructure framework is introduced, to secure IoT communication privacy and trustworthiness in smart cities. This framework uses blockchain for smart city security along with deep learning model and optimization algorithm to optimize smart city infrastructure resource use. Blockchain technology was incorporated into a smart home scenario in (Dorri et al., 2017) and the newly developed framework was introduced to can meet the goals of privacy, trustworthiness, and accessibility. Another study conducted that the current cloud infrastructure is not capable of meeting the growing demands of the Internet of Things (IoT) networks of the future. They created a new distributed architecture that adheres to the necessary design criteria, including security, scalability, efficiency, adaptability, and resilience, by combining blockchain with fog computing and software defined networking (SDN) technologies (Sharma et al., 2018).

Evidently, Blockchain technology is a potential safeguard that provides a powerful solution to strengthen the foundation of the growing ecosystems of smart cities resulting in more dependable and convenient applications. We must take steps to improve the use of this technology in order to address severe privacy and security concerns. Figure 7 shows the different layers present in the blockchain technology.

Ontology Based Technology

For the purpose of strengthening the security framework within Internet of Things (IoT)-enabled smart cities, ontology-based technology also plays a crucial role. Effective management and protection of the intricate network of interconnected Internet of Things devices and systems can be achieved through the utilization of ontology, which is a structured representation of knowledge (Takizaki et al., 2023). The use of ontologies allows for the exact identification and authentication of persons and devices inside the ecosystem of the city. Ontologies establish the links and classifications that exist between the various elements. In (Mozzaquatro et al., 2018) authors present an ontology-based cybersecurity system using knowledge reasoning for IoT with two approaches: design time, which uses a model-driven methodology to build security services based on enterprise processes, and run time, which monitors the IoT environment, classifies threats and vulnerabilities, and actuates to ensure proper adaptation This technology makes it possible to establish a standardized framework for communication and the exchange of data, which guarantees that information is interpreted correctly across a variety of devices and platforms. Further, ontology-based reasoning mechanisms enable smart city infrastructures to identify abnormalities or potential security breaches by examining patterns and deviations from established standards. This is accomplished through the use of pattern recognition and deviation analysis. Through the utilization of ontology, smart cities are able to develop robust authentication procedures, expedite data interoperabil-

Figure 7. Blockchain layers

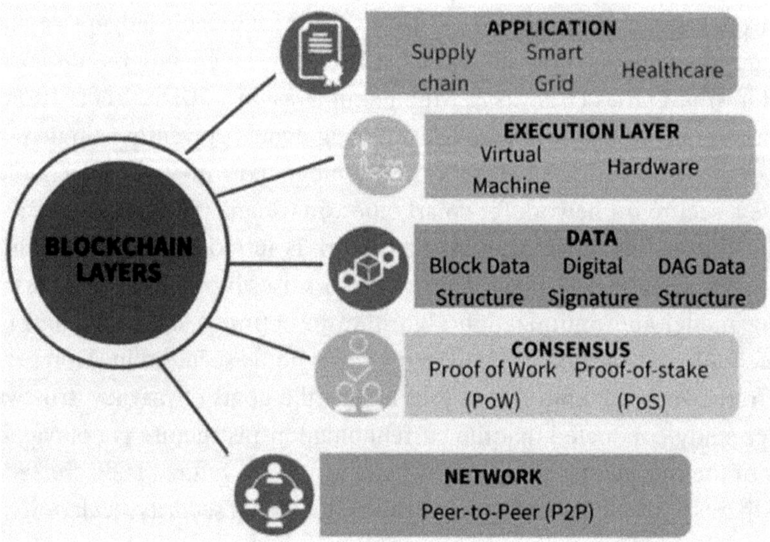

Figure 8. Ontology Based Cybersecurity Framework
(Mozzaquatro et al., 2018)

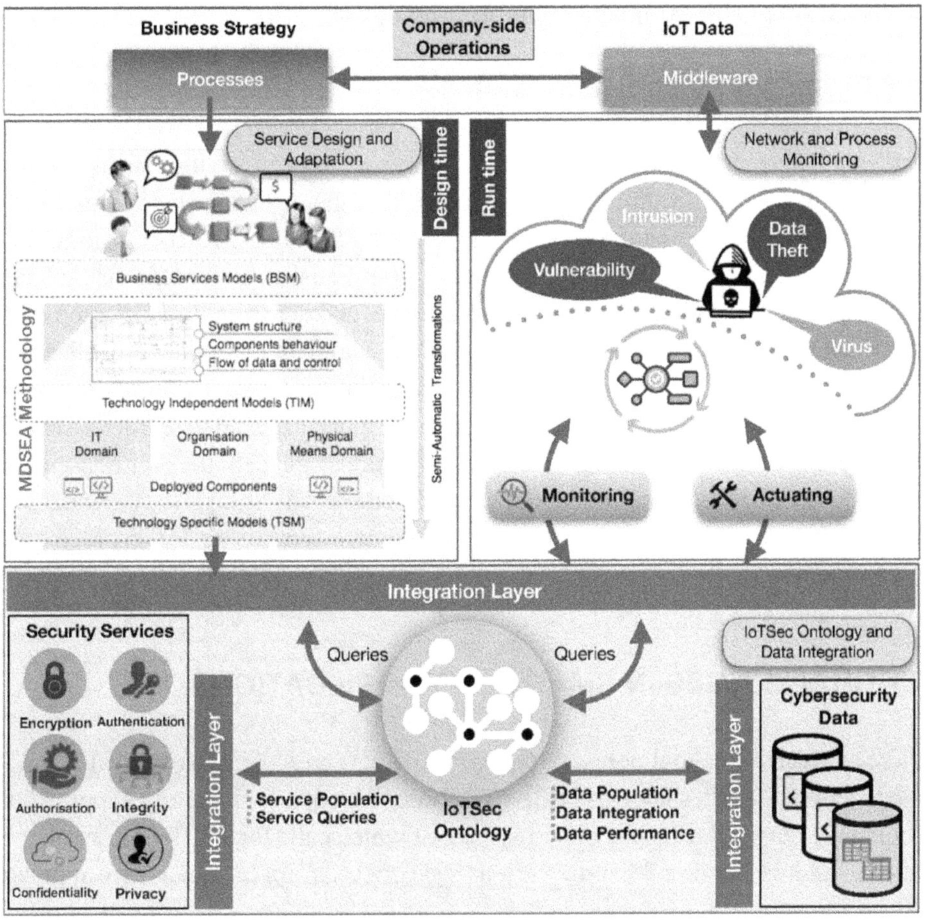

ity, and proactively reduce security threats, hence enhancing the trustworthiness and resilience of their networked systems' capabilities. Fig. 8 represents an ontology-based cybersecurity framework for IoT.

Game Theory

Applying game theory to IoT-enabled smart city security dynamics reveals how varied groups interact to protect these interconnected systems. It helps stakeholders understand how competing or saving money can jeopardize security .Game theory is useful in analysis of the interaction between self-interested smart cars and parcels and malicious smart vehicles and parcels (Abdellaoui alaoui & El Moudden, 2018). Another study investigated a game with smart-home users, stakeholders, and attackers using evolutionary game theory. For this game replicator dynamics was generated and evaluated to establish the evolutionarily stable strategy (ESS) (Douha et al., 2023). Game theory can be utilized to frame the issue of deciding on the connectivity of IoT devices during a malware epidemic as a recurring game. This approach enables individual IoT devices to make connectivity decisions over a period of time (Huang et al., 2019). Game theory also helps manufacturers and service providers to develop incentive structures that encourage collaboration and high security standards. It anticipates and prepares for security threats by monitoring IoT ecosystem activity and intentions. Game theory guides strategic decision-making to protect IoT-enabled smart cities from emerging security threats.

Regulatory Frameworks and Compliance

Protecting IoT-enabled smart cities requires regulatory frameworks and compliance. Connected devices and networks make these cities vulnerable to cybersecurity threats. Data privacy standards like GDPR are needed to secure IoT device data. Security standards like ISO/IEC 27001 (Kitsios et al., 2023) and NIST Cybersecurity Framework (Lefkovitz & Boeckl, 2021) ensure systematic risk management. IoT device regulations require manufacturers to upgrade, secure, and define end-of-life protocols. Standards encourage network cohesion, and certifications and audits validate compliance. Collaboration among stakeholders helps share threats and best practices. Strong incident response strategies, education, and ethics strengthen these systems. Dynamic regulations that respond to new dangers are essential. Enforcing compliance with these regulations through audits, certifications, and penalties for non-compliance. This ensures that IoT devices and systems adhere to the specified security and privacy standards. Regulatory frameworks improve compliance, mitigate risks, and promote security in IoT-enabled smart cities by integrating these features.

SECURITY CHALLENGES IN SMART CITY APPLICATIONS

Although there are many potential points of failure in a smart city, the most critical is the Internet and the various devices linked to it, since this is the vital component of any smart city. Applications for smart cities present a wide range of security concerns, each of which calls for a different set of considerations and techniques to address. Figure 9 list the various security issues in the smart city applications.

Privacy Issues of Autonomous Vehicles in Smart Cities

Data protection is the primary challenge in autonomous vehicles as a huge amount of passenger data including personal details, routes are obtained by driverless cars. It is essential to ensure the encryption and safe transmission of sensitive passenger data to prevent breaches of privacy. Robust cybersecurity protections are also required to prevent unwanted access or control, which can occur due to vulnerabilities in the software or communication networks of autonomous vehicles (Hataba et al., 2022).

Threats Posed by AI in Smart Cities

AI systems are crucial for smart applications including automation of trade systems, appliance control, and pacemaker devices. However, the increasing usage of AI creates security issues such as service providers and device manufacturers using data mining technology to analyse personal data and extract sensitive information beyond the intended aims of associated services. AI system datasets must be secured to prevent biased choices or adjustments that could affect smart city activities (Rjab et al., 2023). To ensure the reliability of AI-driven services, it is crucial to protect AI systems against cyber-attacks such as data poisoning or model manipulation.

Figure 9. Security challenges in smart city applications

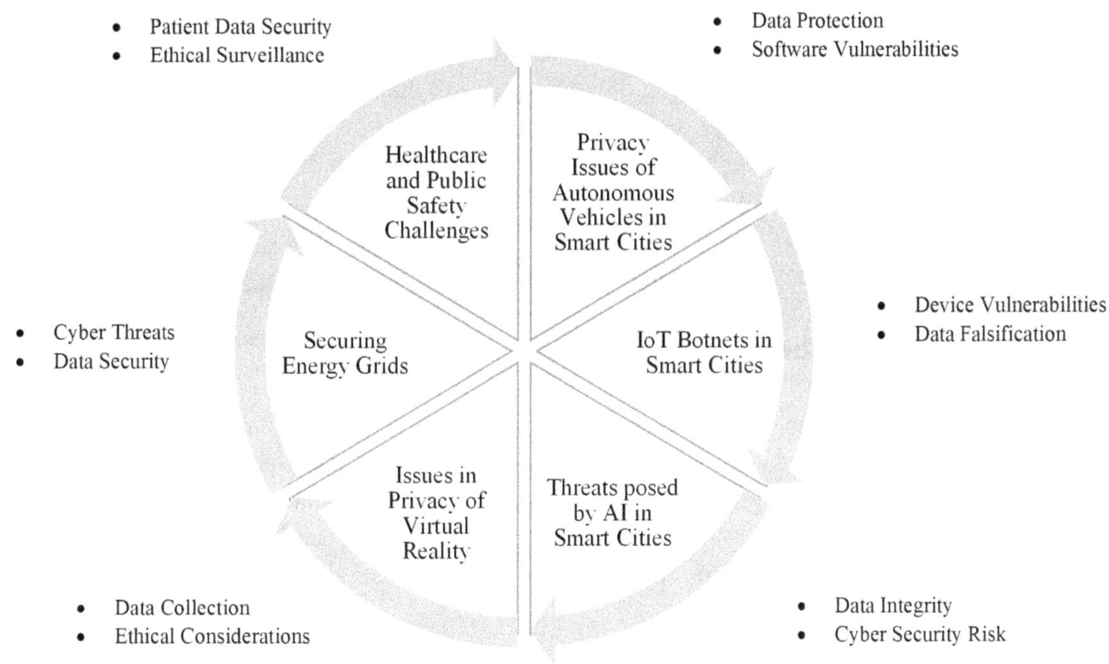

IoT Botnets in Smart Cities

IOT devices in smart cities are vulnerable to botnet attacks, turning them into weapons capable of launching distributed denial of service strikes. The establishment of IoT botnets in a smart city setting can result in widespread denial-of-service (DOS) attacks, which can affect the availability of the city's functions. One such example is the mirai botnet attack designed to hack the IoT devices and leads to DOS attack (Margolis et al., 2017). IoT device security must be improved to avoid botnets from disrupting metropolitan infrastructure. To support reliable smart city decision-making, compromised IoT devices must not transmit erroneous or modified data.

Issues in Privacy of Virtual Reality in Smart Cities

Many businesses, including municipal planning departments, healthcare providers, and engineering firms, have adopted virtual reality (VR) technology in smart cities. However, sensitive information transmitted with third parties, unencrypted VR device communications, and sensor data pose privacy leakage risks. To ensure the privacy of individuals, it is essential to secure user data acquired by virtual reality apps, particularly in the transportation or healthcare industries. It is critical to preserve citizens' right to privacy by ensuring that VR-enhanced technologies adhere to ethical norms, especially in public safety applications.

Securing Energy Grids

The IoT-based Smart Grid faces multifaceted security threats. Numerous and serious vulnerabilities exist, including those that allow for eavesdropping, data manipulation, and illegal access, as well as identity spoofing. . Some of the threats are changing dynamic prices to make people use more energy, tampering with smart meters to pay for energy, and intercepting data that shows how much energy people use. Smart appliances collect extensive data that may reveal user habits and actions, raising privacy concerns (Bekara, 2014). Smart energy systems must be protected from cyberattacks to avoid energy supply interruptions with serious social and economic consequences. Data security is also crucial for smart energy systems to avoid unwanted access and manipulation, which could impair energy distribution.

Healthcare and Public Safety Challenges

There are various challenges in digital healthcare system including data security, inter-realm authentication, health information exchange barriers and device communication in implemented connected health (Zeadally et al., 2019). To prevent breaches of sensitive medical data, smart healthcare systems must have strict security measures to protect patient data. To balance security needs without violating residents' private rights, public safety monitoring systems must be ethical.

MITIGATING RISKS: STRATEGIES AND BEST PRACTICES

The reduction of risks that are linked with Smart Cities is of the utmost importance in the context of the fast-changing environment of Smart Cities, where the incorporation of technology is being used to alter urban living. A comprehensive collection of Smart City Risk Mitigation Strategies is presented in Figure 10. These strategies, when taken as a whole, contribute to the development of an urban environment that is both secure and resilient.

- Cybersecurity Awareness and Education is at the center of these strategies now being used. The level of sophistication of cyber-attacks is growing at an alarming rate, making it absolutely necessary for citizens and stakeholders to have a comprehensive understanding of the potential dangers and the most effective methods for protecting digital assets. Within the context of the Smart City setting, this educational component functions as a basic pillar for the entire security situation.
- Implementing strong Incident Response and Recovery systems complements this awareness. It is crucial for cities to establish effective policies to reduce the impact of cyber events and unexpected disruptions and get back to normal operations quickly. The operation and reliability of Smart City infrastructure depend on the ability to respond efficiently to problems.
- Emphasizing the significance of open communication and information sharing, transparency emerges as another crucial tactic. Because of this openness, both citizens and companies are more likely to trust the Smart City ecosystem, which in turn makes them feel safer. Cities can foster a cooperative atmosphere that encourages community participation in risk management by keeping stakeholders apprised of progress and possible dangers.
- The importance of cooperation among different entities is emphasized by collaborative approaches. To successfully address and mitigate risks, communities, private sectors, and governments

Figure 10. Smart city risk mitigation strategies

must collaborate. In addition to encouraging everyone to do their part, this cooperative spirit makes it easier to combine forces in order to solve difficult problems.

- To guarantee that people's rights are not infringed upon by technological progress, privacy and anonymity measures are crucial. Secure data storage and the preservation of individual rights should be top priorities for smart city planners. The long-term viability of Smart City programs depends on finding a happy medium between privacy concerns and technological advancement.
- Finally, the importance of accountability as a core value is stressed. Everyone with a stake in creating or overseeing a Smart City needs to answer for their activities. This transparency promotes a sense of duty by making those in charge and those carrying out their decisions aware of how their decisions can affect the safety and health of city dwellers.

Incorporating these Smart City Risk Mitigation Strategies into city planning allows cities to anticipate problems, build resilience, and prepare for a future without smart city security threats.

EMERGING TECHNOLOGIES FOR IOT SECURITY

Emerging technologies are often the newest and most cutting edge. They could help solve the growing security problems that come with the growing number of IoT devices. Figure 11 shows the newest

Figure 11. Emerging technology for IOT security

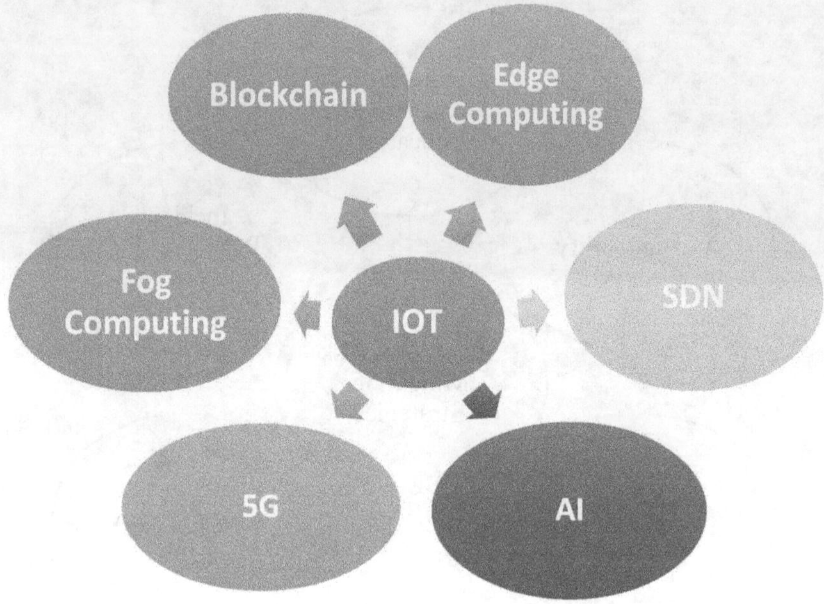

technologies for IoT security (Tawalbeh et al., 2020). Subsequently, detailed explanations of each one will be provided below.

IoT Security Using Blockchain

The technologies of blockchain and IoT are crucial and will significantly influence the IT and telecom industries. Both of these technologies aim to enhance the overall clarity, visibility, user comfort, and level of confidence. IOT devices offer instantaneous data from sensors, while blockchain ensures data security through a distributed, decentralized, and shared ledger. The utilization of blockchain offers numerous benefits in Internet of Things (IoT) applications.

The following paragraphs outline the primary advantages of utilizing blockchain technology in Internet of Things (IoT) applications.

a. **Data coming from IOT devices can be stored in Block chain:** A lot of different devices are linked together in IOT apps. These things are linked to and managed by other things. This setup is also linked to the cloud, which lets IOT apps be used from anywhere. Because it gives data a lot of room to move, blockchain looks like a good way to store data and keep it from being abused. No matter what level of an IOT application it is, blockchain can be used to store and send data.
b. **Distributed nature of block chain allowing secure data storage:** In contrast to other cloud-based IoT systems, blockchain architecture is distributed; therefore, it cannot be a single point of failure. The data produced by the devices can be safely kept on the blockchain regardless of their distance from each other.
c. **Data encryption using the hash key and verified by miners:** Blockchain technology allows for the storage of simply the 256-bit hash key associated with data, rather than the data itself. You can

use cloud storage for the actual data and then use the hash key to map it to the original data. The data hash will be updated whenever the data is modified. The data is protected and kept confidential in this way. Since the block chain simply stores hash values, its size is unaffected by the amount of data. Using the data's hash, only the designated users with permission to access the data can retrieve it from the cloud. It is less likely that devices will store erroneous data while using block chain since every set of data stored on the network is appropriately validated by several miners.

d. **Prevention from data loss and spoofing attacks:** During spoofing attacks on IOT applications, a novel adversary node infiltrates the IOT network and begins impersonating a legitimate member of the original network. Through the act of spoofing, the attacker can effortlessly seize, monitor, or introduce data into the network. The use of blockchain serves as a viable approach to mitigate such threats. Every authorized user or device is enrolled on the blockchain, enabling devices to readily recognize and verify each other without relying on central intermediaries or certification entities. Due to their low power nature, Internet of Things (IoT) devices are susceptible to data loss. In certain instances, data loss can occur for both the transmitter and the receiver as a result of external environmental factors. The utilization of blockchain technology can effectively mitigate such losses, as once a block is appended to the chain, it becomes immutable and cannot be removed.

e. **Block chain to prevent unauthorized access:** Several Internet of Things (IoT) applications necessitate extensive and regular connectivity among multiple nodes. Communication in blockchain occurs through the utilization of public and private keys, ensuring that only the intended recipient or node is able to retrieve the data. Even if an unauthorized person manages to gain access to the data, they will be unable to understand its contents because the data is encrypted using keys. Hence, the blockchain data format endeavors to address diverse security concerns encountered by Internet of Things (IoT) applications.

f. **Proxy-based architecture in blockchain for resource constrained devices:** Even though block-chain offers many security benefits for a spread setting, the Internet of Things (IoT) faces a unique problem: it lacks resources. IOT devices don't have a lot of resources, so they can't store big ledgers. A lot of work has been done in this area to make it easier to use blockchain in IoT. One interesting way to help IoT devices use blockchain is through proxy-based design. The data can be stored in an encrypted form on proxy servers that can be set up in the network. The client can get the encrypted data from the proxy servers.

g. **Elimination of centralized cloud servers:** In the end, blockchain gets rid of centralized cloud services and makes the network peer-to-peer, which makes IOT systems safer. The main thing that data thieves are after are centralized cloud systems. All the nodes in the network will receive the data through block chain, which will secure it with a cryptographic hash function.

h. **Merkle Tree:** To make Internet of Things (IoT) devices even more secure, one can add a Merkle tree to the blockchain data structure. Ralph Merkle came up with the idea for the Merkle tree in the year 1980. There will be fewer blocks added to the chain overall if this is done. A Merkle tree resembles a binary tree in that, with the exception of leaf nodes, every node has two child nodes. Data and transactions are stored on leaf nodes, and their hash values are called roots. It is possible to aggregate numerous transactions into a single root hash, depending on the size of the tree. You can think of each root hash as a block in the chain instead of each transaction. We may use this to decrease the number of blocks. The security of the data is further improved at each level of the tree because of the many layers of hashing (Tawalbeh et al., 2020). Because there are a lot of little communications between IoT devices, combining Merkle trees with blockchain technology could be a good answer.

Figure 12. The Structure of Merkle Hash Tree and Blockchain
(Jiang et al., 2020)

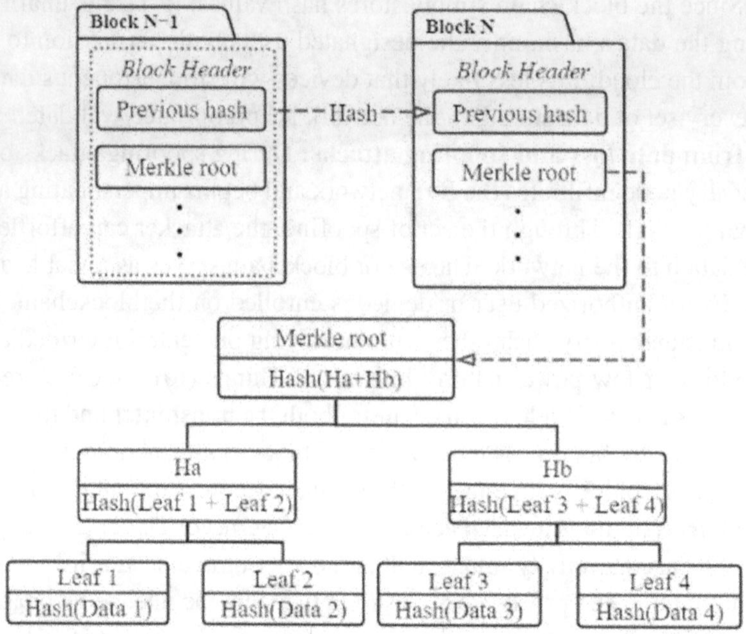

IoT Security using Fog Computing

The Internet of Things (IoT) and cloud computing are distinct technologies with several applications. The Internet of Things (IoT) has facilitated the proliferation of a wide array of intelligent devices and apps for consumers. Likewise, a cloud offers a highly efficient means of storing and organizing data that can be accessed from any location, and is extensively utilized by numerous enterprises. The Internet of Things (IoT) is producing an unparalleled volume of data, placing significant pressure on the infrastructure of the Internet. The convergence of cloud computing and the Internet of Things (IoT) has ushered in a new era of possibilities and complexities in the realm of processing, storing, managing, and safeguarding data with greater efficiency. Efforts have been made by industry and research groups to address the challenges encountered by the Internet of Things (IoT) by incorporating it with cloud technology. The advantages of this integration are insufficient to effectively tackle all the challenges encountered by IoT. Thus, Cisco established the concept of fog computing in 2012. Fog computing serves as a supplement to cloud computing instead of serving as a replacement for it.

Here are some of the ways that fog computing can help you deal with these security threats:

a. **Man-in-the-middle attack:** Fog is a layer of protection between the user and the cloud or IoT system. All attacks or risks on IoT systems have to go through the fog layer first. This layer can spot and stop any strange activity before it reaches the system.
b. **Data transit attacks:** When it comes to data storage and control, secure fog nodes are much better than IoT devices. If you keep data on fog nodes instead of end-user devices, it will be safer. This is another way that fog nodes help make user info more accessible.

Figure 13. Fog computing security solution with block chain
(Chen et al., 2023)

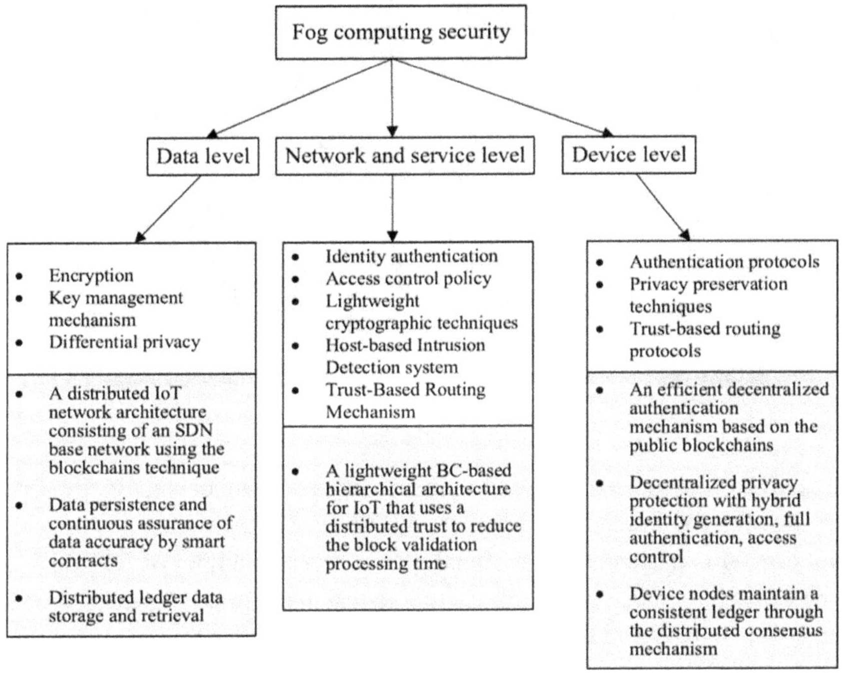

c. **Eavesdropping:** When fog nodes are used, contact only happens between the end user and the fog node. The information doesn't go through the whole network. Because there is less activity on the network, there is a much smaller chance that an enemy will try to listen in.

d. **Resource-constraint issues:** Attackers take advantage of the fact that most IoT devices don't have a lot of resources. For entry, they try to damage the edge devices. The edge devices can be helped by fog nodes, which can also protect them from threats like these. A fog node close by can handle the more complex security tasks that are needed to keep people safe.

e. **Incident response services:** It is possible to set up fog nodes to provide incident reaction services in real time. When fog nodes find data or requests that don't seem right, they can send a flag to the IOT system or the end users. Fog computing makes it possible to find bugs and fix problems while they are in transit. In a lot of important programs, stopping the whole system to fix malware problems might not be possible. In these situations, fog nodes can help while the system is still running.

Artificial Intelligence for Anomaly Detection

Artificial Intelligence (AI) has become an indispensable tool in enhancing the security of Internet of Things (IOT) devices, which are increasingly integral in our daily lives. IOT networks, owing to their extensive data collection and transmission, present attractive targets for cyber-attacks (Jo et al., 2019). AI excels in pattern recognition, allowing it to effectively identify deviations from normal behaviour in IOT systems, signalling potential security breaches. This capability is critical in anomaly detection, as it enables early identification of unusual activities that could indicate cyber threats. Beyond just detection,

Figure 14. Illustrations of an AI-powered cyber security agent in action

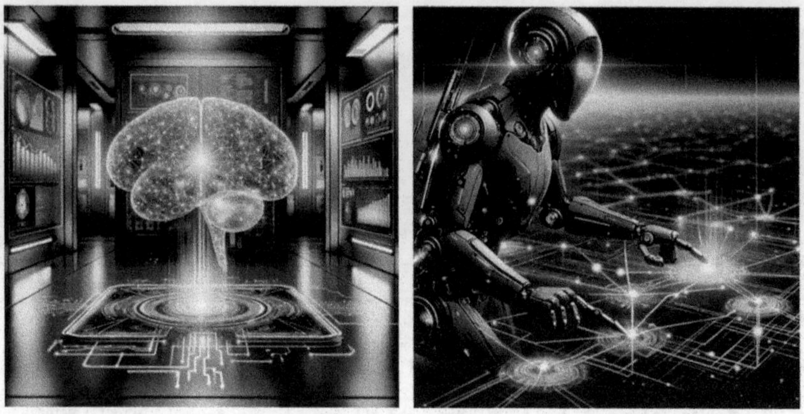

AI's predictive analysis can foresee potential vulnerabilities and attack vectors by scrutinizing trends within the data, allowing for a proactive approach to IOT security.

The scalability of AI is particularly beneficial given the vast number of IOT devices in operation; manual monitoring of such extensive networks is impractical, if not impossible. AI algorithms can simultaneously manage and analyse data from countless devices, ensuring comprehensive security coverage. Moreover, the real-time monitoring and rapid response features of AI are crucial in mitigating the impact of any security breach, offering immediate action against identified threats. This aspect is particularly vital in minimizing potential damage from cyber-attacks. Furthermore, AI systems are equipped with adaptive learning capabilities. They evolve by continuously learning from new threats, thereby enhancing their detection and response strategies over time. This adaptability is essential in keeping pace with the ever-evolving landscape of cyber threats. AI also plays a key role in maintaining the privacy of data collected by IoT devices, promptly identifying and addressing unauthorized data accesses or leaks. Overall, AI's role in anomaly detection for IoT security is multi-faceted, offering pattern recognition, predictive analysis, scalability, real-time response, adaptive learning, and privacy enhancement, making it a critical component in safeguarding emerging IoT technologies against complex and continually advancing cyber threats. The solutions provided by ML to overcome these security threats are discussed below (Harahsheh & Chen, 2023):

a. **DoS Attack:** DoS attacks on Internet of Things devices or assaults that originate from Internet of Things devices are a major cause for concern. The utilization of a Multilayer Perceptron (MLP) based protocol that protects networks against denial-of-service attacks is one method that can be utilized to mitigate attacks of this nature. A particle swarm optimization and back propagation approach has been suggested by the authors of in order to train a multilayer perceptron (MLP) that contributes to the improvement of the security pertaining to wireless networks. The use of machine learning techniques helps to improve the accuracy of deductions and secure Internet of Things devices that are susceptible to denial-of-service assaults.
b. **Eavesdropping:** Attackers could listen in on texts while data is being sent. ML methods, like the Q-learning based offloading strategy or non-parametric Bayesian techniques, can be used to protect against these kinds of attacks. Machine learning methods like Q-learning and Dyna-Q can also be

used to keep devices safe from being spied on. Experiments and reinforcement learning are used to test these methods.

c. **Spoofing:** To prevent spoofing attacks, one can employ many strategies such as Q-learning, Dyna-Q, Support Vector Machines (SVM), Deep Neural Network (DNN) model, incremental aggregated gradient (IAG), and distributed FrankWolfe (dFW). These strategies not only enhance the accuracy of detection and classification, but also contribute to reducing the average error rate and false alarm rate.
d. **Privacy Leakage:** The gathering of personal information, such as health data, location, or images, jeopardizes the user's privacy. To prevent the disclosure of private information, it is advisable to utilize privacy-preserving scientific computations (PPSC). Another method proposed to establish trust in IoT applications is the Commodity Integrity Detection Algorithm (CIDA), which utilizes the Chinese Remainder Theorem (CRT).
e. **Digital Fingerprinting:** Digital fingerprinting is an emerging and promising method for enhancing the security of IoT systems and instilling confidence in end users regarding the reliability of apps. Fingerprints are extensively utilized for purposes such as unlocking cell phones, authorizing payments, accessing vehicles and homes, and so on. Digital fingerprinting is becoming a prominent type of biometric identification due to its affordability, dependability, widespread acceptance, and strong security measures. In addition to the advantages of digital fingerprinting, there exist some obstacles to effectively utilize this method in the Internet of Things (IoT), including fingerprint categorization, image enhancement, and feature matching. Several machine learning algorithms have been created to offer alternative options for addressing these difficulties.

Securing all interconnected systems and devices is the primary requirement in the field of IoT. The primary function of machine learning (ML) is to employ and train algorithms to identify anomalies in IoT devices or detect any unauthorized activity occurring within an IoT system, in order to mitigate the risk of data loss or other related problems. Hence, machine learning offers a viable framework to address the challenges encountered in ensuring the security of IoT devices. Additional contributions in this domain are necessary to sustain the expansion of IoT.

Software Defined Networking (SDN)

SDN plays a crucial role in enhancing IoT security by providing a dynamic and programmable framework for managing network resources. Here's how SDN contributes to improving the security of Internet of Things (IoT) environments:

a. **Dynamic Network Segmentation:** SDN allows for dynamic network segmentation, enabling the isolation of IoT devices into distinct segments based on their security requirements. This ensures that even if one segment is compromised, the impact is limited, and the lateral movement of threats is restricted.
b. **Adaptive Access Control:** SDN enables adaptive access control policies. Policies can be dynamically adjusted based on real-time threat intelligence, device behaviour, and security postures. This ensures that access permissions are continuously aligned with the evolving security landscape.

c. **Centralized Network Visibility:** SDN provides a centralized view of the entire network. This visibility allows security administrators to monitor and analyse traffic patterns, detect anomalies, and respond swiftly to potential security incidents across the IoT infrastructure.
d. **Enhanced Incident Response:** SDN facilitates rapid incident response by allowing security policies to be adjusted programmatically. In the event of a security breach or abnormal behaviour, automated responses can be triggered, such as isolating affected devices or redirecting traffic for further analysis.
e. **Secure Device Onboarding:** SDN assists in the secure onboarding of IoT devices. Network policies can be applied dynamically as devices connect to the network, ensuring that only authorized and properly authenticated devices gain access. This prevents unauthorized devices from joining the network and posing security risks.
f. **Traffic Encryption and Monitoring:** SDN can be used to implement encryption for data in transit between IoT devices and other network components. Additionally, by centralizing network monitoring, SDN allows for the inspection of encrypted traffic, enabling the detection of potential threats and vulnerabilities.
g. **Resource Optimization:** With SDN, network resources are optimized according to security objectives. By allocating more resources and bandwidth to the most important Internet of Things devices first, we can make the network more resistant to assaults from different angles.
h. **Network Virtualization:** SDN enables network virtualization, allowing the creation of isolated virtual networks for specific IoT applications or services. This isolation ensures that compromise in one virtual network does not affect the security of others.
i. **Policy-Based Security Orchestration:** SDN allows for the orchestration of security policies based on predefined rules. These policies can be adjusted dynamically to respond to changing security requirements, ensuring that security measures are aligned with the evolving threat landscape.
j. **Reduced Attack Surface:** SDN helps in minimizing the attack surface by providing granular control over network configurations. Unnecessary services or communication channels can be disabled, reducing the avenues available for attackers to exploit.

Integration of 5G Technology

The integration of 5G technology into the Internet of Things (IoT) marks a significant advancement in terms of emerging technologies for IoT security. 5G's impact on IoT security is multi-dimensional:

a. **Increased Bandwidth and Speed**: 5G provides much higher bandwidth and speed compared to its predecessors. This enables IoT devices to communicate and transmit data more efficiently. Faster data transfer means that security protocols and updates can be implemented swiftly, reducing the window of vulnerability.
b. **Enhanced Connectivity**: 5G technology allows a far greater number of devices to be connected simultaneously. While this increases the complexity of the IoT ecosystem, it also facilitates more integrated and cohesive security strategies, where multiple devices can be coordinated more effectively.
c. **Low Latency**: One of the key features of 5G is its low latency, which is crucial for real-time data processing and immediate response to security threats. This is particularly important for IoT ap-

Figure 15. Multi-Dimensional impact of 5G on IOT security

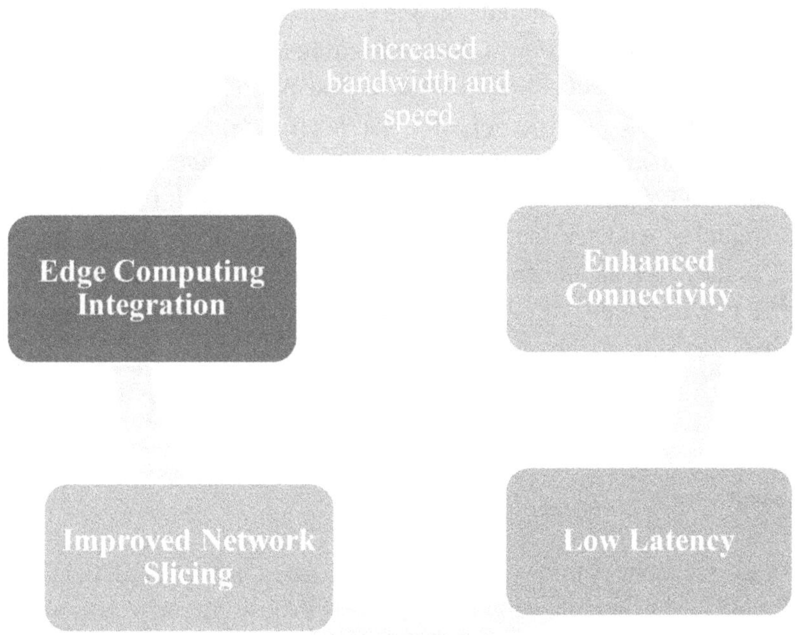

plications requiring instant data analysis and reaction, such as autonomous vehicles or industrial control systems.

d. **Improved Network Slicing**: With 5G, the idea of network slicing is introduced, enabling virtual network segmentation for specific purposes. Depending on the requirements of various Internet of Things (IoT) applications, each slice might have its own unique set of security protocols and settings. By separating various parts of the network, this modification improves security and lessens the likelihood of widespread vulnerabilities.

e. **Edge Computing Integration**: Because 5G works with edge computing, less data will have to be sent to the cloud, which is safer because cloud computing can process massive amounts of data. The security of sensitive information can be greatly enhanced by processing it closer to its point of generation.

SECURING EMERGENCY VEHICLE ROUTES IN HEALTHCARE: A BLOCKCHAIN-DRIVEN APPROACH FOR ENHANCED TRUST AND EFFICIENCY - A CASE STUDY

Concerns about security in the context of healthcare that is integrated with the Internet of Things (IoT) are a major issue in the healthcare sector. One chance to improve emergency vehicle routing is the arrival of next-gen cars with autonomous driving features and accurate decision-making abilities. In this case study(Kaurav et al., 2021), we look at how one company used Blockchain to improve the safety of their emergency healthcare logistics by collecting reliable data on their road networks.

The main goal is to create and implement a reliable and effective strategy for routing emergency vehicles that prioritizes security. This entails the integration of each vehicle with the Ethereum Blockchain, along with the utilization of the Open-Source Routing Machine (OSRM) to ascertain the shortest and most dependable routes. The suggested methodology seeks to mitigate transit delays for emergency vehicles, thereby enhancing the provision of vital healthcare services. Our concept is to offer reliable information and the most efficient route with little traffic for emergency vehicles. The prevention of a single point of failure is a significant priority for ensuring the availability of the proposed routing service in emergency vehicles. Another issue pertains to the security and trustworthiness of data provided by public devices, as they lack an authentication mechanism when transmitting information regarding temporary traffic blocks, accidents, or other incidents. In order to tackle these problems, we provide a method that combines Blockchain technology with the Open-Source Routing Machine (OSRM). Integrating Blockchain with OSRM in emergency vehicles will ensure the secure and authenticated transmission of information to OSRM, enabling the provision of more reliable congestion-aware routes.

Proposed System

The proposed system incorporates three entities: (1) Vehicular clients (VCs), (2) Open-Source Routing Machine (OSRM), and (3) Decentralized Application (DAPP). Automotive customers (VCs): The VCs refer to those who are either seated within or operating the vehicles. Every entity fulfils a distinct function inside the emergency vehicle routing system.

Vehicular Clients (VCs)

VCs represent individuals inside or driving vehicles equipped with advanced features like a Digital screen dashboard and Global Positioning System (GPS).

- **OSRM-Generated Routes Display:** The digital screen presents routes calculated by OSRM, a routing engine utilizing open-source software. Users view these routes on the digital screen interface, providing a visual representation of the most efficient paths based on factors like distance, traffic, and user preferences.
- **Real-time Route Requests by VCs:** Vehicle Controllers (VCs) can interact with OSRM, requesting real-time information for either the shortest or alternative routes. OSRM responds by considering factors like traffic conditions, providing VCs with dynamic routing options tailored to their preferences and operational needs.

Open-Source Routing Machine (OSRM)

OSRM is a routing engine designed to generate the shortest and congestion-aware routes from a given source to a destination.

- **VCs Request Route Information:** Vehicle Controllers (VCs), responsible for managing vehicles, can request route information from OSRM, which generates optimal and congestion-aware routes based on their specific needs.

- **Scalable and Secure OSRM Infrastructure**: OSRM utilizes locally stored maps from OpenStreetMap, and its servers are deployed region-wise for scalability. It ensures secure data sharing through encryption and respects privacy preferences and regulations of individual countries where it operates.

Decentralized Application (DAPP)

DAPP is an advanced application based on a Peer-to-Peer, decentralized network, and Blockchain.

- **Backend Automation with Smart Contracts:** The system employs smart contracts in the backend, executing predefined functions automatically when specific criteria are met. This ensures efficient processing, ranging from transaction execution to decentralized business logic implementation.
- **User-Friendly Interface with Robust Security Measures:** The system offers an interface similar to common web or mobile applications, promoting user-friendly interactions. Simultaneously, it prevents a single point of failure through resilient architecture and incorporates robust security protocols, including the use of Ethereum to store Vehicle Controllers' account information in encrypted form, enhancing decentralized and secure data management.

Challenges Faced and Overcome

Many obstacles may arise during the implementation of a system that combines Open-Source Routing Machine (OSRM) with a decentralized application (DAPP) for reliable information exchange in emergency vehicle routing. Presented here is a list of possible obstacles and proposals for overcoming them:

Decentralized Application Security

- **Challenge:** Security vulnerabilities in the DAPP.
- **Overcoming:** The implementation of stringent security measures, such as encryption, secure coding methods, and routine security audits has been recommended. Increasing the DAPP's resilience can be accomplished by the use of well-established security frameworks.

User Device Authorization

- **Challenge:** Verifying the legitimacy of user devices
- **Overcoming:** Strong security methods for devices should be used, like multi-factor authentication (MFA) and device certificates. To stay ahead of possible threats, keep your security measures up to date and patched on a regular basis.

Human Inputs and OSRM Collaboration

- **Challenge:** Ensuring accurate integration of human inputs into the OSRM.
- **Overcoming:** Implement algorithms and validation checks within the DAPP to verify the accuracy and relevance of human inputs. Continuous monitoring and feedback mechanisms can improve the quality of input data.

Figure 16. Flowchart of the proposed system
(Kaurav et al., 2021)

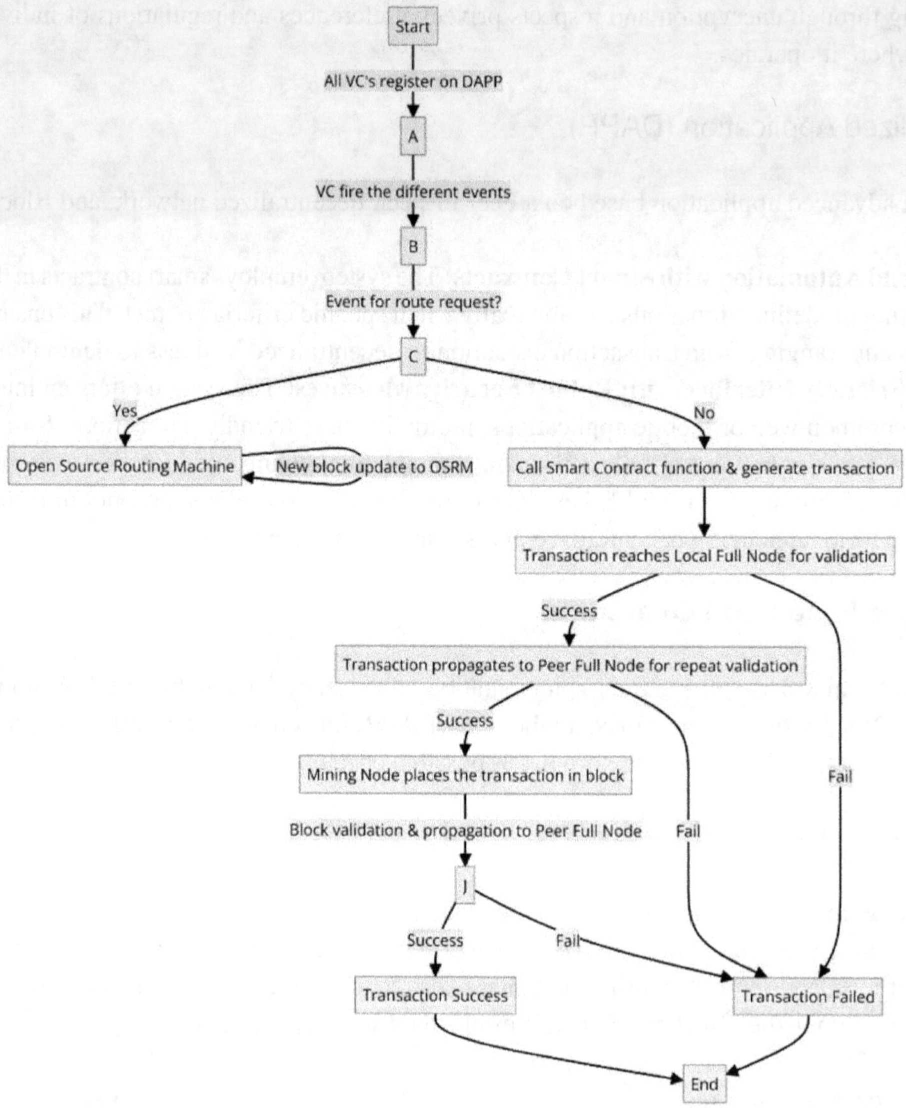

Congestion-Free Route Generation

- **Challenge:** Ensuring efficient and accurate route generation.
- **Overcoming:** Regularly update the OSRM with real-time traffic data and employ machine learning algorithms to improve route prediction accuracy. Conduct periodic reviews and adjustments to algorithms based on the performance of generated routes.

Authentication of Route Information on OSRM

- **Challenge:** Seamless integration of Blockchain-authenticated route information with OSRM.

- **Overcoming:** Establish clear communication protocols and standardized interfaces between the Blockchain and OSRM. Regularly test and optimize integration mechanisms to ensure consistent and reliable authentication of route information.

Evaluation of Proof-of-Stack (PoS)

- **Challenge:** Assessing security, transaction delay, and cost with PoS.
- **Overcoming:** Conduct thorough pilot testing to evaluate PoS suitability for the specific use case. Collaborate with blockchain and security experts to analyze the performance metrics and make informed decisions on whether to proceed with PoS or explore alternative consensus mechanisms.

Transaction Delay

- **Challenge:** Mitigating delays in Blockchain transactions.
- **Overcoming:** Optimize Blockchain protocols, choose consensus mechanisms carefully, and explore solutions like off-chain processing for non-critical transactions. Implement parallel processing and use advanced queuing mechanisms to reduce transaction latency.

Cost Evaluation

- **Challenge:** Balancing the cost of the application with security needs.
- **Overcoming:** Conduct a comprehensive cost-benefit analysis considering infrastructure, maintenance, and transaction fees. Optimize resource usage, explore cost-effective hosting solutions, and ensure that the chosen blockchain approach aligns with the budget constraints.

Scalability

- **Challenge:** Ensuring the system can handle increased demand.
- **Overcoming:** Develop the system with scalability as a primary consideration, utilizing cloud-based solutions that can automatically adjust resource allocation according to demand. Consistently monitor the operation of the system and adjust the infrastructure as needed to accommodate changes in demand.

Regulatory Compliance

- **Challenge:** Adhering to healthcare sector regulations.
- **Overcoming:** Collaborate with legal experts to ensure compliance with healthcare regulations. Implement data protection measures, anonymize sensitive information, and keep abreast of changes in relevant laws.

Overcoming these challenges requires a multidisciplinary approach, involving technology experts, security specialists, and legal professionals. Regular testing, updates, and collaboration with stakeholders are essential for maintaining the effectiveness and reliability of the emergency vehicle routing system.

CONTINUOUS MONITORING AND ADAPTIVE SECURITY MEASURES

Continuous monitoring and adaptive security measures are critical components of a comprehensive cyber security strategy. These practices involve ongoing surveillance, analysis, and adjustment of security measures to address emerging threats and vulnerabilities in real-time. Continuous monitoring is an approach to cybersecurity that involves the constant surveillance of an organization's information systems, networks, and assets to identify and respond to security events.

The Evolving Nature of Cyber Threats

The evolving nature of cyber threats is a constant and dynamic challenge, driven by advancements in technology, changes in the digital landscape, and the ever-increasing interconnectedness of systems. Several key trends highlight the ongoing evolution of cyber threats:

Advanced Persistent Threats

APTs are sophisticated, stealthy cyber threats launched by well-funded and organized adversaries over time. Nation-states, cyber espionage groups, and financially motivated corporations often conduct APTs for long-term infiltration and espionage. APTs aim to stay unnoticed and gain unauthorized access to sensitive systems or networks to steal data, perform surveillance, or disrupt operations.

APTs use complex TTPs to bypass traditional security mechanisms. Zero-day exploits, bespoke malware, and social engineering are used by APT threat actors to obtain initial access and continually maneuver within the targeted environment. APT campaigns typically involve reconnaissance, initial compromise, foothold establishment, privilege escalation, and data exfiltration.

Organizations must use advanced threat detection, continuous monitoring, threat intelligence exchange, and incident response to defend against APTs. APT resilience can be improved by frequent security audits, personnel training, and least privilege access. The cybersecurity community must share information and collaborate to build effective countermeasures against APTs as they evolve.

Ransomware

Ransomware has evolved from opportunistic attacks to extremely complex and targeted operations that threaten individuals, corporations, and key infrastructure. Ransomware has become a lucrative and strategic business for cybercriminals in recent years.

Modern ransomware operations use advanced encryption, making data recovery difficult without paying the ransom. To get initial access, attackers use software vulnerabilities, use polymorphic malware that modifies its code to avoid detection, and use sophisticated social engineering in phishing campaigns. Ransomware-as-a-service (RaaS) platforms allow even novices to launch ransomware attacks with the help of professional criminal networks. Cryptocurrency ransom payments provide cybercriminals more anonymity.

Organizations must prioritize data backups, personnel training, network segmentation, and improved threat detection to combat this changing danger. Staying ahead of sophisticated ransomware assaults requires cybersecurity community collaboration, threat intelligence sharing, and best practices.

Supply Chain Attacks

Supply chain attacks are a sophisticated form of cyber threat that target an organization's interconnected systems and networks. Supply chain attacks use vulnerabilities in third-party software, hardware, and services to compromise the target. These attacks affect many supply chain companies and have far-reaching effects.

Attackers can compromise the supply chain during manufacturing, software development, or distribution. Threat actors can sneak harmful components, backdoors, or compromised software upgrades into the supply chain.

Supply chain hacks include injecting malicious code into legal software upgrades to disseminate compromised software. These attacks exploit supplier-organization trust, making detection difficult.

Organizations must vet third-party vendors, monitor the supply chain for suspicious activity, and create incident response plans to quickly identify and contain breaches to reduce supply chain attack risks. Industry collaboration and information exchange are essential to defending against this complex cyber threat.

Zero-Day Exploits and Vulnerabilities

Zero-day exploits and vulnerabilities are a persistent cyber security concern. Zero-day vulnerabilities are software flaws without a vendor patch. Zero-day exploits occur when cybercriminals exploit vulnerabilities before developers provide a fix. Zero-day attacks are powerful because typical security procedures may fail against unknown attackers.

Zero-day exploits allow hackers to compromise systems, data, and code. These assaults generally target popular software, operating systems, and apps, putting individuals and companies at danger.

Cybercriminals use zero-day vulnerabilities to make money or conduct further cyber espionage. Companies must prioritize proactive security measures including security audits, threat monitoring, and instantaneous security fixes to reduce zero-day attack risks. Creating a strong cyber security culture that values quick response and cooperation

Deepfake Technology

Deepfake technology advances artificial intelligence and machine learning by creating convincing but fake audio, video, and graphics. Deepfakes modify and synthesis content using deep neural networks, frequently replacing a person's image or voice. The technology has great uses in the entertainment business, but it also risks misinformation, identity theft, and digital media trust.

Deepfakes can be used to propagate false information, manipulate public opinion, or impersonate people in targeted attacks. Creating lifelike, realistic content presents ethical, legal, and security concerns. GANs—two neural networks—generate content and detect fakes in deepfake technology. As technology advances, convincing deepfakes become easier to make, threatening digital media credibility. To effectively combat deepfakes, a comprehensive strategy must be adopted, including the creation of sophisticated detection mechanisms, public awareness and education, and legislative frameworks to combat their malicious use. To stay ahead of deepfake technology and its potential effects on society, the technology industry, academics, and politicians must work together.

Emergence of Quantum Computing Threats

Quantum computing could transform cyber security or harm it. Due to superposition and entanglement, quantum computer qubits can exist in several states. This contrasts with classical computers, which encode information as 0s or 1s using bits. Quantum computing promises to solve challenging problems at unprecedented speeds, but it also challenges current cryptography approaches. Quantum computing's ability to solve mathematical problems, which underpin encryption approaches, makes it a threat. Shor's algorithm on a massive quantum computer could break RSA and ECC. This compromises the confidentiality and integrity of sensitive data protected by these algorithms. Researchers are working on quantum-resistant or post-quantum cryptography approaches to mitigate quantum computing's risks. These algorithms defy classical and quantum computer attacks to ensure digital communications safety in the post-quantum era.

Before large-scale, fault-tolerant quantum computers can breach current encryption standards, the cybersecurity sector is transitioning to quantum-resistant algorithms. To prepare for quantum computing's transformational impact, researchers, industry stakeholders, and regulators collaborate to create and adopt new cryptographic standards.

Social Engineering and Phishing Tactics

Regular cyber security training, simulated phishing exercises, and the promotion of a security-conscious culture within organizations are crucial for building resilience against evolving social engineering and phishing tactics. The collaborative efforts of individuals, organizations, and cyber security professionals are essential to stay ahead of these deceptive and continually advancing cyber threats. Cybercriminals employ deceptive tactics such as social engineering and phishing to manipulate individuals into revealing sensitive information or engaging in security-compromising actions. Social engineering exploits trust, authority, fear, or urgency, employing techniques like pretexting, baiting, and quid pro quo. Phishing involves posing as legitimate entities through emails, texts, or websites to trick victims into disclosing confidential details. Spear phishing tailors' attacks for specific individuals or groups, using personalized content for increased credibility. Cybercriminal tactics evolve with sophisticated approaches, including lifelike deepfake technology and reconnaissance for personalized attacks. Mitigating these threats necessitates a combination of technology, awareness, and education. Countermeasures include deploying email filtering, spam detection, and endpoint protection solutions, alongside user education programs to raise awareness and teach individuals how to recognize and report suspicious activities.

Importance of Regular Security Audits

Regular security audits play a crucial role in maintaining a robust and effective cybersecurity posture for individuals, organizations, and systems. These audits involve systematic assessments and examinations of security policies, procedures, controls, and technologies to identify vulnerabilities, assess risks, and ensure compliance with security standards. The importance of conducting regular security audits can be outlined in several key aspects:

Vulnerability Identification

Security audits help in the identification of vulnerabilities in networks, systems, and applications. By systematically reviewing configurations, access controls, and software, organizations can proactively address potential weaknesses before they can be exploited by malicious actors.

Risk Assessment

Through security audits, organizations can evaluate and quantify risks associated with their information systems. Understanding the potential impact and likelihood of security incidents enables the prioritization of resources for risk mitigation strategies.

Compliance Assurance

Various sectors and organizations must adhere to regulatory regulations and compliance standards. Regular security audits guarantee that security procedures are in accordance with these requirements, thereby assisting firms in avoiding legal and financial repercussions linked to non-compliance.

Security Policy Validation

Security audits validate the implementation and effectiveness of security policies. This includes reviewing access controls, encryption practices, incident response plans, and other security measures to ensure that they align with organizational policies and best practices.

Incident Response Preparedness

Audits help organizations assess the effectiveness of their incident response plans and procedures. Regular testing and simulation of security incidents during audits contribute to better preparedness for handling real-world security incidents.

User Awareness and Training

Security audits provide an opportunity to assess the level of security awareness among users. Identifying areas where additional training or awareness efforts are needed can enhance the overall security posture by reducing the human factor in security incidents.

Continuous Improvement

The dynamic nature of cyber threats necessitates continuous improvement of security measures. Security audits serve as a feedback loop, allowing organizations to refine their security strategies based on the evolving threat landscape and changing organizational needs.

Protection of Assets and Reputation

Regular security audits contribute to safeguarding an organization's assets, including sensitive data and intellectual property. By maintaining a strong security posture, organizations protect their reputation and build trust with clients, partners, and stakeholders.

Types of Security Audits

Security audits come in two forms, internal and external audits, that involve the following procedures:

- **Internal audits.** During these audits, a company utilizes its own assets and internal audit division. Internal audits are conducted to verify the adherence of corporate systems to policies and procedures.
- **External audits.** For these kinds of audits, an outside group is brought in to do the work. External audits are also done when a business needs to make sure it is following government rules or industry standards.

External audits can be classified into two types: second-party audits and third-party audits. An organization's supplier may perform a second-party audit. An impartial third party conducts the audit, and its auditors are not associated with the company being audited.

What Systems Does an Audit Cover?

A security audit may check all of a company's systems for weaknesses in the following domains:

- **Network vulnerabilities:** An auditor's job is to find any point of failure in a network that a malicious actor could use to get unauthorized access to data or systems. Data is especially at risk while in transit from one location to another. Regular network monitoring and security audits record all communications throughout the network, whether they be emails, instant messaging, files, or anything else. Part of this audit also includes checking the network's accessibility and availability.
- **Security controls.** The auditor evaluates the efficiency of the company's security controls during this phase of the audit. Part of this process involves checking in on the efficacy of the measures put in place to keep sensitive data and computer systems safe. A company's ability to maintain administrative control over its mobile devices is one factor that auditors may look into. The purpose of the audit is to verify that the controls in place are adequate and that the business is adhering to its own protocols.
- **Encryption.** This section of the audit checks if the company has procedures to oversee the encryption of sensitive data.
- **Software systems.** To make sure they are functioning correctly and giving correct data, software systems are tested here. Additional checks are conducted to guarantee that safeguards are in place to avoid unauthorized individuals obtaining sensitive information. Data processing, software development, and computer systems are some of the subjects that are studied.
- **Architecture management capabilities.** The auditors make sure that the management of the information technology department has established organizational structures and procedures in order to produce a controlled and effective environment for the processing of information.

- **Telecommunications controls.** The controls of telecommunications are examined by auditors to ensure that they are functioning properly on both the client and server sides, as well as on the network that connected them.
- **Systems development audit.** This area of audits ensures that all systems being developed meet the organization's security goals. Making ensuring that systems in development are adhering to standards is another reason for this portion of the audit.
- **Information processing.** Data processing security procedures are confirmed by these audits.

Steps involved in a security audit: These five steps are generally part of a security audit:

a. **Agree on goals:** Discuss the desired outcomes of the audit with all relevant parties.
b. **Define the scope of the audit:** In order to conduct an audit, it is necessary to catalogue all assets, such as computers, internal documents, and processed data.
c. **Conduct the audit and identify threats:** The loss of information due to acts of nature, malicious software, or unauthorized individuals is just one example of the many possible dangers listed for each section.
d. **Evaluate security and risks:** Evaluate the organization's preparedness for potential threats and the likelihood that each one will materialize.
e. **Determine the needed controls:** Figure out what safety precautions need to be put in place or enhanced to reduce danger.

Figure 17. Holistic cyber-security audit framework

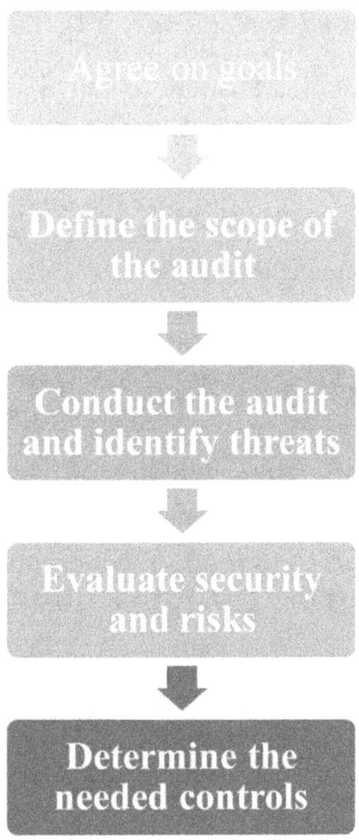

CONCLUSION

This chapter emphasizes the crucial requirement for a watchful strategy in tackling the security issues that exist in the growing domain of IoT-enabled smart cities. An in-depth analysis of possible risks is essential due to the interconnectedness of IoT devices, which range from sensors to edge computing. The primary concern is to protect citizen data and maintain the integrity of key infrastructure. The discussion focuses on the importance of data security and privacy, exploring topics such as encryption, authentication, and the need for regulatory frameworks to assure thorough protection.

Furthermore, the article promotes pragmatic methodologies and optimal strategies for efficiently controlling risks, with a specific focus on strengthening awareness of cybersecurity, reinforcing the ability to respond to incidents, and promoting cooperation among those involved. This chapter offers a thorough analysis and practical insights, making it an essential resource for understanding and addressing security risks in the ever-changing environment of IoT-enabled smart cities. It aims to provide a path towards a future urban environment that is both secure and robust, where the advantages of technology are utilized responsibly for the welfare of individuals and the continuous progress of our linked communities.

REFERENCES

Abdellaoui Alaoui, E. A., & El Moudden, M. (2018). A Game Theoretic Approach to Analyse Security between Smart Vehicles and Parcels in Smart Cities. *MATEC Web of Conferences, 200*. IEEE. doi:10.1051/matecconf/201820000002

Ahmed, Z., Rawat, A., & Kumari, P. (2021). An Anaylsis of Iot Based Smart Cities. [IJETA]. *International Journal of Engineering Trends and Applications*, *8*(4), 30–35. www.ijetajournal.org

Aslam, M., Khan Abbasi, M. A., Khalid, T., Shan, R., Ullah, S., Ahmad, T., Saeed, S., Alabbad, D. A., & Ahmad, R. (2022). Getting Smarter about Smart Cities: Improving Data Security and Privacy through Compliance. *Sensors (Basel)*, *22*(23), 9338. doi:10.3390/s22239338 PMID:36502039

Bekara, C. (2014). Security Issues and Challenges for the IoT-based Smart Grid. *Procedia Computer Science*, *34*, 532–537. doi:10.1016/j.procs.2014.07.064

Ben Rjab, A., Mellouli, S., & Corbett, J. (2023). Barriers to artificial intelligence adoption in smart cities: A systematic literature review and research agenda. *Government Information Quarterly*, *40*(3), 101814. doi:10.1016/j.giq.2023.101814

Biswas, K., & Muthukkumarasamy, V. (2016). Securing Smart Cities Using Blockchain Technology. *2016 IEEE 18th International Conference on High Performance Computing and Communications; IEEE 14th International Conference on Smart City; IEEE 2nd International Conference on Data Science and Systems (HPCC/SmartCity/DSS)*, (pp. 1392–1393). IEEE. 10.1109/HPCC-SmartCity-DSS.2016.0198

Chen, H., Lei, S., Zhang, Y., Han, X., Cao, Y., & Zhang, Y. (2023). Blockchain-based internet of things security architecture and applications. *Journal of Ambient Intelligence and Humanized Computing*, *14*(12), 16703–16714. doi:10.1007/s12652-023-04675-w

Dorri, A., Kanhere, S. S., Jurdak, R., & Gauravaram, P. (2017). Blockchain for IoT security and privacy: The case study of a smart home. *2017 IEEE International Conference on Pervasive Computing and Communications Workshops (PerCom Workshops)*, (pp. 618–623). IEEE. 10.1109/PERCOMW.2017.7917634

Douha, N. Y.-R., Sasabe, M., Taenaka, Y., & Kadobayashi, Y. (2023). An Evolutionary Game Theoretic Analysis of Cybersecurity Investment Strategies for Smart-Home Users against Cyberattacks. *Applied Sciences (Basel, Switzerland)*, *13*(7), 4645. doi:10.3390/app13074645

Ferrag, M. A., Maglaras, L., & Ahmim, A. (2017). Privacy-Preserving Schemes for Ad Hoc Social Networks: A Survey. *IEEE Communications Surveys and Tutorials*, *19*(4), 3015–3045. doi:10.1109/COMST.2017.2718178

Gong, T., Huang, H., Li, P., Zhang, K., & Jiang, H. (2015). A Medical Healthcare System for Privacy Protection Based on IoT. *2015 Seventh International Symposium on Parallel Architectures, Algorithms and Programming (PAAP)*, (pp. 217–222). IEEE. 10.1109/PAAP.2015.48

Harahsheh, K., & Chen, C. H. (2023). A Survey of Using Machine Learning in IoT Security and the Challenges Faced by Researchers. *Informatica (Slovenia)*, *47*(6), 1–54. doi:10.31449/inf.v47i6.4635

Hataba, M., Sherif, A., Mahmoud, M., Abdallah, M., & Alasmary, W. (2022). Security and Privacy Issues in Autonomous Vehicles: A Layer-Based Survey. *IEEE Open Journal of the Communications Society*, *3*, 811–829. doi:10.1109/OJCOMS.2022.3169500

Huang, C.-T., Sakib, M. N., Njilla, L., & Kamhoua, C. (2019). A Game Theoretic Approach for Making IoT Device Connectivity Decisions During Malware Outbreak. *2019 International Conference on Computing, Networking and Communications (ICNC)*, (pp. 457–462). IEEE. 10.1109/ICCNC.2019.8685493

Jiang, N., Wang, W., Wu, J., & Wang, J. (2020). Traceable Method for Personal Information Registration Based on Blockchain. *IEEE Access : Practical Innovations, Open Solutions*, *8*, 52700–52712. doi:10.1109/ACCESS.2020.2981175

Jing, Q., Vasilakos, A. V., Wan, J., Lu, J., & Qiu, D. (2014). Security of the Internet of Things: Perspectives and challenges. *Wireless Networks*, *20*(8), 2481–2501. doi:10.1007/s11276-014-0761-7

Jo, J. H., Sharma, P. K., Sicato, J. C. S., & Park, J. H. (2019). Emerging technologies for sustainable smart city network security: Issues, challenges, and countermeasures. *Journal of Information Processing Systems*, *15*(4), 765–784. doi:10.3745/JIPS.03.0124

Kaurav, R. S., Rout, R. R., & Vemireddy, S. (2021). Blockchain for Emergency Vehicle Routing in Healthcare Services: An Integrated Secure and Trustworthy System. *2021 International Conference on COMmunication Systems and NETworkS, COMSNETS 2021*, (pp. 623–628). IEEE. 10.1109/COMSNETS51098.2021.9352903

Khan, L. U., Yaqoob, I., Tran, N. H., Kazmi, S. M. A., Dang, T. N., & Hong, C. S. (2020). Edge-Computing-Enabled Smart Cities: A Comprehensive Survey. *IEEE Internet of Things Journal*, *7*(10), 10200–10232. doi:10.1109/JIOT.2020.2987070

Kitsios, F., Chatzidimitriou, E., & Kamariotou, M. (2023). The ISO/IEC 27001 Information Security Management Standard: How to Extract Value from Data in the IT Sector. *Sustainability (Basel)*, *15*(7), 5828. doi:10.3390/su15075828

Lefkovitz, N., & Boeckl, K. (2021). *Portuguese Translation of the NIST Privacy Framework Version 1.0*. doi:10.6028/NIST.CSWP.01162020pt

Li, N., Liu, D., & Nepal, S. (2017). Lightweight Mutual Authentication for IoT and Its Applications. *IEEE Transactions on Sustainable Computing*, 2(4), 359–370. doi:10.1109/TSUSC.2017.2716953

Margolis, J., Oh, T. T., Jadhav, S., Kim, Y. H., & Kim, J. N. (2017). An In-Depth Analysis of the Mirai Botnet. *2017 International Conference on Software Security and Assurance (ICSSA)*, (pp. 6–12). IEEE. 10.1109/ICSSA.2017.12

Mozzaquatro, B., Agostinho, C., Goncalves, D., Martins, J., & Jardim-Goncalves, R. (2018). An Ontology-Based Cybersecurity Framework for the Internet of Things. *Sensors (Basel)*, *18*(9), 3053. doi:10.3390/s18093053 PMID:30213085

Poy, A. (2009). Smart Cities: Threat and Countermeasures. *Philosophical Magazine*, *27*, 77.

Poy, A. (2022). Statista. *Philosophical Magazine*, *27*, 77.

Poy, A. (2023). Gartner Reports. *Philosophical Magazine*, *27*, 77.

Radanliev, P., De Roure, D., Van Kleek, M., Santos, O., & Ani, U. (2021). Artificial intelligence in cyber physical systems. *AI & Society*, *36*(3), 783–796. doi:10.1007/s00146-020-01049-0 PMID:32874020

Rai, H. M., Atik-Ur-Rehman, Pal, A., Mishra, S., & Shukla, K. K. (2023). Use of Internet of Things in the context of execution of smart city applications: A review. *Discover Internet of Things*, *3*(1), 8. doi:10.1007/s43926-023-00037-2

Shankar, A., & Maple, C. (2023). Securing the Internet of Things-enabled smart city infrastructure using a hybrid framework. *Computer Communications*, *205*, 127–135. doi:10.1016/j.comcom.2023.04.008

Sharma, P. K., Chen, M.-Y., & Park, J. H. (2018). A Software Defined Fog Node Based Distributed Blockchain Cloud Architecture for IoT. *IEEE Access : Practical Innovations, Open Solutions*, *6*, 115–124. doi:10.1109/ACCESS.2017.2757955

Takizaki, N., Kido, Y., Masuda, Y., Toshima, Y., Yamamoto, M., & Shimojo, S. (2023). Ontology-Based Access Control Framework for Smart Building IoT Devices. *2023 IEEE International Conference on Consumer Electronics (ICCE)*, (pp. 1–2). IEEE. 10.1109/ICCE56470.2023.10043384

Talpur, M. S. H., Bhuiyan, M. Z. A., & Wang, G. (2015). Shared-node IoT network architecture with ubiquitous homomorphic encryption for healthcare monitoring. *International Journal of Embedded Systems*, *7*(1), 43. doi:10.1504/IJES.2015.066141

Tawalbeh, L., Muheidat, F., Tawalbeh, M., & Quwaider, M. (2020). IoT Privacy and Security: Challenges and Solutions. *Applied Sciences (Basel, Switzerland)*, *10*(12), 4102. doi:10.3390/app10124102

Wala, T., Chand, N., & Sharma, A. K. (2020). Energy Efficient Data Collection in Smart Cities Using IoT. *Advances in Intelligent Systems and Computing*, *1132*(February), 632–654. doi:10.1007/978-3-030-40305-8_30

Wang, Y., Wan, J., Guo, J., Cheung, Y.-M., & Yuen, P. C. (2018). Inference-Based Similarity Search in Randomized Montgomery Domains for Privacy-Preserving Biometric Identification. *IEEE Transactions on Pattern Analysis and Machine Intelligence*, *40*(7), 1611–1624. doi:10.1109/TPAMI.2017.2727048 PMID:28715325

Watch, M. (2023). Security of IoT Devices Statistics. *Philosophical Magazine*, *27*, 77.

Zeadally, S., Siddiqui, F., Baig, Z., & Ibrahim, A. (2019). Smart healthcare. *PSU Research Review*, *4*(2), 149–168. doi:10.1108/PRR-08-2019-0027

Zhou, L., Su, C., Chiu, W., & Yeh, K.-H. (2020). You Think, Therefore You Are: Transparent Authentication System with Brainwave-Oriented Bio-Features for IoT Networks. *IEEE Transactions on Emerging Topics in Computing*, *8*(2), 303–312. doi:10.1109/TETC.2017.2759306

Chapter 13
Securing the Foundations:
IoT Infrastructure in Smart Cities

T. Premavathi
Marwadi University, India

Ayush Shekhar
Marwadi University, India

Aayush Raj
Marwadi University, India

Shreya Agrawal
Marwadi University, India

Damodharan Palaniappan
Marwadi University, India

Madhu Shukla
Marwadi University, India

ABSTRACT

Rapid IoT device integration in smart cities is transforming urban environments, delivering unparalleled efficiency, sustainability, and connection. This book chapter tackles smart city IoT infrastructure security, a top priority. It begins with an exploration of how IoT technologies are changing urban living and the pros and cons of their widespread adoption. IoT equipment including sensors, actuators, connected vehicles, and public infrastructure pose security vulnerabilities. IoT implementations, the chapter examines smart city cyber and privacy concerns. The next section presents a technical and policy-based framework for smart city IoT infrastructure security. Collaboration between government, industry, and the public is key to this framework's success. Blockchain for secure transactions, machine learning for anomaly detection, and encryption protocols are also explored in smart city IoT installations. The chapter finishes with a look ahead at smart city IoT infrastructure security, emphasizing the necessity for constant adaptation and improvement to combat new threats.

DOI: 10.4018/979-8-3693-2373-1.ch013

INTRODUCTION

In the ever-evolving landscape of urban development, the rise of smart cities stands as a testament to the transformative power of technology. Central to this paradigm shift is the integration of the Internet of Things (IoT), a network that interconnects a myriad of everyday objects, systems, and infrastructure to facilitate seamless data exchange and communication discussed by zanella et al. (2014). Smart cities leverage the capabilities of IoT technologies to revolutionize various facets of urban living, including transportation, energy management, public services, and environmental sustainability. As urban centers embark on this journey towards greater connectivity, the widespread deployment of diverse IoT devices becomes the linchpin, shaping the very foundation of these smart city ecosystems refered by caragliubet al. (2022).

However, the promising potential of smart cities, with their real-time data insights and improved resource management, is accompanied by an intricate web of security concerns. The extensive network of sensors, actuators, and interconnected systems that define the IoT landscape in smart cities also introduces vulnerabilities, making them susceptible to cyber threats and privacy breaches. In Borgoa (2014) discussed about securing the foundational infrastructure of IoT in smart cities becomes paramount for the long-term success and sustainability of these technological advancements.

This chapter seeks to unravel the delicate equilibrium between the promises inherent in urban IoT deployments and the pressing need for robust security measures. The discussion delves into the multifaceted vulnerabilities arising from the sheer scale and complexity of IoT integrations in urban environments. A profound understanding and effective mitigation of these risks emerge as pivotal factors for steering the sustainable development of smart cities. The narrative progresses to unveil a comprehensive framework that not only acknowledges these challenges but actively addresses them through a synergy of technical solutions and policy-oriented strategies. Advocating for collaboration among government entities, industry stakeholders, and the public, this framework underscores the significance of standardization and the implementation of best practices to establish a resilient security posture for smart cities.

SECURITY CHALLENGES IN IOT INFRASTRUCTURE

Inherent Vulnerabilities in IoT Systems

The deployment of IoT systems in Smart Cities introduces a myriad of security challenges rooted in the inherent vulnerabilities of these interconnected devices. A critical concern is the susceptibility of IoT devices to both physical and remote tampering, posing significant risks to the confidentiality and integrity of the data they manage refered by Chettri et al. (2019). Common vulnerabilities include insufficient authentication mechanisms, insecure device configurations, and the absence of standardized security protocols, leaving these devices open to exploitation by malicious actors.

Risks of Unauthorized Access

Unauthorized access remains a formidable security challenge in the realm of Smart City IoT infrastructure. Malicious actors exploit weaknesses in authentication mechanisms and unsecured communication channels to gain unauthorized control over IoT devices. This not only compromises the individual devices but also poses a systemic threat to the entire Smart City infrastructure. Ensuring robust authentication methods is crucial to mitigating the risks associated with unauthorized access discussed by Conti et al. (2018).

Data Breaches and System Manipulations

Wagmer et al. (2019) discussed about the interconnected nature of IoT devices in Smart Cities amplifies the risks associated with data breaches and system manipulations. A compromised device can serve as a gateway for unauthorized access to sensitive data, leading to potential privacy violations and disruptions in essential urban services. Data integrity and confidentiality emerge as critical concerns, necessitating robust encryption methods and continuous monitoring to detect and thwart potential breaches.

Real-World Examples

In **Figure 1.** refers real-world examples is crucial in understanding the tangible consequences of inadequate IoT security measures. The [Name of Incident] serves as a poignant illustration, highlighting the potential fallout when security vulnerabilities are exploited in a Smart City context referred by Syed et al. (2021). Such incidents underscore the urgency for a proactive and comprehensive approach to secure IoT infrastructure.

SECURITY MEASURES AND BEST PRACTICES

Robust Authentication Protocols

The robustness of Smart City IoT infrastructure begins with the implementation of sophisticated authentication protocols. Multifactor Authentication (MFA) emerges as a gold standard, requiring users to verify their identity through multiple layers of authentication discussed by Rejeb et al. (2022). Biometric identifiers, such as fingerprints or facial recognition, complement traditional password mechanisms, enhancing the overall security posture. MFA significantly fortifies Smart City networks against the persistent threat of unauthorized access, ensuring that only authenticated and authorized users can interact with IoT devices.

Encryption Methods

Securing the transmission of sensitive data within Smart City networks is a paramount concern, and Advanced Encryption Standard (AES) stands as a robust solution. Widely Al-Qarafi et al. (2022) adopted for its efficiency and security, AES ensures end-to-end encryption, safeguarding data from potential interception and manipulation. By employing strong encryption algorithms, Smart Cities can instill confidence in the integrity and confidentiality of the information exchanged among IoT devices, reinforcing the trustworthiness of the entire urban infrastructure.

Intrusion Detection Systems

The dynamic and interconnected nature of Smart City IoT environments necessitates continuous monitoring for potential threats. Intrusion Detection Systems (IDS) play a pivotal role in this regard, employing

Figure 1. Integration of IoT devices in smart cities

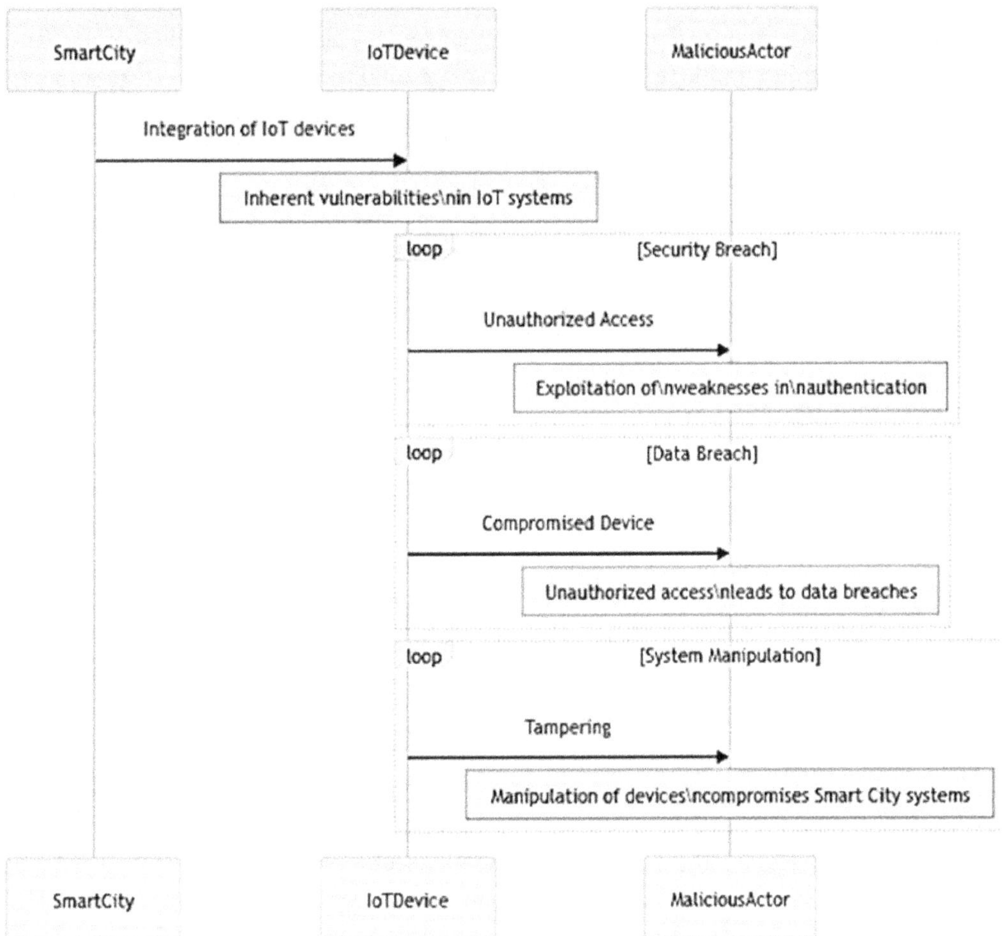

sophisticated algorithms to analyze network traffic in real-time by Bauer et al. (2021). By utilizing both anomaly detection and signature-based approaches, IDS can effectively identify and respond to suspicious activities, thwarting unauthorized access and potential data breaches. The proactive deployment of IDS is indispensable for maintaining the integrity and security of Smart City infrastructure.

Regular Updates and Patches

The longevity of IoT security relies on a proactive approach to addressing vulnerabilities through regular updates and patches. Smart Cities must establish a systematic process for monitoring security advisories and promptly applying updates to IoT devices discussed by Zaidi et al. (2023). This iterative process not only addresses known vulnerabilities but also fortifies the overall resilience of Smart City networks against emerging cyber threats. Collaborative partnerships with device manufacturers and software developers are crucial to ensuring a timely and coordinated response to evolving security challenges.

Public Awareness and Education

In the realm of smart cities and IOT, fostering public awareness and education is imperative cultivate to cyber resilient community. Public engagement should extend to city officials, stakeholders, and the general populace, elucidating the criticality of robust IoT security practices. This entails disseminating information about the intricacies of authentication protocols, encryption standards. A well-informed public is crucial for the responsible utilization of IoT devices, understanding data privacy implications, and actively participating in adherence to regulatory compliance discussed by Abinaya et al. (2023).

NETWORK SECURITY IN SMART CITIES

Network security in smart cities is a pivotal aspect of ensuring the robustness and resilience of the complex web of interconnected devices and systems. The secure communication infrastructure forms the backbone of smart cities, and as such, it must be fortified with advanced measures to protect against a myriad of cyber threats refered by Pandian et al. (2023). A key challenge in network security stems from the diverse nature of devices and systems integrated into the smart city framework. These range from sensors and actuators to critical infrastructure such as transportation systems and energy grids, each with its unique communication protocols and security requirements. Establishing a comprehensive and standardized approach to network security becomes imperative to safeguard against potential vulnerabilities discussed by Pdemiappan et al. (2023).

One critical component of network security is the implementation of secure communication protocols. Ensuring that data exchanged between devices and systems is encrypted and authenticated mitigates the risk of eavesdropping and unauthorized access. Advanced encryption standards, coupled with robust authentication mechanisms, form the cornerstone of a secure network infrastructure. Additionally, the deployment of intrusion detection and prevention systems adds an extra layer of defense, actively monitoring network traffic for anomalous patterns and swiftly responding to potential security incidents.

Mhala et al. (2023) referred about network segmentation emerges as another crucial strategy in enhancing smart city network security. Dividing the network into isolated segments or zones helps contain potential security breaches, preventing the lateral movement of attackers within the infrastructure. This segmentation ensures that even if one part of the network is compromised, the impact is limited, reducing the risk of a widespread security incident. Damodharan et al. (2019) discussed how properly configured firewalls and access controls play a pivotal role in implementing effective network segmentation.

The integration of emerging technologies, such as 5G networks, further introduces both opportunities and challenges in smart city network security. While 5G promises faster and more reliable connectivity, it also expands the attack surface. Ensuring the security of 5G networks involves robust encryption, authentication mechanisms, and proactive monitoring to detect and mitigate potential vulnerabilities. Additionally, network security must adapt to the increasing prevalence of edge computing in smart cities, where computing resources are distributed closer to the devices generating data. Securing these distributed computing nodes is crucial to prevent potential points of compromise.

Ongoing monitoring and timely incident response mechanisms are paramount in smart city network security. Implementing real-time monitoring tools that analyze network traffic for suspicious activities and potential security threats allows for swift identification and mitigation of risks referred by Damodharan and Ravichandran (2019). This proactive approach is essential in the dynamic and evolving landscape of smart cities, where new threats may emerge rapidly. Collaborative efforts between public and private stakeholders also play a critical role in addressing network security challenges, fostering information sharing and collective responses to emerging cyber threats.

In conclusion, network security in smart cities demands a comprehensive and adaptive approach that addresses the unique challenges posed by diverse devices, emerging technologies, and the dynamic nature of urban environments. By implementing robust encryption, authentication mechanisms, network segmentation, and proactive monitoring, smart cities can build a resilient network infrastructure that forms the foundation for secure and interconnected urban ecosystems.

POLICY FRAMEWORKS AND REGULATORY MEASURES

Exploration of Policy Frameworks

Policy frameworks are essential instruments that guide the secure integration of IoT devices into the fabric of Smart Cities. These frameworks set out comprehensive guidelines, standards, and principles that govern the use, deployment, and management of IoT technologies within urban environments.

Components of Policy Frameworks

- Data Ownership and Usage: Establishing clear ownership and usage guidelines for the data generated by IoT devices is critical. Policies may dictate how data is collected, processed, and shared, ensuring transparency and protecting citizens' privacy.
- Access Controls: Defining access controls within policy frameworks helps determine who has permission to interact with specific IoT devices. This involves outlining user roles, authentication mechanisms, and authorization protocols.
- Device Lifecycle Management: Policies should address the entire lifecycle of IoT devices, from procurement and installation to decommissioning. This includes standards for secure device provisioning, periodic security audits, and responsible disposal practices.

Governmental Role in Formulating Policy Frameworks

Governments and city administrations take a central role in formulating policy frameworks. Their involvement ensures a cohesive and standardized approach to IoT security across Smart Cities.

Regulatory Measures Enforcing Security Requirements

While policy frameworks provide overarching principles, regulatory measures serve as the enforcement arm, ensuring that IoT devices adhere to predefined security requirements. These measures involve regulatory bodies, certifications, and adherence to industry standards.

Specific Security Requirements

- Security Assessments: Mandating security assessments ensures that IoT devices undergo thorough evaluations before deployment. This involves vulnerability assessments, penetration testing, and risk analysis to identify and mitigate potential security threats.
- Certifications: Regulatory bodies may issue certifications to IoT devices that meet specific security standards. Certifications provide a tangible indicator of a device's adherence to security protocols and can instill trust in both consumers and Smart City administrators.
- Industry Standards: Aligning regulatory measures with established industry standards ensures consistency and interoperability. Adopting widely recognized standards allows Smart Cities to benefit from a collective knowledge base and best practices in IoT security.

Role of Regulatory Bodies

Regulatory bodies, often established by governmental agencies, play a critical role in overseeing and enforcing compliance with regulatory measures. They provide the necessary oversight to ensure that IoT devices entering the Smart City ecosystem meet stringent security criteria.

The Symbiotic Relationship Between Innovation and Regulation

Achieving a balance between innovation and regulation is crucial for the continued advancement of Smart Cities. This section explores how policy frameworks and regulatory measures can support innovation without compromising security.

Innovation Hubs and Sandboxes

Establishing innovation hubs and sandboxes creates controlled environments where new IoT technologies can be tested and refined. This fosters innovation by providing a space for experimentation without exposing the entire city to potential security risks.

Dynamic Regulatory Ecosystem

A dynamic regulatory ecosystem is characterized by the adaptability of regulations to emerging technologies. It involves periodic reviews and updates to regulatory measures to address new security challenges while supporting ongoing innovation.

Emphasis on Compliance for a Secure Urban Ecosystem

Emphasizing compliance is crucial to ensuring that policy frameworks and regulatory measures translate into tangible security improvements within the Smart City environment.

Monitoring Mechanisms

Governments may implement compliance monitoring mechanisms, including regular audits and inspections. This proactive approach ensures that stakeholders comply with security protocols throughout the lifecycle of IoT devices.

Incentivizing Compliance

Incentivizing compliance can involve offering benefits or recognition to entities that go beyond the minimum requirements. This encourages a culture of exceeding security standards, contributing to a safer and more resilient urban ecosystem.

Shared Responsibility

Compliance emphasizes the shared responsibility of stakeholders, from city planners to IoT device manufacturers, in upholding security standards. It fosters a culture of accountability where the collective commitment to security is integral to Smart City development.

METHODOLOGY

Stakeholder Interview

Stakeholder interviews form a crucial element, facilitating a direct and qualitative engagement with key players in the smart city ecosystem. These are selected to represent a diverse cross section of the smart city landscape, which includes city officials, urban planners, technology providers, cybersecurity experts, IoT device manufacturers, and representatives from relevant regulatory bodies. The selection ensures that a comprehensive range of perspectives is considered, reflecting the complexity and interconnectedness of the smart city environment. Through structured conversations, we intend to gather firsthand perspectives on the challenges, requirements, and opportunities associated with securing IoT infrastructure in smart cities.

Stakeholder interviews contribute to a holistic understanding of the multifaceted dimensions of IoT security, In **Figure 2.** Illustrate various ways of cyber threat, to ensuring that the proposed security measures align with practical needs and industry expectations. Additionally, open-ended questions are incorporated to encourage stakeholders to share unique insights and perspectives.

Comparative Analysis

The comparative analysis involves a systematic examination and comparison of various IoT security frameworks, protocols, and implementations across different smart cities globally. This analysis entails scrutinizing the strengths, weaknesses, and overall effectiveness of different security frameworks adopted by smart cities. It also extends to assessing the practical implementations of these security measures in real-world scenarios within smart city infrastructures.

Figure 2. Illustrating various ways of cyber threat intelligence sharing

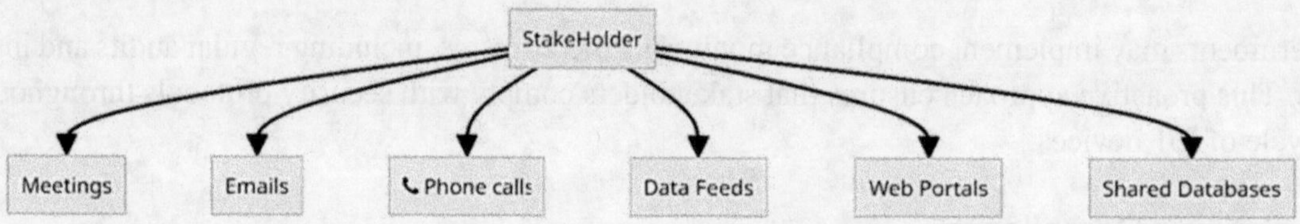

In **Table 1.** Shows the potential impacts of attack on confidentiality, integrity and availability. "Security incidents can impact the fundamental objectives of maintaining the Confidentiality, Integrity, and Availability (the CIA triad) of information".

- Low Impact: Minimal effect on operations, assets, or individuals.
- Moderate Impact: Significantly affects operations, assets, or individuals.
- High Impact: Results in severe or catastrophic consequences for operations, assets, or individuals.
- Not applicable: Pertains exclusively to Confidentiality.

Trend Analysis

- **Integration of Blockchain Technology:**

As smart cities continue to expand their IoT ecosystem, the integration of blockchain technology is emerging as a prominent trend for enhancing security. Blockchain's decentralized and immutable ledger capabilities provide a robust framework for securing data and transactions and IoT networks. This trend signifies a shit towards more tamper- resistant and transparent system, reducing the risk unauthorized access and data manipulation.

Table 1. Potential impacts of attack on confidentiality, integrity and availability

Sample Attacks	Potential Impact on Confidentiality of User Information		Potential Impact on Integrity of User Information		Potential Impact on Availability of User Information	
	Smart Home Heating Control	Smart Health Control	Smart Home Heating Control	Smart Health Control	Smart Home Heating Control	Smart Health Control
GPS location tracking	Low/Mod	Low/Mod	Low	Low/Mod	Low	Low/Mod
Service Disruption (SD)	Low	Low/Mod	Low	Low	Low	Low/Mod
Eavesdropping	Low/Mod	Low/Mod	Low	Low/Mod	Low	Low/Mod
Data Interception	Low/Mod	Low/Mod	Low	Low	Low	Low/Mod
Social Engineering	Low/Mod	Low/Mod	Low	Low/Mod	Low	Low
Malicious ransomware	Low/Mod	Low/Mod	Low	Low/Mod	Low	Low/Mod

- **AI and Machine Learning for Threat Detection:**

The incorporation of Artificial Intelligence and Machine Learning in IoT security is gaining traction for proactive threat detection and response. These technologies enable the analysis of vast amounts of data generated by IoT devices in real-time breaches. The trend emphasizes the importance of predictive security measures to stay ahead of evolving cyber threats in smart city environments.

- **Standardization of Security Protocols:**

With the proliferation of IoT devices and platforms, there is a growing need for standardization in security protocols. The trend involves the development and adoption of common security standards to ensure interoperability and consistent security measures across diverse IoT devices. This approach simplifies management, facilitates collaboration, and promotes a more unified and secure smart city infrastructure.

- **Collaborative Cybersecurity Initiatives:**

The complexity of IoT security challenges necessitates collaborative efforts among stakeholders. A trend is emerging where cities, technology vendors, and cybersecurity experts are forming partnerships to share threat intelligence, best practices, and collectively address evolving cybersecurity risks. This collaborative approach enhances the overall resilience of smart city IoT infrastructures.

- **Zero Trust Security Architecture:**

The Zero Trust security model is becoming a fundamental approach to securing IoT infrastructure in smart cities. In this model, trust is never assumed, and verification is required from everyone trying to access resources in the network, regardless of their location. This trend reflects the acknowledgment of the constantly changing threat landscape and the need for continuous authentication and authorization processes to protect sensitive data and critical infrastructure.

Regulatory Landscape Analysis

The implementation and use of IoT technologies in urban settings are governed by a number of legal and regulatory frameworks, which must be carefully examined as part of a regulatory landscape analysis for smart city security. Regulations at the national and international levels that affect how security measures are implemented for Internet of Things devices and systems in smart cities are taken into account in this research. Laws pertaining to data protection and privacy, cybersecurity, interoperability and resilience requirements, and incident response and reporting rules are important components.

The investigation of data protection laws is the first step in the study to make sure that IoT devices' gathering, handling, and archiving of private and sensitive data complies with legal standards. In order to protect IoT devices from potential cyber attacks, cybersecurity rules are also carefully examined to determine the minimum-security requirements and procedures that must be followed. Interoperability standards play a crucial role in enabling devices made by various manufacturers to function together effortlessly, which in turn promotes a safe and coherent Internet of Things environment.

Figure 3. Stakeholder interview and comparative analysis

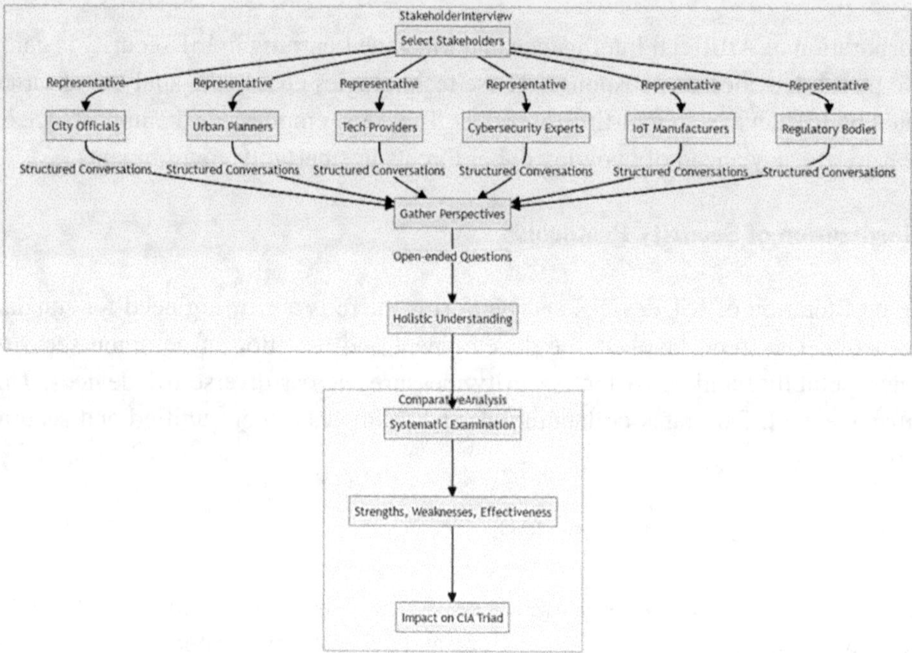

In **Figure 3.** refers stakeholder interview and comparative analysis to recognize the worldwide scope of IoT installations and the necessity of unified rules, international standards and agreements are also taken into consideration. This report gives stakeholders and legislators a thorough understanding of the regulatory environment, points out any gaps or inconsistencies, and makes recommendations for improving the laws pertaining to IoT security in smart cities.

Synthesis of Findings

In **Figure 4.** refers the synthesis of findings on IoT infrastructure security in smart cities shows a complex environment that necessitates thoughtful consideration and creative solutions. Comparative research conducted across a number of smart cities worldwide has brought to light both shared problems and different approaches to IoT security. The results highlight the vital significance of strong security systems above all else. In order to secure IoT devices and data, prosperous smart cities typically incorporate extensive frameworks that include access controls, authentication, and encryption. Furthermore, it became clear that striking a balance between centralized and decentralized security measures was important. While some cities adopted decentralized structures to divide security tasks efficiently, others displayed centralized security operations centres to guarantee a cohesive strategy.

The synthesis revealed that successful implementations often hinge on collaboration between public and private sectors. Cities that fostered partnerships and information sharing demonstrated greater resilience against cyber threats. Additionally, continuous monitoring and threat intelligence were recurring themes in effective IoT security. Smart cities that employed real-time monitoring and incorporated threat intelligence feeds were better equipped to detect and respond to emerging risks promptly.

Figure 4. Synthesis finding

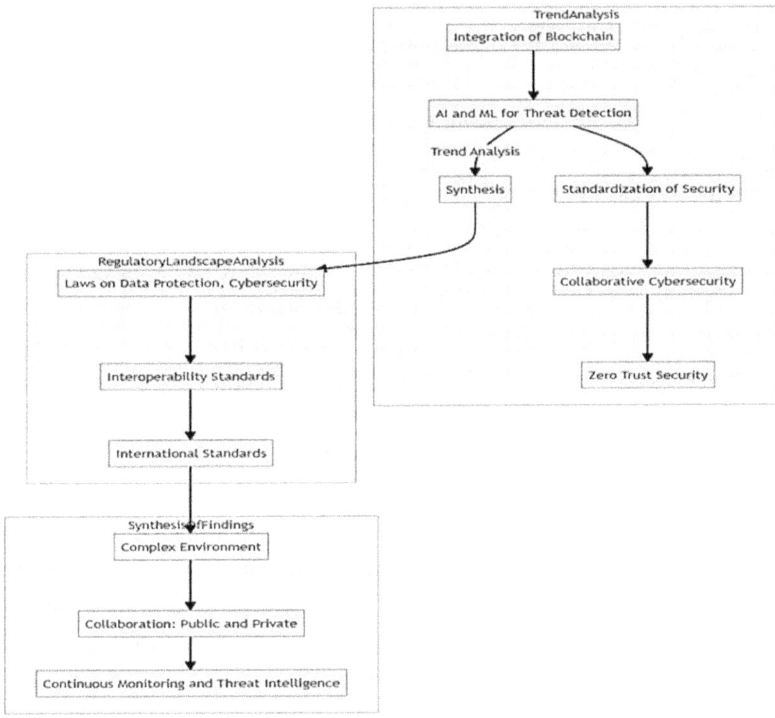

DATA PRIVACY AND GOVERNANCE

Data privacy and governance are critical considerations in the implementation of Internet of Things (IoT) technology within the framework of smart cities. As these interconnected devices collect and process vast amounts of sensitive data, preserving individual privacy becomes paramount. A foundational aspect of data privacy is the establishment of clear and comprehensive data governance frameworks. This involves defining the scope of data collection, specifying the purposes for which the data will be used, and outlining the protocols for data storage and retention. A transparent and well-defined governance structure ensures that data is handled responsibly and ethically.

An essential component of data privacy in smart cities is the implementation of robust data anonymization techniques. Given the often-sensitive nature of the data collected, ensuring that personally identifiable information is adequately protected is crucial. Anonymization methods, such as pseudonymization and data aggregation, help in minimizing the risk of re-identification, enabling the extraction of valuable insights from the data while safeguarding individual privacy

Furthermore, compliance with data protection regulations, such as the General Data Protection Regulation (GDPR) and other regional or national laws, is integral to effective data privacy in smart cities. Adhering to these regulations involves obtaining informed consent from individuals for data collection and processing, providing mechanisms for data access and correction, and notifying authorities in the event of a data breach. A commitment to legal compliance ensures that smart city initiatives respect the rights of individuals and maintain the highest standards of data privacy.

In the context of data governance, data ownership and sharing mechanisms also come to the forefront. Clarifying the ownership of data generated by IoT devices and establishing transparent frameworks for data sharing among stakeholders, including government entities, private organizations, and citizens, helps build trust in the smart city ecosystem. This involves striking a delicate balance between promoting innovation through data sharing and protecting the rights and interests of individuals.

Educating both the public and stakeholders about data privacy is a crucial aspect of successful implementation. Promoting awareness about the types of data collected, the purposes for which it is used, and the security measures in place fosters a culture of informed consent and trust. User-friendly interfaces that allow individuals to manage their privacy preferences and easily understand the implications of data sharing contribute to a more privacy-aware and engaged community.

Regular audits and assessments of data privacy practices within smart city initiatives ensure ongoing compliance with evolving privacy standards and regulations. This proactive approach involves evaluating the effectiveness of privacy safeguards, identifying potential vulnerabilities, and implementing necessary adjustments to mitigate risks. Continuous improvement in data privacy measures is essential to address emerging challenges and maintain the integrity of the smart city's data ecosystem.

In summary, data privacy and governance are foundational pillars in the development of smart cities. **Figure 5.** refers architectural diagram that encompasses transparent governance structures, effective anonymization techniques, legal compliance, clear data ownership, and public awareness is essential to strike a harmonious balance between leveraging data for the benefit of the community and safeguarding individual privacy rights. This comprehensive approach ensures that smart cities not only thrive in technological innovation but also uphold the highest standards of ethical data handling.

SECURITY ATTACKS AND IMPLEMENTATIONS

In the landscape of IoT infrastructure in smart cities, understanding potential security attacks and implementing robust measures to mitigate them is paramount to ensure the resilience and integrity of urban systems. Various types of security attacks pose significant threats to the interconnected networks and devices within smart cities, highlighting the need for comprehensive security strategies and proactive defenses.

One of the most prevalent security threats facing IoT infrastructure is malware attacks. Malicious software can infiltrate IoT devices and networks, compromising their functionality and potentially granting unauthorized access to sensitive data. Implementation of stringent access controls, regular security updates, and the use of reputable antivirus and antimalware solutions are crucial measures to mitigate the risk of malware attacks.

Another significant concern is distributed denial-of-service (DDoS) attacks, where malicious actors flood IoT networks with a high volume of traffic, causing service disruptions and rendering critical systems inaccessible. To counteract DDoS attacks, smart cities can employ traffic filtering mechanisms, rate limiting, and traffic analysis tools to identify and block malicious traffic in real-time. Additionally, leveraging cloud-based DDoS protection services can help absorb and mitigate the impact of volumetric attacks.

Furthermore, IoT devices are susceptible to exploitation through vulnerabilities in their firmware or software. Attackers may exploit these vulnerabilities to gain unauthorized access, manipulate device functionality, or extract sensitive information. Regular vulnerability assessments, penetration testing,

Figure 5. Architectural diagram

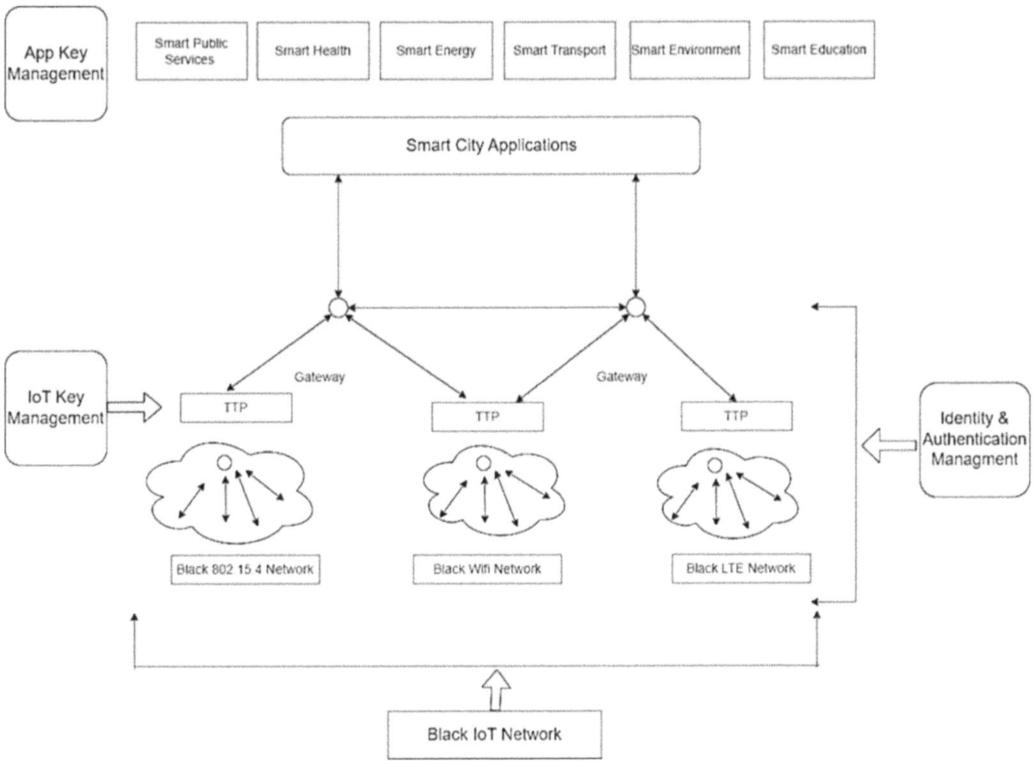

and timely patch management are essential practices to address and remediate known vulnerabilities in IoT devices and systems.

Man-in-the-middle (MitM) attacks represent another significant threat to IoT security in smart cities. In MitM attacks, adversaries intercept and manipulate communication between IoT devices and backend systems, potentially eavesdropping on sensitive data or injecting malicious code into transmitted data packets. Implementation of end-to-end encryption protocols, mutual authentication mechanisms, and secure communication channels can help mitigate the risk of MitM attacks and ensure the confidentiality and integrity of data transmissions.

Moreover, insider threats, whether intentional or accidental, pose a considerable risk to IoT security. Unauthorized access by employees, contractors, or third-party vendors can compromise sensitive data or disrupt critical operations within smart city infrastructure. Implementation of role-based access controls, stringent authentication procedures, and continuous monitoring of user activities can help detect and mitigate insider threats before they escalate into significant security incidents.

Malware Attacks

Implementation: Implement stringent access controls to limit unauthorized access to IoT devices and networks. Ensure regular security updates and patches to address known vulnerabilities. Deploy reputable antivirus and antimalware solutions across the IoT ecosystem to detect and mitigate malware threats.

Distributed Denial-of-Service (DDoS) Attacks

Implementation: Deploy traffic filtering mechanisms and rate limiting to identify and block malicious traffic during DDoS attacks. Utilize traffic analysis tools to detect anomalous patterns and divert legitimate traffic. Consider leveraging cloud-based DDoS protection services to absorb and mitigate the impact of volumetric attacks.

Vulnerabilities Exploitation

Implementation: Conduct regular vulnerability assessments and penetration testing to identify and remediate vulnerabilities in firmware and software. Implement a robust patch management process to ensure timely updates and fixes for known vulnerabilities. Employ intrusion detection systems to monitor for signs of exploitation and unauthorized access.

Man-in-the-Middle (MitM) Attacks

Implementation: Implement end-to-end encryption protocols to secure communication channels between IoT devices and backend systems. Utilize mutual authentication mechanisms to verify the identity of communicating parties. Employ secure communication protocols, such as Transport Layer Security (TLS), to prevent interception and manipulation of data packets by adversaries.

Insider Threats

Implementation: Implement role-based access controls to limit access to sensitive data and critical systems based on user roles and privileges. Enforce stringent authentication procedures, including multi-factor authentication, to verify the identity of users accessing IoT infrastructure. Deploy continuous monitoring and auditing tools to detect and mitigate suspicious activities by insiders.

In conclusion, addressing potential security attacks in IoT infrastructure requires a multifaceted approach that encompasses proactive threat detection, robust access controls, encryption protocols, and ongoing security monitoring. By implementing comprehensive security measures and staying vigilant against emerging threats, smart cities can fortify their defenses and safeguard the reliability, privacy, and security of their interconnected systems and services. Collaboration between stakeholders, ongoing education and awareness initiatives, and adherence to best practices are essential for maintaining the resilience and integrity of IoT infrastructure in the evolving landscape of smart cities.

CASE STUDIES AND BEST PRACTICES

The exploration of case studies and best practices is instrumental in gleaning insights into successful implementations and drawing valuable lessons for the integration of the Internet of Things (IoT) in smart cities. Examining real-world examples provides a practical understanding of challenges faced and effective strategies employed. One noteworthy case study is the city of Barcelona, which has implemented an extensive IoT infrastructure to enhance urban services. From smart street lighting that adapts to real-time conditions to waste management systems optimizing collection routes, Barcelona's approach showcases the transformative potential of IoT in improving the quality of life for its residents.

Another illuminating example is the city of Singapore, renowned for its innovative adoption of smart technologies. Singapore's deployment of IoT in the realm of transportation, with a comprehensive network of sensors and smart traffic management systems, has significantly reduced congestion and enhanced overall traffic flow. This case study underscores the impact of data-driven decision-making in optimizing urban mobility and creating more sustainable, efficient transportation networks.

In the context of best practices, one overarching principle is the importance of collaboration between various stakeholders. Successful smart city initiatives often involve partnerships between government entities, private organizations, academia, and citizens. For instance, in Songdo, South Korea, a city built with smart infrastructure from the ground up, collaboration between the government and private developers has been crucial. Engaging citizens in the planning and decision-making processes is another best practice, ensuring that smart city initiatives align with the needs and preferences of the community.

Effective data governance emerges as a best practice that is consistently observed in successful smart city implementations. Singapore, for example, places a strong emphasis on data security and privacy, implementing stringent measures to protect citizen data. This commitment to robust data governance builds trust among residents and facilitates the responsible use of data for urban planning and improvement.

The integration of sustainability practices is another key best practice in smart city development. The city of Copenhagen exemplifies this approach by leveraging IoT technologies for environmental monitoring and resource management. Through smart grids, efficient waste management, and sustainable energy solutions, Copenhagen has set a benchmark for cities aspiring to blend technological advancement with environmental responsibility.

Furthermore, flexibility and adaptability in the face of evolving technologies and urban challenges represent critical best practices. Smart city initiatives should be designed with scalability and resilience in mind. For instance, the city of Amsterdam has embraced an open data policy, allowing for the continuous evolution of its smart city applications as technology advances and new opportunities emerge.

In conclusion, delving into case studies and best practices provides a wealth of knowledge for those navigating the complexities of implementing IoT in smart cities. Barcelona, Singapore, Songdo, Copenhagen, and Amsterdam exemplify how strategic planning, collaboration, robust data governance, sustainability practices, and adaptability contribute to successful and sustainable smart city initiatives. These examples serve as beacons for other cities seeking to harness the transformative potential of IoT for the benefit of their communities.

Case Study: Securing IoT Infrastructure in Smart City X

Overview

Smart City X has embarked on a comprehensive initiative to deploy IoT infrastructure across various sectors, including transportation, energy management, public safety, and environmental monitoring. The integration of IoT devices promises to enhance efficiency, sustainability, and citizen well-being. However, ensuring the security of this interconnected ecosystem is paramount to safeguarding critical services and data.

Challenges

- ➢ Diverse IoT device ecosystem with varying security capabilities.
- ➢ Potential vulnerabilities in firmware and software of IoT devices.
- ➢ Threat of malware attacks, DDoS attacks, and data breaches.
- ➢ Privacy concerns regarding the collection and usage of sensitive data.
- ➢ Need for compliance with data protection regulations.

Implementation

Vulnerability Assessment and Patch Management

Utilize historical vulnerability data from past security assessments and penetration tests to identify potential weaknesses in IoT devices and systems.

Implement a centralized patch management system to ensure timely updates and fixes for known vulnerabilities.

Monitor vulnerability databases and threat intelligence feeds to stay informed about emerging threats and security patches.

Intrusion Detection and Prevention

Deploy intrusion detection systems (IDS) and intrusion prevention systems (IPS) to monitor network traffic and detect suspicious activities.

Utilize datasets from network traffic logs and anomaly detection algorithms to identify patterns indicative of potential security breaches.

Implement real-time alerts and automated response mechanisms to mitigate threats before they escalate.

Encryption and Secure Communication

Implement end-to-end encryption protocols for data transmission between IoT devices and backend systems.

Utilize datasets on encryption standards and cryptographic algorithms to select the most secure encryption mechanisms.

Conduct regular audits and assessments to ensure compliance with encryption standards and best practices.

Data Privacy and Governance

Establish clear data governance policies and procedures outlining the collection, storage, and usage of citizen data.

Utilize datasets on privacy regulations and compliance requirements to inform policy development and implementation.

Implement anonymization techniques and pseudonymization practices to protect personally identifiable information (PII) and sensitive data.

User Authentication and Access Control

Implement multi-factor authentication (MFA) mechanisms to verify the identity of users accessing IoT devices and systems.

Utilize datasets on user access logs and authentication attempts to detect unauthorized access attempts and suspicious behavior.

Enforce role-based access controls (RBAC) to limit user privileges based on job roles and responsibilities.

Outcomes

- Enhanced resilience and security of IoT infrastructure against potential cyber threats and attacks.
- Improved compliance with data protection regulations and privacy standards.
- Strengthened trust and confidence among citizens regarding the security and privacy of their data.
- Mitigation of security vulnerabilities and proactive response to emerging threats through continuous monitoring and assessment.

In conclusion, the implementation of robust security measures in Smart City X's IoT infrastructure demonstrates a proactive approach to safeguarding critical services and citizen data. By leveraging relevant datasets and adopting best practices in vulnerability management, intrusion detection, encryption, data privacy, and access control, Smart City X sets a benchmark for securing the foundations of IoT infrastructure in the context of smart cities.

ANTICIPATING FUTURE CHALLENGES AND ADVANCEMENTS

In the ever-evolving landscape of Smart Cities, anticipating future challenges in securing IoT infrastructure is imperative for sustained urban development. As cities embrace emerging technologies, including 5G, edge computing, and quantum computing, the paradigm of security faces new complexities. The integration of these technologies not only provides novel opportunities but also introduces unprecedented vulnerabilities that demand innovative security measures.

The increasing complexity of Smart City networks, fueled by the proliferation of IoT devices, presents a multifaceted challenge. As the number and diversity of connected devices grow, managing the security of this intricate ecosystem becomes a critical concern. Securing such a diverse array of devices, each with its unique characteristics and potential vulnerabilities, requires advanced solutions for threat detection, response, and recovery.

Furthermore, the advent of artificial intelligence (AI) introduces a dual-edged sword in the realm of cybersecurity. While AI holds promise for enhancing security measures, it also presents the risk of AI-driven threats. Malicious actors may leverage AI algorithms to orchestrate sophisticated cyber-attacks, necessitating a proactive approach to developing AI-driven defence mechanisms. Understanding and mitigating the potential misuse of AI in the context of Smart Cities is essential for building a robust and adaptive security infrastructure.

In this dynamic landscape, anticipating future challenges is not only about addressing known threats but also about fostering a mindset of continual adaptation and innovation. As Smart Cities advance, the ability to foresee potential security challenges and integrate advancements in technology and policy will be pivotal in ensuring the long-term sustainability and resilience of urban ecosystems.

LIMITATIONS

Embarking on the exploration of securing IoT infrastructure in Smart Cities, it is imperative to acknowledge the contours of our understanding and the boundaries that delineate the scope of this inquiry. While the insights shared herein aim to illuminate the path to a more secure urban future, it's crucial to recognize the limitations that inherently shape the narrative.

Complexity of the Smart City Ecosystem

The very essence of a Smart City lies in its complexity—an intricate tapestry woven with diverse technologies, urban systems, and citizen interactions. Acknowledging this complexity, the chapter takes a panoramic view, offering generalized principles. However, the nuanced intricacies of individual Smart City ecosystems may not be exhaustively addressed, prompting further exploration at the local level.

Technological Evolution Outpacing Documentation

In the dynamic world of technology, innovation is ceaseless. While this chapter endeavors to capture the essence of securing IoT infrastructure, the rapid evolution of technologies may outpace the documentation. Future advancements, unforeseen developments, and emerging threat landscapes are all factors that might influence the relevance of the insights provided.

Resource and Implementation Constraints

Implementing robust security measures requires resources—financial, technological, and human. The chapter underscores the importance of various strategies, yet it recognizes the reality of resource constraints. Not every Smart City may have the same capacity to implement the recommended measures comprehensively. Hence, the practical application of these strategies might vary based on the available resources.

Cultural and Regional Specificities

Smart Cities are not one-size-fits-all entities; they are reflections of diverse cultures, governance structures, and regional nuances. The chapter offers overarching principles, but the effectiveness of security measures might be influenced by cultural variations and regional specificities. Tailoring strategies to align with local contexts becomes a crucial consideration.

Unpredictable Regulatory Landscape

The regulatory environment surrounding IoT security is a dynamic landscape, subject to legislative changes and policy evolution. While the chapter emphasizes the significance of policy frameworks and regulatory measures, the specifics may undergo transformations, necessitating readers to stay abreast of the latest developments in the legal realm.

In navigating the fascinating terrain of Smart City security, these limitations serve as guideposts, urging us to acknowledge the boundaries of our current understanding. As we peer into the future of urban innovation, embracing the unknowns becomes a part of the journey, motivating continuous exploration, adaptation, and refinement in our quest to secure the pulsating heartbeat of Smart Cities.

FUTURE SCOPE

As we delve into the future of securing IoT infrastructure in Smart Cities, this chapter serves as both a reflection of the present challenges and a prologue to the ever-evolving narrative that will shape urban security landscapes. Looking forward, a primary focus will be on the continuous exploration of technological advancements poised to redefine the very fabric of Smart City security. The imminent integration of artificial intelligence (AI) into urban systems presents a profound paradigm shift. Future discussions will delve into the intricate relationship between AI and cybersecurity, unraveling the potential of machine learning algorithms in enhancing threat detection and response mechanisms.

Anticipating the technological trajectory is essential, but equally pivotal is the adaptability of policy frameworks and regulatory measures. The future scope encompasses not only responses to current challenges but proactive strategies to address unforeseen intricacies. The discourse will evolve to provide nuanced insights into the dynamic interplay between technological innovation and the regulatory environment. Considerations for cross-border data governance and collaborative approaches to international cybersecurity standards will be integral components of this ongoing narrative, ensuring a resilient and globally interconnected urban ecosystem.

Human-centric considerations emerge as a crucial facet of the evolving discourse. Beyond technological advancements, understanding the social and ethical dimensions of security becomes imperative. Future discussions will explore how Smart Cities can leverage technology while ensuring inclusivity in digital transformations. Addressing potential societal impacts and ensuring that advanced security measures contribute to the well-being of urban communities will be central to this exploration. Striking a balance between innovation and ethical considerations is paramount in shaping the future narrative of Smart City security.

The future scope also extends to collaborative efforts and knowledge exchange. Recognizing that Smart City challenges are often shared across borders, the narrative will emphasize collaborative frameworks. International platforms for information sharing, the exchange of best practices, and learning from experiences will be essential. This collaborative narrative aims to transcend geographical boundaries, ensuring that the insights gained from one urban landscape can benefit others facing similar challenges.

As the narrative unfolds, the dynamic nature of technological evolution may outpace existing documentation. Continuous updates and future iterations of this discourse will be vital to keep pace with emerging technologies and evolving threat landscapes. The future of securing IoT infrastructure in Smart Cities demands an iterative, responsive, and collaborative approach, ensuring that urban environments remain at the forefront of innovation while navigating the complexities of a secure digital future.

In conclusion, the future scope of this book chapter envisions a continuous and adaptive exploration of securing IoT infrastructure in Smart Cities. Beyond the pages of this discourse lies an unfolding narrative that responds to the cadence of technological evolution, the dynamics of policy landscapes, and the collective aspirations of urban communities towards a secure, inclusive, and resilient future.

CONCLUSION

The exploration of "Securing the Foundations: IoT Infrastructure in Smart Cities" underscores the imperative of addressing multifaceted challenges and embracing best practices to realize the transformative potential of the Internet of Things (IoT) in urban environments. The diversity of IoT devices, inherent vulnerabilities, and privacy concerns necessitate a comprehensive and adaptive security approach. Establishing standardized security measures, robust network security protocols, and effective data privacy governance frameworks are fundamental prerequisites for building a resilient IoT infrastructure. Case studies from pioneering smart cities, such as Barcelona and Singapore, offer valuable insights into successful implementations, emphasizing the importance of collaboration, data governance, and sustainability. Best practices, including citizen engagement, scalability, and adaptability, further illuminate the path toward creating innovative and secure smart cities. As the evolution of technology continues, this chapter serves as a guide for policymakers, urban planners, and technologists to navigate the intricate landscape of IoT implementation, ensuring that smart cities not only thrive in efficiency and connectivity but also prioritize the privacy, security, and well-being of their inhabitants.

Drawing inspiration from successful case studies in cities like Barcelona, Singapore, Songdo, Copenhagen, and Amsterdam, the chapter illuminates the transformative impact of strategic planning and collaborative efforts. The highlighted best practices, from citizen engagement to sustainability and flexibility, offer a roadmap for other urban centers embarking on the journey toward becoming smart cities.

As cities worldwide strive to harness the potential of IoT for improved services, resource efficiency, and citizen well-being, this chapter serves not only as a diagnostic tool for understanding the challenges but also as a blueprint for building resilient, secure, and citizen-centric smart city ecosystems. In this era of technological advancement, the lessons learned from this exploration provide a foundation for creating intelligent urban landscapes that prioritize both innovation and the fundamental rights and values of the communities they serve.

REFERENCES

Abinaya, K., Palaniappan, D., & Vedaraj, M. (2023). A Novel Hyper-Spectral Model to Optimize the Prediction Rate for Heart Disease in Modern Healthcare Networks. *Engineering Proceedings*, *59*(1), 59081.

Al-Qarafi, A., Alsolai, H., Alzahrani, J. S., Negm, N., Alharbi, L. A., Al Duhayyim, M., Mohsen, H., Al-Shabi, M., & Al-Wesabi, F. N. (2022). Artificial jellyfish optimization with deep-learning-driven decision support system for energy management in smart cities. *Applied Sciences (Basel, Switzerland)*, *12*(15), 7457. doi:10.3390/app12157457

Bauer, M., Sanchez, L., & Song, J. (2021). IoT-enabled smart cities: Evolution and outlook. *Sensors (Basel)*, *21*(13), 4511. doi:10.3390/s21134511 PMID:34209436

Borgia, E. (2014). The Internet of Things vision: Key features, applications and open issues. *Computer Communications*, *54*, 1–31. doi:10.1016/j.comcom.2014.09.008

Caragliu, A., & Del Bo, C. F. (2022). Smart cities and urban inequality. *Regional Studies*, *56*(7), 1097–1112. doi:10.1080/00343404.2021.1984421

Chettri, L., & Bera, R. (2019). A comprehensive survey on Internet of Things (IoT) toward 5G wireless systems. *IEEE Internet of Things Journal*, *7*(1), 16–32. doi:10.1109/JIOT.2019.2948888

Conti, M., Dargahi, T., & Dehghantanha, A. (2018). *Cyber threat intelligence: challenges and opportunities*. Springer International Publishing.

Damodharan, P., & Ravichandran, C. S. (2019). Applicability evaluation of web mining in healthcare E-commerce towards business success and a derived cournot model. *Journal of Medical Systems*, *43*(8), 1–10. doi:10.1007/s10916-019-1395-1 PMID:31273541

Damodharan, P., & Ravichandran, C. S. (2019). Inclusive strategic techno-economic framework to incorporate essential aspects of web mining for the perspective of business success. *International Journal of Enterprise Network Management*, *10*(3-4), 329–349. doi:10.1504/IJENM.2019.103159

Mhala, A., Davda, Y., & Palaniappan, D. (2023). A Mobile Social App for Better Life of Poor People Based on Perceived Similarity and Trust Using Supply Chain Management. In *Government Impact on Sustainable and Responsible Supply Chain Management* (pp. 202–222). IGI Global. doi:10.4018/978-1-6684-9062-4.ch011

Palaniappan, D., Davda, Y., & Premavathi, T. (2023). Digital Marketing Based on Machine Learning. In Government Impact on Sustainable and Responsible Supply Chain Management (pp. 143-170). IGI Global. doi:10.4018/978-1-6684-9062-4.ch009

Pandian, M. T., & Damodharan, P. (2023). Forming the Cluster in the RFID Network for Improving the Efficiency and Investigation of the Unkind Attacks. In Computational Intelligence in Analytics and Information Systems (pp. 295-304). Apple Academic Press. doi:10.1201/9781003332367-25

Rejeb, A., Rejeb, K., Simske, S., Treiblmaier, H., & Zailani, S. (2022). The big picture on the internet of things and the smart city: A review of what we know and what we need to know. *Internet of Things : Engineering Cyber Physical Human Systems*, *19*, 100565. doi:10.1016/j.iot.2022.100565

Syed, A. S., Sierra-Sosa, D., Kumar, A., & Elmaghraby, A. (2021). IoT in smart cities: A survey of technologies, practices and challenges. *Smart Cities*, *4*(2), 429–475. doi:10.3390/smartcities4020024

Wagner, T. D., Mahbub, K., Palomar, E., & Abdallah, A. E. (2019). Cyber threat intelligence sharing: Survey and research directions. *Computers & Security*, *87*, 101589. doi:10.1016/j.cose.2019.101589

Zaidi, A., Ajibade, S. S. M., Musa, M., & Bekun, F. V. (2023). New insights into the research landscape on the application of artificial intelligence in sustainable smart cities: A bibliometric mapping and network analysis approach. *International Journal of Energy Economics and Policy*, *13*(4), 287–299. doi:10.32479/ijeep.14683

Zanella, A., Bui, N., Castellani, A., Vangelista, L., & Zorzi, M. (2014). Internet of things for smart cities. *IEEE Internet of Things Journal*, *1*(1), 22–32. doi:10.1109/JIOT.2014.2306328

Chapter 14
Security and Its Implications on Healthcare in an IoT-Enabled Smart City

N. Rajathi Natarajan
Kumaraguru College of Technology, India

Vanitha Veerasamy
Kumaraguru College of Technology, India

ABSTRACT

Smart cities offer the usage of digital technology to enhance the quality of life for city residents. The goal of these cities is to deal with some of the issues that are projected to arise in future cities, enabling more efficient and sustainable resource management, among other benefits. Through technology innovation and data-driven decision-making, smart cities have the potential to make societies safer, more efficient, and more resilient. Healthcare is important for the thriving growth of smart cities, and providing high-quality medical care is the municipal government's most difficult duty. Smart healthcare is a realistic solution for the health care industry to intelligently manage patient flow systems. Adoption of smart healthcare reduces costs and improves illness management. However, as the scale of wearable medical devices increases, preserving privacy and security becomes more difficult. However, clever security measures will be required to ensure that these advancements are not jeopardized. This chapter aims to examine the role of cyber security in the development of smart city healthcare, as well as the key challenges and benefits of the cyber security in the smart city healthcare systems.

INTRODUCTION

The smart city (Sanchez-Corcuera et al., 2019) ecosystem makes use of communicationand information technology to offer a variety of e-government services to ensure the quality and smooth access to participating residents with these services. However, at the same time, this advancement had drawbacks as well, altering society in terms of global warming, air pollution, etc. According to NATO, these consequences could eventually cause significant issues for both the population and the ecology. These include things like population expansion, global warming, and air pollution (NATO Review, 2011).

DOI: 10.4018/979-8-3693-2373-1.ch014

A city is considered intelligent when traditional infrastructure and human resource investments support a strong economy and high quality of life through the utilization of integrated technologies. The smart cities provide a networked urban civilization that gains from intelligent operation management of its operations while accumulating minimum financial, administrative, and social costs. (Caragliu et al., 2011). Any nation whose smart city is penetrated would face major threats to its national security because of this.

As more people relocate to urban regions in search of better economic and educational opportunities, this number is expected to increase. Resource conservation, environmental protection, and a better quality of life for city residents are all benefits of smart cities. A vast variety of services are offered to residents of smart cities including transportation, environment, healthcare, tourism, safety, security etc. Data is gathered on a huge scale using a variety of Internet of Things (IoT) devices. This will produce enormous amounts of data that can be applied to public services as well as applications for efficiency, safety, and entertainment.

The quality of life for urban dwellers may be improved by IoT. With the world's population growing at an incredible rate and the prevalence of chronic diseases rising, it is becoming more and more vital to design affordable healthcare systems that can offer a wide range of medical services while lowering-totalcosts (Rathi et al., 2021). IoT has recently emerged as a major area of development, paving the way for the advancement of healthcare monitoring systems. Accurately tracking individuals and connecting disparate services and objects globally over the internet is the goal of the IoT healthcare monitoring system. Data created by these devices will be gathered, shared, monitored, stored, and analyzed (Bhatia et al., 2021).

Through technology innovation and data-driven decision-making, smart cities have the potential to build communities that are safer, more efficient, and resilient. The public's safety and health, national security, economic security, and the operation of vital infrastructure could all be impacted by potential vulnerabilities that could be exploited. Managing this large volume of data over the course of its existence is essential to the realization of healthcare in smart cities. The data management process, which includes data collection, data processing, and gathering, is depicted in Figure 1. Every new city infrastructure or technology presents an entirely new chance for cyberattacks. One of the areas of smart cities that are expanding the fastest is healthcare, although the development of such systems is hampered by security and privacy issues by the authors Barrett (2018) and Balasubramanlan (Bhatia et al., 2018).

A crucial area in smart cities is urban population health management. To provide unwell residents with top-notch medical care, precise patient health data analysis is necessary for health administration. Large-scale IoT devices, including sensors, wearable technology, IoT, and many others, are employed for this (Datta, 2016). By using cutting-edge technologies to enhance different facets of daily life, such as healthcare services, smart cities are revolutionizing urban living. Healthcare systems in smart cities are becoming more networked and dependent on digital infrastructure, but this also makes them more open to cyber threats. Doctors collaborate on patient health information to provide each patient with a precise diagnosis and curative treatment. Data on patient health are stored with many personal facts.

A better level of confidentiality, availability, and integrity can only be ensured in intelligent cities by ensuring information security. Additionally, it provides the safety needed for national organizations and agencies to produce livable, intelligent ecosystems that are sustainable. The goal of smart cities is to increase production and efficiency, if cyber security is not effectively addressed, both residents and authorities may face serious risks. The major obstacle to safeguarding the wider smart city ecosystem, however, is the inclusion of third parties. These include companies that create consumer goods that

Figure 1. Healthcare data management lifecycle in smart city environment

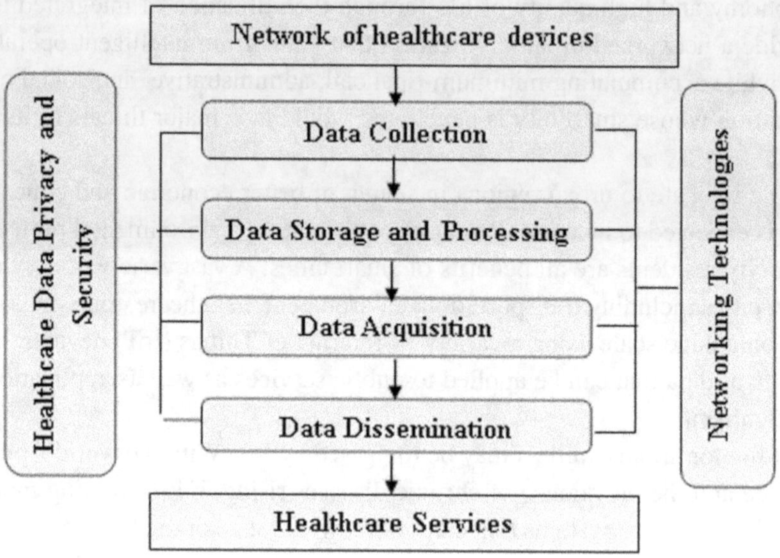

people can integrate directly into the ecosystem. The management of the smart city is powerless to address these security threats and is forced to rely only on their own defenses.

To protect private patient information, security is essential in the healthcare industry. Healthcare organizations maintain a substantial amount of sensitive patient data, including medical histories, diagnoses, and treatments. Sensitive data is vulnerable to a variety of cyber security flaws and unauthorized use. People may be put in jeopardy if sensitive data is exploited by an individual or a formalized group (Khatoun, 2016). Additionally, the increased connectivity creates potential for major cyber security issues that have not yet been adequately identified and resolved (Elmaghraby et al., 2014).

This chapter is structured as follows: The next section discusses the most recent literatures. The challenges and issues in the healthcare industry are covered in Section 3. In section 4, strategies for enhancing cyber security in smart city healthcare are discussed. Section 5 discusses the numerous research directions. In section 6, concluding remarks are offered.

LITERATURE SURVEY

This section reviews the literature on cyber security in smart city healthcare. The goal of smart health is to make medical services available to people wherever they are and at any time.

Habibzadeh et al. (2019) looked at new developments in healthcare applications and important technological advances that effects directly on these transitions. The authors also looked at a number of security issues with smart healthcare systems, as well as their results and solutions. Cyberattacks are possible on wireless networks, which are widely used to link smart health monitoring equipment. However, a number of suspicions about these health monitoring systems and applications raise the possibility of risk (Sharma Bhatia et al., 2019). These include timing and fingerprint-based eavesdropping, router attacks, forwarding assaults, sensor and replay attacks, denial-of-service (DoS) attacks, and sensor attacks by Qiu (2018) and Cook (2018). The authors of this article (Butt et al., 2019) assess the impact of these attacks affect health monitoring systems and offer few potential solutions.

In order to assess people's concerns about security in smart homes and to initiate a conversation on how healthcare technology is included with future homes is vulnerable to cyberattacks that lead to data breaches, this review paper will examine people's concerns. This paper (Safavi et al., 2018) suggests using blockchain to boost security and privacy in smart healthcare.

Continuing the confidentiality and privacy of patient health data is one of the most challenging challenges facing smart healthcare systems. This article (Nidhya et al., 2022) examines the security issues posed by the IoT in healthcare as well as the laws and guidelines necessary to set up a smart healthcare system. Along with describing the numerous general principles and threats to corporate digital assets and patient health information, it also discusses the required fixes for the existing problems, including acommunication protocol and cryptographic function.

In the field of smart healthcare, for instance, this work (Gamundani et al., 2015) offers a thorough analysis of potential authentication concerns and attacks on IoT healthcare devices. A safe cloud storage solution for medical data was also built by the authors of (Chinnasamy, 2018) using a hybrid cryptographic method. The authors in (Quamara, 2021) focus on several levels of security related to the transmission and storage of medical data. Based on the elliptic curve cryptography method, this paper (Poonguzhali, 2020)suggests a blockchain architecture for electronic medical records to protect sensitive data. In contrast, this study offers a workable approach based on blockchain's distinct qualities in cases when distributed ledger technology is believed to be unsupportable.

Based on the seven key smart city areas, the authors provide a summary of the serious cyber threats, attacks and countermeasures in (Sharma et al., 2022). One promising solution that can help the healthcare industry combat the security issues in smart cities is the adoption of blockchain (Giffinger et al., 2010). The health care system can now store patient data more safely and securely thanks to block chain technology.

The security and privacy of healthcare services and concepts in smart cities is an essential part of the complete minimal disclosure of data and information security architecture (Qiu et al., 2018). The study by Alromaihi et al. (2017) and de Fuentes (2028) highlighted the growing use of sensors for medical and healthcare applications over the past ten years. The study revealed significant risks from sensors that collect personal health information, such as blood pressure and heart rate, and stressed the significance of an integrated security solution.

The authors make a case for the benefit of data sharing in secured mobile healthcare systems (Huang et al., 2017). The study created a method for re-encrypting identity-based broadcast encryption and attribute-based encryption, which allowed a data owner to approve third-party healthcare provider data analysis. A summary of the pertinent literature in the area of healthcare security is highlighted in Table 1.

In (Barua et al., 2022), the authors proposed a P2P Smart Contract-based Intelligent Smart City Architecture for Vaccine Manufacturing. The provision of high-quality, affordable healthcare services are a key problem for the present healthcare system. These issues are made worse by the growing older population, which results in a plethora of chronic illnesses and an increase in the need for healthcare services. A proper healthcare service is also difficult to find in some cities due to a lack of resources. With billions of connected "things" placed in smart cities around the world, there are numerous potential weaknesses and strategies.

Table 1. Literatures related to healthcare security

Author	Title of the work	Methodology
Bhardwaj et al. (2021)	IoT based Healthware and Healthcare Monitoring System in India	Addressed about several wearables and how they can revolutionize healthcare in India in the future.
Khor et al. (2021)	Public Blockchains for Resource-Constrained IoT Devices—A State-of-the-Art Survey	Discussed about the applications of blockchain technology in devices with limited resources
Al-Garati et al. (2020)	A Survey of Machine and Deep Learning Methods for Internet of Things (IoT) Security	Machine learning and deep learning based solutions for IoT security issues.
Alromaihiet al. (2018)	Cyber Security Challenges of Deploying IoT in Smart Cities for Healthcare Applications	An overview of several IoT applications and their cyber risks, as well as security and privacy in the context of smart cities healthcare are presented.
Arora et al. (2022)	Machine Learning-Based Security Solutions for Healthcare: An Overview	Machine learning solutions for healthcare security.
Barua et al. (2022)	Security and Privacy Threats for Bluetooth Low Energy in IoT and Wearable Devices: A Comprehensive Survey	Threats to security, classification, and countermeasures for Bluetooth-based attacks. Case studies that demonstrate how various vulnerabilities in actual Bluetooth devices can be attacked
Gaurav et al., (2023)	A comprehensive survey on machine learning approaches for malware detection in IoT-based enterprise information system	Machine learning is employed for malware detection in IoT networks.

IOT BASED HEALTHCARE SYSTEM

Healthcare applications and systems powered by IoT improve people's lives in a variety of ways. One such application is remote healthcare, which uses wireless IoT-driven solutions to deliver patients with medical treatments. Data is safely gathered using Internet of Things (IoT)-based sensors, which are then processed and shared with healthcare providers for appropriate recommendations. The IoT powered non-invasive monitoring sensors gather extensive psychological data in real-time monitoring and used cloud based data storage. IoT healthcare systems use sensor data for preventive care, which helps with early emergency detection and notifies family members (Singh et al., 2022). Figure 2 shows the architecture of IoT based health monitoring system.

In IoT healthcare systems, a number of fruitful research projects have been completed, and numerous others are still in progress. Because of the constantly rising number of aged people and patients with chronic illnesses, there are a growing number of gaps in the treatment that healthcare practitioners deliver. The main advantages of automating healthcare systems are lower healthcare costs, early detection of chronic diseases, quick access to medical services, and improved treatment.

CYBER SECURITY CHALLENGES AND ISSUES IN HEALTHCARE

Due to technological developments, several cyber security issues that must be resolved to ensure the privacy and security of patient data as well as the overall efficacy of the healthcare infrastructure. Figure 3 shows some key cybersecurity challenges in smart city healthcare. Securing

Figure 2. IoT driven health monitoring system

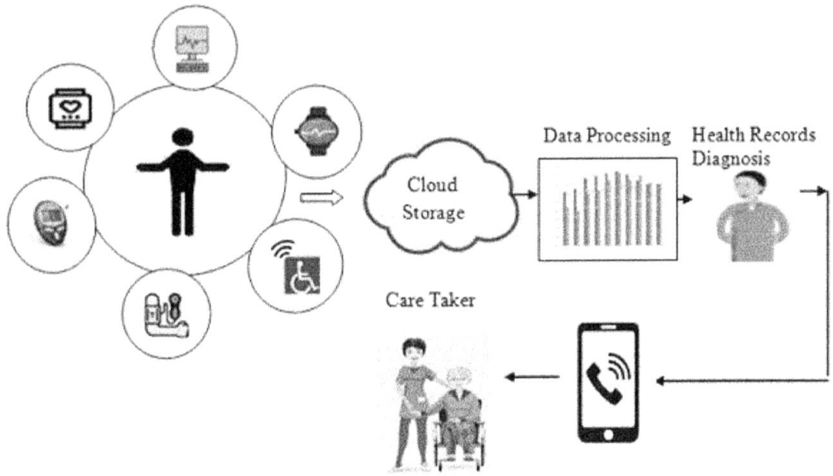

smart city healthcare systems poses a myriad of challenges, each demanding careful attention to safeguard the sensitive nature of patient data. One prominent concern lies in the potential for data breaches, given the vast amounts of health records and individual patient information collected by these systems. Protecting against unauthorized access is imperative to maintain privacy. Furthermore, the interconnected networks integral to these systems create vulnerabilities in infrastructure, necessitating robust security measures to prevent data breaches and service interruptions. Insider attacks pose a persistent threat, with the risk of employees compromising sensitive data either inadvertently or intentionally. Implementing access controls and effective monitoring is crucial to mitigate this risk. The complex supply chain supporting smart city healthcare systems introduces additional challenges, as attackers may exploit vulnerabilities within the supply chain. Interoperability issues also emerge, requiring careful integration of various healthcare systems to prevent security flaws.

The proliferation of IoT devices, including wearable health monitors, contributes to an expanded attack surface, with security flaws that could be exploited by malicious actors. Denial of service attacks, aimed at overwhelming healthcare systems with excessive network traffic, pose a significant risk to patient care and professional collaboration. Unsecured health records, if poorly protected or left unencrypted, may inadvertently be exposed online, providing an opportunity for threat actors and hackers. As cyber threats evolve rapidly, healthcare organizations must stay vigilant against emerging attack strategies such as ransomware, phishing attacks, and insider threats to ensure the resilience of their security measures.

To address the cyber security issues, healthcare organizations in smart cities must create a complex security strategy that incorporates rigorous access controls, regular security audits, intrusion detection systems, incident response plans etc. Cooperation between healthcare institutions, businesses and government agencies is crucial to develop and implement comprehensive cybersecurity measures.

Figure 3. Cyber security challenges in smart city healthcare

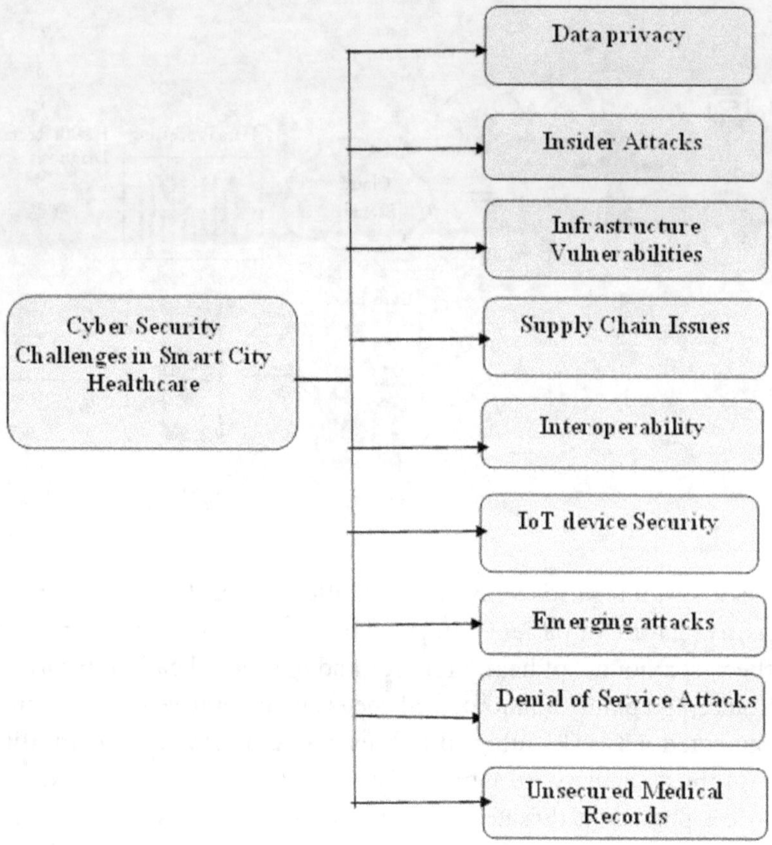

STRATEGIES FOR ENHANCING CYBERSECURITY IN SMART CITY HEALTHCARE

Technology and healthcare are closely related today. It's incredibly challenging to manage any healthcare organization today without substantially relying sophisticated machines for disease diagnosis and maintain patient records. Threats to cyber security pose the largest dangers in these businesses. Figure 4gives an insight on various strategies to ensure the cyber security in the smart healthcare systems.

Ensuring the robust security of healthcare systems is paramount, and several key measures must be implemented to safeguard sensitive patient information. Strong encryption is imperative, employing end-to-end encryption for both data transmission and storage to thwart potential eavesdropping on confidential information. To guarantee that only authorised individuals can access patient data, access control methods are essential. Regular security audits and penetration tests are essential components of a proactive cybersecurity strategy, helping identify vulnerabilities and promptly addressing them to fortify the system against potential threats. Employee training is indispensable, emphasizing cybersecurity best practices and instilling a culture of vigilance to recognize and report potential threats.

Figure 4. Cyber security measures for healthcare domain

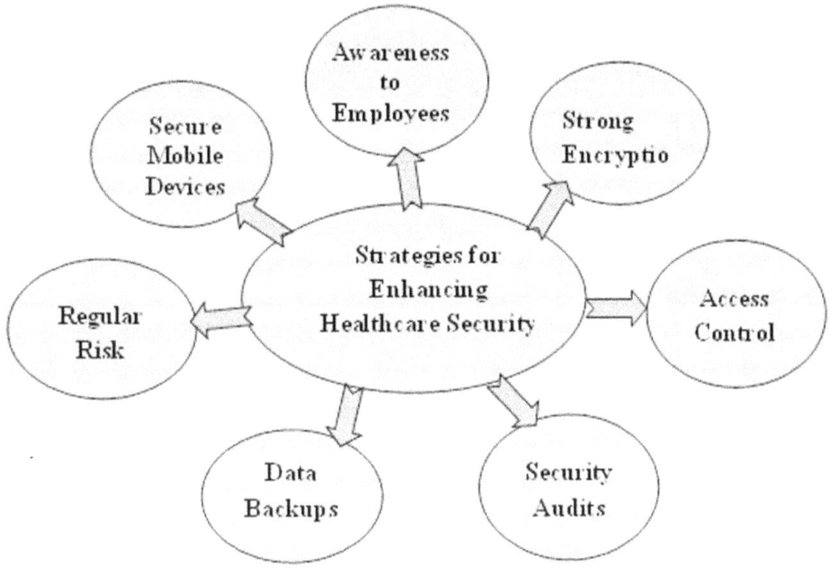

As the healthcare sector increasingly relies on connected devices for monitoring health metrics, the security of these devices becomes paramount, especially in the context of IoT. Risk assessment through regular analyses is vital, providing insights into security flaws or vulnerabilities that need attention. Additionally, data backups are critical in the face of cyber attacks, with regular off-site backups featuring stringent encryption and access controls to preserve the confidentiality and integrity of patient data. These comprehensive security measures collectively contribute to a resilient healthcare infrastructure capable of withstanding evolving cyber security challenges.

RESEARCH DIRECTION IN CREATING SECURED HEALTHCARE FOR SMART CITY ECOSYSTEM

The healthcare sector increasingly relies on digital technologies to store and manage sensitive patient data, cybersecurity in healthcare is a crucial and developing topic. Research in this area is essential for maintaining patient confidentiality and the reliability of healthcare systems. Here are a few topics for future healthcare cyber security research is shown in table 2.

CONCLUSION

Healthcare in smart cities has a huge potential to improve patient care and hospital operations. IoT technology plays a key role in healthcare industry by giving patients with a real-time platform to communicate health information with the physicians. Prioritizing cyber security is essential to maximizing these advantages. Smart city healthcare systems may offer effective, safe, and secure services to residents while defending sensitive patient data from online threats by putting in place strong cyber security safeguards,

Table 2. Challenges and solutions in smart city secured healthcare

S.No.	Research challenge	Solutions
1	Cyber Threat Discovery	■ Deploying network monitoring tools/intrusion detection systems to spot unusual activities. In addition, conducting vulnerability scans on a regular basis to identify system weaknesses. ■ Advanced techniques such as machine learning and artificial intelligence are utilized in cyber threat detection.
2	Protecting Patient Data	■ Use strong encryption algorithms to secure sensitive information and implement robust access controls to prevent from unauthorized users. ■ Utilize secure storage solutions to safeguard patient data ■ Implement regular data backup procedures to ensure that patient data is securely backed up and can be restored
3	Medical IoT Security	■ With a growing number of IoT medical devices, it is essential to investigate and create strong security solutions for these devices.
4	Telehealth Security	■ Telehealth enables medical professionals to assess, diagnose, educate, and treat patients virtually. ■ With the growth of telemedicine and remote patient monitoring, safeguarding the telecommunication channels is an important are of research.
5	Interoperability Standards	■ Research on creating cybersecurity standards that are interoperable in healthcare organizations can assist in ensuring various healthcare entities can securely exchange and interact with patient data
6	Privacy Protecting Techniques	■ An important area of research is the development of privacy-preserving technology that protect patient data. Utilizing a range of cryptographic and access control methods becomes instrumental in ensuring the confidentiality of sensitive healthcare information.
7	Blockchain for healthcare data	■ It has the potential to secure patient data. Research is still being carried out on blockchain applications for managing and exchanging secure healthcare data.

remaining vigilant against emerging threats, and establishing a culture of security awareness. This study provides a comprehensive review of healthcare security problems and challenges in IoT enabled smart cities. Furthermore, more research to be carried out to address theunresolved security risks associated with IoTto enhance the healthcare system. The future research will incorporate machine learning and artificial intelligence techniques to create smart, safe systems specifically designed for Internet of Thing-senabled healthcare applications.

REFERENCES

Al-Garadi, M. A., Mohamed, A., Al-Ali, A. K., Du, X., Ali, I., & Guizani, M. (2020). A survey of machine and deep learning methods for internet of things (IoT) security. *IEEE Communications Surveys and Tutorials*, *22*(3), 1646–1685. doi:10.1109/COMST.2020.2988293

Alromaihi, S., Elmedany, W., & Balakrishna, C. (2018, August). Cyber security challenges of deploying IoT in smart cities for healthcare applications. In *2018 6th International Conference on Future Internet of Things and Cloud Workshops (FiCloudW)* (pp. 140-145). IEEE. 10.1109/W-FiCloud.2018.00028

Alromaihi, S., Elmedany, W., & Balakrishna, C. (2018, August). Cyber security challenges of deploying IoT in smart cities for healthcare applications. In *2018 6th International Conference on Future Internet of Things and Cloud Workshops (FiCloudW)* (pp. 140-145). IEEE. 10.1109/W-FiCloud.2018.00028

Arora, P., Kaur, B., & Teixeira, M. A. (2022). Machine Learning-Based Security Solutions for Healthcare: An Overview. *Emerging Technologies for Computing, Communication and Smart Cities. Proceedings of ETCCS, 2021*, 649–659.

Balasubramanlan, S. (2018). *The Global Cyberattack and the Need to Revisit Health Care Cybersecurity*. Research Gate.

Barrett, B., & Brief, H. (2018). *Hackers are Holding an LA Hospital's Computers Hostage*. Research Gate.

Barua, A., Al Alamin, M. A., Hossain, M. S., & Hossain, E. (2022). Security and privacy threats for bluetooth low energy in iot and wearable devices: A comprehensive survey. *IEEE Open Journal of the Communications Society*, *3*, 251–281. doi:10.1109/OJCOMS.2022.3149732

Bhardwaj, R., Gupta, S. N., Gupta, M., & Tiwari, P. (2021, March). IoT based healthware and healthcare monitoring system in india. In *2021 International Conference on Advance Computing and Innovative Technologies in Engineering (ICACITE)* (pp. 406-408). IEEE. 10.1109/ICACITE51222.2021.9404633

Bhatia, H., Panda, S. N., & Nagpal, D. (2020, June). Internet of Things and its Applications in Healthcare-A Survey. In *2020 8th International Conference on Reliability, Infocom Technologies and Optimization (Trends and Future Directions)(ICRITO)* (pp. 305-310). IEEE. 10.1109/ICRITO48877.2020.9197816

Butt, S. A., Diaz-Martinez, J. L., Jamal, T., Ali, A., De-La-Hoz-Franco, E., & Shoaib, M. (2019, July). IoT smart health security threats. In *2019 19th International conference on computational science and its applications (ICCSA)* (pp. 26-31). IEEE. 10.1109/ICCSA.2019.000-8

Caragliu, A., Del, B., & C–Nijkamp, P. (2011). Smart cities in Europe. *Journal of Urban Technology, 18* (2), 65–82.

Chinnasamy, P., & Deepalakshmi, P. (2018, April). Design of secure storage for health-care cloud using hybrid cryptography. In *2018 second international conference on inventive communication and computational technologies (ICICCT)* (pp. 1717-1720). IEEE. 10.1109/ICICCT.2018.8473107

Cook, D. J., Duncan, G., Sprint, G., & Fritz, R. L. (2018). Using smart city technology to make healthcare smarter. *Proceedings of the IEEE*, *106*(4), 708–722. doi:10.1109/JPROC.2017.2787688 PMID:29628528

Datta, S. K., Da Costa, R. P. F., Bonnet, C., & Härri, J. (2016, June). oneM2M architecture based IoT framework for mobile crowd sensing in smart cities. In *2016 European conference on networks and communications (EuCNC)* (pp. 168-173). IEEE. 10.1109/EuCNC.2016.7561026

de Fuentes, J. M., Gonzalez-Manzano, L., Solanas, A., & Veseli, F. (2018). Attribute-based credentials for privacy-aware smart health services in IoT-based smart cities. *Computer*, *51*(7), 44–53. doi:10.1109/MC.2018.3011042

Elmaghraby, A. S., & Losavio, M. M. (2014). Cyber security challenges in Smart Cities: Safety, security and privacy. *Journal of Advanced Research*, *5*(4), 491–497. doi:10.1016/j.jare.2014.02.006 PMID:25685517

Gamundani, A. M. (2015, May). An impact review on internet of things attacks. In 2015 international conference on emerging trends in networks and computer communications (ETNCC) (pp. 114-118). IEEE. doi:10.1109/ETNCC.2015.7184819

Gaurav, A., Gupta, B. B., & Panigrahi, P. K. (2023). A comprehensive survey on machine learning approaches for malware detection in IoT-based enterprise information system. *Enterprise Information Systems*, *17*(3), 2023764. doi:10.1080/17517575.2021.2023764

Giffinger, R., & Gudrun, H. (2010). Smart cities ranking: an effective instrument for the positioning of the cities?. *ACE: architecture, city and environment, 4*(12), 7-26.

Habibzadeh, H., Nussbaum, B. H., Anjomshoa, F., Kantarci, B., & Soyata, T. (2019). A survey on cybersecurity, data privacy, and policy issues in cyber-physical system deployments in smart cities. *Sustainable Cities and Society*, *50*, 101660. doi:10.1016/j.scs.2019.101660

Huang, Q., Wang, L., & Yang, Y. (2017). Secure and privacy-preserving data sharing and collaboration in mobile healthcare social networks of smart cities. *Security and Communication Networks*, *2017*, 2017. doi:10.1155/2017/6426495

Khatoun, R., & Zeadally, S. (2016). Smart cities: Concepts, architectures, research opportunities. *Communications of the ACM*, *59*(8), 46–57. doi:10.1145/2858789

Khor, J. H., Sidorov, M., & Woon, P. Y. (2021). Public blockchains for resource-constrained IoT devices—A state-of-the-art survey. *IEEE Internet of Things Journal*, *8*(15), 11960–11982. doi:10.1109/JIOT.2021.3069120

Nidhya, R., Kumar, M., Maheswar, R., & Pavithra, D. (2022). Security and privacy issues in smart healthcare system using internet of things. *IoT-Enabled Smart Healthcare Systems, Services and Applications*, 63-85.

Poonguzhali, N., Gayathri, S., Deebika, A., & Suriapriya, R. (2020, July). A framework for electronic health record using blockchain technology. In *2020 International Conference on System, Computation, Automation and Networking (ICSCAN)* (pp. 1-5). IEEE. 10.1109/ICSCAN49426.2020.9262369

Qiu, J., Liang, X., Shetty, S., & Bowden, D. (2018, September). *Towards secure and smart healthcare in smart cities using blockchain. In 2018 IEEE international smart cities conference (ISC2)*. IEEE.

Quamara, M., Gupta, B. B., & Yamaguchi, S. (2021, January). An end-to-end security framework for smart healthcare information sharing against botnet-based cyber-attacks. In *2021 IEEE International Conference on Consumer Electronics (ICCE)* (pp. 1-4). IEEE. 10.1109/ICCE50685.2021.9427753

Rathi, V. K., Rajput, N. K., Mishra, S., Grover, B. A., Tiwari, P., Jaiswal, A. K., & Hossain, M. S. (2021). An edge AI-enabled IoT healthcare monitoring system for smart cities. *Computers & Electrical Engineering*, *96*, 107524. doi:10.1016/j.compeleceng.2021.107524

Safavi, S., Meer, A. M., Melanie, E. K. J., & Shukur, Z. (2018, November). Cyber vulnerabilities on smart healthcare, review and solutions. In 2018 Cyber Resilience Conference (CRC) (pp. 1-5). IEEE. doi:10.1109/CR.2018.8626826

Sanchez-Corcuera, R., Nunez-Marcos, A., Sesma-Solance, J., Bilbao-Jayo, A., Mulero, R., Zulaika, U., & Almeida, A. (2019). Smart cities survey: Technologies, application domains and challenges for the cities of the future. *International Journal of Distributed Sensor Networks*, *15*(6), 1550147719853984. doi:10.1177/1550147719853984

Sharma, H. K., Kumar, A., Pant, S., & Ram, M. (2022). 7 Security and Privacy challenge in Smart Healthcare and Telemedicine systems.

Singh, S. K., Lee, C., & Park, J. H. (2022). CoVAC: A P2P smart contract-based intelligent smart city architecture for vaccine manufacturing. *Computers & Industrial Engineering*, *166*, 107967. doi:10.1016/j.cie.2022.107967 PMID:35136280

Chapter 15

IoT-Enabled Secure and Intelligent Smart Healthcare: Beyond 5G in Enabling Smart Cities

Wasswa Shafik
https://orcid.org/0000-0002-9320-3186
School of Digital Science, Universiti Brunei Darussalam, Brunei & Dig Connectivity Research Laboratory (DCRLab), Kampala, Uganda

ABSTRACT

This study examines the complex array of impediments and potential advantages of internet of things (IoT)-enabled secure and intelligent smart healthcare devices (IESISHDs) associated with the shift towards enabling smart cities, motivated by the pressing necessity to address climate change and promote sustaining smart healthcare systems. This study looks at the technological, economic, and social problems that need to be solved in order to make cities smarter with IoT. It does this by reading a lot of scholarly sources. Most stupendously, it emphasizes the environmentally sustainable merits, potential for economic growth, and improvements in societal well-being that can arise from this transition. It further depicts selected case studies to demonstrate sustainable empirical evidence and provide policy recommendations. The paradigm is to assist governments and other stakeholders in effectively managing human-associated challenges to attain maximum sustainable value and an innovative healthcare future that guarantees worldwide prosperity and ecological welfare.

INTRODUCTION

The notion of 'smart cities' has emerged as a significant and promising advancement within the scope of our research, which delves into the potentials and challenges of the Internet of Things (IoT)-enabled secure and intelligent smart healthcare devices (IESISHDs) beyond 5G' in facilitating the realization of smart cities (Lee et al., 2023; Shafik and Kassim, 2023). The primary aim of intelligent healthcare, as investigated in our study, is to attain a nuanced balance by mitigating greenhouse gas emissions, which is a crucial factor in the broader endeavor to establish more intelligent and sustainable urban areas (Z.

DOI: 10.4018/979-8-3693-2373-1.ch015

Ali et al., 2023). This transition represents a notable shift in the methods by which we produce, utilize and manage resources, resulting in enormous implications for healthcare, our society, economics, and the ecological health of our planet. Explores the possibilities and obstacles related to integrating IoT technology in healthcare, specifically within the framework of developing intelligent and sustainable urban environments (Sadhu et al., 2023).

Integrated energy systems with improved sustainability and greenhouse gas reduction supports IESISHDs encompass a resolute dedication to attaining a condition whereby the net emissions of greenhouse gases (GHGs), namely carbon dioxide (CO2), are successfully offset by endeavors aimed at GHG reduction thus contributing to the well-being of the general population (Jamshidi et al., 2023; Shafik, 2024a). Achieving this complex goal requires a thorough overhaul of all economic sectors, including the reconceptualization of energy generation, resource management, industrial procedures, and other elements. Adopting IESISHDs has profound ramifications for the global environmental landscape and human life and is crucial in the broader fight against climate change (Abbas et al., 2023). It presents a comprehensive strategy for attaining enduring, sustaining smart healthcare systems.

In the late 20th century, we witnessed a pervasive recognition of climate change as a global environmental concern. The establishment of scientific research and global deliberations, exemplified by the United Nations Framework Convention on Climate Change (UNFCCC) in 1992, provided the groundwork for tackling issues on climate change (Xu et al., 2023; Shafik, 2024b). Similarly, the Kyoto Protocol represents a notable milestone in global endeavors to address climate change. The agreement introduced legally enforceable greenhouse gas (GHG) reduction objectives for wealthy nations, therefore pioneering the notion of pledges to reduce emissions (Alabdan et al., 2023).

During the early 2000s, there was a notable increase in investments directed toward clean energy and renewable technology, encompassing various sources such as hydropower, wind, and solar. The advancements in these technologies have resulted in increased accessibility and economic viability (Shafik, 2023a; Liu et al., 2023). This is more evident when numerous enterprises have integrated sustainability into their corporate plans, motivated by environmental apprehensions and market exigencies for environmentally conscious products and practices (Bera et al., 2023).

The Paris Agreement[1], ratified in 2015, signifies a substantial international dedication to mitigating global warming. The objective was to establish a goal of maintaining global temperature rises at levels much below 2 degrees Celsius above those observed during the pre-industrial era to restrict the increase to 1.5 degrees Celsius (Samuel et al., 2023; Shafik et al., 2023). The countries that have signed the agreement have committed to implementing actions aimed at decreasing emissions and strengthening their efforts in adapting to the impacts of climate change.

In recent times, there has been a prominent increase in pledges made to attain brilliant healthcare performance by the middle of the century. Several nations, including prominent emitters such as the United States, China, and India, have declared aggressive objectives for sustainable healthcare management (Datta Gupta et al., 2023; Shafik, 2023b). Likewise, many organizations adopt innovative healthcare commitments concerning their operational activities and supply chains. Incorporating environmental, social, and governance (ESG) factors is progressively becoming an ultimate aspect of investment IESISHDS decision-making (Karagiannis et al., 2023; Fahim et al., 2023). There is a growing trend among investors to seek out investment options that are sustainable and responsible, hence exerting pressure on corporations to align their operations with sustainability objectives, as demonstrated in Figure 1.

There is an increasing recognition of the significance of communal and individual actions in attaining a smart healthcare system in the future. The adoption of behavioral change, encompassing the reduction

Figure 1. Global total IoT and non-IoT active devices between 2015 to 2025 connections

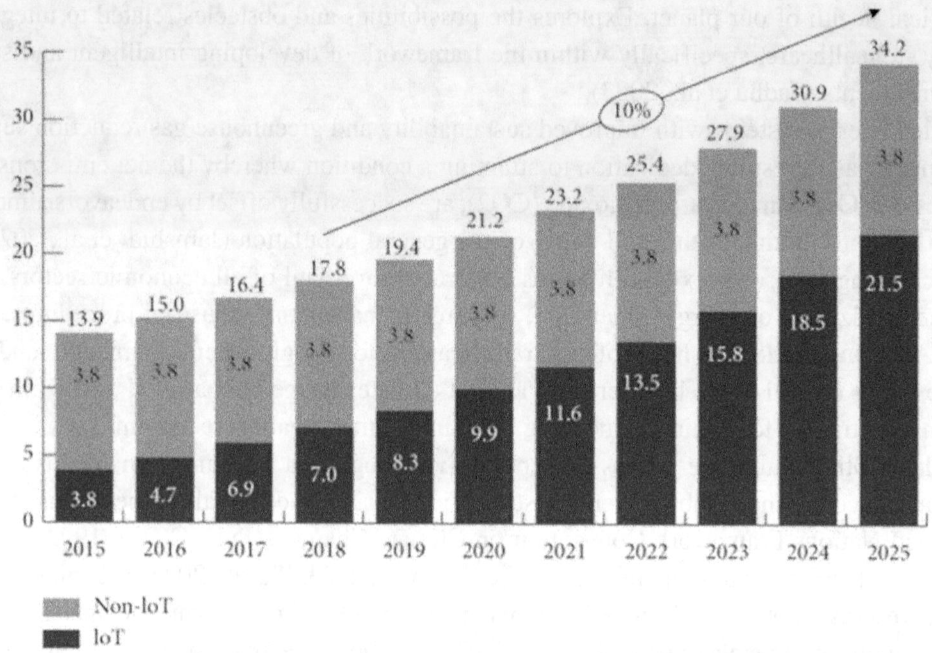

of consumption, the enhancement of energy efficiency, and the selection of sustainable transportation options, is seeing a growing trend (Karar et al., 2023; Shafik et al., 2024 Alnssyan et al., 2023). Therefore, to create a more sustainable climate and future, we must let go of fossil fuel usage in our operations so we are more capable of attaining IESISHDS because necessary technologies and business solutions are already available or almost within reach. Solar and wind are free compared to new fossils that can generate 90% electricity (Riya et al., 2023). As this study illustrates, within global awareness and readiness to attain IESISHDS, there are persisting and existing challenges amidst more opportunities.

The Chapter Contributions

The study mainly presents the following contributions as listed below.

- Discuss the significant obstacles and difficulties faced in transitioning to smart health operations from traditional approaches, including technological, economic, and social challenges.
- Explores the opportunities an IESISHDs presents regarding environmental benefits, economic growth, and social well-being. If not carefully managed, some emissions reduction strategies, such as large-scale tree planting, may have unintended consequences for ecosystems and biodiversity.
- The study stresses and discusses the IESISHDS implications in request to attain sustaining smart healthcare systems, like the extraction of minerals for renewable technologies, which can harm local ecosystems and communities, raising questions about the environmental and social costs of the transition.

- It provides real-world case studies that illustrate challenges and opportunities in the context of IESISHDS and projects on future research trends and developments in achieving a net-zero economy and their potential impact on sustaining smart healthcare systems.
- Finally, it demonstrates that emissions require deploying negative emissions technologies (NETs) that contribute to the longevity of people's direct air usage and enhanced weathering, which are still in the early stages of development and face significant economic, technical, and environmental complexities.

The Chapter Structure

Section 1.2 broadly illustrates the challenges encountered in achieving IESISHDs, including social, human, technological, economic, and other challenges. Section 1.2 illustrates and explores the opportunities a net-zero economy presents regarding environmental benefits, economic growth, and social well-being. Section 1.3 avails the impacts of these advancements and recommendations, including recommendations for governments, businesses, and other stakeholders. Section 1.4 presents case studies that illustrate both challenges and opportunities in the context of a net-zero economy. Section 1.5 demonstrates the future research trends and recommendations for achieving a net-zero economy and their potential impact on sustaining smart healthcare systems. Finally, Section 1.6 presents the chapter conclusion reiterating the importance of addressing challenges and seizing opportunities in transitioning to a net-zero economy.

CHALLENGES IN ACHIEVING A SMART HEALTHCARE SYSTEMS

In the quest to achieve an IESISHDS, where the balance between greenhouse gas emissions and removals is maintained, faces and poses several formidable challenges to sustaining smart healthcare systems, as illustrated below.

Technological Innovation

The effective transition towards an IESISHDS is contingent upon substantial advancements in technological innovation. The goal of implementing and operationalizing sustainable energy technologies, like wind, solar, and improved storage systems, on a scale that is sufficient to supplant healthcare facilities is an immense undertaking (Abikoye et al., 2023; Alaziz et al., 2023). This problem entails the creation of state-of-the-art healthcare-enabled technologies and the imperative to ensure their economic feasibility and seamless integration into established energy systems. In addition, it is imperative to emphasize the significance of carbon capture and storage (CCS) technologies in sectors characterized by substantial emissions, such as cement and steel manufacturing (Villegas-Ch et al., 2023).

Economic Implications

The financial ramifications associated with attaining a IESISHDs are of considerable magnitude. Transitioning to a more sustainable healthcare system may necessitate significant initial investments in renewable energy infrastructure, energy-efficient buildings, and sustainable transportation

Figure 2. Application artificial intelligence and internet of things in smart cities

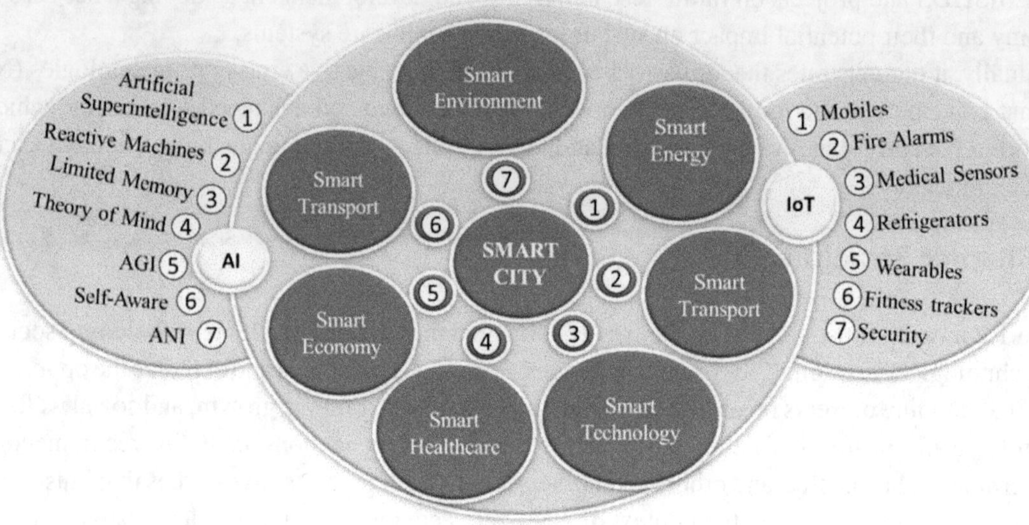

networks (Alshehri, 2023; Kassim et al., 2023). The potential short-term economic disruptions resulting from these expenditures must be carefully weighed against the long-term economic advantages, for example, the reduction of environmental and health-related expenses (Shankar et al., 2023; Shafik, 2024c).

Industrial Transformation

Industries characterized by significant scale and intensity, like steel production, cement manufacturing, and aviation, are among the primary sources of greenhouse gas emissions. Transitioning these sectors towards achieving net-zero emissions presents substantial hurdles that greatly impact human life (Rafique et al., 2023). Often, implementing cleaner alternatives necessitates substituting traditional processes, a task that may include technical intricacies and substantial financial requirements (Alsemmeari et al., 2023). It is imperious for industries to allocate resources towards advancing research, development, and expanding technologies like carbon capture, hydrogen production, and sustainable materials in fourteen growing sector countries, as presented in Figure 2.

Behavioral Change

This encompasses strategies at individual and societal levels like minimizing energy usage for healthcare, promoting the utilization of public transportation for sick people who might not be accepted by the public, embracing sustainable dietary practices, and mitigating waste generation (Prasad et al., 2023). Promoting and maintaining these modifications in behavior frequently necessitates educational initiatives, awareness-raising endeavors, and the implementation of regulations that provide incentives for environmentally conscious decisions and the societal attitudes and conventions surrounding consumption and waste.

Equity, Constitution Justice

The equitable distribution of the constitutional life on land and ecosystem management and rewards associated with a net-zero transition is a pivotal problem (F. Khan et al., 2023). Policy changes, such as the escalation of energy costs or the displacement of employment in carbon-intensive sectors, can disproportionately impact low-income and vulnerable people. It is, therefore, important to establish comprehensive policies that safeguard these communities and guarantee their advantageous involvement in the healthcare transition process (Dar & Kashyap, 2023; Shafik, 2023c). This can be achieved through employment training programs, cheap access to clean energy, and various supportive measures.

Infrastructure Overhaul

A significant portion of global infrastructure, encompassing power generation facilities, transportation systems, and architectural structures, was primarily conceived and developed to utilize fossil fuel resources (Ghubaish et al., 2021). The attainment of smart healthcare may necessitate significant enhancements or even substitutions of the existing infrastructure. This necessitates a substantial monetary commitment and a meticulous equilibrium between immediate expenditures and enduring advantages in terms of sustainability (Wagan et al., 2023).

Political and Policy Consensus

The attainment of intelligent healthcare systems necessitates the implementation of enduring and consistent policies that transcend the temporal limitations associated with individual political tenures, which are not the current state in most underdeveloped and developing countries (K. Kim et al., 2023). The attainment of consensus among policymakers and governments is of utmost importance to mitigate policy reversals and establish the necessary stability for firms and investors to strategize for long-term effectiveness (C. M. Chen et al., 2023). In an ever-evolving political environment, upholding this agreement poses considerable difficulty.

International Cooperation

Climate change is a pervasive worldwide phenomenon that necessitates concerted efforts on an international scale to accomplish substantial advancements. Negotiating and upholding international agreements, like the Paris Agreement, while also assuring adherence to emission reduction targets poses considerable diplomatic and political complexities that affect people directly (Ahila et al., 2023). Establishing cooperative efforts is crucial in effectively addressing transnational challenges such as transboundary contamination and the equitable distribution of resources in medical operations, as demonstrated in Figure 3.

Resource Availability and Accessibility

Certain renewable technologies, particularly those that depend on using rare earth elements in the battery systems of most IESISHDs, may encounter possible limitations in resource availability. Establishing a sustainable supply chain for vital commodities is paramount (Rahmadika et al., 2023). To address this

Figure 3. IoMT architecture with comprehensive growth
(Petrellis et al., 2019)

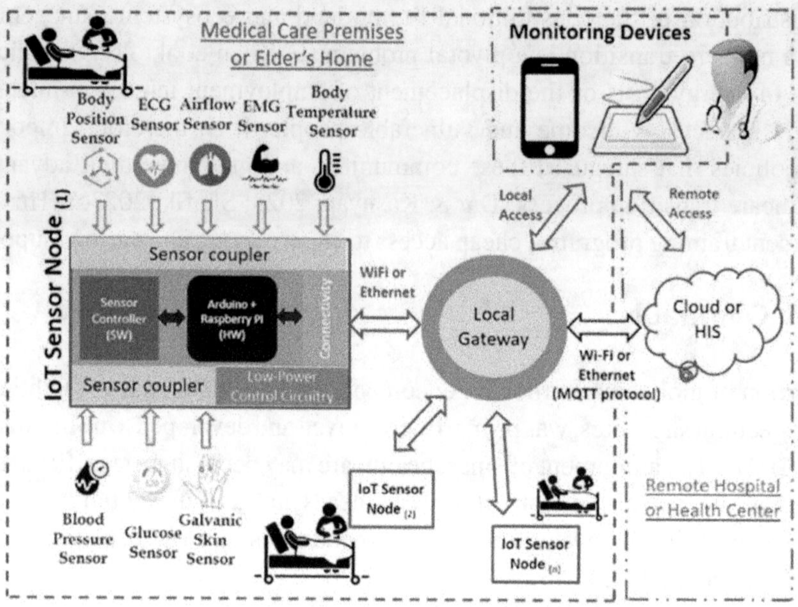

challenge, it is imperative to employ several strategies, including but not limited to recycling, diversifying supply sources, and finding alternative materials.

Natural Carbon Removal

This is one of the most complex challenges to IESISHDS in environmental management and sustainability. Natural processes, for example, afforestation and reforestation, support carbon removal (Singh et al., 2023). However, these approaches may face challenges related to land availability, biodiversity conservation, and competition with other land-use demands, for example, agriculture or urban development. Striking a balance between carbon removal and other land uses while preserving ecosystems requires several interventions combining technological innovation, policy support, societal engagement, and international collaboration (Wang & Song, 2023). Amidst all the above-identified challenges, there are decent merit indicators of IESISHDs to sustain smart healthcare systems, as presented in the following section.

OPPORTUNITIES FOR SUSTAINING SMART HEALTHCARE SYSTEMS

This section explores the IESISHs opportunities presented regarding environmental benefits, economic growth, and social well-being, even if it has not been experienced globally. Capitalizing on these opportunities requires concerted efforts from governments, businesses, and civil society.

Environmental Reimbursements

The attainment of a IESISHDS holds the potential for significant reductions in greenhouse gas emissions. A substantial reduction in the impact of climate change can be achieved through the gradual elimination of fossil fuels and the adoption of sustainable energy alternatives like hydropower, wind, and solar (Singh et al., 2023). Hence, this phenomenon can result in heightened climate stability, diminishing the occurrence and intensity of extreme meteorological occurrences, mitigating the elevation of sea levels, and safeguarding ecosystems that are susceptible to damage (Rahmadika et al., 2023). Reducing emissions leads to enhanced air quality, thereby mitigating health concerns linked to air pollution and yielding financial savings in healthcare expenditures.

Economic Growth

The move towards achieving an IESISHDS paradigm assures various economic prospects. Investments in clean energy infrastructure, encompassing solar and wind farms, energy-efficient buildings, and smart medical electric vehicle[2] (EV) charging networks, can generate employment opportunities and foster technological advancements (S. Kim, 2023). The emerging green economy has the potential to contribute to sustainable economic development in the long term, especially in areas that are shifting away from businesses that heavily rely on carbon emissions. This transition can substantially grow manufacturing, technology, and renewable energy sectors.

Technological Advancements

Achieving smart healthcare reduces emissions and catalyzes technical innovation, ensuring responsible consumption and growth. Research and development endeavors in domains, for example, advanced battery technology, carbon capture and utilization, and sustainable agriculture methods have yielded significant advancements that extend beyond the scope of emissions reduction (Alshammari, 2023). These technological advancements improve industrial production, enhance energy efficiency, and reinforce industries' competitiveness in various sectors.

Good Health and Well-Being Benefits

This IESISHD transition has demonstrated improved air quality and decreased pollution levels. This intervention yields tangible health advantages by reducing the prevalence of respiratory ailments and associated healthcare expenditures (Hossen et al., 2023). Public health enhancement yields several benefits, including increased workforce productivity and reduced burden on healthcare systems, contributing to overall societal well-being.

Energy Independence

Shifting from fossil fuels to renewable energy sources has significantly improved energy security. An economy that sustains smart healthcare, relying on domestically produced renewable energy sources, mitigates susceptibility to swings in the international energy market and geopolitical tensions (Bakkaiahgari & Prasad, 2023). This initiative fosters energy autonomy and enhances energy price stability, yielding advantages for consumers and enterprises.

Sustainable Medical Transportation

Promoting sustainable mobility solutions is critical in fostering a IESISHDS; for example, medical EVs can mitigate emissions, decrease operational expenses, and diminish reliance on imported oil (Vela et al., 2023). Implementing improved public transportation systems reduces emissions and helps ease urban congestion, promoting more efficient and sustainable mobility alternatives.

Enhanced Resilience

Communities and ecosystems can enhance their resilience to the adverse effects of climate change by implementing sustainable practices and mitigating emissions (Yıldırım et al., 2023). Resilience is crucial in protecting vital infrastructure, such as coastal defenses and water supplies, by maintaining operational effectiveness and durability when confronted with climate-induced adversities, the contemporary state of computation entailing digital health care as presented in Figure 4.

Biodiversity Conservation

Transitioning towards a IESISHDS frequently includes adopting measures that yield positive outcomes for biodiversity activities. Implementing reforestation and afforestation initiatives augments the preservation of natural habitats, safeguards endangered species, and mitigates the adverse effects of deforestation (Lee et al., 2023). Sustainable agriculture techniques can potentially mitigate habitat damage, safeguard ecosystems, and foster biodiversity.

Circular Economy

This transition ideally corresponds to the change towards adopting a circular economy model. This model significantly emphasizes reducing waste, reusing materials, and practicing recycling, effectively avoiding resource depletion and mitigating environmental harm (Z. Ali et al., 2023). The use of circular economy concepts facilitates the advancement of sustainability in several sectors, encompassing manufacturing and waste management.

Global Leadership

Countries and agencies leading in the transition towards a IESISHDS can wield influence on the global platform. Through the establishment of ambitious objectives for emissions reduction and the implementation of effective policies, these nations can serve as influential examples for other countries like UN sustainable development goals, thereby assuming a crucial role in shaping global climate debates and agreements (Sadhu et al., 2023). These goals will generally positively impact the climate and save lives on land and below water.

Figure 4. The current state of computation entails digital health care
(Quy et al., 2022)

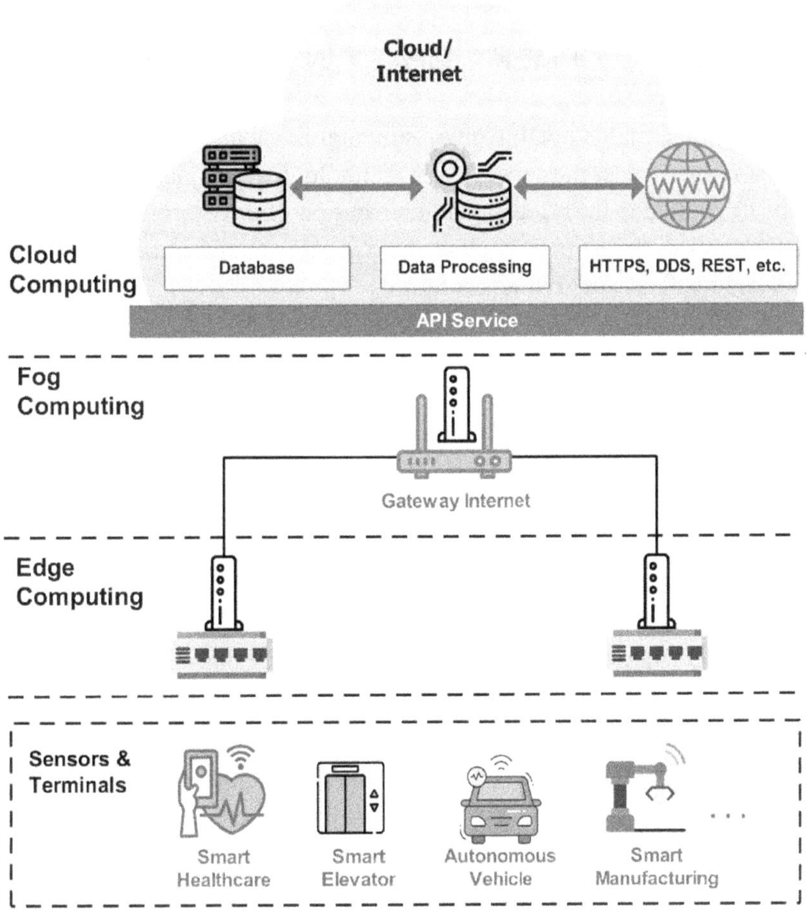

Social and Corporate Equity

The establishment of a IESISHDS presents potential avenues for addressing issues related to social fairness. Implementing equitable policies can effectively facilitate the inclusion of vulnerable populations in the transition process, enabling them to avail themselves of the advantages of clean energy, green employment opportunities, and inexpensive, energy-efficient housing (Villegas-Ch et al., 2023). These policies mitigate inequities and foster an inclusive approach to sustaining smart healthcare systems.

Sustainable and Precision Agriculture

Agriculture or farming has a substantial role in emissions generation, but adopting sustainable and artificial intelligence-assisted farming techniques has the potential to trap carbon effectively, mitigate water use, and mitigate pollutants (Alshehri, 2023). The transition towards a net-zero economy entails promoting techniques that guarantee global food security, foster sustainable, intelligent healthcare systems, and stimulate rural economic development by early plant disease detection and classification (F. Khan et al., 2023).

TECHNOLOGICAL DEVELOPMENT IMPACT IN ENVIRONMENTAL CONTEXT

The process of transitioning entails notable environmental advantages; nonetheless, it is not devoid of obstacles. These factors encompass the necessity for technological advancements, economic adaptations, and fair regulations to guarantee the widespread distribution of environmental and societal advantages (Jiang et al., 2023). However, as illustrated below, the transition signifies a crucial milestone in pursuing a more sustainable and resilient environmental future.

Mitigating Climate Change

Global temperatures are stabilized by substantially reducing greenhouse gas emissions, specifically carbon dioxide (CO2) from fossil fuels, industry, and land use. Consequently, it mitigates the severity and occurrence rate of extreme meteorological phenomena, such as storms, droughts, and heat waves (Ahmed et al., 2023; Singh and Park, 2022). Moreover, it decelerates the inevitable increase in sea level, safeguarding coastal communities and ecosystems. The mitigation of greenhouse gas emissions additionally serves to mitigate the negative impacts on biodiversity and minimize ocean acidification, thereby protecting marine ecosystems (Ghosh & Ghosh, 2023). Thus contributing to the UN's sustainable development climate action goal.

Air Quality Improvement

The shift from fossil fuels to clean energy sources significantly impacts air quality. The immediate and long-term advantages for public health are evident when there is a decrease in the release of harmful pollutants, for example, nitrogen oxides (NOx) and sulfur dioxide (SO2) particulate matter (Tian et al., 2023). Enhancements in air quality have been observed to result in a reduction in respiratory ailments, a decrease in healthcare expenses, and an overall improvement in the well-being of both the environment and human beings (Mu et al., 2023). It mitigates the production of ground-level ozone, a significant constituent of smog, enhancing respiratory well-being inside metropolitan regions, thus ensuring good health and well-being for humans.

Renewable Energy Expansion

Achieving a net-zero economy necessitates a rapid and widespread expansion of renewable energy sources, such as wind, solar, and hydropower. This clean energy transition reduces carbon emissions and curtails dependence on finite fossil fuel resources (Chang et al., 2023). It mitigates the environmental degradation associated with resource extraction, transportation, and combustion, lessening the strain on ecosystems and habitats.

Carbon Removal and Capture

These technologies can extract surplus carbon dioxide from the environment or collect emissions directly from the source, explicitly targeting the cement and steel production sectors. Through the carbon sequestration process, these methodologies can potentially mitigate some of the carbon emissions that have occurred (Lakhan et al., 2023). This has the potential to enhance the well-being of ecosystems and reinforce the effectiveness of natural carbon sinks like forests and wetlands.

Conservation of Natural Habitats

The endeavor to achieve net-zero emissions often entails the adoption of reforestation, afforestation, and sustainable land-use approaches. These efforts contribute to conserving natural habitats, protecting endangered species, and promoting biodiversity (S. E. Ali et al., 2023; Ullah et al., 2023). By actively mitigating deforestation, habitat destruction, and land degradation, individuals and groups play a crucial role in preserving and enhancing ecosystem health while ensuring the protection of places with high levels of biodiversity.

Circular Economy Promotion

The transition towards achieving an IESISHDS regularly corresponds with the fundamental concepts of a circular economy that is supposed to advocate for it. This involves implementing waste reduction, material reuse, and recycling practices to minimize the environmental consequences of resource extraction and production procedures. Promoting circularity in the transition to net-zero emissions leads to developing more sustainable consumption and production patterns, mitigating resource depletion, and minimizing waste formation (Al-Hajjar & Al-Qurabat, 2023). Table 1 summarizes the comparison within the surveyed literature.

Sustainable Agriculture Practices

These practices encompass low-carbon farming techniques, agroforestry, and regenerative agriculture. These activities serve the dual purpose of mitigating emissions from agriculture while improving soil health, conserving water, and enhancing crop resilience (Wang & Wu, 2023). Sustainable agriculture plays a crucial role in safeguarding food security by concurrently fostering sustaining smart healthcare systems and facilitating the growth of rural economies.

Enhanced Ecosystem Resilience

Integrating emission reduction measures and adopting sustainable land-use strategies within a net-zero economy bolsters ecosystem and community resilience in the face of climate change consequences (Zhou et al., 2023). Resilience is crucial in safeguarding vital infrastructure, water supplies, and coastal regions, ensuring their sustained existence and operational efficiency, even against escalating temperatures and heightened severe weather phenomena (Lakhan et al., 2023).

Table 1. IoT-enabled secure and intelligent smart healthcare

Parameters	Merits	Demerits	Security	Technology
Cross-platform Compatibility	Seamless operation across different devices	Compatibility issues with certain platforms	Standardized communication protocols	Cross-platform development frameworks
Supply Chain Security in Healthcare	Ensured the integrity of pharmaceutical supply	Vulnerability to counterfeit medications	Blockchain for traceability, supply chain audits	Blockchain, RFID technology
Telehealth Accessibility and Inclusivity	Increased accessibility to healthcare	Limited access to some demographics	User-friendly interfaces, digital literacy efforts	Telehealth platforms, accessible design
Predictive Maintenance for Healthcare Devices	Proactive device maintenance and reliability	Implementation costs for predictive systems	Secure remote monitoring, predictive analytics	IoT sensors, predictive maintenance algorithms
Real-time Monitoring and Response	Timely detection and intervention	Resource-intensive for constant monitoring	Secure communication, rapid response systems	Wearables, sensors, AI-driven monitoring
Data Integration and Analytics	Comprehensive insights from integrated data	Integration challenges with legacy systems	Data encryption, secure APIs	Data lakes, analytics platforms
Patient Empowerment and Engagement	Enhanced patient involvement in healthcare	Variable digital literacy among patients	Secure patient portals, privacy controls	Mobile apps, patient portals, telemedicine tools
Regulatory Compliance in Healthcare Data	Adherence to healthcare data regulations	Complexity in navigating diverse regulations	Data encryption, compliance monitoring	Compliance management systems, legal frameworks

Global Leadership and Cooperation

Nations and regions that achieve net-zero emissions become global leaders in sustaining smart healthcare systems. They set an example for others, fostering international cooperation and agreements crucial for collectively addressing global environmental challenges (Kumaran et al., 2023). Their leadership helps drive innovation, influence global policies, and encourage other nations to adopt similar measures, amplifying the positive environmental impact of the transition to IESISHDS.

CASE STUDIES

This section presents six real-world case studies illustrating challenges and opportunities in a net-zero economy and its effect on human life.

Wind Power and Energy Transition (Denmark)

Denmark has made significant investments in wind power and renewable energy, thereby capitalizing on the opportunity to advance its sustainable energy sector (C. Chen et al., 2023). The company has emerged as a prominent global frontrunner in wind energy technology, facilitating the advancement of novel ideas, generating employment opportunities, and mitigating carbon emissions. The wind sector in Denmark has successfully garnered investments and created substantial export earnings. The intermittent nature of wind power poses significant issues in managing electrical grids and energy storage (Alizadehsani et al., 2023). Denmark has been compelled to establish sophisticated grid infrastructure and energy storage mechanisms to address energy supply and demand changes efficiently.

Energiewende (Germany)

The Energiewende[3] program in Germany seeks to move from nuclear and fossil fuel-based energy sources to renewable alternatives, presenting a significant opportunity for the country. The transformation has resulted in a notable augmentation in renewable energy capacity, particularly in solar and wind energy, and has effectively mitigated carbon emissions (Dhasarathan et al., 2023). Furthermore, it has generated employment opportunities and stimulated growth within the renewable energy sector. The process of transitioning has incurred significant costs, resulting in elevated energy prices for consumers (Rani et al., 2023). Likewise, Germany encounters various obstacles concerning the integration of the grid, storage of energy, and the preservation of grid stability as the proportion of renewable energy in the overall energy composition grows.

Medical Electric Vehicles and Clean Transportation (California)

California has emerged as a leading proponent of the EV movement like Tesla[4]. Implementing policies aimed at encouraging the adoption of EVs has resulted in significant advancements in technology, the generation of employment opportunities, and a notable decrease in the emission of greenhouse gases (Kumaran et al., 2023). The state's prominent role in the advancement of environmentally friendly transportation has had significant ramifications on a global scale. The broad implementation of EVs poses issues with establishing adequate charging infrastructure and effectively managing the subsequent surge in electricity consumption (Lakhan et al., 2023). The imperative of guaranteeing fair access to EVs and effectively addressing affordability concerns are significant challenges that warrant attention.

Renewable Energy Expansion (China)

China has experienced significant growth in renewable energy capacity, establishing itself as a prominent player in the worldwide solar panel and wind turbine production market. These activities have resulted in the generation of employment opportunities, the mitigation of atmospheric pollution, and the facilitation of international endeavors aimed at addressing the issue of climate change (Zhou et al., 2023). Despite the substantial expansion of renewable energy sources, China largely depends on coal as its primary source for electricity production. The shift away from coal presents significant challenges, mainly from the entrenched infrastructure and economic interests associated with the coal sector (Lakhan et al., 2023). Reconciling economic expansion with decreased emissions presents a multifaceted and intricate dilemma.

Renewable Energy Success (Costa Rica)

Costa Rica has made notable strides in renewable energy production, particularly emphasizing hydropower, wind, and geothermal resources. The nation has successfully generated a significant proportion of its electrical power from sustainable sources, thereby showcasing the capacity of smaller countries to attain a net-zero energy impact (H. U. Khan et al., 2023). The country's significant dependence on hydropower makes it susceptible to fluctuations in meteorological conditions, including extended periods of aridity. The difficulty of maintaining energy security in the face of climate variability persists (Kumaran et al., 2023).

Commitment to Net Zero Emissions (Google)

Technology enterprises such as Google have committed to attaining a state of net-zero emissions while concurrently allocating resources toward acquiring renewable energy and establishing energy-efficient data centers. These actions not only serve to decrease company carbon emissions but also serve as a model for other corporations (Dhasarathan et al., 2023). The difficulty at hand pertains to acquiring clean energy on a large scale and mitigating carbon emissions associated with energy-intensive data centers (Yıldırım et al., 2023). The persistent hurdles lie in attaining round-the-clock utilization of renewable energy sources and addressing the environmental consequences associated with the manufacturing of electronic devices.

OPEN RESEARCH CHALLENGES, FUTURE RESEARCH TRENDS AND RECOMMENDATIONS

This section presents the open research challenges, future research trends, and developments in achieving IESISHDS, and their potential impact on sustaining smart healthcare systems.

Open Research Challenges

Within this section, explicitly identified open research challenges are presented.

Interoperability and Standardization

Interoperability and standardization remain vital difficulties in the combination of varied healthcare tools and systems. With the spread of IoT gadgets, making certain smooth interactions and information exchanges between various systems becomes complicated. The influence of this difficulty is really felt in the fragmented medical care ecological community, impeding the development of a combined and effective clever medical care framework (Karar et al., 2023). Standardization initiatives are critical for accomplishing compatibility, advertising cooperation, and making it possible for reliable information sharing amongst different medical care stakeholders.

Data Security and Privacy

With the increasing interconnectivity of healthcare systems, the amount of confidential patient data expands rapidly. The task of guaranteeing resilient data security and privacy protections directly affects the reliability of intelligent healthcare systems. Unauthorized entry, security breaches, and improper utilization of personal health data present substantial hazards (Wang & Song, 2023). It is essential to tackle these difficulties to establish and uphold public confidence in intelligent healthcare technology, particularly in the setting of smart cities where the gathering of extensive data is prevalent.

Scalability and Network Reliability

One of the most critical challenges that must be addressed is the scalability of smart healthcare solutions within the context of Beyond 5G technology. It is of the utmost importance to guarantee a dependable network infrastructure that manages the growing number of connected devices and data traffic (Z. Ali et al., 2023). One of the ways in which scaling difficulties manifest themselves is in the limited accessibility of healthcare services, which is especially prevalent in smart cities with dense populations. When it comes to providing real-time healthcare services, remote patient monitoring, and prompt interventions, having a network that is both scalable and resilient is necessary (Khatib et al., 2023).

Ethical Considerations in AI and Machine Learning

In the context of smart healthcare, the incorporation of artificial intelligence and machine learning algorithms presents ethical issues, particularly in the context of decision-making processes. The influence of biased algorithms and opaque decision models can lead to unexpected consequences, which can influence the results for patients and exacerbate the gaps that already exist in access to healthcare. Addressing these ethical problems is critical for guaranteeing justice, transparency, and accountability in smart healthcare systems, which are crucial for the acceptance and success of these systems in smart cities.

Regulatory Compliance and Governance

To accommodate the ever-changing nature of IoT-enabled smart healthcare technologies, legal frameworks and governance structures need to be flexible. The sluggish adoption of new solutions because of ambiguities surrounding compliance is a clear indication of the influence that regulatory challenges have (Rani et al., 2023). The establishment of unambiguous criteria for the security of data, the certification of devices, and the ethical utilization of technology are very necessary to encourage innovation while also guaranteeing the responsible deployment of intelligent healthcare solutions (Liu et al., 2023). It is essential to overcome legislative obstacles to expedite the adoption of smart healthcare enabled by Beyond 5G in smart cities, which will be to the advantage of both healthcare providers and people.

Edge Computing and Latency

To provide timely decision assistance in the healthcare industry, the reliance on real-time data processing presents issues that are associated with edge computing and latency. In instances where prompt reactions are required, such as in emergency healthcare situations, the impact of latency concerns is of the utmost importance. It is necessary to put into action efficient edge computing solutions that can process and analyze data at the network's periphery (Khatib et al., 2023). To ensure that smart healthcare systems give timely and actionable information, it is essential to overcome these issues. This will contribute to improved patient outcomes and enhanced healthcare services in smart cities (Rani et al., 2023).

Energy Efficiency of IoT Devices

In healthcare ecosystems, the number of IoT devices is growing, which means that the energy requirements of these devices are becoming a big concern. Inefficient use of energy has a negative influence on the long-term viability of smart healthcare solutions, particularly in smart cities that are working toward achieving environmental sustainability (Alizadehsani et al., 2023). To reduce the impact that smart healthcare systems have on the environment, it is essential to develop Internet of Things devices that are capable of conserving energy and investigate alternate power sources (Khatib et al., 2023). It is vital, for the long-term viability of IoT-enabled healthcare in smart cities, to strike a balance between the requirement for constant monitoring and data transmission and the implementation of sustainable energy practices (Rani et al., 2023).

User Acceptance and Digital Literacy

For smart healthcare technologies to be successfully adopted, both healthcare professionals and the public must acknowledge and comprehend the introduction of these advances (Rahmadika et al., 2023). There is a clear indication of the influence of low user acceptance and limited digital literacy, which manifests itself in resistance to change and optimal exploitation of the technologies that are accessible. It is necessary to encourage awareness, education, and training programs to improve digital literacy among individuals and healthcare providers (Wang & Wu, 2023). Key elements in fostering inclusivity and maximizing the benefits of smart healthcare solutions in varied smart city populations include ensuring user-friendly interfaces and resolving concerns connected to technology-induced anxiety or mistrust (Rani et al., 2023).

Future Research Trends and Recommendations

To tackle these difficulties, researchers, politicians, and industry stakeholders must work together to establish a strong and morally sound basis for the future of healthcare and implement the suggested recommendation.

Advanced Clean Energy Technologies

The investigation of breakthrough clean energy technologies holds the utmost significance in pursuing an IESISHDS. The advancement of solar panels, next-generation batteries, and green hydrogen production holds great potential in improving energy efficiency and mitigating emissions (Hossen et al., 2023). To enhance the pace of advancement, governmental bodies, research institutions, and enterprises must engage in collaborative endeavors to allocate financial resources and offer assistance for research and development initiatives in these domains (Alshammari, 2023). These collaborative alliances have the potential to expedite the implementation of these cutting-edge technologies, thereby revolutionizing the energy sector and fostering the pursuit of sustainable practices (Rani et al., 2023).

Grid Integration and Energy Storage

The effective incorporation of intermittent renewable energy sources into the energy grid is a significant obstacle in trailing IESISHDS. The research should focus on energy storage technology and strategies for smart grid management (Wang & Song, 2023). Efficient research endeavors should prioritize enhancing scalability and dependability in energy storage systems, with the concurrent advancement of grid management technologies that can effectively handle a substantial proportion of intermittent renewable energy sources (Rahmadika et al., 2023). It is imperative to foster advancements in these domains to establish a dependable and robust energy infrastructure.

Carbon Capture and Removal Technologies

Novel techniques such as direct air collection and accelerated weathering exhibit the potential to mitigate atmospheric carbon dioxide levels. Establishing joint research endeavors involving researchers, industry players, and policymakers is imperative to facilitate advancements (C. M. Chen et al., 2023). New collaborative efforts can effectively support the initial testing and improvement of new technologies while simultaneously tackling obstacles related to cost-efficiency, scalability, and potential environmental consequences (Liu et al., 2023).

Circular Economy and Sustainable Materials

The achievement of an IESISHDS requires a fundamental reconsideration of both material utilization and the generation of trash. Current research trends should focus on exploring circular economy models, utilizing sustainable resources, and developing innovative recycling processes (Wagan et al., 2023). To achieve these objectives, it is suggested that efforts be made towards advancing environmentally sustainable materials, implementing efficient recycling mechanisms, and comprehensively examining the environmental and economic consequences associated with adopting circular economies (Wagan et al., 2023). These initiatives have the potential to cultivate a more sustainable approach to the processes of production and consumption.

Social and Behavioral Change

The attainment of a IESISHDS necessitates alterations in behavior at the individual, community, and organizational levels. Academic research should aim to explore the underlying factors that influence sustained behavior modification (Alshammari, 2023). It is advisable to implement collaborative research endeavors to develop efficacious interventions and policies that promote sustainable behavior. These activities should consider several aspects, including education, incentives, and the impact of social norms, which collectively contribute to a more extensive societal transition towards sustainability (Alizadehsani et al., 2023).

Environmental and Equity Justice

The prioritization of equity and environmental justice is crucial in transitioning towards a net-zero economy. The research trends should prioritize examining the equity concerns associated with this transformation, explicitly emphasizing its impact on marginalized populations (H. U. Khan et al., 2023). One recommendation is to do research that contributes to formulating fair and inclusive policies and initiatives, guaranteeing that sustainability advantages are available to a broad range of individuals (Khatib et al., 2023). The primary objective of this study should be to examine and analyze social differences, with a particular focus on elucidating the underlying mechanisms that contribute to inclusion.

Ecosystem Resilience and Biodiversity Conservation

The conservation of ecosystems and safeguarding of biodiversity are of utmost importance in pursuing sustaining smart healthcare systems (Lakhan et al., 2023). Current research trends should investigate ecosystem-based initiatives, such as reforestation and habitat restoration, to enhance resilience and biodiversity. The recommendations emphasize the importance of research to better understand the most effective conservation measures, their ecological consequences, and the enduring advantages of preserving natural environments (Rani et al., 2023). These endeavors can contribute to the protection and preservation of vital ecosystems and the diversity of species.

Climate Adaptation and Resilience Strategies

Adjusting to the consequences of climate change presents a complex and multidimensional task. Research trends should investigate various techniques for enhancing resilience. These strategies should span numerous areas, including developing robust infrastructure, adopting sustainable agriculture practices, and implementing adequate disaster preparedness measures (Dhasarathan et al., 2023). The significance of researching to support policies and practices aimed at improving societal and ecological resilience in the face of climate change is emphasized by recommendations (Vela et al., 2023). This study has the potential to make a valuable contribution towards advancing efficient adaptation strategies.

International Collaboration and Policy Frameworks

The attainment of net-zero emissions is a worldwide undertaking that requires collaboration among nations and establishing comprehensive policy frameworks. Emphasis should be on assessing the efficacy of international climate agreements and examining the significance of global collaboration in attaining smart healthcare objectives (Rani et al., 2023). The recommendations pertain to conducting research centered on assessing and improving the execution of global climate accords. Scholarly investigations have the potential to cultivate international cooperation, promoting the exchange of knowledge and the formulation of collective approaches to address the issue of climate change (Wang & Wu, 2023).

Business and Corporate Sustainability

The current research landscape should prioritize exploring sustainable business models, corporate social responsibility, and supply chain sustainability. The recommendations encompass research that offers valuable insights into implementing effective ways for businesses to mitigate their environmental impact, synchronize their operations with sustainability objectives, and foster private sector involvement in the transition towards achieving net-zero emissions (Zhou et al., 2023). Establishing partnerships among businesses, academia, and politicians is paramount to effectively implement sustainable practices within the corporate sector and expand their influence.

CONCLUSION

The advent of next-generation batteries and renewable energy technologies is fundamentally transforming the transition towards a net-zero future. Further investigation is required to incorporate renewable energy sources into existing power networks effectively, enhance energy storage capabilities, and tackle challenges related to cost-effectiveness and scalability. In addition to these aspects, the transition necessitates a dedicated emphasis on circular economy principles, utilizing sustainable resources, and implementing innovative recycling practices. In addition to being of utmost importance, ethical policies, ecosystem preservation, and climate adaptation are also deemed critical. The achievement of this shift necessitates global cooperation and the establishment of adequate policy frameworks. Establishing partnerships among corporations, academia, and policymakers is crucial to expand sustainability initiatives effectively.

REFERENCES

Abbas, S., Sampedro, G. A., Abisado, M., Almadhor, A., Yousaf, I., & Hong, S. P. (2023). Harris-Hawk-Optimization-Based Deep Recurrent Neural Network for Securing the Internet of Medical Things. *Electronics (Basel)*, *12*(12), 2612. doi:10.3390/electronics12122612

Abikoye, O. C., Oladipupo, E. T., Imoize, A. L., Awotunde, J. B., Lee, C. C., & Li, C. T. (2023). Securing Critical User Information over the Internet of Medical Things Platforms Using a Hybrid Cryptography Scheme. *Future Internet*, *15*(3), 99. doi:10.3390/fi15030099

Ahila, A., Dahan, F., Alroobaea, R., & Alghamdi, W. Y. (2023). A smart IoMT based architecture for E-healthcare patient monitoring system using artificial intelligence algorithms. *Frontiers in Physiology*, *14*, 1125952. doi:10.3389/fphys.2023.1125952 PMID:36793418

Ahmed, J., Nguyen, T. N., Ali, B., Javed, M. A., & Mirza, J. (2023). On the Physical Layer Security of Federated Learning Based IoMT Networks. *IEEE Journal of Biomedical and Health Informatics*, *27*(2), 691–697. doi:10.1109/JBHI.2022.3173947 PMID:35536821

Al-hajjar, A. L. N., & Al-Qurabat, A. K. M. (2023). An overview of machine learning methods in enabling IoMT-based epileptic seizure detection. *The Journal of Supercomputing*, *79*(14), 16017–16064. doi:10.1007/s11227-023-05299-9 PMID:37359338

Alabdan, R., Alruban, A., Hilal, A. M., & Motwakel, A. (2023). Artificial-Intelligence-Based Decision Making for Oral Potentially Malignant Disorder Diagnosis in Internet of Medical Things Environment. *Healthcare (Basel)*, *11*(1), 113. doi:10.3390/healthcare11010113 PMID:36611573

Alaziz, S. N., Albayati, B., El-Bagoury, A. A. A. H., & Shafik, W. (2023). Clustering of COVID-19 Multi-Time Series-Based K-Means and PCA With Forecasting. [IJDWM]. *International Journal of Data Warehousing and Mining*, *19*(3), 1–25. doi:10.4018/IJDWM.317374

Ali, S. E., Tariq, N., Khan, F. A., Ashraf, M., Abdul, W., & Saleem, K. (2023). BFT-IoMT: A Blockchain-Based Trust Mechanism to Mitigate Sybil Attack Using Fuzzy Logic in the Internet of Medical Things. *Sensors (Basel)*, *23*(9), 4265. doi:10.3390/s23094265 PMID:37177468

Ali, Z., Naz, S., Zaffar, H., Choi, J., & Kim, Y. (2023). An IoMT-Based Melanoma Lesion Segmentation Using Conditional Generative Adversarial Networks. *Sensors (Basel)*, *23*(7), 3548. doi:10.3390/s23073548 PMID:37050607

Alizadehsani, R., Roshanzamir, M., Izadi, N. H., Gravina, R., Kabir, H. M. D., Nahavandi, D., Alinejad-Rokny, H., Khosravi, A., Acharya, U. R., Nahavandi, S., & Fortino, G. (2023). Swarm Intelligence in Internet of Medical Things: A Review. *Sensors (Basel)*, *23*(3), 1466. doi:10.3390/s23031466 PMID:36772503

Alnssyan, B., Ahmad, Z., Malela-Majika, J. C., Seong, J. T., & Shafik, W. (2023). On the identifiability and statistical features of a new distributional approach with reliability applications. *AIP Advances*, *13*(12), 125211. doi:10.1063/5.0178555

Alsemmeari, R. A., Dahab, M. Y., Alsulami, A. A., Alturki, B., & Algarni, S. (2023). Resilient Security Framework Using TNN and Blockchain for IoMT. *Electronics (Basel)*, *12*(10), 2252. doi:10.3390/electronics12102252

Alshammari, B. M. (2023). A Framework For Developing Secure Internet Of Medical Things: A Comprehensive Roadmap From An Artificial Intelligence Perspective. *Journal of Theoretical and Applied Information Technology*, *101*(4).

Alshehri, M. (2023). Blockchain-assisted cyber security in medical things using artificial intelligence. *Electronic Research Archive*, *31*(2), 708–728. doi:10.3934/era.2023035

Bakkaiahgari, P. V. D., & Prasad, K. V. (2023). Prim based link quality and thermal aware adaptive routing protocol for IoMT using SigFox network in WBAN. *Evolving Systems*, *14*(3), 533–544. doi:10.1007/s12530-022-09451-3

Bera, B., Mitra, A., Das, A. K., Puthal, D., & Park, Y. H. (2023). Private Blockchain-Based AI-Envisioned Home Monitoring Framework in IoMT-Enabled COVID-19 Environment. *IEEE Consumer Electronics Magazine*, *12*(3), 62–71. doi:10.1109/MCE.2021.3137104

Chang, S. H., Hsia, C. H., & Hong, W. Z. (2023). A secured internet of robotic things (IoRT) for long-term care services in a smart building. *The Journal of Supercomputing*, *79*(5), 5276–5290. doi:10.1007/s11227-022-04845-1 PMID:36258682

Chen, C., He, D., Khan, M. K., Luo, M., & Peng, C. (2023). A Secure Certificateless Signcryption Scheme Without Pairing for Internet of Medical Things. *IEEE Internet of Things Journal*, *10*(10), 9136–9147. doi:10.1109/JIOT.2022.3233180

Chen, C. M., Liu, S., Li, X., Islam, S. H., & Das, A. K. (2023). A provably-secure authenticated key agreement protocol for remote patient monitoring IoMT. *Journal of Systems Architecture*, *136*, 102831. doi:10.1016/j.sysarc.2023.102831

Dar, H., & Kashyap, K. (2023). Smart Healthcare System (SHS): Medical Tourism Delivering, Consumption, and Elevating Tool in the Ages of Smart Technologies. *Tourism Planning & Development, 20*(3), 397–415. doi:10.1080/21568316.2022.2109206

Datta Gupta, K., Sharma, D. K., Ahmed, S., Gupta, H., Gupta, D., & Hsu, C. H. (2023). A Novel Lightweight Deep Learning-Based Histopathological Image Classification Model for IoMT. *Neural Processing Letters, 55*(1), 205–228. doi:10.1007/s11063-021-10555-1 PMID:34121912

Dhasarathan, C., Hasan, M. K., Islam, S., Abdullah, S., Khapre, S., Singh, D., Alsulami, A. A., & Alqahtani, A. (2023). User privacy prevention model using supervised federated learning-based block chain approach for internet of Medical Things. *CAAI Transactions on Intelligence Technology*, cit2.12218. doi:10.1049/cit2.12218

El Khatib, M., Alzoubi, H. M., Hamidi, S., Baydoun, A., Al-Nakeeb, A., & Alshurideh, M. (2023). Impact of Using the Internet of Medical Things on e-Healthcare Performance: Blockchain Assist in Improving Smart Contract. *ClinicoEconomics and Outcomes Research, 15*, 397–411. doi:10.2147/CEOR.S407778 PMID:37287899

Fahim, K. E., Kalinaki, K., & Shafik, W. (2023). Electronic Devices in the Artificial Intelligence of the Internet of Medical Things (AIoMT). In Handbook of Security and Privacy of AI-Enabled Healthcare Systems and Internet of Medical Things (pp. 41-62). CRC Press. https://doi.org/ doi:10.1201/9781003370321-3

Ghosh, S., & Ghosh, S. K. (2023). FEEL: FEderated LEarning Framework for ELderly Healthcare Using Edge-IoMT. *IEEE Transactions on Computational Social Systems, 10*(4), 1800–1809. doi:10.1109/TCSS.2022.3233300

Ghubaish, A., Salman, T., Zolanvari, M., Unal, D., Al-Ali, A., & Jain, R. (2021). Recent Advances in the Internet-of-Medical-Things (IoMT) Systems Security. *IEEE Internet of Things Journal, 8*(11), 8707–8718. doi:10.1109/JIOT.2020.3045653

Hossen, M. N., Panneerselvam, V., Koundal, D., Ahmed, K., Bui, F. M., & Ibrahim, S. M. (2023). Federated Machine Learning for Detection of Skin Diseases and Enhancement of Internet of Medical Things (IoMT) Security. *IEEE Journal of Biomedical and Health Informatics, 27*(2), 835–841. doi:10.1109/JBHI.2022.3149288 PMID:35133971

Jamshidi, M., Moztarzadeh, O., Jamshidi, A., Abdelgawad, A., El-Baz, A. S., & Hauer, L. (2023). Future of Drug Discovery: The Synergy of Edge Computing, Internet of Medical Things, and Deep Learning. *Future Internet, 15*(4), 142. doi:10.3390/fi15040142

Jiang, J., Guo, J., Khan, M., Cui, Y., & Lin, W. (2023). Energy-saving Service Offloading for the Internet of Medical Things Using Deep Reinforcement Learning. *ACM Transactions on Sensor Networks, 19*(3), 1–20. doi:10.1145/3560265

Kalinaki, K., Fahadi, M., Alli, A. A., Shafik, W., Yasin, M., & Mutwalibi, N. (2023). Artificial Intelligence of Internet of Medical Things (AIoMT) in Smart Cities: A Review of Cybersecurity for Smart Healthcare. Handbook of Security and Privacy of AI-Enabled Healthcare Systems and Internet of Medical Things, 271-292. Springer. https://doi.org/ doi:10.1201/9781003370321-11

Karagiannis, S., Ribeiro, L. L., Ntantogian, C., Magkos, E., & Campos, L. M. (2023). Chidroid: A Mobile Android Application for Log Collection and Security Analysis in Healthcare and IoMT. *Applied Sciences (Basel, Switzerland)*, *13*(5), 3061. doi:10.3390/app13053061

Karar, M. E., Khan, Z. F., Alshahrani, H., & Reyad, O. (2023). Smart IoMT-based segmentation of coronavirus infections using lung CT scans. *Alexandria Engineering Journal*, *69*, 571–583. doi:10.1016/j.aej.2023.02.020

Khan, F., Jan, M. A., Alturki, R., Alshehri, M. D., Shah, S. T., & Rehman, A. U. (2023). A Secure Ensemble Learning-Based Fog-Cloud Approach for Cyberattack Detection in IoMT. *IEEE Transactions on Industrial Informatics*, *19*(10), 10125–10132. doi:10.1109/TII.2022.3231424

Khan, H. U., Ali, Y., & Khan, F. (2023). A Features-Based Privacy Preserving Assessment Model for Authentication of Internet of Medical Things (IoMT) Devices in Healthcare. *Mathematics*, *11*(5), 1197. doi:10.3390/math11051197

Kim, K., Ryu, J., Lee, Y., & Won, D. (2023). An Improved Lightweight User Authentication Scheme for the Internet of Medical Things. *Sensors (Basel)*, *23*(3), 1122. doi:10.3390/s23031122 PMID:36772160

Kim, S. (2023). Learning and Game Based Spectrum Allocation Model for Internet of Medical Things (IoMT) Platform. *IEEE Access : Practical Innovations, Open Solutions*, *11*, 48059–48068. doi:10.1109/ACCESS.2023.3266331

Kumaran, D., Prasad, K. L., & Rohith, K. (2023). Internet of Medical Things (IoMT) for Cardio-vascular Disease. *International Journal for Research in Applied Science and Engineering Technology*, *11*(5), 2651–2663. doi:10.22214/ijraset.2023.52187

Lakhan, A., Mohammed, M. A., Nedoma, J., Martinek, R., Tiwari, P., Vidyarthi, A., Alkhayyat, A., & Wang, W. (2023). Federated-Learning Based Privacy Preservation and Fraud-Enabled Blockchain IoMT System for Healthcare. *IEEE Journal of Biomedical and Health Informatics*, *27*(2), 664–672. doi:10.1109/JBHI.2022.3165945 PMID:35394919

Lakhan, A., Mohammed, M. A., Ibrahim, D. A., & Abdulkareem, K. H. (2023). Bio-inspired robotics enabled schemes in blockchain-fog-cloud assisted IoMT environment. *Journal of King Saud University - Computer and Information Sciences, 35*(1). . doi:10.1016/j.jksuci.2021.11.009

Lee, H. Y., Lee, K. H., Lee, K. H., Erdenbayar, U., Hwang, S., Lee, E. Y., Lee, J. H., Kim, H. J., Park, S., Park, J. W., Chung, T. Y., Kim, T. H., & Youk, H. (2023). Internet of medical things-based real-time digital health service for precision medicine: Empirical studies using MEDBIZ platform. *Digital Health*, *9*. doi:10.1177/20552076221149659 PMID:36644659

Liu, W., He, Y., Wang, X., Duan, Z., Liang, W., & Liu, Y. (2023). BFG: Privacy protection framework for internet of medical things based on blockchain and federated learning. *Connection Science*, *35*(1), 2199951. doi:10.1080/09540091.2023.2199951

Mu, T., Ren, Q., Shao, B. L., Bian, G., & Song, J. (2023). A secure and lightweight cloud-centric intelligent medical system based on Internet of Medical Things. *The Journal of Supercomputing*, *79*(16), 18820–18848. doi:10.1007/s11227-023-05363-4

Petrellis, N., Birbas, M., & Gioulekas, F. (2019). On the Design of Low-Cost IoT Sensor Node for e-Health Environments. *Electronics (Basel)*, *8*(2), 178. doi:10.3390/electronics8020178

Prasad, V. K., Bhattacharya, P., Maru, D., Tanwar, S., Verma, A., Singh, A., Tiwari, A. K., Sharma, R., Alkhayyat, A., Ţurcanu, F. E., & Raboaca, M. S. (2023). Federated Learning for the Internet-of-Medical-Things: A Survey. *Mathematics*, *11*(1), 151. doi:10.3390/math11010151

Quy, V. K., Hau, N. V., Anh, D. V., & Ngoc, L. A. (2022). Smart Healthcare IoT Applications Based on Fog Computing: Architecture, Applications and Challenges. *Complex & Intelligent Systems*, *8*(5), 3805–3815. doi:10.1007/s40747-021-00582-9 PMID:34804767

Rafique, W., Khan, M., Khan, S., & Ally, J. S. (2023). SecureMed: A Blockchain-Based Privacy-Preserving Framework for Internet of Medical Things. *Wireless Communications and Mobile Computing*, *2023*, 1–14. doi:10.1155/2023/2558469

Rahmadika, S., Astillo, P. V., Choudhary, G., Duguma, D. G., Sharma, V., & You, I. (2023). Blockchain-Based Privacy Preservation Scheme for Misbehavior Detection in Lightweight IoMT Devices. *IEEE Journal of Biomedical and Health Informatics*, *27*(2), 710–721. doi:10.1109/JBHI.2022.3187037 PMID:35763469

Rani, S., Kataria, A., Kumar, S., & Tiwari, P. (2023). Federated learning for secure IoMT-applications in smart healthcare systems: A comprehensive review. *Knowledge-Based Systems*, *274*, 110658. doi:10.1016/j.knosys.2023.110658

Riya, K. S., Surendran, R., Romero, C. A. T., & Sendil, M. S. (2023). Encryption with User Authentication Model for Internet of Medical Things Environment. *Intelligent Automation & Soft Computing*, *35*(1). doi:10.32604/iasc.2023.027779

Sadhu, P. K., Yanambaka, V. P., Abdelgawad, A., & Yelamarthi, K. (2023). NAHAP: PUF-Based Three Factor Authentication System for Internet of Medical Things. *IEEE Consumer Electronics Magazine*, *12*(3), 107–115. doi:10.1109/MCE.2022.3176420

Samuel, O., Omojo, A. B., Onuja, A. M., Sunday, Y., Tiwari, P., Gupta, D., Hafeez, G., Yahaya, A. S., Fatoba, O. J., & Shamshirband, S. (2023). IoMT: A COVID-19 Healthcare System Driven by Federated Learning and Blockchain. *IEEE Journal of Biomedical and Health Informatics*, *27*(2), 823–834. doi:10.1109/JBHI.2022.3143576 PMID:35041615

Shafik, W. (2023a). A Comprehensive Cybersecurity Framework for Present and Future Global Information Technology Organizations. In *Effective Cybersecurity Operations for Enterprise-Wide Systems* (pp. 56–79). IGI Global., doi:10.4018/978-1-6684-9018-1.ch002

Shafik, W. (2023b). Making Cities Smarter: IoT and SDN Applications, Challenges, and Future Trends. In Opportunities and Challenges of Industrial IoT in 5G and 6G Networks (pp. 73-94). IGI Global. doi:10.4018/978-1-7998-9266-3.ch004

Shafik, W. (2023c). *Artificial intelligence and Blockchain technology enabling cybersecurity in telehealth systems*. Artificial Intelligence and Blockchain Technology in Modern Telehealth Systems. doi:10.1049/PBHE061E_ch11

Shafik, W. (2024a). Wearable Medical Electronics in Artificial Intelligence of Medical Things. Handbook of Security and Privacy of AI-Enabled Healthcare Systems and Internet of Medical Things, 21-40. Springer. https://doi.org/ doi:10.1201/9781003370321-2

Shafik, W. (2024b). Introduction to ChatGPT. In *Advanced Applications of Generative AI and Natural Language Processing Models* (pp. 1–25). IGI Global. doi:10.4018/979-8-3693-0502-7.ch001

Shafik, W. (2024c). Artificial intelligence and Blockchain technology enabling cybersecurity in telehealth systems. In *Artificial Intelligence and Blockchain Technology in Modern Telehealth Systems* (pp. 285–326). IET. doi:10.1049/PBHE061E_ch11

Shafik, W., & Kalinaki, K. (2023). Smart City Ecosystem: An Exploration of Requirements, Architecture, Applications, Security, and Emerging Motivations. In Handbook of Research on Network-Enabled IoT Applications for Smart City Services (pp. 75-98). IGI Global. doi:10.4018/979-8-3693-0744-1.ch005

Shafik, W., Matinkhah, S. M., & Shokoor, F. (2022). Recommendation system comparative analysis: Internet of things aided networks. *EAI Endorsed Transactions on Internet of Things*, *8*(29), e5. doi:10.4108/eetiot.v8i29.1108

Shafik, W., Tufail, A., Liyanage, C. D. S., & Apong, R. A. A. H. M. (2024). Medical Robotics and AI-Assisted Diagnostics Challenges for Smart Sustainable Healthcare. In AI-Driven Innovations in Digital Healthcare: Emerging Trends, Challenges, and Applications (pp. 304-323). IGI Global. doi:10.4018/979-8-3693-3218-4.ch016

Shankar, N., Nallakaruppan, M. K., Ravindranath, V., Senthilkumar, M., & Bhagavath, B. P. (2023). Smart IoMT Framework for Supporting UAV Systems with AI. *Electronics (Basel)*, *12*(1), 86. doi:10.3390/electronics12010086

Singh, P., Gaba, G. S., Kaur, A., Hedabou, M., & Gurtov, A. (2023). Dew-Cloud-Based Hierarchical Federated Learning for Intrusion Detection in IoMT. *IEEE Journal of Biomedical and Health Informatics*, *27*(2), 722–731. doi:10.1109/JBHI.2022.3186250 PMID:35816521

Singh, S. K., & Park, J. H. (2022). TaLWaR: Blockchain-based trust management scheme for smart enterprises with augmented intelligence. *IEEE Transactions on Industrial Informatics*, *19*(1), 626–634. doi:10.1109/TII.2022.3204692

Tian, D., Yu, N., Yu, J., Zhang, H., Sun, J., & Bai, X. (2023). Research on Dual-Line Array Subpixel Scanning Imaging for IoMT-Based Blood Cell Analysis System. *IEEE Internet of Things Journal*, *10*(1), 367–377. doi:10.1109/JIOT.2022.3201571

Ullah, R., Asghar, I., & Griffiths, M. G. (2023). An Integrated Methodology for Bibliometric Analysis: A Case Study of Internet of Things in Healthcare Applications. *Sensors (Basel)*, *23*(1), 67. doi:10.3390/s23010067 PMID:36616665

Vela, L. M., Crandall, H., Lim, T., Zhang, F., Gibbs, A., Mitchell, A. R. J., Condon, A., Diamond, L. M., Zhang, H., & Sanchez, B. (2023). IoMT-Enabled Stress Monitoring in a Virtual Reality Environment and at Home. *IEEE Internet of Things Journal*, *10*(12), 10649–10661. doi:10.1109/JIOT.2023.3240099

Villegas-Ch, W., García-Ortiz, J., & Urbina-Camacho, I. (2023). Framework for a Secure and Sustainable Internet of Medical Things, Requirements, Design Challenges, and Future Trends. *Applied Sciences (Basel, Switzerland), 13*(11), 6634. doi:10.3390/app13116634

Wagan, S. A., Koo, J., Siddiqui, I. F., Qureshi, N. M. F., Attique, M., & Shin, D. R. (2023). A Fuzzy-Based Duo-Secure Multi-Modal Framework for IoMT Anomaly Detection. *Journal of King Saud University. Computer and Information Sciences, 35*(1), 131–144. doi:10.1016/j.jksuci.2022.11.007

Wang, X., & Song, Y. (2023). Edge-Assisted IoMT-Based Smart-Home Monitoring System for the Elderly With Chronic Diseases. *IEEE Sensors Letters, 7*(2), 1–4. doi:10.1109/LSENS.2023.3240670

Wang, X., & Wu, Y. (2023). Fog-Assisted Internet of Medical Things for Smart Healthcare. *IEEE Transactions on Consumer Electronics, 69*(3), 391–399. doi:10.1109/TCE.2023.3253896

Xu, Y., Gao, H., Li, R., Jiang, Y., Mumtaz, S., Jiang, Z., Fang, J., & Dong, L. (2023). Adversarial Learning-Based Sentiment Analysis for Socially Implemented IoMT Systems. *IEEE Transactions on Computational Social Systems, 10*(4), 1691–1700. doi:10.1109/TCSS.2023.3252028

Yıldırım, E., Cicioğlu, M., & Çalhan, A. (2023). Fog-cloud architecture-driven Internet of Medical Things framework for healthcare monitoring. *Medical & Biological Engineering & Computing, 61*(5), 1133–1147. doi:10.1007/s11517-023-02776-4 PMID:36670240

Zhou, X., Ye, X., Wang, K. I. K., Liang, W., Nair, N. K. C., Shimizu, S., Yan, Z., & Jin, Q. (2023). Hierarchical Federated Learning with Social Context Clustering-Based Participant Selection for Internet of Medical Things Applications. *IEEE Transactions on Computational Social Systems, 10*(4), 1742–1751. doi:10.1109/TCSS.2023.3259431

ENDNOTES

1. https://world101.cfr.org/global-era-issues/climate-change/paris-agreement
2. https://www.normet.com/en/discover-normet/innovations/smartdrive/
3. https://www.iea.org/reports/germany-2020
4. https://www.tesla.com/

Chapter 16
Green Healthcare in Smart Cities:
Harnessing IoT for Sustainable Transformation of Healthcare Systems

Jaspreet Kaur
Chandigarh University, India

ABSTRACT

The amalgamation of healthcare, sustainability, and internet of things (Io T) technology offers a significant prospect for effectively tackling urgent issues in the provision of healthcare services in metropolitan areas inside smart cities. The present research investigates the incorporation of IoT technology in order to advance environmental sustainability, augment healthcare accessibility, and boost health outcomes within the framework of smart city endeavors. This study seeks to enhance our comprehension of the interconnections between green healthcare and smart city development by employing a comprehensive strategy that includes healthcare delivery, technology innovation, urban planning, and community involvement. The research taxonomy encompasses multiple dimensions of the study, such as the examination of environmental sustainability in healthcare, the use of IoT applications, the integration of smart city infrastructure, policy and governance considerations, community participation, health equity, and effect evaluation. This research aims to clarify the intricacies of green healthcare in smart cities and develop strategies for improving sustainability, equality, and resilience in urban healthcare systems by analyzing these characteristics. This study's findings represent a valuable contribution to the academic conversation surrounding green healthcare, IoT technology, and the development of smart cities. The study provides practical recommendations that may be implemented by policymakers, healthcare practitioners, technology developers, urban planners, and community stakeholders. This project seeks to facilitate sustainable transformation in healthcare delivery and enhance holistic well-being in the rapidly urbanizing settings of smart cities through the promotion of interdisciplinary collaboration, stakeholder involvement, and evidence-based decision-making.

DOI: 10.4018/979-8-3693-2373-1.ch016

INTRODUCTION

Due to the urgent need for sustainable development and the increasing effects of urbanization on human and environmental health, the idea of green healthcare in smart cities is attracting a lot of attention. "Smart cities" employ information-driven tactics and contemporary technology to improve living conditions while reducing their adverse environmental consequences. Green healthcare supports patient care and facility management techniques that are environmentally friendly by integrating sustainable practices and innovations into healthcare systems. Contemporary urban areas employ state-of-the-art technologies and analytical methods to enhance quality of life, encourage environmental consciousness, and optimize municipal functions. It necessitates the integration of several industries, such as infrastructure, energy, transportation, healthcare, and cooperation (Adi, 2020).

Figure 1 displays a few of the key components and characteristics of smart cities that have been found in earlier research: Smart cities require a robust ICT infrastructure, which includes sensors, data networks, communication systems, and high-speed internet access. It is now possible to collect and analyze data from several sources thanks to these technologies. By retrieving relevant data, artificial intelligence (AI) and sophisticated analytical techniques assist in the decision-making process (Ahad, 2020).

Smart cities prioritize sustainability by integrating renewable energy sources, optimizing resource utilization, and reducing carbon emissions. This covers initiatives such as energy-efficient building designs, eco-friendly transportation choices, and smart grids. Smart cities seek to enhance their transportation systems through the use of technology such as intelligent traffic management, integrated mobility platforms, smart parking systems, and real-time public transit information.

This attempts to promote ecologically friendly transit options, reduce traffic, and increase safety. When creating smart cities, infrastructure systems such as public facilities, waste management, electrical grids, and water supplies are prioritized. Sensors and monitoring systems enable real-time issue detection, facilitating efficient resource management and preventative maintenance. Involving individuals in decision-making is a key component of smart city development. Thanks to technological advancements like social media, online platforms, and mobile applications, residents may voice concerns, offer suggestions, and actively engage in urban planning and government. The ultimate goal of smart cities is to improve the quality of life for their residents. This entails guaranteeing that individuals have access to essential services, improving security and safety, promoting health, and creating inclusive and livable communities (Ahvenniemi, 2017).

To establish a smart city, cooperation between public agencies, commercial companies, academic institutions, and citizens is required. Trans sector collaboration and public-private partnerships are crucial for implementing novel concepts and promoting sustainable urban growth. It's important to keep in mind that the concept of "smart cities" is always evolving, and that, depending on their unique needs and limits, each cities may have different priorities and approaches. Smart city technology adoption is a dynamic process aimed at creating more efficient, sustainable, and livable urban environments (Al, 2012). As figure 2 illustrates, incorporating eco-friendly practices into healthcare facilities, cutting waste, conserving resources, and maintaining the environment are all part of the concept of "green healthcare," also known as "sustainable healthcare" or "eco-friendly healthcare."

Healthcare facilities can reduce energy use by using energy-saving technologies including robotics, motion sensors, LED lighting, and efficient HVAC (heating, ventilation, and air conditioning) systems. Solar panels and other renewable energy sources can power healthcare buildings as well. By putting waste management

Figure 1. Characteristics of smart cities

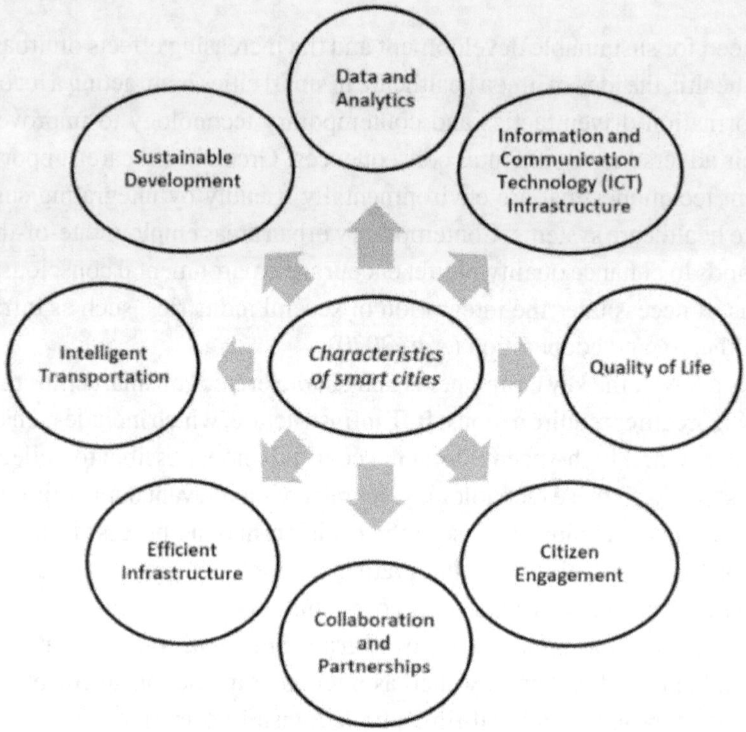

strategies into place, healthcare facilities may significantly reduce the amount of trash they produce. Paper, plastic, glass, and other materials should all have well-established recycling programs, and if possible, efforts should be taken to cut down on the use of single-use goods (Alabadi, 2022). Furthermore, disposal of hazardous trash must follow tight criteria to preserve the environment. Additionally, using sustainable building materials, like recycled or locally produced materials, helps reduce the environmental impact of construction.

Natural lighting, vegetation, and rainwater collection systems can all be used to create a more sustainable and healthful environment. Water-saving measures that healthcare facilities can implement include low-flow toilets, faucets, and efficient irrigation systems. Rainwater collection systems and gray water recycling can also be employed to reduce reliance on freshwater sources. Healthcare institutions should prioritize buying ecologically friendly products and equipment. This includes purchasing eco-friendly cleaning products, environmentally friendly packaging materials, and energy-efficient medical equipment and robots. Promoting green healthcare practices among medical personnel, patients, and other healthcare providers is crucial. Education programs can improve awareness of the importance of sustainability, the impact on the environment, and personal responsibility in medical settings (Ali, 2022).

IMPACT OF IO T-ENABLED SUSTAINABLE PRACTICES ON HEALTHCARE COSTS

A significant shift in the healthcare sector has been brought about by the use of Internet of Things (Io T) technology to support sustainable practices, which has resulted in significant savings in healthcare

Figure 2. Key aspects and practices associated with green healthcare

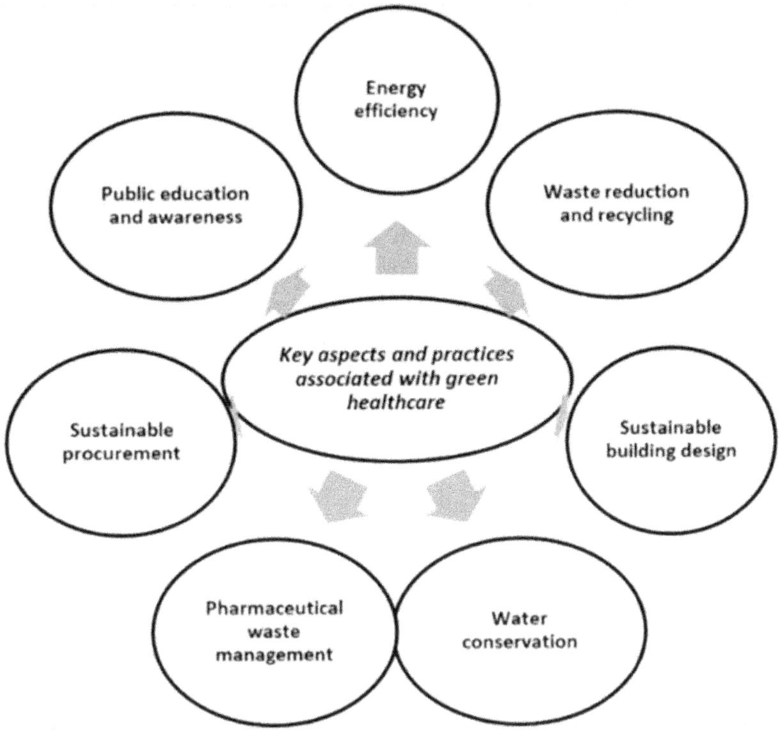

costs. By employing Io T technology, healthcare providers can optimize resources, improve operational efficiency, and cut costs. The capacity to continuously monitor and manage medical facilities and equipment in real-time is a significant outcome. By using Io T devices, medical equipment may be remotely monitored, which makes preventative maintenance easier and reduces the likelihood of costly problems. Additionally, integrating Io T into patient treatment may make it easier to implement personalized and preventative healthcare plans, which could lessen the burden on the healthcare system as a whole. People can take an active role in maintaining their health with wearable technology and connected health monitoring tools, which encourage early diagnosis of health issues and stop the progression of chronic conditions. The shift to preventive care reduces the financial burden associated with treating complicated and costly medical issues while simultaneously improving patient outcomes (Almalki, 2023).

Healthcare organizations can effectively monitor their energy use by adopting sustainable practices made possible by the deployment of Internet of Things (Io T) technology. Smart building technologies may effectively control heating, cooling, and lighting systems based on occupancy and consumption patterns by utilizing Internet of Things (Io T) sensors. This can lead to significant energy savings and lower operating costs. Additionally, the utilization of telemedicine and remote patient monitoring, made possible by Io T connectivity, can lessen the need for in-person appointments, which will save costs associated with infrastructure and travel for both patients and doctors.

In the end, the healthcare industry's adoption of Internet of Things (Io T) technology in conjunction with environmentally friendly procedures provides a thorough cost-cutting plan. Io T technologies improve patient care by encouraging preventative care, streamlining resource management, and boosting energy efficiency, all of which contribute to the sustainability and financial sustainability of the healthcare system. The objective of enhancing the industry's financial and environmental sustainability is in line with these developments (Anzanpour et al., 2015; Baskar, 2024).

RELATED WORK

In recent years, there has been a growing focus on the convergence of healthcare, sustainability, and technology, notably in the realm of smart city development. The rapid pace of urbanization and increasing environmental concerns necessitate a reevaluation of healthcare delivery systems in urban areas, with a focus on achieving both environmental sustainability and technical advancement. This literature review offers a thorough examination of current research and academic conversations around "Green Healthcare in Smart Cities: Utilizing Io T for Sustainable Health System Transformation." This study explores several significant themes, namely environmental sustainability in the healthcare sector, applications of the Internet of Things (Io T), integration of smart city infrastructure, policy frameworks, community participation, and effect assessment (Batty, 2012).

The primary objective of green healthcare efforts is to mitigate the ecological impact of healthcare facilities and operations, while concurrently advancing the welfare and promoting public health. Numerous scholarly investigations have underscored the noteworthy ecological ramifications associated with healthcare operations, encompassing energy consumption, waste production, and water utilization (Belli, 2020; Bhatt & Chakraborty, 2023). Possible approaches to enhance environmental sustainability in healthcare environments encompass the implementation of energy-efficient architectural designs, the adoption of renewable energy sources, waste minimization, the establishment of recycling initiatives, and the adoption of water conservation measures, the utilization of Internet of Things (Io T) technology presents potential for real-time monitoring and optimization of resource allocation. This capability facilitates enhanced energy management, waste tracking, and water usage monitoring (Burange & Misalkar, 2015; Chen & Han, 2018).

The widespread adoption of Internet of Things (Io T) devices, sensors, and connectivity solutions has significantly transformed the provision of healthcare by facilitating remote monitoring, individualism care, and evidence-based decision-making. The applications of the Internet of Things (Io T) in healthcare cover various scenarios, such as monitoring patients remotely, using wearable health technology, using smart medical devices, and providing telemedicine services . These technologies enable people to engage actively in the management of their healthcare, aid in the early identification of health concerns, and assist healthcare providers in implementing timely interventions and tailored treatment strategies. Furthermore, healthcare solutions provided by the Internet of Things (Io T) show potential for enhancing healthcare accessibility, especially in metropolitan regions that lack sufficient services, by overcoming geographical obstacles and decreasing the necessity for face-to-face consultations (Chourabi et al., 2012).

Healthcare accessibility, efficiency, and sustainability can be improved by integrating healthcare services with smart city infrastructure. The utilization of digital health platforms and interoperable data systems facilitates the smooth transmission of information between healthcare practitioners, public health authorities, and community organizations. The utilization of Internet of Things (Io T) connection and digital communication technology enables the provision of remote healthcare consultations, monitoring, and education through telemedicine and telehealth services. Furthermore, the implementation of smart city initiatives, including intelligent transportation systems, urban planning, and environmental monitoring, plays a significant role in the development of urban settings that are both healthier and more livable (Chías & Abad, 2017).

The acceptance and implementation of green healthcare projects in smart cities necessitate the presence of effective governance frameworks and policy interventions. The adoption of sustainable practices and investment in Io T-enabled technology in healthcare is significantly influenced by regulatory frameworks, standards, and incentives. In order to establish public confidence and uphold ethical standards in the utilization of healthcare data within Io T-driven environments, it is imperative for policymakers to give precedence to issues pertaining to data privacy, security, and interoperability. In addition, it is imperative to employ collaborative governance strategies that include stakeholders from all sectors in order to collectively formulate and execute policies that effectively tackle the intricate dynamics between healthcare, technology, and urban development (Eckelman et al., 2020; Das et al., 2022).

The success of green healthcare projects relies heavily on community engagement, as it guarantees that interventions are customized to address the varied needs and preferences of local communities. The involvement of residents, community leaders, and stakeholders in decision-making processes promotes a sense of ownership, accountability, and sustainability in healthcare programme. In addition, it is crucial to prioritize the resolution of health equity issues in order to guarantee that green healthcare initiatives have a positive impact on all demographic groups, with a special focus on vulnerable and marginalized communities. In order to mitigate inequities in healthcare access and outcomes within smart city contexts, it is imperative to employ culturally sensitive approaches, provide language accessibility, and implement targeted outreach initiatives (Fadda, 2020).

It is crucial to monitor and evaluate the effects of green healthcare treatments in order to determine their effectiveness, pinpoint areas that need improvement, and guide decision-making based on evidence. The measurement of the environmental, social, and economic effect of Io T-enabled healthcare solutions in smart cities can be facilitated by the utilization of performance metrics and outcome indicators. To gain useful insights into the lived experiences, views, and preferences of end-users and community members, stakeholders can utilize feedback mechanisms, surveys, and participatory evaluations. In order to evaluate the enduring viability and expand-ability of green healthcare projects in various urban settings, it is imperative to conduct longitudinal research and comparative analysis (Kamel & Al-Shorbaji, 2014).

In summary, the research domain titled "Green Healthcare in Smart Cities: Harnessing Io T for Sustainable Transformation of Healthcare System" encompasses several aspects of healthcare delivery, technological advancements, urban planning, policy formulation, and community involvement. This literature review offers a complete overview of significant issues, difficulties, and opportunities in the discipline by synthesizing insights from existing literature and scholarly discourse. In order to advance knowledge, promote innovation, and achieve sustainable change in urban healthcare systems, it is crucial to have coordinated efforts among researchers, policymakers, healthcare providers, technology developers, and community stakeholders.

METHODS

The present study utilizes a research methodology that integrates qualitative and quantitative approaches to thoroughly examine the convergence of environmental sustainability, healthcare delivery, and Io T technology in the context of smart city environments. To begin with, conducting a comprehensive examination of the current body of literature pertaining to green healthcare initiatives, Internet of Things

(Io T) applications in the healthcare sector, and sustainable practices in smart cities serves to establish a fundamental comprehension and guide the development of the study framework. In order to obtain valuable insights from a range of stakeholders, including healthcare practitioners, patients, technology experts, and urban planners, primary data gathering methods such as surveys, interviews, and maybe focus groups are employed. These methodologies facilitate the acquisition of intricate viewpoints, obstacles, and prospects linked to the incorporation of Internet of Things (Io T) technology into healthcare systems with the aim of fostering sustainability in smart cities. Statistical analysis and modeling are commonly utilized in quantitative data analysis to detect correlations and patterns in extensive datasets.

Conversely, qualitative data analysis approaches, such as theme analysis, are employed to reveal profound insights and narratives inherent in qualitative data. The research seeks to provide practical recommendations for policymakers, healthcare practitioners, technology developers, and urban planners to promote the implementation and improvement of Io T-enabled green healthcare solutions in smart cities. This will be achieved through a process of iterative interpretation and analysis of findings, supported by theoretical frameworks and contextual analysis. To assure the legitimacy and validity of the study's conclusions, the research methodology places a high emphasis on rigor, transparency, and ethical considerations throughout the entire process.

RESULTS AND DISCUSSION

Interview Insights

The objective of the research project titled "Green Healthcare in Smart Cities: Harnessing Io T for Sustainable Transformation of Healthcare System" is to gain an understanding of the obstacles, possibilities, and approaches that are associated with the incorporation of Internet of Things (Io T) technology for the purpose of providing sustainable healthcare delivery within the context of smart city environments. The researchers were able to gain these insights by conducting interviews with various stakeholders that were participating in the study. The course of conversations with healthcare professionals, technology specialists, parliamentarians, urban planners, and community stakeholders brought to light a wide variety of perspectives on significant issues such as the availability of healthcare, the sustainability of the environment, technological innovation, and the expansion of urban areas.

In the healthcare industry, there is a significant amount of emphasis placed on the potential of solutions that are made possible by the Internet of Things (Io T) to improve patient care, speed up operational procedures, and make the most of the resources that are available inside healthcare facilities. and emphasize the relevance of monitoring and evaluating data in real time for the aim of effectively managing diseases, putting preventative healthcare interventions into place, and devising treatment programme that are personalize to the individual patient. Furthermore, healthcare professionals stress the relevance of interoperability and data security protocols in order to perform seamless integration and safeguard patient privacy inside healthcare systems driven by the Internet of Things (Io T).

Experts in the field of technology are highlighting the revolutionary capabilities of Internet of Things (Io T) devices, sensors, and data analytic. This is due to the fact that these technologies contribute to the improvement of healthcare delivery, resource management, and environmental sustainability. It is essential to emphasize the significance of robust infrastructure, platforms that are flexible, and collaborative activities that span a wide range of areas when it comes to fully leveraging the potential of the

Internet of Things (Io T) for the purpose of accomplishing sustainable healthcare transformation in smart cities. This is because the Io T has the potential to transform healthcare in a way that is both sustainable and sustainable. A further point to consider is that proponents of technology urge for the deployment of user-centered design principles and the pursuit of continuous innovation as viable solutions to handle the ever-changing demands that are placed on healthcare and the complexities of society.

Policymakers are placing a heavy emphasis on the importance of legislative frameworks, standards, and additional incentives in order to encourage the adoption and implementation of environmentally friendly healthcare solutions that are enabled by the Internet of Things (Io T). This is being done in order to stimulate the adoption and implementation of these solutions. A significant factor that highlights the value of these types of collaborations is the potential for public-private partnerships, financial mechanisms, and policy interventions to facilitate systemic transformation and foster fair and equitable provision of sustainable healthcare services in urban regions. This potential is a significant highlight of the value of these types of collaborations. The importance of utilizing evidence-based policy making, engaging stakeholders, and utilizing participatory decision-making procedures is something that policymakers emphasize on a regular basis when it comes to the effective implementation and expansion of green healthcare projects in smart city settings.

When it comes to the process of building cities that are both habitable and resilient, urban planners place a significant amount of importance on the significance of healthcare, urban infrastructure, and environmental sustainability. Within the context of urban environments, the primary focus is on the promotion of health equity, social inclusion, and environmental stewardship. This is accomplished through the incorporation of green building design, sustainable transportation systems, and green spaces. The incorporation of green spaces is the means by which this objective is fulfilled. Furthermore, urban planners emphasize the significance of utilizing data-driven decision-making, spatial planning, and community interaction in order to design neighbourhood that are both accessible and healthy, while also promoting sustainability. This is done in order to create neighbourhood that are sustainable. In order to construct neighbourhood that are the result of a collective effort, this behaviour is carried out. In order to achieve better health outcomes for their communities, these communities have the potential to make effective use of technology that are connected to the Internet of Things (Io T).

Community advocates advocate for the application of practices that are inclusive and participatory in the planning, delivery, and governance of healthcare. The fundamental objective of these advocates is to ensure that the requirements, desires, and aspirations of the community in relation to healthcare are given precedence. They place an emphasis on the significance of healthcare services that are sensitive to the diverse cultures that are there, interventions that are rooted in the community, and activities that originate at the grassroots level in order to address the inequities that exist in terms of access to healthcare and results. Within the framework of smart city environments, community leaders lay an emphasis on the significance of education, knowledge, and empowerment in the context of the development of health literacy, environmental consciousness, and community resilience.

The data that were gathered from interviews, in general, provided light on the intricate connection that exists between healthcare, technology, urban development, and community involvement in terms of the influence that these factors have on the construction of sustainable healthcare systems in smart cities. By cultivating multidisciplinary collaboration, actively including stakeholders, and adopting inclusive decision-making procedures, stakeholders have the ability to jointly utilize the revolutionary capabilities of Internet of Things (Io T) technology. This is possible due to the fact that stakeholders have the capacity to utilize these capabilities. For the purpose of achieving the intended results, this is an essential ingredient. By promoting environmental sustainability, expanding accessibility to healthcare, and ultimately improving accessibility to healthcare, the ultimate objective of this collaborative effort is to improve health outcomes for all residents of smart cities. This will be accomplished by eventually enhancing accessibility to healthcare.

TAXONOMY OF THE RESEARCH

The research topic "Green Healthcare in Smart Cities: Harnessing Io T for Sustainable Transformation of Healthcare System" calls for the creation of a thorough taxonomy that classifies a range of dimensions, aspects, and constituents pertaining to the confluence of smart city initiatives, Io T technology, healthcare, and sustainability. This taxonomy offers a methodical framework for classifying research questions, pinpointing areas of incomplete information, and directing the creation of research approaches and plans targeted at promoting the transition of sustainable healthcare in smart city settings.

Health Care's Environmental Sustainability

In the healthcare industry, environmental sustainability refers to a range of programme that are designed to minimize environmental effect, reduce carbon footprint, and conserve resources. This comprises (Kaur, 2024):

Energy Efficiency: Techniques for maximizing the use of renewable energy sources, smart building management, Io T-enabled systems, and energy-efficient equipment to reduce energy usage in healthcare facilities.

Waste Management: Strategies to reduce the production of medical waste, encourage recycling, and put into practice sustainable waste management techniques including composting, recycling, and waste-to-energy conversion.

Water conservation: Internet of Things applications for tracking water use, finding leaks, and putting water-saving strategies like rainwater collection, gray-water recycling, and low-flow fixtures into healthcare facilities.

Internet of Things Uses in Healthcare

Innovative approaches to proactive healthcare management, personalized treatment, and remote monitoring are made possible by the integration of Io T technology in the healthcare industry. Important uses consist of:

Remote patient monitoring is the use of Internet of Things (Io T) devices and sensors to track vital signs, chronic illnesses, and medication compliance in real-time. This allows for early intervention, individualized treatment plans, and better patient outcomes.

Wearable health technology is the integration of fitness trackers, smartwatches, and wearable gadgets for ongoing behaviour tracking, lifestyle management, and health monitoring. It promotes wellness and preventive healthcare.

Adoption of Io T-enabled medical equipment and devices for diagnosis, treatment, and rehabilitation, improving patient safety, precision medicine, and the effectiveness of healthcare delivery, is known as "smart medical devices (Kaur, 2023).

Integration of Healthcare and Smart City Infrastructure

The integration of healthcare systems and smart city infrastructure enables smooth data transfer, interoperability, and real-time decision-making. Important points of integration consist of:

- Digital health platforms: When smart city infrastructure is integrated with electronic health records (EHRs), telemedicine platforms, and health information exchange (HIE) networks, secure data sharing, analytic, and collaborative care delivery are made possible.
- Telemedicine and telehealth refer to the use of digital communication technologies, Io T connectivity, and telehealth platforms to improve healthcare access and lower geographical boundaries through remote consultations, tele monitoring, and virtual care delivery.
- Health Information Exchange: To enable smooth information sharing, care coordination, and population health management, healthcare providers, public health organizations, and community organizations should establish interoperable data exchange networks (Kaur, 2023).

Green Healthcare Policy and Governance

In order to ensure data security, equal access to healthcare services, and environmental sustainability, policy frameworks and governance procedures are essential. Important things to think about are:

- Regulatory Frameworks: Creating guidelines, rules, and standards to control the adoption of Io T-enabled medical technologies while guaranteeing adherence to environmental sustainability, privacy, and security standards.
- Financing and Incentives: Providing funds, grants, and other forms of encouragement to green healthcare projects, technology uptake, and smart city infrastructure improvements in order to promote sustainability and creativity.
- In order to serve a variety of requirements, objectives, and interests, stakeholders are involved in collaborative governance processes, decision-making, and policy development. These stakeholders include healthcare providers, legislators, technology vendors, community organizations, and individuals (Kaur, 2024).

Involvement of the Community and Health Equity

Initiatives aimed at promoting health literacy, empowering locals, and addressing gaps in healthcare outcomes and access are the goals of community engagement and health equity. Important tactics consist of:

The enhancement of health literacy, promotion of preventive care, and raising of knowledge of environmental health risks and sustainable lifestyle choices are all achieved through the implementation of community outreach programme, health campaigns, and educational activities.

Equity in Healthcare Access: Methods for lowering obstacles to receiving healthcare, enhancing health equity, and tackling socioeconomic determinants of health via focused interventions, neighbourhood collaborations, and the provision of treatment that is sensitive to cultural differences.

In order to guarantee exclusivity, openness, and responsiveness to community needs and preferences, participatory planning involves involving residents, community leaders, and stakeholders in urban planning, healthcare delivery, and decision-making processes (Kim et al., 2015).

Assessment and Impact Evaluation

For green healthcare programme and Io T-enabled healthcare solutions to be effective, efficient, and sustainable, evaluation and impact assessment approaches are critical. Important things to think about are:

- Performance Metrics: The creation of key performance indicators (KPIs) and metrics to evaluate how green healthcare interventions—such as energy conservation, waste reduction, patient outcomes, and healthcare access—affect the environment, society, and economy.
- Outcome Evaluation: Establishing frameworks for tracking the development, results, and long-term impacts of Io T-enabled healthcare interventions in order to facilitate scalability, continuous improvement, and evidence-based decision-making.
- Stakeholder Feedback: To evaluate user satisfaction, identify obstacles, and inform iterative improvements and innovations in green healthcare programme and smart city initiatives, feedback is gathered from healthcare providers, patients, policymakers, and other stakeholders through surveys, focus groups, and stakeholder consultations (Letaifa, 2015).

To put it briefly, this taxonomy offers an all-inclusive structure for classifying research questions, pinpointing areas of incomplete information, and directing the creation of research approaches and tactics meant to promote sustainable healthcare transformation in smart city settings as depicted in figure 3 above (Liu et al., 2019). Through the consideration of important factors like community involvement, policy and governance, Io T applications, environmental sustainability, and impact assessment, researchers and stakeholders can work together to realize resilient, equitable, and green healthcare systems in the context of smart cities (Nimlyat, 2018); Muhammad et al., 2019; Nassereddine & Khang, 2024).

The key performance indicators (KPIs) used to evaluate the effectiveness and impact of Internet of Things (Io T) installations in the fields of smart city development and green healthcare are depicted in Figure 4 above (Pinzone et al., 2012; Silva et al., 2018; Richie, 2020).

This research investigates the impact of security systems based on the Internet of Things (Io T) and continuous surveillance on enhancing public safety and mitigating criminal activity in smart cities. This study centers its attention on the surveillance and utilization of Internet of Things (Io T) technologies within the framework of smart urban infrastructure. This includes a range of elements, including networked gadgets, environmental monitoring devices, and smart systems for handling waste (Singh & Ahmed, 2021). This research evaluates the effectiveness of remote patient monitoring facilitated by the Internet of Things (Io T) within the framework of green healthcare, with the objective of reducing the need for frequent hospitalizations and improving patient outcomes. Cities have the potential to improve their assessment of the overall effects and benefits of their Internet of Things (Io T) initiatives by incorporating performance data collected from smart cities and green healthcare. The systematic observation and examination of these essential performance metrics (KPIs) might facilitate evidence-based decision-making, leading to improved healthcare provisions (Singh et al., 2019; Sinha et al., 2021). The utilization of technology in the establishment of sustainable and environmentally pleasant surroundings is a common objective of the Internet of Things (Io T) within the domains of smart towns and green healthcare. The challenges and possibilities range among various industries, but they are driven by the objective of establishing an era that is more integrated, efficient, and environmentally conscious (Sodhro et al., 2019; Syed et al., 2021; Stamopoulos et al., 2024). The objectives, applications, and challenges

Figure 3. Diagram illustrating the taxonomy of IoT-enabled smart cities and green healthcare

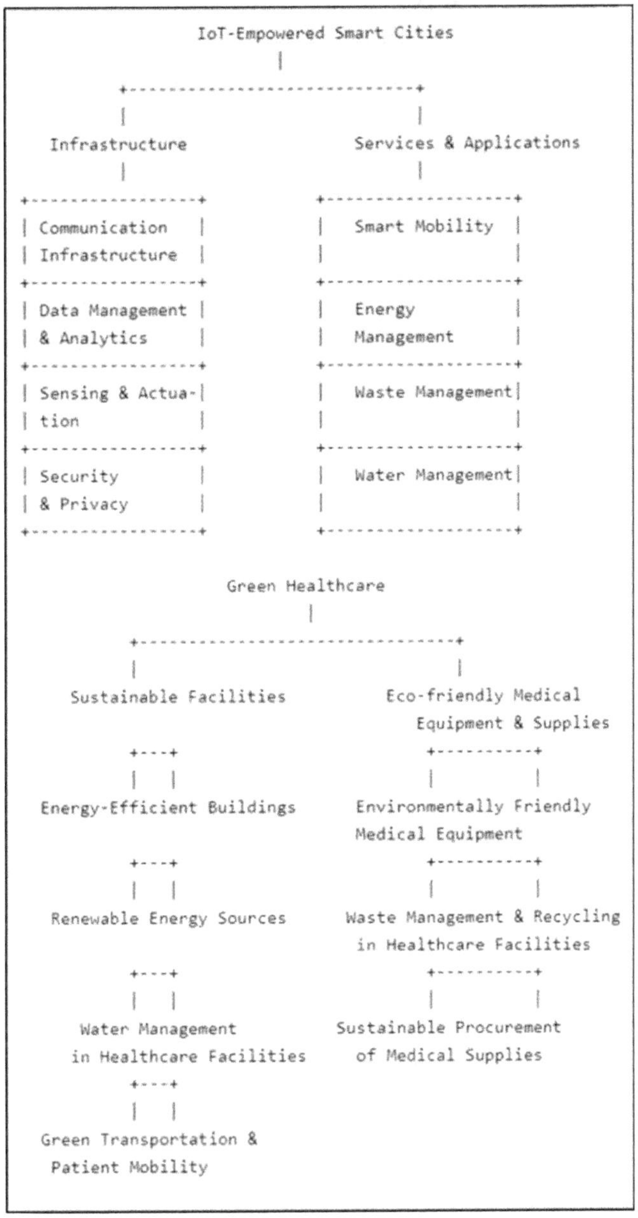

associated with the Internet of Things (Io T) in Smart Cities and Green Healthcare exhibit variations based on their distinct areas of focus, as depicted in Table 1.

REAL-WORLD EXAMPLES

Although there may be a scarcity of precise case studies or real-world examples that specifically highlight the use of Internet of Things (Io T) in promoting environmentally-friendly healthcare in smart cities, there

Figure 4. Intelligence cities and sustainable healthcare performance metric diagram for the internet of thingsL Important measures of performance

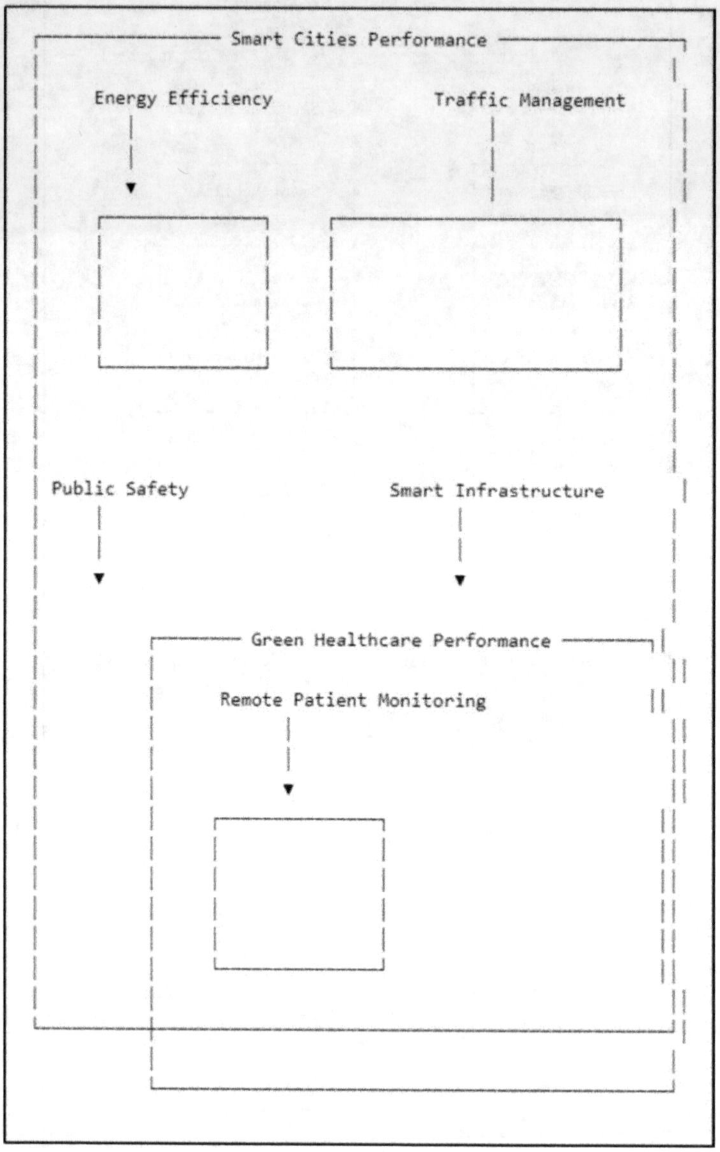

are occasions when Io T technologies play a role in fostering sustainable healthcare practices within the larger framework of smart cities. Here are a few demonstrative instances (Tomar & Kaur, 2019; Ullo & Sinha, 2020; Sudha et al., 2024).

Singapore's Intelligent Healthcare Aides

Singapore is widely recognized for its dedication to becoming into a smart city, and it has successfully incorporated Internet of Things (Io T) technologies into multiple industries, including healthcare. The nation has deployed intelligent healthcare aides, wearable gadgets, and sensors that track health metrics.

Table 1. Comparative examination of the internet of things in green healthcare and smart cities

Aspect	Smart Cities	Green Healthcare
Objective	❖ Enhance the quality of urban living, optimize efficiency, and minimize resource usage by utilizing data-driven decision-making and automation.	❖ Enhance the provision of healthcare services by using more effective and environmentally-friendly practices, such as remote patient monitoring, asset management, and energy-efficient healthcare facilities.
Scope	❖ Encompassing a wide array of uses, such as the management of transportation, trash, energy, public safety, and citizen involvement.	❖ The main focal points include the electronic surveillance of patients, the efficient management of medical assets and resources, and the creation of healthcare facilities that prioritize environmental sustainability.
Key Applications	❖ Enhancing traffic flow, implementing intelligent lighting systems, managing trash, improving energy efficiency in buildings, and implementing advanced public safety measures.	❖ The suggested remedies involve the implementation of remote patient monitoring, the continuous monitoring of healthcare data, the predictive repair of medical devices, and the energy-efficient administration of hospitals.
Impact on Environment	❖ Can result in decreased energy usage, improved trash disposal, and streamlined mobility, therefore promoting a more sustainable urban setting.	❖ Facilitates the monitoring of patients from a distance and the use of energy-efficient healthcare facilities, thereby mitigating the environmental consequences of the healthcare industry.
Key Performance Indicators	❖ Efficiency in energy use ❖ The mitigation of traffic congestion ❖ The Efficiency of Waste Management ❖ The utilization of smart infrastructure ❖ Public Safety Involvement of Citizens	❖ Patient results ❖ The reduction of energy consumption and the management of assets and inventory. ❖ Anticipatory Maintenance ❖ Sustainable Healthcare Facilities
Benefits	❖ Improved urban services and quality of life for residents. ❖ Reduced environmental footprint through optimized resource utilization. ❖ Enhanced public safety and emergency response.	❖ Enhanced patient care with remote monitoring and timely interventions. ❖ More sustainable healthcare practices, leading to cost savings. ❖ Improved energy efficiency in healthcare facilities.
Challenges	❖ Privacy and security concerns related to data collection. ❖ Integration and interoperability of diverse Io T systems. ❖ High initial implementation costs.	❖ Ensuring data privacy and security of patient information. ❖ Integrating Io T devices with existing healthcare infrastructure. - ❖ Training healthcare professionals to use Io T-enabled systems.
Future Potential	❖ Further integration with AI and big data analytic for smarter decision-making. ❖ Expansion of Io T applications in smart infrastructure and services. ❖ Advancements in autonomous vehicles and smart transportation.	❖ Wider adoption of Io T in telemedicine and remote patient care. ❖ Development of Io T-enabled wearable medical devices. ❖ Integration of Io T with electronic health records (EHR) for seamless data exchange.

These gadgets have the capability to gather health data in real-time and send it to healthcare specialists, allowing for proactive healthcare actions. Not only does this enhance patient outcomes, but it also decreases the necessity for unnecessary hospital visits, hence reducing energy consumption linked to conventional healthcare delivery.

Barcelona's Urban Lab

Barcelona has enthusiastically adopted the idea of a smart city through its urban lab programs. Barcelona's utilization of Io T in other industries indirectly promotes sustainable healthcare practices, while it is not solely dedicated to the healthcare industry. As an illustration, the city utilizes intelligent waste management technologies that optimize the routes for rubbish pickup, so minimizing fuel use and emissions. The enhancement of environmental circumstances has an indirect positive impact on public health, leading to the development of a more sustainable and healthier urban environment.

Copenhagen's Climate Adaptation Plan

Copenhagen, Denmark, has enacted an all-encompassing climate adaption strategy that incorporates Internet of Things (Io T) technology to tackle the consequences of climate change. Although this effort does not primarily revolve around healthcare, its emphasis on establishing a robust and enduring urban environment might indirectly enhance public health. Copenhagen wants to improve overall well-being, including healthcare outcomes, by utilizing Io T technology for climate monitoring, pollution management, and infrastructure resilience.

These examples illustrate how the implementation of Io T technology in smart cities can help to the overarching objective of sustainability and indirectly bolster environmentally-friendly healthcare practices. Data-driven technologies integration enables optimized resource allocation, minimized environmental footprint, and enhanced overall quality of life, hence fostering the development of intelligent, sustainable, and healthy urban environments.

ETHICAL IMPLICATIONS

The adoption of Internet of Things (Io T) technology into healthcare systems for the purpose of improving sustainable practices gives rise to noteworthy ethical problems. The utilization of Io T in healthcare can result in enhanced resource allocation, less waste, and an overall improvement in sustainability. Smart gadgets and sensors have the capability to monitor and optimize energy usage in healthcare facilities, thereby reducing their environmental impact. Moreover, the implementation of Internet of Things (Io T) solutions has the potential to optimize healthcare delivery, resulting in improved patient outcomes and perhaps decreasing the overall environmental footprint of the healthcare sector. Nevertheless, ethical issues emerge about the protection and confidentiality of data. Robust measures are necessary to ensure patient confidentiality and prevent unauthorized access to the vast volume of sensitive health data generated by Io T devices. Ensuring the ethical adoption of Io T technologies in healthcare requires a careful balance between utilizing them for sustainable healthcare practices and protecting patient privacy. Additionally, it is important to take accessibility and inclusiveness into account while developing Io T-enabled healthcare solutions. This means ensuring that these solutions are beneficial to all sectors of the population and do not worsen current healthcare inequities. In order to effectively address the ethical considerations associated with the use of Io T in sustainable healthcare, it is crucial to adopt a meticulous and all-encompassing strategy that places equal importance on environmental conservation and safeguarding individual rights and welfare (Yigitcanlar, 2015; Yin et al., 2015;Yuehong et al., 2016; Zekhnini et al., 2022).

CONCLUSION

Potentially beneficial and ecologically conscious, the combination of the Io T, smart cities, and green healthcare offers a way to enhance healthcare systems. Internet of Things (Io T) technology has the potential to make cities more efficient, environmentally conscious, and adaptable. In addition, hospitals and other medical centers may do more to put patients first and highlight the significance of environmental sustainability. With the help of the Io T, smart cities may maximize the effectiveness and efficiency of vital infrastructure and services, which benefits city planners, governments, and citizens alike. Cities may lessen their negative effects on the environment and make life better for its residents by using IoT solutions in sectors such as transportation, energy management, waste control, and water conservation. The well-being of society as a whole and environmental protection are both enhanced by participation in environmentally conscious pursuits. When it comes to environmentally friendly healthcare, the Internet of Things (Io T) is mainly concerned with improving healthcare facilities and services. Medical professionals can greatly reduce their impact on the environment by using sustainable medical equipment, implementing energy-efficient building systems, and following proper waste management protocols. Smart cities, green healthcare, and the Internet of Things (Io T) all work together to offer additional benefits. Healthcare institutions stand to gain from more efficient energy networks in a number of ways, including the provision of sustainable power, the integration of smart transport systems to increase patient mobility, and better access to healthcare services. Smart city environmental monitoring systems can provide doctors and nurses with a wealth of information on possible risks to public health and prevailing patterns. To conquer challenges like data security, interoperability, regulatory compliance, and stakeholder engagement, it is essential to stick to a sustainable trajectory. Successfully navigating these challenges is crucial for the effective implementation of Io T in both industries.

Innovative solutions in various industries, particularly healthcare, have been made possible by combining Internet of Things (Io T) technologies with the idea of smart cities. With its many advantages in conservation of resources, effectiveness, availability, and patient-centered care, the Internet of Things (Io T) might significantly impact healthcare services. The delivery of medical treatment might undergo a dramatic shift in smart cities.

Thanks to the coming together of a number of factors, a theoretical framework called "Green Healthcare" has emerged. In order to create healthcare organizations that are known for being sustainable and environmentally beneficial, the suggested framework uses smart city infrastructure that is enabled by the Internet of Things (Io T). When it comes to green healthcare, in particular, the incorporation of networked gadgets and sensors into smart city frameworks is crucial within the context of the Internet of Things (Io T). By collecting and transmitting data in real-time, Internet of Things (Io T) devices let healthcare providers keep tabs on the environment, evaluate patients' health from afar, and distribute resources efficiently. Wearable health gadgets, for instance, can keep tabs on vital physiological markers all the time, allowing for preventative healthcare interventions and cutting down on office visits.

Reduced greenhouse gas emissions in health care institutions are mostly attributable to the Internet of Things (Io T) and smart grid integration in smart cities, which in turn reduce energy use. Improved energy efficiency, power consumption monitoring, and the integration of renewable energy sources into hospital infrastructure are all possible outcomes of systems for managing energy that make use of the Internet of Things. This might lead to a more sustainable future. Furthermore, healthcare service accessibility is enhanced through the synergistic use of Internet of Things (Io T) and smart city technologies. Internet of Things (Io T) gadgets and high-speed internet have made telemedicine, which enables the remote delivery of assessments, diagnostics, and treatments, much easier to deploy. For people who reside in remote places or have mobility issues, this method offers substantial benefits. This technical development removes geographical barriers, allowing more people to have access to healthcare.

Additionally, the Internet of Things (Io T) enables the deployment of predictive analytic and AI algorithms, which have advantages in the area of early illness identification and prevention. By sifting through mountains of data generated by Io T devices, AI can spot trends and predict prospective health issues. Healthcare providers can take preventative actions. Improved patient outcomes and slower disease progression are two additional benefits of this intervention that work together to save healthcare costs. However, there are a lot of things to think about and hurdles to overcome when integrating the Internet of Things (Io T) into smart cities in order to provide healthcare that is both affordable and environmentally friendly. Because medical records are inherently sensitive, it is critical that all data be kept secure and private. Implementing strict privacy standards and utilizing strong security measures are crucial for maintaining patient confidentiality and protecting sensitive data. One major issue with the Internet of Things is the difficulty of making all of its constituent platforms and devices work together. To achieve seamless data transfer and integration, it is essential to implement standards and interoperability across many platforms and devices.

Information silos are a major obstacle to effective healthcare delivery, and this program aims to break down those barriers. In addition, it should be mentioned that the initial investment needed to establish Io T technology in smart towns could be substantial. In order to devote resources to healthcare solutions that are measurable, economically practical, and helpful to the overall system, it is necessary for governments, commercial groups, and stakeholders to develop partnerships. Also, smart city implementations of Io T technology show great potential to advance sustainable healthcare. Healthcare systems that put patients first, are efficient, and don't harm the environment can advance because to the merging of the Io T with smart city infrastructure. Healthcare providers can lessen their impact on the environment while increasing patient safety and satisfaction through the use of Io T-enabled proactive and tailored healthcare services. Using networked devices, processing data in real-time, and integrating remote monitoring capabilities allows us to accomplish the stated goal.

Security of data, connectivity, and early engagement are three hurdles that stakeholders must overcome before smart cities can fully utilize the Internet of Things (Io T) for environmentally sustainable healthcare. Smart city governments, healthcare providers, tech companies, and residents must work together for green healthcare that is enabled by the Internet of Things (Io T) to be adopted and advanced. Utilizing the trans-formative potential of the Internet of Things in smart cities can make the delivery of environmentally friendly healthcare both feasible and livable. In addition to protecting the environment for years to come, this will boost human health in general.

REFERENCES

Adi, E., Anwar, A., Baig, Z., & Zeadally, S. (2020). Machine learning and data analytics for the Io T. *Neural Computing & Applications*, *32*(20), 16205–16233. doi:10.1007/s00521-020-04874-y

Ahad, M. A., Paiva, S., Tripathi, G., & Feroz, N. (2020). Enabling technologies and sustainable smart cities. *Sustainable Cities and Society*, *61*, 102301. doi:10.1016/j.scs.2020.102301

Ahvenniemi, H., Huovila, A., Pinto-Seppä, I., & Airaksinen, M. (2017). What are the differences between sustainable and smart cities? *Cities (London, England)*, *60*, 234–245. doi:10.1016/j.cities.2016.09.009

Al Nuaimi, A. J. J., Al Neyadi, H., Mohamed, N., & Al-Jaroodi, J. (2015). Applications of big data to smart cities. *Journal of Internet Services and Applications*, *6*(1), 25. doi:10.1186/s13174-015-0041-5

Alabadi, M., Habbal, A., & Wei, X. (2022). Industrial internet of things: Requirements, architecture, challenges, and future research directions. *IEEE Access : Practical Innovations, Open Solutions*, *10*, 66374–66400. doi:10.1109/ACCESS.2022.3185049

Ali, M. H., Jaber, M. M., Abd, S. K., Alkhayyat, A., & Albaghdadi, M. F. (2022). Big data analysis and cloud computing for smart transportation system integration. *Multimedia Tools and Applications*, 1–18. doi:10.1007/s11042-022-13700-7

Almalki, F. A., Alsamhi, S. H., Sahal, R., Hassan, J., Hawbani, A., Rajput, N. S., Saif, A., Morgan, J., & Breslin, J. (2023). Green Io T for eco-friendly and sustainable smart cities: Future directions and opportunities. *Mobile Networks and Applications*, *28*(1), 178–202. doi:10.1007/s11036-021-01790-w

Anzanpour, A., Rahmani, A. M., Liljeberg, P., & Tenhunen, H. (2015, December). Internet of things enabled in-home health monitoring system using early warning score. In *Proceedings of the 5th EAI international conference on wireless mobile communication and healthcare* (pp. 174-177). EUDL. 10.4108/eai.14-10-2015.2261616

Baskar, P., Khang, A., Annadurai, S., Amritha, S. S., & Annadurai, P. (2024). Quantum Computing Smart City: Fostering Sustainability and Green Infrastructure With Smart City. In Applications and Principles of Quantum Computing (pp. 162-213). IGI Global.

Batty, M., Axhausen, K. W., Giannotti, F., Pozdnoukhov, A., Bazzani, A., Wachowicz, M., Ouzounis, G., & Portugali, Y. (2012). Smart cities of the future. *The European Physical Journal. Special Topics*, *214*(1), 481–518. doi:10.1140/epjst/e2012-01703-3

Belli, L., Cilfone, A., Davoli, L., Ferrari, G., Adorni, P., Di Nocera, F., Dall'Olio, A., Pellegrini, C., Mordacci, M., & Bertolotti, E. (2020). Io T-enabled smart sustainable cities: Challenges and approaches. *Smart Cities*, *3*(3), 1039–1071. doi:10.3390/smartcities3030052

Bhatt, V., & Chakraborty, S. (2023). Improving service engagement in healthcare through internet of things based healthcare systems. *Journal of Science and Technology Policy Management*, *14*(1), 53–73. doi:10.1108/JSTPM-03-2021-0040

Burange, A. W., & Misalkar, H. D. (2015, March). Review of Internet of Things in development of smart cities with data management & privacy. In *2015 International Conference on Advances in Computer Engineering and Applications* (pp. 189-195). IEEE. 10.1109/ICACEA.2015.7164693

Chen, Y., & Han, D. (2018). Water quality monitoring in smart city: A pilot project. *Automation in Construction*, *89*, 307–316. doi:10.1016/j.autcon.2018.02.008

Chías, P., & Abad, T. (2017). Green hospitals, green healthcare. *International Journal of Energy Production and Management*, *2*(2), 196–205. doi:10.2495/EQ-V2-N2-196-205

Chourabi, H., Nam, T., Walker, S., Gil-Garcia, J. R., Mellouli, S., Nahon, K., & Scholl, H. J. (2012, January). Understanding smart cities: An integrative framework. In *2012 45th Hawaii international conference on system sciences* (pp. 2289-2297). IEEE.

Das, J., Ghosh, S., Mukherjee, A., Ghosh, S. K., & Buyya, R. (2022). RESCUE: Enabling green healthcare services using integrated Io T-edge-fog-cloud computing environments. *Software, Practice & Experience, 52*(7), 1615–1642. doi:10.1002/spe.3078

Eckelman, M. J., Huang, K., Lagasse, R., Senay, E., Dubrow, R., & Sherman, J. D. (2020). Health Care Pollution And Public Health Damage In The United States: An Update: Study examines health care pollution and public health damage in the United States. *Health Affairs, 39*(12), 2071–2079. doi:10.1377/hlthaff.2020.01247 PMID:33284703

Fadda, J. (2020). Green healthcare system: Main features in supporting sustainability of healthcare system—A review. In *Green Buildings and Renewable Energy: Med Green Forum 2019-Part of World Renewable Energy Congress and Network* (pp. 113-128). Springer International Publishing.

Kamel Boulos, M. N., & Al-Shorbaji, N. M. (2014). On the Internet of Things, smart cities and the WHO Healthy Cities. *International Journal of Health Geographics, 13*(1), 1–6. doi:10.1186/1476-072X-13-10 PMID:24669838

Kaur, J. (2023). Robotic Process Automation in Healthcare Sector. In *E3S Web of Conferences* (Vol. 391, p. 01008). EDP Sciences.

Kaur, J. (2023, May). How is Robotic Process Automation Revolutionising the Way Healthcare Sector Works? In *International Conference on Information, Communication and Computing Technology* (pp. 1037-1055). Singapore: Springer Nature Singapore. 10.1007/978-981-99-5166-6_70

Kaur, J. (2024). Green Finance 2.0: Pioneering Pathways for Sustainable Development and Health Through Future Trends and Innovations. In Sustainable Investments in Green Finance (pp. 294-319). IGI Global.

Kaur, J. (2024). Towards a Sustainable Triad: Uniting Energy Management Systems, Smart Cities, and Green Healthcare for a Greener Future. In Emerging Materials, Technologies, and Solutions for Energy Harvesting (pp. 258-285). IGI Global.

Kim, S. K., Hwang, Y., Lee, Y. S., & Corser, W. (2015). Occupant comfort and satisfaction in green healthcare environments: A survey study focusing on healthcare staff. *Journal of Sustainable Development, 8*(1), 156. doi:10.5539/jsd.v8n1p156

Letaifa, S. B. (2015). How to strategize smart cities: Revealing the SMART model. *Journal of Business Research, 68*(7), 1414–1419. doi:10.1016/j.jbusres.2015.01.024

Liu, Y., Kashef, M., Lee, K. B., Benmohamed, L., & Candell, R. (2019). Wireless network design for emerging IIo T applications: Reference framework and use cases. *Proceedings of the IEEE, 107*(6), 1166–1192. doi:10.1109/JPROC.2019.2905423 PMID:31555010

Muhammad, K., Lloret, J., & Baik, S. W. (2019). Intelligent and energy-efficient data prioritization in green smart cities: Current challenges and future directions. *IEEE Communications Magazine, 57*(2), 60–65. doi:10.1109/MCOM.2018.1800371

Nassereddine, M., & Khang, A. (2024). Applications of Internet of Things (Io T) in smart cities. In *Advanced Io T Technologies and Applications in the Industry 4.0 Digital Economy* (pp. 109–136). CRC Press.

Nimlyat, P. S. (2018). Indoor environmental quality performance and occupants' satisfaction [IEQPOS] as assessment criteria for green healthcare building rating. *Building and Environment*, *144*, 598–610. doi:10.1016/j.buildenv.2018.09.003

Pinzone, M., Lettieri, E., & Masella, C. (2012). Sustainability in healthcare: Combining organizational and architectural levers. *International Journal of Engineering Business Management*, *4*, 38. doi:10.5772/54841

Richie, C. (2020). Can United States healthcare become environmentally sustainable? towards green healthcare reform. *The Journal of Law, Medicine & Ethics*, *48*(4), 643–652. doi:10.1177/1073110520979371 PMID:33404336

Silva, B. N., Khan, M., & Han, K. (2018). Towards sustainable smart cities: A review of trends, architectures, components, and open challenges in smart cities. *Sustainable Cities and Society*, *38*, 697–713. doi:10.1016/j.scs.2018.01.053

Singh, M., & Ahmed, S. (2021). Io T based smart water management systems: A systematic review. *Materials Today: Proceedings*, *46*, 5211–5218. doi:10.1016/j.matpr.2020.08.588

Singh, P., Dixit, V., & Kaur, J. (2019). Green healthcare for smart cities. *Green and Smart Technologies for Smart Cities*, 91-130.

Sinha, M., Chacko, E., Makhija, P., & Pramanik, S. (2021). Energy-Efficient smart cities with green internet of things. *Green Technological Innovation for Sustainable Smart Societies: Post Pandemic Era,* 345-361.

Sodhro, A. H., Pirbhulal, S., Luo, Z., & De Albuquerque, V. H. C. (2019). Towards an optimal resource management for Io T based Green and sustainable smart cities. *Journal of Cleaner Production*, *220*, 1167–1179. doi:10.1016/j.jclepro.2019.01.188

Stamopoulos, D., Dimas, P., Siokas, G., & Siokas, E. (2024). Getting smart or going green? Quantifying the Smart City Industry's economic impact and potential for sustainable growth. *Cities (London, England)*, *144*, 104612. doi:10.1016/j.cities.2023.104612

Sudha, C. N., Nayahi, J. J. V., Saravanan, S., & Renugadevi, N. (2024). The Future of Sustainable Green Smart Cities. In *Green Computing for Sustainable Smart Cities* (pp. 313–340). CRC Press. doi:10.1201/9781003388814-16

Syed, A. S., Sierra-Sosa, D., Kumar, A., & Elmaghraby, A. (2021). Io T in smart cities: A survey of technologies, practices and challenges. *Smart Cities*, *4*(2), 429–475. doi:10.3390/smartcities4020024

Tomar, P., & Kaur, G. (Eds.). (2019). *Green and smart technologies for smart cities*. CRC Press. doi:10.1201/9780429454837

Ullo, S. L., & Sinha, G. R. (2020). Advances in smart environment monitoring systems using Io T and sensors. *Sensors (Basel)*, *20*(11), 3113. doi:10.3390/s20113113 PMID:32486411

Yigitcanlar, T. (2015). Smart cities: An effective urban development and management model? *Australian Plants*, *52*(1), 27–34. doi:10.1080/07293682.2015.1019752

Yin, C., Xiong, Z., Chen, H., Wang, J., Cooper, D., & David, B. (2015). A literature survey on smart cities. *Science China. Information Sciences*, *58*(10), 1–18. doi:10.1007/s11432-015-5397-4

Yuehong, Y. I. N., Zeng, Y., Chen, X., & Fan, Y. (2016). The internet of things in healthcare: An overview. *Journal of Industrial Information Integration*, *1*, 3–13. doi:10.1016/j.jii.2016.03.004

Zekhnini, K., Cherrafi, A., Bouhaddou, I., Chaouni Benabdellah, A., & Bag, S. (2022). A model integrating lean and green practices for viable, sustainable, and digital supply chain performance. *International Journal of Production Research*, *60*(21), 6529–6555. doi:10.1080/00207543.2021.1994164

Chapter 17
Sustainable Smart Transportation:
Technologies, Benefits, Challenges to Urbanisation Concept

Chandan Kumar Shiva
SR University, India

B. Vedik
SR University, India

Geetha Manoharan
https://orcid.org/0000-0002-8644-8871
SR University, India

ABSTRACT

In smart city planning and development, smart transportation integrates advanced technology with traditional transportation systems to maximise sustainability, safety, and efficiency. Intelligent transportation systems collect and analyse vehicle movement, traffic patterns, and other data using sensors, data analytics, and AI. This data can then be utilised to optimise transport systems, decreasing emissions, enhancing safety, alleviating traffic, and boosting quality of life. Intelligent transport, which improves transport network sustainability, efficiency, and security, could transform urban mobility, and elevate living standards. In this chapter, intelligent transportation systems and their benefits are extensively covered. Mobility-as-a-service platforms, connected and autonomous vehicles, and intelligent transportation networks are investigated as emerging transportation technologies. This chapter also discusses the policies and norms needed to install intelligent transport systems and the obstacles to their implementation.

DOI: 10.4018/979-8-3693-2373-1.ch017

INTRODUCTION

"Smart transportation" is the term used to describe the integration of advanced technologies into traditional transportation systems with the intention of improving them. Concurrently enhancing the safety, efficiency, and sustainability of conveyance is the aim of these technologies, which are designed to optimize the user experience. The components of smart transportation systems (Jan et al., 2019; Saarika et al., 2017) include intelligent transportation systems, connected and autonomous vehicles, and mobility-as-a-service platforms. There are numerous benefits to intelligent transportation. The aforementioned benefits include improved road safety, reduced traffic congestion, average emissions, and universal transportation service accessibility. Moreover, intelligent transportation has the potential to yield cost reductions and improved service quality by enhancing the overall efficiency of transportation networks (Dewi & Putra, 2021; Jimenez, 2018). However, there are various challenges that hinder the successful integration of intelligent transportation systems. Impediments to the implementation of intelligent transportation systems include technological challenges, infrastructure requirements, regulatory and policy barriers, and societal acceptance issues. To guarantee the secure, efficient, and equitable implementation of intelligent transportation systems (Aamir et al., 2019; Fantin Irudaya Raj & Appadurai, 2022), it is critical that policymakers and transportation stakeholders work together to effectively address these challenges.

The benefits that intelligent transportation systems, the transformational technologies that support this industry, and intelligent transportation systems themselves are examined in detail in this chapter. The paper also investigates the policies and regulations that are crucial for the successful deployment of intelligent transportation systems, in addition to the obstacles and difficulties that arise during their implementation. Case studies of successfully implemented smart transportation systems from around the world conclude the chapter.

Motivation

The purpose of this chapter is to provide a comprehensive overview of the latest developments and emerging trends in the field of transportation technology with respect to intelligent transportation. The purpose of this chapter is to analyze the profound and far-reaching effects that various technologies have had on the movement of people and goods, in addition to the benefits and challenges that these technologies present. Furthermore, the report examines the function of diverse stakeholders in promoting the execution of intelligent transportation solutions, as well as the requisite policies and regulations that support this process.

The primary aim of this chapter is to provide a valuable resource for industry professionals, policymakers, and researchers who have an interest in intelligent transportation. This chapter serves as an introductory overview of the latest developments and trends in the field, laying the groundwork for subsequent analyses and inquiries. Moreover, the chapter provides insightful viewpoints regarding the challenges and opportunities associated with the implementation of intelligent transportation solutions. The implications of these insights for policy and industry-level decision-making are substantial.

Contribution

The chapter's contribution pertaining to intelligent transportation is threefold:

The chapter commences by conducting a comprehensive examination of the diverse technologies that are revolutionizing the transportation sector. This includes, among other innovations, a comprehensive discussion of autonomous vehicles, intelligent infrastructure, and mobility-as-a-service platforms. Through an analysis of the advantages and difficulties linked to these technologies, the chapter imparts significant perspectives on the trajectory of transportation in the future.

The chapter then examines the regulations and policies required to facilitate the implementation of intelligent transportation solutions. This includes an examination of funding mechanisms, public-private partnerships, and government policies, regulations, and standards. The chapter advises policymakers and industry professionals by delineating the critical elements that are indispensable for facilitating the implementation of intelligent transportation solutions.

The chapter concludes with a collection of case studies showcasing intelligent transportation initiatives from various countries. The chapter demonstrates how smart transportation solutions can be practically implemented through the analysis of successful initiatives like Singapore's Smart Mobility 2030 and London's Congestion Charge. This can inspire forthcoming smart transportation initiatives and aid in the formation of policies and industries that make decisions.

Definition of Smart Transportation

Intelligent transportation systems (ITS), alternatively referred to as smart transportation, encompass the amalgamation of cutting-edge communication systems and technologies with conventional transportation infrastructure and vehicles. In addition to enhancing the overall user experience, smart transportation aims to improve the security, efficiency, and sustainability of transportation networks (Fantin Irudaya Raj & Appadurai, 2022; Zichichi et al., 2020).

Smart transportation fundamentally entails the acquisition, processing, and distribution of data pertaining to transportation. This includes information on weather patterns, traffic flow, vehicle location, and road conditions, among other things. Through real-time analysis and interpretation of this data, it is possible to optimize transportation systems with the aim of enhancing safety, efficiency, and sustainability (Boukerche & Coutinho, 2019; Yan et al., 2020).

Intelligent transportation systems comprise a variety of technologies, including mobility-as-a-service platforms, intelligent transportation systems, and connected and autonomous vehicles. By virtue of their communication systems and sensors, connected vehicles are capable of exchanging information with other vehicles and transportation infrastructure, including road signs and traffic signals. This capability empowers vehicles to avoid collisions by adapting to shifting traffic conditions (Mrityunjaya et al., 2017; Zantalis et al., 2019).

Autonomous vehicles, also known as self-driving automobiles, navigate roads and make decisions without human intervention by utilizing sophisticated sensors and artificial intelligence. This technology possesses the capacity to substantially enhance road safety and efficiency, while also expanding transportation accessibility for individuals incapable of operating a motor vehicle.

Figure 1. The three key transportations essentially for a smart city

Optimization of transportation networks through the utilization of communication technologies and data analytics constitutes ITS. This includes freight logistics, traffic management, and transit operations systems. ITS can enhance safety, reduce congestion, and optimize traffic flow through the utilization of real-time data (Azgomi & Jamshidi, 2018; Ding et al., 2015).

Mobility-as-a-service (MaaS) platforms offer a unified interface through which users can access a variety of transportation alternatives, including bike sharing, ride-sharing, and public transportation. This can contribute to the reduction of single-occupancy vehicles on the road and the improvement of universal transportation accessibility (Möller & Vakilzadian, 2016; Shukla et al., 2016).

In essence, intelligent transportation comprises a collection of communication and technological systems designed to enhance the sustainability, efficiency, and safety of transportation networks. Intelligent transportation systems, connected and autonomous vehicles, and mobility-as-a-service platforms are examples of these technologies. Intelligent transportation systems have the capability to enhance the overall user experience and optimize transportation networks through the real-time collection and analysis of data.

Benefits of Smart Transportation

Smart transportation systems offer a wide range of benefits across multiple areas of transportation. In this section, we will discuss these benefits in more detail (Bacciu et al., 2017; Finger & Audouin, 2019; Stefansson & Lumsden, 2009; Xu et al., 2017; Zhang et al., 2018).

Safety

Safety enhancements on roadways are among the most substantial advantages of intelligent transportation systems. The implementation of cutting-edge technologies, such as autonomous and connected vehicles, has the potential to significantly mitigate road accidents and fatalities. Connected vehicles are furnished with communication systems and sensors that facilitate the exchange of data with transportation infrastructure, including road signs and traffic signals. This enables collision avoidance and real-time detection of potential hazards. Conversely, autonomous vehicles significantly mitigate the likelihood of human error by navigating the road and making decisions without human intervention using sophisticated sensors and artificial intelligence.

By providing traffic management centers with real-time data on conditions, intelligent transportation systems can additionally enhance safety by facilitating prompt responses to incidents and emergencies. For instance, drivers can be promptly notified of perilous road conditions or impending collisions through the use of advanced warning systems, whereas traffic signals can be modified to alleviate congestion and enhance traffic flow.

Efficiency

By decreasing travel expenses and durations, intelligent transportation systems can improve the efficacy of transportation networks significantly. Intelligent transportation systems have the capability to enhance travel times, minimize congestion, and optimize traffic flow through the provision of up-to-date information regarding traffic conditions to vehicles and traffic management centers. The aforementioned data may be utilized to modify traffic signals, redirect vehicles, and offer alternate modes of transportation such as bike-sharing or public transportation. Additionally, petroleum consumption and emissions can be reduced through the implementation of these enhancements, which decrease congestion and idling time.

Additionally, mobility-as-a-service platforms can increase productivity by offering users a variety of transportation options that are customized to their particular requirements. MaaS platforms can improve traffic flow and decrease emissions by accommodating a variety of modes of transportation, including ride-sharing, public transit, bike-sharing, and others, thereby decreasing the number of single-occupancy vehicles on the road.

Sustainability

Intelligent transportation systems possess the capacity to alleviate the environmental repercussions associated with transportation by encouraging the use of sustainable modalities of travel and minimizing emissions. The number of single-occupancy vehicles on the road can be reduced through the use of public transportation, while electrified vehicles have the potential to substantially mitigate emissions and improve air quality. Moreover, through the promotion of shared transportation alternatives, MaaS platforms have the potential to mitigate emissions and curb the overall vehicle fleet.

Improved User Experience

Intelligent transportation systems have the capacity to greatly improve the overall user experience by providing more dependable, accommodating, and personalized transportation options. MaaS platforms have the capability to streamline the transportation experience for users by integrating multiple modes of transportation into a single platform. This integration enables users to conveniently plan and pay for their transportation needs through a unified application. Information Technology (ITS) possesses the capacity to provide users with current data concerning the availability of parking spaces, traffic conditions, and transit schedules. This capability aids in travel planning and ultimately saves time.

In summary, intelligent transportation systems have the potential to substantially improve various aspects of transportation networks, including but not limited to safety, efficiency, sustainability, and user experience. By integrating state-of-the-art technologies and communication systems, intelligent transportation has the potential to optimize transportation networks while simultaneously mitigating the environmental consequences of transportation.

TECHNOLOGIES TRANSFORMING TRANSPORTATION

The transportation industry is undergoing a rapid transformation thanks to the integration of various technologies. In this section, we will discuss some of the key technologies that are transforming transportation.

Connected Vehicles

Through the utilization of sensor technology and communication systems, connected vehicles possess the ability to exchange data with both other vehicles and the transportation infrastructure. Thus, collision avoidance and real-time detection of potential dangers are made possible. Connected vehicles can contribute to timely responses to incidents and emergencies, as well as furnish traffic management centres with up-to-date information on prevailing conditions.

Autonomous Vehicles

Autonomous vehicles operate without human intervention on the road by utilizing advanced sensors and artificial intelligence to determine their own course of action. This technological advancement has the potential to significantly reduce the occurrence of human error and improve the safety of roadways. Automobile-driven transportation can optimize traffic flow, thereby mitigating travel disruptions and congestion.

Mobility-as-a-Service Platforms

Mobility-as-a-service (MaaS) platforms provide consumers with an extensive array of personalized transportation options. By accommodating a variety of modalities of transportation (e.g., bike-sharing, public transit, and ride-sharing), MaaS platforms can reduce emissions and optimize traffic flow; consequently, this will reduce the quantity of single-occupancy vehicles on the road. MaaS platforms have the capability to expedite the transportation experience for users by integrating multiple modes of transportation onto a single platform. This integration enables users to conveniently plan and pay for their transportation needs via a unified application.

Intelligent Transportation Systems

ITS enhance road safety and optimize transportation networks through the use of cutting-edge technologies. ITS has the capability to furnish users with up-to-date information regarding parking availability, traffic conditions, and transit schedules, thereby facilitating trip planning and time reduction. By enabling traffic management centers to react swiftly to incidents and emergencies, ITS can also be used to optimize traffic flow, decrease congestion, and enhance safety.

Figure 2. Security in intelligent transport systems for smart cities

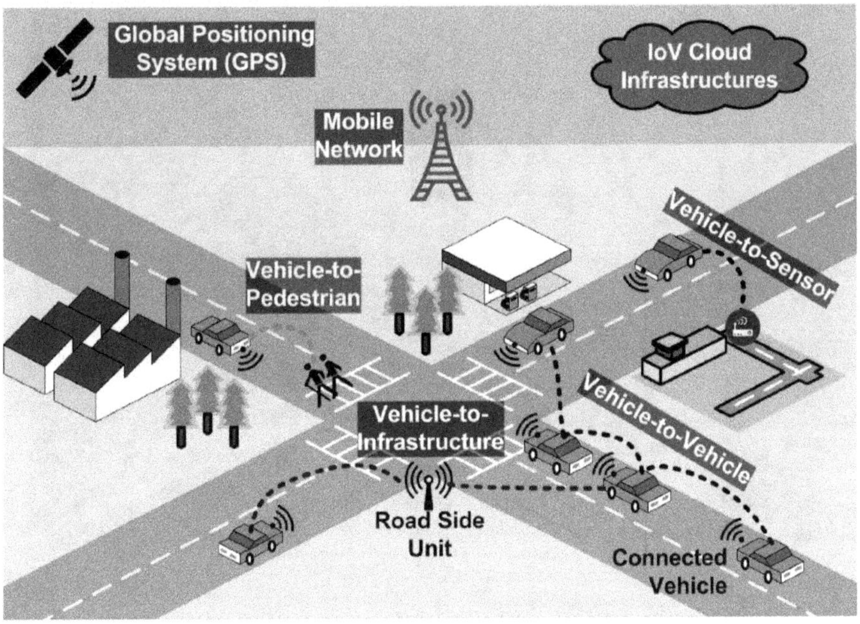

Electric Vehicles

Electric vehicles (EVs) derive the majority of their power from electricity, which significantly reduces emissions and enhances air quality. With the construction of additional charging infrastructure and the continuous improvement of battery technology, electric vehicles are gaining in popularity.

5G Technology

5G technology represents an advancement in mobile internet connectivity, presenting enhanced connectivity for a greater number of devices concurrently, improved connection reliability, and accelerated download and upload rates. The implementation of 5G technology has the potential to significantly augment the functionalities of autonomous and connected vehicles, facilitating expedited information exchange and enhanced responsiveness to potential hazards.

Blockchain Technology

The utilization of blockchain technology in the development of transparent and secure data exchange systems enables the transportation industry's various stakeholders to conduct secure transactions and share information. Additionally, decentralized ride-sharing platforms that eliminate the need for intermediaries and reduce user costs can be developed using blockchain technology.

Overall, the transportation industry is undergoing a significant transformation due to the integration of diverse technologies, which enables the creation of safer, more sustainable, and more efficient transportation systems. Prominent technologies propelling this paradigm shift include intelligent trans-

Figure 3. An image of smart transportation system

portation systems, connected and autonomous vehicles, blockchain technology, intelligent transportation platforms, and 5G technology.

BENEFITS OF SMART TRANSPORTATION

Intelligent transportation provides numerous advantages, such as enhanced user experience, safety, efficiency, and sustainability. A detailed discussion of each of these benefits will be provided in this section.

Safety

In addition to reducing the probability of human error, intelligent transportation can substantially improve road safety by providing up-to-date information on potential hazards. Connected and autonomous vehicles utilize advanced communication systems and sensors in order to detect potential hazards and respond promptly in order to prevent collisions. Smart transportation systems have the capability to expedite responses to incidents and emergencies by furnishing traffic management centers with up-to-date information on conditions. In addition to saving lives, intelligent transportation can lessen the financial repercussions of traffic collisions by enhancing road safety.

Efficiency

By optimizing traffic flow and reducing congestion, intelligent transportation can increase the efficiency of transportation systems. Through the reduction of single-occupancy vehicles in circulation, mobility-as-a-service platforms have the potential to mitigate traffic congestion and accelerate travel durations. Intelligent transportation systems can facilitate the reduction of congestion and the optimization of traffic flow by furnishing traffic management centers with real-time data on traffic conditions. Electric vehicles can reduce the environmental impact of transportation by enhancing air quality and decreasing emissions.

Sustainability

Intelligent transportation has the potential to contribute to the development of a more sustainable transportation system through the achievement of increased energy efficiency and decreased emissions. Electric vehicles substantially improve air quality and reduce emissions by making extensive use of electricity for propulsion. By reducing the number of single-occupant vehicles on the road, mobility-as-a-service platforms can aid in the reduction of traffic congestion and emissions. Intelligent transportation systems can reduce emissions and petroleum consumption by optimizing traffic flow. Smart transportation can contribute to the mitigation of climate change effects through the facilitation of a more sustainable transportation infrastructure.

User Experience

The implementation of intelligent transportation systems holds the capacity to greatly improve the overall user experience by offering individualized and more efficient alternatives. Platforms for mobility-as-a-service can streamline the transportation planning and payment process by providing users with a diverse selection of customized options that meet their specific needs. The implementation of autonomous and connected vehicles holds promise for improving the convenience and comfort of passengers' trips by decreasing travel times and eliminating the need for human driver intervention. Intelligent transportation systems have the capability to enhance travel planning through the provision of up-to-date information regarding transit schedules, parking availability, and traffic conditions.

Fundamentally, intelligent transportation offers a wide range of benefits, including improvements in sustainability, safety, efficiency, and user experience. By employing state-of-the-art technologies like intelligent transportation systems, connected and autonomous vehicles, and mobility-as-a-service platforms, smart transportation has the capacity to establish an environmentally sustainable, efficient, and user-centric transportation system.

BARRIERS AND OBSTACLES TO THE IMPLEMENTATION OF INTELLIGENT TRANSPORTATION

There are numerous obstacles and challenges that smart transportation technology implementation must surmount. Four main categories of obstacles will be examined in this section: infrastructure, technical, regulatory and policy, and societal acceptance.

Technical Obstacles

The complexity of intelligent transportation technologies is one of the greatest obstacles to their widespread adoption. In order to operate efficiently, these technologies necessitate sophisticated sensors, communication systems, and algorithms. As an illustration, in order to detect and react to their surroundings, connected and autonomous vehicles necessitate intricate sensor systems. Similarly, mobility-as-a-service

Figure 4. A preliminary work on predicting travel times and optimal routes

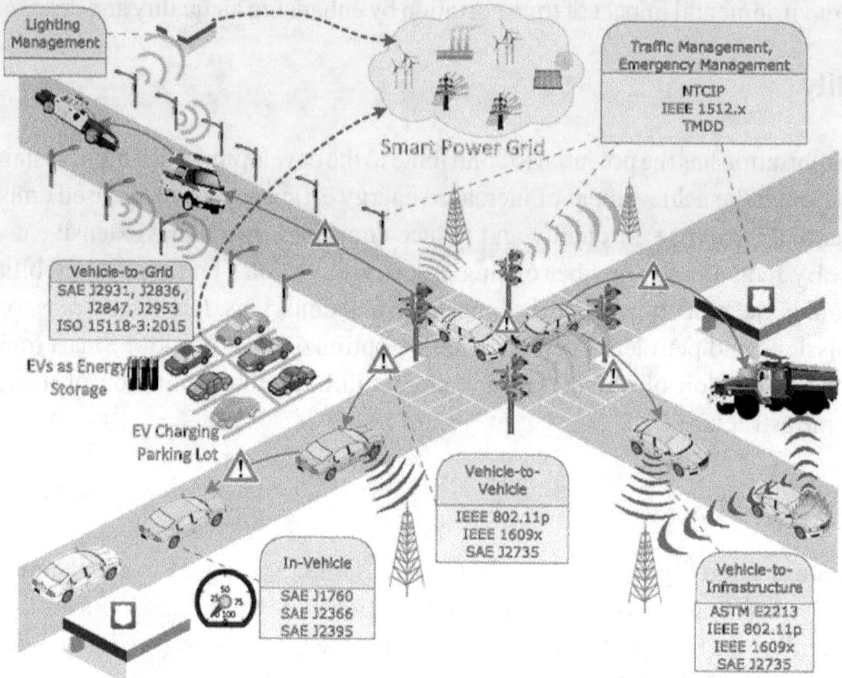

platforms operate on sophisticated algorithms that pair passengers with suitable transportation alternatives. In addition, these technologies must have the capability to exchange information both internally and with other transportation system components; this necessitates a resilient communication infrastructure.

Infrastructure Difficulties

Infrastructure enhancements are also crucial for the successful integration of intelligent transportation technologies. Connected and autonomous vehicles, for instance, necessitate high-speed communication networks in order to exchange information with one another and with other transportation system components. Transportation options and digital payment systems in real-time are essential components for mobility-as-a-service platforms. In order to operate electric vehicles, charging infrastructure is necessary. Significant investment and coordination between public and private sector stakeholders are required to construct this infrastructure.

Elaborate Regulatory and Policy Obstacles

Additionally, intelligent transportation technologies encounter regulatory and policy obstacles. The development and deployment of connected and autonomous vehicles, for instance, necessitates the establishment of novel safety regulations and standards. In order to incorporate mobility-as-a-service platforms into pre-existing transportation systems, modifications to the regulations that regulate transportation providers are necessary. To facilitate the deployment of charging infrastructure for electric vehicles, new policies and regulations are necessary. Coordination between multiple levels of government and stakeholders, in addition to the creation of new policies and regulations, are required to implement these modifications.

Elementary Obstacles to Societal Acceptance

Additionally, societal acceptability is critical to the success of intelligent transportation technologies. Due to safety or privacy concerns, some individuals may be hesitant to utilize new modes of transportation, such as ride-sharing or autonomous vehicles. There are individuals who might exhibit resistance towards modifications in transportation policies or infrastructure enhancements due to the potential for such to interfere with their daily routines. Efforts must be made to resolve concerns regarding privacy and equity, in addition to implementing successful communication and outreach strategies to inform the public about the safety and advantages of these technologies, in order to surmount these obstacles.

In essence, the integration of intelligent transportation technologies encounters numerous obstacles and challenges, encompassing technological intricacy, infrastructure modernization, alterations in regulations and policies, and societal reception. Coordination between multiple levels of government and stakeholders, in addition to the development of effective communication and dissemination strategies to garner public support for these technologies, are required to address these challenges.

REGULATIONS AND POLICIES REGARDING INTELLIGENT TRANSPORTATION

For intelligent transportation technologies to be implemented successfully, policies and regulations must be formulated to facilitate their deployment. Government policies, regulations, and standards; public-private partnerships; and funding mechanisms will be examined in this section.

Official Government Policies

Government policies that facilitate the implementation of intelligent transportation technologies may be indispensable. For instance, numerous governments provide fiscal incentives and rebates to promote the adoption of electric vehicles. To increase efficiency and safety, governments may also mandate the use of particular technologies, such as connected vehicle technology. In addition, governments have the ability to formulate policies that facilitate the implementation of mobility-as-a-service platforms. This may involve allocating public funds to aid in the advancement of these systems.

Standards and Regulations

It is essential that regulations and standards be established to guarantee the interoperability and security of intelligent transportation technologies. For instance, the implementation of regulations that oversee the development and operation of autonomous vehicles contributes to their compliance with safety standards for public roads. Communication protocol standards guarantee interoperability among various components of the transportation system. Furthermore, the implementation of regulations pertaining to the utilization of data in transportation systems can serve to safeguard the privacy of consumers and guarantee the ethical and responsible application of data.

Collaborations between Governance and the Private Sector

Public-private collaborations have the potential to significantly contribute to the implementation of intelligent transportation technologies. By capitalizing on the respective advantages of the public and private sectors, these alliances can effectively tackle obstacles pertaining to finances, infrastructure, and technological advancement. For instance, public-private partnerships may be utilized to support the deployment of novel mobility-as-a-service platforms or to finance the development of charging infrastructure for electric vehicles.

Funding Approaches

Intelligent transportation technology deployment frequently necessitates substantial financial investment. In bolstering these investments, funding mechanisms may serve a pivotal function. For instance, governments may support the deployment of new mobility-as-a-service platforms or the development of charging infrastructure for electric vehicles through the provision of grants or loans. Collaborations with public sector organizations or venture capital funding from the private sector can also be instrumental in facilitating the deployment of these technologies.

In essence, the establishment of policies and regulations is indispensable for facilitating the implementation of intelligent transportation technologies. Regulations and standards can guarantee the security and interoperability of these technologies, public-private partnerships can capitalise on the respective sectors' strengths to tackle obstacles, and funding mechanisms can facilitate investments in such technologies. Government policies have the capacity to encourage the adoption of novel technologies. The resolution of these policy concerns necessitates the cooperation of various stakeholders, such as governmental bodies, private sector organizations, and consumers.

ILLUSTRATIONS OF INTELLIGENT TRANSPORTATION

Case studies pertaining to smart transportation offer significant insights into the technological strategies implemented by cities globally in order to tackle transportation-related obstacles. Four case studies will be examined in this section: Smart Mobility 2030 in Singapore, Congestion Charge in London, Intelligent Transportation System in New York City, and Mobility-as-a-Service Platform in Los Angeles.

Intelligent Mobility in Singapore 2030

Smart Mobility 2030 is a strategic plan outlining the progression of an intelligent transportation infrastructure in Singapore. The implementation of autonomous vehicles, the creation of a real-time traffic management system, and the establishment of a nationwide electronic payment system for transportation services are among the initiatives outlined in the road map. The purpose of these initiatives is to enhance the sustainability and efficacy of Singapore's transportation system, as well as to provide residents with more mobility options.

An essential undertaking outlined in the Smart Mobility 2030 strategic plan is the advancement of autonomous vehicles. Since 2015, Singapore has conducted trials of autonomous vehicles on public highways with the objective of implementing a fleet of autonomous taxis by 2022. It is anticipated that the integration of autonomous vehicles into Singapore's transportation system will increase safety and efficacy, decrease emissions, and alleviate congestion.

Congestion Charge in London

Congestion Charge is a pricing structure that imposes a toll on motorists who wish to travel through the heart of London during congested periods. Implemented in 2003, the initiative aimed to mitigate traffic congestion and enhance the urban environment's air quality. Due to the effectiveness of the Congestion Charge in reducing traffic congestion, traffic volume in the charging zone has decreased by 30% since the program's inception.

Other beneficial effects of the Congestion Charge include an improvement in air quality and a reduction in emissions in the city center. Furthermore, the revenue produced through the initiative has been allocated towards financing enhancements to the public transportation infrastructure, such as the establishment of a bike-sharing initiative and the augmentation of the city's bus network.

Intelligent Transportation System of New York City

The Information Technology System (ITS) of the New York metropolitan area comprises an interconnected system of cameras and sensors designed to collect data pertaining to traffic conditions within the city. The data is employed to improve road safety, alleviate traffic congestion, and streamline traffic circulation within the municipality. The system incorporates a variety of technologies, including signal coordination, real-time traffic monitoring, and incident detection and response.

As a result of the ITS's implementation in the city, travel times have been reduced and traffic circulation has been improved. Further enhancing road safety, the number of traffic fatalities in the municipality has decreased by 33% since its implementation in 2010.

Mobility-as-a-Service Platform of Los Angeles

The Mobility-as-a-Service (MaaS) platform in Los Angeles functions as a mobile application that empowers users to plan and transfer funds for trips involving diverse transportation options, including bike-sharing, public transit, and ride-sharing. The application not only provides up-to-date information regarding transit schedules and availability but also enables users to compare prices across different modes of transportation.

The MaaS platform has significantly improved the range of mobility options available to residents, particularly those who do not possess private vehicles. It has enhanced the efficiency of the city's transportation system by reducing the reliance on single-occupancy vehicle trips and by providing users with real-time information on alternatives to driving.

Fundamentally, these case studies serve to demonstrate the potential of intelligent transportation technologies to alleviate challenges in transportation and improve the range of mobility options available to residents. The accomplishments of these initiatives highlight the importance of collaboration among diverse stakeholders—including government agencies, private sector organizations, and consumers—in the development and implementation of intelligent transportation solutions.

CONCLUSION AND PROSPECTS FOR THE FUTURE

Synopsis of Principal Arguments

We have examined the notion of intelligent transportation and its prospective advantages for municipalities and inhabitants throughout this chapter. A range of transportation-transforming technologies have been examined, alongside the obstacles and difficulties associated with the implementation of intelligent transportation solutions. Case studies of successful smart transportation system implementations in cities around the globe and policies and regulations that can facilitate their development have also been analyzed. A concise overview of the chapter's main arguments is as follows:

(1) Intelligent transportation technologies may increase inhabitants' mobility options, decrease congestion and emissions, and improve the safety and effectiveness of transportation systems.
(2) Mobility-as-a-Service platforms, autonomous vehicles, and real-time traffic management systems are transforming the transportation sector.
(3) It is imperative to confront technical, infrastructure, regulatory, policy, and societal adoption obstacles in order to successfully implement smart transportation solutions.
(4) Funding mechanisms, public-private partnerships, governmental policies, and regulations can all contribute to the advancement of intelligent transportation systems.
(5) The potential of these solutions is demonstrated by successful implementations of smart transportation technologies, including Smart Mobility 2030 in Singapore, Congestion Charge in London, Intelligent Transportation System in New York City, and Mobility-as-a-Service Platform in Los Angeles.

Prospective Trajectories

In the foreseeable future, intelligent transportation solutions are anticipated to further develop and proliferate across various domains. These consist of:

(a) The advancement and implementation of more sophisticated autonomous vehicles, such as lorries and buses, could contribute to additional emission reductions and enhanced road safety.
b) The incorporation of nascent technologies like blockchain and artificial intelligence, which have the potential to bolster the effectiveness and safeguarding of transportation systems.
(c) The proliferation of shared mobility alternatives and Mobility-as-a-Service platforms, which can offer residents more adaptable and environmentally friendly modes of transportation.

Urgent Action Request for Stakeholders in the Transportation Sector

For the full potential of intelligent transportation technologies to be realized, it is critical that transportation industry stakeholders collaborate and act. Consumers, governments, and private sector organizations are all stakeholders in the development and implementation of intelligent transportation solutions. Particular measures that stakeholders may undertake encompass:

To advance intelligent transportation solutions, governments may invest in transportation infrastructure, form public-private partnerships, and enact policies and regulations that are conducive to their objectives.

By investing in research and development of intelligent transportation technologies, collaborating with other stakeholders, and developing novel approaches to transportation challenges, private sector organizations can contribute to the field.

Advocacy for sustainable transportation alternatives, including but not limited to walking, cycling, and public transit, can be observed among consumers, who should also adopt emergent technologies that augment their mobility choices.

Intelligent transportation has the capacity to revolutionize urban mobility and enhance the standard of living in locales across the globe. Despite the obstacles and difficulties associated with their implementation, these solutions are worthwhile to pursue due to the benefits they provide. Stakeholders in the transportation industry can contribute to the development of a more sustainable, equitable, and efficient transportation system for all by cooperating and taking action.

REFERENCES

Aamir, M., Masroor, S., Ali, Z. A., & Ting, B. T. (2019). Sustainable framework for smart transportation system: A case study of karachi. *Wireless Personal Communications, 106*(1), 27–40. doi:10.1007/s11277-019-06259-4

Azgomi, H. F., & Jamshidi, M. (2018, November). A brief survey on smart community and smart transportation. In *2018 IEEE 30th international conference on tools with artificial intelligence (ICTAI)* (pp. 932-939). IEEE. 10.1109/ICTAI.2018.00144

Bacciu, D., Carta, A., Gnesi, S., & Semini, L. (2017). An experience in using machine learning for short-term predictions in smart transportation systems. *Journal of Logical and Algebraic Methods in Programming, 87*, 52–66. doi:10.1016/j.jlamp.2016.11.002

Boukerche, A., & Coutinho, R. W. (2019). Crowd management: The overlooked component of smart transportation systems. *IEEE Communications Magazine, 57*(4), 48–53. doi:10.1109/MCOM.2019.1800641

Dewi, N. K., & Putra, A. S. (2021, March). Law enforcement in smart transportation systems on highway. In *International Conference on Education of Suryakancana (IConnects Proceedings)*. IEEE.

Ding, Z., Yang, B., Chi, Y., & Guo, L. (2015). Enabling smart transportation systems: A parallel spatio-temporal database approach. *IEEE Transactions on Computers, 65*(5), 1377–1391. doi:10.1109/TC.2015.2479596

Fantin Irudaya Raj, E., & Appadurai, M. (2022). Internet of things-based smart transportation system for smart cities. In *Intelligent Systems for Social Good: Theory and Practice* (pp. 39–50). Springer Nature Singapore. doi:10.1007/978-981-19-0770-8_4

Finger, M., & Audouin, M. (2019). *The governance of smart transportation systems*. Academic Press.

Jan, B., Farman, H., Khan, M., Talha, M., & Din, I. U. (2019). Designing a smart transportation system: An internet of things and big data approach. *IEEE Wireless Communications, 26*(4), 73–79. doi:10.1109/MWC.2019.1800512

Jimenez, J. A. (2018). Smart transportation systems. *Smart Cities: Applications, Technologies, Standards, and Driving Factors*, 123-133.

Möller, D. P., & Vakilzadian, H. (2016, May). *Cyber-physical systems in smart transportation. In 2016 IEEE international conference on electro information technology (EIT) (pp. 776-781)*. IEEE.

Mrityunjaya, D. H., Kumar, N., Ali, S., & Kelagadi, H. M. (2017, February). Smart transportation. In *2017 International Conference on I-SMAC (IoT in Social, Mobile, Analytics and Cloud)(I-SMAC)* (pp. 1-5). IEEE.

Saarika, P. S., Sandhya, K., & Sudha, T. (2017, August). Smart transportation system using IoT. In *2017 International Conference On Smart Technologies For Smart Nation (SmartTechCon)* (pp. 1104-1107). IEEE. 10.1109/SmartTechCon.2017.8358540

Shukla, S., Balachandran, K., & Sumitha, V. S. (2016, November). A framework for smart transportation using Big Data. In *2016 International Conference on ICT in Business Industry & Government (ICTBIG)* (pp. 1-3). IEEE. 10.1109/ICTBIG.2016.7892720

Stefansson, G., & Lumsden, K. (2009). Performance issues of smart transportation management systems. *International Journal of Productivity and Performance Management*.

Xu, H., Lin, J., & Yu, W. (2017). Smart transportation systems: Architecture, enabling technologies, and open issues. *Secure and trustworthy transportation cyber-physical systems*, 23-49.

Yan, J., Liu, J., & Tseng, F. M. (2020). An evaluation system based on the self-organizing system framework of smart cities: A case study of smart transportation systems in China. *Technological Forecasting and Social Change*, *153*, 119371. doi:10.1016/j.techfore.2018.07.009

Zantalis, F., Koulouras, G., Karabetsos, S., & Kandris, D. (2019). A review of machine learning and IoT in smart transportation. *Future Internet*, *11*(4), 94. doi:10.3390/fi11040094

Zhang, Y., Zhang, G., Fierro, R., & Yang, Y. (2018). Force-driven traffic simulation for a future connected autonomous vehicle-enabled smart transportation system. *IEEE Transactions on Intelligent Transportation Systems*, *19*(7), 2221–2233. doi:10.1109/TITS.2017.2787141

Zichichi, M., Ferretti, S., & D'Angelo, G. (2020, January). A distributed ledger based infrastructure for smart transportation system and social good. In 2020 IEEE 17th Annual Consumer Communications & Networking Conference (CCNC) (pp. 1-6). IEEE. doi:10.1109/CCNC46108.2020.9045640

Chapter 18
A Comprehensive Exploration of the "Umber" Mobile App's IoT-Infused Revolution in Umbrella Technology

Sophia Mosalla
Sun Moon University, South Korea

Rahul Ranjan
https://orcid.org/0000-0003-4549-5118
Sun Moon University, South Korea

Saurabh Singh
Woosong University, South Korea

ABSTRACT

The 'Umber' mobile app stands as a pioneering technological advancement, reshaping the traditional usage of umbrellas. This abstract encapsulates the app's diverse objectives, focusing on elevated user convenience, technological innovation, environmental sustainability, and increased accessibility. Through seamless integration of technology, 'Umber' revolutionizes the umbrella experience, introducing on-demand services, reducing forgetfulness, and promoting sustainability. Drawing inspiration from successful applications like GCOO, Kakao T, and Panda Korea, 'Umber' adopts a proven model to address umbrella-related challenges. This chapter delves into the innovative development of the 'Umber' mobile app, a paradigm-shifting solution at the intersection of global mobility, Internet of Things (IoT) integration, and cutting-edge technologies. The core of the technological architecture involves the incorporation of Firebase for real-time data management, ESP32 microcontrollers, and Reed switches for seamless interaction, GPS tracking for precise location awareness, and map integration to enhance user experience. The 'Umber' app not only redefines traditional umbrella usage but also serves as a testament to the transformative potential of thoughtful, purpose-driven technology development on a global scale. Future research endeavors may entail augmenting the technological capabilities of the 'Umber' app through the exploration of advanced sensor technologies and machine learning algorithms. This could

DOI: 10.4018/979-8-3693-2373-1.ch018

lead to an enhanced user experience and increased adaptability to diverse weather conditions, potentially manifested in a compact screen on the umbrella box. Users could conveniently access real-time weather updates, monitor the condition of the box, and receive information about the umbrella housed inside. Additionally, there is potential for further innovation by upgrading each umbrella to include features such as a built-in flashlight, providing users with added convenience and safety for nighttime walks.

INTRODUCTION

The integration of IoT technology in the 'Umber' mobile app represents a significant advancement in the way everyday objects are utilized. By incorporating smart sensors within the umbrella, real-time data on weather conditions, user behavior, and location is collected, thereby enhancing the overall user experience. This aligns with the broader trend of IoT applications, which have the potential to revolutionize various industries and daily activitie. The 'Umber' app's technological architecture, utilizing Firebase for real-time data management, ESP32 microcontrollers, Reed switches, GPS tracking, and map integration, exemplifies a comprehensive and innovative approach to mobility solutions (IoTGuard, 2019).

Furthermore, the use of IoT in mobile applications has been recognized as valuable for citizens, health professionals, and decision makers, particularly in addressing critical challenges such as reducing the burden on hospitals, providing access to credible information, and tracking individuals' symptoms and mental health. This underscores the broader impact of IoT-enabled mobile apps in enhancing user convenience and accessibility, which are key principles driving the development of the 'Umber' app. The increasing ubiquity of IoT has the potential to drastically alter the way healthcare systems are utilized, both at home and in care environments. This highlights the broader societal implications of IoT integration, including its potential to transform how individuals interact with technology in various contexts, including mobility applications like 'Umber' (al A. K., 2020). The mobile application called 'Umber' has integrated IoT technology, making it a pioneer in the field of global mobility. It aligns with the broader trend of IoT applications reshaping various industries and daily activities. The comprehensive technological architecture of the 'Umber' app reflects a paradigm shift in how everyday objects are used. It emphasizes user convenience, technological innovation, environmental sustainability, and increased accessibility.

This chapter contributes to the existing literature by presenting a comprehensive overview of the 'Umber' mobile app, which is a pioneering technological advancement in the field of umbrella usage. It provides an in-depth understanding of the app's multifaceted objectives, technological architecture, and the development process. The chapter also highlights the app's contribution to promoting user convenience, technological innovation, environmental sustainability, and accessibility. The chapter is organized in a systematic manner, beginning with an introduction that outlines the importance of IoT technology and its role in the app. The following sections provide a detailed explanation of the related work, work methodology, experimental setup, and results. The chapter concludes with a summary of Prototype 1's primary features and outlines future research directions. Overall, the chapter provides a valuable resource for researchers and practitioners interested in the development of purpose-driven technology that enhances user experiences and addresses evolving needs.

RELATED WORK

In the rapidly evolving landscape of future mobility services, several key players have emerged, each contributing uniquely to the paradigm shift in transportation and convenience. The following section explores notable precedents and contemporaries in the industry, shedding light on their distinctive features and contributions.

GCOO: Mobility Evolution for All

GCOO, a pioneering brand in the global markets of North America and Asia Pacific, has set a bold trajectory for the future of mobility. The brand's commitment to evolution is encapsulated in its new slogan, "Mobility Evolution for All." GCOO has strategically expanded its offerings beyond traditional E-Scooter and E-Bike services. The inclusion of various sub-services, such as battery services and rentals, reflects the brand's comprehensive approach to mobility solutions. The goal to become a leading future mobility company underscores GCOO's dedication to safe, reliable, and technologically advanced mobility (https://gcoo.io/en/team).

Kakao T: Revolutionizing Transportation Services

Kakao T, introduced in 2015 by Kakao, stands as a testament to the transformative power of technology in the transportation sector. This app seamlessly integrates call taxi and public transportation services, offering users the convenience of a nationwide service linked to their Kakao accounts. The implementation of a robust evaluation system for both drivers and passengers ensures a reliable and trustworthy experience. With a staggering 13.71 million passengers within three years of launch and an extensive cumulative operating distance, Kakao T has become a cornerstone in the realm of ride-hailing and public transportation (https://www.kakaocorp.com/page/service/service/KakaoT?lang=en).

Panda Korea: IoT-Powered Smartphone Charging Solutions

Panda Korea, operating as a professional IoT service provider, addresses a ubiquitous challenge in the modern era—smartphone battery shortage. The company's IoT technology facilitates the easy location of charging points, termed "Charging Pigs," in various public spaces such as convenience stores, theaters, cafes, and subways. By providing a systematic and stable service, Panda Korea ensures customers can conveniently charge their smartphones anytime, anywhere. The commitment to quality service and technical support highlights the brand's dedication to enhancing customer satisfaction and convenience (http://ww.piggycell.com).

WORK METHODOLOGY OR PROPOSED METHOD

Tracking

The significance of GPS location tracking transcends personal navigation, finding application in diverse fields such as emergency services, transportation logistics, and scientific research. In emergency scenarios, GPS assumes a pivotal role by precisely identifying the location of individuals in distress, facilitating

Figure 1. Architecture diagram

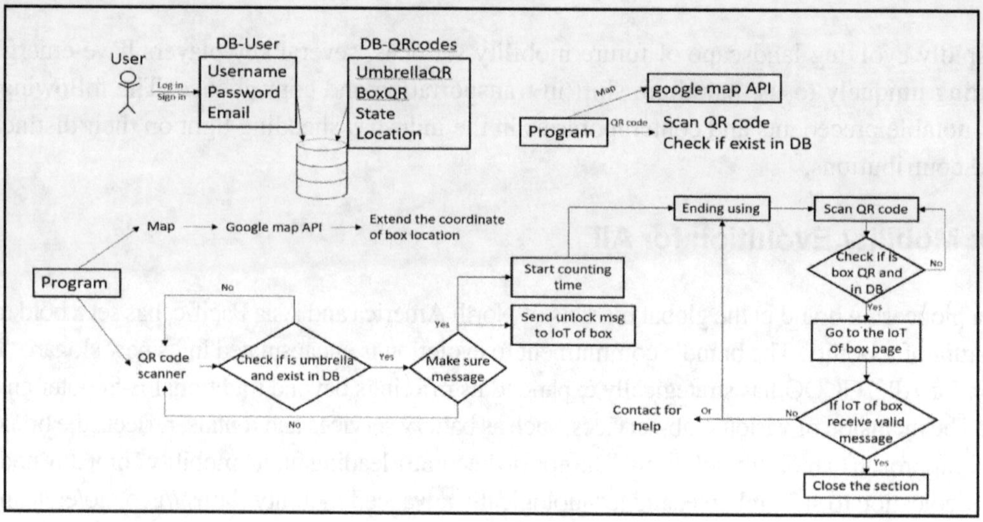

swift and effective rescue operations. Furthermore, GPS contributes to route optimization and real-time monitoring of goods in transportation logistics, thereby fostering cost-saving measures and ensuring timely deliveries Singh et al., (2023). In outdoor settings, GPS commonly serves as a navigation aid for vehicles, assisting in locating destinations and determining current positions. It is essential to note, however, that this sensor's functionality is contingent upon the availability of an existing GPS network. This underscores the reliance on a robust infrastructure to support the seamless operation of GPS technology, thereby reinforcing its indispensable role in diverse applications Singh et al., (2024) shown in figure 1.

GPS Neo-6

The NEO-6 module series comprises stand-alone GPS receivers featuring the high-performance u-blox 6 positioning engines. These receivers, known for their flexibility and cost-effectiveness, provide a variety of connectivity options in a compact 16 x 12.2 x 2.4 mm package. Tailored for battery-operated mobile devices with strict cost and space constraints, the NEO-6 modules excel in power efficiency and memory utilization (NEO-6 u-blox 6 GPS Modules). Powered by a 50-channel u-blox 6 positioning engine, the modules boast a Time-To-First Fix (TTFF) of under 1 second. The dedicated acquisition engine, equipped with 2 million correlators, conducts parallel time/frequency space searches, ensuring rapid satellite detection. Notably, the innovative design and advanced technology of the NEO-6 series effectively counteract jamming sources and mitigate multipath effects, providing excellent navigation performance even in challenging environments (Shunfu Hu). all the GPS Neo-6 performance are in table1.

The NEO-6 GPS module will play a pivotal role in the real-time tracking of the box's location. Leveraging the advanced capabilities of the NEO-6, we intend to implement a sophisticated tracking system that ensures accurate and reliable location data. This technology will not only enable precise monitoring of the box's movements but also contribute to enhanced logistics management, providing valuable insights into the box's journey, transit times, and overall efficiency. By utilizing the NEO-6 GPS module for location tracking, we aim to optimize operational processes, improve resource allocation, and enhance the overall efficiency of the tracking system.

Table 1. Neo-6 GPS performance

Parameter	Specification			
Receiver type	50 Channels GPS L1 frequency, C/A Code SBAS: WAAS, EGNOS, MSAS			
Time-To-First-Fix[1]		NEO-6G/Q/T	NEO-6M/V	NEO-6P
	Cold Start[2]	26 s	27 s	32 s
	Warm Start[2]	26 s	27 s	32 s
	Hot Start[2]	1 s	1 s	1 s
	Aided Starts[3]	1 s	<3 s	<3 s
Sensitivity[4]		NEO-6G/Q/T	NEO-6M/V	NEO-6P
	Tracking & Navigation	-162 dBm	-161 dBm	-160 dBm
	Reacquisition[5]	-160 dBm	-160 dBm	-160 dBm
	Cold Start (without aiding)	-148 dBm	-147 dBm	-146 dBm
	Hot Start	-157 dBm	-156 dBm	-155 dBm
Maximum Navigation update rate		NEO-6G/Q/M/T	NEO-6P/V	
		5Hz	1 Hz	
Horizontal position accuracy[6]	GPS	2.5 m		
	SBAS	2.0 m		
	SBAS + PPP[7]	< 1 m (2D, R50)[8]		
	SBAS + PPP[7]	< 2 m (3D, R50)[8]		
Configurable Timepulse frequency range		NEO-6G/Q/M/P/V	NEO-6T	
		0.25 Hz to 1 kHz	0.25 Hz to 10 MHz	
Accuracy for Timepulse signal	RMS	30 ns		
	99%	<60 ns		
	Granularity	21 ns		
	Compensated[9]	15 ns		
Velocity accuracy[6]		0.1m/s		
Heading accuracy[6]		0.5 degrees		
Operational Limits	Dynamics	≤ 4 g		
	Altitude[10]	50,000 m		
	Velocity[10]	500 m/s		

Leveraging Google Maps API for Dynamic Location Visualization

Google Maps API has revolutionized online mapping services since its inception in 2005. It has introduced a new client/server interaction model based on Asynchronous JavaScript and XML (AJAX), which allows for seamless connectivity between the client and server for the immediate downloading of additional map information Kumar et al., (2024). The API also empowers developers through its Application Programming Interface, which provides a rich repository of data structures, object classes, and functions accessible to programmers deploying JavaScript, PHP, or other scripting languages (2009).

This paper presents a comprehensive approach to real-time location tracking using the NEO-6 GPS module. The process entails acquiring coordinates from the NEO-6 module and transmitting this data to the Firebase Database for efficient storage and retrieval. The pivotal aspect of this location tracking system is the integration with the Google Maps platform, which dynamically visualizes the received coordinates. The integration with Google Maps is achieved through the utilization of JavaScript facilitated by a dedicated library. This strategic implementation enhances the functionality of the system, allowing for an interactive and user-friendly display of the tracked location on the Google Maps interface (al J. S., 2012).

The workflow involves the NEO-6 module capturing location coordinates, which are then transmitted to the Firebase Database in a structured and organized manner. The Firebase Database serves as a robust backend, facilitating the seamless storage and retrieval of location data. Concurrently, the Google Maps integration, driven by JavaScript, empowers the system to translate these coordinates into a visually intuitive map interface. This integration holds paramount significance as it amalgamates cutting-edge technologies, transforming raw GPS data into a tangible and interactive map representation. The use of Firebase as the backend database ensures data integrity and accessibility, while Google Maps, through its JavaScript library, serves as the dynamic canvas for presenting the real-time location updates Park et al., (2024).

This paper provides a detailed exposition of this integrated system, which not only contributes to the understanding of GPS-based location tracking but also highlights the synergy between hardware components like the NEO-6 module, cloud-based databases like Firebase, and sophisticated mapping interfaces provided by Google Maps. The amalgamation of these elements serves as a testament to the advancement in location-based technologies, opening avenues for enhanced applications in fields such as logistics, asset tracking, and geospatial analytics (2019).

EXPERIMENTAL SETUP

IOT Of Box

Within each container, an ESP32 microcontroller is intricately incorporated to facilitate the acquisition of data from both the GPS NEO-6 module and reed switches. The ESP32 acts as the central intelligence unit, seamlessly orchestrating the integration of diverse components for a comprehensive tracking system.

One noteworthy element within this intricate setup is the utilization of reed switches. Reed switches represent a specialized category of electrical switches, uniquely responsive to magnetic fields for activation and deactivation. Typically, these switches comprise two slender, flexible ferromagnetic wires or blades known as reeds, strategically positioned with a slight separation within a hermetically sealed glass enclosure. This physical arrangement defines the reed switch contacts, with the change-over type featuring three reeds instead of the more common two (RSC). The specific configuration of reed switches in this context is purposeful: they are strategically arranged within the container to effectively detect the presence or absence of umbrellas. By leveraging the magnetism-driven actuation of reed switches, the system can discern whether an umbrella is positioned within the container, providing valuable data for tracking and inventory management.

Functionally, the ESP32 microcontroller seamlessly interfaces with both the reed switches and the GPS NEO-6 module. When reed switches detect the open or close status within the box, this information, coupled with GPS coordinates from the NEO-6 module, is diligently transmitted to a real-time database hosted on Firebase. This dynamic database becomes a repository of live information, constantly updated by the ESP32 microcontroller as it receives and processes data from the reed switches and GPS module.

This comprehensive integration of hardware components and sophisticated sensors underscores the meticulous design of the tracking system. The ESP32, acting as the nerve center, not only manages the concurrent reception of data from reed switches and the GPS module but also orchestrates the seamless transmission of this information to the Firebase real-time database. This holistic approach to data collection and transmission serves to enhance the efficiency and accuracy of the tracking system, making it a robust solution for real-time monitoring of the presence and location of umbrellas within the designated containers. The amalgamation of advanced hardware components and purposeful sensor configurations

Table 2. Box connections

esp32	GPS neo-6	reed switch 1	reed switch 2
5V	-	VCC	VCC
3V	VCC	-	-
GRD	GRD	GRD	GRD
G17		do	
G18			do
G21	RX		
G20	TX		

showcases a sophisticated and well-engineered system poised for practical applications in inventory management and tracking scenarios. Box connections Table 2.

RESULTS

Map

Utilizing the robust capabilities of the Google Maps JavaScript API, this study leverages a powerful tool for seamlessly embedding interactive maps within web applications. The integration of markers within the API enables the precise highlighting of specific locations on the map. Building upon this functionality, the 'Umber' mobile app project aims to harness the dynamic and user-friendly mapping interfaces offered by the Google Maps API.

To initiate the second phase of the project, involving the creation of a map displaying both user and box locations, a series of essential steps are undertaken. This process begins with the installation of requisite libraries through the following commands: in figure 3.

These commands facilitate the incorporation of essential libraries, paving the way for the seamless integration of the Google Maps functionality into the 'Umber' mobile app. By following these steps, the project ensures a robust foundation for the development of an interactive and visually intuitive map interface, thereby enhancing user experience and providing real-time location insights. The result in the application in the figure 4.

QR Code Scanner

To ensure optimal identification and interpretation by users, tailored QR codes are generated for each 'Umber' box and umbrella, with embedded specific text values for efficient storage and retrieval. The implementation of this QR code system necessitates camera permissions to enable users to scan the QR codes seamlessly.

The QR scanning functionality is realized through the integration of JavaScript libraries, notably the jsqr library. This library empowers the device to scan QR codes using the device's camera, facilitating a streamlined and user-friendly experience.

Figure 2. Box hardware

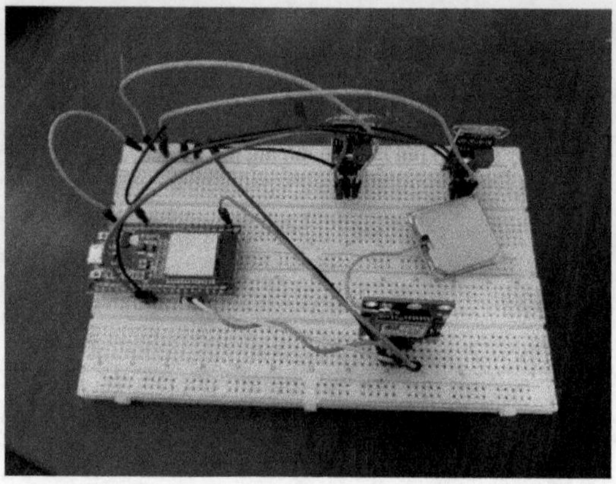

Figure 3. Necessary package for installation

```
npx expo install expo-task-manager
npx expo install expo-location
npx expo install react-native-maps
```

Figure 4. Mapping the user and umbrella box locations in the app

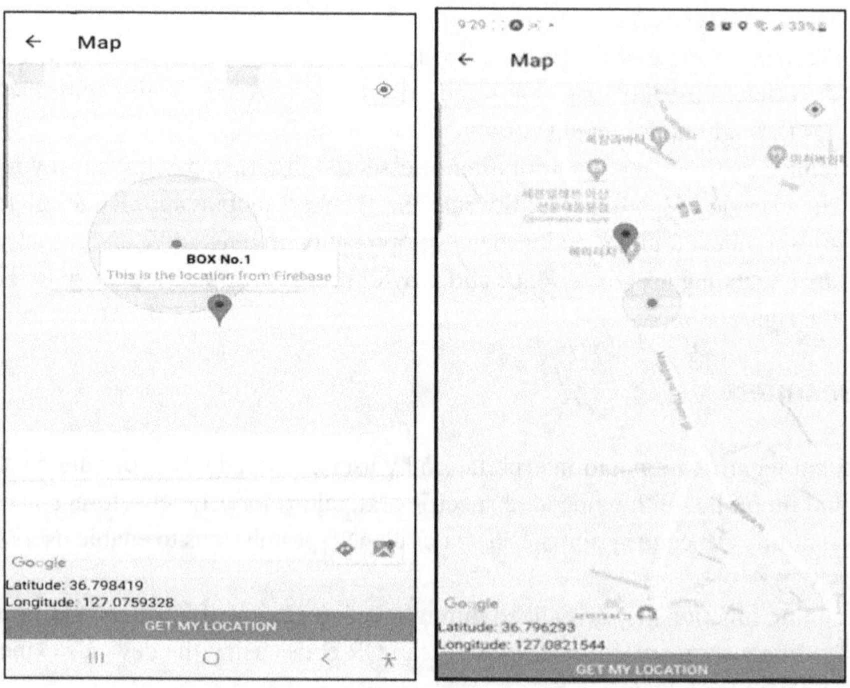

Figure 5. The result in the application

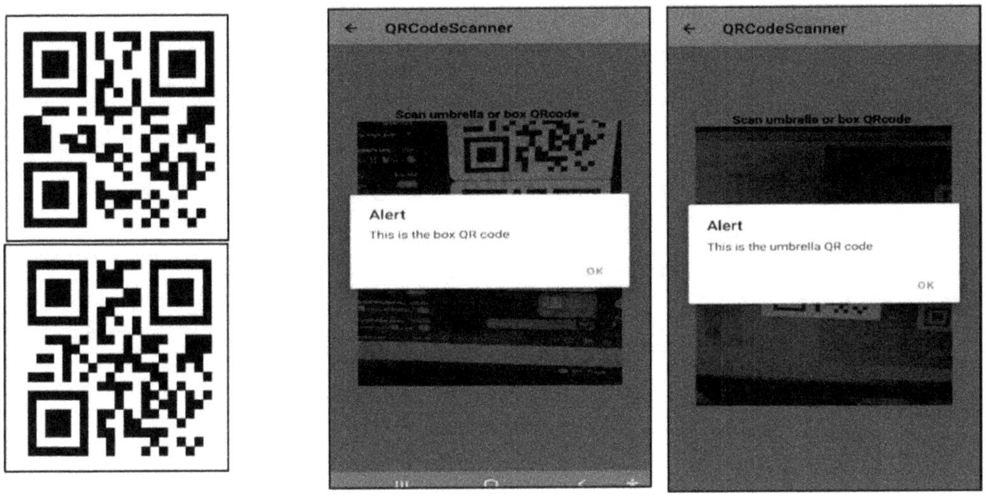

Expanding the scope of this functionality to Internet of Things (IoT) applications,

ESP32 microcontrollers, equipped with camera modules, play a pivotal role. This extension of QR code scanning to IoT applications, showcasing the versatility and adaptability of the 'Umber' mobile app's QR scanning feature.

- using'expo-barcode-scanner'library for QRcode scanning

box QR code
151121
umbrella QR code
151123

Box IOT (Dashboard)

The 'Umber' system includes umbrellas that are equipped with magnets to activate their corresponding reed switch. The system also has a GPS module, such as the neo-6, to capture precise location data. This location data is transmitted to Firebase through the integrated WiFi module of the ESP32 microcontroller. The JavaScript code interacts with Firebase to fetch real-time data to determine the status of each hole in the umbrella box, whether open or closed. Based on this information, the code dynamically adjusts the color representation for each hole, providing users with an intuitive visual cue.

During the project, a transition was made from using hardwareSerial to softwareSerial because it is more convenient to retrieve data from the GPS module. To use SoftwareSerial, we needed to install the SoftwareSerial library specifically tailored for ESP32. This change streamlined the data retrieval process from the GPS, contributing to the overall efficiency and functionality of the 'Umber' system.

Figure 6. The results in application: A) When umbrella insert, B) When there is no umbrella inside of the box

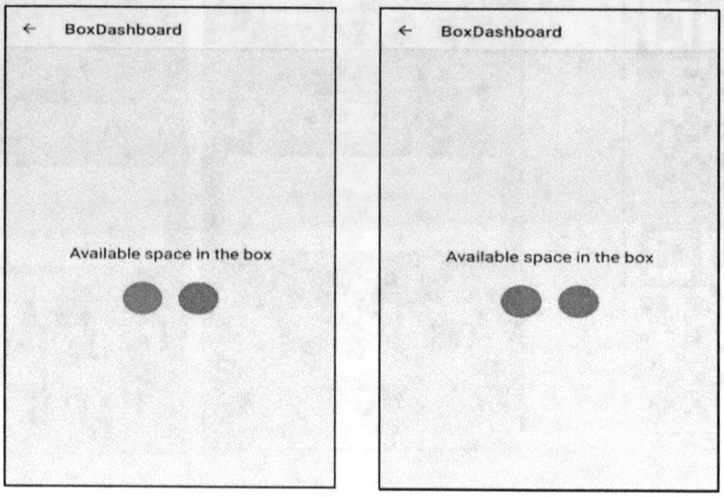

Server and Database

MySQL serves as a secure repository for user data within the 'Umber' system, encompassing encrypted storage of emails and passwords through a robust hash algorithm. Additionally, the database houses QR codes associated with umbrellas and boxes, enabling administrators to monitor the current utilization status of each umbrella. This comprehensive data management strategy ensures the confidentiality of user information while providing real-time insights into umbrella usage in figure 7.

Figure 7. The database diagram

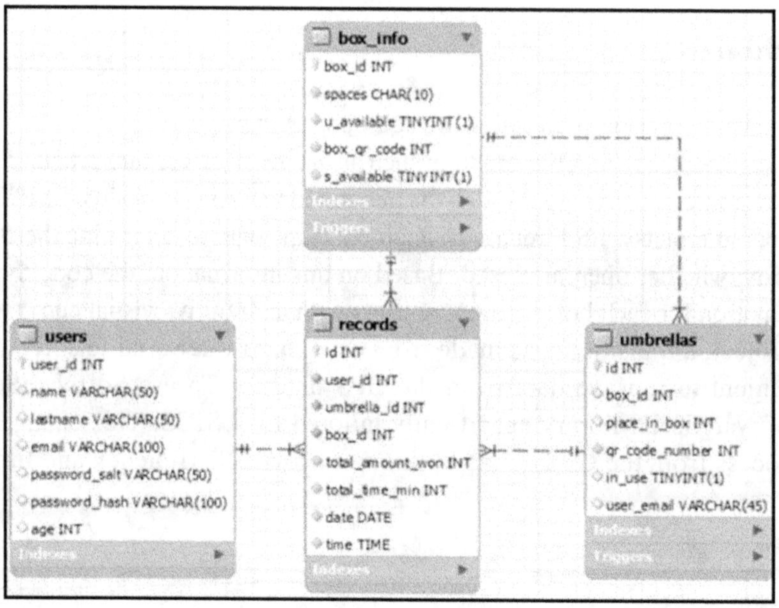

Figure 8. Store all the data, time, and amount in DB

id	user_id	umbrella_id	box_id	total_amount_won	total_time_min	date	time
1	1	1	1	20	2	2023-12-11	15:00:01
2	1	1	1	70	7	2023-12-11	16:33:44
3	1	1	1	40	4	2023-12-11	16:38:31
4	1	1	1	40	4	2023-12-11	16:44:21
5	1	1	1	20	2	2023-12-11	16:46:24
6	1	1	1	50	5	2023-12-11	16:49:15
7	1	1	1	50	5	2023-12-11	16:49:15
8	1	1	1	20	2	2023-12-11	16:53:58
9	1	1	1	20	2	2023-12-11	16:54:03
10	1	1	1	30	3	2023-12-11	16:55:20
11	1	1	1	30	3	2023-12-11	16:55:24
12	1	1	1	30	3	2023-12-11	16:56:46
13	1	1	1	90	9	2023-12-11	16:59:23
14	1	1	1	30	3	2023-12-11	17:00:35
15	1	1	1	10	1	2023-12-11	17:02:36
16	1	1	1	10	1	2023-12-11	17:10:47

Figure 9. Recording the usage of umbrella in DB

id	box_id	place_in_box	qr_code_number	in_use	user_email
1	1	1	151123	0	NULL
2	NULL	NULL	151122	1	sophiatest@test...
NULL	NULL	NULL	NULL	NULL	NULL

box_id	spaces	u_available	box_qr_code	s_available
1	10	1	151121	1
NULL	NULL	NULL	NULL	NULL

In the database, all umbrella QR codes, box states, and locations are systematically recorded based on user email. As users engage with the umbrellas, the state of each umbrella in the database dynamically updates, facilitating accurate tracking of the umbrella's status throughout its usage figure 8.

Figure 10. Showcases the umbrella box prototype printed using a PLA 3D printer

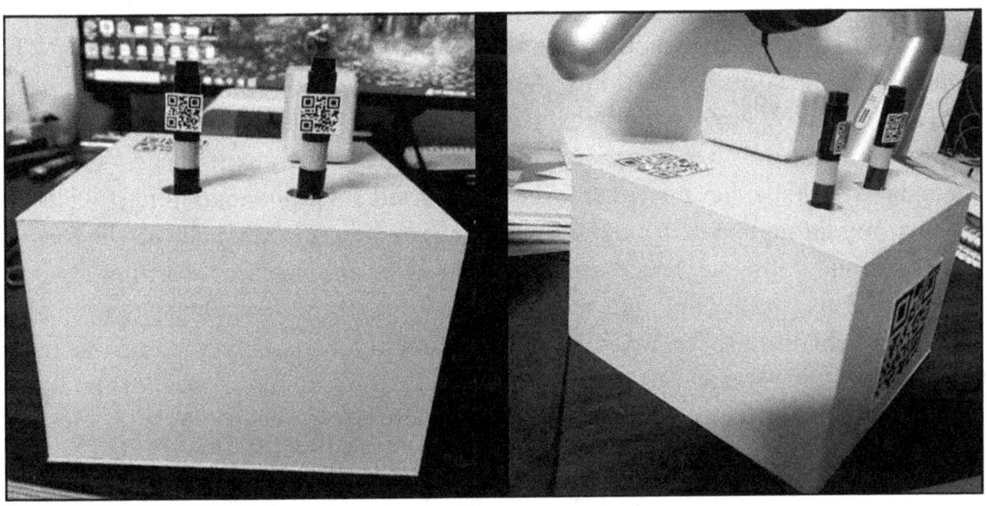

Password security is further fortified through the implementation of salt and password hashing using the bcrypt library. During user registration, the entered password undergoes a process where it is combined with a newly generated salt and hashed, mitigating vulnerabilities to brute force attacks. The resultant hashed password and salt are then securely stored in the database.

On the server side, robust security measures are applied, with password hashing and salting executed to enhance protection. During user registration, the server-side process involves hashing and salting the entered password, and during user sign-in, the server-side comparison ensures secure access for the user.

The server architecture includes endpoints facilitating communication between clients and the MySQL database. This functionality empowers the server to retrieve and authorize user information, as well as manage umbrella and box-related data. All variables are meticulously parameterized to prevent SQL injection, reinforcing the overall security posture of the 'Umber' system shown in figure 9.

CONCLUSION

In conclusion, Prototype 1 serves as a detailed exhibition of the key features of the 'Umber mobile app project. It encompasses crucial elements such as the user interface (UI) and a seamless login process, which makes it easier for users to access the app. The prototype adeptly illustrates its capacity to track user and box locations, calculate usage time, and autonomously conclude usage upon the umbrella's return to its designated box. This feature is particularly useful for people who tend to forget their umbrellas or misplace them since it ensures that the umbrella is always in the right place when not in use. The 'Umber' app is proficient in reading and scanning QR codes, which contributes to a user-friendly and efficient experience. This feature enables users to quickly access the app and use its functionalities without any hassle. The inclusion of user data storage for login purposes adds a personalized touch, ensuring a tailored experience for each user. This feature also makes it easier for users to access the app since they don't have to log in every time they want to use it.

Moreover, the app empowers users to track their location while visualizing the positions of 'Umber' boxes on a map. This feature is particularly useful for people who are unfamiliar with the area they're in and need help finding the nearest 'Umber' box. The app also facilitates the reception and display of real-time box status data, augmenting user awareness and convenience. This feature enables users to know whether a box is available or not, making it easier for them to plan their activities. The development of the 'Umber' mobile app aligns with its overarching objective of introducing an on-demand umbrella service, redefining user convenience, and reshaping the traditional use of umbrellas. This innovative approach reflects the broader trend of integrating technology into daily life, highlighting the transformative impact of innovation on everyday experiences. The 'Umber' app effectively addresses challenges related to forgetfulness and environmental impact while contributing to sustainability through tracking and search functionalities. Looking ahead, the focus of future research involves integrating advanced sensor technologies and machine learning algorithms into the 'Umber' app. This exploration aims to enhance the user experience and improve adaptability to various weather conditions. The potential introduction of a compact screen on the umbrella box could showcase real-time weather updates, AI assistants, box condition monitoring, and information about the umbrella inside. Additionally, there is room for innovation by upgrading umbrellas to include practical features such as a built-in flashlight, further enhancing user convenience and safety during nighttime walks. These technological enhancements align with the overarching goal of 'Umber' to consistently elevate user experience and address evolving needs, reflecting a commitment to purpose-driven technology development that enriches daily life.

REFERENCES

Celik, Z. B. (2019). IoTGuard: Dynamic Enforcement of Security and Safety Policy in Commodity IoT. *Network and Distributed System Security Symposium*. 10.14722/ndss.2019.23326

GCOO. (2024). *Asia Pacific's Leading Personal Mobility Startup*. GCOO. gcoo.io/team

Hlaing, N. N. S., Naing, M., & Naing, S. S. (2019). GPS and GSM Based Vehicle Tracking System. [IJTSRD]. *International Journal of Trend in Scientific Research and Development*, *3*(4), 271–275. https://www.ijtsrd.com/papers/ijtsrd23718.pdf. doi:10.31142/ijtsrd23718

Hu, S., & Dai, T. (2013). *Online Map Application Development Using Google Maps API, SQL Database, and ASP*. NET.

Hudson-Smith, A., Crooks, A., Gibin, M., Milton, R., & Batty, M. (2009). NeoGeography and Web 2.0: Concepts, Tools and Applications. *Journal of Location Based Services*, *3*(2), 118–145. doi:10.1080/17489720902950366

KakaoTalk. (n.d.). *Where People and the World Come to Get Connected*. Kakaocorp.com. www.kakaocorp.com/page/service/service/KakaoTalk?lang=en

Khanna, A., & Kaur, S. (2020). Internet of Things (IoT), Applications and Challenges: A Comprehensive Review. *Wireless Personal Communications*, *114*(2), 1687–1762. doi:10.1007/s11277-020-07446-4

Kumar, M., Kim, C., Son, Y., Singh, S. K., & Kim, S. (2024). Empowering Cyberattack Identification in IoHT Networks With Neighborhood Component-based Improvised Long Short-Term Memory. *IEEE Internet of Things Journal*, 1. doi:10.1109/JIOT.2024.3354988

Park, J. H., Yotxay, S., Singh, S. K., & Park, J. H. (2024). PoAh-Enabled Federated Learning Architecture for DDoS Attack Detection in IoT Networks. *Human-Centric Computing and Information Sciences, 14*(3).

Singh, S. K., Azzaoui, A. E., Choo, K. K. R., Yang, L. T., & Park, J. H. (2023). A Comprehensive Survey on Blockchain for Secure IoT-enabled Smart City beyond 5G: Approaches, Processes, Challenges, and Opportunities. *Human-Centric Computing and Information Sciences, 13*(51).

Singh, S. K., Kumar, M., Tanwar, S., & Park, J. H. (2024). GRU-based digital twin framework for data allocation and storage in IoT-enabled smart home networks. *Future Generation Computer Systems*, *153*, 391–402. doi:10.1016/j.future.2023.12.009

Stückler, J., & Behnke, S. (2021). Model Learning and Real-Time Tracking Using Multi-Resolution Surfel Maps. *Proceedings of the ... AAAI Conference on Artificial Intelligence*, *26*(1), 2081–2087. 10.1609/aaai.v26i1.8388

U-blox. (2015). *NEO-6 Series*. U-Blox. www.u-blox.com/en/product/neo-6-series

Compilation of References

Aamir, M., Masroor, S., Ali, Z. A., & Ting, B. T. (2019). Sustainable framework for smart transportation system: A case study of karachi. *Wireless Personal Communications*, *106*(1), 27–40. doi:10.1007/s11277-019-06259-4

Abbas, S., Sampedro, G. A., Abisado, M., Almadhor, A., Yousaf, I., & Hong, S. P. (2023). Harris-Hawk-Optimization-Based Deep Recurrent Neural Network for Securing the Internet of Medical Things. *Electronics (Basel)*, *12*(12), 2612. doi:10.3390/electronics12122612

Abbeel, P., & Ng, A. Y. (2004, July). Apprenticeship learning via inverse reinforcement learning. In *Proceedings of the twenty-first international conference on Machine learning* (p. 1). ACM. 10.1145/1015330.1015430

Abdelhady, A. M., Amin, O., Alouini, M. S., & Shihada, B. (2022). Revolutionizing optical wireless communications via smart optics. *IEEE Open Journal of the Communications Society*, *3*, 654–669. doi:10.1109/OJCOMS.2022.3164790

Abdellaoui Alaoui, E. A., & El Moudden, M. (2018). A Game Theoretic Approach to Analyse Security between Smart Vehicles and Parcels in Smart Cities. *MATEC Web of Conferences, 200*. IEEE. doi:10.1051/matecconf/201820000002

Abi Sen, A. A., Aljohani, Y. M., Hakami, A. A. H., Bahbouh, N. M., Alkhodre, A., & Alghamdi, M. S. (2023, March). A Framework for Moving from Traditional to Smart University. In *2023 10th International Conference on Computing for Sustainable Global Development (INDIACom)* (pp. 562-569). IEEE.

Abikoye, O. C., Oladipupo, E. T., Imoize, A. L., Awotunde, J. B., Lee, C. C., & Li, C. T. (2023). Securing Critical User Information over the Internet of Medical Things Platforms Using a Hybrid Cryptography Scheme. *Future Internet*, *15*(3), 99. doi:10.3390/fi15030099

Abinaya, K., Palaniappan, D., & Vedaraj, M. (2023). A Novel Hyper-Spectral Model to Optimize the Prediction Rate for Heart Disease in Modern Healthcare Networks. *Engineering Proceedings*, *59*(1), 59081.

Adi, E., Anwar, A., Baig, Z., & Zeadally, S. (2020). Machine learning and data analytics for the Io T. *Neural Computing & Applications*, *32*(20), 16205–16233. doi:10.1007/s00521-020-04874-y

Aggarwal, S., Chaudhary, R., Aujla, G. S., Kumar, N., Choo, K. K. R., & Zomaya, A. Y. (2019). Blockchain for smart communities: Applications, challenges and opportunities. In Journal of Network and Computer Applications, 144. doi:10.1016/j.jnca.2019.06.018

Aghimien, D. O., Aigbavboa, C., Edwards, D. J., Mahamadu, A. M., Olomolaiye, P., Nash, H., & Onyia, M. (2022). A fuzzy synthetic evaluation of the challenges of smart city development in developing countries. *Smart and Sustainable Built Environment*, *11*(3), 405–421. doi:10.1108/SASBE-06-2020-0092

Ahad, M. A., Paiva, S., Tripathi, G., & Feroz, N. (2020). Enabling technologies and sustainable smart cities. *Sustainable Cities and Society*, *61*, 102301. doi:10.1016/j.scs.2020.102301

Ahila, A., Dahan, F., Alroobaea, R., & Alghamdi, W. Y. (2023). A smart IoMT based architecture for E-healthcare patient monitoring system using artificial intelligence algorithms. *Frontiers in Physiology*, *14*, 1125952. doi:10.3389/fphys.2023.1125952 PMID:36793418

Ahmad, T., Madonski, R., Zhang, D., Huang, C., & Mujeeb, A. (2022). Data-driven probabilistic machine learning in sustainable smart energy/smart energy systems: Key developments, challenges, and future research opportunities in the context of smart grid paradigm. *Renewable & Sustainable Energy Reviews*, *160*, 112128. doi:10.1016/j.rser.2022.112128

Ahmed, E., Yaqoob, I., Gani, A., Imran, M., & Guizani, M. (2016). Internet-of-things-based smart environments: State of the art, taxonomy, and open research challenges. *IEEE Wireless Communications*, *23*(5), 10–16. doi:10.1109/MWC.2016.7721736

Ahmed, I., Zhang, Y., Jeon, G., Lin, W., Khosravi, M. R., & Qi, L. (2022). A Blockchain- and artificial intelligence-enabled smart IoT framework for sustainable city. *International Journal of Intelligent Systems*, *37*(9), 6493–6507. doi:10.1002/int.22852

Ahmed, J., Nguyen, T. N., Ali, B., Javed, M. A., & Mirza, J. (2023). On the Physical Layer Security of Federated Learning Based IoMT Networks. *IEEE Journal of Biomedical and Health Informatics*, *27*(2), 691–697. doi:10.1109/JBHI.2022.3173947 PMID:35536821

Ahmed, Z., Rawat, A., & Kumari, P. (2021). An Anaylsis of Iot Based Smart Cities. [IJETA]. *International Journal of Engineering Trends and Applications*, *8*(4), 30–35. www.ijetajournal.org

Ahuja, N. J., Srikanth, P., Konstantinou, C., & Kaust, C. (2021). *Blockchain and Autonomous Vehicles: Recent Advances and Future Directions*. Research. Gate.

Ahvar, E., Ahvar, S., Raza, S. M., Manuel Sanchez Vilchez, J., & Lee, G. M. (2021). Next generation of SDN in cloud-fog for 5G and beyond-enabled applications: Opportunities and challenges. *Network*, *1*(1), 28-49.28-49. doi:10.3390/network1010004

Ahvenniemi, H., Huovila, A., Pinto-Seppä, I., & Airaksinen, M. (2017). What are the differences between sustainable and smart cities? *Cities (London, England)*, *60*, 234–245. doi:10.1016/j.cities.2016.09.009

Al Nuaimi, A. J. J., Al Neyadi, H., Mohamed, N., & Al-Jaroodi, J. (2015). Applications of big data to smart cities. *Journal of Internet Services and Applications*, *6*(1), 25. doi:10.1186/s13174-015-0041-5

Al Sharif, R., & Pokharel, S. (2022). Smart city dimensions and associated risks: Review of literature. *Sustainable Cities and Society*, *77*, 103542. doi:10.1016/j.scs.2021.103542

Alabadi, M., Habbal, A., & Wei, X. (2022). Industrial internet of things: Requirements, architecture, challenges, and future research directions. *IEEE Access : Practical Innovations, Open Solutions*, *10*, 66374–66400. doi:10.1109/ACCESS.2022.3185049

Alabdan, R., Alruban, A., Hilal, A. M., & Motwakel, A. (2023). Artificial-Intelligence-Based Decision Making for Oral Potentially Malignant Disorder Diagnosis in Internet of Medical Things Environment. *Healthcare (Basel)*, *11*(1), 113. doi:10.3390/healthcare11010113 PMID:36611573

Alahi, M. E. E., Sukkuea, A., Tina, F. W., Nag, A., Kurdthongmee, W., Suwannarat, K., & Mukhopadhyay, S. C. (2023). Integration of IoT-enabled technologies and artificial intelligence (AI) for smart city scenario: Recent advancements and future trends. *Sensors (Basel)*, *23*(11), 5206. doi:10.3390/s23115206 PMID:37299934

Alamri, B., Crowley, K., & Richardson, I. (2022). Blockchain-Based Identity Management Systems in Health IoT: A Systematic Review. *IEEE Access : Practical Innovations, Open Solutions*, *10*, 59612–59629. doi:10.1109/ACCESS.2022.3180367

Alawadhi, S., & Aldama-Nalda, A. (2019). The impact of smart city applications on the quality of life in Smart Dubai city. *Telematics and Informatics*, *44*, 101271.

Alaziz, S. N., Albayati, B., El-Bagoury, A. A. A. H., & Shafik, W. (2023). Clustering of COVID-19 Multi-Time Series-Based K-Means and PCA With Forecasting. [IJDWM]. *International Journal of Data Warehousing and Mining*, *19*(3), 1–25. doi:10.4018/IJDWM.317374

Aleksandrovičs, V., Filičevs, E., & Kampars, J. (2016). Internet of things: Structure, features and management. *Information Technology and Management Science*, *19*(1), 78–84. doi:10.1515/itms-2016-0015

Al-Garadi, M. A., Mohamed, A., Al-Ali, A. K., Du, X., Ali, I., & Guizani, M. (2020). A survey of machine and deep learning methods for internet of things (IoT) security. *IEEE Communications Surveys and Tutorials*, *22*(3), 1646–1685. doi:10.1109/COMST.2020.2988293

Al-hajjar, A. L. N., & Al-Qurabat, A. K. M. (2023). An overview of machine learning methods in enabling IoMT-based epileptic seizure detection. *The Journal of Supercomputing*, *79*(14), 16017–16064. doi:10.1007/s11227-023-05299-9 PMID:37359338

Ali, M. H., Jaber, M. M., Abd, S. K., Alkhayyat, A., & Albaghdadi, M. F. (2022). Big data analysis and cloud computing for smart transportation system integration. *Multimedia Tools and Applications*, 1–18. doi:10.1007/s11042-022-13700-7

Ali, S. E., Tariq, N., Khan, F. A., Ashraf, M., Abdul, W., & Saleem, K. (2023). BFT-IoMT: A Blockchain-Based Trust Mechanism to Mitigate Sybil Attack Using Fuzzy Logic in the Internet of Medical Things. *Sensors (Basel)*, *23*(9), 4265. doi:10.3390/s23094265 PMID:37177468

Ali, Z., Naz, S., Zaffar, H., Choi, J., & Kim, Y. (2023). An IoMT-Based Melanoma Lesion Segmentation Using Conditional Generative Adversarial Networks. *Sensors (Basel)*, *23*(7), 3548. doi:10.3390/s23073548 PMID:37050607

Alizadehsani, R., Roshanzamir, M., Izadi, N. H., Gravina, R., Kabir, H. M. D., Nahavandi, D., Alinejad-Rokny, H., Khosravi, A., Acharya, U. R., Nahavandi, S., & Fortino, G. (2023). Swarm Intelligence in Internet of Medical Things: A Review. *Sensors (Basel)*, *23*(3), 1466. doi:10.3390/s23031466 PMID:36772503

Al-Kahtani, M. S., Khan, F., & Taekeun, W. (2022). Application of internet of things and sensors in healthcare. *Sensors (Basel)*, *22*(15), 5738. doi:10.3390/s22155738 PMID:35957294

Al-Kashoash, H. A., & Kemp, A. H. (2016). Comparison of 6LoWPAN and LPWAN for the Internet of Things. *Australian Journal of Electrical and Electronics Engineering*, *13*(4), 268–274. doi:10.1080/1448837X.2017.1409920

Almalki, F. A., Alsamhi, S. H., Sahal, R., Hassan, J., Hawbani, A., Rajput, N. S., Saif, A., Morgan, J., & Breslin, J. (2023). Green Io T for eco-friendly and sustainable smart cities: Future directions and opportunities. *Mobile Networks and Applications*, *28*(1), 178–202. doi:10.1007/s11036-021-01790-w

Alnssyan, B., Ahmad, Z., Malela-Majika, J. C., Seong, J. T., & Shafik, W. (2023). On the identifiability and statistical features of a new distributional approach with reliability applications. *AIP Advances*, *13*(12), 125211. doi:10.1063/5.0178555

Al-Qarafi, A., Alsolai, H., Alzahrani, J. S., Negm, N., Alharbi, L. A., Al Duhayyim, M., Mohsen, H., Al-Shabi, M., & Al-Wesabi, F. N. (2022). Artificial jellyfish optimization with deep-learning-driven decision support system for energy management in smart cities. *Applied Sciences (Basel, Switzerland)*, *12*(15), 7457. doi:10.3390/app12157457

Alqarni, M. A., Alkatheiri, M. S., Chauhdary, S. H., & Saleem, S. (2023). Use of Blockchain-Based Smart Contracts in Logistics and Supply Chains. *Electronics (Basel)*, *12*(6), 1340. doi:10.3390/electronics12061340

Alromaihi, S., Elmedany, W., & Balakrishna, C. (2018, August). Cyber security challenges of deploying IoT in smart cities for healthcare applications. In *2018 6th International Conference on Future Internet of Things and Cloud Workshops (FiCloudW)* (pp. 140-145). IEEE. 10.1109/W-FiCloud.2018.00028

Alsaig, A., & Alagar, V. (2023, August). Dependable Service-Oriented Design of Healthcare IoT. In *2023 IEEE International Conference on Smart Internet of Things (SmartIoT)* (pp. 257-264). IEEE. 10.1109/SmartIoT58732.2023.00046

Alsemmeari, R. A., Dahab, M. Y., Alsulami, A. A., Alturki, B., & Algarni, S. (2023). Resilient Security Framework Using TNN and Blockchain for IoMT. *Electronics (Basel)*, *12*(10), 2252. doi:10.3390/electronics12102252

Alshammari, A., & Fayez Alanazi, M. (2023). Use of Technology in Enhancing Learning Among Nurses in Saudi Arabia; a Systematic Review. *Journal of Multidisciplinary Healthcare*, *16*, 1587–1599. doi:10.2147/JMDH.S413281 PMID:37313273

Alshammari, B. M. (2023). A Framework For Developing Secure Internet Of Medical Things: A Comprehensive Roadmap From An Artificial Intelligence Perspective. *Journal of Theoretical and Applied Information Technology*, *101*(4).

Alshehri, M. (2023). Blockchain-assisted cyber security in medical things using artificial intelligence. *Electronic Research Archive*, *31*(2), 708–728. doi:10.3934/era.2023035

Al-Turjman, F., & Lemayian, J. P. (2020). Intelligence, security, and vehicular sensor networks in internet of things (IoT)-enabled smart-cities: An overview. *Computers & Electrical Engineering*, *87*, 106776. doi:10.1016/j.compeleceng.2020.106776

AlZubi, A. A., Alarifi, A., Al-Maitah, M., & Alheyasat, O. (2021). Multi-sensor information fusion for Internet of Things assisted automated guided vehicles in smart city. *Sustainable Cities and Society*, *64*, 102539. doi:10.1016/j.scs.2020.102539

Anantrasirichai, N., & Bull, D. (2022). Artificial intelligence in the creative industries [review]. *Artificial Intelligence Review*, *55*(1), 589–656. doi:10.1007/s10462-021-10039-7

Andoni, M., Robu, V., Flynn, D., Abram, S., Geach, D., Jenkins, D., McCallum, P., & Peacock, A. (2019). Blockchain technology in the energy sector: A systematic review of challenges and opportunities. In Renewable and Sustainable Energy Reviews, 100. doi:10.1016/j.rser.2018.10.014

Andreani, S., Kalchschmidt, M., Pinto, R., & Sayegh, A. (2019). Reframing technologically enhanced urban scenarios: A design research model towards human centered smart cities. *Technological Forecasting and Social Change*, *142*, 15–25. doi:10.1016/j.techfore.2018.09.028

Andrews, J. G., Buzzi, S., Choi, W., Hanly, S. V., Lozano, A., Soong, A. C. K., & Zhang, J. C. (2014). What will 5G be? *IEEE Journal on Selected Areas in Communications*, *32*(6), 1065–1082. doi:10.1109/JSAC.2014.2328098

Ang, K. L. M., Seng, J. K. P., & Ngharamike, E. (2022). Towards crowdsourcing internet of things (crowd-iot): Architectures, security and applications. *Future Internet*, *14*(2), 49. doi:10.3390/fi14020049

Angrishi, K. (2017). Turning internet of things (iot) into internet of vulnerabilities (iov): Iot botnets. *arXiv preprint arXiv:1702.03681.*

Anzanpour, A., Rahmani, A. M., Liljeberg, P., & Tenhunen, H. (2015, December). Internet of things enabled in-home health monitoring system using early warning score. In *Proceedings of the 5th EAI international conference on wireless mobile communication and healthcare* (pp. 174-177). EUDL. 10.4108/eai.14-10-2015.2261616

Ardakani, S. P., & Cheshmehzangi, A. (2023). *Big Data Analytics for Smart Urban Systems*. Springer Nature. doi:10.1007/978-981-99-5543-5

Arora, P., Kaur, B., & Teixeira, M. A. (2022). Machine Learning-Based Security Solutions for Healthcare: An Overview. *Emerging Technologies for Computing, Communication and Smart Cities. Proceedings of ETCCS, 2021*, 649–659.

Ashokrao, P. R., Radhakrishna, D. D., Sharma, M., & Bhad, S. (2023, May). Health Disease Prediction Using Machine Learning and Internet of Things. In *2023 4th International Conference on Intelligent Engineering and Management (ICIEM)* (pp. 1-6). IEEE. 10.1109/ICIEM59379.2023.10165903

Ashraf, S. (2021). A proactive role of IoT devices in building smart cities. *Internet of Things and Cyber-Physical Systems*, *1*, 8–13. doi:10.1016/j.iotcps.2021.08.001

Aslam, M., Khan Abbasi, M. A., Khalid, T., Shan, R., Ullah, S., Ahmad, T., Saeed, S., Alabbad, D. A., & Ahmad, R. (2022). Getting Smarter about Smart Cities: Improving Data Security and Privacy through Compliance. *Sensors (Basel)*, *22*(23), 9338. doi:10.3390/s22239338 PMID:36502039

Astarita, V., Giofrè, V. P., Mirabelli, G., & Solina, V. (2020). A Review of Blockchain-Based Systems in Transportation. *Information (Basel)*, *11*(1), 21. doi:10.3390/info11010021

Ateya, A. A., Algarni, A. D., Hamdi, M., Koucheryavy, A., & Soliman, N. F. (2021). Enabling heterogeneous IoT networks over 5G networks with ultra-dense deployment—Using MEC/SDN. *Electronics (Basel)*, *10*(8), 910. doi:10.3390/electronics10080910

Attar, H., Issa, H., Ababneh, J., Abbasi, M., Solyman, A. A. A., Khosravi, M., & Agieb, R. S. (2022). 5G System Overview for Ongoing Smart Applications: Structure, Requirements, and Specifications. *Computational Intelligence and Neuroscience 2022*. doi:10.1155/2022/2476841

Atzori, L., Iera, A., & Morabito, G. (2010). The Internet of Things: A survey. *Computer Networks*, *54*(15), 2787–2805. doi:10.1016/j.comnet.2010.05.010

Aydin, S., & Aydin, M. N. (2020). A sustainable multi-layered open data processing model for agriculture: IoT based case study using semantic web for hazelnut fields. *Adv. Sci. Technol. Eng. Syst. J*, *5*(2), 309–319. doi:10.25046/aj050241

Azgomi, H. F., & Jamshidi, M. (2018, November). A brief survey on smart community and smart transportation. In *2018 IEEE 30th international conference on tools with artificial intelligence (ICTAI)* (pp. 932-939). IEEE. 10.1109/ICTAI.2018.00144

Bacciu, D., Carta, A., Gnesi, S., & Semini, L. (2017). An experience in using machine learning for short-term predictions in smart transportation systems. *Journal of Logical and Algebraic Methods in Programming*, *87*, 52–66. doi:10.1016/j.jlamp.2016.11.002

BaconD. (2017). Federated learning: Strategies for improving communication efficiency. Available:arXiv:1610.05492.

Bagga, P., Das, A. K., Chamola, V., & Guizani, M. (2022). Blockchain-envisioned access control for internet of things applications: A comprehensive survey and future directions. *Telecommunication Systems*, *81*(1), 125–173. doi:10.1007/s11235-022-00938-7 PMID:35879968

Bakkaiahgari, P. V. D., & Prasad, K. V. (2023). Prim based link quality and thermal aware adaptive routing protocol for IoMT using SigFox network in WBAN. *Evolving Systems*, *14*(3), 533–544. doi:10.1007/s12530-022-09451-3

Balasubramanlan, S. (2018). *The Global Cyberattack and the Need to Revisit Health Care Cybersecurity*. Research Gate.

Bandara, E., Shetty, S., Rahman, A., Mukkamala, R., & Liang, X. (2022). Moose: A Scalable Blockchain Architecture for 5G Enabled IoT with Sharding and Network Slicing. *IEEE Wireless Communications and Networking Conference, WCNC,* (pp. 1194–1199). IEEE. 10.1109/WCNC51071.2022.9771885

Bansod, S., & Ragha, L. (2022). Challenges in making Blockchain privacy compliant for the digital world: some measures. *Sadhana - Academy Proceedings in Engineering Sciences, 47*(3), 1–17. https://doi.org/. doi:10.1007/S12046-022-01931-1/FIGURES/9

Bao, Z., He, D., Wang, H., Luo, M., & Peng, C. (2023). A Group Signature Scheme with Selective Linkability and Traceability for Blockchain-Based Data Sharing Systems in E-health Services. *IEEE Internet of Things Journal, 10*(23), 21115–21128. doi:10.1109/JIOT.2023.3284968

Barrett, B., & Brief, H. (2018). *Hackers are Holding an LA Hospital's Computers Hostage.* Research Gate.

Barros, T., Silva, R., Quevedo, J., Corujo, D., & Aguiar, R. L. (2023, November). Flexible Aether Slice Provisioning for 5G Enterprise Connected Edge. In *2023 IEEE Conference on Network Function Virtualization and Software Defined Networks (NFV-SDN)* (pp. 227-232). IEEE. 10.1109/NFV-SDN59219.2023.10329728

Barua, A., Al Alamin, M. A., Hossain, M. S., & Hossain, E. (2022). Security and privacy threats for bluetooth low energy in iot and wearable devices: A comprehensive survey. *IEEE Open Journal of the Communications Society, 3*, 251–281. doi:10.1109/OJCOMS.2022.3149732

Baskar, P., Khang, A., Annadurai, S., Amritha, S. S., & Annadurai, P. (2024). Quantum Computing Smart City: Fostering Sustainability and Green Infrastructure With Smart City. In Applications and Principles of Quantum Computing (pp. 162-213). IGI Global.

Batty, M., Axhausen, K. W., Giannotti, F., Pozdnoukhov, A., Bazzani, A., Wachowicz, M., Ouzounis, G., & Portugali, Y. (2012). Smart cities of the future. *The European Physical Journal. Special Topics, 214*(1), 481–518. doi:10.1140/epjst/e2012-01703-3

Bauer, M., Sanchez, L., & Song, J. (2021). IoT-enabled smart cities: Evolution and outlook. *Sensors (Basel), 21*(13), 4511. doi:10.3390/s21134511 PMID:34209436

Bekara, C. (2014). Security Issues and Challenges for the IoT-based Smart Grid. *Procedia Computer Science, 34*, 532–537. doi:10.1016/j.procs.2014.07.064

Belli, L., Cilfone, A., Davoli, L., Ferrari, G., Adorni, P., Di Nocera, F., & Bertolotti, E. (2020). IoT-enabled smart sustainable cities: Challenges and approaches. *Smart Cities, 3*(3), 1039-1071.*3*(3), 1039-1071.

Belli, L., Cilfone, A., Davoli, L., Ferrari, G., Adorni, P., Di Nocera, F., Dall'Olio, A., Pellegrini, C., Mordacci, M., & Bertolotti, E. (2020). IoT-enabled smart sustainable cities: Challenges and approaches. *Smart Cities, 3*(3), 1039–1071. doi:10.3390/smartcities3030052

Ben Rjab, A., Mellouli, S., & Corbett, J. (2023). Barriers to artificial intelligence adoption in smart cities: A systematic literature review and research agenda. *Government Information Quarterly, 40*(3), 101814. doi:10.1016/j.giq.2023.101814

Benedict, S., Rumaise, P., & Kaur, J. (2019). IoT Blockchain Solution for Air Quality Monitoring in SmartCities. *International Symposium on Advanced Networks and Telecommunication Systems, ANTS, 2019-December.* IEEE. 10.1109/ANTS47819.2019.9118148

Bennis, M., Taleb, T., & Debbah, M. (2018). Ultra-reliable and low latency wireless communication: Tail, risk, and scale. *Proceedings of the IEEE, 106*(10), 1834–1853. doi:10.1109/JPROC.2018.2867029

Bera, B., Mitra, A., Das, A. K., Puthal, D., & Park, Y. H. (2023). Private Blockchain-Based AI-Envisioned Home Monitoring Framework in IoMT-Enabled COVID-19 Environment. *IEEE Consumer Electronics Magazine, 12*(3), 62–71. doi:10.1109/MCE.2021.3137104

Bernard, S., Mawad, F., & Kim, Y. (2020). From human-computer interaction to human- computer co-creation: A symbiotic approach to designing AI systems. *ACM Transactions on Interactive Intelligent Systems, 10*(2), 1–29.

Bertino, E., & Jahanshahi, M. R. (2018). Adaptive and cost-effective collection of high- quality data for critical infrastructure and emergency management in smart cities—Framework and challenges. [JDIQ]. *ACM Journal of Data and Information Quality, 10*(1), 1–6. doi:10.1145/3190579

Bhardwaj, R., Gupta, S. N., Gupta, M., & Tiwari, P. (2021, March). IoT based healthware and healthcare monitoring system in india. In *2021 International Conference on Advance Computing and Innovative Technologies in Engineering (ICACITE)* (pp. 406-408). IEEE. 10.1109/ICACITE51222.2021.9404633

Bhatia, H., Panda, S. N., & Nagpal, D. (2020, June). Internet of Things and its Applications in Healthcare-A Survey. In *2020 8th International Conference on Reliability, Infocom Technologies and Optimization (Trends and Future Directions) (ICRITO)* (pp. 305-310). IEEE. 10.1109/ICRITO48877.2020.9197816

Bhattacharjee, Y., Arief, I., & Bose, S. (2017). Recent trends in multi-layered architectures towards screening electromagnetic radiation: Challenges and perspectives. *Journal of Materials Chemistry. C, Materials for Optical and Electronic Devices, 5*(30), 7390–7403. doi:10.1039/C7TC02172K

Bhatt, V., & Chakraborty, S. (2023). Improving service engagement in healthcare through internet of things based healthcare systems. *Journal of Science and Technology Policy Management, 14*(1), 53–73. doi:10.1108/JSTPM-03-2021-0040

Bibri, S. E., & Bibri, S. E. (2018). Conceptual, theoretical, disciplinary, and discursive foundations: A multidimensional framework. *Smart Sustainable Cities of the Future: The Untapped Potential of Big Data Analytics and Context–Aware Computing for Advancing Sustainability*, (pp. 39-131). Research Gate.

Bibri, S. E. (2018). The IoT for smart sustainable cities of the future: An analytical framework for sensor-based big data applications for environmental sustainability. *Sustainable Cities and Society, 38*, 230–253. doi:10.1016/j.scs.2017.12.034

Bibri, S. E., & Jagatheesaperumal, S. K. (2023). Harnessing the Potential of the Metaverse and Artificial Intelligence for the Internet of City Things: Cost-Effective XReality and Synergistic AIoT Technologies. *Smart Cities, 6*(5), 2397–2429. doi:10.3390/smartcities6050109

Biswas, K., & Muthukkumarasamy, V. (2016). Securing Smart Cities Using Blockchain Technology. *2016 IEEE 18th International Conference on High Performance Computing and Communications; IEEE 14th International Conference on Smart City; IEEE 2nd International Conference on Data Science and Systems (HPCC/SmartCity/DSS)*, (pp. 1392–1393). IEEE. 10.1109/HPCC-SmartCity-DSS.2016.0198

Boccardi, F., Heath, R. W., Lozano, A., Marzetta, T. L., & Popovski, P. (2014). Five disruptive technology directions for 5G. *IEEE Communications Magazine, 52*(2), 74–80. doi:10.1109/MCOM.2014.6736746

Bokhari, S. A. A., & Myeong, S. (2022). Use of artificial intelligence in smart cities for smart decision-making: A social innovation perspective. *Sustainability (Basel), 14*(2), 620. doi:10.3390/su14020620

Bolukbasi, T., Chang, K.-W., Zou, J. Y., Saligrama, V., & Kalai, A. T. (2016). Man is to computer programmer as woman is to homemaker? Debiasing word embeddings. *Advances in Neural Information Processing Systems.*

Bommu, S., M, A. K., Babburu, K., N, S., Thalluri, L. N., G, V. G., Gopalan, A., Mallapati, P. K., Guha, K., Mohammad, H. R., & S, S. K. (2023). Smart City IoT System Network Level Routing Analysis and Blockchain Security Based Implementation. *Journal of Electrical Engineering & Technology*, *18*(2), 1351–1368. doi:10.1007/s42835-022-01239-4 PMID:37521954

Borcoci, E., Drăgulinescu, A. M., Li, F. Y., Vochin, M. C., & Kjellstadli, K. (2021). An overview of 5G slicing operational business models for Internet of vehicles, maritime IoT applications and connectivity solutions. *IEEE Access : Practical Innovations, Open Solutions*, *9*, 156624–156646. doi:10.1109/ACCESS.2021.3128496

Borgia, E. (2014). The Internet of Things vision: Key features, applications and open issues. *Computer Communications*, *54*, 1–31. doi:10.1016/j.comcom.2014.09.008

Botez, R., Sferle, A. T., Ivanciu, I. A., & Dobrota, V. (2023, July). Work-in-Progress: KubeUT: A Cloud-Agnostic Kubernetes Management Platform. In *2023 IEEE International Black Sea Conference on Communications and Networking (BlackSeaCom)* (pp. 384-389). IEEE. 10.1109/BlackSeaCom58138.2023.10299745

Bouaouad, A. E., Cherradi, A., Assoul, S., & Souissi, N. (2020). The key layers of IoT architecture. In *2020 5th International Conference on Cloud Computing and Artificial Intelligence: Technologies and Applications (CloudTech)* (pp. 1-4). IEEE. 10.1109/CloudTech49835.2020.9365919

Boukerche, A., & Coutinho, R. W. (2019). Crowd management: The overlooked component of smart transportation systems. *IEEE Communications Magazine*, *57*(4), 48–53. doi:10.1109/MCOM.2019.1800641

Bruce, Z. (2017, February, 9). Overview of networking technologies used to build IoT solutions. *Intelligent CIO*. https://www.intelligenttechchannels.com/2017/02/09/overview-of-networking-technologies-used-to-build-iot-solutions/

Brunetta, G., & Caldarice, O. (2020). Spatial resilience in planning: Meanings, challenges, and perspectives for urban transition. *Sustainable Cities and Communities*, 628-640.

Burange, A. W., & Misalkar, H. D. (2015, March). Review of Internet of Things in development of smart cities with data management & privacy. In *2015 International Conference on Advances in Computer Engineering and Applications* (pp. 189-195). IEEE. 10.1109/ICACEA.2015.7164693

Butt, S. A., Diaz-Martinez, J. L., Jamal, T., Ali, A., De-La-Hoz-Franco, E., & Shoaib, M. (2019, July). IoT smart health security threats. In *2019 19th International conference on computational science and its applications (ICCSA)* (pp. 26-31). IEEE. 10.1109/ICCSA.2019.000-8

Cabanillas-Carbonell, M., Pérez-Martínez, J., & Yáñez, J. (2023). 5G Technology in the Digital Transformation of Healthcare, a Systematic Review. *Sustainability*, *15*, 3178. doi:10.3390/su15043178

Cappa, F., Franco, S., & Rosso, F. (2022). Citizens and cities: Leveraging citizen science and big data for sustainable urban development. *Business Strategy and the Environment*, *31*(2), 648–667. doi:10.1002/bse.2942

Caragliu, A., Del, B., & C–Nijkamp, P. (2011). Smart cities in Europe. *Journal of Urban Technology, 18* (2), 65–82.

Caragliu, A., & Del Bo, C. (2023). Smart cities and the urban digital divide. *NPJ Urban Sustainability*, *3*(1), 43. doi:10.1038/s42949-023-00117-w

Caragliu, A., & Del Bo, C. F. (2022). Smart cities and urban inequality. *Regional Studies*, *56*(7), 1097–1112. doi:10.1080/00343404.2021.1984421

Caragliu, A., Del Bo, C., & Nijkamp, P. (2011). Smart cities in Europe. *Journal of Urban Technology*, *18*(2), 65–82. doi:10.1080/10630732.2011.601117

Cardullo, P. (2020). *Citizens in the'smart City': Participation, Co-production, Governance*. Routledge. doi:10.4324/9780429438806

Car, T., Stifanich, L. P., & Kovačić, N. (2022). The role of 5G and IoT in smart cities. *ENTRENOVA-ENTerprise REsearch InNOVAtion*, *8*(1), 377–389. doi:10.54820/entrenova-2022-0032

Cath, C., Wachter, S., Mittelstadt, B., Taddeo, M., & Floridi, L. (2021). Artificial intelligence and the 'good society': The US, EU, and UK approach. *Science & Public Policy*, *48*(1), 1–14.

Cekerevac, Z., Dvorak, Z., Prigoda, L., & Cekerevac, P. (2017). Internet of things and the man-in-the-middle attacks–security and economic risks. *MEST Journal*, *5*(2), 15–25. doi:10.12709/mest.05.05.02.03

Celik, Z. B. (2019). IoTGuard: Dynamic Enforcement of Security and Safety Policy in Commodity IoT. *Network and Distributed System Security Symposium*. 10.14722/ndss.2019.23326

Centobelli, P., Cerchione, R., Del Vecchio, P., Oropallo, E., & Secundo, G. (2022). Blockchain technology for bridging trust, traceability and transparency in circular supply chain. *Information & Management*, *59*(7), 103508. doi:10.1016/j.im.2021.103508

Chakraborty, T., Naik, S. M., Panja, M., & Manvitha, B. (2023). Ten Years of Generative Adversarial Nets (GANs): A survey of the state-of-the-art. arXiv preprint arXiv:2308.16316. https://doi.org//arXiv.2308.16316 doi:10.48550

Chakravarthi, P. K., Yuvaraj, D., & Venkataramanan, V. (2022). IoT-based smart energy meter for smart grids. *ICDCS 2022 - 2022 6th International Conference on Devices, Circuits and Systems*, 360–363. 10.1109/ICDCS54290.2022.9780714

Chaloupková, M., & Janurová, M. (2019, June). Applications of the Smart Cities Concept. In *Proceedings of FEB Zagreb International Odyssey Conference on Economics and Business* (Vol. 1, No. 1, pp. 532-546). University of Zagreb, Faculty of Economics and Business.

Chang, S. H., Hsia, C. H., & Hong, W. Z. (2023). A secured internet of robotic things (IoRT) for long-term care services in a smart building. *The Journal of Supercomputing*, *79*(5), 5276–5290. doi:10.1007/s11227-022-04845-1 PMID:36258682

Chen, H., Yuan, L., & Jing, G. (2020). *5G Boosting Smart Cities Development.* 2020 2nd International Conference on Artificial Intelligence and Advanced Manufacture (AIAM), Manchester, UK. 10.1109/AIAM50918.2020.00038

Chen, C. M., Liu, S., Li, X., Islam, S. H., & Das, A. K. (2023). A provably-secure authenticated key agreement protocol for remote patient monitoring IoMT. *Journal of Systems Architecture*, *136*, 102831. doi:10.1016/j.sysarc.2023.102831

Chen, C., He, D., Khan, M. K., Luo, M., & Peng, C. (2023). A Secure Certificateless Signcryption Scheme Without Pairing for Internet of Medical Things. *IEEE Internet of Things Journal*, *10*(10), 9136–9147. doi:10.1109/JIOT.2022.3233180

Chen, H., Lei, S., Zhang, Y., Han, X., Cao, Y., & Zhang, Y. (2023). Blockchain-based internet of things security architecture and applications. *Journal of Ambient Intelligence and Humanized Computing*, *14*(12), 16703–16714. doi:10.1007/s12652-023-04675-w

Chen, X., Zhang, S., Ding, X., Kadry, S. N., & Hsu, C. H. (2021). IoT cloud platform for information processing in smart city. *Computational Intelligence*, *37*(3), 1428–1444. doi:10.1111/coin.12387

Chen, Y., & Han, D. (2018). Water quality monitoring in smart city: A pilot project. *Automation in Construction*, *89*, 307–316. doi:10.1016/j.autcon.2018.02.008

Chen, Y., Yao, Z., Zhao, Y., & Liu, K. (2018). A survey of big data architectures and machine learning algorithms in healthcare. *Journal of King Saud University. Computer and Information Sciences*.

Chettri, L., & Bera, R. (2019). A comprehensive survey on Internet of Things (IoT) toward 5G wireless systems. *IEEE Internet of Things Journal*, *7*(1), 16–32. doi:10.1109/JIOT.2019.2948888

Chías, P., & Abad, T. (2017). Green hospitals, green healthcare. *International Journal of Energy Production and Management*, *2*(2), 196–205. doi:10.2495/EQ-V2-N2-196-205

Chi, M.-H. (2022). IC Technologies and Systems for Green Future. *2022 China Semiconductor Technology International Conference (CSTIC)*, Shanghai, China. 10.1109/CSTIC55103.2022.9856769

Chinnasamy, P., & Deepalakshmi, P. (2018, April). Design of secure storage for health-care cloud using hybrid cryptography. In *2018 second international conference on inventive communication and computational technologies (ICICCT)* (pp. 1717-1720). IEEE. 10.1109/ICICCT.2018.8473107

Choi, M., Azzaoui, A. E., Singh, S. K., Salim, M. M., Jeremiah, S. R., & Park, J. H. (2022). The future of metaverse: Security issues, requirements, and solutions. *Human-Centric Computing and Information Sciences*, *12*(60), 1–14.

Choi, Y., Lim, D., Kim, M., & Chung, J. (2021). DeepFake and AI-based multimedia forgery detection: A review. *IEEE Access : Practical Innovations, Open Solutions*, *9*, 3599–3622.

Chourabi, H., Nam, T., Walker, S., Gil-Garcia, J. R., Mellouli, S., Nahon, K., & Scholl, H. J. (2012). Understanding smart cities: An integrative framework. *2012 45th Hawaii international conference on system sciences* (pp. 2289-2297). IEEE.

Chourabi, H., Nam, T., Walker, S., Gil-Garcia, J. R., Mellouli, S., Nahon, K., & Scholl, H. J. (2012, January). Understanding smart cities: An integrative framework. In *2012 45th Hawaii international conference on system sciences* (pp. 2289-2297). IEEE.

Chrysikos, T., Gourna, S., & Skouroliakou, A. (2023). RF Coverage Design for the Implementation of a Broadband Monitoring Service in the Context of 5G-Enabled Smart Cities. *Information (Basel)*, *14*(3), 156. doi:10.3390/info14030156

Cisco. (2020). *Cisco Global Cloud Index: Forecast and Methodology, 2016-2021* (White Paper). Cisco. https://www.cisco.com/c/en/us/solutions/executive-perspectives/annual-internet-report/index.html

Coman, C. M., D'amico, G., Coman, A. V., & Florescu, A. (2021). Techniques to improve reliability in an IoT architecture framework for intelligent products. *IEEE Access : Practical Innovations, Open Solutions*, *9*, 56940–56954. doi:10.1109/ACCESS.2021.3072168

Conti, M., Dargahi, T., & Dehghantanha, A. (2018). *Cyber threat intelligence: challenges and opportunities*. Springer International Publishing.

Cook, D. J., Duncan, G., Sprint, G., & Fritz, R. L. (2018). Using smart city technology to make healthcare smarter. *Proceedings of the IEEE*, *106*(4), 708–722. doi:10.1109/JPROC.2017.2787688 PMID:29628528

Cui, L., Xie, G., Qu, Y., Gao, L., & Yang, Y. (2018). Security and privacy in smart cities: Challenges and opportunities. *IEEE Access : Practical Innovations, Open Solutions*, *6*, 46134–46145. doi:10.1109/ACCESS.2018.2853985

Damodharan, P., & Ravichandran, C. S. (2019). Applicability evaluation of web mining in healthcare E-commerce towards business success and a derived cournot model. *Journal of Medical Systems*, *43*(8), 1–10. doi:10.1007/s10916-019-1395-1 PMID:31273541

Damodharan, P., & Ravichandran, C. S. (2019). Inclusive strategic techno-economic framework to incorporate essential aspects of web mining for the perspective of business success. *International Journal of Enterprise Network Management*, *10*(3-4), 329–349. doi:10.1504/IJENM.2019.103159

Dange, S., & Chatterjee, M. (2019). IoT botnet: The largest threat to the IoT network. In *Data Communication and Networks* [Singapore: Springer Singapore.]. *Proceedings of GUCON, 2019*, 137–157.

Dangi, R., Lalwani, P., Choudhary, G., You, I., & Pau, G. (2021). Study and Investigation on 5G Technology: A Systematic Review. *Sensors (Basel)*, *22*(1), 26. doi:10.3390/s22010026 PMID:35009569

Dar, H., & Kashyap, K. (2023). Smart Healthcare System (SHS): Medical Tourism Delivering, Consumption, and Elevating Tool in the Ages of Smart Technologies. *Tourism Planning & Development*, *20*(3), 397–415. doi:10.1080/21568316.2022.2109206

Darwish, D. (Ed.). (2024). *Emerging Trends in Cloud Computing Analytics*. Scalability, and Service Models.

Das, J., Ghosh, S., Mukherjee, A., Ghosh, S. K., & Buyya, R. (2022). RESCUE: Enabling green healthcare services using integrated Io T-edge-fog-cloud computing environments. *Software, Practice & Experience*, *52*(7), 1615–1642. doi:10.1002/spe.3078

Datta Gupta, K., Sharma, D. K., Ahmed, S., Gupta, H., Gupta, D., & Hsu, C. H. (2023). A Novel Lightweight Deep Learning-Based Histopathological Image Classification Model for IoMT. *Neural Processing Letters*, *55*(1), 205–228. doi:10.1007/s11063-021-10555-1 PMID:34121912

Datta, S. K., Da Costa, R. P. F., Bonnet, C., & Härri, J. (2016, June). oneM2M architecture based IoT framework for mobile crowd sensing in smart cities. In *2016 European conference on networks and communications (EuCNC)* (pp. 168-173). IEEE. 10.1109/EuCNC.2016.7561026

Dawood, M. S., Margaret, M. J., & Devika, R. (2018). Review on applications of internet of things (IoT). [IJARCET]. *International Journal of Advanced Research in Computer Engineering and Technology*, *7*(12).

de Fuentes, J. M., Gonzalez-Manzano, L., Solanas, A., & Veseli, F. (2018). Attribute-based credentials for privacy-aware smart health services in IoT-based smart cities. *Computer*, *51*(7), 44–53. doi:10.1109/MC.2018.3011042

Deebak, B. D., & Fadi, A. T. (2022). A robust and distributed architecture for 5G-enabled networks in the smart blockchain era. *Computer Communications*, *181*, 293–308. doi:10.1016/j.comcom.2021.10.015

Delson, T. R., & Jose, I. (2022, October). Study on 5G Massive MIMO Technology Key Parameters for Spectral Efficiency Improvement Including SINR Mapping on Rural Area Test Case. In *2022 IEEE 3rd Global Conference for Advancement in Technology (GCAT)* (pp. 1-6). IEEE.

Demertzi, V., Demertzis, S., & Demertzis, K. (2023). An Overview of Cyber Threats, Attacks and Countermeasures on the Primary Domains of Smart Cities. *Applied Sciences (Basel, Switzerland)*, *13*(2), 790. doi:10.3390/app13020790

Demirel, E. (2023). Application of Blockchain-Based Smart Contract in Sustainable Tourism Finance. *Blockchain for Tourism and Hospitality Industries,* 122–138. Springer. . doi:10.4324/9781003351917-9

Dewi, N. K., & Putra, A. S. (2021, March). Law enforcement in smart transportation systems on highway. In *International Conference on Education of Suryakancana (IConnects Proceedings)*. IEEE.

Dhasarathan, C., Hasan, M. K., Islam, S., Abdullah, S., Khapre, S., Singh, D., Alsulami, A. A., & Alqahtani, A. (2023). User privacy prevention model using supervised federated learning-based block chain approach for internet of Medical Things. *CAAI Transactions on Intelligence Technology*, cit2.12218. doi:10.1049/cit2.12218

Dieye, M., Valiorgue, P., Gelas, J. P., Diallo, E. H., Ghodous, P., Biennier, F., & Peyrol, E. (2023). A Self-Sovereign Identity Based on Zero-Knowledge Proof and Blockchain. *IEEE Access : Practical Innovations, Open Solutions*, *11*, 49445–49455. doi:10.1109/ACCESS.2023.3268768

Ding, Z., Yang, B., Chi, Y., & Guo, L. (2015). Enabling smart transportation systems: A parallel spatio-temporal database approach. *IEEE Transactions on Computers*, *65*(5), 1377–1391. doi:10.1109/TC.2015.2479596

Dlimi, Z., Ezzati, A., & Ben Alla, S. (2021). A Lightweight Blockchain for IoT in Smart City (IoT-SmartChain). *Computers, Materials & Continua*, *69*(2), 2687–2703. doi:10.32604/cmc.2021.018942

Dong, J., Song, C., Liu, S., Yin, H., Zheng, H., & Li, Y. (2022). Decentralized peer-to-peer energy trading strategy in energy Blockchain environment: A game-theoretic approach. *Applied Energy*, *325*, 119852. doi:10.1016/j.apenergy.2022.119852

Dorri, A., Kanhere, S. S., Jurdak, R., & Gauravaram, P. (2017). Blockchain for IoT security and privacy: The case study of a smart home. *2017 IEEE International Conference on Pervasive Computing and Communications Workshops (PerCom Workshops)*, (pp. 618–623). IEEE. 10.1109/PERCOMW.2017.7917634

dos Santos, Y. L., & Dias Canedo, E. (2019). On the design and implementation of an IoT based architecture for reading ultra high frequency tags. *Information (Basel)*, *10*(2), 41. doi:10.3390/info10020041

Douha, N. Y.-R., Sasabe, M., Taenaka, Y., & Kadobayashi, Y. (2023). An Evolutionary Game Theoretic Analysis of Cybersecurity Investment Strategies for Smart-Home Users against Cyberattacks. *Applied Sciences (Basel, Switzerland)*, *13*(7), 4645. doi:10.3390/app13074645

Dutta, A., & Hammad, E. (2020). 5G Security Challenges and Opportunities: A System Approach, *2020 IEEE 3rd 5G World Forum (5GWF)*, (pp. 109-114). IEEE. 10.1109/5GWF49715.2020.9221122

Dwivedi, Y. K., Hughes, L., Ismagilova, E., Aarts, G., Coombs, C., Crick, T., Duan, Y., Dwivedi, R., Edwards, J., Eirug, A., Galanos, V., Ilavarasan, P. V., Janssen, M., Jones, P., Kar, A. K., Kizgin, H., Kronemann, B., Lal, B., Lucini, B., & Williams, M. D. (2021). Artificial Intelligence (AI): Multidisciplinary perspectives on emerging challenges, opportunities, and agenda for research, practice and policy. *International Journal of Information Management*, *57*, 101994. doi:10.1016/j.ijinfomgt.2019.08.002

Ech-Chaitami, T., Mrabet, R., & Berbia, H. (2011). Interoperability of LoWPANs Based on the IEEE802. 15.4 Standard through IPV6. [IJCSI]. *International Journal of Computer Science Issues*, *8*(2), 315.

Eckelman, M. J., Huang, K., Lagasse, R., Senay, E., Dubrow, R., & Sherman, J. D. (2020). Health Care Pollution And Public Health Damage In The United States: An Update: Study examines health care pollution and public health damage in the United States. *Health Affairs*, *39*(12), 2071–2079. doi:10.1377/hlthaff.2020.01247 PMID:33284703

Ejreaw, A. M. A. (2023). The Integration of 5G Technology in Smart Cities: Challenges and Solutions. [AJAPAS]. *African Journal of Advanced Pure and Applied Sciences*, *2*(4), 289–297.

El Azzaoui, A., Singh, S. K., Pan, Y., & Park, J. H. (2020). Block5GIntell: Blockchain for AI-enabled 5G networks. *IEEE Access : Practical Innovations, Open Solutions*, *8*, 145918–145935. doi:10.1109/ACCESS.2020.3014356

El Khatib, M., Alzoubi, H. M., Hamidi, S., Baydoun, A., Al-Nakeeb, A., & Alshurideh, M. (2023). Impact of Using the Internet of Medical Things on e-Healthcare Performance: Blockchain Assist in Improving Smart Contract. *ClinicoEconomics and Outcomes Research*, *15*, 397–411. doi:10.2147/CEOR.S407778 PMID:37287899

Elmaghraby, A. S., & Losavio, M. M. (2014). Cyber security challenges in Smart Cities: Safety, security and privacy. *Journal of Advanced Research*, *5*(4), 491–497. doi:10.1016/j.jare.2014.02.006 PMID:25685517

El-Shorbagy, A. (2021). 5G Technology and the Future of Architecture. *Procedia Computer Science*, *182*, 121–131. doi:10.1016/j.procs.2021.02.017

Elwy, F., Aburukba, R., & Al-Ali, A. R. (2022). Role of Fog Computing in Smart Spaces. *2022 IEEE International Conference on Edge Computing and Communications (EDGE)*, Barcelona, Spain. 10.1109/EDGE55608.2022.00021

Englund, C., Aksoy, E. E., Alonso-Fernandez, F., Cooney, M. D., Pashami, S., & Åstrand, B. (2021). AI perspectives in Smart Cities and Communities to enable road vehicle automation and smart traffic control. *Smart Cities*, *4*(2), 783–802. doi:10.3390/smartcities4020040

Ergen, S. C. (2004). ZigBee/IEEE 802.15. 4 Summary. *UC Berkeley, September, 10*(17), 11.

Fabrègue, B. F. G., & Bogoni, A. (2023). Privacy and Security Concerns in the Smart City. *Smart Cities*, *6*(1), 586–613. doi:10.3390/smartcities6010027

Fadda, J. (2020). Green healthcare system: Main features in supporting sustainability of healthcare system—A review. In *Green Buildings and Renewable Energy: Med Green Forum 2019-Part of World Renewable Energy Congress and Network* (pp. 113-128). Springer International Publishing.

Fahim, K. E., Kalinaki, K., & Shafik, W. (2023). Electronic Devices in the Artificial Intelligence of the Internet of Medical Things (AIoMT). In Handbook of Security and Privacy of AI-Enabled Healthcare Systems and Internet of Medical Things (pp. 41-62). CRC Press. https://doi.org/ doi:10.1201/9781003370321-3

Fang, H., Lo, S., & Lo, J. T. (2021). Building fire evacuation: An IoT-aided perspective in the 5G era. *Buildings*, *11*(12), 643. doi:10.3390/buildings11120643

Fantin Irudaya Raj, E., & Appadurai, M. (2022). Internet of things-based smart transportation system for smart cities. In *Intelligent Systems for Social Good: Theory and Practice* (pp. 39–50). Springer Nature Singapore. doi:10.1007/978-981-19-0770-8_4

Fernandez-Carames, T. M., & Fraga-Lamas, P. (2018). A review on the use of blockchain for the Internet of Things. *IEEE Access : Practical Innovations, Open Solutions*, *6*, 32979–33001. doi:10.1109/ACCESS.2018.2842685

Ferrag, M. A., Maglaras, L., & Ahmim, A. (2017). Privacy-Preserving Schemes for Ad Hoc Social Networks: A Survey. *IEEE Communications Surveys and Tutorials*, *19*(4), 3015–3045. doi:10.1109/COMST.2017.2718178

Finger, M., & Audouin, M. (2019). *The governance of smart transportation systems*. Academic Press.

Floridi, L., Cowls, J., Beltrametti, M., Chatila, R., Chazerand, P., Dignum, V., & Madelin, R. (2018). AI4People—an ethical framework for a good AI society: Opportunities, risks, principles, and recommendations. *Minds and Machines*, *28*(4), 689–707. doi:10.1007/s11023-018-9482-5 PMID:30930541

Fruhlinger, J. (2018). The Mirai botnet explained: How teen scammers and CCTV cameras almost brought down the internet. *CSO online, 9*.

Fysarakis, K., Askoxylakis, I., Katos, V., Ioannidis, S., & Marinos, L. (2017). Security Concerns in Cooperative Intelligent Transportation Systems. *Intrusion Detection and Prevention for Mobile Ecosystems*, 487-522.

Gai, R., Du, X., Ma, S., Chen, N., & Gao, S. (2021, March). A Summary of 5G applications and prosprcts of 5G in the Internet of Things. In *2021 IEEE 2nd International Conference on Big Data, Artificial Intelligence and Internet of Things Engineering (ICBAIE)* (pp. 858-863). IEEE. 10.1109/ICBAIE52039.2021.9389985

Gal, R., Alaluf, Y., Atzmon, Y., Patashnik, O., Bermano, A. H., Chechik, G., & Cohen-Or, D. (2022). *An image is worth one word: Personalizing text-to-image generation using textual inversion*. arXiv preprint arXiv:2208.01618.

Gamundani, A. M. (2015, May). An impact review on internet of things attacks. In 2015 international conference on emerging trends in networks and computer communications (ETNCC) (pp. 114-118). IEEE. doi:10.1109/ETNCC.2015.7184819

Gansky, L. (2010). *The mesh: Why the future of business is sharing*. Penguin.

Gardašević, G., Veletić, M., Maletić, N., Vasiljević, D., Radusinović, I., Tomović, S., & Radonjić, M. (2017). The IoT architectural framework, design issues and application domains. *Wireless Personal Communications*, *92*(1), 127–148. doi:10.1007/s11277-016-3842-3

Gaurav, A., Gupta, B. B., & Panigrahi, P. K. (2023). A comprehensive survey on machine learning approaches for malware detection in IoT-based enterprise information system. *Enterprise Information Systems*, *17*(3), 2023764. doi:10.1080/17517575.2021.2023764

Gaur, L., & Sahoo, B. M. (2022). *Explainable Artificial Intelligence for Intelligent Transportation Systems: Ethics and Applications*. Springer Nature. doi:10.1007/978-3-031-09644-0

GCOO. (2024). *Asia Pacific's Leading Personal Mobility Startup*. GCOO. gcoo.io/team

Gebremariam, Y. E., Duguma, D. G., Park, H. Y., Kim, Y. N., Kim, B., & You, I. (2021, August). 5G and beyond telco cloud: architecture and cybersecurity challenges. In *2021 World Automation Congress (WAC)* (pp. 1-6). IEEE. 10.23919/WAC50355.2021.9559450

Gebremichael, T., Ledwaba, L. P., Eldefrawy, M. H., Hancke, G. P., Pereira, N., Gidlund, M., & Akerberg, J. (2020). Security and privacy in the industrial internet of things: Current standards and future challenges. *IEEE Access : Practical Innovations, Open Solutions*, *8*, 152351–152366. doi:10.1109/ACCESS.2020.3016937

Georgiou, K. E., Georgiou, E., Satava, R. M. (2021). 5G Use in Healthcare: The Future is Present. *Journal of the Society of Laparoscopic & Robotic Surgeons. 25*(4), e2021.00064. . doi:10.4293/JSLS.2021.00064

Ghosh, S., & Ghosh, S. K. (2023). FEEL: FEderated LEarning Framework for ELderly Healthcare Using Edge-IoMT. *IEEE Transactions on Computational Social Systems*, *10*(4), 1800–1809. doi:10.1109/TCSS.2022.3233300

Ghubaish, A., Salman, T., Zolanvari, M., Unal, D., Al-Ali, A., & Jain, R. (2021). Recent Advances in the Internet-of-Medical-Things (IoMT) Systems Security. *IEEE Internet of Things Journal*, *8*(11), 8707–8718. doi:10.1109/JIOT.2020.3045653

Giffinger, R., & Gudrun, H. (2010). Smart cities ranking: an effective instrument for the positioning of the cities?. *ACE: architecture, city and environment, 4*(12), 7-26.

Giourka, P., Sanders, M. W., Angelakoglou, K., Pramangioulis, D., Nikolopoulos, N., Rakopoulos, D., Tryferidis, A., & Tzovaras, D. (2019). The smart city business model canvas—A smart city business modeling framework and practical tool. *Energies*, *12*(24), 4798. doi:10.3390/en12244798

Gkagkas, G., Vergados, D. J., & Michalas, A. (2021, September). The advantage of the 5G network for enhancing the Internet of Things. In *2021 6th South-East Europe Design Automation, Computer Engineering, Computer Networks and Social Media Conference (SEEDA-CECNSM)* (pp. 1-7). IEEE. 10.1109/SEEDA-CECNSM53056.2021.9566239

Goddard, M. (2017, November). The EU general data protection regulation (GDPR): European regulation that has global impact. *International Journal of Market Research*, *59*(6), 703–705. doi:10.2501/IJMR-2017-050

Gohar, A., & Nencioni, G. (2021). The Role of 5G Technologies in a Smart City: The Case for Intelligent Transportation System. *Sustainability (Basel)*, *13*(9), 5188. doi:10.3390/su13095188

Gong, T., Huang, H., Li, P., Zhang, K., & Jiang, H. (2015). A Medical Healthcare System for Privacy Protection Based on IoT. *2015 Seventh International Symposium on Parallel Architectures, Algorithms and Programming (PAAP)*, (pp. 217–222). IEEE. 10.1109/PAAP.2015.48

Goodin, D. (2017, October 28). Assessing the threat, the Reaper botnet poses to the Internet—what we know now. *Ars Technica*. https://arstechnica.com/information-technology/2017/10/assessing-the-threat-the-reaper-botnet-poses-to-the-internet-what-we-know-now/

Goundar, S., Purwar, A., & Singh, A. (Eds.). (2022). *Applications of Artificial Intelligence, Big Data and Internet of Things in Sustainable Development*. CRC Press. doi:10.1201/9781003245469

Gracias, J. S., Parnell, G. S., Specking, E., Pohl, E. A., & Buchanan, R. (2023). Smart Cities—A Structured Literature Review. *Smart Cities*, *6*(4), 1719–1743. doi:10.3390/smartcities6040080

Grigg, N. S. (2010). *Infrastructure finance: the business of infrastructure for a sustainable future* (Vol. 536). John Wiley & Sons. doi:10.1002/9781118266182

Gubbi, J., Buyya, R., Marusic, S., & Palaniswami, M. (2013). Internet of Things (IoT): A review. *Future Generation Computer Systems*, *29*(7), 1645–1660. doi:10.1016/j.future.2013.01.010

Guevara, L., & Auat Cheein, F. (2020). The role of 5G technologies: Challenges in smart cities and intelligent transportation systems. *Sustainability (Basel)*, *12*(16), 6469. doi:10.3390/su12166469

Gupta, P., Sinha, A., & Srivastava, Kr., P., Perti, A., & Singh, A. K. (2021). Security implementations in IoT using digital signature. In *Innovations in Electrical and Electronic Engineering: Proceedings of ICEEE 2020* (pp. 523-535). Springer Singapore. 22.

Gupta, A., & Jha, R. K. (2015). A survey of 5G network: Architecture and emerging technologies. *IEEE Access : Practical Innovations, Open Solutions*, *3*, 1206–1232. doi:10.1109/ACCESS.2015.2461602

Gupta, A., Tripathi, M., & Sharma, A. (2020, July). A provably secure and efficient anonymous mutual authentication and key agreement protocol for wearable devices in WBAN. *Computer Communications*, *160*, 311–325. doi:10.1016/j.comcom.2020.06.010

Habibzadeh, H., Nussbaum, B. H., Anjomshoa, F., Kantarci, B., & Soyata, T. (2019). A survey on cybersecurity, data privacy, and policy issues in cyber-physical system deployments in smart cities. *Sustainable Cities and Society*, *50*, 101660. doi:10.1016/j.scs.2019.101660

Hanes, D., Salgueiro, G., Grossetete, P., Barton, R., & Henry, J. (2017). *IoT fundamentals: Networking technologies, protocols, and use cases for the internet of things*. Cisco Press.

Haque, A. K. M. B., Zihad, M. O. M., & Hasan, M. R. (2023). 5G and Internet of Things-Integration Trends, Opportunities, and Future Research Avenues. In: Bhushan, B., Sharma, S.K., Kumar, R., Priyadarshini, I. (eds) 5G and beyond. Springer Tracts in Electrical and Electronics Engineering. Springer, Singapore. doi:10.1007/978-981-99-3668-7_11

Harahsheh, K., & Chen, C. H. (2023). A Survey of Using Machine Learning in IoT Security and the Challenges Faced by Researchers. *Informatica (Slovenia)*, *47*(6), 1–54. doi:10.31449/inf.v47i6.4635

Harvey, A. C., Strong, R., & Liu, B. (2019). Generating Credible Fake News. *The Journal of Economic Perspectives*, *33*(2), 173–196. doi:10.48550/arXiv.2208.01618

Hassanein, A. A., El-Tazi, N., & Mohy, N. N. (2022). Blockchain, smart contracts, and decentralized applications: an introduction. *Implementing and leveraging Blockchain programming*, 97-114. Springer.. doi:10.1007/978-981-16-3412-3_6

Hataba, M., Sherif, A., Mahmoud, M., Abdallah, M., & Alasmary, W. (2022). Security and Privacy Issues in Autonomous Vehicles: A Layer-Based Survey. *IEEE Open Journal of the Communications Society*, *3*, 811–829. doi:10.1109/OJCOMS.2022.3169500

He, Y., & Zhang, X. (2023). Retracted Article: Key technologies of massive concurrent data processing in smart city based on cloud computing. *International Journal of Computers and Applications*, *45*(2), 204–211. doi:10.1080/1206212X.2020.1743040

Hirota, Y. (2021 End-to-End Management of All Optical Disaggregated Network and Applications with Cloud Native Environment for the Smart World Network Infrastructure. *2021 Opto-Electronics and Communications Conference (OECC)*, Hong Kong, Hong Kong. 10.1364/OECC.2021.M4A.4

Hlaing, N. N. S., Naing, M., & Naing, S. S. (2019). GPS and GSM Based Vehicle Tracking System. [IJTSRD]. *International Journal of Trend in Scientific Research and Development*, *3*(4), 271–275. https://www.ijtsrd.com/papers/ijtsrd23718.pdf. doi:10.31142/ijtsrd23718

Horijon, T. (2017). *Paving the road towards intelligent transportation systems: A governmentality analysis of smart traffic management in the Netherlands.* Wageningen University & Research.

Hossen, M. N., Panneerselvam, V., Koundal, D., Ahmed, K., Bui, F. M., & Ibrahim, S. M. (2023). Federated Machine Learning for Detection of Skin Diseases and Enhancement of Internet of Medical Things (IoMT) Security. *IEEE Journal of Biomedical and Health Informatics*, *27*(2), 835–841. doi:10.1109/JBHI.2022.3149288 PMID:35133971

Howell, J. (2017). Number of connected iot devices will surge to 125 billion by 2030, ihs markit says. *IHS Markit Technology*, (Oct), 24.

Hsu, W. L., Wu, X., Yu, F. C., & Sun, K. S. (2021, December). Research on Shanghai smart city evaluation system in the era of 5G Internet of Things. In *2021 IEEE 3rd International Conference on Architecture, Construction, Environment and Hydraulics (ICACEH)* (pp. 1-4). IEEE.10.1109/ICACEH54312.2021.9768847

Huang, C.-T., Sakib, M. N., Njilla, L., & Kamhoua, C. (2019). A Game Theoretic Approach for Making IoT Device Connectivity Decisions During Malware Outbreak. *2019 International Conference on Computing, Networking and Communications (ICNC)*, (pp. 457–462). IEEE. 10.1109/ICCNC.2019.8685493

Huang, Q., Wang, L., & Yang, Y. (2017). Secure and privacy-preserving data sharing and collaboration in mobile healthcare social networks of smart cities. *Security and Communication Networks*, *2017*, 2017. doi:10.1155/2017/6426495

Hudson-Smith, A., Crooks, A., Gibin, M., Milton, R., & Batty, M. (2009). NeoGeography and Web 2.0: Concepts, Tools and Applications. *Journal of Location Based Services*, *3*(2), 118–145. doi:10.1080/17489720902950366

Hughes, R. T., Zhu, L., & Bednarz, T. (2021). Generative adversarial networks–enabled human–artificial intelligence collaborative applications for creative and design industries: A systematic review of current approaches and trends. *Frontiers in Artificial Intelligence*, *4*, 604234. doi:10.3389/frai.2021.604234 PMID:33997773

Huh, M. A.-N. (2014). Fog computing and smart gateway based communication for cloud of things. *2nd IEEE Interenational Conference on Future Internet of Things and Cloud.* IEEE.

Humayun, M., Hamid, B., Jhanjhi, N. Z., Suseendran, G., & Talib, M. N. (2021). 5G Network Security Issues, Challenges, Opportunities and Future Directions: A Survey. *Journal of Physics: Conference Series*, *979*(1), 012037. doi:10.1088/1742-6596/1979/1/012037

Hu, S., & Dai, T. (2013). *Online Map Application Development Using Google Maps API, SQL Database, and ASP.* NET.

Huseien, G. F., & Shah, K. W. (2022). A review on 5G technology for smart energy management and smart buildings in Singapore. *Energy and AI*, *7*, 100116. doi:10.1016/j.egyai.2021.100116

Huzaifah, M., & Wyse, L. (2021). Deep generative models for musical audio synthesis. *Handbook of Artificial Intelligence for Music: Foundations, Advanced Approaches, and Developments for Creativity*, 639-678. Springer. https://link.springer.com/chapter/10.1007/978- 3-030-72116-9_22

Iqbal, M. A., Olaleye, O. G., &Bayoumi, M. A. (2017). A review on the Internet of Things (IoT): security and privacy requirements and the solution approaches. *Global Journal of Computer Science and Technology.*

Jain, A., Laxmi, V., Tripathi, M., Gaur, M. S., & Bishnoi, R. (2020). TRACK: An algorithm for fault-tolerant, dynamic and scalable 2D mesh network-on-chip routing reconfiguration. *Integration (Amsterdam)*, *72*, 92–110. doi:10.1016/j.vlsi.2020.01.005

Jain, S., Ahuja, N. J., Srikanth, P., Bhadane, K. V., Nagaiah, B., Kumar, A., & Konstantinou, C. (2021). Blockchain and autonomous vehicles: Recent advances and future directions. *IEEE Access : Practical Innovations, Open Solutions*, *9*, 130264–130328. doi:10.1109/ACCESS.2021.3113649

James, P., Astoria, R., Castor, T., Hudspeth, C., Olstinske, D., & Ward, J. (2021). Smart cities: Fundamental concepts. Handbook of smart cities, (pp. 3-33). Springer. https://doi.org/ doi:10.1007/978-3-030 69698-6_2

Jamshidi, M., Moztarzadeh, O., Jamshidi, A., Abdelgawad, A., El-Baz, A. S., & Hauer, L. (2023). Future of Drug Discovery: The Synergy of Edge Computing, Internet of Medical Things, and Deep Learning. *Future Internet*, *15*(4), 142. doi:10.3390/fi15040142

Janani, R. P., Renuka, K., & Aruna, A. (2021). IoT in smart cities: A contemporary survey. *Global Transitions Proceedings*, *2*(2), 187–193. doi:10.1016/j.gltp.2021.08.069

Jan, B., Farman, H., Khan, M., Talha, M., & Din, I. U. (2019). Designing a smart transportation system: An internet of things and big data approach. *IEEE Wireless Communications*, *26*(4), 73–79. doi:10.1109/MWC.2019.1800512

Javed, A. R., Shahzad, F., Rehman, S., Zikria, Y. B., Razzak, I., Jalil, Z., & Xu, G. (2022). Future smart cities: Requirements, emerging technologies, applications, challenges, and future aspects. *Cities (London, England)*, *129*, 103794. doi:10.1016/j.cities.2022.103794

Jensen, C. S., Toftkjær, T., Larsen, A., & Hansen, T. R. (2015). Smart City in a box: Understanding strategic approaches to the smart city concept. In *2015 48th Hawaii international conference on system sciences* (pp. 2334-2343). IEEE.

Jeong, M., & Shin, H. H. (2020). Tourists' experiences with smart tourism technology at smart destinations and their behavior intentions. *Journal of Travel Research*, *59*(8), 1464–1477. doi:10.1177/0047287519883034

Jha, S. K. (2023). Application of Blockchain technology in libraries and information centers services. *Library Hi Tech News*. doi:10.1108/LHTN-02-2023-0020

Jha, S., Nkenyereye, L., Joshi, G. P., & Yang, E. (2020). Mitigating and monitoring smart city using internet of things. *Computers, Materials & Continua*, *65*(2), 1059–1079. doi:10.32604/cmc.2020.011754

Jiang, H., Geertman, S., & Witte, P. (2023). The contextualization of smart city technologies: An international comparison. *Journal of Urban Management*, *12*(1), 33–43. doi:10.1016/j.jum.2022.09.001

Jiang, J., Guo, J., Khan, M., Cui, Y., & Lin, W. (2023). Energy-saving Service Offloading for the Internet of Medical Things Using Deep Reinforcement Learning. *ACM Transactions on Sensor Networks*, *19*(3), 1–20. doi:10.1145/3560265

Jiang, N., Wang, W., Wu, J., & Wang, J. (2020). Traceable Method for Personal Information Registration Based on Blockchain. *IEEE Access : Practical Innovations, Open Solutions*, *8*, 52700–52712. doi:10.1109/ACCESS.2020.2981175

Jiang, Y., Xiao, W., Wang, R., & Barnawi, A. (2020). Smart Urban Living: Enabling Emotion-Guided Interaction With Next Generation Sensing Fabric. *IEEE Access : Practical Innovations, Open Solutions*, *8*, 28395–28402. doi:10.1109/ACCESS.2019.2961957

Jimenez, J. A. (2018). Smart transportation systems. *Smart Cities: Applications, Technologies, Standards, and Driving Factors*, 123-133.

Jing, Q., Vasilakos, A. V., Wan, J., Lu, J., & Qiu, D. (2014). Security of the Internet of Things: Perspectives and challenges. *Wireless Networks*, *20*(8), 2481–2501. doi:10.1007/s11276-014-0761-7

Jo, J. H., Sharma, P. K., Sicato, J. C. S., & Park, J. H. (2019). Emerging technologies for sustainable smart city network security: Issues, challenges, and countermeasures. *Journal of Information Processing Systems*, *15*(4), 765–784. doi:10.3745/JIPS.03.0124

Joshi, K., Sharma, R., Singh, N., & Sharma, B. (2023). Digital World of Cloud Computing and Wireless Networking: Challenges and Risks. In Applications of Artificial Intelligence in Wireless Communication Systems (pp. 36-47). IGI Global.

KakaoTalk. (n.d.). *Where People and the World Come to Get Connected.* Kakaocorp.com. www.kakaocorp.com/page/service/service/KakaoTalk?lang=en

Kalinaki, K., Fahadi, M., Alli, A. A., Shafik, W., Yasin, M., & Mutwalibi, N. (2023). Artificial Intelligence of Internet of Medical Things (AIoMT) in Smart Cities: A Review of Cybersecurity for Smart Healthcare. Handbook of Security and Privacy of AI-Enabled Healthcare Systems and Internet of Medical Things, 271-292. Springer. https://doi.org/doi:10.1201/9781003370321-11

Kalinaki, K., Thilakarathne, N. N., Mubarak, H. R., Malik, O. A., & Abdullatif, M. (2023). Cybersafe Capabilities and Utilities for Smart Cities. In *Cybersecurity for Smart Cities* (pp. 71–86). Springer., doi:10.1007/978-3-031-24946-4_6

Kamel Boulos, M. N., & Al-Shorbaji, N. M. (2014). On the Internet of Things, smart cities and the WHO Healthy Cities. *International Journal of Health Geographics*, *13*(1), 1–6. doi:10.1186/1476-072X-13-10 PMID:24669838

Kang, C. C., Lee, T. Y., Lim, W. F., & Yeo, W. W. Y. (2023). Opportunities and challenges of 5G network technology toward precision medicine. *Clinical and Translational Science*, *16*(11), 2078–2094. doi:10.1111/cts.13640 PMID:37702288

Karagiannis, S., Ribeiro, L. L., Ntantogian, C., Magkos, E., & Campos, L. M. (2023). Chidroid: A Mobile Android Application for Log Collection and Security Analysis in Healthcare and IoMT. *Applied Sciences (Basel, Switzerland)*, *13*(5), 3061. doi:10.3390/app13053061

Karar, M. E., Khan, Z. F., Alshahrani, H., & Reyad, O. (2023). Smart IoMT-based segmentation of coronavirus infections using lung CT scans. *Alexandria Engineering Journal*, *69*, 571–583. doi:10.1016/j.aej.2023.02.020

Kashif, M., & Kalkan, K. (2024). EPIoT: Enhanced privacy preservation based Blockchain mechanism for internet-of-things. *Computer Networks*, *238*, 110107. doi:10.1016/j.comnet.2023.110107

Kataray, T., Nitesh, B., Yarram, B., Sinha, S., Cuce, E., Shaik, S., & Roy, A. (2023). Integration of smart grid with renewable energy sources: Opportunities and challenges–A comprehensive review. *Sustainable Energy Technologies and Assessments*, *58*, 103363. doi:10.1016/j.seta.2023.103363

Kaur, J. (2023, May). How is Robotic Process Automation Revolutionising the Way Healthcare Sector Works? In *International Conference on Information, Communication and Computing Technology* (pp. 1037-1055). Singapore: Springer Nature Singapore. 10.1007/978-981-99-5166-6_70

Kaur, J. (2024). Green Finance 2.0: Pioneering Pathways for Sustainable Development and Health Through Future Trends and Innovations. In Sustainable Investments in Green Finance (pp. 294-319). IGI Global.

Kaur, J. (2024). Towards a Sustainable Triad: Uniting Energy Management Systems, Smart Cities, and Green Healthcare for a Greener Future. In Emerging Materials, Technologies, and Solutions for Energy Harvesting (pp. 258-285). IGI Global.

Kaur, P., & Garg, R. (2021). A survey on key enabling technologies towards 5G. In IOP Conference Series: Materials Science and Engineering (Vol. 1033, No. 1, p. 012011). IOP Publishing. doi:10.1145/3457388.3458614

Kaur, S., & Sharma, S. (2023, April). Internet of Things Enabled Framework for Sustainable Mobility and Clean Environment in Smart Cities. In *International Conference on Recent Trends in Artificial Intelligence and IoT* (pp. 285-298). Cham: Springer Nature Switzerland. 10.1007/978-3-031-37303-9_21

Kaurav, R. S., Rout, R. R., & Vemireddy, S. (2021). Blockchain for Emergency Vehicle Routing in Healthcare Services: An Integrated Secure and Trustworthy System. *2021 International Conference on COMmunication Systems and NETworkS, COMSNETS 2021*, (pp. 623–628). IEEE. 10.1109/COMSNETS51098.2021.9352903

Kaur, J. (2023). Robotic Process Automation in Healthcare Sector. In *E3S Web of Conferences* (Vol. 391, p. 01008). EDP Sciences.

Kaur, M., Sandhu, M., Mohan, N., & Sandhu, P. S. (2011). RFID technology principles, advantages, limitations & its applications. *International Journal of Computer and Electrical Engineering*, *3*(1), 151–157. doi:10.7763/IJCEE.2011.V3.306

Khalid, U., Asim, M., Baker, T., Hung, P. C. K., Tariq, M. A., & Rafferty, L. (2020). A decentralized lightweight Blockchain-based authentication mechanism for IoT systems. *Cluster Computing*, *23*(3), 2067–2087. doi:10.1007/s10586-020-03058-6

Khalil, U., Malik, O. A., Uddin, M., & Chen, C. L. (2022). A Comparative Analysis on Blockchain versus Centralized Authentication Architectures for IoT-Enabled Smart Devices in Smart Cities: A Comprehensive Review, Recent Advances, and Future Research Directions. *Sensors (Basel)*, *22*(14), 5168. doi:10.3390/s22145168 PMID:35890848

Khalil, U., Mueen-Uddin, Malik, O. A., & Hussain, S. (2022). A Blockchain Footprint for Authentication of IoT-Enabled Smart Devices in Smart Cities: State-of-the-Art Advancements, Challenges and Future Research Directions. *IEEE Access : Practical Innovations, Open Solutions*, *10*, 76805–76823. Advance online publication. doi:10.1109/ACCESS.2022.3189998

Khan, F., Jan, M. A., Alturki, R., Alshehri, M. D., Shah, S. T., & Rehman, A. U. (2023). A Secure Ensemble Learning-Based Fog-Cloud Approach for Cyberattack Detection in IoMT. *IEEE Transactions on Industrial Informatics*, *19*(10), 10125–10132. doi:10.1109/TII.2022.3231424

Khan, H. U., Ali, Y., & Khan, F. (2023). A Features-Based Privacy Preserving Assessment Model for Authentication of Internet of Medical Things (IoMT) Devices in Healthcare. *Mathematics*, *11*(5), 1197. doi:10.3390/math11051197

Khanh, Q. V., Hoai, N. V., Manh, L. D., Le, A. N., & Jeon, G. (2022). Wireless communication technologies for IoT in 5G: Vision, applications, and challenges. *Wireless Communications and Mobile Computing*, *2022*, 1–12. doi:10.1155/2022/3229294

Khan, L. U., Yaqoob, I., Tran, N. H., Kazmi, S. A., Dang, T. N., & Hong, C. S. (2020). Edge-computing-enabled smart cities: A comprehensive survey. *IEEE Internet of Things Journal*, *7*(10), 10200–10232. doi:10.1109/JIOT.2020.2987070

Khanna, A., & Kaur, S. (2020). Internet of Things (IoT), Applications and Challenges: A Comprehensive Review. *Wireless Personal Communications*, *114*(2), 1687–1762. doi:10.1007/s11277-020-07446-4

Khan, R. H., & Khan, J. Y. (2013). A comprehensive review of the application characteristics and traffic requirements of a smart grid communications network. *Computer Networks*, *57*(3), 825–845. doi:10.1016/j.comnet.2012.11.002

Khatoun, R., & Zeadally, S. (2016). Smart cities: Concepts, architectures, research opportunities. *Communications of the ACM*, *59*(8), 46–57. doi:10.1145/2858789

Khedekar, I., & Murthy, G. (2015). Internet of Things: A new backbone for education system. *Procedia Computer Science*, *45*, 545–551.

Khor, J. H., Sidorov, M., & Woon, P. Y. (2021). Public blockchains for resource-constrained IoT devices—A state-of-the-art survey. *IEEE Internet of Things Journal*, *8*(15), 11960–11982. doi:10.1109/JIOT.2021.3069120

Khrais, L. T. (2020). IoT and Blockchain in the development of smart cities. *International Journal of Advanced Computer Science and Applications*, *2*(2). doi:10.14569/IJACSA.2020.0110220

Khujamatov, K. E., Toshtemirov, T. K., Lazarev, A. P., & Raximjonov, Q. T. (2021, November). IoT and 5G technology in agriculture. In *2021 International Conference on Information Science and Communications Technologies (ICISCT)* (pp. 1-6). IEEE. 10.1109/ICISCT52966.2021.9670037

Kim, K., Ryu, J., Lee, Y., & Won, D. (2023). An Improved Lightweight User Authentication Scheme for the Internet of Medical Things. *Sensors (Basel)*, *23*(3), 1122. doi:10.3390/s23031122 PMID:36772160

Kim, S. (2023). Learning and Game Based Spectrum Allocation Model for Internet of Medical Things (IoMT) Platform. *IEEE Access : Practical Innovations, Open Solutions*, *11*, 48059–48068. doi:10.1109/ACCESS.2023.3266331

Kim, S. K., Hwang, Y., Lee, Y. S., & Corser, W. (2015). Occupant comfort and satisfaction in green healthcare environments: A survey study focusing on healthcare staff. *Journal of Sustainable Development*, *8*(1), 156. doi:10.5539/jsd.v8n1p156

Kim, S., & Na, W. (2016). Safe data transmission architecture based on cloud for Internet of Things. *Wireless Personal Communications*, *86*(1), 287–300. doi:10.1007/s11277-015-3063-1

Kitchin, R. (2016). The ethics of smart cities and urban science. *Philosophical Transactions. Series A, Mathematical, Physical, and Engineering Sciences*, *374*(2083), 20160115. doi:10.1098/rsta.2016.0115 PMID:28336794

Kitsios, F., Chatzidimitriou, E., & Kamariotou, M. (2023). The ISO/IEC 27001 Information Security Management Standard: How to Extract Value from Data in the IT Sector. *Sustainability (Basel)*, *15*(7), 5828. doi:10.3390/su15075828

Knaap, G. J., Lewis, R., Chakraborty, A., & June-Friesen, K. (2022). Toward a "Smart Growth 2.0". *Handbook on Smart Growth: Promise, Principles, and Prospects for Planning*, 324. Research Gate.

Knieps, G., & Bauer, J. M. (2022). Internet of things and the economics of 5G-based local industrial networks. *Telecommunications Policy*, *46*(4), 102261. doi:10.1016/j.telpol.2021.102261

Kolias, C., Kambourakis, G., Stavrou, A., & Voas, J. (2017). DDoS in the IoT: Mirai and other botnets. *Computer*, *50*(7), 80–84. doi:10.1109/MC.2017.201

Korade, S., Kotak, V., & Durafe, A. (2019). A review paper on internet of things (IoT) and its applications. *Int. Res. J. Eng. Technol*, *6*(6), 1623–1630.

Korzun, D., Balandina, E., Kashevnik, A., Balandin, S., & Viola, F. (Eds.). (2019). Ambient Intelligence Services in IoT Environments: Emerging Research and Opportunities. Springer. doi:10.4018/978-1-5225-8973-0

Krishnamurthy, R., Smith, K. L., & Desouza, K. C. (2017). Urban informatics: critical data and technology considerations. *Seeing Cities Through Big Data: Research, Methods and Applications in Urban Informatics*, (pp. 163-188). Research Gate.

Kumaran, D., Prasad, K. L., & Rohith, K. (2023). Internet of Medical Things (IoMT) for Cardio-vascular Disease. *International Journal for Research in Applied Science and Engineering Technology*, *11*(5), 2651–2663. doi:10.22214/ijraset.2023.52187

Kumar, H., Singh, M. K., Gupta, M. P., & Madaan, J. (2020). Moving towards smart cities: Solutions that lead to the Smart City Transformation Framework. *Technological Forecasting and Social Change*, *153*, 119281. doi:10.1016/j.techfore.2018.04.024

Kumari, A., Patra, M. K., & Sahoo, B. (2023). Data Controlling and Security Issues in Cloud: A Step Towards Serverless. In Perspectives on Social Welfare Applications' Optimization and Enhanced Computer Applications (pp. 105-124). IGI Global. doi:10.4018/978-1-6684-8306-0.ch007

Kumar, M., Kim, C., Son, Y., Singh, S. K., & Kim, S. (2024). Empowering Cyberattack Identification in IoHT Networks with Neighborhood Component-based Improvised Long Short-Term Memory. *IEEE Internet of Things Journal*, 1. doi:10.1109/JIOT.2024.3354988

Kumar, R. L., Pham, Q. V., Khan, F., Piran, M. J., & Dev, K. (2021). Blockchain for securing aerial communications: Potentials, solutions, and research directions. *Physical Communication*, *47*, 101390. doi:10.1016/j.phycom.2021.101390

Kumar, S., Tiwari, P., & Zymbler, M. (2019). Internet of Things is a revolutionary approach.Salman, A. (2020, September 28). Internet of Things (IoT) and its Applications: A Survey. *International Journal of Computer Applications*. doi:10.5120/ijca202091991

Kumar, Y., & Kumar, V. (2023). A Systematic Review on Intrusion Detection System in Wireless Networks: Variants, Attacks, and Applications. *Wireless Personal Communications*, *133*(1), 1–58. doi:10.1007/s11277-023-10773-x

Kushner, D. (2013). The real story of stuxnet. *ieee*. *IEEE Spectrum*, *50*(3), 48–53. doi:10.1109/MSPEC.2013.6471059

Kushwaha, S. S., Joshi, S., Singh, D., Kaur, M., & Lee, H. N. (2022). Systematic Review of Security Vulnerabilities in Ethereum Blockchain Smart Contract. *IEEE Access : Practical Innovations, Open Solutions*, *10*, 6605–6621. doi:10.1109/ACCESS.2021.3140091

Lakhan, A., Mohammed, M. A., Ibrahim, D. A., & Abdulkareem, K. H. (2023). Bio-inspired robotics enabled schemes in blockchain-fog-cloud assisted IoMT environment. *Journal of King Saud University - Computer and Information Sciences, 35*(1). . doi:10.1016/j.jksuci.2021.11.009

Lakhan, A., Mohammed, M. A., Nedoma, J., Martinek, R., Tiwari, P., Vidyarthi, A., Alkhayyat, A., & Wang, W. (2023). Federated-Learning Based Privacy Preservation and Fraud-Enabled Blockchain IoMT System for Healthcare. *IEEE Journal of Biomedical and Health Informatics*, *27*(2), 664–672. doi:10.1109/JBHI.2022.3165945 PMID:35394919

Law, S., & Neira, M. (2019, November). An unsupervised approach to geographical knowledge discovery using street level and street network images. In *Proceedings of the 3rd ACM SIGSPATIAL International Workshop on AI for Geographic Knowledge Discovery* (pp. 56-65). ACM. 10.1145/3356471.3365238

Leal Filho, W., Marisa Azul, A., Brandli, L., Gökçin Özuyar, P., & Wall, T. (Eds.). (2020). *Sustainable cities and communities*. Springer International Publishing.

Lee, H. Y., Lee, K. H., Lee, K. H., Erdenbayar, U., Hwang, S., Lee, E. Y., Lee, J. H., Kim, H. J., Park, S., Park, J. W., Chung, T. Y., Kim, T. H., & Youk, H. (2023). Internet of medical things-based real-time digital health service for precision medicine: Empirical studies using MEDBIZ platform. *Digital Health*, *9*. doi:10.1177/20552076221149659 PMID:36644659

Lee, I., Bagheri, B., & Kao, H. A. (2015). A Cyber-Physical Systems architecture for Industry 4.0-based manufacturing systems. *Manufacturing Letters*, *3*, 18–23. doi:10.1016/j.mfglet.2014.12.001

Lee, J. G., Han, J., Li, X., & Cheng, H. (2010). Mining discriminative patterns for classifying trajectories on road networks. *IEEE Transactions on Knowledge and Data Engineering*, *23*(5), 713–726. doi:10.1109/TKDE.2010.153

Lee, J. Y., & Lee, J. H. (2015). A study on the planning process of ubiquitous city and the case of Songdo IBD in South Korea. *Habitat International*, *46*, 118–125.

Lefebvre, M. (2021). *Reimagining Smart Cities: reconsidering pluralism and data subjectivities* [Doctoral dissertation, University of Oxford].

Lefkovitz, N., & Boeckl, K. (2021). *Portuguese Translation of the NIST Privacy Framework Version 1.0*. doi:10.6028/NIST.CSWP.01162020pt

Lellis, R. (2020). *How IT leaders are turning to employee experience in 2020*. CIO Dive. [Online Article]

Letaifa, S. B. (2015). How to strategize smart cities: Revealing the SMART model. *Journal of Business Research*, *68*(7), 1414–1419. doi:10.1016/j.jbusres.2015.01.024

Liao, Y., & He, J. (2020). Deepfake Detection: A Review. *ACM Computing Surveys*, *53*(5), 1–35. doi:10.1145/3324473

Li, N., Liu, D., & Nepal, S. (2017). Lightweight Mutual Authentication for IoT and Its Applications. *IEEE Transactions on Sustainable Computing*, *2*(4), 359–370. doi:10.1109/TSUSC.2017.2716953

Lin, J., Yu, W., Zhang, N., Yang, X., Zhang, H., & Zhao, W. (2017, October). Asur-vey on Internet of Things: Architecture, enabling technologies, security and privacy, and applications. *IEEE Internet of Things Journal*, *4*(5), 1125–1142. doi:10.1109/JIOT.2017.2683200

Li, S., Da Xu, L., & Zhao, S. (2015). The Internet of Things: A survey. *Information Systems Frontiers*, *17*(2), 243–259. doi:10.1007/s10796-014-9492-7

Littman, M. L., Ajunwa, I., Berger, G., Boutilier, C., Currie, M., Doshi-Velez, F., & Walsh, T. (2022). Gathering strength, gathering storms: The one hundred year study on artificial intelligence (AI100) 2021 study panel report. *arXiv preprint arXiv:2210.15767.*

Liu, F., Fan, H. Y., & Qi, J. Y. (2022). Blockchain technology, cryptocurrency: Entropy-based perspective. *Entropy (Basel, Switzerland)*, *24*(4), 557. doi:10.3390/e24040557 PMID:35455220

Liu, H., Han, S., & Zhu, Z. (2023). Blockchain Technology toward Smart Construction: Review and Future Directions. *Journal of Construction Engineering and Management*, *149*(3), 03123002. Advance online publication. doi:10.1061/JCEMD4.COENG-11929

Liu, Q., Yang, Y., Meng, Q., Man, S., & Wang, Y. (2022). The Multiple Cooperative Mechanism and Globalization Path of Small Inland Cities in China: A Showcase Study of Dunhuang, China. *International Journal of Environmental Research and Public Health*, *19*(18), 11241. doi:10.3390/ijerph191811241 PMID:36141533

Liu, W., He, Y., Wang, X., Duan, Z., Liang, W., & Liu, Y. (2023). BFG: Privacy protection framework for internet of medical things based on blockchain and federated learning. *Connection Science*, *35*(1), 2199951. doi:10.1080/09540091.2023.2199951

Liu, Y., Kashef, M., Lee, K. B., Benmohamed, L., & Candell, R. (2019). Wireless network design for emerging IIo T applications: Reference framework and use cases. *Proceedings of the IEEE*, *107*(6), 1166–1192. doi:10.1109/JPROC.2019.2905423 PMID:31555010

Liu, Y., Peng, M., Shou, G., Chen, Y., & Chen, S. (2020, August). Toward Edge Intelligence: Multiaccess Edge Computing for 5G and Internet of Things. *IEEE Internet of Things Journal*, *7*(8), 6722–6747. doi:10.1109/JIOT.2020.3004500

Liu, Y., Wang, K., Qian, K., Du, M., & Guo, S. (2020). Tornado: Enabling Blockchain in Heterogeneous Internet of Things Through a Space-Structured Approach. *IEEE Internet of Things Journal*, *7*(2), 1273–1286. doi:10.1109/JIOT.2019.2954128

LiuY.YuanX.XiongZ.KangJ.WangX. (2020). Federated learning for 6G communications: Challenges, methods, and future directions. Available:arXiv:2006.02931.

Lu, H. H., Li, C. Y., Tsai, W. S., Chang, P. S., Chen, Y. T., Liu, C. X., Ko, T., & Lin, Y. Y. (2021). Simultaneous transmission of 5G MMW and sub-THz signals through a fiber-FSO-5G NR converged system. *Journal of Lightwave Technology*, *40*(8), 2348–2356. doi:10.1109/JLT.2021.3139620

Lv, Z., Hu, B., & Lv, H. (2019). Infrastructure monitoring and operation for smart cities based on IoT system. *IEEE Transactions on Industrial Informatics*, *16*(3), 1957–1962. doi:10.1109/TII.2019.2913535

Lv, Z., & Xie, S. (2022). Artificial intelligence in the digital twins: State of the art, challenges, and future research topics. *Digital Twin*, *1*, 12. doi:10.12688/digitaltwin.17524.2

Ma, J., Zhang, J., Shen, G., Marshall, A., & Chang, C. H. (2023, May). White-Box Adversarial Attacks on Deep Learning-Based Radio Frequency Fingerprint Identification. In *ICC 2023-IEEE International Conference on Communications* (pp. 3714-3719). IEEE. 10.1109/ICC45041.2023.10278927

Madakam, S., & Date, H. (2016). Security mechanisms for connectivity of smart devices in the internet of things. *Connectivity Frameworks for Smart Devices: The Internet of Things from a Distributed Computing Perspective*. Research Gate.

Madhwal, Y., Yanovich, Y., Balachander, S., Poojaa, K. H., Saranya, R., & Subashini, B. (2023). Enhancing Supply Chain Efficiency and Security: A Proof of Concept for IoT Device Integration With Blockchain. *IEEE Access : Practical Innovations, Open Solutions*, *11*, 121173–121189. doi:10.1109/ACCESS.2023.3328569

Mahamuni, C. V. (2023, November). Exploring IoT-Applications: A Survey of Recent Progress, Challenges, and Impact of AI, Blockchain, and Disruptive Technologies. In *2023 7th International Conference on Electronics, Communication and Aerospace Technology (ICECA),* (pp. 1324-1331). IEEE. 10.1109/ICECA58529.2023.10395064

Mahmoud, H. H. H., Amer, A. A., & Ismail, T. (2021). 6G: A comprehensive survey on technologies, applications, challenges, and research problems. *Transactions on Emerging Telecommunications Technologies*, *32*(4), e4233. doi:10.1002/ett.4233

Majeed, M. (2018). Internet of Things (IoT) applications in healthcare: A review. *Journal of King Saud University. Computer and Information Sciences*.

Majeed, U., Khan, L. U., Yaqoob, I., Kazmi, S. M. A., Salah, K., & Hong, C. S. (2021). Blockchain for IoT-based smart cities: Recent advances, requirements, and future challenges. *Journal of Network and Computer Applications*, *181*, 103007. doi:10.1016/j.jnca.2021.103007

Makani, S., Pittala, R., Alsayed, E., Aloqaily, M., & Jararweh, Y. (2022). A survey of Blockchain applications in sustainable and smart cities. *Cluster Computing*, *25*(6), 3915–3936. doi:10.1007/s10586-022-03625-z

Makhdoom, I., Abolhasan, M., Franklin, D., Lipman, J., Zimmermann, C., Piccardi, M., & Moghadam, N. S. (2023). Detecting compromised IoT devices: Existing techniques, challenges, and a way forward. *Computers & Security*, *132*, 103384. doi:10.1016/j.cose.2023.103384

Ma, L., & Sun, B. (2020). Machine learning and AI in marketing–Connecting computing power to human insights. *International Journal of Research in Marketing*, *37*(3), 481–504. doi:10.1016/j.ijresmar.2020.04.005

Malini, P., Gowthaman, N., Gautami, A., & Thillaiarasu, N. (2021). Internet of Everything (IoE) in smart city paradigm using advanced sensors for handheld devices and equipment. In *IoT and IoE Driven Smart Cities* (pp. 121–141). Springer International Publishing.

Ma, N., Waegel, A., Hakkarainen, M., Braham, W. W., Glass, L., & Aviv, D. (2023). Blockchain + IoT sensor network to measure, evaluate and incentivize personal environmental accounting and efficient energy use in indoor spaces. *Applied Energy*, *332*, 120443. doi:10.1016/j.apenergy.2022.120443

Manjula, V., & Vijayabanu, C. (2023, April). Predicting the Application of Internet of Things (IoT) a New Wave of Technology for Smart Health Care. In *2023 International Conference on Inventive Computation Technologies (ICICT)* (pp. 1343-1350). IEEE. 10.1109/ICICT57646.2023.10134279

Mansour, M., Gamal, A., Ahmed, A. I., Said, L. A., Elbaz, A., Herencsar, N., & Soltan, A. (2023). Internet of Things: A Comprehensive Overview on Protocols, Architectures, Technologies, Simulation Tools, and Future Directions. *Energies*, *16*(8), 3465. doi:10.3390/en16083465

Manyika, J., Chui, M., Brown, B., Bughin, J., Dobbs, R., Roxburgh, C., & Byers, A. H. (2013). *Big data: The next frontier for innovation, competition, and productivity*. McKinsey Global Institute.

Margolis, J., Oh, T. T., Jadhav, S., Kim, Y. H., & Kim, J. N. (2017). An In-Depth Analysis of the Mirai Botnet. *2017 International Conference on Software Security and Assurance (ICSSA)*, (pp. 6–12). IEEE. 10.1109/ICSSA.2017.12

Maria de Fátima, F. D., & Radwan, A. (2017). *Optical Fiber Sensors for LoT and Smart Devices*. Springer.

Markendahl, J., Lundberg, S., Kordas, O., & Movin, S. (2017). *On the role and potential of IoT in different industries: Analysis of actor cooperation and challenges for introduction of new technology. 2017 Internet of Things Business Models*. Users, and Networks.

Marr, B. (2020). *Tech Trends in Practice: The 25 technologies that are driving the 4th Industrial Revolution*. John Wiley & Sons.

McEwen, A., & Cassimally, H. (2013). *Designing the internet of things*. John Wiley & Sons.

Mehmood, Y., Ahmad, F., Yaqoob, I., Adnane, A., Imran, M., & Guizani, S. (2017). Internet-of-things-based smart cities: Recent advances and challenges. *IEEE Communications Magazine*, *55*(9), 16–24. doi:10.1109/MCOM.2017.1600514

Mendez, D. M., Papapanagiotou, I., & Yang, B. (2017). Internet of things: Survey on security and privacy. *arXiv preprint arXiv:1707.01879*.

Mendonça, S., Damásio, B., Freitas, L., Oliveira, L., Cichy, M., & Nicita, A. (2022). The rise of 5G technologies and systems: A quantitative analysis of knowledge production. *Telecommunications Policy*, *46*(4), 102327. doi:10.1016/j.telpol.2022.102327

Meulen, R. (2017). *Gartner says 8.4 billion connected "things" will be in use in 2017, up 31 percent from 2016*. Gartner. gartner.com/en/newsroom/press-releases/2017-02-07-gartner-says-8-billion-connected-things-will-be-in-use-in-2017-up-31-percent-from-2016

Mhala, A., Davda, Y., & Palaniappan, D. (2023). A Mobile Social App for Better Life of Poor People Based on Perceived Similarity and Trust Using Supply Chain Management. In *Government Impact on Sustainable and Responsible Supply Chain Management* (pp. 202–222). IGI Global. doi:10.4018/978-1-6684-9062-4.ch011

Miglani, A., & Kumar, N. (2019). Deep learning models for traffic flow prediction in autonomous vehicles: A review, solutions, and challenges. *Vehicular Communications*, *20*, 100184. doi:10.1016/j.vehcom.2019.100184

Minoli, D., & Occhiogrosso, B. (2018). Internet of things applications for smart cities. *Internet of things A to Z: technologies and applications*, 319-358.

Minoli, D., & Occhiogrosso, B. (2019). Practical Aspects for the Integration of 5G Networks and IoT Applications in Smart Cities. Environments, Wireless Communications and Mobile Computing. Hindawi. doi:10.1155/2019/5710834

Mishra, P., & Singh, G. (2023). Energy management systems in sustainable smart cities based on the internet of energy: A technical review. *Energies*, *16*(19), 6903. doi:10.3390/en16196903

Misra & van der Maaten. (2020). Self-supervised learning of pretext-invariant representations. *Proceedings of the IEEE/CVF Conference on Computer Vision and Pattern Recognition*, 6707–6717.

Mitieka, D., Luke, R., Twinomurinzi, H., & Mageto, J. (2023). Smart Mobility in Urban Areas: A Bibliometric Review and Research Agenda. *Sustainability (Basel), 15*(8), 6754. doi:10.3390/su15086754

Mohammadi, M., & Al-Fuqaha, A. (2018, February). Enabling cognitive smart cities using big data and machine learning: Approaches and challenges. *IEEE Communications Magazine, 56*(2), 94–101. doi:10.1109/MCOM.2018.1700298

Mohring, K. A. (2018). *Smart streetlights: a feasibility study* [Doctoral dissertation, James Cook University].

Moir, E., Moonen, T., & Clark, G. (2014). What are future cities? Origins, meanings and uses. Government Office for Science, 14.

Mollel, M. S., Abubakar, A. I., Ozturk, M., Kaijage, S. F., Kisangiri, M., Hussain, S., & Abbasi, Q. H. (2021). A survey of machine learning applications to handover management in 5G and beyond. *IEEE Access : Practical Innovations, Open Solutions, 9*, 45770–45802. doi:10.1109/ACCESS.2021.3067503

Möller, D. P., & Vakilzadian, H. (2016, May). *Cyber-physical systems in smart transportation. In 2016 IEEE international conference on electro information technology (EIT) (pp. 776-781).* IEEE.

Mozzaquatro, B., Agostinho, C., Goncalves, D., Martins, J., & Jardim-Goncalves, R. (2018). An Ontology-Based Cybersecurity Framework for the Internet of Things. *Sensors (Basel), 18*(9), 3053. doi:10.3390/s18093053 PMID:30213085

Mrityunjaya, D. H., Kumar, N., Ali, S., & Kelagadi, H. M. (2017, February). Smart transportation. In *2017 International Conference on I-SMAC (IoT in Social, Mobile, Analytics and Cloud)(I-SMAC)* (pp. 1-5). IEEE.

Muhammad, A., Saqib, M., & Song, W.-C. (2021). Sensor Virtualization and Data Orchestration in Internet of Vehicles (IoV*). IFIP/IEEE International Symposium on Integrated Network Management (IM)*, Bordeaux, France.

Muhammad, K., Lloret, J., & Baik, S. W. (2019). Intelligent and energy-efficient data prioritization in green smart cities: Current challenges and future directions. *IEEE Communications Magazine, 57*(2), 60–65. doi:10.1109/MCOM.2018.1800371

Mukherjee, S., Gupta, S., Rawlley, O., & Jain, S. (2022). Leveraging big data analytics in 5G-enabled IoT and industrial IoT for the development of sustainable smart cities. *Transactions on Emerging Telecommunications Technologies, 33*(12), e4618. doi:10.1002/ett.4618

Mukhopadhyay, D., Bhattacharyya, S., Krishnan, B., & Roy, S. (Eds.). (2022). *Blockchain for IoT*. CRC Press. doi:10.1201/9781003188247

Murshed, M. S., Murphy, C., Hou, D., Khan, N., Ananthanarayanan, G., & Hussain, F. (2021). Machine learning at the network edge: A survey. *ACM Computing Surveys, 54*(8), 1–37. doi:10.1145/3469029

Musa, A. A., Malami, S. I., Alanazi, F., Ounaies, W., Alshammari, M., & Haruna, S. I. (2023). Sustainable Traffic Management for Smart Cities Using Internet-of-Things-Oriented Intelligent Transportation Systems (ITS): Challenges and Recommendations. *Sustainability (Basel), 15*(13), 9859. doi:10.3390/su15139859

Mu, T., Ren, Q., Shao, B. L., Bian, G., & Song, J. (2023). A secure and lightweight cloud-centric intelligent medical system based on Internet of Medical Things. *The Journal of Supercomputing, 79*(16), 18820–18848. doi:10.1007/s11227-023-05363-4

Naaz, S., & Parveen, S. (2023, January). An In-Depth Study of 5G-Based Eco-Friendly Smart City. In *International Conference on Smart Trends in Computing and Communications* (pp. 537-548). Singapore: Springer Nature Singapore 10.1007/978-981-99-0769-4_47

Nam, T., & Pardo, T. A. (2011). Conceptualizing smart city with dimensions of technology, people, and institutions. In *Proceedings of the 12th Annual International Digital Government Research Conference: Digital Government Innovation in Challenging Times* (pp. 282-291). ACM. 10.1145/2037556.2037602

Nandyala, C. S., & Kim, H.-K. (2016). Green IoT agriculture and healthcare application (GAHA). *International Journal of Smart Home, 10*(4), 289–300. doi:10.14257/ijsh.2016.10.4.26

Narendra, P., Duquennoy, S., & Voigt, T. (2016). BLE and IEEE 802.15. 4 in the IoT: Evaluation and Interoperability Considerations. In *Internet of Things. IoT Infrastructures: Second International Summit, IoT 360° 2015, Rome, Italy, October 27-29, 2015, Revised Selected Papers, Part II* (pp. 427-438). Springer International Publishing.

Nasiri, M. (2016). *Internet of Things as an enabler in disruptive innovation for sustainability*. Research Gate.

Nassereddine, M., & Khang, A. (2024). Applications of Internet of Things (Io T) in smart cities. In *Advanced Io T Technologies and Applications in the Industry 4.0 Digital Economy* (pp. 109–136). CRC Press.

Naz, H., Nijhawan, R., Ahuja, N. J., Al-Otaibi, S., Saba, T., Bahaj, S. A., & Rehman, A. (2023). Ensembled Deep Convolutional Generative Adversarial Network for Grading Imbalanced Diabetic Retinopathy Recognition. *IEEE Access : Practical Innovations, Open Solutions, 11*, 120554–120568. doi:10.1109/ACCESS.2023.3327900

Nazim, S. F., Danish, M. S. S., & Senjyu, T. (2022). A brief review of the future of smart mobility using 5G and IoT. *Journal of Sustainability Outreach*. doi:10.37357/1068/jso/3.1.02

Nguyen. (2021). Federated learning meets blockchain in edgecomputing: Opportunities and challenges. *IEEE Internet Things J.* . doi:10.1109/JIOT.2021.3072611

Nguyen, D. D., Rohács, J., Rohács, D., & Boros, A. (2020). Intelligent total transportation management system for future smart cities. *Applied Sciences (Basel, Switzerland), 10*(24), 8933. doi:10.3390/app10248933

Nica, E., Popescu, G. H., Poliak, M., Kliestik, T., & Sabie, O. M. (2023). Digital Twin Simulation Tools, Spatial Cognition Algorithms, and Multi-Sensor Fusion Technology in Sustainable Urban Governance Networks. *Mathematics, 11*(9), 1981. Advance online publication. doi:10.3390/math11091981

Nidhya, R., Kumar, M., Maheswar, R., & Pavithra, D. (2022). Security and privacy issues in smart healthcare system using internet of things. *IoT-Enabled Smart Healthcare Systems, Services and Applications*, 63-85.

Nigmatov, A., Pradeep, A., & Musulmonova, N. (2023). Blockchain Technology in Improving Transparency and Efficiency in Government Operations. *15th International Conference on Electronics, Computers and Artificial Intelligence, ECAI 2023 - Proceedings*. IEEE. 10.1109/ECAI58194.2023.10194154

Nimlyat, P. S. (2018). Indoor environmental quality performance and occupants' satisfaction [IEQPOS] as assessment criteria for green healthcare building rating. *Building and Environment, 144*, 598–610. doi:10.1016/j.buildenv.2018.09.003

Nordrum, A. (2016). *Popular Internet of Things Forecast of 50 Billion Devices by 2020 is Outdated*. IEEE.

Nourildean, S. W., Hassib, M. D., & Mohammed, Y. A. (2022). Internet of things based wireless sensor network: A review. *Indonesian Journal of Electrical Engineering and Computer Science, 27*(1), 246–261. doi:10.11591/ijeecs.v27.i1.pp246-261

O'Connell, E., Moore, D., & Newe, T. (2020). Challenges Associated with Implementing 5G in Manufacturing. *Telecom., 1*(1), 48–67. doi:10.3390/telecom1010005

Obiako, I. V. (2022). *Toward a Bio-Inspired System Architecting Framework: Simulation of the Integration of Autonomous Bus Fleets and Alternative Fueling Infrastructures in Closed Sociotechnical Environments* [Doctoral dissertation, University of South Alabama].

Ogbodo, E. U., Abu-Mahfouz, A. M., & Kurien, A. M. (2023). A Survey on 5G and LPWAN-IoT for Improved Smart Cities and Remote Area Applications: From the Aspect of Architecture and Security. *Sensors (Basel)*, *22*(16), 6313. doi:10.3390/s22166313 PMID:36016078

Orabi, M., Al Aghbari, Z., & Kamel, I. (2023). FogLBS: Utilizing fog computing for providing mobile Location-Based Services to mobile customers. *Pervasive and Mobile Computing*, *94*, 101832. doi:10.1016/j.pmcj.2023.101832

Otter, D. W., Medina, J. R., & Kalita, J. K. (2020). A survey of the usages of deep learning for natural language processing. *IEEE Transactions on Neural Networks and Learning Systems*, *32*(2), 604–624. doi:10.1109/TNNLS.2020.2979670 PMID:32324570

Ou, D., Jiang, C., Zheng, M., & Ren, Y. (2023). Container Power Consumption Prediction Based on GBRT-PL for Edge Servers in Smart City. *IEEE Internet of Things Journal, 10*(21), 18799-18807. doi:10.1109/JIOT.2023.3281368

Paiva, S., Ahad, M. A., Tripathi, G., Feroz, N., & Casalino, G. (2021). Enabling technologies for urban smart mobility: Recent trends, opportunities and challenges. *Sensors (Basel)*, *21*(6), 2143. doi:10.3390/s21062143 PMID:33803903

Palaniappan, D., Davda, Y., & Premavathi, T. (2023). Digital Marketing Based on Machine Learning. In Government Impact on Sustainable and Responsible Supply Chain Management (pp. 143-170). IGI Global. doi:10.4018/978-1-6684-9062-4.ch009

Pandian, M. T., & Damodharan, P. (2023). Forming the Cluster in the RFID Network for Improving the Efficiency and Investigation of the Unkind Attacks. In Computational Intelligence in Analytics and Information Systems (pp. 295-304). Apple Academic Press. doi:10.1201/9781003332367-25

Pandiyan, P., Saravanan, S., Usha, K., Kannadasan, R., Alsharif, M. H., & Kim, M. K. (2023). Technological advancements toward smart energy management in smart cities. *Energy Reports*, *10*, 648–677. doi:10.1016/j.egyr.2023.07.021

Papapanagiotou, I., Toumpakaris, D., Lee, J., & Devetsikiotis, M. (2009). A survey on next generation mobile WiMAX networks: Objectives, features and technical challenges. *IEEE Communications Surveys and Tutorials*, *11*(4), 3–18. doi:10.1109/SURV.2009.090402

Park JH, Rathore S, Singh SK, Salim MM, Azzaoui AE, Kim TW, Pan Y, Park JH. A comprehensive survey on core technologies and services for 5G security: Taxonomies, issues, and solutions. Hum.-Centric Comput. Inf. Sci. 2021 Jan 29;11(3).

Park, J. H., Yotxay, S., Singh, S. K., & Park, J. H. (2024). PoAh-Enabled Federated Learning Architecture for DDoS Attack Detection in IoT Networks. *Hum.-Centric Comput. Inf. Sci, 14*(3).

Park, J. H., Yotxay, S., Singh, S. K., & Park, J. H. (2024). PoAh-Enabled Federated Learning Architecture for DDoS Attack Detection in IoT Networks. *Human Centric Computing and Information Science, 14*(3).

Park, J. H., Yotxay, S., Singh, S. K., & Park, J. H. (2024). PoAh-Enabled Federated Learning Architecture for DDoS Attack Detection in IoT Networks. *Human-Centric Computing and Information Sciences, 14*(3).

Park, J. H., Yotxay, S., Singh, S. K., & Park, J. H. (2024). PoAh-Enabled Federated Learning Architecture for DDoS Attack Detection in IoT Networks. *Human-Centric Computing And Information Sciences, 14.*

Park, J. H., Yotxay, S., Singh, S. K., & Park, J. H. (2024). PoAh-Enabled Federated Learning Architecture for DDoS Attack Detection in IoT Networks. *HumCentric Comput. Inf. Sci, 14*(3).

ParkJ. (2020). *Communication-efficient and distributed learning over wireless networks: Principles and applications.* arXiv:2008.02608.

Park, J. H., Singh, S. K., Salim, M. M., Azzaoui, A. E., & Park, J. H. (2022). Ransomware-based Cyber Attacks: A Comprehensive Survey. *Wangji Wanglu Jishu Xuekan*, *23*(7), 1557–1564. doi:10.53106/160792642022122307010

Park, S., Kim, D., Park, Y., Cho, H., Kim, D., & Kwon, S. (2021). 5G Security Threat Assessment in Real Networks. *Sensors (Basel)*, *21*(16), 5524. doi:10.3390/s21165524 PMID:34450971

Parmar, J. K., & Desai, A. (2016). IoT: Networking technologies and research challenges. *International Journal of Computer Applications*, *154*(7), 1–6. doi:10.5120/ijca2016912181

Patel, R. K., Gidwani, P., & Patel, N. R. (2023). Privacy Preservation and Cloud Computing. In Privacy Preservation and Secured Data Storage in Cloud Computing (pp. 88-107). IGI Global. doi:10.4018/979-8-3693-0593-5.ch004

Patra, M. K., Kumari, A., Sahoo, B., & Turuk, A. K. (2023). Challenges and Opportunities Toward Integration of IoT with Cloud Computing. *Integration of IoT with Cloud Computing for Smart Applications*, 81-98.

Patra, M. K., Kumari, A., Sahoo, B., & Turuk, A. K. (2023). Smart Healthcare System Using Cloud-Integrated Internet of Medical Things. In Exploring the Convergence of Computer and Medical Science Through Cloud Healthcare (pp. 60-83). IGI Global.

Patra, M. K., Sahoo, S., Sahoo, B., & Turuk, A. K. (2021). Cloud-Edge Centric Service Provisioning in Smart City Using Internet of Things. In Advances in Parallel & Distributed Processing, and Applications: Proceedings from PDPTA'20, CSC'20, MSV'20, and GCC'20 (pp. 619-631). Springer International Publishing. doi:10.1007/978-3-030-69984-0_44

Patra, M. K. (2017, February). An architecture model for smart city using Cognitive Internet of Things (CIoT). In *2017 Second International Conference on Electrical, Computer and Communication Technologies (ICECCT)* (pp. 1-6). IEEE. 10.1109/ICECCT.2017.8117893

Perera, C., Zaslavsky, A., Christen, P., & Georgakopoulos, D. (2014). Context Aware Computing for The Internet of Things: A Survey. *IEEE Communications Surveys and Tutorials*, *16*(1), 414–454. doi:10.1109/SURV.2013.042313.00197

Pérez-Romero, J., Sallent, O., Ferrús, R., & Agustí, R. (2016, September). Knowledge-based 5G radio access network planning and optimization. In *2016 International Symposium on Wireless Communication Systems (ISWCS)* (pp. 359-365). IEEE 10.1109/ISWCS.2016.7600929

Petrellis, N., Birbas, M., & Gioulekas, F. (2019). On the Design of Low-Cost IoT Sensor Node for e-Health Environments. *Electronics (Basel)*, *8*(2), 178. doi:10.3390/electronics8020178

Pham, Q. V., Fang, F., Ha, V. N., Piran, M. J., Le, M., Le, L. B., Hwang, W.-J., & Ding, Z. (2020). A survey of multi-access edge computing in 5G and beyond: Fundamentals, technology integration, and state-of-the-art. *IEEE Access : Practical Innovations, Open Solutions*, *8*, 116974–117017. doi:10.1109/ACCESS.2020.3001277

Pinzone, M., Lettieri, E., & Masella, C. (2012). Sustainability in healthcare: Combining organizational and architectural levers. *International Journal of Engineering Business Management*, *4*, 38. doi:10.5772/54841

Pitichat, T. (2013). Smartphones in the workplace: Changing organizational behavior, transforming the future. *LUX: A Journal of Transdisciplinary Writing and Research from Claremont Graduate University*, *3*(1), 13.

Plevris, V., Lagaros, N. D., & Zeytinci, A. (2022). Blockchain in Civil Engineering, Architecture and Construction Industry: State of the Art, Evolution, Challenges and Opportunities. In Frontiers in Built Environment, 8. doi:10.3389/fbuil.2022.840303

Politou, E., Alepis, E., Virvou, M., & Patsakis, C. (2022). Privacy in Blockchain. In *Privacy and Data Protection Challenges in the Distributed Era. Learning and Analytics in Intelligent Systems* (Vol. 26, pp. 133–149). Springer. doi:10.1007/978-3-030-85443-0_7

Politou, E., Casino, F., Alepis, E., & Patsakis, C. (2021). Blockchain Mutability: Challenges and Proposed Solutions. *IEEE Transactions on Emerging Topics in Computing*, *9*(4), 1972–1986. doi:10.1109/TETC.2019.2949510

Ponnusamy, M., & Alagarsamy, A. (2023). Traffic monitoring in smart cities using internet of things assisted robotics. *Materials Today: Proceedings*, *81*, 290–294. doi:10.1016/j.matpr.2021.03.192

Pons, M., Valenzuela, E., Rodríguez, B., Nolazco-Flores, J. A., & Del-Valle-Soto, C. (2023). Utilization of 5G Technologies in IoT Applications: Current Limitations by Interference and Network Optimization Difficulties—A Review. *Sensors (Basel)*, *23*(8), 3876. doi:10.3390/s23083876 PMID:37112216

Poonguzhali, N., Gayathri, S., Deebika, A., & Suriapriya, R. (2020, July). A framework for electronic health record using blockchain technology. In *2020 International Conference on System, Computation, Automation and Networking (ICSCAN)* (pp. 1-5). IEEE. 10.1109/ICSCAN49426.2020.9262369

Poy, A. (2009). Smart Cities: Threat and Countermeasures. *Philosophical Magazine*, *27*, 77.

Poy, A. (2022). Statista. *Philosophical Magazine*, *27*, 77.

Poy, A. (2023). Gartner Reports. *Philosophical Magazine*, *27*, 77.

Prasad, V. K., Bhattacharya, P., Maru, D., Tanwar, S., Verma, A., Singh, A., Tiwari, A. K., Sharma, R., Alkhayyat, A., Țurcanu, F. E., & Raboaca, M. S. (2023). Federated Learning for the Internet-of-Medical-Things: A Survey. *Mathematics*, *11*(1), 151. doi:10.3390/math11010151

Pundir, S., Wazid, M., Singh, D. P., Das, A. K., Rodrigues, J. J. P. C., & Park, Y. (2020). Intrusion Detection Protocols in Wireless Sensor Networks Integrated to Internet of Things Deployment: Survey and Future Challenges. *IEEE Access : Practical Innovations, Open Solutions*, *8*, 3343–3363. doi:10.1109/ACCESS.2019.2962829

Qadeer, A., & Lee, M. J. (2022). *DDPG-Edge-Cloud: A Deep-Deterministic Policy Gradient based Multi-Resource Allocation in Edge-Cloud System.* 2022 International Conference on Artificial Intelligence in Information and Communication (ICAIIC), Jeju Island, South Korea. 10.1109/ICAIIC54071.2022.9722676

Qin, X., Huang, Y., Yang, Z., & Li, X. (2021). LBAC: A lightweight blockchain-based access control scheme for the internet of things. *Information Sciences*, *554*, 222–235. doi:10.1016/j.ins.2020.12.035

Qiu, J., Liang, X., Shetty, S., & Bowden, D. (2018, September). *Towards secure and smart healthcare in smart cities using blockchain. In 2018 IEEE international smart cities conference (ISC2).* IEEE.

Qolomany, B., Al-Fuqaha, A., Gupta, A., Benhaddou, D., Alwajidi, S., Qadir, J., & Fong, A. C. (2019). Leveraging machine learning and big data for smart buildings: A comprehensive survey. *IEEE Access : Practical Innovations, Open Solutions*, *7*, 90316–90356. doi:10.1109/ACCESS.2019.2926642

Quamara, M., Gupta, B. B., & Yamaguchi, S. (2021, January). An end-to-end security framework for smart healthcare information sharing against botnet-based cyber-attacks. In *2021 IEEE International Conference on Consumer Electronics (ICCE)* (pp. 1-4). IEEE. 10.1109/ICCE50685.2021.9427753

Quy, V. K., Hau, N. V., Anh, D. V., & Ngoc, L. A. (2022). Smart Healthcare IoT Applications Based on Fog Computing: Architecture, Applications and Challenges. *Complex & Intelligent Systems*, *8*(5), 3805–3815. doi:10.1007/s40747-021-00582-9 PMID:34804767

Radanliev, P., De Roure, D., Van Kleek, M., Santos, O., & Ani, U. (2021). Artificial intelligence in cyber physical systems. *AI & Society*, *36*(3), 783–796. doi:10.1007/s00146-020-01049-0 PMID:32874020

Rafique, W., Khan, M., Khan, S., & Ally, J. S. (2023). SecureMed: A Blockchain-Based Privacy-Preserving Framework for Internet of Medical Things. *Wireless Communications and Mobile Computing*, *2023*, 1–14. doi:10.1155/2023/2558469

Rahmadika, S., Astillo, P. V., Choudhary, G., Duguma, D. G., Sharma, V., & You, I. (2023). Blockchain-Based Privacy Preservation Scheme for Misbehavior Detection in Lightweight IoMT Devices. *IEEE Journal of Biomedical and Health Informatics*, *27*(2), 710–721. doi:10.1109/JBHI.2022.3187037 PMID:35763469

Rahman, M. M., Khatun, F., Sami, S. I., & Uzzaman, A. (2022). The evolving roles and impacts of 5G enabled technologies in healthcare: The world epidemic COVID-19 issues. *Array (New York, N.Y.)*, *14*, 100178. doi:10.1016/j.array.2022.100178 PMID:35571870

Rahul, A., Rao, S., & Raghu, M. E. (2015). Near field communication (NFC) technology: A survey. [IJCI]. *International Journal on Cybernetics & Informatics*, *4*(2), 133–144. doi:10.5121/ijci.2015.4213

Rai, H. M., Atik-Ur-Rehman, Pal, A., Mishra, S., & Shukla, K. K. (2023). Use of Internet of Things in the context of execution of smart city applications: A review. *Discover Internet of Things*, *3*(1), 8. doi:10.1007/s43926-023-00037-2

Rajaei, H., Kanumuri, B., & Narreddi, N. (2020). SBDC: Smart Building Data Center for Iot, Edge, and 5G. *2020 Spring Simulation Conference (SpringSim)*, Fairfax, VA, USA. 10.22360/SpringSim.2020.CNS.004

Rajendran, G., Nivash, R. R., Parthy, P. P., & Balamurugan, S. (2019, October). Modern security threats in the Internet of Things (IoT): Attacks and Countermeasures. In *2019 International Carnahan Conference on Security Technology (ICCST)* (pp. 1-6). IEEE. 10.1109/CCST.2019.8888399

Ramírez-Moreno, M. A., Keshtkar, S., Padilla-Reyes, D. A., Ramos-López, E., García-Martínez, M., Hernández-Luna, M. C., & Lozoya-Santos, J. D. J. (2021). Sensors for sustainable smart cities: A review. *Applied Sciences (Basel, Switzerland)*, *11*(17), 8198. doi:10.3390/app11178198

Ramzan, R., Beg, A., Jawed, S. A., Aaquib, M., & Junaid, M. (2023, September). Quadrature RF-Only Logic Family for Single-Chip Self-Powered Transceivers. In *2023 IEEE 36th International System-on-Chip Conference (SOCC)* (pp. 1-5). IEEE. 10.1109/SOCC58585.2023.10256996

RaneN. (2023) ChatGPT and Similar Generative Artificial Intelligence (AI) for Smart Industry: Role, Challenges and Opportunities for Industry 4.0, Industry 5.0 and Society 5.0. doi:10.2139/ssrn.4603234

Rani, S., Kataria, A., Kumar, S., & Tiwari, P. (2023). Federated learning for secure IoMT-applications in smart healthcare systems: A comprehensive review. *Knowledge-Based Systems*, *274*, 110658. doi:10.1016/j.knosys.2023.110658

Rathi, V. K., Rajput, N. K., Mishra, S., Grover, B. A., Tiwari, P., Jaiswal, A. K., & Hossain, M. S. (2021). An edge AI-enabled IoT healthcare monitoring system for smart cities. *Computers & Electrical Engineering*, *96*, 107524. doi:10.1016/j.compeleceng.2021.107524

Ravindran, A. (2022). *Will AI Dictate the Future?* Marshall Cavendish International Asia Pte Ltd.

Ray, P. P. (2018). A survey on Internet of Things architectures. *Journal of King Saud University. Computer and Information Sciences*, *30*(3), 291–319. doi:10.1016/j.jksuci.2016.10.003

Razzak, F. (2012). Spamming the Internet of Things: A Possibility and its probable Solution. *Procedia Computer Science*, *10*, 658–665. doi:10.1016/j.procs.2012.06.084

Rejeb, A., Rejeb, K., Simske, S. J., & Keogh, J. G. (2021). Blockchain technology in the smart city: A bibliometric review. *Quality & Quantity*. doi:10.1007/s11135-021-01251-2 PMID:34629554

Rejeb, A., Rejeb, K., Simske, S., Treiblmaier, H., & Zailani, S. (2022). The big picture on the internet of things and the smart city: A review of what we know and what we need to know. *Internet of Things : Engineering Cyber Physical Human Systems, 19*, 100565. doi:10.1016/j.iot.2022.100565

Rejeb, A., Rejeb, K., Treiblmaier, H., Appolloni, A., Alghamdi, S., Alhasawi, Y., & Iranmanesh, M. (2023). The Internet of Things (IoT) in healthcare: Taking stock and moving forward. *Internet of Things : Engineering Cyber Physical Human Systems, 22*, 100721. doi:10.1016/j.iot.2023.100721

Richie, C. (2020). Can United States healthcare become environmentally sustainable? towards green healthcare reform. *The Journal of Law, Medicine & Ethics, 48*(4), 643–652. doi:10.1177/1073110520979371 PMID:33404336

Riđić, O., Jukić, T., Riđić, G., Mangafić, J., Bušatlić, S., & Karamehić, J. (2022). Implementation of Blockchain Technologies in Smart Cities, Opportunities and Challenges. In Environmental Footprints and Eco-Design of Products and Processes. Springer. doi:10.1007/978-981-16-6301-7_4

Rito, P. (2023). Aveiro Tech City Living Lab: A Communication, Sensing, and Computing Platform for City Environments. *IEEE Internet of Things Journal, 10*(15), 13489-13510. . doi:10.1109/JIOT.2023.3262627

Riya, K. S., Surendran, R., Romero, C. A. T., & Sendil, M. S. (2023). Encryption with User Authentication Model for Internet of Medical Things Environment. *Intelligent Automation & Soft Computing, 35*(1). doi:10.32604/iasc.2023.027779

Rong, B., Han, S., Kadoch, M., Chen, X., & Jara, A. (2020). Integration of 5G Networks and Internet of Things for Future Smart City, Wireless Communications and Mobile Computing. Hindawi. doi:10.1155/2020/2903525

Saarika, P. S., Sandhya, K., & Sudha, T. (2017, August). Smart transportation system using IoT. In *2017 International Conference On Smart Technologies For Smart Nation (SmartTechCon)* (pp. 1104-1107). IEEE. 10.1109/SmartTechCon.2017.8358540

Sabrina, F., Li, N., & Sohail, S. (2022). A Blockchain Based Secure IoT System Using Device Identity Management. *Sensors, 22*(19), 7535. . doi:10.3390/s22197535

Sadhu, P. K., Yanambaka, V. P., Abdelgawad, A., & Yelamarthi, K. (2023). NAHAP: PUF-Based Three Factor Authentication System for Internet of Medical Things. *IEEE Consumer Electronics Magazine, 12*(3), 107–115. doi:10.1109/MCE.2022.3176420

Safavi, S., Meer, A. M., Melanie, E. K. J., & Shukur, Z. (2018, November). Cyber vulnerabilities on smart healthcare, review and solutions. In 2018 Cyber Resilience Conference (CRC) (pp. 1-5). IEEE. doi:10.1109/CR.2018.8626826

Saini, P., Gupta, L., & Malhotra, S. (2023, June). Internet of Medical Things: Current Applications, Challenges and Future. In *2023 International Conference on IoT, Communication and Automation Technology (ICICAT)* (pp. 1-5). IEEE. 10.1109/ICICAT57735.2023.10263636

Sajjan, R., Chaturvedi, T., Bhanusghare, D., & Bansal, Y. (2023, April). ProHealth–Improvised E-Health Care System. In *2023 IEEE International Conference on Contemporary Computing and Communications (InC4)* (Vol. 1, pp. 1-6). IEEE.

Samuel, O., Omojo, A. B., Onuja, A. M., Sunday, Y., Tiwari, P., Gupta, D., Hafeez, G., Yahaya, A. S., Fatoba, O. J., & Shamshirband, S. (2023). IoMT: A COVID-19 Healthcare System Driven by Federated Learning and Blockchain. *IEEE Journal of Biomedical and Health Informatics, 27*(2), 823–834. doi:10.1109/JBHI.2022.3143576 PMID:35041615

Sanchez-Corcuera, R., Nunez-Marcos, A., Sesma-Solance, J., Bilbao-Jayo, A., Mulero, R., Zulaika, U., & Almeida, A. (2019). Smart cities survey: Technologies, application domains and challenges for the cities of the future. *International Journal of Distributed Sensor Networks*, *15*(6), 1550147719853984. doi:10.1177/1550147719853984

Sarker, I. H. (2021). Data science and analytics: An overview from data-driven smart computing, decision-making and applications perspective. *SN Computer Science*, *2*(5), 377. https://link.springer.com/article/10.1007/s42979-021-00765-8. doi:10.1007/s42979-021-00765-8 PMID:34278328

Sartal, A., Carou, D., & Davim, J. P. (Eds.). (2020). *Enabling technologies for the successful deployment of industry 4.0.* CRC Press. doi:10.1201/9780429055621

Sarwat, A. I., Sundararajan, A., Parvez, I., Moghaddami, M., & Moghadasi, A. (2018). Toward a smart city of interdependent critical infrastructure networks. Sustainable Interdependent Networks: *From Theory to Application*, 21-45. Springer. https://link.springer.com/chapter/10.1007/978-3-319-74412-4_3

Schwartz, R., Dodge, J., Smith, N. A., & Etzioni, O. (2019). Green AI. *Proceedings of the 57th Annual Meeting of the Association for Computational Linguistics*. Springer.

Seung-Yoon, S., Dongwook, K., & Soon, A. C. (2021). Digital Divide in Advanced Smart City Innovations [April.]. *Sustainability, MDPI*, *13*(7), 1–22.

Shackelford, S. J. (2020). *The Internet of Things: What Everyone Needs to Know*. Oxford University Press. doi:10.1093/wentk/9780190943813.001.0001

Shafik, W. (2023b). Cyber Security Perspectives in Public Spaces: Drone Case Study. In Handbook of Research on Cybersecurity Risk in Contemporary Business Systems (pp. 79-97). IGI Global. doi:10.4018/978-1-6684-7207-1.ch004

Shafik, W. (2023c). Making Cities Smarter: IoT and SDN Applications, Challenges, and Future Trends. In Opportunities and Challenges of Industrial IoT in 5G and 6G Networks (pp. 73-94). IGI Global. doi:10.4018/978-1-7998-9266-3.ch004

Shafik, W. (2024a). Wearable Medical Electronics in Artificial Intelligence of Medical Things. Handbook of Security and Privacy of AI-Enabled Healthcare Systems and Internet of Medical Things, 21-40. Springer. https://doi.org/doi:10.1201/9781003370321-2

Shafik, W., & Kalinaki, K. (2023). Smart City Ecosystem: An Exploration of Requirements, Architecture, Applications, Security, and Emerging Motivations. In Handbook of Research on Network-Enabled IoT Applications for Smart City Services (pp. 75–98). IGI Global. doi:10.4018/979-8-3693-0744-1.ch005

Shafik, W., Tufail, A., Liyanage, C. D. S., & Apong, R. A. A. H. M. (2024). Medical Robotics and AI-Assisted Diagnostics Challenges for Smart Sustainable Healthcare. In AI-Driven Innovations in Digital Healthcare: Emerging Trends, Challenges, and Applications (pp. 304-323). IGI Global. doi:10.4018/979-8-3693-3218-4.ch016

Shafik, W. (2023a). A Comprehensive Cybersecurity Framework for Present and Future Global Information Technology Organizations. In *Effective Cybersecurity Operations for Enterprise-Wide Systems* (pp. 56–79). IGI Global., doi:10.4018/978-1-6684-9018-1.ch002

Shafik, W. (2023c). *Artificial intelligence and Blockchain technology enabling cybersecurity in telehealth systems.* Artificial Intelligence and Blockchain Technology in Modern Telehealth Systems. doi:10.1049/PBHE061E_ch11

Shafik, W. (2024a). Introduction to ChatGPT. In *Advanced Applications of Generative AI and Natural Language Processing Models* (pp. 1–25). IGI Global. doi:10.4018/979-8-3693-0502-7.ch001

Shafik, W. (2024b). Predicting Future Cybercrime Trends in the Metaverse Era. In *Forecasting Cyber Crimes in the Age of the Metaverse* (pp. 78–113). IGI Global. doi:10.4018/979-8-3693-0220-0.ch005

Shafik, W. (2024c). *Toward a More Ethical Future of Artificial Intelligence and Data Science. The Ethical Frontier of AI and Data Analysis*. IGI Global. doi:10.4018/979-8-3693-2964-1.ch022

Shafik, W., Matinkhah, S. M., & Shokoor, F. (2022). Recommendation system comparative analysis: Internet of things aided networks. *EAI Endorsed Transactions on Internet of Things*, *8*(29), e5. doi:10.4108/eetiot.v8i29.1108

Shafik, W., Matinkhah, S. M., & Shokoor, F. (2023). Cybersecurity in unmanned aerial vehicles: A review. *International Journal on Smart Sensing and Intelligent Systems*, *16*(1), 20230012. doi:10.2478/ijssis-2023-0012

Shah, S. H., & Yaqoob, I. (2016). A survey: Internet of Things (IOT) technologies, applications and challenges. *2016 IEEE Smart Energy Grid Engineering (SEGE),* (pp. 381-385). IEEE.

Shah, I. A., & Ahmed, M. (2023, March). $$F_K-meansRA$$: Fuzzy K-Means Clustering Routing Algorithm for Load Balancing in Wireless Sensor Networks. *Wireless Personal Communications*, *130*(2), 1071–1083. doi:10.1007/s11277-023-10320-8

ShahzadF.JavedA. R.ZikriaY. B.RehmanS.JalilZ. (2021). Future smart cities: requirements, emerging technologies, applications, challenges, and future aspects. TechRxiv.

Shankar, A., & Maple, C. (2023). Securing the Internet of Things-enabled smart city infrastructure using a hybrid framework. *Computer Communications*, *205*, 127–135. doi:10.1016/j.comcom.2023.04.008

Shankar, N., Nallakaruppan, M. K., Ravindranath, V., Senthilkumar, M., & Bhagavath, B. P. (2023). Smart IoMT Framework for Supporting UAV Systems with AI. *Electronics (Basel)*, *12*(1), 86. doi:10.3390/electronics12010086

Sharma, H. K., Kumar, A., Pant, S., & Ram, M. (2022). 7 Security and Privacy challenge in Smart Healthcare and Telemedicine systems.

Sharma, M., Sharma, M., Sharma, N., & Boopathi, S. (2024). Building Sustainable Smart Cities Through Cloud and Intelligent Parking System. In Handbook of Research on AI and ML for Intelligent Machines and Systems (pp. 195-222). IGI Global.

Sharma, A., & Singh, B. (2022). Measuring Impact of E-commerce on Small Scale Business: A Systematic Review. *Journal of Corporate Governance and International Business Law*, *5*(1).

Sharma, P. K., Chen, M.-Y., & Park, J. H. (2018). A Software Defined Fog Node Based Distributed Blockchain Cloud Architecture for IoT. *IEEE Access : Practical Innovations, Open Solutions*, *6*, 115–124. doi:10.1109/ACCESS.2017.2757955

Sharma, R., & Arya, R. (2023). Security threats and measures in the Internet of Things for smart city infrastructure: A state of art. *Transactions on Emerging Telecommunications Technologies*, *34*(11), e4571. doi:10.1002/ett.4571

Sheller, M. J., Reina, G. A., Edwards, B., & Martin, J. (2019). Multi-Institutional Deep Learning Modeling Without Sharing Patient Data: A Feasibility Study on Brain Tumor Segmentation. Brainlesion.

Shen, G., & Liu, B. (2011, May). The visions, technologies, applications, and security issues of the Internet of Things. In *2011 International Conference on E-Business and E-Government (ICEE)* (pp. 1-4). IEEE. 10.1109/ICEBEG.2011.5881892

Shen, S., Wei, Z. Q., Sun, L. J., Su, Y. Q., Wang, R. C., & Jiang, H. M. (2018). The shared bicycle and its network—internet of shared bicycle (IOSB): A review and survey. *Sensors (Basel)*, *18*(8), 2581. doi:10.3390/s18082581 PMID:30087263

Shihab, S., & AlTawy, R. (2023). Lightweight Authentication Scheme for Healthcare with Robustness to Desynchronization Attacks. *IEEE Internet of Things Journal*, *10*(20), 18140–18153. doi:10.1109/JIOT.2023.3279035

Shin, S.-Y., Kim, D., & Chun, S. A. (2021). Digital Divide in Advanced Smart City Innovations. *Sustainability (Basel)*, *13*(7), 4076. doi:10.3390/su13074076

Shi, W., Dustdar, S., & Pan, Y. (2016). Edge computing: Vision and challenges. *IEEE Internet of Things Journal, 3*(5), 637–646. doi:10.1109/JIOT.2016.2579198

Shourie, P., Kumar, N., Kaushal, R. K., & Verma, S. (2023, May). IoT-based Hybrid Fitness Monitoring Device. In *2023 7th International Conference on Intelligent Computing and Control Systems (ICICCS)* (pp. 1527-1532). IEEE. 10.1109/ICICCS56967.2023.10142333

Shukla, S., Balachandran, K., & Sumitha, V. S. (2016, November). A framework for smart transportation using Big Data. In *2016 International Conference on ICT in Business Industry & Government (ICTBIG)* (pp. 1-3). IEEE. 10.1109/ICTBIG.2016.7892720

Silva, L., Magaia, N., Sousa, B., Kobusińska, A., Casimiro, A., Mavromoustakis, C. X., & De Albuquerque, V. H. C. (2021). Computing paradigms in emerging vehicular environments: A review. *IEEE/CAA Journal of Automatica Sinica, 8*(3), 491-511.

Silva, B. M., Khan, M. A., & Han, K. (2019). *Environmental Internet of Things: Building Smart Environmental Management Systems*. Springer.

Silva, B. N., Khan, M., & Han, K. (2018). Towards sustainable smart cities: A review of trends, architectures, components, and open challenges in smart cities. *Sustainable Cities and Society, 38*, 697–713. doi:10.1016/j.scs.2018.01.053

Silva, B. N., Khan, M., Jung, C., Seo, J., Muhammad, D., Han, J., Yoon, Y., & Han, K. (2018). Urban planning and smart city decision management empowered by real-time data processing using big data analytics. *Sensors (Basel), 18*(9), 2994. doi:10.3390/s18092994 PMID:30205499

Singh, B. (2023). Blockchain Technology in Renovating Healthcare: Legal and Future Perspectives. In Revolutionizing Healthcare Through Artificial Intelligence and Internet of Things Applications (pp. 177-186). IGI Global.

Singh, P., Dixit, V., & Kaur, J. (2019). Green healthcare for smart cities. *Green and Smart Technologies for Smart Cities*, 91-130.

Singh, R., Singh, S. K., Kumar, S., & Gill, S. S. (2022). SDN-Aided Edge Computing-Enabled AI for IoT and Smart Cities. *SDN-Supported Edge-Cloud Interplay for Next Generation Internet of Things*, (pp. 41-70). Research Gate.

Singh, S. K., Azzaoui, A. E., Choo, K. K. R., Yang, L. T., & Park, J. H. (2023). A Comprehensive Survey on Blockchain for Secure IoT-enabled Smart City beyond 5G: Approaches, Processes, Challenges, and Opportunities. *Hum.-Centric Comput. Inf. Sci, 13*(51).

Singh, S. K., Azzaoui, A. E., Choo, K. K. R., Yang, L. T., & Park, J. H. (2023). A Comprehensive Survey on Blockchain for Secure IoT-enabled Smart City beyond 5G: Approaches, Processes, Challenges, and Opportunities. *Human-Centric Computing and Information Sciences, 13*(51).

Singh, S. K., Azzaoui, A. E., Choo, K. K. R., Yang, L. T., & Park, J. H. (2023). Articles A Comprehensive Survey on Blockchain for Secure IoT-enabled Smart City beyond 5G: Approaches, Processes, Challenges, and Opportunities. *Hum.-Centric Comput. Inf. Sci, 13*(51).

Singh, S. K., Azzaoui, A. E., Choo, K. K. R., Yang, L. T., & Park, J. H. (2023b). A Comprehensive Survey on Blockchain for Secure IoT-enabled Smart City beyond 5G: Approaches, Processes, Challenges, and Opportunities. *Human Centric Computing and Information Science, 13*(51).

Singh, S. K., Park, L., & Park, J. H. (2022b). Blockchain-based Federated Approach for Privacy-Preserved IoT-enabled Smart Vehicular Networks. In *2022 13th International Conference on Information and Communication Technology Convergence (ICTC)* (pp. 1995-1999). IEEE. 10.1109/ICTC55196.2022.9952835

Singh, B. (2023). Federated Learning for Envision Future Trajectory Smart Transport System for Climate Preservation and Smart Green Planet: Insights into Global Governance and SDG-9 (Industry, Innovation and Infrastructure). *National Journal of Environmental Law*, *6*(2), 6–17.

Singh, B. (2023). Tele-Health Monitoring Lensing Deep Neural Learning Structure: Ambient Patient Wellness via Wearable Devices for Real-Time Alerts and Interventions. *Indian Journal of Health and Medical Law*, *6*(2), 12–16.

Singh, B. (2024). Legal Dynamics Lensing Metaverse Crafted for Videogame Industry and E-Sports: Phenomenological Exploration Catalyst Complexity and Future. *Journal of Intellectual Property Rights Law*, *7*(1), 8–14.

Singh, B., & Kaunert, C. (2024). Integration of Cutting-Edge Technologies such as Internet of Things (IoT) and 5G in Health Monitoring Systems: A Comprehensive Legal Analysis and Futuristic Outcomes. *GLS Law Journal*, *6*(1), 13–20.

Singh, M., & Ahmed, S. (2021). Io T based smart water management systems: A systematic review. *Materials Today: Proceedings*, *46*, 5211–5218. doi:10.1016/j.matpr.2020.08.588

Singh, P., Gaba, G. S., Kaur, A., Hedabou, M., & Gurtov, A. (2023). Dew-Cloud-Based Hierarchical Federated Learning for Intrusion Detection in IoMT. *IEEE Journal of Biomedical and Health Informatics*, *27*(2), 722–731. doi:10.1109/JBHI.2022.3186250 PMID:35816521

Singh, S. K., Azzaoui, A. E., Choo, K.-K. R., Yang, L. T., & Park, J. H. (n.d.). *ArticlesA Comprehensive Survey on Blockchain for Secure IoT-enabled Smart City beyond 5G: Approaches*. Processes, Challenges, and Opportunities.

Singh, S. K., Azzaoui, A. E., Kim, T. W., Pan, Y., & Park, J. H. (2021b). DeepBlockScheme: A deep learning-based blockchain driven scheme for secure smart city. *Human-centric Computing and Information Sciences*, *11*(12), 1–13.

Singh, S. K., Kumar, M., Tanwar, S., & Park, J. H. (2024). GRU-based digital twin framework for data allocation and storage in IoT-enabled smart home networks. *Future Generation Computer Systems*, *153*, 391–402. doi:10.1016/j.future.2023.12.009

Singh, S. K., Lee, C., & Park, J. H. (2022, April). CoVAC: A P2P smart contract-based intelligent smart city architecture for vaccine manufacturing. *Computers &amp. Industrial Engineering (American Institute of Industrial Engineers)*, *166*, 107967. doi:10.1016/j.cie.2022.107967 PMID:35136280

Singh, S. K., Pan, Y., & Park, J. H. (2021a). OTS scheme based secure architecture for energy-efficient iot in edge infrastructure. *Computers, Materials & Continua*, *66*(3), 2905–2922. doi:10.32604/cmc.2021.014151

Singh, S. K., Pan, Y., & Park, J. H. (2022c). Blockchain-enabled secure framework for energy-efficient smart parking in sustainable city environment. *Sustainable Cities and Society*, *76*, 103364. doi:10.1016/j.scs.2021.103364

Singh, S. K., & Park, J. H. (2022a). TaLWaR: Blockchain-based trust management scheme for smart enterprises with augmented intelligence. *IEEE Transactions on Industrial Informatics*, *19*(1), 626–634. doi:10.1109/TII.2022.3204692

Singh, S. K., Park, J. H., Sharma, P. K., & Pan, Y. (2022, November). BIIoVT: Blockchain-Based Secure Storage Architecture for Intelligent Internet of Vehicular Things. *IEEE Consumer Electronics Magazine*, *11*(6), 75–82. doi:10.1109/MCE.2021.3089992

Singh, S. K., Yang, L. T., & Park, J. H. (2023a). FusionFedBlock: Fusion of blockchain and federated learning to preserve privacy in industry 5.0. *Information Fusion*, *90*, 233–240. doi:10.1016/j.inffus.2022.09.027

Singh, S., Sanwar Hosen, A. S. M., & Yoon, B. (2021). Blockchain Security Attacks, Challenges, and Solutions for the Future Distributed IoT Network. *IEEE Access : Practical Innovations, Open Solutions*, *9*, 13938–13959. doi:10.1109/ACCESS.2021.3051602

Singh, S., Sharma, P. K., Yoon, B., Shojafar, M., Cho, G. H., & Ra, I. H. (2020). Convergence of blockchain and artificial intelligence in IoT network for the sustainable smart city. *Sustainable Cities and Society*, *63*, 102364. doi:10.1016/j.scs.2020.102364

Singh, T., Solanki, A., Sharma, S. K., Nayyar, A., & Paul, A. (2022a). A Decade Review on Smart Cities: Paradigms, Challenges and Opportunities. *IEEE Access : Practical Innovations, Open Solutions*, *10*, 68319–68364. doi:10.1109/ACCESS.2022.3184710

Sinha, M., Chacko, E., Makhija, P., & Pramanik, S. (2021). Energy-Efficient smart cities with green internet of things. *Green Technological Innovation for Sustainable Smart Societies: Post Pandemic Era,* 345-361.

Sodhro, A. H., Pirbhulal, S., Luo, Z., & De Albuquerque, V. H. C. (2019). Towards an optimal resource management for Io T based Green and sustainable smart cities. *Journal of Cleaner Production*, *220*, 1167–1179. doi:10.1016/j.jclepro.2019.01.188

Sohn. (2016). Improved deep metric learning with multi- class n-pair loss objective. Advances in neural information processing systems, 1857–1865.

Solanki, P., Garg, S., & Chhikaniwala, H. (2022). Preserve Privacy on Streaming Data During the Process of Mining Using User Defined Delta Value. In *Innovative Data Communication Technologies and Application* [Springer.]. *Proceedings of ICIDCA*, *2021*, 197–212.

Stamopoulos, D., Dimas, P., Siokas, G., & Siokas, E. (2024). Getting smart or going green? Quantifying the Smart City Industry's economic impact and potential for sustainable growth. *Cities (London, England)*, *144*, 104612. doi:10.1016/j.cities.2023.104612

Stefansson, G., & Lumsden, K. (2009). Performance issues of smart transportation management systems. *International Journal of Productivity and Performance Management.*

Stratigea, A., & Panagiotopoulou, M. (2015). 'Smart'Cities at the Service of Urban Sustainability-A Flavor of the Mediterranean Experience. *Journal of Regional & Socio-Economic Issues*, *5*(3).

Stückler, J., & Behnke, S. (2021). Model Learning and Real-Time Tracking Using Multi-Resolution Surfel Maps. *Proceedings of the ... AAAI Conference on Artificial Intelligence, 26*(1), 2081–2087. 10.1609/aaai.v26i1.8388

Sudha, C. N., Nayahi, J. J. V., Saravanan, S., & Renugadevi, N. (2024). The Future of Sustainable Green Smart Cities. In *Green Computing for Sustainable Smart Cities* (pp. 313–340). CRC Press. doi:10.1201/9781003388814-16

Sullivan, S., Brighente, A., Kumar, S., & Conti, M. (2021). 5G Security Challenges and Solutions: A Review by OSI Layers. *IEEE Access : Practical Innovations, Open Solutions*, *495*, 116294–116314. https://engagedscholarship.csuohio.edu/enece_facpub/495. doi:10.1109/ACCESS.2021.3105396

Su, X., Hu, Y., Liu, W., Jiang, Z., Qiu, C., Xiong, J., & Sun, J. (2023). A Blockchain-based smart contract model for secured energy trading management in smart microgrids. *Security and Privacy*, *341*. doi:10.1002/spy2.341

Syed, A. S., Sierra-Sosa, D., Kumar, A., & Elmaghraby, A. (2021). IoT in smart cities: A survey of technologies, practices and challenges. *Smart Cities*, *4*(2), 429–475. doi:10.3390/smartcities4020024

Takizaki, N., Kido, Y., Masuda, Y., Toshima, Y., Yamamoto, M., & Shimojo, S. (2023). Ontology-Based Access Control Framework for Smart Building IoT Devices. *2023 IEEE International Conference on Consumer Electronics (ICCE)*, (pp. 1–2). IEEE. 10.1109/ICCE56470.2023.10043384

Talpur, M. S. H., Bhuiyan, M. Z. A., & Wang, G. (2015). Shared-node IoT network architecture with ubiquitous homomorphic encryption for healthcare monitoring. *International Journal of Embedded Systems*, *7*(1), 43. doi:10.1504/IJES.2015.066141

Tang, Y., Dananjayan, S., Hou, C., Guo, Q., Luo, S., & He, Y. (2021). A survey on the 5G network and its impact on agriculture: Challenges and opportunities. *Computers and Electronics in Agriculture*, *180*, 105895. doi:10.1016/j.compag.2020.105895

Tang, Y., Yan, J., Chakraborty, C., & Sun, Y. (2023). Hedera: A Permissionless and Scalable Hybrid Blockchain Consensus Algorithm in Multi-Access Edge Computing for IoT. *IEEE Internet of Things Journal*, *10*(24), 21187–21202. doi:10.1109/JIOT.2023.3279108

Tan, L., Xiao, H., Yu, K., Aloqaily, M., & Jararweh, Y. (2021). A blockchain-empowered crowdsourcing system for 5G-enabled smart cities. *Computer Standards & Interfaces*, *76*, 103517. doi:10.1016/j.csi.2021.103517

Tawalbeh, L., Muheidat, F., Tawalbeh, M., & Quwaider, M. (2020). IoT Privacy and Security: Challenges and Solutions. *Applied Sciences (Basel, Switzerland)*, *10*(12), 4102. doi:10.3390/app10124102

Telsaç, C., & Yilmaz, V. (2021). *Smart City Components*. 10th International Conference on Social Sciences, Arapgir -Malatya, Turkey.

Testi, N., Marconi, R., & Pasher, E. (2023). Exploring the potential of Blockchain technology for citizen engagement in smart governance. *Open Research Europe*, *3*, 183. doi:10.12688/openreseurope.16153.2

Tian, D., Yu, N., Yu, J., Zhang, H., Sun, J., & Bai, X. (2023). Research on Dual-Line Array Subpixel Scanning Imaging for IoMT-Based Blood Cell Analysis System. *IEEE Internet of Things Journal*, *10*(1), 367–377. doi:10.1109/JIOT.2022.3201571

Tiwari, P., Ilavarasan, P. V., & Punia, S. (2019). Content analysis of literature on big data in smart cities. *Benchmarking*, *28*(5), 1837–1857. doi:10.1108/BIJ-12-2018-0442

Tokkozhina, U., Mataloto, B. M., Martins, A. L., & Ferreira, J. C. (2023). Decentralizing Online Food Delivery Services: A Blockchain and IoT Model for Smart Cities. *Mobile Networks and Applications*. doi:10.1007/s11036-023-02119-5

Tomar, P., & Kaur, G. (Eds.). (2019). *Green and smart technologies for smart cities*. CRC Press. doi:10.1201/9780429454837

Truong, H. L., Dohler, M., & Charbonnier, D. (2013). Low-cost and highly scalable urban transportation: A market-oriented approach. *IEEE Communications Magazine*, *51*(12), 36–43.

Tsakyridis, A., Ruggeri, E., Kalfas, G., Oldenbeuving, R. M., van Dijk, P. W., Roeloffzen, C. G., Leiba, Y., Miliou, A., Pleros, N., & Vagionas, C. (2021). Reconfigurable fiber wireless IFoF fronthaul with 60 GHz phased array antenna and silicon photonic ROADM for 5G mmWave C-RANs. *IEEE Journal on Selected Areas in Communications*, *39*(9), 2816–2826. doi:10.1109/JSAC.2021.3064649

U-blox. (2015). *NEO-6 Series*. U-Blox. www.u-blox.com/en/product/neo-6-series

Uchani Gutierrez, O. C., & Xu, G. (2023). Blockchain and Smart Contracts to Secure Property Transactions in Smart Cities. *Applied Sciences (Basel, Switzerland)*, *13*(1), 66. doi:10.3390/app13010066

Ullah, F., Sepasgozar, S. M., & Wang, C. (2018). A systematic review of smart real estate technology: Drivers of, and barriers to, the use of digital disruptive technologies and online platforms. *Sustainability (Basel)*, *10*(9), 3142. doi:10.3390/su10093142

Ullah, R., Asghar, I., & Griffiths, M. G. (2023). An Integrated Methodology for Bibliometric Analysis: A Case Study of Internet of Things in Healthcare Applications. *Sensors (Basel), 23*(1), 67. doi:10.3390/s23010067 PMID:36616665

Ullah, Z., Naeem, M., Coronato, A., Ribino, P., & De Pietro, G. (2023). Blockchain Applications in Sustainable Smart Cities. *Sustainable Cities and Society, 97*, 104697. doi:10.1016/j.scs.2023.104697

Ullo, S. L., & Sinha, G. R. (2020). Advances in smart environment monitoring systems using Io T and sensors. *Sensors (Basel), 20*(11), 3113. doi:10.3390/s20113113 PMID:32486411

Umran, S. M., Lu, S. F., Abduljabbar, Z. A., & Nyangaresi, V. O. (2023). Multi-chain Blockchain based secure data-sharing framework for industrial IoTs smart devices in petroleum industry. *Internet of Things : Engineering Cyber Physical Human Systems, 24*, 100969. doi:10.1016/j.iot.2023.100969

Vanzara, R., Sharma, P., Bhatt, H. S., Tanwar, S., Tyagi, S., Kumar, N., & Obaidat, M. S. (2018, November). ADYTIA: Adaptive and Dynamic TCP Interface Architecture for heterogeneous networks. *International Journal of Communication Systems, 32*(2), e3855. doi:10.1002/dac.3855

Varadharajan, V. (2021). Next Generation of Intelligent Cities: Case Studies From Europe. In Developing and Monitoring Smart Environments for Intelligent Cities (pp. 87-111). IGI Global.

Varoudis, T., & Penn, A. (2019, July). Variational Beauty of Space: Machine Intuition and Non-Linear Neural Aggregations. In *12th Space Syntax Symposium* (Vol. 12). IEEE.

Vela, L. M., Crandall, H., Lim, T., Zhang, F., Gibbs, A., Mitchell, A. R. J., Condon, A., Diamond, L. M., Zhang, H., & Sanchez, B. (2023). IoMT-Enabled Stress Monitoring in a Virtual Reality Environment and at Home. *IEEE Internet of Things Journal, 10*(12), 10649–10661. doi:10.1109/JIOT.2023.3240099

Verma, S., & Sheel, A. (2022). Blockchain for government organizations: Past, present and future. *Journal of Global Operations and Strategic Sourcing, 15*(3), 406–430. doi:10.1108/JGOSS-08-2021-0063

Vermesan, O., Friess, P., Guillemin, P., Giaffreda, R., Grindvoll, H., Eisenhauer, M., & Tragos, E. Z. (2022, September). Internet of Things beyond the Hype: Research, Innovation and Deployment. In Building the Hyperconnected Society-Internet of Things Research and Innovation Value Chains, Ecosystems and Markets (pp. 15–118). River Publishers. doi:10.1201/9781003337454-3

Vilalta, R., López, V., Giorgetti, A., Peng, S., Orsini, V., Velasco, L., Serral-Gracia, R., Morris, D., De Fina, S., Cugini, F., Castoldi, P., Mayoral, A., Casellas, R., Martinez, R., Verikoukis, C., & Munoz, R. (2017). TelcoFog: A unified flexible fog and cloud computing architecture for 5G networks. *IEEE Communications Magazine, 55*(8), 36–43. doi:10.1109/MCOM.2017.1600838

Villegas-Ch, W., García-Ortiz, J., & Urbina-Camacho, I. (2023). Framework for a Secure and Sustainable Internet of Medical Things, Requirements, Design Challenges, and Future Trends. *Applied Sciences (Basel, Switzerland), 13*(11), 6634. doi:10.3390/app13116634

Wagan, S. A., Koo, J., Siddiqui, I. F., Qureshi, N. M. F., Attique, M., & Shin, D. R. (2023). A Fuzzy-Based Duo-Secure Multi-Modal Framework for IoMT Anomaly Detection. *Journal of King Saud University. Computer and Information Sciences, 35*(1), 131–144. doi:10.1016/j.jksuci.2022.11.007

Wagner, T. D., Mahbub, K., Palomar, E., & Abdallah, A. E. (2019). Cyber threat intelligence sharing: Survey and research directions. *Computers & Security, 87*, 101589. doi:10.1016/j.cose.2019.101589

Wala, T., Chand, N., & Sharma, A. K. (2020). Energy Efficient Data Collection in Smart Cities Using IoT. *Advances in Intelligent Systems and Computing, 1132*(February), 632–654. doi:10.1007/978-3-030-40305-8_30

Wang, A., Wang, P., Miao, X., Li, X., Ye, N., & Liu, Y. (2020). A review on non-terrestrial wireless technologies for Smart City Internet of Things. *International Journal of Distributed Sensor Networks, 16*(6), 1550147720936824. doi:10.1177/1550147720936824

Wang, X., & Song, Y. (2023). Edge-Assisted IoMT-Based Smart-Home Monitoring System for the Elderly With Chronic Diseases. *IEEE Sensors Letters, 7*(2), 1–4. doi:10.1109/LSENS.2023.3240670

Wang, X., & Wu, Y. (2023). Fog-Assisted Internet of Medical Things for Smart Healthcare. *IEEE Transactions on Consumer Electronics, 69*(3), 391–399. doi:10.1109/TCE.2023.3253896

Wang, Y., Shafik, W., Seong, J. T., Al Mutairi, A., Mustafa, M. S., & Mouhamed, M. R. (2023). Service delay and optimization of the energy efficiency of a system in fog-enabled smart cities. *Alexandria Engineering Journal, 84*, 112–125. doi:10.1016/j.aej.2023.10.034

Wang, Y., Wan, J., Guo, J., Cheung, Y.-M., & Yuen, P. C. (2018). Inference-Based Similarity Search in Randomized Montgomery Domains for Privacy-Preserving Biometric Identification. *IEEE Transactions on Pattern Analysis and Machine Intelligence, 40*(7), 1611–1624. doi:10.1109/TPAMI.2017.2727048 PMID:28715325

Wang, Z., Hu, J., Min, G., Zhao, Z., & Wang, J. (2021, June). Data-Augmentation-Based Cellular Traffic Prediction in Edge-Computing-Enabled Smart City. *IEEE Transactions on Industrial Informatics, 17*(6), 4179–4187. doi:10.1109/TII.2020.3009159

Watch, M. (2023). Security of IoT Devices Statistics. *Philosophical Magazine, 27*, 77.

Wen, J., Nie, J., Kang, J., Niyato, D., Du, H., Zhang, Y., & Guizani, M. (2023). *From generative ai to generative internet of things: Fundamentals, framework, and outlooks.* arXiv preprint arXiv:2310.18382.

Wen, M., Li, Q., Kim, K. J., López-Pérez, D., Dobre, O. A., Poor, H. V., Popovski, P., & Tsiftsis, T. A. (2021). Private 5G networks: Concepts, architectures, and research landscape. *IEEE Journal of Selected Topics in Signal Processing, 16*(1), 7–25. doi:10.1109/JSTSP.2021.3137669

Williams, K. (2019). *Smart cities and climate change: Digital low carbon cities.* Routledge.

Xie, H., Huang, R., Sun, H., Han, Z., Jiang, M., Zhang, D., Goh, H. H., Kurniawan, T. A., Han, F., Liu, H., & Wu, T. (2023). Wireless energy: Paving the way for smart cities and a greener future. *Energy and Building, 297*, 113469. doi:10.1016/j.enbuild.2023.113469

Xiong, C., Song, T., & Zhou, C. (2022). A Study on the Relationship between Artificial Intelligence and 5G Network Construction and the Level of Economic Development of Regional Cities. *Wireless Communications and Mobile Computing, 2022*, 1–9. doi:10.1155/2022/8020388

Xu, H., Lin, J., & Yu, W. (2017). Smart transportation systems: Architecture, enabling technologies, and open issues. *Secure and trustworthy transportation cyber-physical systems*, 23-49.

Xu, Y., & Jia, S. (2021). Application of 5G to Smart City. *The 2nd International Conference on Civil, Architecture and Pollution Control (ICCAPC 2021).* IOP Conference Series: Earth and Environmental Science.

Xu, S., Liu, X., Guo, S., Qiu, X., & Meng, L. (2021, July/August). MECC: A Mobile Edge Collaborative Caching Framework Empowered by Deep Reinforcement Learning. *IEEE Network, 35*(4), 176–183. doi:10.1109/MNET.011.2000663

Xu, T., Wendt, J. B., & Potkonjak, M. (2014, November). Security of IoT systems: Design challenges and opportunities. In *2014 IEEE/ACM International Conference on Computer-Aided Design (ICCAD)* (pp. 417-423). IEEE. 10.1109/ICCAD.2014.7001385

Xu, Y., Gao, H., Li, R., Jiang, Y., Mumtaz, S., Jiang, Z., Fang, J., & Dong, L. (2023). Adversarial Learning-Based Sentiment Analysis for Socially Implemented IoMT Systems. *IEEE Transactions on Computational Social Systems*, *10*(4), 1691–1700. doi:10.1109/TCSS.2023.3252028

Yadav, M., Agarwal, U., Rishiwal, V., Tanwar, S., Kumar, S., Alqahtani, F., & Tolba, A. (2023). Exploring Synergy of Blockchain and 6G Network for Industrial Automation. *IEEE Access : Practical Innovations, Open Solutions*, *11*, 137163–137187. doi:10.1109/ACCESS.2023.3338861

Yang, C., Liang, P., Fu, L., Cui, G., Huang, F., Teng, F., & Bangash, Y.A. (2022). Using 5G in Smart Cities: A Systematic Mapping Study. ArXiv, abs/*2202.04312*.

Yang, C., Liang, P., Fu, L., Cui, G., Huang, F., Teng, F., & Bangash, Y. A. (2022). Using 5G in smart cities: A systematic mapping study. *Intelligent Systems with Applications*, *14*, 200065. doi:10.1016/j.iswa.2022.200065

Yang, T., Ning, J., Lan, D., Zhang, J., Yang, Y., Wang, X., & Taherkordi, A. (2022, April). Kubeedge Wireless for Integrated Communication and Computing Services Everywhere. *IEEE Wireless Communications*, *29*(2), 140–145. doi:10.1109/MWC.004.2100038

Yang, Y., Wu, L., Yin, G., Li, L., & Zhao, H. (2017). A survey on security and privacy issues in Internet-of-Things. *IEEE Internet of Things Journal*, *4*(5), 1250–1258. doi:10.1109/JIOT.2017.2694844

Yang, Z., Jianjun, L., Faqiri, H., Shafik, W., Talal Abdulrahman, A., Yusuf, M., & Sharawy, A. M. (2021). Green internet of things and big data application in smart cities development. *Complexity*, *2021*, 1–15. doi:10.1155/2021/4922697

Yan, J., Liu, J., & Tseng, F. M. (2020). An evaluation system based on the self-organizing system framework of smart cities: A case study of smart transportation systems in China. *Technological Forecasting and Social Change*, *153*, 119371. doi:10.1016/j.techfore.2018.07.009

Yarahmadi, H., Shiri, M. E., Challenger, M., Navidi, H., & Sharifi, A. (2023, June). On the Use of Multi-agent Reinforcement Learning in Cyber-physical and Internet of Thing Systems. In *2023 12th Mediterranean Conference on Embedded Computing (MECO)* (pp. 1-8). IEEE. 10.1109/MECO58584.2023.10154952

Yigitcanlar, T. (2015). Smart cities: An effective urban development and management model? *Australian Plants*, *52*(1), 27–34. doi:10.1080/07293682.2015.1019752

Yıldırım, E., Cicioğlu, M., & Çalhan, A. (2023). Fog-cloud architecture-driven Internet of Medical Things framework for healthcare monitoring. *Medical & Biological Engineering & Computing*, *61*(5), 1133–1147. doi:10.1007/s11517-023-02776-4 PMID:36670240

Yin, C., Xiong, Z., Chen, H., Wang, J., Cooper, D., & David, B. (2015). A literature survey on smart cities. *Science China. Information Sciences*, *58*(10), 1–18. doi:10.1007/s11432-015-5397-4

Yu, S., Chen, X., Zhou, Z., Gong, X., & Wu, D. (2021). When Deep Reinforcement Learning Meets Federated Learning: Intelligent Multitimescale Resource Management for Multiaccess Edge Computing in 5G Ultradense Network. *IEEE Internet of Things Journal, 8*(4), 2238-2251. . doi:10.1109/JIOT.2020.3026589

Yu, S., Gong, X., Shi, Q., Wang X., & Chen, X. (2022). EC-SAGINs: Edge-Computing-Enhanced Space–Air–Ground-Integrated Networks for Internet of Vehicles. *IEEE Internet of Things Journal, 9*(8), 5742-5754. . doi:10.1109/JIOT.2021.3052542

Yuehong, Y. I. N., Zeng, Y., Chen, X., & Fan, Y. (2016). The internet of things in healthcare: An overview. *Journal of Industrial Information Integration*, *1*, 3–13. doi:10.1016/j.jii.2016.03.004

Yuen, B., & Jiang, Y. (2019). Singapore's smart nation initiative: A critical perspective. *Cities (London, England)*, *87*, 80–90.

Yu, Z., Song, L., Jiang, L., & Khold Sharafi, O. (2022). Systematic literature review on the security challenges of Blockchain in IoT-based smart cities. *Kybernetes*, *51*(1), 323–347. doi:10.1108/K-07-2020-0449

Zaidi, A., Ajibade, S. S. M., Musa, M., & Bekun, F. V. (2023). New insights into the research landscape on the application of artificial intelligence in sustainable smart cities: A bibliometric mapping and network analysis approach. *International Journal of Energy Economics and Policy*, *13*(4), 287–299. doi:10.32479/ijeep.14683

Zakari, R. Y., Lawal, Z. K., & Abdulmumin, I. (2021). A Systematic Literature Review of Hausa Natural Language Processing. *International Journal of Computer and Information Technology*, *10*(4), 2279–0764. doi:10.24203/ijcit.v10i4.86

Zanella, A., Bui, N., Castellani, A., Vangelista, L., & Zorzi, M. (2014). Internet of things for smart cities. *IEEE Internet of Things Journal*, *1*(1), 22–32. doi:10.1109/JIOT.2014.2306328

Zantalis, F., Koulouras, G., Karabetsos, S., & Kandris, D. (2019). A review of machine learning and IoT in smart transportation. *Future Internet*, *11*(4), 94. doi:10.3390/fi11040094

Zeadally, S., Siddiqui, F., Baig, Z., & Ibrahim, A. (2019). Smart healthcare. *PSU Research Review*, *4*(2), 149–168. doi:10.1108/PRR-08-2019-0027

Zekhnini, K., Cherrafi, A., Bouhaddou, I., Chaouni Benabdellah, A., & Bag, S. (2022). A model integrating lean and green practices for viable, sustainable, and digital supply chain performance. *International Journal of Production Research*, *60*(21), 6529–6555. doi:10.1080/00207543.2021.1994164

Zhang, P., Yang, X., Chen, J., & Huang, Y. (2019). A survey of testing for 5G: Solutions, opportunities, and challenges. *China Communications*, *16*(1), 69–85.

Zhang, Y., Zhang, G., Fierro, R., & Yang, Y. (2018). Force-driven traffic simulation for a future connected autonomous vehicle-enabled smart transportation system. *IEEE Transactions on Intelligent Transportation Systems*, *19*(7), 2221–2233. doi:10.1109/TITS.2017.2787141

Zhang, Y., Zhang, J., Chen, W., & You, I. (2016). A survey on the edge computing for the Internet of Things. *IEEE Access : Practical Innovations, Open Solutions*, *4*, 2169–2179.

Zhang, Y., Zhang, J., Chen, W., & You, I. (2019). Security and privacy in the era of IoT and 5G: Challenges and solutions. *IEEE Internet of Things Journal*, *6*(3), 1606–1616.

Zhao, Q. (2023). *Customizable Cloud-Native Infrastructure for Private 5G*. 2023 26th Conference on Innovation in Clouds, Internet and Networks and Workshops (ICIN), Paris, France. 10.1109/ICIN56760.2023.10073479

Zhao, W., Liang, Z., & Li, B. (2022). Realizing a Rural Sustainable Development through a Digital Village Construction: Experiences from China. *Sustainability (Basel)*, *14*(21), 14199. doi:10.3390/su142114199

Zhao, X., Askari, H., & Chen, J. (2021). Nanogenerators for smart cities in the era of 5G and Internet of Things. *Joule*, *5*(6), 1391–1431. doi:10.1016/j.joule.2021.03.013

Zhou, L., Su, C., Chiu, W., & Yeh, K.-H. (2020). You Think, Therefore You Are: Transparent Authentication System with Brainwave-Oriented Bio-Features for IoT Networks. *IEEE Transactions on Emerging Topics in Computing*, *8*(2), 303–312. doi:10.1109/TETC.2017.2759306

Zhou, S., Wei, C., Song, C., Pan, X., Chang, W., & Yang, L. (2023, February). Short-Term Traffic Flow Prediction of the Smart City Using 5G Internet of Vehicles Based on Edge Computing. *IEEE Transactions on Intelligent Transportation Systems*, *24*(2), 2229–2238. doi:10.1109/TITS.2022.3147845

Zhou, X., Ye, X., Wang, K. I. K., Liang, W., Nair, N. K. C., Shimizu, S., Yan, Z., & Jin, Q. (2023). Hierarchical Federated Learning with Social Context Clustering-Based Participant Selection for Internet of Medical Things Applications. *IEEE Transactions on Computational Social Systems*, *10*(4), 1742–1751. doi:10.1109/TCSS.2023.3259431

Zhou, Y. (2021). Material foundation for future 5G technology. *Accounts of Materials Research*, *2*(5), 306–310. doi:10.1021/accountsmr.0c00087

Zhu, L., Li, H., Dang, R., Yao, Y., & Wang, H. (2023). A Review of Approaches for Detecting Vulnerabilities in Smart Contracts within Web 3.0 Applications. *Blockchains, 1*(1), 3–18.

Zichichi, M., Ferretti, S., & D'Angelo, G. (2020, January). A distributed ledger based infrastructure for smart transportation system and social good. In 2020 IEEE 17th Annual Consumer Communications & Networking Conference (CCNC) (pp. 1-6). IEEE. doi:10.1109/CCNC46108.2020.9045640

Zikria, Y. B., Kim, S. W., Hahm, O., Afzal, M. K., & Aalsalem, M. Y. (2019). Internet of Things (IoT) operating systems management: Opportunities, challenges, and solution. *Sensors (Basel)*, *19*(8), 1793. doi:10.3390/s19081793 PMID:30991658

About the Contributors

Sushil Kumar Singh (Member, IEEE) is an Associate Professor in the Department of Computer Engineering at Marwadi University, Rajkot, India. He received Ph.D. degree from Seoul National University of Science and Technology, Seoul, South Korea. He received M.Tech. Degree in Computer Science and Engineering from Uttarakhand Technical University, Dehradun, India. He also received an M.E. degree in Information Technology from Karnataka State University, Mysore, India. He has also been the lab leader of the UCS Lab at the Department of Computer Science Engineering, Seoul National University of Science and Technology, Seoul, South Korea. He has received the Best Lab Leadership Award from UCS Lab for 2019-2021. He has more than 12 years of experience teaching in the field of computer science. He has published Four Books: Computer C Programming, Cyber Security, Big Data Analytics, and Mobile Computing. He has also published many high-quality papers (Q1, Top 10% JCR Rank) in international journals and conferences. He has already delivered international lectures in many countries. His research interests include Blockchain, Artificial Intelligence, Big Data, Internet of Things, Smart City Security, and Cyber-Physical Systems. He is an Associate Editor in the HCIS (Human-centric Computation and Information Sciences) Journal and Editor in IGI Global Publication. He is a reviewer of the IEEE Wireless Communication Magazine, IEEE SYSTEMS, IEEE Internet of Things, FGCS, TETT, EXSY, JISA, Computer Network, MDPI, CIE, HCIS, JIPS, Computing (COMP), Multimedia Tools & Applications, and SCIS Journal.

Sudeep Tanwar (Senior Member, IEEE) is working as a professor at the Nirma University, India. He is also a Visiting Professor with WSG University, Bydgoszczy, Poland, Jan Wyzykowski University, Poland, WSG University, Bydgoszcz, and the University of Pitesti, Romania. He is senior member of IEEE and also Vice Chair of IEEE Computer Society Gujarat Section. He received B.Tech in 2002 from Kurukshetra University, India, M.Tech (Honor's) in 2009 from Guru Gobind Singh Indraprastha University, Delhi, India and Ph.D. in 2016 with specialization in Wireless Sensor Network. He has authored 05 books and edited 25 books, more than 400 technical articles, including top cited journals and conferences, such as IEEE TNSE, IEEE TVT, IEEE TII, IEEE TGCN, IEEE TCSC, IEEE IoTJ, IEEE NETWORKS, IEEE WCM, ICC, IWCMC, GLOBECOM, CITS, and INFOCOM. He initiated the research field of blockchain technology adoption in various verticals in the year 2017. His H-index as per Google Scholar and Scopus is 71 and 57, respectively. His research interests include blockchain technology, D2D communication, Deep Learning/ machine Learning, wireless sensor networks, fog computing, smart grid, and the IoT. He is a member of the Technical Committee on Tactile Internet of IEEE Communication Society. Recently, He has been awarded cash prize of Rs, 50,000 for publishing papers with 5+ Impact factor and publication of books with Springer, IET & CRC under the scheme of "Faculty Awards and Incentives" of Nirma University for the year 2019-2020. He has been awarded the Best Research Paper Awards from IEEE SCIoT

2022, IEEE IWCMC-2021, IEEE ICCCA-2021, IEEE GLOBECOM 2018, IEEE ICC 2019, and Springer ICRIC-2019. He has won Dr KW Wong Annual Best Paper Prize (with 750 USD) for 2021 sponsored by Elsevier (publishers of JISA). He has served many international conferences as a member of the Organizing Committee, such as the Publication Chair for FTNCT-2020, ICCIC 2020, and WiMob2019, and a General Chair for IC4S 2019, 2020, 2021, 2022, ICCSDF 2020, FTNCT 2021. He is also serving the editorial boards of COMCOM-Elsevier, IJCS-Wiley, Cyber Security and Applications- Elsevier, Frontiers of blockchain, SPY, Wiley, IJMIS journal of Inderscience, JCCE, and JSSS. He is also leading the ST Research Laboratory, where group members are working on the latest cutting-edge technologies.

Zdzislaw Polkowski is a professor of UJW at Faculty of Technical Sciences and Rector's Representative for International Cooperation and Erasmus+ Program at the Jan Wyzykowski University Polkowice. Since 2019 he is also Adjunct Professor in Department of Business Intelligence in Management, Wroclaw University of Economics and Business, Poland. Moreover, he is visiting professor in Univeristy of Pitesti, Romania, WSG University Bydgoszcz, Poland and adjunct professor in Marwadi University, India. He is the former dean of the Technical Sciences Faculty during the period 2009 -2012 at UZZM in Lubin. He holds a PhD degree in Computer Science and Management from Wroclaw University of Technology, Post Graduate degree in Microcomputer Systems in Management from University of Economics in Wroclaw and Post Graduate degree IT in Education from Economics University in Katowice. He obtained his Engineering degree in Computer Systems in Industry from Technical University of Zielona Gora. He has published more than 75 papers in journals, 25 conference proceedings, including more than 20 papers in journals indexed in the Web of Science, Scopus, IEEE. He served as a member of Technical Program Committee in many International conferences in Poland, India, China, Iran, Romania and Bulgaria. Till date he has delivered 24 invited talks at different international conferences across various countries. He is also the member of the Board of Studies and expert member of the doctoral research committee in many universities in India. He is also the member of the editorial board of several journals and served as a reviewer in a wide range of international journals. His area of interests includes IT in Business, IoT in Business and Education Technology. He has successfully completed a research project on Developing the innovative methodology of teaching Business Informatics funded by the European Commission. He also owns an IT SME consultancy company in Polkowice and Lubin, Poland.

Saurabh Singh received the Ph.D. degree from Jeonbuk National University, Jeonju-si, South Korea, carrying out his research in the field of ubiquitous security. He was a Postdoctoral Researcher with Kunsan National University, South Korea. He also worked at Dongguk University, Seoul, South Korea, as an Assistant Professor. Currently he is working as a post of Assistant professor in Woosong University, Daejeon South Korea. He has published many SCI/SCIE journals and conference papers. His research interests include Blockchain technology, Cloud computing and Security, the IoT, Deep learning, and Cryptography.

***

Purnima Gupta is working as Assistant Professor at IMS Ghaziabad, University Courses Campus. She has an experience of more than nine years in the field of Academics. She is pursuing Ph.D from Amity University. She did M.Tech from Abdul Kalam Technical University. She is a member of IEEE and Oracle Academy. She has Qualified four times UGC NET (June 2014, June 2018 & Dec 2018, June

2019) and two times AWES PRT exam in 2014 & 2015 in Computer Science. She has received three appreciation awards from Indian railway ECR for working on their five projects (RRM, GHI, TROMGS, LAR, PSS & RMS). She has received WOW award by IMS Noida. She has done BIG Data and Hadoop Course from IITR and multiple online Courses. She has many publication (more than 10) research papers in reputed journals and conference. She has published two patents. She has been a Resource person in many workshops and FDPs. She has organized multiple events.

Archana Gupta is working as an Assistant Professor at IMS Ghaziabad, University Courses Campus. She has an experience of 15 years in academics and research. She is pursuing her Ph.D. in Computer Science and Engineering from JJTU, Rajasthan. She completed her MCA from Uttar Pradesh Technical University and M.Tech (IT). She has Qualified UGC NET (June 2012). She has published research papers in reputed national journals. She has attended various faculty development programmers and workshops.

Vishal Jain is presently working as an Associate Professor at Department of Computer Science and Engineering, School of Engineering and Technology, Sharda University, Greater Noida, U. P. India. Before that, he has worked for several years as an Associate Professor at Bharati Vidyapeeth's Institute of Computer Applications and Management (BVICAM), New Delhi. He has more than 15 years of experience in the academics. He obtained Ph.D (CSE), M.Tech (CSE), MBA (HR), MCA, MCP and CCNA. He has authored more than 100 research papers in reputed conferences and journals, including Web of Science and Scopus. He has authored and edited more than 45 books with various reputed publishers, including Elsevier, Springer, IET, Apple Academic Press, CRC, Taylor and Francis Group, Scrivener, Wiley, Emerald, NOVA Science, IGI-Global and River Publishers. His research areas include information retrieval, semantic web, ontology engineering, data mining, ad hoc networks, and sensor networks. He received a Young Active Member Award for the year 2012–13 from the Computer Society of India, Best Faculty Award for the year 2017 and Best Researcher Award for the year 2019 from BVICAM, New Delhi.

Kassim Kalinaki (MIEEE) is a passionate technologist, researcher, and educator with more than ten years of experience in industry and academia. He received his Diploma in Computer engineering from Kyambogo University, a BSc in computer science and engineering, and an MSc. Computer Science and Engineering from Bangladesh's Islamic University of Technology (IUT). Since 2014, He has been lecturing at the Islamic University in Uganda (IUIU), where he most recently served as the Head of Department Computer Science department (2019-2022). Currently, he's pursuing his Ph.D. in Computer Science at the School of Digital Science at Universiti Brunei Darussalam (UBD) since January 2022 and is slated to complete in August 2025. He's the founder and principal investigator of Borderline Research Laboratory (BRLab) and his areas of research include Ecological Informatics, Data Analytics, Computer Vision, ML/DL, Digital Image Processing, Cybersecurity, IoT/AIoMT, Remote Sensing, and Educational Technologies. He has authored and co-authored several published peer-reviewed articles in renowned journals and publishers, including in Springer, Elsevier, Taylor and Francis, Emerald and IEEE.

Christian Kaunert is Professor of International Security at Dublin City University, Ireland. He is also Professor of Policing and Security, as well as Director of the International Centre for Policing and Security at the University of South Wales. In addition, he is Jean Monnet Chair, Director of the Jean Monnet Centre of Excellence and Director of the Jean Monnet Network on EU Counter-Terrorism ().

Jaspreet Kaur is currently working as an Assistant Professor in University Business School,Chandigarh University,Mohali,Punjab.She is a post graduate (MBA-H.R) from Panjab University,Chandigarh.She has also qualified UGC NET JRF in Human Resource Management/Labour and Social Welfare and has done PhD in Business Management from Chandigarh University,Mohali. She has over 8 years of experience in academic and administrative assignments.She also received "Best Teacher of the Department Award " in the year 2019 and 2021 in the field of imparting quality education.Her research interests include Employee Engagement, Management of Organizational Change and Organization Development.She has published several research papers and articles in reputed international and national journals and has presented papers in various national and international conferences.She also contributed one edited book and 10 book chapters on various topics.

Manisha Koranga is an Assistant Professor in the department of Computer Science and Engineering in Graphic Era Hill University, Haldwani.She has 13 years of teaching experience. Her research area interest includes machine learning and Artificial Intelligence.

Om Pal has been working as an assistant professor in CE/IT Department of FoET at Ganpat University from 2020. Having experience more than 15 years. Currently pursuing Ph D from Nirma University Ahmedabad. He is members of various technical society and published papers in many conferences and journals. His research areas are Cyber Security, Network Security, Cloud Security

Damodharan Palaniappan received PhD degree from Anna University, Tamil Nadu, India. Presently he is working as an Associate Professor at Marwadi University, Rajkot, Gujarat. He has more than 17 years teaching experience. His research interests are Web Mining, Machine Learning, Image Processing and Big Data.

Richa Pandey is an Assistant Professor in the department of Computer Science and Engineering in Graphic Era Hill University, Haldwani. She has 3 years of teaching experience. She is currently pursuing Ph.D in the field of Blockchain and Machine Learning.

Roheen Qamar received her (B.S) degree in Computer Science and (M.S) degree in Computer Science in QUEST NAWABSHAH. Her research area includes Artificial Intelligence, DDOS Block chain, Internet of Things Soft Computing, Convolutional Neural Network, Shallow Neural Network, Case Cade Neural Network, Fit Net Neural Network, Recursive Neural Network and Image Processing so on. She Works As A Reviewer In Many International Journals.

Ketan Sarvakar is a highly skilled researcher and professor with a focus on artificial intelligence and computer science. Having worked in academia for more than 20 years, he is currently a professor at Ganpat University. Prof. Sarvakar has received the Staff Excellence Award for Outstanding Faculty and Researcher on several occasions. His extensive research has produced ten patents in the UK, Canada, Australia, and India, as well as more than fifty research papers in journals indexed in the Web of Science, Scopus, IEEE, and other databases covering facial emotion recognition, sentiment analysis, and machine learning. He actively participates in professional organizations and research initiatives, showcasing his creative contributions. Professor Sarvakar is a prominent and esteemed member of the academic community in his field. He was also a member of the IEEE Gujarat Section's Ex-COM in 2021, and 2022. In addition, he has reviewed articles for a number of international journals and served as a reviewer in a wide range of international journals.

Wasswa Shafik is an IEEE member, P.Eng received a bachelor of science in Information Technology Engineering with a minor in Mathematics in 2016 from Ndejje University, Kampala, Uganda, a PhD and master of engineering in Information Technology Engineering (MIT) in 2020, from the Computer Engineering Department, Yazd University, Islamic Republic of Iran. He is an associate researcher at the Computer Science department, Network interconnectivity Lab at Yazd University, Islamic Republic of Iran, and at Information Sciences, Prince Sultan University, Saudi Arabia. His areas of interest are Computer Vision, Anomaly Detection, Drones (UAVs), Machine/Deep Learning, AI-enabled IoT/IoMTs, IoT/IIoT/OT Security, Cyber Security and Privacy. Shafik is the chair/co-chair/program chair of some Scopus/EI conferences. Also, academic editor/ associate editor for set of indexed journals (Scopus journals' quartile ranking). He is the founder and lead investigator of Digital Connectivity Research Laboratory (DCR-Lab) since 2019, the Managing Executive director of Asmaah Charity Organisation (ACO).

Praveen Kumar Sharma received his B.E. degree (Hons.) in Electronics and Communication Engineering from the University of Rajasthan, Jaipur, India, and the M.E. degree in Electronics and Communication Engineering from the National Institute of Technical Teachers Training and Research (NITTTR), Chandigarh, India. He did his PhD from BITS Pilani, India in the field of Flexible antennas. He is currently working as a Research Scientist at the Research Center for Electrical and Information Technology, Seoul National University of Science and Technology, Seoul Republic of Korea. His research interests include antennas, material science, microwaves, and electromagnetics.

Deepak Kumar Verma has professional and research experience spanning over 16 years and is currently working as an associate professor in the department of computer engineering at Marwadi University, Rajkot, Gujarat, India. He has a Ph.D. in CSE from the Dr. APJ Abdul Kalam Technical University, Lucknow, Uttar Pradesh, India. He is a member of many international and national technical societies, such as IEEE, IEEE CS, IACSIT, IAENG, CSI, IETE, and ISTE. Through these societies, he actively contributes to the development of professional studies. He has been a reviewer for many popular international journals and conferences. He has delivered many invited lectures and keynote addresses at many workshops and conferences. He has organized and participated in many workshops. His research interests are cloud computing and data security. He has many publications (over 20) in peer-reviewed international journals and international and national conferences (including those published by IEEE, ACM, and Springer). He is also supervising three Ph.D. students in related research areas.

Baqar Ali Zardari received a (B.S) degree in Computer Science, (M.S) in Information Technology and (PhD) From QUEST Nawab shah His Area Of Interest Includes HCI, Distributed Databases, User Experience, Artificial Intelligence, DDOS And Shallow Neural Network.

Index

D

E

F

G

H

I

T

U

W

Z

www.ingramcontent.com/pod-product-compliance
Lightning Source LLC
LaVergne TN
LVHW060358300926
849162LV00006B/1294